THE FIRST LAWS
OF THE STATE OF
VIRGINIA

THE FIRST LAWS OF THE ORIGINAL THIRTEEN STATES

Compiled by: JOHN D. CUSHING

Virginia.
...

THE FIRST LAWS
OF THE STATE OF
VIRGINIA

Michael Glazier, Inc.
Wilmington, Delaware

This edition published in 1982 by:
MICHAEL GLAZIER, INC., 1723 Delaware Avenue
Wilmington, Delaware 19806

Library of Congress Catalog Card Number: 81-81270

International Standard Book Number
  Series: 0-89453-211-1
  This Volume: 0-89453-221-9

Printed in the United States of America

Editorial Note

THIS FACSIMILE SERIES is undertaken for the sole purpose of making available to researchers from many disciplines the texts of the first compilations of laws issued by the North American states. In many instances, original editions of those laws are to be found only in major research libraries where, more often than not, they must be used under restrictions governing the use of rare books. The present series should help provide better access to those texts and, at the same time, contribute to the conservation of the rare original editions. The "NOTE" prefacing each of these volumes is confined to the absolute minimum necessary to set each in reasonable bibliographical context.

Obviously, the "first" printed laws of most states were session laws. Unfortunately, many of them were never printed in full sequence, and when they were they invariably lack tables of contents or indexes. The present series, therefore, will give first consideration to issuing facsimile copies of the first retrospective compilations issued by the various states after their emergence from colonial status. In some instances those compilations will be supplemented by session laws in order to present a more useful text, and when no satisfactory compilation exists, digests will be used.

The traditional system for publishing the laws in Virginia varied markedly from that in most other colonies in that heavy reliance was long placed upon circulating manuscript copies at the conclusion of each legislative session. Printed laws were scarce and, according to contemporary observers, usually unsatisfactory. Following the appearance in 1612 of William Strachey's *Lavves Diuine Morall and Martiall*—a crude, quasi-military code—six retrospective compilations were published between 1662 and 1728, all of them in London. Thereafter another compilation was published at Glasgow and five editions of abridgements or acts then in force were issued locally, the last of them before the American Revolution appearing in 1769.

Very few separate acts are known to have been printed in the

pre-revolutionary years, and no session laws at all appear to have been printed before 1730. Thereafter, they were issued with reasonable frequency, some of them being substantial publications, but many of them consisting of no more than two or four pages each. With the conclusion of the March session of the Assembly in 1773, nothing further appears to have been issued until October of 1776, when session laws began to appear on a regular basis. Taken with the necessarily expurgated compilation of 1769, they constituted the body of printed laws for the state. As was the case in most other states, a large number of the session laws issued during the wartime years were devoted to military matters, security, and the establishment of a new government.

As the war drew to a close, it became evident that an entirely new order had been created in the former American colonies, and that it would be necessary to revise the legislative relics of the old regime, and to bring some order out of fourteen years of legislative chaos. Accordingly, in June of 1783, the Assembly ordered a new compilation that would contain all viable legislation enacted since 1769. Two years later, the new work emerged under the title *A Collection of all Such Acts of the General Assembly...Passed Since the Year 1768 as are Now in Force*. The 235 page edition, the title page proclaims, was prepared under the supervision of the Judges of the High Court of Chancery, and was published at Richmond by Thomas Nicholson and William Prentis. It fell well below the standards of similar publications issued in most other states at the time. Indeed, it would not be until 1809, when William Waller Henning began to issue his monumental 13 volume *Statutes at Large*, that Virginia possessed a satisfactory compilation of its statutes.

The 1785 edition, reproduced in this facsimile edition, contained no prefatory material to enlighten the reader concerning the history of its preparation or its arrangement. Perhaps it was thought that none was needed, because the statutes were simply arranged according to legislative session, with each chapter being assigned a number. Private and expired acts were published by title only; the material in the 1769 edition that had been repealed or amended appeared in the order that such legislation had been considered. At the end appeared a "Table," or rudimentary index, arranged by subject headings, that leads the user to specific pages.

The present facsimile edition is copied from that in the Historical Society of Pennsylvania through the kindness of its Director, Dr. James E. Mooney.

Publisher's Note

THE ORIGINAL COPIES of the books reproduced in this series range from large folios that are difficult to handle, to small octavos printed from small type that is difficult to read. In the interest of convenience and legibility some of the facsimile volumes have been enlarged in size while others have been reduced.

A
COLLECTION

OF ALL SUCH

PUBLIC ACTS

OF THE

GENERAL ASSEMBLY,

AND

ORDINANCES

OF THE

CONVENTIONS

OF

VIRGINIA,

Paſſed ſince the year 1768, as are now in force;

With a TABLE of the PRINCIPAL MATTERS.

Publiſhed under inſpeſtion of the JUDGES of the HIGH COURT of CHANCERY, by a reſolution of GENERAL ASSEMBLY, the 16th day of June 1783.

RICHMOND.

Printed by *THOMAS NICOLSON* and *WILLIAM PRENTIS*.
M.DCC.LXXXV.

ANNO REGNI

GEORGII III.

Regis, Magnæ Britanniæ, Franciæ, et Hiberniæ,

decimo.

At a GENERAL ASSEMBLY, begun and held at the CAPITOL, in the City of WILLIAMSBURG, on Tuesday the 7th Day of November, Anno Domini, 1769, in the 10th Year of the Reign of *GEORGE* III. of Great Britain, France, and Ireland, King, Defender of the Faith, &c. being the first Session of this present General Assembly.

CHAP. I.

An act for regulating the election of Burgesses, for declaring their privileges and allowances, and for fixing the rights of electors. **(a)**

CHAP. II.

An act to continue and amend the act entitled an act for amending the staple of tobacco, and for preventing frauds in his Majesty's customs.

Expired.

CHAP. III.

An act to amend an act entitled an act declaring the law concerning executions, and for relief of insolvent debtors. **(b)**

I. WHEREAS by an act of General Assembly made in the twenty-second year of the reign of his late Majesty King *George* the second, entitled *An act declaring the law concerning executions, and for relief of insolvent debtors,* it was among other things enacted, that if the owner of goods and chattels taken by any sheriff, or other officer, by virtue of a writ of *fieri facias,* should give

Recital.

(a) This act is omitted, because the King's approbation thereof until which the execution of it was suspended, never was signified.

(b) See 22 Geo. II. (1748) Chap. 8. of the Edit. in 1769.

A. D. 1769.

sufficient security to such sheriff, or officer, to have the same goods and chattels forth coming at the day of sale, it should be lawful for such sheriff, or other officer, to accept the security, and suffer the goods and chattels to remain in the possession, and at the risk of the debtor, until the time aforesaid: But in case the debtor refused to deliver up the goods and chattels accordingly, no remedy was therein provided for the creditor or officer, who being therefore obliged to commence a new suit on such bond, was compellable, on serving another *fieri facias* again, to accept security, to have the estate taken forth coming, and might be thereby prevented from ever recovering the debt: For remedy herein,

Goods taken in execution by fi' fa' may remain in possession of the owner tendering security to have them forth coming, till the day of sale.

II. BE it enacted, by the Governour, Council, and Burgesses, of this present General Assembly, and by the authority of the same, that if the owner of any goods or chattels which shall be taken by any sheriff, or other officer, by virtue of a writ of *fieri facias*, shall tender sufficient security to have the same goods and chattels forth coming at the day of sale, it shall be lawful for the sheriff or officer to take a bond from such debtor and securities, payable to the creditor, reciting the service of such execution, and the amount of the money of tobacco due thereon, and with condition to have the goods or chattels forth coming at the day of sale, appointed by such sheriff or officer, and shall thereupon suffer the said goods and chattels to remain in the possession, and at the risk of the debtor until that time.

Bond for delivering goods taken in execution, to be returned to clerk's office, and have the force of a judgment; and execution upon it not to be delayed.

III. AND be it further enacted, that if the owner of such goods or chattels shall fail to deliver up the same, according to the condition of the bond, or pay the money or tobacco mentioned in the execution, such sheriff or officer shall return the bond to the office of the clerk of the court from whence the execution issued, to be there safely kept, and to have the force of a judgment, and thereupon it shall be lawful for the court where such bond shall be lodged, upon motion of the person to whom the same is payable, his executors or administrators, to award execution for the money and tobacco therein mentioned, with interest thereon from the date of the bond, till payment, and costs, provided the obligors, their executors or administrators, or such of them against whom execution is awarded, have ten days previous notice of such motion; and upon such execution, or on any execution awarded, on a bond given to replevy an estate taken by a former execution, the sheriff or officer shall not take any security, either to have the goods forth coming at the day of sale, or for the payment of the money at a future day, according to the further directions of the said recited act, but shall levy the same immediately, and keep in his hands the goods and chattels taken thereupon, until he shall have sold sufficient thereof to raise the money and tobacco mentioned in the execution, or the same be otherwise satisfied; any thing in the said recited act to the contrary notwithstanding. And for the better direction of such sheriff or officer, the

Clerk to endorse on the execution, no security to be taken.

clerk shall endorse upon every such execution, that no security of any kind is to be taken. And for settling what fees the sheriffs or other officers shall receive for executing writs of *distringas* upon judgments, in actions of detinue, or attachments on decrees in chancery for the payment of money;

Officers fees for serving writ of distringas, or attachment on decree in Chancery.

IV. BE it further enacted, that the sheriff or officer for executing any such writ of *distringas*, or attachment on such decree, shall be entitled to the same fee or commissions upon the amount of the value of the goods and chattels recovered, or money mentioned in such decree, as is by law allowed for serving any other execution.

Coroner to give bond, &c. for faithful executing office;

not paying money levied by execution, or suffering defendant to escape, judgment and execution may be awarded against him, on motion.

V. AND be it further enacted, by the authority aforesaid, that every coroner, before he shall be at liberty to serve any writ of execution, shall, in the court of his county, enter into bond, with good and sufficient security, payable to our Lord the King, in the penalty of five hundred pounds with condition for the true and faithful execution of his office; and if such coroner shall thereafter make return upon any writ of *fieri facias* or *venditioni exponas*, that he hath levied the debt, damages and costs, as in such writ is required, or any part thereof, and shall not immediately pay the same to the party to whom it is payable, or his attorney, or shall return upon any writ of *capias ad satisfaciendum*, or attachment for not performing a decree in chancery, for payment of money or tobacco, that he hath taken the body of the defendant or defendants, and hath the same ready to satisfy, the money and tobacco in the said writ mentioned and shall actually have received such money or tobacco of the defendant or defendants, or have suffered him, her, or them, to have escaped, with his consent, and shall not immediately pay such money or tobacco to the party to whom the same is payable, or his attorney, that then, or in either of the said cases, it shall be lawful for the court, from whence such writ issued, upon the motion of the creditor, to give judgment against such coroner, his executors or administrators, for the amount of the money and tobacco therein mentioned, and costs, and thereon to award execution; provided such coroner, his executors, or administrators, have ten days previous notice of such motion; and upon such execution no security for payment of the money or tobacco therein mentioned at a future day, or to have the goods forth coming at the day of sale, shall be taken or received; and the clerk shall endorse thereon that no security of any kind is to be taken.

Estate of sheriff, &c. taken in execution upon judgment for money levied, &c. not repleviable.

VI. AND be it further enacted, that when execution shall issue against the estate of any sheriff, or under sheriff, or their securities, upon a judgment obtained against such sheriff, or under sheriff, and securities, for money or tobacco received by such sheriff, or under sheriff, by virtue of any execution, or process levied or executed by him, or them, or for any money collected or received by them, in any manner as sheriffs, no security for payment of the money or tobacco mentioned in such execution at a future day, or to have the goods forth coming at the day of sale, shall be taken or received; but the officer taking such estate in execution, shall proceed immediately to the sale thereof, notwithstanding such security shall be tendered; and for the better direction of such officer, the clerk issuing such execution shall endorse thereon, that no security of any kind is to be taken.

Insolvent debtor in execution how to be discharged

VII. AND for the more speedy relief of insolvent debtors, Be it further enacted, by the authority aforesaid, that when any person shall be committed to jail in execution, in any suit commenced or prosecuted in any county court, and shall have remained in prison twenty days, it shall be lawful for any justice of such court, by warrant under his hand and seal, to command the jailer or keeper of the said prison to bring before the said court, if sitting, or if not sitting, before any two justices of the said court, at their county courthouse, on a certain day, to be appointed in such warrant, the body of such person to in prison, together with a list of the several executions with which he or she shall stand charged in the said jail, of which day, so appointed in the said warrant, reasonable notice shall be given to the creditor or creditors, his or their executors, administrators, or agents, at whose suit or suits such prisoner shall be in execution, in manner herein after directed, which warrant such jailer is hereby required to obey; and every such prisoner coming before the said court, or justices, as the case shall be, shall subscribe and deliver in a schedule of his whole estate, and take the same oath as is prescribed by one act of Assembly, entitled An act declaring the law concerning executions, and for relief of insolvent debtors; which schedule being so subscribed, shall be by the justices, when taken out of court, returned to the clerk of the court, there to remain for the better information of the creditors; and after delivering in such schedule, and taking such oath, such prisoner shall be by warrant from such court, or two justices, as the case shall be, discharged from his imprisonment, and the jailer shall be indemnified, in like manner as in the said act is directed.

See 12 Geo. II. chap. 8. sect. 24.

A. D. 1769.

VIII. *PROVIDED always*, that notwithstanding such discharge, it shall be lawful for any creditor or creditors, at whose suit such insolvent prisoner was imprisoned, at any time afterwards to sue out a writ of *scieri facias*, to have execution against any lands or tenements, goods or chattels, which such insolvent person shall thereafter acquire or be possessed of.

His lands, &c. notwithstanding aischarged, liable to execution.

IX. *AND be it further enacted, by the authority aforesaid*, that all the estate contained in such schedule and any other estate which may be discovered to belong to the prisoner, for such interest therein as such prisoner hath, and may lawfully depart withal, shall be vested in the sheriff of the county, to be by him sold, and the money paid and disposed of as in the said act is directed; but for as much as the schedules to be subscribed, and delivered in by insolvent debtors, may often contain articles of money and tobacco due to such debtors, and goods, chattels, and estates, in the possession of others, which cannot be recovered without new suits, and the sheriffs may decline commencing such suits, on account of the trouble and expence in which they may be involved, whereby such debts, goods, chattels, and estates, may be lost to the creditors: For remedy herein,

His estate how to be disposed of.

Sect. 25.

X. *BE it further enacted, by the authority aforesaid*, that when any insolvent debtor shall be discharged, pursuant to this, or to the act above mentioned, or according to the directions of an act of Assembly made in the twenty seventh year of the reign of king *George* the second, entitled *An act for reducing the several laws made for establishing the general court, and for regulating and settling the proceedings therein into one act of Assembly*, and the schedule subscribed and delivered in by such prisoner, shall contain articles of money or tobacco due to such prisoner, or of goods, chattels, or estates, to him belonging, and in the possession of any other, in that case the clerk of the court with whom such schedule is directed to remain, shall immediately issue a summons against each of the persons named as debtors in the said schedule, and against such others as are therein said to have possession of any goods, chattels, or estates, of the property of the prisoner, reciting the sum of money or the quantity of tobacco, he or she is charged with, or the particular goods, chattels, or estates, said to be in his possession, and requiring him or her to appear at the next court, and to declare on oath whether the said money or tobacco, or any part thereof, be really due to such prisoner, or whether such goods, chattels or estates, or any of them be really in his or her possession, and are the property of such prisoner; and if the person so summoned shall fail to attend according to such summons, or to shew good cause for his non-attendance, it shall be lawful for the court to enter judgment against every such person, for the money, tobacco, goods, chattels, or estates, in such schedule mentioned, together with costs of suit, a lawyer's fee excepted. And if any such person, so summoned, shall appear and be sworn, judgment shall be entered for so much of the money, tobacco, goods, chattels, or estates, as he or she shall acknowledge to be due, or to be of the property of such prisoner, and in his possession with costs as aforesaid, which judgments shall be entered in the name of the sheriff, who may, thereupon proceed to levy executions, as in other cases, and to dispose of the money, tobacco, goods, chattels, or estates, so recovered, in the same manner as by the said acts he is directed to dispose of the other effects.

His estate in possession of, or due from others, how recoverable.

27 Geo. II. (1753) *chap.* 1, *s. 8.* 31.

XI. *PROVIDED always*, that where any such garnishee shall not acknowledge the whole money or tobacco to be due, or all the goods, chattels, and estates, mentioned in the schedule, to be of the property of the prisoner, and in his possession, the sheriff or such prisoner, at any time after (unless barred by any of the several acts, limiting the times of the commencement of actions) shall be at liberty to claim the residue, by legal process; and the former judgment, as to such garnishee, shall be no further bar in such process, than for so much money or tobacco, or such goods, chattels, and estates, as the garnishee is thereby ordered to pay or deliver.

Not barred by judgment against garnishee for past, from claiming the residue.

XII. *AND be it further enacted, by the authority aforesaid*, that every sheriff shall be allowed to retain out of the effects of such insolvent debtor, before the distribution thereof, all reasonable expences, in recovering such money, tobacco, goods, chattels, and estates as aforesaid, including such fee to a lawyer, for the proceeding against the garnishees, as shall be judged reasonable by the court; and if such effects be not sufficient, he shall be reimbursed such expences by the creditor, or creditors if more than one, in proportion to their demands.

Allowance to sheriff out of the estate or, if that is not sufficient, to be paid by the creditors.

XIII. *AND* whereas it is unreasonable that sheriffs should be obliged to go out of their counties, to give notice to creditors at whose suit any person may be in custody of such sheriff, or to pay money levied by executions: *Be it further enacted*, that where any execution shall be delivered to the sheriff of any other county than that wherein the creditor resides, such creditor shall name some person resident in the county where the execution is to be levied, to be his, her, or their agent, for the particular purpose of receiving the money on such execution, and for giving to and receiving from the sheriff any notices which may be necessary relating thereto; and payments made and notices given to such agent, shall be as effectual as if made or given to the creditor. And if any creditor shall fail to appoint such agent, no judgment shall be entered against the sheriff for non-payment of the money and tobacco mentioned in such execution, unless a demand thereof shall have been first made of such sheriff, in his county, by the creditor or some other person having a written order from him: Nor in case of failure, in appointing such agent, shall the sheriff or prisoner be obliged to give notice previous to the discharge of such prisoner, either for want of security for his prison fees, or upon his taking the oath of an insolvent debtor as aforesaid; but such prisoner may be discharged in those cases respectively, without any notice to be given to the creditor so failing.

Creditor not resident in the county to which execution is sent to appoint an agent there for receiving the money &c. failing to appoint an agent not to recover judgment against sheriff for non-payment, without previous demand, &c. not to have notice before discharge of debtor for want of security for prison fees, &c.

XIV. *PROVIDED always*, that the execution of this act shall be, and the same is suspended until his majesty's approbation thereof shall be obtained.   *(a)*

Suspending clause.

(a) *The king's approbation, which was likewise requisite to give this act validity, was published by the governor's proclamation in the* Virginia Gazette, *as the persons who were appointed to inspect this work have been credibly informed. The reader may apply this note to the 4th, 18th, 19th, 29th, and 37th chapters of this session, which are in the same predicament.*

A. D. 1769.

CHAP. IV

An act to regulate the practice of suing out and prosecuting Writs of Replevin, in cases of distress for Rents.

Recital.

22 Geo. II. (1748) chap. 10 of the edit. in 1769.

Goods distrained for rent not to be replevied, without bond and security.

I. WHEREAS very great and unjust delays have arisen, from the suing out writs of replevin, in cases of goods distrained for rent, contrary to the true intent and meaning of the act of the General Assembly made in the twenty-second year of the reign of his late Majesty, entitled *An act for the better securing the payment of rents, and preventing the fraudulent practices of tenants:* For remedy whereof, Be it enacted by the Governor, Council, and Burgesses, of this present General Assembly, and it is hereby enacted by the authority of the same, that from and after the passing of this act, before any writ of replevin shall be granted, in case of goods and chattels distrained for rent, the person or persons praying such writ, shall enter into bond, with one or more sufficient securities, in the clerk's office, in the penalty of at least double the value, of the rent distrained for, and costs of suit, to perform and satisfy the judgment of the court in such suit, in case he, she, or they, shall be cast therein; and if upon the trial of such suit, it shall be found that the rent distrained for, was justly due, the party injured or delayed by suing forth the said writ, shall recover against the party suing forth and prosecuting the same, double the value of the rent in arrear, and distrained for, with full costs of suit; to be recovered in the same manner as judgments are by law recovered, on executing a writ of *fieri facias,* where the clerk is directed to endorse on the back of the writ, no security is to be taken.

Rent being found due, &c.

Person other than the tenant may sue out a writ of replevin, and if cast, judgment shall be given against him for double value and costs.

II. AND be it further enacted, by the authority aforesaid, that where any person shall suggest that the goods distrained, are his or her property, and not the property of the tenant, nor held in trust for the use of the tenant in any manner whatsoever, and that the same in his or her opinion is not liable to such distress, he or she giving bond and security, in manner herein before directed, may sue out a writ of replevin for such goods, but not otherwise; and in case the person or persons suing out the said writ shall be cast in such suit, judgment shall be given against him for double the value of the rent in arrear, and distrained for, with full costs as aforesaid. And for the more speedy determination of all such writs of replevin,

Suits in replevin to be speedily tried.

III. BE it further enacted, by the authority aforesaid, that every such writ shall be returnable to the next court after the same shall be issued; and such court shall, at their next sitting after the return, cause an issue to be made up therein, which shall be tried at the following court, without waiting for its turn in the order of priority in regard to other suits.

Not to extend to replevins on giving bond to pay in 3 months, whereon judgment to be in the same manner as on bond upon executing fi fa

IV. PROVIDED always, that this act shall not extend to prevent the replevying goods or chattels, distrained for rent, where the tenant shall give bond and security for payment thereof at the end of three months, in the manner directed by the above-mentioned act.

V. PROVIDED also, that judgment shall and may be recovered on such last mentioned bond, in the same manner as on bonds taken upon executing a writ of *fieri facias.*

Suspending clause.

VI. PROVIDED always, that the execution of this act shall be, and the same is hereby suspended until his Majesty's approbation thereof shall be obtained.   *(a)*

CHAP. V.

An act for further continuing the act, entitled An act for reducing the several acts of Assembly for making provision against invasions and insurrections into one act.

Expired.

CHAP. VI.

An act to continue and amend an act entitled An act for reducing the several acts made for laying a duty upon liquors into one act.

Expired.

CHAP. VII.

An act for continuing certain acts of Assembly, imposing duties on slaves

Expired.

CHAP. VIII.

An act for laying an additional duty upon slaves, imported into this Colony.

Expired.

CHAP. IX.

An act for further continuing the act, entitled An act for the better regulating and collecting certain officers fees, and for other purposes therein mentioned.

Expired.

CHAP. X.

An act for paying officers fees due from the inhabitants of other counties, for services done in the counties therein mentioned.   *(b)*

Recital.

I. WHEREAS by an act of the General Assembly, passed in the twenty-seventh year of the reign of his late Majesty *George* the second, the inhabitants of the counties of *Halifax* and *Bedford,* were allowed to pay all officers fees at twelve shillings and six pence *per* hundred on the nett tobacco, and by an act passed in the thirty-second year of the reign of his said late Majesty *George* the

---

(a) See note to chap. 3, sect. 14.
(b) See 19 Geo. II. (1745) chap. 1, of edit. 1769, with notes subjoined.

second, the inhabitants of the county of *Loudoun* were allowed to discharge all officers fees, payable in the said county, in money for tobacco at the rate of twelve shillings and six pence *per* hundred; and by an act passed in the first year of his present Majesty's reign, the inhabitants of the counties of *Frederick*, *Augusta*, and *Hampshire*, were allowed to pay all officers fees at the rate of eight shillings and four pence for every hundred weight of gross tobacco; and by an act passed in the seventh year of his present Majesty's reign, the inhabitants of *Pittsylvania* were allowed to pay all officers fees at twelve shillings and six pence *per* hundred; and by an act passed this present General Assembly, the inhabitants of the county of *Botetourt* are allowed to pay all officers fees at the rate of eight shillings and four pence for every hundred weight of gross tobacco; and for as much as the inhabitants of the other counties, within this colony, are by law compellable to pay the fees due from them to the respective officers of the said counties of *Halifax*, *Bedford*, *Loudoun*, *Frederick*, *Augusta*, *Hampshire*, *Pittsylvania*, and *Botetourt*, in tobacco or money at the rate of two pence *per* pound, although upon judgments obtained by them against the inhabitants of the before mentioned counties, they are obliged to receive money for the tobacco fees taxed upon such judgments, according to the rates by which the same are payable in the said counties respectively, which is unequal and unjust:

A. D 1769.
10 Geo. III.
chap. 10.

II. BE it therefore enacted, by the *Governor, Council, and Burgesses*, of this present General Assembly, and it is hereby enacted by the authority of the same, that from and after the passing of this act, it shall and may be lawful for all and every person or persons to pay all fees due from them to the respective officers of the said counties of *Halifax*, *Bedford*, *Loudoun*, *Frederick*, *Augusta*, *Hampshire*, *Pittsylvania*, and *Botetourt*, in money for tobacco, according to the rates the inhabitants of the said counties respectively are by law allowed to pay the same; any law, to the contrary thereof, in any wise notwithstanding.

*Tobacco fees due
to officers of several
counties payable in
money at certain
rates;*

III. AND be it further enacted, by the authority aforesaid, that when any inhabitant of the said counties of *Halifax*, *Bedford*, *Loudoun*, *Frederick*, *Augusta*, *Hampshire*, *Pittsylvania*, or *Botetourt*, shall recover in any action or suit brought by them against the inhabitants of any other county, the person against whom judgment shall be obtained in such action or suit, may pay and discharge all the tobacco fees, taxed upon the judgment in such action or suit, at the same rate the plaintiff in such action or suit is entitled to discharge the same; any law, custom, or usage, to the contrary thereof, in any wise, notwithstanding.

*recovered by party
to be discharged at
the same rate as
Plaintiff is intitled
to discharge them.*

CHAP. XI.

An act for laying a public levy.

Executed.

CHAP. XII.

An act for the better support of the contingent charges of government.

Expired.

CHAP. XIII.

An act to prevent forging the Treasury notes of this colony in circulation.

*The subject of its
operation annihilated.*

CHAP. XIV.

An act for the more speedy and effectual recovery of the debt due to the public from the estate of the late Treasurer.

Executed.

CHAP. XV.

An act to amend an act, entitled An act for inspecting pork, beef, flour, tar, pitch, and turpentine.

Repealed.

CHAP. XVI.

An act to continue an act, entitled An act for establishing pilots, and regulating their fees.

Expired.

CHAP. XVII.

An act for preventing and suppressing private lotteries.

I. WHEREAS many pernicious games, called lotteries, have been set up in this colony, which have a manifest tendency to the corruption of morals, and the impoverishment of families; and whereas such pernicious practices may not only give opportunities to defraud the honest and industrious, but may be productive of all manner of vice, idleness, and immorality, and against the common good and welfare of the community: For remedy whereof, Be it enacted by the *Governor, Council, and Burgesses, of this present General Assembly, and it is hereby enacted by the authority of the same,* that from and after the first day of *May* next, no person or persons whatever, shall, on his own account, or that of another, either publicly or privately, set up, erect, make, exercise, keep open, shew, expose, or cause to be played at, drawn or thrown at, any such lotteries, or shall procure the same to be done, either by dice, lots, cards, tickets, or any other numbers or figures, or any other way whatever; and every person or persons herein offending, shall forfeit and pay to the parish, for the use of the poor of such parish, where such offence shall be committed, the whole of the sum or sums to be raised by such lottery; to be recovered by action of debt, or information, in any court within this colony.

Recital.

*No person shall
set up a lottery,*

under a penalty.

A. D. 1769.

CHAP. XVIII.

An act to repeal an act, made in the twenty-second year of his late Majesty's reign, entitled An act concerning strays, and to establish a more effectual method to prevent frauds committed by persons taking up strays.

Recital.

I. WHEREAS the act of Assembly made in the twenty-second year of the reign of his late Majesty, *George* the second, entitled *An act concerning strays*, hath been found ineffectual to answer the purposes for which it was intended; and great frauds have been committed, under colour of the said act, by ill disposed people, in taking up and concealing stray horses from the knowledge of the proprietors, and afterwards advertising them by false and imperfect descriptions, so as to make them their own property, under pretence of pursuing the directions of the said act: *Be it therefore enacted by the Governor, Council, and Burgesses, of this present General Assembly, and it is hereby enacted by the authority of the same,* that the said act of Assembly, entitled *An act concerning strays,* shall be, and the same is hereby repealed, and made void, to all intents and purposes.

*22 Geo. II.
(1748) cap. 36 of
the Edit. in 1769,
repealed.*

*In what manner
stray horses, &c.
taken up, shall be
viewed, appraised,
registered, and
advertised;*

II. AND be it further enacted, by the authority aforesaid, that every person within this colony and dominion, who shall hereafter take up any stray horse, mare, or colt, shall immediately carry the same before some Justice of the Peace of the county where such stray shall be taken up, and make oath before such Justice that the same was taken up at his plantation or place of residence in the said county, and that the marks or brands thereof have not been altered since the taking up; and then such Justice shall take a particular and exact description in writing of the marks, brands, stature, colour, and age, of such horse, mare, or colt, together with the name of the taker up, and his place of abode, and such Justice is required immediately to issue his warrant to three disinterested freeholders of the neighbourhood, who, after taking an oath before him for that purpose, shall view and appraise such stray; which description and valuation shall, by such Justice, be transmitted to the clerk of the court of such county in twenty days after the same is taken, who shall enter the same in a book, to be by him kept for that purpose. And the taker-up shall pay to the clerk ten pounds of tobacco for making such entry, to be paid and collected in the same manner as his other fees are by law directed to be collected. And every person who shall hereafter take up any neat cattle, sheep, hog, or goat, shall cause the same to be viewed by a freeholder of the county where the same shall happen, and shall immediately go with such freeholder before a Justice of the said county, and make oath before him that the same was taken up at his plantation or place of residence in the said county, and that the marks or brands of such stray have not been altered since the taking up; and then such Justice shall take from the said freeholders, upon oath, a particular and exact description of the marks, brand, stature, colour, and age, of every such neat cattle, and the mark and colour of every such sheep, hog, or goat, and such Justice shall, in like manner, issue his warrant for the appraisement of such stray; which description and valuation shall, in like manner, be transmitted by such Justice to the clerk of his county, to be by him entered in the aforesaid book; and the taker up shall pay such clerk five pounds of tobacco for every head of neat cattle, and three pounds of tobacco for every sheep, hog, or goat, so entered, to be paid and collected as aforesaid; and every such clerk shall moreover cause a copy of every such description and valuation to be publicly affixed at the court-house of his county, on two several court days next after the same shall be transmitted to him. And for a reward for taking up, there shall be paid by the owner five shillings for every horse, mare, colt, or head of neat cattle, and one shilling for every sheep, hog, or goat.

*where they shall
be vested in the
taker-up,*

III. AND be it further enacted, by the authority aforesaid, that if no owner shall appear after notice twice published at the court-house, as aforesaid, the property thereof shall, immediately after such publication, be vested in the taker-up, where the valuation is under twenty shillings.

*or may be reclaim-
ed by the owner.
Stray valued to
20s. shall be ad-
vertised in the Vir-
ginia Gazette, and
may be recovered
by owner paying
reward, &c.*

IV. PROVIDED nevertheless, that the former owner thereof shall, at any time afterwards, have it in his option to demand and recover such stray, or the valuation money, deducting the reward for taking up, and the clerk's fees. And where the valuation amounts to twenty shillings, the taker-up shall, within one month after such appraisement, send to the printer a particular description of such stray or strays, together with the name of his county, and place of residence, certified by the clerk of his said county, to be advertised three times in the *Virginia Gazette,* for which the printer may demand and take two shillings for every horse, mare, colt, or head of neat cattle, mentioned in such advertisement for the first, and one shilling for every advertisement thereafter, and no more; and one shilling for every sheep, hog, or goat, so advertised. And if no person shall claim such stray or strays, within six months after such publication, the property shall be vested in the taker-up: But it shall and may be lawful for the former owner, at any time afterwards, upon proving his property, and paying the reward for taking up, and the clerk's and printer's fees, to demand and recover such stray or strays, or the valuation money, at the option of the said former owner. And every person taking up any stray horse, mare, or colt, and failing to carry the same immediately before some Justice as aforesaid, or if any other stray, failing to cause a particular description thereof to be given to a Justice, in manner aforesaid, in three days after taking up the same, or failing to send a description thereof to the printer, certified by the clerk, within the time, and according to the directions of this act, or making use of any such stray before the same shall be appraised, as aforesaid, shall, for every such offence, forfeit and pay to the informer the sum of ten pounds, to be recovered, with costs, in any court of record, wherein the same shall be cognizable; and moreover shall be liable to the action of the owner of such stray or strays, and, upon conviction, shall pay double damages.

*Taker-up failing
to carry stray be-
fore a Justice, &c.
or refusing it, sub-
ject to penalty, and
liable to action of
owner.*

*Proceedings in case
of vessels adrift,
taken up.*

V. AND be it further enacted, by the authority aforesaid, that if any person whatsoever, whether he be a freeholder, tenant for years, or otherwise, shall take up any boat, or other vessel, adrift, he shall, in like manner, cause the same to be viewed by some freeholder of the county where the same shall be taken up, and shall immediately go with such freeholder before some Justice of the county, and make oath when and where the same was taken up, and that the marks thereof have not been altered or defaced since the taking up; and then such Justice shall take from such freeholder, upon oath, an exact description of such vessel, and the burthen and built thereof, and thereupon the like proceedings shall be pursued, and the taker-up shall be entitled to the same rewards, and be subject to the same penalties, fines, and forfeitures, to be recovered and appropriated in the same manner as are herein before directed, prescribed, and appointed, with respect to stray horses.

*Stray dying, &c.
before claim, taker
up not answerable.
Who may not
take up a stray,
without being sub-
ject to penalty.*

VI. PROVIDED always, that if, after notice published, as aforesaid, any stray shall happen to die, or get away, before the owner shall claim and prove his or her right, the taker-up shall not be answerable for the same. And if any person, not being a freeholder, or tenant by lease for the term of three years at least, shall presume to take up any stray, or if any such freeholder or tenant for years shall take up any such stray, at any other place than on his own plantation, or at his place of residence, he or she shall, for every offence, forfeit and pay to the informer the sum of twenty shillings, recoverable, with costs, before any Justice of the county where the offence shall be committed: And upon failure of payment, or giving security for payment, within ten days after conviction, every such offender shall, by order of such Justice, receive twenty lashes on his or her bare back, well laid on.

VII. *PROVIDED always*, that the execution of this act shall be, and the same is hereby suspended, until his Majesty's approbation thereof shall be obtained.

Suspending clause.

C H A P. XIX.

An act to amend the act, entitled An act to amend the act for the better government of servants and slaves. (a)

I. WHEREAS by an act of the General Assembly made in the twenty second year of his late Majesty George the second, entitled *An act directing the trial of slaves committing capital crimes, and for the more effectually punishing conspiracies and insurrections of them, and for the better government of negroes, mulattoes, and Indians, bond or free,* the county courts within this dominion are empowered to punish outlying slaves who cannot be reclaimed, by dismembering such slaves, which punishment is often disproportioned to the offence, and contrary to the principles of humanity: *Be it therefore enacted, by the Governor, Council, and Burgesses, of this present General Assembly, and it is hereby enacted, by the authority of the same,* that it shall not be lawful for any county court to order and direct castration of any slave, except such slave shall be convicted of an attempt to ravish a white woman, in which case they may inflict such punishment; any thing in the said recited act to the contrary notwithstanding.

Castration of a slave, except for attempt to ravish a white woman, unlawful.

II. AND whereas the act passed in the fifth year of his present Majesty's reign, *(b)* entitled *An act to amend the act for the better government of servants and slaves,* as to so much thereof as relates to the method of taking up and proceeding with runaway servants and slaves, is found ineffectual, and it is necessary the same should be further amended:

III. BE it therefore enacted, by the authority aforesaid, that from and after the commencement of this act, the taker-up of every runaway servant or slave, who shall discover the name of his or her master or owner, shall immediately carry such servant or slave before a Justice of the Peace of the county where such servant or slave shall be taken up, to be examined; and if thereupon, and upon the oath of the taker-up, such servant or slave appears to be a runaway, the Justice shall grant the taker-up a certificate of his having made such oath, reciting his or her proper name and surname, the county of his or her residence, the name of the runaway, the proper name and surname of his or her owner, and the county where he or she resides, the time and place when and where the runaway was taken up, and the distance of miles, in the judgment of the Justice, from the place of residence of the owner, or from the house or quarter where the runaway was usually kept and upon delivery of such runaway, and producing the certificate as aforesaid, the taker-up shall be entitled to a reward of ten shillings for taking up, and sixpence per mile, mentioned in the certificate, to be paid by the owner; and upon such owner's neglecting or refusing to pay the said reward, the taker up may sue for and recover the same, with costs, either by warrant before a single Justice, where the reward shall not exceed twenty five shillings, or, where the reward shall exceed that sum, by petition or action, as the case may require, in any court of record within this colony.

Taker up of runaway servant &c. to carry him before a Justice, who shall grant a certificate.

Reward of taker-up; how to be recovered.

IV. *PROVIDED always, and be it further enacted, by the authority aforesaid,* that the taker up shall have it in his option either to convey such runaway to the owner or overseer of the plantation where such runaway is usually kept, as aforesaid, or to carry him or her to jail; and in the latter case the Justice shall issue his warrant, directed to the sheriff or jailer of the county wherein the runaway is taken up, commanding him to receive such runaway into his custody, and to commit him or her to prison, and the sheriff or jailer shall give the taker-up a receipt for the body of such runaway, which receipt the taker-up producing to the Justice, the Justice shall thereupon grant his certificate to entitle the taker up to the reward aforesaid, for taking up and conveying such runaway; and the sheriff or jailer shall forthwith cause notice of such commitment, with a description of the runaway, to be advertised in the *Virginia* ..tte three weeks; and if no owner shall appear, at the expiration of two months from the time of the commitment, such runaway shall be conveyed to the public jail, according to the directions of the act passed in the twenty-seventh year of his late Majesty *George* the second, entitled *An act for the better government of servants and slaves.*   *(c)*

Taker-up may convey runaway to owner, &c or carry him to jail.

Sheriff or jailer, by Justices warrant, to commit runaway, and give receipt, and advertise in the gazette.

V. *PROVIDED also,* that if the owner or overseer of such runaway shall be an inhabitant of the county where such runaway is taken up, the taker up shall, in that case, convey and deliver him or her to the owner or overseer as aforesaid, and shall not be at liberty to carry such runaway to the jail of the county, as is before directed.

Runaway to be carried to owner, &c. resident in the county where taken up.

VI. AND be it further enacted, by the authority aforesaid, that before any runaway shall be delivered out of custody of the sheriff or jailer, the person claiming such runaway shall pay down the reward aforesaid, for taking up, and the charge for advertising, with the fees for keeping and maintaining the runaway, as the same are now settled by law; and every sheriff or jailer receiving the reward aforesaid for taking up, and refusing or neglecting to pay the same, the taker-up may recover the same, with costs, by warrant, before a single Justice, where the reward shall not exceed twenty five shillings, or where the reward shall exceed that sum, then by petition or action, as the case may require, in any court of record within this colony.

Reward for taking up, &c. to be paid to sheriff, &c. recoverable by taker-up.

VII. *AND be it further enacted, by the authority aforesaid,* that where such runaway servant or slave cannot or will not declare the name of his or her owner, the same proceedings shall be pursued as are directed by the last recited act of Assembly.

How runaway, not declaring his name, to be dealt with.

VIII. AND whereas many owners of slaves, in consideration of stipulated wages to be paid by such slaves, licence them to go at large, and to trade as freemen, which is found to be a great encouragement to the commission of thefts and other evil practices by such slaves, in order to enable them to fulfil their agreements with their masters or owners: For prevention whereof, *Be it further enacted, by the authority aforesaid,* that from and after the commencement of this act, if any master or owner of a slave shall licence such slave to go at large, and trade as a freeman as aforesaid, the master or owner shall forfeit and pay the sum of ten pounds current money, for the use of the poor of that parish, where such slave shall be found going at large, and trading as aforesaid, to be recovered by the Churchwardens by action of debt,

Master licencing slave to go at large and trade, subject to penalty.

(a) See 22 Geo. II. (1748) chap. 31, of the edit. in 1769.
(b) 5 Geo. III. (1764) chap. 9, of the edit. in 1769.
(c) 27 Geo. II. (1753) chap. 2, of the edit. in 1769.

A. D. 1769.

in any court of record within this dominion. And if, after conviction, such slave shall be found so going at large, and trading, the master or owner shall again be liable to the like penalty, to be recovered and applied as aforesaid, and so as often after conviction as such slave shall be found so going at large, and trading.

Part of 5 Geo. III. chap. 9, repealed.

IX. AND be it further enacted, by the authority aforesaid, that so much of the said recited act, entitled *An act to amend the act for the better government of servants and slaves,* concerning the apprehending and conveying such runaway servants and slaves, and paying for the same, as is contrary to this act, shall be, and the same is hereby repealed and made void.

Suspending clause.

X. PROVIDED always, that the execution of this act shall be, and the same is hereby suspended, until his Majesty's approbation thereof shall be obtained.   *(a)*

CHAP. XX.

Private.

An act to oblige the owners of mills, hedges, or stops, on the rivers therein mentioned, to make openings or slopes therein for the passage of fish.

CHAP. XXI.

Expired.

An act for encouraging the making hemp.

CHAP. XXII.

Repealed.

An act for encouraging the making wine.

CHAP. XXIII.

Repealed.

An act to suspend the execution of an act entitled An act to amend an act entitled an act for the inspection of pork, beef, flour, tar, pitch, and turpentine.

CHAP. XXIV.

Executed.

An act for appointing commissioners to meet with commissioners, who are or may be appointed by the legislatures of the neighbouring colonies, to form and agree upon a general plan for the regulation of the Indian trade.

CHAP. XXV.

An act for appointing several new ferries, and for other purposes therein mentioned.

Ferries and rates of ferriage at certain places, for men, &c.

I. WHEREAS it is represented to this present General Assembly, that public ferries at the places hereafter mentioned will be of great advantage to travellers and others : *Be it therefore enacted, by the Governor, Council, and Burgesses, of this present General Assembly, and it is hereby enacted by the authority of the same,* that public ferries be constantly kept at the following places, and that the rates for passing the same shall be as follows : that is to say, from the land of *Benjamin Foreman,* in *Frederick* county, over *Potowmack* river, to the land of the right honourable lord *Baltimore,* in *Maryland,* the price for a man three pence three farthings, and the price for a horse the same; from the land of *Benjamin Howard,* in the county of *Buckingham,* across the *Fluvanna* river, to the land of *Neil Campbell,* in the county of *Albemarle,* the price for a man three pence, and the price for a horse the same; from the land of *William Simms,* in the county of *Halifax,* across *Staunton* river, to the land of *John Randolph,* in the county of *Charlotte,* the price for a man three pence, and the price for a horse the same; from the land of *John Nicholas,* in the county of *Buckingham,* across *Slate* river, to the land of the said *Nicholas,* opposite thereto, the price for a man three pence, and the price for a horse the same; from the land of *Harman Miller,* in the county of *Halifax,* across *Dan* river, to the land of *James Legrand,* opposite thereto, the price for a man three pence, and for a horse the same; from the land of *Thomas Aubrey,* in the county of *Loudoun,* across *Potowmack* river, to the land of *James Hook,* in *Maryland,* the price for a man three pence three farthings, and for a horse the same; from the land of *Daniel Cargill,* in the county of *Charlotte,* across *Staunton* river, to the land of *John Foushee,* in the county of *Halifax,* the price for a man three pence, and for a horse the same; from the land of *Richard Jones,* in the county of *Halifax,* across *Dan* river, to the land of the reverend *Miles Selden,* opposite thereto, the price for a man three pence, and for a horse the same. And for the transportation of wheel carriages, tobacco, cattle, and other

Carriages, &c.

beasts, at any of the ferries aforesaid, the ferry keepers may demand and take the following rates ; that is to say, for every coach, chariot, or waggon, and the driver thereof, the same as for six horses ; for every cart or four wheeled chaise, the same as for four horses ; for every two wheeled chaise or chair the same as for two horses ; for every hogshead of tobacco as for one horse ; for every head of neat cattle as for one horse; for every sheep, goat, or lamb, one fifth part of the ferriage of one horse ; and for every hog, one fourth part of the ferriage of one horse, according to the prices herein before settled at such ferries respectively, and no more. And if any of the said ferry keepers shall presume to demand or receive

Penalty on ferry keeper demanding more than legal rates.

County courts may appoint opposite ferries, &c.

from any person or persons whatsoever, any greater rates than is hereby allowed for the carriage or ferriage of any thing whatsoever, he, she, or they, for such offence, shall forfeit and pay to the party grieved the ferriage demanded or received, and ten shillings, to be recovered, with costs, before any Justice of the Peace, where the offence shall be committed. And where a ferry is by this act appointed on one side of a river, and none on the other side answerable thereto, it shall and may be lawful for the respective county courts to appoint an opposite ferry, and to allow the respective rates herein before directed : And such courts shall and may, and are hereby required to order and direct what boat or boats, and

Ferry keeper to enter into bond.

what number of hands shall be kept at each ferry respectively : And every such ferry keeper shall enter into

---

(a) See note to chap. 3, sect. 14.

bond in the manner directed by one act of Assembly, made in the twenty-second year of his late Majesty's reign, (a) entitled *An act for the settlement and regulation of ferries, and for dispatch of public expresses*, and shall be liable to the penalties thereby inflicted for any neglect or omission of their duty.

A. D. 1769.

II. AND whereas by an act of the General Assembly, passed in the seventh year of his present Majesty's reign, (b) the rates of ferriage at *Swan's Point*, *James-town*, and *Crouche's* creek, were increased, which hath been since found burthensome to divers inhabitants of this colony: *Be it therefore enacted, by the authority aforesaid*, that so much of the act of the General Assembly, entitled *An act for increasing the rates of ferriage at Swan's Point*, James-town, *and Crouche's creek, and for other purposes therein mentioned*, as relates to the increase of the said ferriage be, and the same is hereby repealed, and made void.

III. AND whereas by an act of the General Assembly, passed in the twenty-second year of his late Majesty's reign, ferries were established from *Tappahannock* town, in the county of *Essex*, to the land of *Landon Carter*, Esq; in the county of *Richmond*; from *Hackley's* land, on the north side of *Rappahannock* river, to the land of *Richard Corbin*, Esq; in the county of *Caroline*: from the land of *William Lowry*, in the county of *Essex*, to the land of *Benjamin Rust*, in the county of *Richmond*, and from the said *Rust's* to the said *Lowry's*; and from the land of *Richard Eppes*, at *City Point*, in the county of *Prince George*, to the ship-landing at *Shirley Hundred*, in the county of *Charles City*, and from the said ship-landing to the *City Point*, which said several ferries are now become useless and inconvenient: *Be it therefore enacted by the authority aforesaid*, that so much of the act of the General Assembly, entitled *An act for the settlement and regulation of ferries, and dispatch of public expresses*, as relates to the appointment of the said several last mentioned ferries be, and the same is hereby repealed and made void.

Former ferries discontinued.

IV. *AND be it further enacted*, that so much of the act of General Assembly made in the fourth year of the reign of his present Majesty, entitled *An act for exempting the inhabitants of* Elizabeth City *county, and also the Ministers and other parishoners of* Suffolk *in* Nansemond, *and of* Antrim *parish, in* Halifax, *from the payment of ferriage, and for other purposes therein mentioned*, as exempts all the inhabitants of the said parish of *Suffolk*, except the Minister thereof, from the payment of ferriage over *Nansemond* river, be and is repealed.

Part of 4 Geo. III. (1764) chap. 11, repealed.

V. AND whereas doubts and disputes have often arisen, to the great delay and hindrance of passengers, about the right which a person appointed to keep a ferry on one side of a river or creek hath to take in a fare on the opposite shore, and to receive the pay for ferrying over: *Be it therefore enacted, by the authority aforesaid*, that it shall and may be lawful for any keeper of a ferry to take into his boat or boats, any passenger or passengers, carriage, horses and cattle of any kind whatsoever, on either side, to convey them over, and to receive the ferriage for the same; any law, usage, or custom, to the contrary, in any wise notwithstanding.

Ferry-keepers may bring passengers, &c. from opposite shore and receive the ferriage.

CHAP. XXVI.

An act to regulate the inoculation of the small-pox within this Colony. (c)

I. WHEREAS the wanton introduction of the small-pox into this colony by inoculation, when the same was not necessary, hath, of late years, proved a nuisance to several neighbourhoods, by disturbing the peace and quietness of many of his Majesty's subjects, and exposing their lives to the infection of that mortal distemper, which, from the situation and circumstances of the colony, they would otherwise have little reason to dread: To prevent which for the future, *Be it enacted, by the Governor, Council, and Burgesses, of this present General Assembly, and it is hereby enacted, by the authority of the same*, that if any person or persons whatsoever, shall wilfully, or designedly, after the first day of *September* next ensuing, presume to import or bring into this colony, from any country or place whatever, the small-pox, or any variolous or infectious matter of the said distemper, with a purpose to inoculate any person or persons whatever, or by any means whatever, to propagate the said distemper within this colony, he, or she, so offending, shall forfeit and pay the sum of one thousand pounds, for every offence so committed; one moiety whereof shall be to the informer, and the other moiety to the Churchwardens of the parish where the offence shall be committed, for the use of the poor of the said parish; to be recovered, with costs, by action of debt, bill, plaint, or information, in any court of record within this dominion.

Penalty for importing matter to inoculate the small-pox.

II. BUT forasmuch as the inoculation of the small pox may, under peculiar circumstances, be not only a prudent but necessary means of securing those who are unavoidably exposed to the danger of taking the distemper in the natural way, and for this reason it is judged proper to tolerate it, under reasonable restrictions and regulations:

III. BE it therefore enacted, *by the authority aforesaid*, that from and after the said first day of *September* next, if any person shall think him or herself, his or her family, exposed to the immediate danger of catching the said distemper, such person may give notice thereof to the Sheriff of any county, or to the Mayor or chief Magistrate of any city or corporation, and the said Sheriff, Mayor, or chief Magistrate, shall, immediately, and without loss of time, summon all the acting Magistrates of the said county, city, or borough, to meet at the most convenient time and place in the said county, city, or borough, and the said Magistrates, or such of them as shall be present, being assembled, shall consider whether, upon the whole circumstances of the case, inoculation may be prudent or necessary, or dangerous to the health and safety of the neighbourhood; and thereupon either grant a licence for such inoculation, under such restrictions and regulations as they shall judge necessary and proper, or prohibit the same, as to them, or a majority of them, shall seem expedient.

Inoculation, necessary, tolerated under restrictions and regulations.

IV. *AND be it further enacted, by the authority aforesaid*, that if any person or persons shall inoculate, or procure inoculation of the small-pox to be performed within this colony, without obtaining a licence in the manner before directed, or shall not conform to the rules and regulations prescribed by such Justices, he, she, or they, shall forfeit and pay respectively, for every such offence, the sum of one hundred pounds: one moiety whereof shall be to the informer, and the other moiety to the Churchwardens of the parish wherein such offence shall be committed, for the use of the poor of the said parish; to be recovered, with costs, by action of debt, bill, plaint, or information, in any court of record within this dominion. And moreover it shall and may be lawful for any Justice of the Peace, upon information given to him, upon oath, to issue his warrant against any person so offending, and upon sufficient proof, before him made, to cause such offender to give security, in such reasonable penalty as such Justice shall think fit, for his or her good behaviour, and, upon failure to give such security, to commit him or her to the jail of his county, there to be confined until such security is given.

Penalty for inoculating without licence, &c.

(a) 22 Geo. II (1748) chap. 11, of the edit. in 1769.
(b) 7 Geo. III (1766) chap. 25, of the edit. in 1769.
(c) See October Sess. 1777, chap. 5.

Expences incur-
red in checking
finall-pox, or in
carrying on inocu-
lation, how to be
defrayed.

V. AND whereas checking of the progress of the said distemper, where it may accidentally break out, or the regulations which may be established for carrying on inoculation, may be attended with some expence: *Be it therefore enacted, by the authority aforesaid,* that it shall and may be lawful for the Justices of the court of every county, at the time of laying their levy, and for the Mayor, Recorder, Aldermen, and Common-Council, of any city or borough, at such time as they shall judge most convenient, to levy on the tithable persons in their said county, city or borough, so much tobacco or money as will be sufficient to defray the expences necessarily incurred for the purposes aforesaid, in any such county, city, or borough.

Penalty upon
Magiftrates, &c.
for breach of duty.

VI. AND *be it further enacted, by the authority aforesaid,* that if any Sheriff, Mayor, or chief Magistrate, shall, upon application to him made, in manner aforesaid, refuse, or unreasonably delay, to summon the Magistrates of any county, city, or borough, for the purpose aforesaid, or if any Magistrate so summoned, shall refuse, or neglect to attend according to such summon, every such Sheriff, Mayor, or chief Magistrate, shall forfeit the sum of one hundred pounds, upon his refusing or neglecting to give such notice, without reasonable excuse, and every other Magistrate so refusing or neglecting, without reasonable excuse, shall forfeit and pay the sum of five pounds, to the person aggrieved: to be recovered, with costs, by action of debt, in any court of record within this dominion.

CHAP. XXVII.

An act for the relief of parishes from such charges as may arise from bastard children born within the same. (a)

Method of pro-
ceeding to compel
the fathers of baf-
tard children, born
of free fingle wo-
men, to indemnify
the parifh from the
charge of their
maintenance.

I. WHEREAS the laws now in force are not sufficient to provide for the security and indemnifying the parishes from the great charges frequently arising from children begotten and born out of lawful matrimony: For remedy whereof, *Be it enacted by the Governor, Council, and Burgesses, of this present General Assembly, and it is hereby enacted by the authority of the same,* that from and after the passing of this act, if any single woman, not being a servant or slave, shall be delivered of a bastard child which shall be chargeable, or likely to become chargeable, to any parish, and shall, upon examination to be taken in writing, upon oath, before any Justice of the Peace of the county wherein such parish shall lie, charge any person, not being a servant, with being the father of such bastard child, it shall and may be lawful for any Justice of the Peace of the county wherein the person so charged shall be a resident or inhabitant, upon application made to him by the Churchwardens of the parish wherein such child shall be born, or by any one of them, to issue his warrant for the immediate apprehending the person so charged as aforesaid, and for bringing him before such Justice, or before any other Justice of the Peace of the county wherein he is a resident or inhabitant; and the Justice before whom such person shall be brought is hereby authorized and required to commit the person so charged as aforesaid to the common jail of his county, unless he shall enter into a recognizance, with sufficient security, in the sum of ten pounds, upon condition to appear at the next court to be held for such county, and to abide by and perform such order or orders as shall be made by the said court; and if, upon the circumstances of the case, such court shall adjudge the person so charged to be the father of such bastard child, and that such child is likely to become chargeable to the parish, they shall, and may, by their discretion, take order for keeping such bastard child, by charging the father with the payment of money or tobacco for the maintenance of such child, in such manner, and in such proportions, as they shall think meet and convenient, and for such time as such child is likely to become chargeable to the parish, and no longer. And the father of such child shall enter into a recognizance, with sufficient securities, before the said court, in such sum as the said court, in their discretion, shall think fit, payable to his Majesty, his heirs and successors, to observe and perform such order or orders of the court as aforesaid. And if the father, charged with the maintenance of such bastard child, as aforesaid, shall make default, and not pay the money or tobacco so as aforesaid charged upon him by order of the said court, to the Churchwardens of the parish, for the maintenance of such child, the court before whom such recognizance was entered into, shall, from time to time, upon the motion of the Churchwardens of the said parish, or any one of them, enter up judgment and award execution for the money or tobacco in such order or orders mentioned, as the same shall become due, against the said father and his securities, their executors or administrators; provided ten days notice be given to the parties against whom such motion is made before the making thereof. And if the father of such child shall refuse to enter into recognizance as aforesaid, such father shall be committed by the said court to the common jail of the county, there to remain, without bail or mainprize, until he shall enter into such recognizance as aforesaid, or until he shall discharge himself by taking the oath of an insolvent debtor, and delivering in a schedule of his estate in manner directed, by the laws now in force, for debtors in execution* (and which estate shall, by order of the court, be applied towards indemnifying the parish as aforesaid) or until the Churchwardens of the parish concerned shall otherwise consent to his discharge.

* *See* 22 Geo.
II. (1748) *chap.* 8.
of the edit. in 1769,
fect. 24.

Woman not com-
pellable before de-
livery, to be exa-
mined, &c.

II. PROVIDED *always,* that it shall not be lawful for any Justice or Justices of the Peace, to send for any woman whatsoever, before she shall be delivered, in order to her being examined concerning her pregnancy, or to compel her to answer any questions relating thereto, before her delivery.

Penalty upon her
for having a baf-
tard;

not to be whipped,
&c.

III. AND *be it further enacted, by the authority aforesaid,* that if any single woman, not being a servant, shall be delivered of a bastard child, she shall be liable to pay the sum of twenty shillings current money of *Virginia,* to the Churchwardens of the parish wherein she shall be delivered; to be recovered, with costs, before a Justice of the Peace, and on such judgment execution may issue as in other cases: But the persons so convicted shall not be liable to be whipped for failing to make payment, or to give security for such fine, any law to the contrary notwithstanding; which fine, recovered as aforesaid, shall be applied by the Churchwardens to the use of the poor of the parish.

Baftard children
to be bound ap-
prentices, how to
be maintained, &c.

IV. AND *be it further enacted, by the authority aforesaid,* that every such bastard child shall be bound apprentice by the Churchwardens of the parish, for the time being, wherein such child shall be born, every male until he shall attain the age of twenty-one years, and every female until she shall attain the age of eighteen years, and no longer; and the master or mistress of every such apprentice shall find and provide for him or her diet, clothes, lodging, and accommodations fit and necessary, and shall teach, or cause him or her to be taught to read and write, and at the expiration of his or her apprenticeship, shall pay every such apprentice the like allowance as is by law* appointed for servants, by indenture or custom, and on refusal, shall be compellable thereto in like manner. And if, upon complaint made to the county court, it shall appear that any such apprentice is ill used, or not taught the trade or profession to which he or she may be bound, it shall be lawful for such court to remove and bind him or her to such other person or persons as they shall think fit.

* 27 Geo. II.
(1753) *chap.* 2, *of*
the edit. in 1769,
fect. 8.

(a). *See* 1 Geo. II. (1727) *chap.* 1 *of the edit. in* 1769.

V. AND whereas by an act of Assembly made in the twenty seventh year of the reign of King *George* the second, entitled *An act for the better government of servants and slaves*, it is amongst other things enacted,* if any woman servant shall be delivered of a bastard child, within the time of her service, that, in recompence for the loss and trouble occasioned her master or mistress thereby, she shall, for every such offence, serve her said master or owner one whole year, after her time, by indenture, custom, or former order of court, shall be expired, or pay her master or owner one thousand pounds of tobacco; and the reputed father, if free, shall give security to the Churchwardens of the parish to maintain the child, and keep the parish indemnified, or be compelled thereto, by order of the county court, upon the complaint of the Churchwardens. And whereas it frequently happens that convict servants are delivered of such bastard children, who, being disabled to give testimony, cannot be examined, nor for that reason can the reputed father of such bastard child be discovered, and the parish indemnified from the charge of its maintenance: For remedy whereof,

A. D. 1760.
* *Sect. 13.*

VI. BE it enacted, that where any convict servant woman shall be delivered of a bastard child, during the time of her service, the master or owner of such servant shall be obliged to maintain such child, or be compelled thereto by the county court, on complaint of the Churchwardens, and, in consideration of such maintenance, shall be entitled to the service of such child, if a male until he shall arrive to the age of twenty one years, if a female until she shall arrive to the age of eighteen years.

Master of convict servant women to maintain their bastard children, and be entitled to their service till certain ages;

VII. *PROVIDED always*, that such master or owner shall find and provide for such child, the like accommodations, education, and freedom dues, and shall be compelled to answer his or her complaint made to the county court, for default therein, or for ill usage, in like manner, as is before directed in the case of other apprentices.

and provide for their education &c.

VIII. *AND be it further enacted*, that all and every act and acts, clause and clauses, heretofore made, as to so much thereof as is contrary to this act, be, and the same are hereby repealed.

Repealing clause.

C H A P. XXVIII.

An act to make provision for the support and maintenance of Ideots, Lunatics, and other persons of unsound minds. (a)

I. WHEREAS several persons of insane and disordered minds, have been frequently found wandering in different parts of this colony, and no certain provision having been yet made either towards effecting a cure of those whose cases are not become quite desperate, nor for restraining others who may be dangerous to society: *Be it therefore enacted, by the Governour, Council, and Burgesses of this present General Assembly, and it is hereby enacted, by the authority of the same,* that the honourable *John Blair, William Nelson, Thomas Nelson, Robert Carter,* and *Peyton Randolph*, Esquires, and *Robert Carter Nicholas, John Randolph, Benjamin Waller, John Blair,* jun. *George Wythe, Dudley Digges,* jun. *Lewis Burwell, Thomas Nelson,* jun. *Thomas Everard,* and *John Tazewell*, Esquires, be, and they are hereby constituted trustees for founding and establishing a public hospital, for the reception of such persons as shall from time to time, according to the rules and orders established by this act, be sent thereto. And the said trustees shall be called and known by the name and style of the court of directors of the public hospital, for persons of insane and disordered minds.

Trustees appointed.

To found a public hospital for reception of ideots, &c.

Their style;

II. AND for the better and more regular ordering the business of the said hospital, the said directors shall, at their first meeting, proceed to the choice of a president, who, with any six of the other directors, shall hold a court for the despatch of business, and in case of the absence, sickness, or death of the said president, the other members of the said court may choose another president, either perpetual or temporary, as the exigency of affairs may require; and in case of the death, resignation, or absence out of the colony for the space of two years of one or more of the said directors, the president, for the time being, and the rest of the directors, continuing in office, shall and may proceed to the choice of other fit and able persons, to supply all such vacancies.

To choose a president,

and supply vacancies happening by death, &c.

III. *AND be it further enacted, by the authority aforesaid,* that the said court of directors be, and they are hereby impowered to purchase a piece or parcel of land, not exceeding four acres, the most healthy in situation that can be procured, and as convenient as may be to the city of *Williamsburg*, and to contract for the building thereon a commodious house or houses, fit for the reception and accommodation of such disordered persons as are described by this act, and to provide a proper keeper and matron of the said hospital, with necessary nurses and guards, and, as occasion may require, to call on any physicians or surgeons for the assistance and relief of such poor patients, and to provide all necessaries for their comfortable support and maintenance, and in general, from time to time, to make and ordain all such rules, orders, and regulations, for the better establishing and governing such hospital, as to them shall seem fit and necessary. And for the better and more regular determining who are the proper objects of this act,

To purchase ground, &c. build houses, provide keeper &c. employ physicians, &c.

and ordain rules.

IV. BE it further enacted, by the authority aforesaid, that any Magistrate of the quorum, in any county within this colony, or any chief Magistrate of any city or borough, either upon his own knowledge, or on proper information, that any such disordered person is going at large in his county, city, or borough, shall, and he is hereby required to issue his warrant to the sheriff, or any one of the constables of the said county, city, or borough, commanding him to bring such person before him, or any other Justice of the quorum, and any other two Magistrates, which three Magistrates being assembled, may examine the said person supposed to be disordered in his or her senses, and take such evidence in writing, touching his or her insanity, and the causes of it, as they can procure; and if it shall appear expedient and necessary to such Magistrates, or a majority of them, they shall forthwith, by warrant under their hands and seals, transmit such disordered person, together with the depositions taken before them, either with or without a guard, as may seem necessary, to the public hospital, to be delivered to the keeper of the said hospital, who shall give a receipt for such person, and immediately give notice to the president of the directors, who shall in convenient time summon his court to consider what is further necessary to be done; and if it shall appear to such court, that such person is a proper object of this act, they shall enter his name in a book to be kept for this purpose, and pursue such measures as his or her case may require.

Who to be received into the hospital,

and how to be sent thither;

received, and registered.

V. *PROVIDED always*, if any friend of such person will appear before such Magistrates, or such court of directors, and give sufficient security that proper care shall be taken of such person, and that he or she shall be restrained, or secured from going at large till he or she is restored to his or her senses, it shall and may be lawful for such Justices, or such court, to deliver such insane person to his or her friend.

Person of insane mind may be delivered to a friend, giving security &c.

(a) See (1772) chap. 46, and acts in 1777, 1779, 1781, and 1782.

D

Officer's allowance for removing.

VI. *AND be it further enacted, by the authority aforesaid,* that the sheriff or other officer conveying such disordered person to the public hospital, shall receive such compensation for his trouble and expences as to the court of directors shall seem reasonable, having regard to the quality of such person.

Money to be paid for purchasing and building, and for support of ideots, &c.

VII. *AND be it further enacted, by the authority aforesaid,* that the Treasurer of this colony for the time being is hereby empowered and required to pay, upon the Governor's warrant, to the court of directors, for purchasing the land, building the hospital, and other incidental charges, any sum or sums of money, not exceeding the sum of twelve hundred pounds, and for each person removed, to be maintained and supported in the said hospital, any sum not exceeding twenty five pounds *per annum.*

Persons of unsound minds, having estate may be removed to the hospital,

VIII. AND whereas it may happen, that some persons may fall into the unhappy circumstances described by this act, whose estates may be sufficient to defray the expence of their support and maintenance in the said hospital, where they may be more securely kept and managed, and with much less anxiety to their friends: *BE it further enacted, by the authority aforesaid,* that it shal and may be lawful for the court of any county, city, or borough, within this colony, upon application to them made by the friend or guardian of any such insane or disordered person, to appoint three or more of their members to inquire, upon oath to be taken before such court, into the state and condition of such person, and also into the circumstances of his or her estate; and if, upon the report of the person so appointed, it shall appear to such court necessary or expedient, that such person should be placed in the said hospital, the said court is hereby empowered and required to order and direct such person to be forthwith removed thereto, and at the same time to settle the allowance to be made to the said hospital for such person's support and maintenance out of his or her estate, having regard to the neat profits thereof.

and received by the trustees, who may ordain rules for their government, and allowances out of the estate.
Trustees to lay their accounts before the General Assembly.
When a person taken into the hospital may be discharged.

IX. *AND be it further enacted, by the authority aforesaid,* that the said court of directors are hereby empowered and required to receive such person into the said hospital, and, from time to time. to make and ordain such rules and orders for the better government of such person, according to his or her quality, and the allowance made out of his or her estate, as to them shall seem necessary or expedient. And the said court of directors are hereby directed and required to keep distinct and proper accounts of the expenditure of all such monies which shall be paid into their hands, to be laid before the General Assembly, when the same shall be called for.

X. *AND be it further enacted, by the authority aforesaid,* that if any person who shall be taken into the said hospital, shall recover his or her perfect senses, so that he or she, in the opinion of the said court of directors, may be safely released, it shall and may be lawful for the said court to discharge such person, giving him or her a proper certificate thereof.

Continuance.

XI. *AND be it further enacted, by the authority aforesaid,* that this act shall continue and be in force for and during the term of five years, and from thence to the end of the next session of Assembly.

C H A P.   XXIX.

An act to prevent the exorbitant exactions of the collectors of the county and parish levies.

Recital.

I. WHEREAS many of the inhabitants of this colony do not make tobacco to pay their levies, and others are so remote from the public warehouses, that they cannot conveniently carry their tobacco to be inspected before the tenth day of *April* yearly *(a)* when distress may be made for such levies, whereby such persons are subject to great oppression from the sheriffs and other collectors, who exact an unreasonable and exorbitant price for such levies in money, and afterwards purchase transfer tobacco at an under rate, to pay the county and parish creditors, taking to themselves the whole gain they so unjustly extort from the people: For remedy whereof, *Be it enacted, by the Governor, Council, and Burgesses, of this present General Assembly, and it is hereby enacted, by the authority of the same,* that from and after the first day of *August* next, all allowances now directed to be levied by the county courts, for the secretary, clerks, and sheriffs, for public and other services, be levied and assessed in money, in lieu of tobacco, after the rate of two pence *per* pound; and all contracts hereafter to be made by any county court or vestry shall be made payable in money, and such courts and vestries shall lay their levies in money, and proportion the same upon the tithable persons within their counties and parishes; but such courts and vestries respectively shall also, at the same time, settle what quantity of tobacco may be paid for each tithable, in lieu of the said money levy, and it shall and may be lawful for all persons chargeable with such county and parish levies to pay the same in money or tobacco, at their option, according to such proportions; and if any person chargeable with such levies shall neglect or refuse to pay the same to the sheriffs or other collectors, in money or tobacco as aforesaid, before the tenth day of *May* yearly, such sheriffs or collectors shall and may distrain for the same, in manner as is now directed by law.

Allowances to be levied by county courts for secretary &c shall be levied and assessed in money for tobacco at 2 d. per lb. and contracts by courts and vestries shall be payable in money, and the levies may be paid in money, or tobacco, to be rated by the courts or vestries, and shall be collected before 10th of May.

Distress shall be sold for money.

II. *PROVIDED always,* that any distress taken and sold for such levies, shall be sold for money.

Sheriff, &c. shall in June lay an account before the court of his collection; and sell the tobacco and pay the money to the creditors.
Penalty upon sheriff, &c. refusing or delaying to pay.

III. *AND be it further enacted, by the authority aforesaid,* that every sheriff or collector shall, at the court held for his county, in the month of *June* yearly, or if there shall be no court in that month, then at the next succeeding court, lay before the court an account, upon oath, of all tobacco and money which he shall have received for levies, expressing in such list of whom the same was received; and after such account exhibited, and oath made, such sheriff or other collector shall sell all the tobacco by him received at public auction, at the door of the courthouse, between the hours of two and four, and shall, within ten days after such sale, pay each creditor their respective demands in money; and if any sheriff or other collector shall refuse or delay to make payment accordingly, when required, it shall be lawful for the court of his county, and they are hereby authorised and required, upon the motion of any creditor unpaid, to give judgment for the amount of any such claim, if the same exceeds twenty five shillings, together with costs, and thereon to award execution; provided such sheriff or collector have ten days previous notice of such motion; and if such claim be of the value of twenty five shillings, or under, the same shall be recoverable before any Justice of the Peace, in the same manner as small debts are now recovered.

Tobacco selling for more or less than the price estimated, how the sheriff shall be reimbursed or account for surplus.

IV. *PROVIDED always,* that if the tobacco shall sell for less than the price estimated as aforesaid by the court or vestry when the levy was laid, the deficiency shall be levied for the sheriff or collector at the laying of the next levy; and if the tobacco shall sell for more than such estimate, the county and parish, respectively, shall take credit for the same, in the hands of the sheriff, or collector, at the laying of the next levy.

(a) See 5. Geo. III (1764) chap. 4, of the edit. in 1769, sect. 56.

A. D. 1769.

V. *AND be it further enacted, by the authority aforesaid*, that if any sheriff or other collector shall fail to account for and sell the tobacco by him received as aforesaid, such sheriff or other collector shall be answerable to each creditor for his full demand, to be recovered as aforesaid, and shall moreover be chargeable to the county or parish for the full value of the tobacco by him received, accounting for the whole levies (insolvents excepted) as if the same had been wholly paid in tobacco, to be recovered, with costs, by and in the names of the Justices and vestrymen respectively, in any court of record within this dominion, upon motion as aforesaid, to and for the use of their county or parish respectively, to be applied in discharge of their next levy; and if it shall appear to the court upon the account, to be rendered as aforesaid, or by the oaths of two or more credible witnesses, that any sheriff or collector hath demanded or received a greater price for tobacco from any person chargeable therewith than the price so as aforesaid proportioned by the court or vestry, such court shall and may, and they are hereby authorized and required immediately to give judgment, and award execution against the estate of such sheriff or collector, for double the value of such overplus and costs, in favour of the person aggrieved.

Sheriff, &c. failing to account for and sell the tobacco, what he shall be answerable for; demanding more than the price estimated, subject to penalty.

VI. *PROVIDED always*, that nothing in this act shall be construed to extend to the salary of any Minister now received, or hereafter to be received, into any parish within this colony, who is or shall be entitled to receive their salary in tobacco. But if any Minister shall, at the laying of the parish levy, agree with his vestry to receive his salary in money, in lieu of tobacco, such vestry shall and may, and they are hereby authorized and required to make such agreement with their Ministers, and levy the same accordingly; and every collector shall be answerable to such Minister in the same manner as to other creditors aforesaid; and if such Ministers shall not choose to enter into such agreement, the vestry shall levy so much money, as in their judgment will be sufficient, and shall direct their Churchwardens or collector to purchase tobacco at some of the warehouses, the notes of which are directed to pass in payment of levies in such parish; and if the Churchwardens or collector shall fail to pay such tobacco to their Minister, by the time aforesaid, it shall and may be lawful for the court of the county where such Minister shall reside, and they are hereby authorized and required to give judgment against the Churchwardens or collector for such tobacco and costs, upon the motion of the said Minister.

Minister not obliged to receive money for his salary; but may agree to do so; and in that case, the money shall be levied, &c.

If no agreement, money to be levied to purchase tobacco.

VII. *PROVIDED always*, that such Churchwardens or collectors shall have ten days previous notice of such motion.

VIII. *PROVIDED also*, that nothing in this act contained, shall be construed to extend to alter the rate of tobacco in such counties, in which the inhabitants thereof are now allowed to discharge the same in money for tobacco, at certain prices by law directed.

Rates of tobacco settled by former acts not altered. See 27 Geo II. chap. 3. 3 Geo. II. chap. 5. 34 Geo. II. chap. 1.

IX. *AND be it further enacted, by the authority aforesaid*, that all and every other act and acts, clause and clauses, heretofore made, contrary to the purview of this act, shall be, and are hereby repealed.

X. *AND be it further enacted*, that this act shall continue and be in force from the passing thereof for three years, and from thence to the end of the next session of Assembly.

Continuance.

XI. *PROVIDED always*, that the execution of this act shall be, and is hereby suspended until his Majesty's approbation thereof shall be obtained. *(a)*

Suspending clause.

CHAP. XXX.

An act to amend an act, entitled An act against stealing hogs.

I. WHEREAS the act of Assembly now in force against stealing hogs hath been found defective, in that the offenders cannot be ruled to give special bail, and, being generally people of no property, do, on the commencement of suits, remove away, leaving the prosecutor to pay the costs, to the great discouragement of such prosecutions: For remedy whereof,

II. BE it enacted, by the Governor, Council, and Burgesses, of this present General Assembly, and it is hereby enacted by the authority of the same, that from and after the first day of October next, in all suits to be brought, or informations filed, against any persons, not being a slave, for hog-stealing, it shall be lawful for the court to rule the defendant to give special bail, and to commit him or her to prison, until he or she shall give such bail; any law to the contrary notwithstanding.

In prosecution for hog-stealing, defendant may be ruled to give special bail.

CHAP. XXXI.

An act to continue an act, entitled An act for regulating the practice of Attornies.

Expired.

CHAP. XXXII.

An act to compel persons to find security for payment of costs in certain cases.

I. WHEREAS divers litigious persons have, of late, preferred petitions to the Governor or Commander in Chief for grants of lands, under pretence that they were forfeited for non-payment of his Majesty's quitrents, or for want of seating and planting, which petitions are heard in the General Court; others have entered caveats in the Secretary's office against the issuing out of patents to those who have surveyed lands, in order to the obtaining such patents, pretending that the rules of government have not been complied with, in the progress of making and returning the surveys, which caveats are heard before the Governor and Council; and others have causelessly procured indictments to be preferred to the Grand Juries for assaults and batteries, and other offences, not capital; in defending which several proceedings the defendants are often put to great expence, which they cannot be reimbursed, although the complaint shall appear groundless, the person prosecuting the same being either unable, or not subject, to repay such costs: For remedy whereof, Be it enacted, by the Governor, Council, and Burgesses, of this present General Assembly, and it is hereby enacted by the authority of the same, that upon the determination of any caveat, now depending, or hereafter to be entered and heard, before the Governor or Commander in Chief, and the Council of this colony, it shall be lawful for the said Governor and Council to award costs (to be settled by such person as they shall appoint for that purpose,

Recital.

Governor, &c. may award costs to defendants in caveats;

A. D. 1769.

And county courts may give judgments for them on motion.

Governor, &c. may rule petitioners in caveats, and for lapsed lands; and prosecutors of certain indictments to find security for costs.

and by them approved) to the defendant in such caveat, in case he shall prevail, and upon a certificate thereof, it shall be lawful for the court of the county, in which the party resides, against whom such costs shall be awarded, upon motion of the other party, to enter judgment for the amount of such costs, with the costs of the motion, and thereon to award execution; provided that the person or persons, against whom such judgment is entered, have ten days previous notice of such motion. And in all such caveats it shall be lawful for the Governor and Council, upon good cause to them shewn, to rule the person entering the same to find security for payment of costs; and if such person or persons shall fail to give security accordingly, such caveat shall be dismissed, with costs. And in all petitions for lapsed land and indictments as aforesaid, now depending, or hereafter to be brought or prosecuted, it shall be lawful for the court, before whom the same shall be depending, upon good cause to them shewn, to compel the petitioner or prosecutor to find security for payment of the costs; and if such petitioner or prosecutor should fail to give security accordingly, the petition or indictment shall be dismissed, with costs.

II. AND whereas divers such litigious persons have given notice to the proprietors of lands, to survey the same, under pretence of their being surplus lands within the bounds of their grants, in order to obtain patents for such surplus lands, according to the directions of an act passed in the twenty-second year of the reign of King *George* the second, entitled *An act for settling the titles and bounds of lands, and for preventing unlawful hunting and ranging (a)* and when such lands have been surveyed at considerable expence, and found to contain no more than the quitrents had been paid for, the person giving notice was wholly unable to repay the charges of survey, to which he is made liable by the said act.

Person not obliged to survey his lands upon notice, unless bond for payment of costs be tendered.

III. BE it therefore further enacted, that from and after the first day of *August* next, no person shall be obliged to survey his land, upon notice as aforesaid; nor shall the person, giving such notice, derive to himself any advantage therefrom unless, at the time of giving the same, he or she shall tender to the person, to whom the notice is given, a bond, with good and sufficient security, for repaying the charges of survey, in case the lands shall be found to contain no more than the quantity for which quitrents have been usually paid.

C H A P. XXXIII.

Expired.

An act for further continuing and amending the act, entitled An act for increasing the rewards for killing wolves, within certain counties, to be paid by the respective counties wherein the services shall be performed.

C H A P. XXXIV.

Expired.

An act for destroying crows and squirrels in certain counties therein mentioned.

C H A P. XXXV.

Executed.

An act to appoint Commissioners to state and settle the damages done by the late storm in several warehouses.

C H A P. XXXVI.

An act to repeal an act of the General Assembly exempting the inhabitants of Mecklenburg *county from the payment of ferriage on certain days.*

I. WHEREAS by an act of the General Assembly passed in the seventh year of his present Majesty's reign, entitled *An act for exempting the inhabitants of* Mecklenburg *county, and also the Minister and other parishioners of* St. James's *parish, in the said county, from the payment of ferriage on* Sundays, court days, and on the days appointed for general musters, the inhabitants of *Mecklenburg* county were exempted from the payment of ferriage on certain days, and the court of the said county were empowered and required to contract and agree with the ferry keepers for an annual allowance to be paid them, which was directed to be levied upon the people.

7 Geo. III. (1765) chap. 37, repealed.

II. AND whereas it is represented to this present General Assembly, that the said act is burthensome to the inhabitants of the said county, and no ways expedient: Be it therefore enacted, by the Governor, Council, and Burgesses, of this present General Assembly, and it is hereby enacted by the authority of the same, that the said act, and all and every the clause or clauses therein contained, shall be, and the same are hereby repealed.

C H A P. XXXVII.

An act for exempting free negro, mulatto, and Indian *women, from the payment of levies.*

I. WHEREAS by an act of the General Assembly passed in the twenty-second year of the reign of his late Majesty *George* the second, entitled *An act concerning tithables,* it is among other things enacted, *that all free negro, mulatto, and* Indian women, of the age of fifteen years, except *Indians* tributary to this government, and all wives of free negroes, mulattoes, and *Indians,* except as is before excepted, should be, and are thereby declared tithables, and chargeable for defraying the public, county, and parish levies, of this colony and dominion, which is found very burthensome to such negroes, mulattoes, and *Indians,* and is moreover derogatory of the rights of free born subjects: For remedy whereof, Be it enacted, by the Governor, Council, and Burgesses, of this present General Assembly, and it is hereby enacted, by the authority of the same, that from and after the ninth day of *June* next, all free negro, mulatto, and *Indian* women, and all wives other than slaves, of free negroes, mulattoes, and *Indians,* shall be, and are hereby exempted from being listed as tithables, and from the payment of any public, county, or parish levies.

* 22 Geo. II. (1748) chap. 16, sect. 1.

Free negro women, &c. exempt from paying levies.

II. AND be it further enacted, by the authority aforesaid, that so much of the said recited act as declares free negro, mulatto, and *Indian* women, to be chargeable with public, county, and parish levies, shall be, and the same is hereby repealed.

Repealing clause.

III. PROVIDED always, that the execution of this act shall be, and the same is hereby suspended until his Majesty's approbation thereof shall be obtained. *(b)*

Suspending clause.

(a) See 22 Geo. II. (1748) *chap.* 1, *sect.* 41.

(b) See note to chap. 3, *sect.* 14.

C H A P.   XXXVIII.

An act for giving a salary to the Speaker of the House of Burgesses.

Expired.

C H A P.   XXXIX.

An act for continuing the act, entitled An act for appointing a Treasurer.

Expired.

C H A P.   XL.

An act for dividing the county and parish of Augusta, *and for adding certain islands, in the* Fluvanna river, *to the counties of* Albemarle *and* Amherst.

Private.

C H A P.   XLI.

An act for dividing the parish of St. George, *in the county of* Spotsylvania, *and for other purposes therein mentioned.*

Private.

C H A P.   XLII.

An act for altering the court days of several counties therein mentioned.

Private.

C H A P.   XLIII.

An act to explain certain doubts touching the jurisdiction of the Court of Hustings of the city of Williamsburg.

Supposed to have been disallowed by the King.

C H A P.   XLIV.

An act for settling the fees of the Clerk and Serjeant of the Court of Hustings for the City of Williamsburg.

I. **B**E it enacted, by the Governor, Council, and Burgesses, of this present General Assembly, and it is hereby enacted, by the authority of the same, that from and after the passing of this act, the clerk of the Court of Hustings for the city of *Williamsburg,* shall be entitled to the same fees for services by him done, as are by law allowed for the like services to the clerks of county courts, to be collected, levied, and accounted for, in the same manner, and under the like regulations, as are provided in the case of the clerk of the county court of *York.*

II. AND be it further enacted, by the authority aforesaid, that the serjeant of the said Court of Hustings shall be entitled to the same fees for services by him done, as are by law allowed for the like services to the sheriffs of the several counties, to be collected, levied, and accounted for, in the same manner, and under the like regulations, as are provided in the case of the sheriff of *York* county.

C H A P.   XLV.

An act to divide the parish of Hamilton, *in the counties of* Fauquier *and* Prince William.

Private.

C H A P.   XLVI.

An act for adding part of the county of Nansemond *to the county of* Isle of Wight, *and for ascertaining part of the boundary between the county of* James City *and* York.

Private.

C H A P.   XLVII.

An act for adding part of the parish of Southfarnham *to the parish of* Saint Anne.

Private.

C H A P.   XLVIII.

An act for reimbursing the inhabitants of King William *and* Hanover *counties the expence of clearing* Pamunkey *river.*

Private.

C H A P.   XLIX.

An act to empower the vestry of Meherrin *parish, in the county of* Brunswick, *to sell the glebe of the said parish, and lay out the money in purchasing a more convenient glebe.*

Private.

C H A P.   L.

An act to empower the vestry of Dettingen *parish, in the county of* Prince William, *to sell the glebe of the said parish, and lay out the money in purchasing a more convenient glebe.*

Private.

E

A. D 1769.

CHAP. LI.

Private,

An act to empower the Vestry of Saint Mark's parish, in the county of Culpeper, to sell the glebe of the said parish, and lay out the money in purchasing a more convenient glebe.

CHAP. LII.

Private,

An act to amend an act entitled An act for establishing a town near Warwick, in the county of Henrico.

CHAP. LIII.

Private,

An act for adding twenty acres of land, whereof Patrick Ramsay is seized, to the town of Blandford.

CHAP. LIV.

Private.

An act to impower the Churchwardens and Vestry of the parish of Hungars, in the county of Northampton to lease certain lands therein mentioned.

CHAP. LV.

Private,

An act for reimbursing the late Vestry of the parish of Frederick, in the county of Frederick, the amount of a judgment therein mentioned.

CHAP. LVI.

Private.

An act to amend an act, passed in the former part of this session of Assembly, for reimbursing the counties of Hanover and King William the expence of clearing Pamunkey river.

CHAP. LVII.

Private.

An act for establishing a town in the county of Pittsylvania.

CHAP. LVIII.

Private,

An act for continuing and amending an act, entitled An act for reviving and amending the acts for allowing fairs to be kept in the towns of Fredericksburg and Richmond, and for enlarging the town of Fredericksburg.

CHAP. LIX.

Private,

An act to annex part of the county of York to the county of James City, and for other purposes therein mentioned.

CHAP. LX.

Private,

An act for establishing towns at Rockey Ridge, Gloucester courthouse, and Layton's warehouse, and for other purposes therein mentioned.

CHAP. LXI.

Private.

An act for dividing the parishes of Frederick, in the county of Frederick, and Cameron, in the county of Loudoun, and for other purposes therein mentioned.

CHAP. LXII.

Private,

An act to explain and amend an act of this present session of Assembly, entitled an Act to divide the parish of Hamilton, in the counties of Fauquier and Prince William.

CHAP LXIII.

Private,

An act to repeal an act for increasing the salary of the Minister of the parish of Frederick, in the county of Frederick.

CHAP. LXIV.

Private,

An act to impower the Vestry of Bristol parish, in the counties of Dinwiddie and Prince George, to sell their glebe.

CHAP. LXV.

Private.

An act for dissolving the several Vestries therein mentioned.

CHAP. LXVI.

Private,

An act to appoint Trustees, in the room of those who are dead, for the Pamunkey Indians, and with further power to hear and determine controversies among them.

Private.

CHAP. LXXXIII.

An act to vest certain intailed lands therein mentioned in George Brooke, Gentleman, in fee simple, and for settling other lands of greater value, in lieu thereof.

Private.

CHAP. LXXXIV.

An act to vest certain lands whereof Bernard Moore, Esquire, is seized in fee tail, in trustees, to be sold, and the money laid out in the purchase of other lands and slaves, to be settled to the same uses.

Private.

CHAP. LXXXV.

An act to vest certain intailed lands whereof Charles Lewis, Gentleman, is seized, in John Lewis, Gentleman, in fee simple, and settle other lands to the same uses.

Private.

CHAP. LXXXVI.

An act to dock the intail of four thousand acres of land in the county of Isle of Wight, whereof James Burwell is seized in fee tail, and for vesting the same in trustees in fee simple, for certain purposes therein mentioned.

Private.

CHAP. LXXXVII.

An act to dock the intail of five hundred and fifty acres of land in the county of Gloucester, whereof Sarah, the wife of John Rootes, Gentleman, is seized, and for vesting the same in trustees, for the purposes therein mentioned.

Private.

CHAP. LXXXVIII.

An act to vest certain intailed lands, whereof William and John Armistead, Gentlemen, are seized, in trustees, to be sold for payments of the debts due from the estate of their father.

Executed.

CHAP. LXXXIX.

An act for the ease and relief of the people, by paying the Burgesses in money for the last Convention and present session of Assembly.

William Nelson, Esquire, President.

At a GENERAL ASSEMBLY, begun and held at the Capitol, in the City of *Williamsburg*, the seventh day of *November*, *Anno Domini* one thousand seven hundred and sixty-nine, in the tenth year of the reign of GEORGE, III. of *Great Britain*, *France*, and *Ireland*, King, Defender of the Faith, *&c.* and from thence continued by several prorogations, and convened by proclamation the eleventh day of *July*, in the year of our Lord one thousand seven hundred and seventy-one, being the second session of this present General Assembly.

Executed.

CHAP. I.

An act for the relief of the sufferers by the loss of tobacco damaged or burnt in several warehouses.

Expired.

CHAP. II.

An act for further continuing the act, entitled an act for the better regulating and disciplining the militia.

Private.

CHAP. III.

An act to impower the inhabitants of the parish of Augusta, in the county of Augusta, to elect a vestry.

Executed.

CHAP. IV.

An act for the ease and relief of the people, by paying the Burgesses wages in money for this present session of Assembly.

A.D. 1772.

At a GENERAL ASSEMBLY, begun and held at the Capitol, in the City of *Williamsburg*, on *Monday* the tenth day of *February*, *Anno Domini* one thousand seven hundred and seventy-two, in the twelfth year of the reign of GEORGE, III. of *Great Britain, France*, and *Ireland*, King, Defender of the Faith, &c. being the first session of this present General Assembly.

Lord DUNMORE, Governor.

CHAP. I.

An act to continue and amend the act, entitled An act to continue and amend the act, entitled an act for amending the staple of tobacco, and for preventing frauds in his Majesty's customs.

Expired.

CHAP. II.

An act to amend so much of an act of Assembly, entitled An act for the inspection of pork, beef, flour, tar, pitch, and turpentine, as relates to the inspection of flour.

Expired.

CHAP III.

An act for further continuing the act, entitled An act for reducing the several acts of Assembly, for making provision against invasions and insurrections, into one act.

Expired.

CHAP. IV.

An act for further continuing and amending the act entitled An act for the better regulating and collecting certain officers fees, and for other purposes therein mentioned.

Expired.

CHAP. V.

An act to impower the clerks of county courts to issue certain writs of execution into other counties.   (a)

I. WHEREAS the laws concerning executions are defective in not authorizing the clerks of county courts to issue all manner of legal and proper writs of execution upon judgments, decrees in chancery, and final orders, duly recovered and obtained in such courts, into other counties, as is done in writs of capias ad satisfaciendum and fieri facias: Be it therefore enacted, by the Governor, Council, and Burgesses, of this present General Assembly, and it is hereby enacted, by the authority of the same, that the clerks of the several county courts in this colony, shall be, and they are hereby impowered and required, upon the application of any party who hath obtained, or shall obtain, any judgment, decree, or final order, in such courts, to issue any legal or proper writ of execution or attachment thereupon, as the case may require; as also to issue attachments against executors, administrators, or guardians, who shall fail to account when ordered so to do by such court, directed to the sheriff of the same, or any other county, provided there be fifteen days at least, and not more than ninety days between the teste and return of such writ.

Recital.

Execution, &c. may be issued by clerk of one county to sheriff of another.

II. *AND be it further enacted, by the authority aforesaid,* that the sheriff to whom such writ shall be directed and delivered, shall duly execute and return the same, or in default therein shall be liable to the like penalties as are by law inflicted, respectively, for the not executing or returning other writs of execution; and upon failing to pay the money by him received upon any such writ, or suffering a voluntary or negligent escape of the debtor, shall be subject to the same remedy and proceedings as are prescribed by the laws now in force for the like defaults in other executions.

Duty of, and remedy against sheriffs.

CHAP. VI.

An act for altering the method of suing out writs of alias capias, and other process, in the county courts, for regulating certain expences on attachments, and writs of execution, and for altering the court days of certain counties.   (b)

I. WHEREAS the laws, as they now stand, restrain the clerks of the county courts within this colony from issuing any writs of alias capias, renewing any petitions, or other process, where the original process hath not been executed, until such new process shall be ordered by the court of such county; and whereas it frequently happens that such courts, neglecting to sit to order such new process, the honest creditor is obliged to pay the costs of his original process, or run the risk of losing his just debt: To remedy which evil, Be it enacted, by the Governor, Council, and Burgesses, of this present General Assembly, and it is hereby enacted, by the authority of the same, that when the sheriff or any other officer, of any county within this colony, shall return any writ, petition, or other process to him directed, into the clerk's office of such county, by which return it shall appear to the clerk that the said process hath not been executed, it shall and may be lawful for such clerk, and he is hereby required, at the request of the party at whose instance the same was originally sued out, or his attorney, to issue an alias capias, or renew such process, without the formality of having such suit called in court; any law, custom, or usage, to the contrary notwithstanding.

Recital.

Process returned, not executed, clerk may issue subsequent process although the suit be not called in court.

(a) See acts of 1769 chap. 3.
(b) See note to the last act.

F

A. D. 1772.

Recital.

Maintenance of live stock taken in execution, &c. to be provided by officer, and expence thereof to be taxed in bill of costs.

II. AND whereas the sheriffs, and other officers, of the several counties within this colony, do frequently serve attachments, and writs of execution, upon horses, cattle, hogs, sheep, and other live stock, which such officers are obliged to retain in their custody for a length of time before an order of court can be obtained for the sale of such live stock, or for want of buyers, during which time such stock frequently perish for want of proper food, or are greatly impoverished, to the great detriment both of the creditor and his debtor: For remedy whereof, *Be it further enacted, by the authority aforesaid,* that when any sheriff or other officer, shall serve an attachment, or any writ of execution, on horses, or other live stock, and the same shall not be immediately replevied or restored to the debtor, it shall and may be lawful for such officers, and they are hereby required, to provide sufficient sustenance for the support of such live stock, until such stock shall be sold, or otherwise legally discharged from such attachment, or writ of execution; and upon the trial of any attachment, or return of any execution, the court before whom such attachment shall be tried, or such execution returned, may and shall, upon the motion of the officer serving the same, settle and adjust what such officer shall be allowed for his expences incurred by supporting such stock, to be taxed in the bill of costs against the party against whom judgment shall be given on such attachment, and the same shall be retained by the officer out of the money arising from the sale of such stock; and the said officer shall and may retain the expences of supporting such stock, taken by execution, as aforesaid, out of the money arising from the sale, to be settled in manner aforesaid. And where the plaintiff in any attachment shall be cast, the expences aforesaid shall be taxed in the bill of costs against such plaintiff, for which the defendant may take execution, with the other costs.

Court days of Loudoun & Pittsylvania.

III. AND whereas it is represented to this present General Assembly, that the court days of the counties of *Loudoun* and *Pittsylvania,* as they are now appointed, are found to be inconvenient, as well to the inhabitants of the said counties, as to others who attend the said courts. For remedy whereof, *Be it enacted,* that from and after the first day of *May* next, the court of the said county of *Loudoun* shall be constantly held on the fourth *Monday,* and the court of the said county of *Pittsylvania* on the fourth *Thursday* in every month; any law, custom, or usage, to the contrary, notwithstanding.

CHAP. VII.

Private.

An act for altering the court days of the counties of Surry, Bedford, *and* Princess Anne.

CHAP. VIII.

Repealed.

An act to amend an act, entitled An act to prevent malicious maiming and wounding.

CHAP. IX.

An act for amending the acts concerning the trials and outlawries of slaves.

Recital.
Slave convicted of house breaking in the night, not excluded from clergy, unless a free man, in the like case would be so.
Sentence of death not to be passed upon a slave unless four of his judges, &c. concur.

I. WHEREAS it has been doubted whether slaves convicted of breaking and entering houses in the night time, without stealing goods or chattels from thence, are entitled to the benefit of clergy: For explaining the law in this point, *Be it enacted, by the Governor, Council, and Burgesses, of this present General Assembly, and it is hereby enacted by the authority of the same,* that a slave who shall break any house in the night time, shall not be excluded from clergy, unless the said breaking, in the case of a freeman, would be a burglary.

II. *AND be it further enacted,* that from and after the passing of this act, sentence of death shall in no case be passed upon any slave, unless four of the court, before whom such slave is arraigned and tried, being a majority, shall concur in their opinion of his or her guilt; any law, custom, or usage, to the contrary thereof, notwithstanding.

Slaves not to be outlawed, unless outlying and doing mischief; nor paid for by the public.

III. AND whereas doubts have arisen, and various opinions have prevailed, touching the proper construction of part of an act of Assembly, made in the twenty second year of the reign of his late Majesty, directing the method of proceeding against outlying slaves, and in what manner they shall be paid for by the public, when killed or destroyed, in pursuance of the said act: For removing such doubts, and that the said act may hereafter receive one uniform interpretation, *Be it enacted by the authority aforesaid,* that no Justice or Justices of the Peace of this colony shall, by virtue of the said act, issue a proclamation against any slave, authorizing any person to kill or destroy such slave, unless it shall appear to the satisfaction of such Justice or Justices that such slave is outlying and doing mischief; and if any slave shall hereafter be killed or destroyed, by virtue of any proclamation, issued contrary to this act, the owner or proprietor of such slave shall not be paid for such slave by the public; any thing in the said recited act to the contrary, or seeming to the contrary, in any wise, notwithstanding.

CHAP. X.

An act to amend an act, entitled an act concerning seamen.

Recital.

In actions against masters of vessels for putting sick sailors, &c. on shore, defendants may be ruled to give bail.

I. WHEREAS the act, passed in the twenty second year of the reign of his late Majesty King *George* the second entitled *An act concerning seamen,* hath been found insufficient to restrain masters or commanders of vessels from discharging sick, or disabled sailors or servants, and is often evaded by such commanders leaving the country before any suit brought against them can be determined, and without effects whereon to levy execution: *Be it therefore enacted, by the Governor, Council, and Burgesses, of this present General Assembly, and it is hereby enacted, by the authority of the same,* that from and after the passing of this act, if any suit shall be brought by the Churchwardens of any parish against any master or commander of a vessel, for putting on shore any sick or disabled sailor or servant, contrary to the said recited act, it shall and may be lawful for the court, before whom such suit is depending, upon a motion of the plaintiffs, to rule the defendant, on his appearance, to special bail; any law, custom, or usage, to the contrary, in any wise, notwithstanding.

Upon affidavit certified, the clerk shall endorse on writ, 'bail to be taken.'
Remedy against bail and sheriff.

II. *PROVIDED always,* that the said Churchwardens, or either of them, shall make affidavit of the cause of action before a Magistrate, and the same being certified to the clerk of the court, such clerk shall endorse upon the writ to be issued, that good bail is to be taken, and such bail, or the sheriff, if he takes none or insufficient bail, shall be subject to the same proceedings, and entitled to the like remedy as is provided by law in other cases, and the special bail to be given in any such suit shall be liable in the same manner as in other cases.

CHAP. XI.

An act to amend the act entitled An act prescribing the method of appointing Sheriffs, and for limiting the time of their continuance in office, and directing their duty therein, and for other purposes. (a)

I. WHEREAS by the long continuance of under sheriffs in office they gain an undue influence, and by that means are induced to commit many acts of oppression and injustice to his Majesty's subjects: For prevention whereof, Be it enacted and declared, by the Governor, Council, and Burgesses, of this present General Assembly, and it is hereby enacted, by the authority of the same, that no person whatever shall be capable to serve or execute the office of under sheriff, or deputy sheriff, of any county, for any longer time than two years successively, without the consent and approbation of the court of the said county; any law, custom, or usage, to the contrary thereof, in any wise, notwithstanding.

Recital.

Under sheriff may not continue more than two years in office without consent of the court.

II. AND whereas it frequently happens, from the inclemency of weather, or other accidents, that the county courts are not held at the time the high sheriffs are by law to qualify under the commissions granted to them, which has occasioned various disputes touching the legality of the execution of the office by the preceding sheriff, after the granting of any new commission: For remedy whereof, Be it further enacted, by the authority aforesaid, that if no court shall be held for any county in the month next after the date of any new commission granted to the sheriff, the preceding sheriff shall continue to act and execute the office of sheriff, till a court shall be held for the county, so as to qualify the sheriff appointed by such new commission.

Until a new sheriff be qualified, his predecessor shall act.

III. AND whereas the inhabitants of this colony are liable to be, and in many instances have been, imposed upon by the sheriffs, or collectors of the several counties, for want of an account stated separately and distinctly of the several fees by them collected for different officers, and also a clear account of the quitrents, public, county, or parish levies, which the said sheriffs, or their deputies, often refuse to give, and often do make distress, if immediate payment be not made of a sum demanded by them in gross, which practices are productive of great inconveniences: For remedy whereof, Be it further enacted, by the authority aforesaid, that every sheriff, deputy sheriff, or collector, who shall hereafter receive from any person, or persons, any officers fees, quitrents, public, county, or parish levies, shall deliver to the person, so paying, a fair and distinct account of the several articles, for which he shall receive the same, and also a receipt for what shall be so paid him; and every sheriff, deputy sheriff, or collector, failing herein, shall forfeit and pay to the person by whom such payment shall be made, the sum of twenty shillings for each offence, to be recovered, with costs, before any Justice of the Peace of the county where such sheriff, deputy sheriff, or collector, shall reside; and such sheriff or other officer, shall moreover be liable to the party grieved for all damages he may sustain by means of such officers demanding and receiving a greater sum than shall be really due, to be recovered by action of trespass on the case, before any court of record within this colony, in which action, where the plaintiff shall recover, he shall also recover his full costs.

Sheriff, &c. receiving fees, &c. shall deliver to the party a distinct account of the articles with a receipt, or be subject to a penalty, and liable to the party's action.

IV. AND whereas by an act of the General Assembly, passed in the tenth year of his present Majesty's reign, the inhabitants of the county of *Botetourt* are allowed to discharge all secretary's, clerk's, and other officers fees, at the rate of eight shillings and four pence for every hundred weight of gross tobacco, and it is reasonable that the same liberty should be granted to the county of *Fincastle*: Be it therefore further enacted, by the authority aforesaid, that from and after the first day of *December* next, the inhabitants of the said county of *Fincastle* shall discharge all fees due from them to the secretary, clerks, and other officers, in the said county, at the rate of eight shillings and four pence for every hundred weight of gross tobacco.

Tobacco fees due in Fincastle may be discharged in money at 8s. 4d. per cent.

CHAP. XII.

An act to amend an act, entitled An act directing the duty of Surveyors of land. (b)

I. WHEREAS many inconveniencies have arisen from the inattention of surveyors to the variation of the magnetic needle, in resurveying lands which were formerly surveyed, when the variation was very different from what it is now, and many mistakes and much confusion may arise in comparing future surveys with the present: For remedy whereof, Be it enacted, by the Governor, Council, and Burgesses, of this present General Assembly, and it is hereby enacted, by the authority of the same, that from and after the first day of *June*, in the year of our Lord one thousand seven hundred and seventy three, every surveyor of this colony shall, under the penalty of five pounds, return all his or their original or new surveys, and protract and lay down their plats by the true, and not by the artificial or magnetic meridian, and shall moreover express and declare, in or on the plat and return of each survey, by him or them taken or made, the true quantity or degree of the variation aforesaid, and whether it be east or west.

Recital.

In new surveys plats to be laid down by the true, not artificial meridian, with the variation.

II. PROVIDED always, that when any surveyor shall be called upon or ordered to resurvey any lands, that may have been surveyed before the commencement of this act, such surveyor shall or may resurvey such lands according to the present mode of surveying by the magnetic meridian, but shall, nevertheless, under the penalty aforesaid, return and certify, in his plat, the quantity or degree of the variation of the magnetic needle from the true meridian, at the time of making such resurvey, and shall also, in the said plat, and return, certify (where the same can be done) the quantity or degree of variation between the original lines of such former survey from the true meridian aforesaid.

In resurveys, the present mode by the magnetic meridian may be observed, but the variation shall be certified.

III. AND be it further enacted, that the penalties inflicted by this act may be recovered by any person, or persons, who shall sustain any damage by the surveyors failing to comply with the directions of this act, who will inform or sue for the same by action of debt, bill, plaint, or information, in any court of record within this dominion.

Penalty how to be recovered, and appropriated.

CHAP. XIII.

An act for regulating the allowances to the Keeper of the Public Prison for the maintenance of poor prisoners for debt, and for other purposes therein mentioned.

I. WHEREAS by one clause of an act, passed in the twenty-second year of the reign of his late Majesty King *George* the second, entitled *An act declaring the law concerning executions, and for relief of insolvent debtors*, it is amongst other things enacted, that where any person shall be committed to prison, for any debt or damages whatsoever, and shall not be able to satisfy and pay his or her ordinary prison fees, such of the said fees as shall become due for the first twenty days imprison-

Recital.

(a) See October session 1782, chap. 29, and May session 1783, chap. 32.
(b) This officers duty in other particulars prescribed in several acts.

A. D. 1772.

Part of 22 Geo. II. chap. 8, sect. 23 repealed.

Party liable for insolvent prisoner's fees; refusing to pay them, &c. officer may discharge prisoner.

ment shall be discharged by the county, which is unreasonable, and frequently occasions the imprisonment of poor and indigent persons by their creditors, who are not compellable, by the said act, to reimburse the county the fees due on such imprisonment: *Be it therefore enacted, by the Governor, Council, and Burgesses, of this present General Assembly, and it is hereby enacted, by the authority of the same,* that so much of the said act which directs that the prison fees, due for the first twenty days, of the imprisonment of any person committed to prison, for any debt or damages, who are not able to pay and satisfy such fees, shall be discharged by the county, be, and the same is hereby repealed. And the sheriff or jailer may demand and receive of the party or parties, at whose suit such insolvent person shall be imprisoned, all such fees as shall become due, until the creditor shall agree to release such prisoner; and if the creditor, upon notice given to him or her, his or her attorney or agent, shall refuse to give security to the sheriff or jailer for the payment of such prison fees, or shall fail to pay the same, when demanded, it shall and may be lawful for such sheriff or jailer to discharge such debtor out of prison, according to the directions of the said recited acts.

One shilling and sixpence per day for maintenance of poor imprisoned debtors, for first 20 days, to be paid by public, and levied on creditor.

II. AND whereas, by one other act, passed the same session, entitled *An act concerning the public prison, and directing the method of appointing the keeper thereof,* the keeper of the said public jail is empowered to demand and receive of all prisoners committed to his custody by the General Court, on mesne process, or in execution, the fees and allowances settled or to be settled by law, but where any such prisoner should be so poor as not to be able to maintain him or herself in prison, there should be allowed six pence *per* day, and paid by the General Assembly, for the maintenance of such poor prisoner, which, from the high price of provisions is found to be insufficient for such maintenance, and doubts have also arisen whether the public or counties are to pay the public jailer for the maintenance of such poor prisoners, who, being committed to a county jail, are removed to the public prison by habeas corpus: *Be it therefore enacted, by the authority aforesaid,* that the allowance to the keeper of the public jail, for all poor prisoners, who are unable to pay his or her ordinary prison fees, whether committed on execution, or by order of the General Court, or removed by habeas corpus, shall, for the first twenty days, be paid by the public, and levied on the creditor, and that such allowance, for such poor prisoners, shall be one shilling and six pence *per* day.

One shilling per day for runaways.

III. AND be it further enacted, by the authority aforesaid, that the keeper of the said public jail shall also be entitled to receive one shilling *per* day for the keeping every runaway servant or slave, committed to the said jail, pursuant to the laws now in force.

£. 100 to be paid by Treasurer to Jailer annually.

IV. AND the better to enable the said keeper of the public jail to provide for the prisoners under his care, *Be it enacted, by the authority aforesaid,* that the Treasurer of this colony, for the time being, shall advance and pay to the said jailer, out of the public money in his hands, by warrant from the Governor or Commander in Chief, for the time being, the sum of one hundred pounds, at four equal payments, to be deducted out of the tobacco that shall be levied for the said jailer in the book of claims by the succeeding session of Assembly.

CHAP. XIV.

Expired.

An act to continue an act, entitled An act to continue and amend an act, entitled An act for reducing the several acts made for laying a duty upon liquors, into one act.

CHAP. XV.

Expired.

An act for continuing and amending several acts, and reviving one act, for laying duties upon slaves imported.

CHAP. XVI.

Executed.

An act for laying a public levy.

CHAP. XVII.

Executed.

An act to amend the several acts of Assembly respecting the currency of copper money in this colony.

CHAP. XVIII.

Executed.

An act for the ease and relief of the people by paying the Burgesses wages in money for the present session of Assembly.

CHAP. XIX.

Repealed.

An act to compel ships importing convicts, servants, or slaves, infected with the jail fever, or small-pox, to perform quarentine.

CHAP. XX.

An act for erecting a Lighthouse on Cape Henry.   *(a)*

Recital.

I. WHEREAS the erecting and maintaining a lighthouse at Cape *Henry,* and fixing buoys on the shoals, in the bay of *Chesapeak,* will greatly conduce to the safety and preservation of ships, and other vessels, coming into, and going out of, the said bay, and the expence of such building and keeping a light therein, and fixing such buoys, may be defrayed by a small and inconsiderable duty on the tonnage of such ships, and vessels, to be paid by their owners, or masters, in consideration of the immediate benefits arising to them: And whereas the lower House of Assembly, of the province of *Maryland,* which province will be equally benefited thereby, hath signified the resolution of that House to concur in the expence thereof: To the end, therefore, that a work of such use may be

(a) See May *session,* 1782, *chap.* 31.

compleated with all convenient speed, *Be it enacted, by the Governor, Council, and Burgesses, of this present General Assembly, and it is hereby enacted, by the authority of the same,* that the honourable *William Nelson, Thomas Nelson,* and *William Byrd,* Esquires, and *Severn Eyre, Joseph Hutchings, Thomas Newton,* junior, *James Holt, Paul Loyal, John Hutchings, Matthew Phripp,* and *Thomas Reynolds Walker,* Esquires, shall be, and are hereby appointed, directors and managers for erecting and finishing, or causing to be erected and finished, at such convenient place, on the head land of Cape *Henry,* as to them, in their discretion, shall appear most proper for that purpose, a good and substantial lighthouse, of such height and dimensions as they shall think best. And the said directors or managers, or any seven of them, as soon as the Assembly of *Maryland* shall pass an act of the same import with this act, shall have power and authority, by virtue hereof, in conjunction with such person, or persons, as by the said Assembly shall be appointed for the purposes aforesaid, to contract and agree with any person, or persons, for building and finishing such lighthouse, in the best and most substantial manner, upon such terms as to them shall seem reasonable; also for placing, and constantly keeping, a light therein, and furnishing the same with such necessaries as they shall think proper; and for purchasing and placing buoys on such shoals of the bay of *Chesapeak* as may be necessary, which agreement, or agreements, being by them certified to the Governor or Commander in Chief of this dominion, and a warrant thereupon obtained from him to the Treasurer of this colony for the time being, the said Treasurer is hereby authorized and required, out of the public money in his hands, to pay the sum or sums so certified to be due unto the person, or persons, to whom the same shall be ordered by the said directors, not exceeding the sum of six thousand pounds current money of *Virginia;* and to enable them to carry on the said building, and to repay so much as shall be expended in erecting the said lighthouse, and to provide a proper fund for lighting and supporting the same, *Be it further enacted, by the authority aforesaid,* that from and after the first day of *November* next, there shall be paid by the masters, or owners, of all ships, and other vessels, coming into, or going out of, this colony, other than from *Maryland,* once in every voyage, at the time of clearing out, the duty of four pence *per* tun of the burthen of each ship, or vessel, until such duty shall amount to a sum sufficient to reimburse the money hereby directed to be paid by the treasurer of this colony, and thereafter a duty of one penny half-penny *per* tun, for and towards the support of the said lighthouse, to be collected by the naval officers of the several districts within this colony, who are hereby directed and required to receive the same, which duties shall be to our Sovereign Lord the King, his heirs, and successors, for ever, for the uses and purposes hereafter mentioned, and by them to be accounted for and paid to the Treasurer of this colony, appointed by, or pursuant to, an act of Assembly, in the same manner, and with the like salary for collecting, as they are by law directed to account for the duties upon liquors, and by the said Treasurer shall be accounted for to the General Assembly, to be by them applied and ordered for repaying so much as shall be expended in erecting the said lighthouse, and fixing necessary buoys on the shoals, in the bay of *Chesapeak,* and to provide a proper fund for lighting and supporting the said lighthouse, and keeping in repair such buoys.

II. AND *be it further enacted, by the authority aforesaid,* that the said directors, or any seven of them, shall and may, and they are hereby empowered, from time to time, to appoint a keeper of such lighthouse, and to allow him such compensation, or salary, as to the said directors shall appear reasonable, to be paid upon the Governor's warrant, by the Treasurer of this colony, for the time being, out of the money in his hands, which shall arise from the duties aforesaid. And in case of the death, resignation, or misconduct of the said keeper, the said directors shall have power and authority to appoint another in his room. And the said keeper shall keep good and sufficient lights in the night time in the said lighthouse; and if he shall fail or neglect so to do, he shall forfeit and pay, for every such offence, two hundred pounds, one moiety whereof shall be to the informer, and the other to the said directors, to be applied to the purposes of this act, to be recovered by action of debt, bill, plaint, or information, in any court of record in this dominion,

III. AND *be it enacted, by the authority aforesaid,* that all ships and vessels, liable to the payment of the duties imposed by this act, shall, by the several naval officers, be measured according to the directions of one act of Assembly, made in the ninth year of the reign of her late Majesty Queen *Anne,* entitled *An act for raising a public revenue for the better support of the government of her Majesty's colony and dominion of* Virginia.

IV. AND *be it further enacted, by the authority aforesaid,* that every keeper of the said lighthouse, before he enters on the execution of his office, shall give bond, with sufficient security (to be approved of by the said directors) in the sum of five hundred pounds, payable to our Sovereign Lord the King, his heirs, and successors, for the due performance of his said office.

V. AND whereas the taking away, removing, sinking, or destroying the buoys to be fixed, according to the directions of this act, may have very fatal effects: *Be it therefore enacted, by the authority aforesaid,* that if any person or persons, shall take away or remove, without leave of the said directors, or shall wilfully sink or destroy any of the said buoys, he or they on being convicted thereof, shall be adjudged guilty of felony, and shall suffer death, without benefit of clergy.

Marginal notes:
- A. D. 1772.
- Directors,
- in conjunction with persons appointed by the Assembly of Maryland, to build a lighthouse at Cape Henry, &c.
- A sum not exceeding 6000l to be paid for the work by the Treasurer.
- Duty of 4d. per tun on vessels to defray the expense of building, &c. and afterwards one penny half penny for repairing, &c.
- Keeper, his salary, and duty.
- Penalty on him for neglect.
- Manner of ascertaining the tunnage of vessels.
- Keeper to give security.
- Taking away buoys, &c. felony.

CHAP. XXI.

An act to continue an act, entitled An act for establishing Pilots, and regulating their fees.   (a)

Expired.

CHAP. XXII.

An act to revive and continue the acts for the more effectual keeping the public roads and bridges in repair.

Expired.

CHAP. XXIII.

An act for keeping in repair several roads, and for other purposes therein mentioned.

Expired.

CHAP XXIV.

An act for clearing a road from the Warm Springs *in* Augusta, *and for other purposes therein mentioned.*

Private.

(a) See May session, 1783, chap. 1.

G

A. D. 1772.
Executed.

C H A P. XXV.

An act to appoint Commissioners to view a place proposed for a road through the South Mountain.

C H A P. XXVI.

Private.

An act for building a bridge over the Western Branch of Nansemond *river by subscription.*

C H A P. XXVII.

An act for establishing several new ferries, and for other purposes.

Recital.

I. WHEREAS it is represented to the present General Assembly, that public ferries, at the places hereafter mentioned, will be of great advantage to travellers and others: *Be it therefore enacted, by the Governor, Council, and Burgesses, of this present General Assembly, and it is hereby enacted by the authority of the same,* that public ferries be constantly kept at the following places, and the rates for passing the same shall be as follows, that is to say, from the land of the right honourable the Earl of *Tankerville,* in *Loudoun* county, in the tenure and occupation of *John Farrow,* and *Alexander Reame,* over *Potowmack* river, to the opposite shore, in *Maryland,* the price for a man three pence three farthings, and for a horse the same; from the town of *Cobham,* on the lower side of *Gray's* creek, in the county of *Surry,* to *James Town,* in *James City* county, the price for a man seven pence half penny, and for a horse the same; from the land of *William Crow,* over *James* river, to the land of *Andrew Boyd,* in the county of *Botetourt,* the price for a man two pence, and for a horse the same; from the land of *Walter Coles,* in the county of *Halifax,* over *Staunton* river, to the land of *Joseph Fuqua,* in the county of *Charlotte,* the price for a man three pence, and for a horse the same.

New ferries and their respective rates.

Rates for coaches, &c. settled.

Penalty for receiving greater rates, how to be recovered.

II. *AND be it further enacted, by the authority aforesaid,* that from and after the passing this act, it shall and may be lawful to and for the ferry keeper, from the land of *Edward Booker,* deceased, in the county of *Halifax,* to the land of *John Fuqua,* deceased, in the county of *Charlotte,* over *Staunton* river, to demand and take, for the transportation of a man over the said ferry, three pence, and for a horse the same; any law, custom, or usage, to the contrary thereof, in any wise, notwithstanding. And for the transportation of wheel carriages, tobacco, cattle, and other beasts, at any of the places aforesaid, the ferry keeper may demand and take the following rates, that is to say, for every, coach, chariot, or waggon, and the driver thereof, the same as for six horses, for every cart or four wheeled chaise, and the driver thereof, the same as for four horses, for every two wheeled chaise, or chair, the same as for two horses, for every hogshead of tobacco as for one horse, for every head of neat cattle as for one horse, for every sheep, goat, or lamb, one fifth part of the ferriage for one horse, and for every hog one fourth part of the ferriage for one horse, according to the prices herein before settled at such ferries respectively, and no more. And if any ferry keeper shall presume to demand and receive from any person or persons whatsoever any greater rates than is hereby allowed for the carriage or ferriage of any thing whatsoever, he, or they, for every such offence, shall forfeit and pay to the party grieved the ferriages demanded and received, and ten shillings, to be recovered with costs, before any Justice of the Peace of the county where such offence shall be committed. And where a ferry is, by this act, appointed on one side of a river, and none on the other side, answerable thereto, it shall and may be lawful for the respective county courts to appoint an opposite ferry, and to allow the respective rates herein before directed; and such courts shall and may, and are hereby required to order and direct what boat or boats, and what number of hands shall be kept at each ferry, respectively; and every such ferry keeper shall enter into bond, in the manner directed by an act of Assembly made in the twenty second year of the reign of his late Majesty King *George* the second, for the settlement and regulation of ferries, and dispatch of public expresses, and shall be subject and liable to the penalties thereby inflicted for any neglect or omission of their duty.

County courts may appoint an opposite ferry, and direct boats, &c.
Ferry keeper to give bond, &c.

Several ferries discontinued.

III. AND whereas the several ferries following, that is to say, from *Crouche's* creek, on the land of *William Edwards,* in the county of *Surry,* across *James* river to *James Town,* in *James City* county, from the land of *Cornelius Thomas,* in the county of *Amherst,* over the *Fluvanna* river, to the land of *Nicholas Davies,* opposite thereto, in the county of *Bedford,* and from the land of the said *Nicholas Davies,* to the land of the said *Cornelius Thomas,* and from the land of *William Fuqua,* deceased, in the county of *Charlotte,* to the land of *Walter Coles,* in the county of *Halifax,* opposite thereto, have become useless and unnecessary: *Be it therefore enacted by the authority aforesaid,* that so much of the several acts of Assembly, made in the twenty second year of the reign of his late Majesty King *George* the second, and in the first and fifth years of the reign of his present Majesty, as establishes those ferries, respectively, be, and the same is hereby repealed and made void.

Ferry from Cobham, vested in trustees, who may let to the highest bidder, and make rules concerning boats, &c.
Trustees to give bond, and be liable for neglect.
Application of the profits.

IV. *AND be it further enacted by the authority aforesaid,* that the ferry from the town of *Cobham,* on the lower side of *Gray's* creek, to *James Town,* herein before mentioned and established, be, and the same is hereby vested in the trustees for the said town, appointed by an act of this present session of Assembly, and they, the said trustees, or any five of them, are hereby authorized and empowered to let the same to the highest bidder, for any number of years, and to make such rules, orders, and regulations therein, with respect to the number of boats and hands, landing places and wharfs, as to them shall seem expedient; and the said trustees shall, within two months from and after the passing this act, give bond in the same manner the other ferry keepers, herein mentioned, are directed to give bond, and shall, in the like manner be liable for any neglect or omission of duty; and the profits arising from the said ferry, shall, by the said trustees, be applied towards building and keeping in repair proper and convenient houses for the accommodation of passengers and travellers, and for erecting and maintaining wharfs, if necessary, and for such other public purposes within the said town, as to them shall seem meet and expedient.

C H A P. XXVIII.

Private.

An act for cutting a navigable canal from Archer's Hope *creek to* Queen's *creek, through or near the city of* Williamsburg.

C H A P. XXIX.

Private.

An act to enlarge the power of the trustees appointed to carry into execution an act, passed this present session of Assembly, entitled an act for cutting a navigable canal from Archer's Hope *creek to* Queen's *creek, through or near the city of* Williamsburg.

C H A P. XXX.

An act for opening the falls of James river by subscription, and for other purposes.

C H A P. XXXI.

An act for opening and extending the navigation of the river Potowmack, from fort Cumberland to tide water.

Private.

C H A P. XXXII.

An act to amend an act, entitled An act for clearing Mattapony river.

Private.

C H A P. XXXIII.

An act to explain and amend an act, entitled An act to oblige the owners of mills, hedges, or stops, on the rivers therein mentioned, to make openings or slopes therein for the passage of fish.

Private.

C H A P. XXXIV.

An act to amend an act, entitled an act to amend an act, entitled An act to oblige the owners of mills, hedges, or stone stops, on sundry rivers therein mentioned, to make openings or slopes therein for the passage of fish, and for other purposes therein mentioned.

Private.

C H A P. XXXV.

An act for appointing trustees to regulate the making of slopes for the passage of fish in the mill dams within the county of Bedford,

Private.

C H A P. XXXVI.

An act to revive the act, entitled An act for giving a salary to the Speaker of the House of Burgesses.

Expired.

C H A P. XXXVII.

An act for further continuing the act, entitled An act for appointing a Treasurer.

Expired.

C H A P. XXXVIII.

An act to enable the Nottoway Indians to lease certain lands, and for other purposes therein mentioned.

Private.

C H A P. XXXIX.

An act to amend an act, entitled An act for the better preservation of the breed of deer, and preventing unlawful hunting.

I. WHEREAS the act passed in the twelfth year of his late Majesty King *George* the second, entitled *An act for the better preservation of the breed of deer, and preventing unlawful hunting,* and one other act, passed in the first year of his present Majesty, for amending the said act, have been found insufficient to prevent the mischiefs thereby intended to be remedied, many idle people making a practice in severe frozen weather, and deep snows, to destroy deer in great numbers, with dogs, so that the whole breed is likely to be destroyed, in the inhabited parts of this colony: For remedy of which, Be it enacted, by the Governor, Council, and Burgesses, of this present General Assembly, and it is hereby enacted by the authority of the same, that from and after the passing of this act, every person who shall kill any deer, contrary to the tenor of the said acts, shall forfeit and pay the sum of fifty shillings, for every deer so killed; to be recovered with costs, by petition, where the penalty complained for, at one time, does not exceed five pounds, and by action of debt, or information, where the same shall exceed five pounds, brought in the court of the county where the offence was committed, by any person suing for the same.

Recital.

Penalty.
How to be recovered.

II. AND for the more effectual discovery of persons offending against this and the before recited acts, Be it further enacted, by the authority aforesaid, that the presiding Justice of every court in this colony, at the time the grand jury, for his county, shall be sworn, shall give it in charge to the said grand jury, to make enquiry and presentment of all such offenders, and, on conviction, the penalty shall go to the use of the poor of the parish where the offence was committed, towards lessening the said parish levy.

Grand Jury to be charged to present.

Penalty applied.

III. AND be it further enacted, that every grand jury shall take an oath, at the time they are impannelled, to make due presentment of all and every person within their county, whom they shall know to have been guilty of a breach of this act.

Grand Jury to be sworn to present.

IV. AND whereas numbers of disorderly persons, not regarding the laws, now in force, for the preservation of the breed of deer, have, during the late great snows, in many parts of this colony, almost destroyed the breed, by which the inhabitants will not only be deprived of that wholesome and agreeable food, but the trade in the article of skins, will be greatly diminished, as well as the revenue of the College, unless, for a time, all persons be prohibited from killing of deer: Therefore, be it further enacted, by the authority aforesaid, that from and after the passing of this act, no person shall hunt, shoot, or kill, in any manner, any wild deer, until the first day of *August,* which shall be in the year of our Lord Christ one thousand seven hundred and seventy-six; and every person, so offending, shall be liable

A. D. 1772.

to the fame penalty, and to be recovered and applied in the fame manner as the penalty before inflicted by this act for killing deer out of feafon.

Unlawful to kill tame deer, having bell or collar.

Remedy to owner, faving to inhabitants of frontier counties.

General faving.

V. AND whereas doubts have arifen whether an action will lie againft any perfon who fhall kill a tame deer, the property of another, that fhall be found ranging on any uncultivated lands, other than thofe of the owner of the deer, which prevents many perfons from attempting to raife tame deer : For fettling fuch doubts, Be it enacted, by the authority aforefaid, that if any perfon fhall fhoot, or otherwife kill, any tame deer, having a bell or collar on its neck, every perfon, fo offending, fhall be liable to an action of trefpafs, to the perfon whofe property the fame fhall be, to be profecuted in the court of the county where the offence fhall be committed. Provided neverthelefs, that nothing in this act fhall be conftrued to prevent any perfon refiding in the frontier counties of this colony, from killing deer for food for themfelves and families, as is allowed by the before recited acts of Affembly, nor any other perfons, from killing deer in their own enclofed lands, at fuch time and times as deer are allowed to be killed by the faid firft recited act.

Penalty not paid or fecured, offender to be whipped.

Summary remedy on bonds for penalty.

VI. AND be it further enacted, by the authority aforefaid, that if any perfon, or perfons, not being a freeholder, fhall, on conviction, fail to make prefent payment of the penalties and forfeitures, by this act inflicted, to the perfon or perfons, entitled to receive the fame, or give fecurity to pay the fame, within fix months after fuch conviction, or where the penalty fhall be to the parifh, at the laying of the next parifh levy, where fuch offence fhall be committed, then, or in either cafe, he or they, fo offending, fhall, by order of fuch Juftice, or the court, before whom the conviction fhall be made, receive, for every fuch offence, twenty lafhes, on his or their bare back, well laid on ; and if any fuch offenders fhall refufe to pay the money on the bonds aforefaid, when the fame fhall become due, it fhall and may be lawful for fuch Juftice, or the court of the county where fuch offender, or offenders, refide, on a motion to them made by the informer, or the Churchwardens, as the cafe may be, to give judgment on the faid bonds, and thereon to award execution ; provided fuch offender or offenders, and his or their fecurities, his and their heirs, executors, or adminiftrators, have ten days previous notice, in writing.

Repealing claufe.

VII. AND be it further enacted, by the authority aforefaid, that fo much of the faid recited acts, as is within the purview of this act, be, and the fame is hereby repealed, and made void.

C H A P.   XL.

Executed.

An act for making further provifion for the fupport and maintenance of Ideots, Lunatics, and other perfons of unfound minds.

C H A P.   XLI.

Expired.

An act for further continuing and amending the act, entitled An act for increafing the reward for killing wolves within certain counties, to be paid by the refpective counties wherein the fervices fhall be performed.

C H A P.   XLII.

Expired.

An act for continuing and amending the act, entitled An act for deftroying crows and fquirrels in certain counties therein mentioned.

C H A P.   XLIII.

Private.

An act for dividing the county of Frederick into three diftinct counties.

C H A P.   XLIV.

Private.

An act for dividing the county of Botetourt into two diftinct counties.

C H A P.   XLV.

Private.

An act to appoint Commiffioners to ftrike a dividing line between the counties of Stafford and King George.

C H A P.   XLVI.

Private.

An act for adding part of the county of Nanfemond, to the county of Ifle of Wight.

C H A P.   XLVII.

Private.

An act for dividing the parifhes of Southam, in the county of Cumberland, and Dale, in the county of Chefterfield.

C H A P.   XLVIII.

Private.

An act for diffolving the Veftries of the parifhes of Saint Martin, in the counties of Hanover and Louifa, and of Saint John, in the county of King William.

C H A P.   XLIX.

Private.

An act to impower the Veftry of the parifh of Saint George, in Spotfylvania, to fell part of the churchyard.

C H A P.   L.

Private.

An act to allow the Minifter of the parifh of Antrim, in the county of Halifax, the fame falary as other Minifters are entitled to receive.

A. D. 1772.

At a CONVENTION of DELEGATES for the Counties and Corporations in the Colony of *Virginia*, held at *Richmond* Town, in the County of *Henrico*, on *Monday* the seventeenth day of *July*, in the Year of our Lord one thousand seven hundred and seventy-five.

C H A P.   I.

Executed.

An ordinance for raising and embodying a sufficient force, for the defence and protection of this Colony.

C H A P.   II.

Expired.

An ordinance for the better government of the forces to be raised and employed in the service of the Colony and Dominion of Virginia.

C H A P.   III.

Expired.

An ordinance appointing a Committee of Safety for the more effectual carrying into execution the several rules and regulations established by this Convention for the protection of this Colony.

C H A P.   IV.

An ordinance for regulating the election of Delegates, and ascertaining their allowances, and also for regulating the election of Committee-men, in the several Counties and Corporations within this Colony, and for other purposes therein mentioned.   (a)

Preamble.

I. WHEREAS by the unhappy differences subsisting between *Great Britain* and this colony, the usual meetings of the General Assembly, deliberations on the situation of the country, and making provision for the exigencies of government in the constitutional way, are altogether obstructed: For these reasons, it has become indispensably necessary for the oppressed people of this country, at a crisis so alarming, to adopt such other mode of consulting and providing for the general safety as may seem most conducive to that great end:

For what places and by whom Delegates, who must be resident, may be elected.

II. THEREFORE, be it declared and ordained, by the Delegates of the several counties and corporations in the colony of Virginia, assembled in General Convention, and it is hereby declared and ordained, that the freeholders of every county within this colony, who are by law properly qualified to vote for Burgesses *(b)* shall have the liberty and privilege of choosing annually two of the most fit and able men, being freeholders of such county respectively, to be present and to act and vote in all General Conventions, which from time to time, and at any time thereafter, shall be held within this dominion; and also, that the freeholders of the several and respective corporations, and town of *James City (c)* and others by law qualified to vote for a Citizen or Burgess, shall have the liberty of electing one Delegate to be present, and to act and vote in the General Convention; and the landholders of the district of *West Augusta* shall be considered as a distinct county, and have the liberty of sending two Delegates to represent them in General Convention, as aforesaid.

Rules to be observed in elections.

III. AND for the more regular and proper electing the said Delegates, It is hereby declared, and ordained, that the following rules and methods shall be observed, to wit: The elections of Delegates in the several counties and corporations, and the town of *James City*, within this colony, shall be in the month of *April* annually, on the several days appointed by law for the holding of the county or corporation courts respectively, and at the places where such courts are accustomed to be held, and shall be conducted by the sheriffs of the respective counties, and mayors of the city of *Williamsburg* and borough of *Norfolk;* or in case any sheriff shall neglect or refuse to act, or there be no sheriff or mayor, then the clerk of the Committee for such county or corporation, in the same manner as is directed by law in the election of Burgesses in this colony: And the sheriff or mayor, or clerk of the Committee, shall have the same privilege of preferring and returning any Delegate, regularly elected, as by law is given to the sheriff in the election of Burgesses, in case any two candidates may happen to have an equal number of votes.

IV. PROVIDED always, that the election of Delegates for the town of *James City*, and the college of *William* and *Mary, (d)* shall be on the same day and place appointed for the county of *James City,* and shall be conducted by the sheriff or clerk of the committee for such county, in manner herein before directed; and after the election shall be made, in manner as is herein before directed, the sheriff or mayor, or clerk of the Committee as aforesaid, shall deliver to each of the Delegates elected a certificate, under his hand and seal, that such Delegate was duly elected for his county or corporation, to serve in General Convention for one year then next following. And further, the said sheriff or mayor, or clerk of the Committee, shall deliver to any candidate requiring the same, as soon as may be, a fair attested copy of the poll taken by him.

Vacancies, how filled up.

V. AND it is hereby further declared and ordained, that in case of the death or incapacity of any member of the General Convention, the President of the said Convention for the time being shall have full power and authority to issue his order, under his hand and seal, for the election of a Delegate to fill up such vacancy, to be directed to the sheriff, mayor, or clerk of the Committee of that county or cor-

---

(a) See May 1776, chap. 2, sect. 7.

(b) See 4, Ann. chap. 1.

(c) James City *deprived of a representative by* May 1776, chap. 2, sect. 5.

(d) The college *deprived of a representative by* May 1776, chap. 2, sect. 5.

poration where such vacancy has happened; and thereupon such sheriff, mayor, or clerk, shall appoint some day, not exceeding twenty, nor under ten days, after the receipt of such order, for the election of a Delegate accordingly, and shall publish notice, and proceed to the election of a Delegate, in the same manner as is by law directed in the case of an election of a Burgess, to be made during the fitting of any General Assembly.

A. D. 1775.

VI. AND be it further declared and ordained, that the Delegates so elected shall meet annually in General Convention, on the first Monday in May, and shall have power to adjourn from time to time; and if, during the recess, it shall appear to the President, or, in case of his death or absence, to Robert Carter Nicholas, Esquire, or to the Committee of Safety, that a meeting of the Convention is necessary, sooner than the time to which they stand adjourned, he or they shall have full power and authority, by advertisement published in the Virginia Gazette, or in case of exigency, by expresses dispatched to the Delegates of the respective counties and corporations within this colony, to summon the said Delegates to meet and sit in Convention, at such time as he shall appoint; the place of each meeting to be appointed by the Convention, at their session next preceding. And every Delegate attending in Convention, if the same shall be appointed and held at Williamsburg, shall be paid for his attendance, in the same manner as by law the Burgesses are allowed for attending the General Assembly; and where the Convention shall be at any other place than Williamsburg, then the said Delegates shall be allowed respectively for their attendance in the same manner, and for travelling, at the rate of four pence per mile for coming, and the same for returning, and all ferriages by them actually advanced, which allowances to the said Delegates shall be paid as by law the payment of the Burgesses wages is directed.

Delegates shall meet the first Monday in May annually (see May 1784 ch. 20) and may adjourn from time to time (see May 1776, ch. 2, sect. 10) the residue of this sect. expired.

VII. AND whereas the critical and dangerous state of this country made it expedient to hold two former Conventions, to wit, the one in the city of Williamsburg, on the first day of August, one thousand seven hundred and seventy-four, and the other in the town of Richmond, on the twentieth day of March last, and it is reasonable and just that the members who attended the said Conventions should be allowed for the same: Be it hereby ordained, that the Delegates respectively shall have the same allowance for attending the two Conventions aforesaid, and also this present Convention, that are herein provided for, and allowed, to the Delegates who may attend any future Convention.

Executed.

VIII. AND it is hereby declared and ordained, that any person who now is, or hereafter may be, appointed sheriff or mayor of any county or corporation in this colony, or clerk of any county or corporation Committee, or collector of any taxes, duties, or levies, that may be imposed by the General Convention, or any person that is already appointed to, or shall accept of, any military post of profit, except in any regiment or battalion of minute-men which may be hereafter established, shall not be capable of sitting or voting as a member of the General Convention; and in all such cases, there shall be a new election of a member, to fill up the vacancy, in the same manner as if such person was naturally dead.

Persons disqualified to be elected, or to sit and vote in Convention or

IX. AND it is hereby further declared and ordained, that all clergymen of the church of England, and all dissenting ministers or teachers, shall be incapable of being elected as a Delegate, or fitting and voting in Convention. And any person who shall hereafter accept any office of profit, or pecuniary appointment, under the crown, or shall have procured himself to be elected by bribery, in giving money, or any public entertainment of meat or drink, or made any promise to do so to the electors, or by any other corrupt practices, shall be disqualified from sitting or voting in the General Convention, the General Congress, Council of Safety, or county or corporation Committees; and in all such cases, the same proceedings shall be had as if the person so accepting was naturally dead.

in General Congress

X. AND whereas the mode hitherto pursued in electing Committee-men in the several counties and corporations in this colony, under the continental association, has not been uniformly the same, and many inconveniencies have arisen by the supernumerary Committee-men elected in some counties; and whereas also no limitation has been fixed for their continuing to discharge that duty, and they may assume to themselves a power of acting under their present appointments at all times in future, which is incompatible with the principles of representation, and the just control that the electors ought to have over them: For the removing the present inconveniencies, and better regulating the elections of Committee-men hereafter, It is hereby declared and ordained, that the freeholders of every county and corporation within this colony, and others who are by law qualified to vote at an election of Burgesses, and the landholders in the district of West Augusta, as hereafter described, shall have the liberty and privilege of electing annually twenty-one of the most discreet, fit, and able men, of their county or corporation, being freeholders, to act as a committee for carrying into execution the association, and such other measures as the Continental Congress, or General Convention of this colony, have, or hereafter may, from time to time, direct and ordain, and forwarding all public expresses of importance, the expence of which shall be paid by the public. And the said Committees shall have power to appoint out of their members a Committee of Correspondence, and such other sub-committees as may be found necessary, to superintend the different districts of their respective counties or corporations; with an appeal where any person shall think himself aggrieved, to the county or corporation Committee at large, and accountable to them for all their proceedings.

Determined.

XI. AND for the more regular electing such Committee, It is hereby declared and ordained, that the following rules and methods shall be observed, that is to say: The elections of Committee-men in the several counties and corporations within this colony shall be in the month of November annually, on the several days appointed by law for the holding of the county or corporation courts respectively, and at the places where such courts are accustomed to be held; at which elections the freeholders, and others qualified as aforesaid, shall appear and deliver in to the chairman, or, in case of his absence, to the clerk of the Committee, a list of such persons as may be judged the most discreet, fit, and able, to serve as Committee-men as aforesaid, which several lists shall be fairly counted by the chairman, or clerk of the Committee, in the presence of so many of the Committee as may choose to attend the same, and publication shall be made of the several persons that appear to have a majority of votes, who are hereby declared, in such case, to be duly elected a Committee to serve as aforesaid.

Determined.

XII. AND whereas the inhabitants of the county of Fincastle, and the district of West Augusta, although long possessed of their lands, under surveys, entries, or orders of Council, have few of them obtained patents for the same, which have been obstructed without any default in them, who, having performed what is required on their part, have an equitable interest in their lands, and ought to share in the representation, in Conventions and Committees, with other landholders in this colony: Be it therefore declared and ordained, that every free white man who, at the time of elections for Delegates or Committee men, in the said county or district respectively, shall have been for one year preceding in possession of twenty-five acres of land with a house and plantation thereon, or one hundred acres of land without a house or plantation, in such county or district, claiming an estate for life at least in the said land, in his own right, or in right of his wife, shall have a vote, or be capable of being chosen at such elections respectively, although no legal title in the land shall have been conveyed to such possessor. And to the end

Qualifications of electors in Fincastle in West Augusta.

A. D. 1775.

that no perfons fhall vote at fuch elections who are not qualified to do fo, the committee of the county or corporation fhall previoufly appoint three fit perfons to fuperintend the election, who, being firft fworn, fhall determine all difputes about the right of a perfon to vote who fhall offer any lift; and if he fhall be adjudged not to have fuch right, his lift fhall not be received.

Determined.   XIII. AND *it is hereby declared and ordained,* that a committee elected as aforefaid, or a majority of them, fhall have full power to elect one of their body as chairman, to prefide at all their meetings; and may appoint any perfon willing to undertake the fame, to officiate as clerk to them, who fhall have fuch annual allowance as the committee fhall think reafonable, to be levied by the court of the county or corporation, and may at any time or times, during their appointment, convene themfelves, and hear, confider, and determine, on all fuch matters as may fall properly under their cognizance, according to the nature and intention of their inftitution; and fhall keep a true and faithful journal of their proceedings, which fhall be read by the clerk, and figned by the chairman, at every meeting of fuch committee. And moreover, in cafe of the death or refignation of the chairman, or clerk appointed as aforefaid, the faid committee or a majority of them, fhall have full authority to fill up any vacancy occafioned thereby, by election or appointment, in manner as aforefaid. *Provided neverthelefs,* that the committees elected as aforefaid, fhall, in all their inquiries and decifions, confine themfelves within the line of duty prefcribed by the Continental Congrefs and the General Convention, and fhall not affume to themfelves any other power or authority whatever.

Determined.   XIV. AND for preventing the interruption to bufinefs that may frequently happen through the neceffary or unavoidable abfence of the chairman or clerk of the committee, *It is hereby declared and ordained,* that when any meeting of a committee fhall be regularly appointed, and it may fo happen, through ficknefs or other caufes, that the chairman or clerk fhall fail to attend fuch meeting, the committee fhall have the liberty and full power, to choofe or appoint, in manner as aforefaid, fome other chairman or clerk to act *pro tempore.*

Determined.   XV. AND to the end this ordinance may be duly carried into execution, and the duties required of certain perfons therein named faithfully difcharged, *It is hereby further declared and ordained,* that if any fheriff, mayor, chairman or clerk of a committee, or any other perfon herein named who is required to do any particular act, or perform any certain duty, fhall perverfely, obftinately, or wilfully refufe or neglect to comply with the directions of this ordinance, fuch perfon fo offending, and being adjudged guilty thereof by the committee of the county or corporation, where fuch delinquency may happen, fhall be deemed an enemy to *American* liberty and the welfare of this country, and be fubject to the cenfures of the continental affociation, in fuch cafes provided.

XVI. AND *it is hereby further declared and ordained,* that all and every other cafe or cafes, matters or things, within the purview of this ordinance, and not hereby particularly provided for, fhall be ordered, governed, judged, and decided, according to the law *(a)* for regulating the election of Burgeffes, and not otherwife.

C H A P. V.

Executed.

An ordinance for appointing Commiffioners to fettle the accounts of the militia lately drawn out into actual fervice, and for making provifion to pay the fame, as well as the expence of raifing and providing for the forces and minute men directed to be embodied for the defence of this colony.

C H A P. VI.

Executed.

An ordinance for providing arms and ammunition for the ufe of this colony.

C H A P. VII.

Repealed.

An ordinance to provide for paying the expences of the Delegates from this colony to the General Congrefs.

At a CONVENTION of DELEGATES held at the Town of *Richmond,* in the Colony of *Virginia,* on *Friday* the firft of *December,* in the Year of our Lord one thoufand feven hundred and feventy-five, and afterwards, by adjournment, in the City of *Williamsburg.*

C H A P. I.

Executed.

An ordinance for raifing an additional number of forces for the defence and protection of this colony, and for other purpofes therein mentioned.

C H A P. II.

Determined.

An ordinance for appointing Sheriffs.

C H A P. III.

Executed.

An ordinance for amending an ordinance, entitled An ordinance for providing arms and ammunition for the ufe of this colony.

C H A P. IV.

Expired.

An ordinance for reviving and amending an ordinance appointing a Committee of Safety.

C H A P. V.

Determined.

An ordinance for eftablifhing tobacco payments, during the difcontinuance of the infpection law, and for other purpofes therein mentioned.

C H A P. VI.

Executed.

An ordinance to amend an ordinance, entitled An ordinance for regulating the election of Delegates, and afcertaining their allowances, and alfo for regulating the election of Committee-men, in the feveral counties and corporations within this colony, and for other purpofes therein mentioned.

C H A P. VII.

Determined.

An ordinance for eftablifhing a mode of punifhment for the enemies of America in this colony.

(a) See 4, Ann. chap. 1.

A. D. 1776.

At a GENERAL CONVENTION of Delegates and Representatives, from the feveral Counties and Corporations of *Virginia,* held at the Capitol in the City of *Williamsburg,* on *Monday* the 6th of *May* 1776.

CHAP. I.

A Declaration of Rights made by the reprefentatives of the good people of Virginia, affembled in full and free Convention; which rights do pertain to them, and their pofterity, as the bafis and foundation of government.

I. THAT all men are by nature equally free and independent, and have certain inherent rights, of which, when they enter into a ftate of fociety, they cannot, by any compact, deprive or deveft their pofterity; namely, the enjoyment of life and liberty, with the means of acquiring and poffeffing property, and purfuing and obtaining happinefs and fafety.

II. THAT all power is vefted in, and confequently derived from, the people; that Magiftrates are their truftees and fervants, and at all times amenable to them.

III. THAT government is, or ought to be, inftituted for the common benefit, protection and fecurity, of the people, nation, or community; of all the various modes and forms of government, that is beft, which is capable of producing the greateft degree of happinefs and fafety, and is moft effectually fecured againft the danger of mal-adminiftration; and that when any government fhall be found inadequate or contrary to thefe purpofes, a majority of the community hath an indubitable, unalienable, and indefeafible right, to reform, alter, or abolifh it, in fuch manner as fhall be judged moft conducive to the public weal.

IV. THAT no man, or fet of men, are entitled to exclufive or feparate emoluments or privileges from the community, but in confideration of public fervices; which not being defcendible, neither ought the offices of Magiftrate, Legiflator, or Judge, to be hereditary.

V. THAT the Legiflative, and Executive powers of the ftate fhould be feparate and diftinct from the Judiciary; and that the members of the two firft may be reftrained from oppreffion, by feeling and participating the burthens of the people, they fhould, at fixed periods, be reduced to a private ftation, return into that body from which they were originally taken, and the vacancies be fupplied by frequent certain, and regular elections, in which all, or any part of the former members, to be again eligible, or ineligible, as the laws fhall direct.

VI. THAT elections of members to ferve as reprefentatives of the people, in Affembly, ought to be free; and that all men, having fufficient evidence of permanent common intereft with, and attachment to, the community, have the right of fuffrage, and cannot be taxed or deprived of their property for public ufes without their own confent, or that of their reprefentatives fo elected, nor bound by any law to which they have not, in like manner, affented, for the public good.

VII. THAT all power of fufpending laws, or the execution of laws, by any authority without confent of the reprefentatives of the people, is injurious to their rights and ought not to be exercifed.

VIII. THAT in all capital or criminal profecutions a man hath a right to demand the caufe and nature of his accufation, to be confronted with the accufers and witneffes, to call for evidence in his favour, and to a fpeedy trial by an impartial jury of his vicinage, without whofe unanimous confent he cannot be found guilty, nor can he be compelled to give evidence againft himfelf; that no man be deprived of his liberty except by the law of the land, or the judgment of his peers.

IX. THAT exceffive bail ought not to be required, nor exceffive fines impofed, nor cruel and unufual punifhments inflicted.

X. THAT general warrants, whereby an officer or meffenger may be commanded to fearch fufpected places without evidence of a fact committed, or to feize any perfon or perfons not named, or whofe offence is not particularly defcribed and fupported by evidence, are grievous and oppreffive, and ought not to be granted.

XI. THAT in controverfies refpecting property, and in fuits between man and man, the ancient trial by jury is preferable to any other, and ought to be held facred.

XII. THAT the freedom of the prefs is one of the great bulwarks of liberty, and can never be reftrained but by defpotick governments.

XIII. THAT a well regulated militia, compofed of the body of the people, trained to arms, is the proper, natural and fafe defence of a free ftate; that ftanding armies, in time of peace, fhould be avoided, as dangerous to liberty; and that in all cafes, the military fhould be under ftrict fubordination to, and governed by, the civil power.

XIV. THAT the people have a right, to uniform government; and therefore, that no government feparate from, or independent of, the government of *Virginia,* ought to be erected or eftablifhed within the limits thereof.

XV. THAT no free government, or the bleffing of liberty, can be preferved to any people but by a firm adherence to juftice, moderation, temperance, frugality, and virtue, and by frequent recurrence to fundamental principles.

XVI THAT religion, or the duty which we owe to our Creator, and the manner of difcharging it, can be directed only by reafon and conviction, not by force or violence, and therefore all men are equally entitled to the free exercife of religion, according to the dictates of confcience; and that it is the mutual duty of all to practife Chriftian forbearance, love, and charity, towards each other.

I

CHAP. II.

The Conſtitution or Form of Government, agreed to and reſolved upon by the Delegates and Repreſentatives of the ſeveral Counties and Corporations of Virginia.

I. WHEREAS *George* the third, King of *Great Britain* and *Ireland*, and electer of *Hanover*, heretofore entruſted with the exerciſe of the kingly office in this government, hath endeavoured to pervert the ſame into a deteſtable and inſupportable tyranny, by putting his negative on laws the moſt wholeſome and neceſſary for the public good: By denying his Governors permiſſion to paſs laws of immediate and preſſing importance, unleſs ſuſpended in their operation for his aſſent, and, when ſo ſuſpended, neglecting to attend to them for many years: By refuſing to paſs certain other laws, unleſs the perſons to be benefited by them would relinquiſh the ineſtimable right-of repreſentation in the Legiſlature: By diſſolving Legiſlative Aſſemblies repeatedly and continually, for oppoſing with manly firmneſs his invaſions of the rights of the people: When diſſolved, by refuſing to call others for a long ſpace of time, thereby leaving the political ſyſtem without any Legiſlative head: By endeavouring to prevent the population of our country, and, for that purpoſe, obſtructing the laws for the naturalization of foreigners: By keeping among us, in time of peace, ſtanding armies and ſhips of war: By affecting to render the military independent of, and ſuperiour to, the civil power: By combining with others to ſubject us to a foreign juriſdiction, giving his aſſent to their pretended acts of Legiſlation: For quartering large bodies of armed troops among us: For cutting off our trade with all parts of the world: For impoſing taxes on us without our conſent: For depriving us of the benefits of trial by jury: For tranſporting us beyond ſeas, to be tried for pretended offences: For ſuſpending our own Legiſlatures, and declaring themſelves inveſted with power to legiſlate for us in all caſes whatſoever: By plundering our ſeas, ravaging our coaſts, burning our towns, and deſtroying the lives of our people: By inciting inſurrections of our fellow ſubjects, with the allurements of forfeiture and confiſcation: By prompting our negroes to riſe in arms among us, thoſe very negroes whom, by an inhuman uſe of his negative, he hath refuſed us permiſſion to exclude by law: By endeavouring to bring on the inhabitants of our frontiers, the mercileſs *Indian* ſavages, whoſe known rule of warfare is an undiſtinguiſhed deſtruction of all ages, ſexes, and conditions of exiſtence: By tranſporting, at this time, a large army of foreign mercenaries, to complete the works of death, deſolation, and tyranny, already begun with circumſtances of cruelty and perfidy unworthy the head of a civilized nation: By anſwering our repeated petitions for redreſs with a repetition of injuries: And finally, by abandoning the helm of government, and declaring us out of his allegiance and protection. By which ſeveral acts of miſrule, the government of this country, as formerly exerciſed under the crown of *Great Britain*, is totally diſſolved.

II. WE therefore, the Delegates and Repreſentatives of the good people of *Virginia*, having maturely conſidered the premiſes, and viewing with great concern the deplorable condition to which this once happy country muſt be reduced, unleſs ſome regular adequate mode of civil polity is ſpeedily adopted, and in compliance with a recommendation of the General Congreſs, do ordain and declare the future form of government of *Virginia* to be as followeth:

III. THE Legiſlative, Executive, and Judiciary departments, ſhall be ſeparate and diſtinct, ſo that neither exerciſe the powers properly belonging to the other; nor ſhall any perſon exerciſe the powers of more than one of them at the ſame time, except that the Juſtices of the county courts ſhall be eligible to either Houſe of Aſſembly.

IV. THE Legiſlative ſhall be formed of two diſtinct branches, who, together, ſhall be a complete Legiſlature. They ſhall meet once or oftener, every year, and ſhall be called the General Aſſembly of *Virginia*.

V. ONE of theſe ſhall be called the Houſe of Delegates, and conſiſt of two Repreſentatives to be choſen for each county, and for the diſtrict of *Weſt Auguſta*, annually, of ſuch men as actually reſide in and are freeholders of the ſame, or duly qualified according to law, and alſo one Delegate or Repreſentative to be choſen annually for the city of *Williamſburg*, and one for the borough of *Norfolk*, and a Repreſentative for each of ſuch other cities and boroughs as may hereafter be allowed particular repreſentation by the Legiſlature; but when any city or borough ſhall ſo decreaſe as that the number of perſons having right of ſuffrage therein ſhall have been for the ſpace of ſeven years ſucceſſively leſs than half the number of voters in ſome one county in *Virginia*, ſuch city or borough thenceforward ſhall ceaſe to ſend a Delegate or Repreſentative to the Aſſembly.

VI. THE other ſhall be called the Senate, and conſiſt of twenty four members, of whom thirteen ſhall conſtitute a Houſe to proceed on buſineſs, for whoſe election the different counties ſhall be divided into twenty four diſtricts, and each county of the reſpective diſtrict, at the time of the election of its Delegates, ſhall vote for one Senator, who is actually a reſident and freeholder within the diſtrict, or duly qualified according to law, and is upwards of twenty five years of age; and the ſheriffs of each county, within five days at fartheſt after the laſt county election in the diſtrict, ſhall meet at ſome convenient place, and from the poll ſo taken in their reſpective counties return as a Senator the man who ſhall have the greateſt number of votes in the whole diſtrict. To keep up this Aſſembly by rotation, the diſtricts ſhall be equally divided into four claſſes, and numbered by lot. At the end of one year after the general election, the ſix members elected by the firſt diviſion ſhall be diſplaced, and the vacancies thereby occaſioned ſupplied from ſuch claſs or diviſion, by new election, in the manner aforeſaid. This rotation ſhall be applied to each diviſion, according to its number, and continued in due order annually.

VII. THAT the right of ſuffrage in the election of members of both Houſes ſhall remain as exerciſed at preſent, and each Houſe ſhall chooſe its own Speaker, appoint its own officers, ſettle its own rules of proceeding, and direct writs of election for ſupplying intermediate vacancies.

VIII. ALL laws ſhall originate in the Houſe of Delegates, to be approved or rejected by the Senate, or to be amended with the conſent of the Houſe of Delegates; except money bills, which in no inſtance ſhall be altered by the Senate, but wholly approved or rejected.

IX. A Governor, or Chief Magiſtrate, ſhall be choſen annually, by joint ballot of both Houſes, to be taken in each Houſe reſpectively, depoſited in the conference room, the boxes examined jointly by a Committee of each Houſe, and the numbers ſeverally reported to them, that the appointments may be entered (which ſhall be the mode of taking the joint ballot of both Houſes in all caſes) who ſhall not continue in that office longer than three years ſucceſſively, nor be eligible until the expiration of four years after he ſhall have been out of that office. An adequate, but moderate ſalary, ſhall be ſettled on him during his continuance in office; and he ſhall, with the advice of a Council of State, exerciſe the executive powers of government according to the laws of this commonwealth; and ſhall not, under any pretence, exerciſe any power or prerogative by virtue of any law, ſtatute, or cuſtom, of *England*: But

Marginal notes

Preamble Enumerating inſtances of royal miſrule.

Former government diſſolved.

Another declared. Legiſlative, Executive, and Judiciary ſeparated, with an exception. Legiſlative formed of two Houſes, called General Aſſembly, ſhall meet every year, once or oftener; one of them to be called the Houſe of Delegates, members of which, how qualified, and for what places choſen. When a corporation's right to repreſentation ſhall ceaſe. Of what number of members the other, called the Senate, ſhall conſiſt, and how they ſhall be choſen.

Each Houſe may chooſe its Speaker and officers, and iſſue writs for ſupplying vacancies. Laws ſhall originate in the Houſe of Delegates, but, if not money bills, amendable by the Senate. Governor, how choſen, method of balloting in this, and other caſes; his ſalary and powers; reſtrained from

be fhall, with the advice of the Council of State, have the power of granting reprieves or pardons, except where the profecution fhall have been carried on by the Houfe of Delegates, or the law fhall otherwife particularly direct; in which cafes, no reprieve or pardon fhall be granted, but by refolve of the Houfe of Delegates. *granting reprieves or pardons in certain cafes,*

X. EITHER Houfe of the General Affembly may adjourn themfelves refpectively. The Governor fhall not prorogue or adjourn the Affembly during their fitting, nor diffolve them at any time; but he fhall, if neceffary, either by advice of the Council of State, or on application of a majority of the Houfe of Delegates, call them before the time to which they fhall ftand prorogued or adjourned. *When he may convoke the General Affembly,*

XI. A Privy Council or Council of State, confifting of eight members, fhall be chofen by joint ballot of both Houfes of Affembly, either from their own members or the people at large, to affift in the adminiftration of government. They fhall annually choofe out of their own members a Prefident, who, in cafe of the death, inability, or neceffary abfence of the Governor from the government, fhall act as Lieutenant Governor. Four members fhall be fufficient to act, and their advice and proceedings fhall be entered of record, and figned by the members prefent (to any part whereof any member may enter his diffent) to be laid before the General Affembly, when called for by them. This Council may appoint their own clerk, who fhall have a falary fetled by law, and take an oath of fecrecy in fuch matters as he fhall be directed by the Board to conceal. A fum of money appropriated to that purpofe fhall be divided annually among the members, in proportion to their attendance; and they fhall be incapable during their continuance in office, of fitting in either Houfe of Affembly. Two members fhall be removed by joint ballot of both Houfes of Affembly at the end of every three years, and be ineligible for the three next years. Thefe vacancies, as well as thofe occafioned by death or incapacity, fhall be fupplied by new elections, in the fame manner. *Privy Council, number of: their duty, power, and time of continuance in office.*

XII. THE Delegates for *Virginia* to the Continental Congrefs fhall be chofen annually, or fuperfeded in the mean time by joint ballot of both Houfes of Affembly, *Delegates to Congrefs, how chofen,*

XIII. THE prefent militia officers fhall be continued, and vacancies fupplied by appointment of the Governor, with the advice of the Privy Council, or recommendations from the refpective county courts; but the Governor and Council fhall have a power of fufpending any officer, and ordering a court-martial on complaint of mifbehaviour or inability, or to fupply vacancies of officers happening when in actual fervice. The Governor may embody the militia, with the advice of the Privy Council, and when embodied, fhall alone have the direction of the militia under the laws of the country. *Military regulations,*

XIV. THE two Houfes of Affembly fhall, by joint ballot, appoint Judges of the Supreme Court of Appeals, and General Court, judges in Chancery, Judges of Admiralty, Secretary, and the Attorney General, to be commiffioned by the Governor, and continue in office during good behaviour. In cafe of death, incapacity, or refignation, the Governor, with the advice of the Privy Council, fhall appoint perfons to fucceed in office, to be approved or difplaced by both Houfes. Thefe officers fhall have fixed and adequate falaries, and, together with all others holding lucrative offices, and all Minifters of the Gofpel of every denomination, be incapable of being elected members of either Houfe of Affembly, or the Privy Council. *Courts of Appeals, General, of Equity, and Admiralty, Judges of; Secretary, and Attorney General, how appointed; falaries of: excluded with fome others, from the Legiflative and Executive.*

XV. THE Governor, with the advice of the Privy Council, fhall appoint Juftices of the Peace for the counties; and in cafe of vacancies, or a neceffity of increafing the number hereafter, fuch appointments to be made upon the recommendation of the refpective county courts. The prefent acting Secretary in *Virginia*, and clerks of all the county courts, fhall continue in office. In cafe of vacancies, either by death, incapacity, or refignation, a Secretary fhall be appointed as before directed, and the clerks by the refpective courts. The prefent and future clerks fhall hold their offices during good behaviour, to be judged of and determined in the General Court. The Sheriffs and Coroners fhall be nominated by the refpective courts, approved by the Governor, with the advice of the Privy Council, and commiffioned by the Governor. The Juftices fhall appoint conftables, and all fees of the aforefaid officers be regulated by law. *Counties, Juftices of, how appointed; fhall nominate their clerks, recommend fheriffs and coroners to be commiffioned by Executive; and appoint conftables,*

XVI. THE Governor, when he is out of office, and others offending againft the ftate, either by mal-adminiftration, corruption, or other means by which the fafety of the ftate may be endangered, fhall be impeachable by the Houfe of Delegates. Such impeachment to be profecuted by the Attorney General, or fuch other perfon or perfons as the Houfe may appoint in the General Court, according to the laws of the land. If found guilty, he or they fhall be either for ever difabled to hold any office under government, or removed from fuch office *pro tempore*, or fubjected to fuch pains or penalties as the law fhall direct. *Impeachment,*

XVII. IF all, or any of the Judges of the General Court, fhall, on good grounds (to be judged of by the Houfe of Delegates) be accufed of any of the crimes or offences before-mentioned, fuch Houfe of Delegates may, in like manner, impeach the Judge or Judges fo accufed, to be profecuted in the Court of Appeals; and he or they, if found guilty, fhall be punifhed in the fame manner as is prefcribed in the preceding claufe.

XVIII. COMMISSIONS and grants fhall run *In the name of the* COMMONWEALTH *of* VIRGINIA, and bear teft by the Governor with the feal of the commonwealth annexed. Writs fhall run in the fame manner, and bear teft by the clerks of the feveral courts. Indictments fhall conclude, *Againft the peace and dignity of the commonwealth.* *Commiffion, grants and writs, ftile, and tefte of. Indictments, conclufion of.*

XIX. A Treafurer fhall be appointed annually, by joint ballot of both Houfes. *Treafurer.*

XX. ALL efcheats, penalties, and forfeitures, heretofore going to the King, fhall go to the commonwealth, fave only fuch as the Legiflature may abolifh, or otherwife provide for. *Efcheats, penalties, forfeitures.*

XXI. THE territories contained within the charters erecting the colonies of *Maryland, Pennfylvania, North* and *South Carolina*, are hereby ceded, releafed, and for ever confirmed to the people of thofe colonies refpectively, with all the rights of property, jurifdiction, and government, and all other rights whatfoever which might at any time heretofore have been claimed by *Virginia*, except the free navigation and ufe of the rivers *Potowmack* and *Pohomoke*, with the property of the *Virginia* fhores or ftrands bordering on either of the faid rivers, and all improvements which have been or fhall be made thereon. The weftern and northern extent of *Virginia* fhall in all other refpects ftand as fixed by the charter of King *James* the firft, in the year one thoufand fix hundred and nine, and by the public treaty of peace between the Courts of *Great Britain* and *France* in the year one thoufand feven hundred and fixty three; unlefs, by act of Legiflature, one or more territories fhall hereafter be laid off, and governments eftablifhed weftward of the *Allegheny* mountains. And no purchafe of lands fhall be made of the *Indian* natives but on behalf of the public, by authority of the General Affembly. *Territorial limits; ceffion to co-terminous ftates; future governments weft of Mount Allegheny how to be eftablifhed. No purchafes from Indian natives, but for republic.*

XXII. In order to introduce this government, the reprefentatives of the people met in Convention fhall choofe a Governor and Privy Council, alfo fuch other officers directed to be chofen by both Houfes as may be judged neceffary to be immediately appointed. The Senate to be firft chofen by the people, to continue until the laft day of *March* next, and the other officers until the end of the fucceeding feffion of Affembly. In cafe of vacancies, the Speaker of either Houfe fhall iffue writs for new elections,

C H A P.   III.

An ordinance prescribing the oaths of office to be taken by the Governor and Privy Council, and other officers of the commonwealth of Virginia, and for other purposes therein mentioned. (a)

I. BE it ordained, by the Delegates or Representatives of the counties and corporations in Virginia, now met in Convention, that the Governor, Privy Council, members of the General Assembly, and officers of government, shall take the oaths herein after prescribed before they shall enter into the execution of their respective offices, in the following manner:

The OATH of the GOVERNOR.

II. I A. B. *elected Governor of Virginia, by the representatives thereof, do solemnly promise and swear, that I will, to the best of my skill and judgment, execute the said office diligently and faithfully, according to law, without favour, affection, or partiality; that I will, to the utmost of my power, support, maintain, and defend, the commonwealth of Virginia, and the constitution of the same, and protect the people thereof in the secure enjoyment of all their rights, franchises, and privileges; and will constantly endeavour that the laws and ordinances of the commonwealth be duly observed, and that law and justice, in mercy, be executed in all judgments. And lastly, I do solemnly promise and swear, that I will peaceably and quietly resign the government, to which I have been elected, at the several periods to which my continuance in the said office is or shall be limited by law and the constitution. So help me* GOD.

The OATH of a PRIVY COUNCELLOR.

III. I A. B. *elected one of the Privy Council of Virginia by the representatives thereof, do solemnly promise and swear, that I will, to the best of my skill and judgment, execute the said office diligently and faithfully according to law, without favour, affection, or partiality; that I will be faithful to the commonwealth of Virginia, and will support and defend the same, according to the constitution thereof, to the utmost of my power; and that I will keep secret such proceedings and orders of the Privy Council as the board shall direct to be concealed, unless when the same shall be called for by either House of Assembly. So help me* GOD. Which oaths shall be administered, that to the Governor, by any four of the Privy Council, and the other by the Governor, on or before the sixth day of this instant *July,* for which purpose he is required to summon the Privy Council to attend him at *Williamsburg;* and until that time the powers of the Committee of Safety, according to the ordinances of Convention, shall continue, and no longer.

The OATH of a SENATOR and DELEGATE.

IV. I A. B. *do solemnly promise and swear, that I will be faithful and true to the commonwealth of Virginia, that I will well and truly demean myself as a Senator (or Delegate, as the case may be) of the General Assembly, to which I have been elected, in all things appertaining to the duties of the same, according to the best of my skill and judgment, and without favour, affection, or partiality. So help me* GOD. Which oath shall be administered by any Privy Councellor.

The OATH of the SECRETARY, ATTORNEY GENERAL, and CLERK of a COUNTY COURT.

V. I A. B. *do solemnly promise and swear, that I will be faithful and true to the commonwealth of Virginia, and that I will well and truly demean myself in the office or Secretary, (Attorney General, or Clerk of the county court of   , as the case may be) to which I have been appointed, in all things appertaining to the duties thereof, according to the best of my skill and judgment, and without favour, affection, or partiality. So help me* GOD. Which oaths shall be administered, those to the Secretary and Attorney General by any four of the Privy Council, and the other by the court of which the officer is clerk.

Oath of an Attorney at Law.

VI. AND every Attorney at Law shall, before he be permitted to practise in any court, take the following oath before such court: I A. B. *do solemnly promise and swear, that I will be faithful and true to the commonwealth of Virginia, and that I will well and truly demean myself in the office of an Attorney at Law. So help me* GOD.

VII. AND every other person, heretofore required by law to take the oaths of government, now taking instead thereof an oath, before some court of record, *that he will be faithful and true to the commonwealth of Virginia, and that he will well and truly demean himself in his office, in all things appertaining to the duties thereof, according to the best of his skill and judgment, and without favour, affection, or partiality,* shall be deemed sufficiently qualified to execute his office.

VIII. AND all members of Committees of Inspection and Observation shall take the like oath, which any two members of such Committees respectively are hereby empowered to administer.

IX. AND whereas doubts may arise concerning the powers of the Governor and Privy Council, to the great injury of the community, in this time of war and public danger: *Be it ordained,* that, superadded, to the powers given to the Governor and Privy Council by the form of government passed this Convention, the Governor, with the advice of the Privy Council, shall have and possess all the powers and authority given to the Committee of Safety by an ordinance appointing a Committee of Safety passed at *Richmond, July* 1775, or by any resolution of Convention; and also to direct such military movements and operations as, in their judgment, shall be necessary for the safety and security of the commonwealth.

X. *PROVIDED always, and be it ordained,* that the powers given by the said ordinance and resolutions hereby transferred to the Governor and Council, and the authority herein also given to direct military movements and operations, shall continue no longer than until the tenth day after the meeting of the next Convention or General Assembly.

XI. *AND be it further ordained,* that *Thomas Everard* and *James Cocke,* Esquires, shall be, and they are hereby appointed Commissioners, to examine, state, and settle all public accounts referred to them for that purpose by the Governor and Privy Council; each of which Commissioners shall be allowed the sum of ten shillings *per* day for his services therein, until the end of the next meeting of the Convention or General Assembly.

C H A P.   IV.

Executed.

An ordinance for erecting Salt Works in this colony, and for encouraging the making of Salt.

(a) Only so much of this as prescribes the oath of an Attorney at Law seems to be in force. *See* May session 1779, chap. 5.

CHAP. V.

An ordinance to enable the present Magistrates and officers to continue the administration of justice, and for settling the general mode of proceedings in criminal and other cases till the same can be more amply provided for.

I. WHEREAS it hath been found indispensably necessary to establish government in this colony, independent of the Crown of Great Britain, or any authority derived therefrom, and a plan of such government hath been accordingly formed by the General Convention, but it will require some considerable time to compile a body of laws suited to the circumstances of the country, and it is necessary to provide some method of preserving peace and security to the community in the meantime:

Preamble.
Reciting necessity of temporary provision for public security.

II. BE it therefore ordained, by the *Representatives of the people now met in General Convention*, that the several persons named in the commission of the peace in each county respectively; having in the court of the county taken the following oath, which shall be administered to the first person named who is present by any two of the others, and then by him administered to all the others, that is to say: *I A.B. do solemnly swear, that I will be faithful and true to the commonwealth of Virginia; that I will, to the utmost of my power, support, maintain, and defend, the constitution and government thereof, as settled by the General Convention; and that I will faithfully execute the office of ____ for the county of ____ and do equal right and justice to all men, to the best of my judgment, and according to law;* shall each and every of them, have full power to execute the office of a Justice of Peace, as well within his county court as without, in all things according to law.

Persons in commission having taken the oath here prescribed, impowered to act as Justices.

III. AND be it further ordained, that where it shall happen that there is not a sufficient number of Magistrates for holding a court in any county already appointed, the Governor may, with the advice of the Privy Council, appoint such and so many Magistrates in such county as may be judged proper and necessary.

Governor and Council to appoint Magistrates, where there is not a sufficient number.

IV. AND whereas courts in the district of *West Augusta* have been hitherto held by writs of adjournment, which writs cannot now be obtained: *Be it therefore ordained*, that the Justices residing in the said district, on taking the same oath aforesaid, shall have the power and authority to hold a court within the said district, on the third *Tuesday* in every month, at such place as they may appoint, and shall exercise their office, both in court and without, in the same manner as the Justices of the several counties are by this ordinance empowered to do.

Justices in West Augusta, on taking the oath, likewise to exercise the office.

V. PROVIDED always, that upon complaint made to the Governor and Privy Council against any Justice of Peace, now in commission, of misfeazance in office, or disaffection to the commonwealth, it shall and may be lawful for the Governor, with advice of the Privy Council, on a full and fair hearing of both parties, to remove such Justice from his office, if they shall be of opinion that the said complaint is just and well founded.

Justices, on complaint, removable by Executive.

VI AND be it further ordained, that the common law of *England*, all statutes or acts of Parliament made in aid of the common law prior to the fourth year of the reign of King *James* the first, and which are of a general nature, not local to that kingdom, together with the several acts of the General Assembly of this colony now in force, so far as the same may consist with the several ordinances, declarations, and resolutions of the General Convention, shall be the rule of decision, and shall be considered as in full force, until the same shall be altered by the Legislative power of this colony.

Common law of England, general statutes in aid thereof prior to 4, Jac. I, in force.

VII. PROVIDED always, and be it further ordained, that all quitrents and arrears thereof, and all duties, aids, penalties, fines, and forfeitures, heretofore made payable to the King, his heirs and successors, shall be and inure to the use of the commonwealth, and all bonds for securing the same shall be made payable to the person or persons having the executive power.

(b) Quitrents, duties, &c to inure to the use of the commonwealth, and bonds for their security to be made payable to Executive.

VIII. AND be it further ordained, that all bonds to be entered into by sheriffs or other public officers, and in all other cases, where the same are required by law, shall be made payable to the Justices of the court taking such bond, and, in the names of them or their successors, may be sued and prosecuted at the costs and for the benefit of the public, or any private person or persons injured by the breach thereof, as often as there may be occasion, until the whole penalty be levied.

Bonds from sheriffs, &c. payable to Justices, &c.

IX. AND be it further ordained, that all the present sheriffs now in office under a commission from the late Governor, upon taking the oath before prescribed in the court of their county, shall continue to act, and have all the powers and authorities of sheriff, according to law, until the 25th day of *October* next.

Sheriffs continued till 25th October.

CHAP. VI.

An ordinance to arrange the Counties in districts, for electing Senators, and to ascertain their wages.

I. FOR the regular election of Senators to this Convention, at the time the same shall be adjourned to, and that the people may be more equally represented in that branch of the Legislature,

Preamble.

II. BE it ordained, by the *Delegates of the counties and corporations of Virginia, now met in Convention, and it is hereby ordained by the authority thereof*, that the counties of *Accomack* and *Northampton* shall be one district; the counties of *Princess Anne, Norfolk*, and *Nansemond*, one other district; the counties of *Isle of Wight, Surry*, and *Prince George*, one other district; the counties of *Dinwiddie, Southampton*, and *Sussex*, one other district; the counties of *Brunswick, Lunenburg*, and *Mecklenburg*, one other district; the counties of *Charlotte, Halifax*, and *Prince Edward*, one other district; the counties of *Chesterfield, Amelia*, and *Cumberland*, one other district; the counties of *Buckingham, Albemarle*, and *Amherst*, one other district; the counties of *Pittsylvania* and *Bedford*, one other district; the counties of *Botetourt* and *Fincastle*, one other district; the counties of *Elizabeth City, Warwick*, and *York*, one other district; the counties of *Charles City, James City*, and *New Kent*, one other district; the counties of *Henrico, Goochland*, and *Louisa*, one other district; the counties of *Hanover* and *Caroline*, one other district; the counties of *East Augusta* and *Dunmore*, one other district; the counties of *Gloucester* and *Middlesex*, one other district; the counties of *Essex, King William*, and *King & Queen*, one other district; the counties of *Lancaster, Richmond*, and *Northumberland*, one other district; the counties of *Westmoreland, Stafford*, and *King George*, one other district; the counties of *Spotsylvania, Orange*, and *Culpeper*, one other district; the counties of *Prince William* and *Fairfax*, one other district; the counties of *Loudoun* and *Fauquier*, one other district; the counties of *Frederick, Berkeley*, and *Hampshire*, one other district; and *West Augusta*, one other district; for every one of which districts one Senator shall be chosen by the

Counties arranged into districts.

Voters, by whom to be summoned.
Times of election.

persons qualified to vote for Delegates, who shall be summoned for that purpose by the sheriffs, or, where there is no such officer, by the clerks of the Committees of Observation and Inspection, to meet at the courthouses of their respective counties, or, where there are no courthouses, at some other convenient places, on the second *Tuesday* in *September* for the first district, on the second *Thursday* in *August* for the second and fourth districts, on the first *Thursday* in *August* for the third, sixteenth, and nineteenth districts, on the first *Monday* in *August* for the eighteenth district, on the fifth *Thursday* in *August* for the sixth district, on the first *Friday* in *August* for the seventh district, on the first *Monday* in *September* for the fifth, eighth, thirteenth, and twenty-first districts, on the fourth *Thursday* in *August* for the ninth and eleventh districts, on the first *Tuesday* in *September* for the tenth, fifteenth, and twenty-fourth districts; on the first *Wednesday* in *September* for the twelfth district, on the third *Thursday* in *August* for the twentieth district, on the second *Monday* in *August* for the seventeenth district, on the second *Monday* in *September* for the twenty-second district, on the second *Tuesday* in *September* for the twenty-third district, and on the second *Tuesday* in *August* for the fourteenth district. And the sheriffs and clerks of each district, having taken the polls in the manner heretofore used in the election of Burgesses, shall within ten days afterwards meet together and return as a Senator the man who shall have the greatest number of votes, certifying their own votes in case each candidate shall have an equal number.

Sheriffs and clerks to compare polls, and return Senator.

Vacancies in Convention, how supplied.

III. AND for supplying vacancies in this Convention, by death, and disqualification of any Delegates thereof, *Be it further ordained, by the authority aforesaid,* that the President of this Convention shall issue warrants to the sheriffs of those counties, the Delegates whereof are or shall be dead or disqualified, for the election of other Delegates in their room.

Wages and allowances of Senators.

IV. AND be it further ordained, by the authority aforesaid, that each and every Senator shall be allowed the like number of travelling days, and the same wages, as are or shall by law be established for Burgesses or Delegates coming to, attending on, and returning from, the General Assembly.

C H A P. VII.

Expired.

An ordinance to amend an ordinance entitled an ordinance for establishing a mode of punishment for the enemies of America in this Colony.

C H A P. VIII.

Determined.

An ordinance to amend an ordinance entitled an ordinance for establishing a mode of making tobacco payments during the discontinuance of the inspection law, and for other purposes therein mentioned.

C H A P. IX.

Repealed.

An ordinance to amend an ordinance entitled an ordinance to provide for paying the expences of the Delegates from this Colony to the General Congress.

C H A P. X.

An ordinance making it felony to counterfeit the continental paper currency, and for other purposes therein mentioned.

Counterfeiting or debasing coin, felony.

I. BE it ordained, by the Delegates of the several counties and corporations in this colony, assembled in Convention, that if any person shall counterfeit, aid or abet in counterfeiting, the continental bills of credit in this colony, or the paper money of any of the United Colonies, or shall counterfeit, aid or abet, in counterfeiting, or making base coin, or who shall pass any such in payment, knowing the same to be counterfeit or base, every such person shall, on legal conviction, suffer death, without benefit of Clergy.

C H A P. XI.

Executed.

An ordinance for augmenting the ninth regiment of regular forces, providing for the better defence of the frontiers of this Colony, and for raising six troops of horse.

C H A P. XII.

Executed.

An ordinance for amending an ordinance for raising and embodying a sufficient force for the defence and protection of this Colony and for other purposes therein mentioned.

C H A P. XIII.

Executed.

An ordinance to supply certain defects in a former ordinance of this Convention, for raising six troops of horse.

C H A P. XIV.

Executed.

An ordinance for making further provision for the defence and protection of this Colony.

C H A P. XV.

Repealed.

An ordinance for establishing a Board of Commissioners, to superintend and direct the naval affairs of this Colony.

At a GENERAL ASSEMBLY begun and held at the Capitol in the City of *Williamsburg*, on *Monday* the 7th day of *October*, in the Year of our Lord 1776.

CHAP. I.

An act for reviving several public warehouses for the reception of tobacco, and other purposes.   Expired.

CHAP. II.

An act for exempting the different societies of Dissenters from contributing to the support and maintenance of the Church as by law established, and its Ministers, and for other purposes therein mentioned.

I. WHEREAS several oppressive acts of Parliament respecting religion have been formerly enacted, and doubts have arisen, and may hereafter arise, whether the same are in force within this commonwealth or not: For prevention whereof, *Be it enacted by the General Assembly of the commonwealth of Virginia, and it is hereby enacted by the authority of the same*, that all and every act of Parliament, by whatever title known or distinguished, which renders criminal the maintaining any opinions in matters of religion, forbearing to repair to church, or the exercising any mode of worship whatsoever, or which prescribes punishments for the same, shall henceforth be of no validity or force within this commonwealth.

Preamble.

Acts of Parliament for punishing religious opinions, &c. declared void.

II. AND whereas there are within this commonwealth great numbers of dissenters from the church established by law who have been heretofore taxed for its support, and it is contrary to the principles of reason and justice that any should be compelled to contribute to the maintenance of a church with which their consciences will not permit them to join, and from which they can therefore receive no benefit: For remedy whereof, and that equal liberty, as well religious as civil, may be universally extended to all the good people of this commonwealth, *Be it enacted by the General Assembly of the commonwealth of Virginia, and it is hereby enacted by the authority of the same*, that all dissenters, of whatever denomination, from the said church, shall, from and after the passing this act, be totally free and exempt from all levies, taxes, and impositions whatever, towards supporting and maintaining the said church, as it now is or may hereafter may be established, and its ministers.

Dissenters exempt from levies towards support of the church.

III. *PROVIDED nevertheless, and it is further enacted, by the authority aforesaid*, that the vestries of the several parishes, where the same hath not been already done, shall and may, and they are hereby authorized and required, at such time as they shall appoint, to levy and assess on all tithables within their respective parishes, as well dissenters as others, all such salaries and arrears of salaries as are or may be due to the ministers or incumbents of their parishes for services to the first day of *January* next; moreover to make such assessments on all tithables as will enable the said vestries to comply with their legal parochial engagements already entered into; and lastly, to continue such future provision for the poor in their respective parishes as they have hitherto by law been accustomed to make.

Exception as to arrears of salary, engagements already entered into by vestries, and provision for the poor.

IV. AND be it further enacted, by the authority aforesaid, that there shall in all time coming be saved and reserved to the use of the church by law established the several tracts of glebe land already purchased, the churches and chapels already built, and such as were begun or contracted for before the passing of this act for the use of the parishes, all books, plate, and ornaments, belonging or appropriated to the use of the said church, and all arrears of money or tobacco arising from former assessments or otherwise; and that there shall moreover be saved and reserved to the use of such parishes as may have received private donations, for the better support of the said church and its ministers, the perpetual benefit and enjoyment of all such donations.

Glebes, &c. saved to the parishes.

V. AND whereas great variety of opinions hath arisen, touching the propriety of a general assessment, or whether every religious society should be left to voluntary contributions for the support and maintenance of the several ministers and teachers of the Gospel who are of different persuasions and denominations, and this difference of sentiments cannot now be well accommodated, so that it is thought most prudent to defer this matter to the discussion and final determination of a future Assembly, when the opinions of the country in general may be better known: To the end, therefore, that so important a subject may in no sort be prejudged, *Be it enacted, by the authority aforesaid*, that nothing in this act contained shall be construed to affect or influence the said question of a general assessment, or voluntary contribution, in any respect whatever.

Question between general assessments and voluntary contributions, deferred.

VI. AND whereas, by the exemptions allowed dissenters, it may be too burthensome in some parishes to the members of the established church if they are still compelled to support the clergy by certain fixed salaries, and it is judged best that this should be done for the present by voluntary contributions: *Be it therefore enacted, by the authority aforesaid*, that so much of an act of the General Assembly made in the twenty-second year of the reign of King *George* the second, entitled *An act for the support of the clergy, and for the regular collecting and paying the parish levies*, or any other act as provides salaries for the ministers, and authorizes the vestries to levy the same, except in the cases before directed, shall be, and the same is hereby suspended, until the end of the next session of Assembly.

The act of 22, Geo. II chap 28, &c. partly suspended.

VII. AND whereas it is represented that in some counties lists of tithables have been omitted to be taken: For remedy whereof, and for the regular listing all tithable persons, *Be it further enacted*, that the court of every county where lists of the tithables, agreeable to the directions of the laws now in force, are not already taken, it shall and may be lawful for the courts of such counties, and they are hereby required, at the first or second court after the end of this session of Assembly, to divide their counties into convenient precincts, and appoint one of the Justices for each precinct to take a list of all the tithables therein; and every such Justice so to be appointed, shall give public notice of his being so appointed, and at what place or places he intends to receive the lists, by advertisements thereof affixed to the doors of the churches and meeting-houses in the parish where the precinct lies, and shall accordingly attend on the said day by him to be appointed, and at the second court next following shall deliver a fair list of the names and number of the tithables by him taken, to the clerk of the court, who on

Expired.

the next court day shall set up fair copies of such lists in his courthouse, there to remain during the sitting of that court, for the better discovery of such as shall be concealed.

VIII. AND if the Justices of any county, where lists of tithables have not been already taken, shall fail to appoint some of their members to take the list of tithables in the manner directed by this act, every such Justice so failing shall forfeit and pay ten pounds; to be recovered in the General Court with costs, by action of debt or information against such Justices jointly. And if any Justice so appointed shall refuse or fail to give notice as aforesaid, and to take and return such list as aforesaid, he shall forfeit and pay two thousand pounds of tobacco, or ten pounds; to be recovered with costs, in any court of record in this commonwealth. And every master or owner of a family, or in his absence or non-residence at the plantation, his or her agent, attorney, or overseer, shall, on the said time appointed by the Justice for taking in the lists, deliver, or cause to be delivered, under his or her hand, to the Justice appointed for that precinct, a list of the names and number of all tithable persons who were abiding in or belonging to his or her family on the ninth day of *June* last. Every master or owner, or in his or her absence or non-residence, every overseer, failing herein, shall be adjudged a concealer of such and so many tithables as shall not be listed and given in, and for every tithable person so concealed shall forfeit and pay five hundred pounds of tobacco, or fifty shillings; to be recovered by action of debt or information, in any court of record. And when any overseer shall fail to list the tithables upon the plantation whereof he is overseer, the master or owner shall be subject to the payment of his levies, in the same manner as he would have been if they had been listed. Every person, at the time of giving in lists of tithables, shall also give in a list of his or her wheel carriages subject to a tax, to the several Justices appointed to take the list of tithables, under the like penalty for each failure, and to be recovered in the same manner as is herein directed for concealing tithables. All the penalties hereby imposed shall be, one moiety to the informer, and the other moiety to the use of the county where the offence shall be committed, towards lessening the county levy.

C H A P. III.

An act declaring what shall be Treason.

I. WHEREAS divers opinions may be what case shall be adjudged treason, and what not: *Be it enacted, by the General Assembly of the commonwealth of* Virginia, that if a man do levy war against this commonwealth in the same, or be adherent to the enemies of the commonwealth within the same, giving to them aid and comfort in the commonwealth or elsewhere, and thereof be legally convicted of open deed by the evidence of two sufficient and lawful witnesses, or their own voluntary confession, the cases above rehearsed shall be judged treason, which extendeth to the commonwealth, and the person so convicted shall suffer death without benefit of clergy, and forfeit his lands and chattels to the commonwealth, saving to the widows of such offenders their dower in the lands.

II. *PROVIDED always, and it is enacted,* that no such attainder shall work any corruption of blood.

III. *AND it is further enacted, by the authority aforesaid,* that the Governor, or in case of his death, inability, or necessary absence, the Councellor who acts as President, shall in no wise have or exercise a right of granting pardon to any person or persons convicted in manner aforesaid, but may suspend the execution until the meeting of the General Assembly, who shall determine whether such person or persons are proper objects of mercy or not, and order accordingly.

C H A P. IV.

An act to entitle the late Sheriffs of those counties which have not recommended Sheriffs to act, until others can be recommended and qualified.

C H A P. V.

An act for the punishment of certain offences.

C H A P. VI.

An act for appointing Commissioners of Oyer and Terminer *for the trial of criminals now in the public jail.*

C H A P. VII.

An act for further continuing the act entitled An act to make provision for the support and maintenance of Ideots, Lunaticks, and other persons of unsound minds.

I. WHEREAS the act of Assembly made in the year 1769, entitled *An act to make provision for the support and maintenance of ideots, lunaticks, and other persons of unsound minds,* will expire at the end of the present session of Assembly, and it is necessary that the same should be farther continued:

II. BE *it therefore enacted by the General Assembly of the commonwealth of* Virginia, *and it is hereby enacted by the authority of the same,* that the said act shall continue and be in force from and after the end of this present session of Assembly for and during the term of one year, and from thence to the end of the next session of Assembly.

C H A P. VIII.

An act to increase the reward for apprehending Horsestealers, and for other purposes therein mentioned.

I. WHEREAS the reward offered for apprehending horsestealers, by an act entitled *An act to prevent losses from drivers passing with horses and cattle through this colony, and for laying a duty on horses imported, and the more effectual preventing horsestealing,* is found not to be a sufficient inducement to persons to undertake the pursuit of those offenders, who are of late greatly multiplied, more especially on the frontier parts of the country, to the great detriment and loss of the inhabitants:

II. BE *it therefore enacted by the General Assembly of the commonwealth of* Virginia, *and it is hereby enacted by the authority of the same,* that all and every person and persons who shall apprehend and take any person guilty of the stealing of any horse, and shall prosecute him, her, or them, so apprehended and taken, until he, she, or they, be convicted thereof, such apprehenders or takers, for his, her, or

their reward, shall have and receive the sum of ten pounds, over and above the reward given by the said *A. D.* 1776.
act, to be paid by the Treasurer for the time being, upon such certificate of the conviction of the felons
as is in the said act directed and required.

III. *PROVIDED always, and be it further enacted,* that no person who is or shall be admitted as a *Witnesses not enti-*
witness against the person or persons so apprehended and prosecuted, upon his, her, or their trial for *tled to, without a*
the said offence, shall be entitled to the rewards given by this and the said recited act, or any part there *certificate.*
of, unless the Judges before whom the criminal shall be tried shall be of opinion there was other sufficient evidence to corroborate the testimony of such apprehender, so as to induce them by their certificate
to entitle him or them to such reward.

IV. *AND be it further enacted, by the authority aforesaid,* that the reward to be paid by this, or the *To be levied upon*
said recited act, shall be by the General Assembly levied upon the estate of the offender, if the same be *the offenders estate.*
sufficient, and paid to the Treasurer for the time being, for the use of the public.

C H A P. IX.
An act for the revision of the Laws. *Executed.*

C H A P. X.
An act for the further continuance of certain powers given to the Governor and Council by an ordinance of the last Convention. *Expired.*

C H A P. XI.
An act for raising six additional battalions of infantry on the continental establishment *Executed.*

C H A P. XII.
An act for the appointment of Naval Officers and ascertaining their fees. *Expired.*

C H A P. XIII.
An act for making a further provision for the internal security and defence of this country. *Executed.*

C H A P. XIV.
An act for appointing a Treasurer.

I. WHEREAS *Robert Carter Nicholas,* Esq; hath been from time to time appointed and continued *Preamble.*
Treasurer of this commonwealth, to receive all taxes and duties imposed by any act of
General Assembly, or ordinance of Convention, and pay the same away in discharge of the
demands against the public, which office he hath faithfully discharged, and the accounts of the treasury
have been examined, and passed by the General Assembly to the nineteenth day of *October* last; and
whereas, by the constitution of Government as settled by the last Convention, all persons holding lucrative offices are declared incapable of being elected members of either House of Assembly, and the said
Robert Carter Nicholas, rather than incur such incapacity, hath made his election to resign the said office
of Treasurer:

II. BE it therefore enacted, *by the General Assembly of the commonwealth of* Virginia, *and it is hereby enacted* *Treasurer, choice*
by the authority of the same, that from and after the end of this present session of Assembly such person as *of how made; con-*
shall be chosen by the joint ballot of the two Houses of Assembly shall be Treasurer of the revenues arising *tinuance of in office;*
from the taxes on lands and tithables, and of all other public money payable into the treasury of this
state for public uses, by virtue of any acts of Assembly or ordinances of Convention, to hold the said
office for one year, and afterwards to the end of the next session of Assembly; and the said Treasurer is *power and duty.*
hereby authorized, impowered, and required, to demand, receive, and take, of and from the several
collectors of the said taxes, all and every the sum or sums of money arising by force and virtue of the
said acts or ordinances of Convention, or any or either of them, and shall apply and utter the same to
and for such uses only, and on such warrants, as by the said acts or ordinances for laying the said taxes,
or by any other act or acts of Assembly, is or shall be appointed or directed, and shall be accountable
for the said money to the General Assembly.

III. *AND be it further enacted, by the authority aforesaid,* that there shall be allowed to the said Trea- *His salary (since*
surer the sum of seven hundred pounds *per annum,* for his trouble in executing the duties of his office. *altered)*

IV. AND to the end a Treasurer may not be wanting, in case of the death, resignation or disability *Successor of, in*
of the Treasurer hereby appointed, *Be it further enacted,* that in either of these cases it shall and may *case of death, &c.*
be lawful for the Governor with the advice of the Council, if the Assembly is not then sitting, to appoint *how appointed.*
some other fit and able person to be Treasurer in his room, who shall have power to act in all things
pertaining to the said office until the meeting of the next General Assembly, and no longer.

V. *AND be it further enacted,* that the said Treasurer, or the Treasurer for the time being appointed
pursuant to this act, shall not be capable of executing the said office of Treasurer until he hath given *Qualifications of;*
bond, with such security as shall be approved by the Governor, with the advice of the Council, in the
sum of four hundred thousand pounds, payable to the Governor and his successors, in trust, for the use
of the commonwealth, and conditioned for the faithful accounting for and paying all such sums of
money as shall be received by him from time to time in virtue of this or any other act of Assembly, or
any ordinance of Convention; to be recovered, upon a breach thereof, on the motion of the succeeding
Treasurer, in any court of record, for the public use, provided that ten days notice be given in writing
of such motion. And moreover, the said Treasurer before he enters into his said office, shall take an
oath before the Governor to the effect following, to wit: *I do swear, that, to the best of my judgment,*
I will truly and faithfully execute the office of Treasurer in all things, according to the true intent and meaning
of the act of Assembly entitled An act for appointing a Treasurer. *So help me GOD.*

Accounts of, how to be kept;

VI. *AND be it further enacted,* that the said Treasurer shall keep, in a book or books to be provided for that purpose, at the public charge, true, faithful, and just accounts of all the money by him received from time to time on the respective taxes and impositions by virtue of any act or acts of Assembly, or ordinance of Convention, and also of all such sum or sums of money as he shall pay out of the treasury pursuant to any act or resolution of Assembly or ordinance of Convention; which accounts shall be so kept as that the nett produce of the several and respective taxes and impositions, and the money paid out of the treasury for every particular service, may appear separate and distinct from each other.

Penalty on, for misapplication of public money.

VII. *AND be it further enacted,* that if the said Treasurer, or the Treasurer for the time being, shall divert or misapply any part of the money paid into the treasury for the public use, contrary to the directions of the acts of Assembly, or ordinances of Convention, by which the same is raised, then the said Treasurer for such offence, shall forfeit his office, and be incapable of any office or place of trust whatsoever, and, moreover shall be liable to pay double the value of any sum or sums of money so diverted or misapplied; to be recovered for the public use, by motion of the succeeding treasurer, in any court of record, provided ten days notice be given in writing of such motion.

Accounts of, how to be examined.

VII. *AND be it further enacted,* that *Richard Cary, Thomas Everard, John Tazewell, Robert Prentis, Joseph Prentis, Edmund Randolph,* and *William Norvell,* Esquires, or any three of them, be, and they are hereby appointed a Committee to examine the accounts of the treasury from the said nineteenth day of *October* last past to the end of this present session of Assembly, and shall give a certificate thereof to the said *Robert Carter Nicholas.* And the said Committee shall, moreover, in the month of *January* in every year, examine into the state of the treasury; and the said Treasurer is hereby required to lay before the said Committee, at the time aforesaid, all the accounts of the treasury, and produce the money in his hands, and thereupon the said Committee shall cause all the treasury notes which appear to have been received for taxes and impositions, appropriated for the redemption of treasury notes, to be burnt and destroyed in their presence, and shall give a certificate thereof to the said Treasurer, who shall be allowed for the same in his account. And if the said Committee shall discover that any sum or sums of money, paid into the treasury upon taxes and impositions aforesaid, hath or have been diverted to any use or uses contrary to the direction of the acts of Assembly, or ordinances of Convention, by virtue whereof the said taxes and impositions were raised, the said Committee shall certify the same to the next session of Assembly.

C H A P.   XV.

An act for appointing a Court of Admiralty.   (a)

C H A P.   XVI.

An act to enable persons living in other countries to dispose of their estates in this Commonwealth with more ease and convenience.

Preamble.

I. WHEREAS the several acts of Assembly which require the recording of deeds, and other conveyances of lands and tenements within this commonwealth, have been found beneficial, and a very great security to creditors and purchasers, but the necessity of an acknowledgment, or proof by witnesses, of the execution of such deeds, being made in open court previous to their admission to record, hath made it very difficult and troublesome for the proprietors of lands who reside in other countries to convey or settle their said lands, and it hath been doubted whether any *feme covert,* being out of the commonwealth can legally pass her estate in lands here by conveyance, in which she may be willing to join with her husband, no certain and determinate method having been provided for the privy examination of such *feme covert,* essentially necessary to give validity to her conveyance:

What certificates will authenticate the acknowledgments or probates of conveyances by non-residents.

II. *Be it therefore enacted, by the General Assembly of this commonwealth, and it is hereby enacted by the authority of the same,* that from and after the passing of this act all deeds and conveyances whatsoever made in writing, indented and sealed by any person or persons whatsoever residing in any other country, for passing any lands and tenements, or other estate situate in this commonwealth, which shall be acknowledged by the party or parties making the same, or proved by three or more witnesses to be his her or their act and deed, before the Mayor or other chief Magistrate, of the city, town, or corporation, wherein, or near to which, he she or they shall reside, and such acknowledgment or proof, certified by the Mayor or other chief Magistrate, under the common seal of the said city, town, or corporation, annexed to the deed, shall be admitted to record in the General Court, or court of the county where the lands or other estate lie, and shall be as effectual for passing the estate therein mentioned as if the conveyance had been acknowledged or proved in such court; or where the parties making such deeds shall reside in any of the states of *America,* and there shall happen to be no city or town corporate within the county wherein they shall dwell, a certificate under the hands and seals of two Justices or Magistrates of the county, that such proof or acknowledgment hath been made before them, together with a certificate from the Governor, under the seal of such state, or from the clerk of the county court, under the common seal of the county, that the persons certifying such proof or acknowledgment are Justices or Magistrates within the same, shall authorise the recording of such deeds, and make them effectual as aforesaid.

The privy examinations and acknowledgments of non-resident femes covert.

III. *PROVIDED always, and be it further enacted,* that where any person, making such conveyance, shall be a *feme covert,* her interest in any lands or tenements shall not pass thereby unless she shall personally acknowledge the same before such Mayor or other chief Magistrate, or before two Justices or Magistrates as aforesaid, according to her place of residence, and be by her or them previously examined, privily and apart from her husband, whether she doth the same freely and voluntarily, and without his persuasions or threats, and a certificate made as before directed of such privy examination, and her free acknowledgment of the deed or conveyance; but upon such certificate annexed to the deed or conveyance being produced to the General Court, or court of the county wherein the lands lie, the same shall be admitted to record, and be as effectual for passing the estate of such *feme covert,* in the lands mentioned in the conveyance, as if such *feme* had acknowledged the same in open court, and been there privily examined.

IV. *AND whereas* many *femes covert,* residing out of this commonwealth, have heretofore joined with their husbands in making deeds or settlements of their estates here, and have acknowledged the conveyances, after a privy examination, before such Mayor or other chief Magistrate, without any commission, or before two Justices or Magistrates of the county where she resided, by virtue of commissions issued

---

(a) *The substance of this comprehended in chap.* 26 *of the acts of* May *session* 1779, *except the clause empowering the court to settle the Register's fees.*

from the courts here, and others have acknowledged deeds without any certificate of their privy examination, and doubts may arise about the validity of such deeds or settlements, whereby *bona fide* purchasers, or persons claiming under family settlements, made upon good and legal considerations, may be involved in great expence and difficulties:

V. FOR prevention whereof, *Be it further enacted, by the authority aforesaid*, that all deeds and settlements heretofore *bona fide* made by any husband and wife residing out of this commonwealth, for conveying or settling the lands of the wife, which have been personally acknowledged by her, and a certificate made thereof, and of her privy examination before the Mayor or other Chief Magistrate of a city, town, or corporation, under the common seal, though no commission hath issued for taking the same, or where a certificate hath been made of such privy examination and acknowledgment before two Justices or Magistrates, by virtue of a commission issued for that purpose from the General Court, or court of the county where the lands lie, and the deeds and certificates have been recorded, in either case such conveyance shall be as effectual for passing the estate of the *feme covert* thereby conveyed as if she had been privily examined, and made the acknowledgment in open court.

Certificates in a certain form, of wives privy examinations and acknowledgments of deeds formerly made by them with their husbands confirmed.

VI. *AND be it further enacted, by the authority aforesaid*, that where any deed hath heretofore been made by any husband and wife residing out of this commonwealth, of her lands, and the same hath been admitted to record, upon proof or certificate of her having acknowledged the same without any certificate of her privy examination, in one of the ways before mentioned, it shall and may be lawful for the clerk of the court where the deed is recorded, at the request of the person or persons claiming under the same, to issue a commission for taking the privy examination and acknowledgment of the *feme*, to be directed to the Mayor or other Chief Magistrate of a city, town, or corporation; or if she resides in *America*, to two Justices or Magistrates, as before directed, whose certificates, under seal as aforesaid, of the privy examination and free acknowledgment of such deed by the *feme*, being returned with the commission and deed annexed, shall be recorded, and be as effectual as if the *feme* had been privily examined, and acknowledged the deed in court.

How certificates, where that form hath been omitted, may be obtained.

VII. AND whereas several persons have purchased lands in this commonwealth, from commissioners and sheriffs who sold the same under decrees and judgments of the courts of this commonwealth whilst it was the colony of *Virginia*, which purchasers, notwithstanding they have conveyances from such commissioners and sheriffs, have only an equitable title to such lands, which in many instances may prejudice the interest of such purchasers, and those claiming under them:

VIII. *BE it further enacted, by the authority aforesaid*, that all conveyances of commissioners and sheriffs heretofore made for lands sold in virtue of any decree or judgment of any court within this commonwealth, as aforesaid, and all such conveyances which shall hereafter be made, shall be, and they are hereby declared to be good and effectual for passing the absolute title of such lands to the purchasers thereof, and all persons claiming under them, any law to the contrary, notwithstanding; saving to the commonwealth, and to all and every other person and persons, bodies politic and corporate, their respective heirs and successors, other than the parties to such conveyances, decrees, or judgments, and those claiming under them, all such right, title, interest, and demand, as they, every, or any of them, would have had in case this act had not been made.

Conveyances by commissioners and sheriffs, in virtue of judgments and decrees, confirmed.

IX. *PROVIDED always*, that nothing in this act contained shall extend to any conveyance now in controversy in any suit commenced, and actually depending, in any court within this commonwealth.

Not to extend to cases now in controversy.

C H A P. XVII.

An act to repeal so much of an ordinance as fixes the stations of the troops raised for the protection of the frontiers.

Executed.

C H A P. XVIII.

An act to empower the Governor to issue commissions without the seal of the commonwealth, and to confirm those already issued.

I. WHEREAS, by an ordinance of Convention, it is declared that all commissions shall run in the name of the commonwealth of *Virginia*, and bear teste by the Governor, with the seal of the commonwealth annexed, and certain persons were directed to provide the said seal, but, from unavoidable delays, they have not been able to execute the same; and whereas, in some instances of great and pressing necessity, the Governor, with advice of Council, hath already granted commissions, the validity of which may be drawn into question, to remedy which inconveniencies, it is necessary that some provision should now be made:

Preamble.

II. *BE it therefore enacted by the General Assembly of the commonwealth of* Virginia, *and it is hereby enacted by the authority of the same*, that the Governor, with the advice of Council, shall have full power and authority henceforth to issue commissions under his signature, without any seal, until the seal of this commonwealth shall be provided, as by the said ordinance is directed; and that all commissions heretofore granted, or which may be hereafter so granted, shall be as efficacious and valid, to all intents and purposes, as if the same had issued according to the above recited ordinance.

Certain commissions without the seal, declared valid.

C H A P. XIX.

An act to empower the eldest Privy Councellor to act as Lieutenant Governor, in case of the death, inability, or necessary absence of the Governor and President of the Council.

I. WHEREAS by the constitution or form of government, it is directed that a Privy Council or Council of State, consisting of eight members, should be chosen by joint ballot of both Houses of Assembly, to assist in the administration of government, which said Council was also directed annually to choose out of their own members a President, who, in case of the death, inability, or necessary absence of the Governor from the government, should act as Lieutenant Governor, but in case of the death, inability, or necessary absence of the Governor and President of the Privy Council at the same time, no provision is made for the exercise of the executive powers of government:

Preamble.

A. D. 1776.

The first Privy Councellor, in certain events, empowered to act as Lieutenant.

II. FOR remedy whereof, *Be it enacted by the General Assembly of the commonwealth of* Virginia, *and it is hereby enacted by the authority of the same,* that in case of the death, inability, or necessary absence of the Governor and President of the Privy Council, as aforesaid, the first Privy Councellor, according to the order of priority in election and nomination, who shall be present and able, is hereby empowered to act as Lieutenant Governor, and be vested with all the powers and authority aforesaid.

CHAP. XX.

An act for giving salaries to the Speakers of the two Houses of the General Assembly.

Preamble.

I. WHEREAS it is necessary, in order to enable the Speakers of the two Houses of the General Assembly to support their dignity, and employ their time in the service of the country, that a proper allowance should be made each of them.

Salaries to the Speakers of the Senate and House of Delegates.

II. BE it therefore enacted by the General Assembly of the commonwealth of Virginia, that the Treasurer, out of the public money in his hands, shall, and he is hereby required to pay to *Archibald Cary,* Esq; Speaker of the Senate, and *Edmund Pendleton,* Esq; Speaker of the House of Delegates, or to the Speakers thereof respectively for the time being, the following sums of money, that is to say: To the Speaker of the Senate, the sum of two hundred pounds annually, and to the Speaker of the House of Delegates, in consideration of the great trouble and constant attendance so necessary for discharging the duties of that office, the sum of four hundred pounds annually, exclusive of their daily allowance as members of the respective Houses of Assembly, to be paid to each of them in four equal payments, to commence from the seventh day of *October* last past.

CHAP. XXI.

Executed.

An act to amend an act entitled An act for raising six additional battalions of infantry on the continental establishment.

CHAP. XXII.

An act to restrain the operations of the acts for limitation of actions and recording deeds in certain cases. (a)

Preamble.

I. WHEREAS during the confusions in this commonwealth, occasioned first by the expiration of the fee bill on the twelfth day of *April* one thousand seven hundred and seventy four, and the suspension of government subsequent thereto, the Justices in many places, omitted to hold their courts, whereby deeds for conveying lands, slaves, or other estate, which by law are required to be recorded within a limited time from the date thereof, could not be proved and recorded, and the titles claimed under such deeds may be drawn into dispute, and although such purchasers in many cases, might have relieved themselves by taking new deeds, yet such persons, through ignorance or mistake, have omitted to use such precaution, and others have been deprived of an opportunity of such renewal, by the removal, death, or refusal of the venders.

Certain deeds, not recorded within the prescribed term, may yet be recorded;

II. FOR remedy herein, *Be it enacted by the General Assembly of the commonwealth of* Virginia, that all deeds, and other conveyances, of lands, slaves, or other estate, made according to the directions of the several acts of Assembly relating thereto, which bear date at any time within the times respectively prescribed by law, next before the said twelfth day of *April,* one thousand seven hundred and seventy four, and also all other such deeds and conveyances bearing date between the said twelfth day of *April* one thousand seven hundred and seventy four, and the end of this present session of Assembly, which have been acknowledged by the parties, or proved by three witnesses, or shall be so acknowledged or proved within eight months from the passing of this act, shall be recorded, and be as effectual for passing the estate thereby conveyed as if such deeds had been recorded within the times respectively prescribed by law from the date thereof, any thing in the said laws to the contrary notwithstanding.

the period between the 12th of April 1774 and the end of this session, to be computed as one day in certain cases.

III. AND whereas it would be unreasonable that persons should be barred of their just rights by acts of limitation in respect to the time which hath occurred during the said confusions, and omissions to hold courts; *Be it therefore enacted,* that in all questions which may arise in any court of record, upon any act for limitation of actions, making entries into lands, or limitation of evidence in the computation of time, the period between the said twelfth day of *April* one thousand seven hundred and seventy four, and the end of this session of Assembly, shall not be accounted any part thereof, so as to bar such action, entry, or evidence, but in all such computations the progression shall be from the said twelfth day of *April* to the day after the end of this session, as one day.

CHAP. XXIII.

An act to amend the act entitled An act for better securing the payment of levies and restraint of vagrants, and for making provision for the poor.

Preamble.

I. WHEREAS it is represented to this present General Assembly that there hath of late been a great increase of idle and disorderly persons in some parts of this commonwealth, who are deemed rogues and vagabonds, as described by an act, entitled *An act for the better securing the payment of levies and restraint of vagrants, and for making provision for the poor,* and that upon such persons being committed to the county jail, by a warrant from a Justice of Peace, according to the direction of the said act, they have been immediately rescued and set at liberty by their associates, whereby the good purposes of the said act are not only defeated, but continual expences are incurred in repairing the jails:

Vagabonds, refusing to give security for betaking themselves to employment, may be committed.

II. FOR remedy whereof, *Be it enacted by the General Assembly of the commonwealth of* Virginia, *and it is hereby enacted by the authority of the same,* that when any person or persons shall, upon examination before a Justice of Peace, appear to be under the description of vagabonds within the said act, it shall and may be lawful for the Justice to require every such vagabond to give sufficient security for his good behaviour, and for betaking himself to some lawful calling or honest labour; and if he shall fail so to do, either to commit him to the common jail of the county, there to remain until such security be given, or until the next court, whereupon such proceedings shall be had as in the said recited act is directed. Or if the Justice shall apprehend there is danger of such person's being rescued, he shall call to his assistance another Justice of Peace in the same county, being of the quorum; and if both shall concur in the

(a) See October 1777, *chap.* 24; May 1781, *chap.* 9.

A. D. 1776.

apprehenfion of danger, they may, by warrant under their hands and feals, order and direct him or them to be conveyed by the fheriff of his county to the public jail, which warrant the fheriff is hereby required to obey, and to convey and deliver the perfon or perfons therein named to the faid public jail in the city of *Williamfburg.* And the keeper of the faid public jail is hereby required to receive fuch perfon or perfons into his cuftody, and him or them fafely keep until fecurity be given, or until they be difcharged in the manner herein after mentioned; and for fuch removal the fheriff fhall be entitled to the like allowance as is by law allowed for removing criminals from the county jail, which allowance, together with the charge of maintaining the vagabonds in the public jail, fhall be levied and paid by the Juftices of the county from whence he is removed, in their county levy, to be repaid them by the public.

III. *AND be it further enacted, by the authority aforefaid,* that if any vagabond, fo committed to the public jail, fhall not within three months after his commitment give fecurity as aforefaid, it fhall and may be lawful for the Governor, with the advice of his Privy Council, to caufe all fuch vagabonds as fhall be able to undergo the fatigues of the fame to be put on board any of the row gallies, or other armed veffels that may be engaged in the fervice of this commonwealth, for and during the term of one year, upon the like wages as landmen receive who voluntarily enlift into the faid fervice; and for the keeper of the public jail, with the confent of the neareft county court to the faid jail, to put all fuch vagabonds committed to his cuftody, who fhall not be able bodied enough to do duty on board the faid row gallies, or other armed veffels, to fervice upon wages, for the term of one year, to any perfon or perfons approved of by the faid court, which wages, in both cafes, fhall be applied in the firft place towards reimburfing the expences of removal and maintenance of fuch vagabonds, and the furplus, if any, in the former cafe, paid to fuch vagabonds as it grows due, and in the latter, upon the expiration of his or her fervice.

And failing with-in three months af-ter to do fo, may be put to labour.

Wages of, how applied.

IV. *AND be it further enacted, by the authority aforefaid,* that all able bodied men who fhall neglect or refufe to pay their public, county, and parifh levies, and who fhall have no vifible eftate whereon fufficient diftrefs may be made for the fame, fhall be held, deemed, and taken to be vagabonds within this and the faid recited act, and may be proceeded againft accordingly.

Defaulters in pay-ing levies, in cer-tain cafes, account-ed fuch.

C H A P. XXIV.

An act for extending the powers of the Commiffioners of Oyer *and* Terminer, *and for other purpofes therein mentioned.*

Expired.

C H A P. XXV.

An act to make provifion, for defraying the expences of erecting fortifications, and for other purpofes therein mentioned.

Executed.

C H A P. XXVI.

An act declaring tenants of lands or flaves in taille to hold the fame in fee fimple. (b)

I. WHEREAS the perpetuation of property in certain families, by means of gifts made to them in fee taille, is contrary to good policy, tends to deceive fair traders, who give a credit on the vifible poffeffion of fuch eftates, difcourages the holder thereof from taking care and improving the fame, and fometimes does injury to the morals of youth, by rendering them independent of and difobedient to their parents; and whereas the former method of docking fuch eftates taille by fpecial act of Affembly, formed for every particular cafe, employed very much of the time of the Legif-lature, and the fame, as well as the method of defeating fuch eftates, when of fmall value, was burthen-fome to the public, and alfo to individuals:

Preamble.

II. *BE it therefore enacted, by the General Affembly of the commonwealth of* Virginia, *and it is hereby enacted, by the authority of the fame,* that any perfon who now hath, or hereafter may have, any eftate in fee taille, general or fpecial, in any lands or flaves in poffeffion, or in the ufe or truft of any lands or flaves in poffeffion, or who now is or hereafter may be entitled to any fuch eftate taille in reverfion or remain-der, after the determination of any eftate for life or lives, or of any leffer eftate, whether fuch eftate taille hath been or fhall be created by deed, will, act of Affembly, or by any other ways or means, fhall from henceforth, or from the commencement of fuch eftate taille, ftand *ipfo facto* feized, poffeffed, or enti:led of, in, or to fuch lands or flaves, or ufe in lands or flaves, fo held or to be held as aforefaid, in poffeffion, reverfion, or remainder, in full and abfolute fee fimple, in like manner as if fuch deed, will, act of Affembly, or other inftrument, had conveyed the fame to him in fee fimple; any words, limita-tions, or conditions, in the faid deed, will, act of Affembly, or other inftrument, to the contrary notwithftanding.

Perfons having eftates taille fhall ftand feized, &c. in abfolute fee.

III. SAVING to all and every perfon and perfons, bodies politick and corporate, other than the iffue in taille, and thofe in reverfion and remainder, all fuch right, title, intereft, and eftate, claim, and demand, as they, every, or any of them, could or might claim if this act had never been made; and faving alfo to fuch iffue in taille, and to thofe in reverfion and remainder, any right or title which they may have acquired by their own contract for good and valuable confideration actually and *bona fide* paid or performed.

Saving rights of ftrangers, and thofe acquirea by iffues in taille, and by them in remainder and reverfion.

C H A P. XXVII.

An act for eftablifhing the places of holding courts in the counties of Stafford *and* King George.

Private.

C H A P. XXVIII.

An act to empower the veftry of the parifh of Weftover, *in the county of* Charles City, *to fell the lands appropriated to the ufe of the poor of the faid parifh.*

Private.

C H A P. XXIX.

An act for altering the place of holding courts in the county of Halifax.

Private.

(b) See May 1783, chap. 27.

M

A. D 1776.

Private.

CHAP. XXX.

An act to empower the late Sheriff of Prince George to take the election of Delegates for the said county.

Private.

CHAP. XXXI.

An act to empower the Justices of the county of Norfolk to hold courts at such place as they shall appoint, and for other purposes therein mentioned.

CHAP. XXXII.

An act for establishing several new ferries, and for discontinuing a former ferry.

I. WHEREAS it is represented to this present General Assembly, that public ferries, at the places hereafter mentioned, will be of great advantage to travellers and others:

Several new ferries established, with their rates.

II. BE it therefore enacted, by the General Assembly of the commonwealth of Virginia, that public ferries be constantly kept at the following places, and the rates for passing the same shall be as follows, that is to say: From the land of *David Brandon*, in the county of *Halifax*, over *Dan* river, to the land of *John Lawson*, on the opposite shore, the price for a man three pence, and for a horse the same; from the land of *John Boyd*, in the said county of *Halifax*, over *Dan* river, to the land of *Patrick Boyd*, on the opposite shore, the price for a man three pence, and for a horse the same; from the land of *Henry Trent*, in the county of *Amherst*, over the *Fluvannah* river, to the land of *Nicholas Davies*, on the opposite shore, in the county of *Bedford*, the price for a man three pence, and for a horse the same; from the point of the fork of the *Rivannah* and *Fluvannah* rivers, across the said *Fluvannah*, to the lands late the property of *Philip Mayo*, deceased, on the south side thereof, the price for a man three pence, and for a horse the same; from the said point of fork across the said river, to the lands of *Samuel Martin*, on the north side thereof, in the county of *Albemarle*, the price for a man two pence, and for a horse the same; from the lands of *Samuel Martin*, across the mouths of the two rivers *Fluvannah* and *Rivannah*, to the lands late the property of the said *Philip Mayo*, on the south side of the said *Fluvannah*, the price for a man three pence, and for a horse the same; from the lands of *William Cannon*, across the said *Fluvannah* river, to the lands of *Walter King*, the price for a man three pence, and for a horse the same; from the lands of *Jacob Bousman*, across the *Monongehela* river, to the town of *Pittsburg*, the price for a man four pence halfpenny, and for a horse the same; from the public landing at the town of *Port Royal*, in the county of *Caroline*, across *Rappahannock* river, to the lands of *Francis Conway*, the price for a man three pence three farthings, and for a horse the same, the keeping of which last mentioned ferry, and emoluments arising therefrom, are hereby given and granted to *James Bowie* the younger, his heirs or assigns, so long as he or they shall well and faithfully keep the same according to the directions of this act.

III. PROVIDED always, that the said *James Bowie*, his heirs or assigns, shall set over the said ferry all such foot passengers as may incline to cross without demanding or receiving any ferriage for the same.

IV. AND for the transportation of wheel carriages, tobacco, cattle, and other beasts, at any of the places aforesaid, the ferry keeper may demand and take the following rates, that is to say: For every coach, chariot, or waggon, and the driver thereof, the same as for six horses; for every cart or four wheeled chaise and the driver thereof, the same as for four horses; for every two wheeled chaise, or chair, the same as for two horses; for every hogshead of tobacco as for one horse; for every head of neat cattle, as for one horse; for every sheep, goat, or lamb, one fifth part of the ferriage for one horse; and for every hog, one fourth part of the ferriage for one horse, according to the prices herein before settled at such ferries respectively, and no more.

Penalty on ferry keeper demanding more than the rate, method of recovery.

V. AND if any ferry keeper shall presume to demand or receive, from any person or persons whatsoever, any greater rates than is hereby allowed for the carriage or ferriage of any thing whatsoever, he or they, for every such offence, shall forfeit and pay to the party grieved the ferriages demanded or received, and ten shillings; to be recovered, with costs, before any Justice of the Peace of the county where such offence shall be committed.

County courts may appoint ferries opposite, shall direct what boats, &c. ferry keeper to give bond, &c

VI. AND where a ferry is by this act appointed on one side of a river, and none on the other side answerable thereto, it shall and may be lawful for the respective county courts to appoint an opposite ferry, and to allow the respective rates herein before directed, and such courts shall and may, and are hereby required to order and direct what boat or boats, and what number of hands, shall be kept at each ferry respectively; and every such ferry keeper shall enter into bond, in the manner directed by an act of Assembly entitled *An act for the settlement and regulation of ferries, and for dispatch of public expresses,* and shall be liable to the penalties thereby inflicted for any neglect or omission of their duty.

A former ferry discontinued.

VII. AND whereas the public ferry from the land of *William Roberts*, across *Dan* river, to the land of *Henry Gaines*, hath been found inconvenient: Be it therefore further enacted, by the authority aforesaid, that the said ferry shall henceforth be discontinued.

CHAP. XXXIII.

An act to establish public storehouses, at the head of Potowmack creek, for the reception of naval stores.

I. WHEREAS it is found necessary that public storehouses, for the reception of naval stores, be established at *Cave's* warehouse, near the head of *Potowmack* creek, in the county of *Stafford*, to be under the care and direction of such person as shall be appointed by the Commissioners of the Navy.

II. BE it therefore enacted, by the General Assembly of the commonwealth of Virginia, that it shall and may be lawful for any two Justices of Peace in the county of *Stafford*, and they are hereby required, to issue their precept to the sheriff of the said county, commanding him to summon a jury of the neighbourhood, to meet the said Justices at the warehouses called *Cave's*, on such day as shall be appointed for that purpose, which jury, being sworn to do impartial justice on the occasion, shall view and examine one acre of land whereon the warehouses aforesaid stand, and value the same exclusive of the said warehouses. And the said Justices shall certify and return the inquisition of the jury to the court of the said county, there to be recorded, and shall give to the proprietor of the land a certificate of the valuation, who shall thereupon receive from the Treasurer of this commonwealth the amount

A. D. 1776

thereof, deducting what such proprietor shall formerly have received from the public for the use of the said land for a public warehouse; and thereafter the said acre of land shall be vested in the Governor of this commonwealth and his successors, for the use of the public. And the Commissioners of the Navy, may either cause proper houses to be built thereon, at the public expence, for the reception and safe keeping of the naval stores and materials for ship building, and appoint a proper person to take care of the houses and stores, or may let the said acre of land to any person or persons for the purposes of building and keeping such storehouses thereon, and contract with them for the receipt, safe keeping, and delivery of such stores and materials, as they shall judge most for the public good; but, in either case, the person contracted with shall not interfere with the public warehouses already built or to be built on the said acre of land for the reception of tobacco, or hinder the free egress or regress to the same for delivering, inspecting, and carrying away tobacco.

One acre of land vested in the Governor, &c. for public use.

CHAP. XXXIV.

An act to empower the Governor and Council to employ persons for working the lead mines to greater advantage.

Private.

CHAP. XXXV.

An act to empower the vestries of the parishes of St. James and Amherst to fix the rate of paying the levies thereof in tobacco.

Private.

CHAP. XXXVI.

An act to appoint Commissioners to dispose of the lands and slaves formerly purchased pursuant to an act entitled An act for encouraging the making wine.

Executed.

CHAP. XXXVII.

An act for vesting certain lots and streets in the town of Patesfield in trustees, and for other purposes therein mentioned.

Private.

CHAP. XXXVIII.

An act for dividing the county of Pittsylvania into two distinct counties.

Private.

CHAP. XXXIX.

An act to establish the places of holding courts in the counties of Pittsylvania and Henry.

Private.

CHAP. XL.

An act for altering and establishing the boundaries of the counties of Stafford and King George.

Private.

CHAP. XLI.

An act to establish Auditors of Public Accounts.

Repealed.

CHAP. LXII.

An act for establishing a town at the Warm Springs in the county of Berkeley.

Private.

CHAP. XLIII.

An act for the inspection of pork, beef, flour, tar, pitch, and turpentine. (a)

I. WHEREAS the act of Assembly made in the year one thousand seven hundred and sixty-two, entitled *An act for the inspection of pork, beef, flour, tar, pitch, and turpentine*, which was amended by five other acts, all which will expire at the end of the present session of Assembly:

Preamble.

II. BE it therefore enacted by the General Assembly of the commonwealth of Virginia, and it is hereby enacted by the authority of the same, that no pork, beef, or flour, shall be exported out of this commonwealth, or tar, pitch, or turpentine, exposed to sale, or exported, until the same shall be packed or filled in barrels under the regulation herein after expressed. And the Justices of every county court within this commonwealth are hereby authorized and required, at their first or second court held after the passing of this act, where application shall be made to them, and in the month of *August* or *September* annually to nominate and appoint in open court one or more (not exceeding six in one county) fit and able person or persons, residing in the same county, to inspect the package and weigh all pork, beef, and flour, and also to inspect the filling of all tar, pitch, and turpentine, packed or filled for sale or exportation in their respective counties; and the said courts may appoint the said person or persons, to be inspectors of pork, beef, flour, tar, pitch, and turpentine, if such person appears to them to be duly qualified, or may appoint several inspectors, as in their discretion shall seem best. And every person so appointed shall, before he enters upon the execution of that office, make oath, before the Justices of his county court, carefully to view, inspect, and examine, when required, all pork, beef, flour, tar, pitch, and turpentine, packed or filled for sale or exportation, and to the best of his skill and judgment, not to pass or stamp any barrel of pork or beef, or any flour, tar, pitch, or turpentine, that is not good, clean, sound, merchantable, and of the weight or gauge by this act directed; and faithfully to discharge the duty of his office, without favour, affection, or partiality; and shall constantly attend, upon notice, at such time and place as the owner of any of the said commodities shall appoint, to inspect the same within his county, but shall not inspect or stamp any

Inspectors, how appointed and qualified; duty of, penalty upon for neglect or malversation.

(a) See May 1780, chap. 32; November 1781, chap. 37; May 1782, chap. 40, 52; May 1783, chap. 7.

A. D. 1776.

tar, pitch, or turpentine, or any pork or beef imported from *Carolina*, until the same shall be brought to some public landing, and shall provide a stamp, or stamps, with the first letter of his county, the letter V for *Virginia*, the first letter of his own christian name, and his whole sirname at length, to be stamped on each barrel or cask by him passed, and on every cask or barrel of flour found to be good and merchantable, the quality of the flour, S F for superfine, and F for fine, and on every barrel of pork the letter L for large, or the letter S for small pork, and on the head of every barrel of tar, pitch, or turpentine, shall distinguish whether the same be tar, pitch, or turpentine, for which he may demand and take, for every barrel of pork or beef by him stamped, six pence, for every barrel of tar, pitch, or turpentine, two pence, for every barrel of flour containing two hundred and twenty pounds nett, or less, one penny half-penny, and in proportion for every cask of greater weight, and no more, to be paid down by the owner. And if any officer so appointed and sworn shall neglect his duty, or stamp any of the commodities aforesaid contrary to this act, he shall forfeit and pay twenty shillings for every barrel of pork or beef, ten shillings for every barrel or cask of flour, and five shillings for every barrel of tar, pitch, or turpentine, which shall be found not duly qualified, or of less weight or contents than this act requires, and also five shillings for every neglect of his duty; recoverable by the informer, with costs, before a Justice of the Peace of the county where such offence shall be committed.

See November 1781, chap. 37, and May 1782, chap. 52.

III. AND be it further enacted, that from and after the first day of *December* next all casks containing flour intended for exportation, before the same is removed from the mill where manufactured, shall be branded with the first letter of the owner's christian name, and with his sirname at length, or the name of the said mill, which brand or mark so used shall be recorded in the court of the county where such owners reside, and the clerk of the court, for recording the same, shall receive one shilling; and for every cask of flour removed before the same shall be branded, as is before directed, the owners thereof shall forfeit and pay one shilling.

Flour to be pure, and how packed, penalty.

IV. AND be it further enacted, that all wheat flour made for exportation shall be genuine and unmixed with any other grain, and shall be all of the same fineness, and faithfully packed in good casks made of seasoned timber, and when delivered, well and securely nailed or pinned, under the penalty of one shilling for every cask, to be recovered of the miller, or if he be a servant or slave, of the owner who shall neglect or fail so to do, in either of the cases aforesaid.

Tare of casks; penalty for false tare; when and how to be reviewed.

V. AND be it further enacted, that the owners of mills and bake-houses shall, on every cask containing flour or bread, mark the true tare of such cask, and for every cask false tared the offender shall forfeit and pay five shillings; and if any inspector of flour, or the purchaser of flour or bread, shall suspect any fraud, such inspector or purchasers may, in the presence of the seller, cause any of the said casks to be unpacked, and if any fraud is discovered, the seller, besides the penalty aforesaid, shall be obliged to pay the expence attending the same, but if no fraud appears, then the said expence shall be paid by the purchaser.

Manifest.

VI. AND be it further enacted, that every owner of a mill or bake-house, or the manager thereof, at the time of the delivery of any flour or bread for exportation, shall make out and deliver therewith a manifest, or invoice, under his hand, of the marks, numbers, and nett weight of every cask, on pain of forfeiting forty shillings for every neglect. And all flour or bread delivered as aforesaid, and put into

Flour, when and how to be secured in the carriage.

any cart, wain, waggon, or boat, to be conveyed to the place of exportation, shall be sufficiently covered and secured from the weather; and if any driver of a cart, wain, or waggon, or skipper of a boat or other vessel, carrying flour or bread as aforesaid, shall neglect to provide such covering, he, or in case he shall be a servant or slave, the owner, shall forfeit and pay one shilling for every cask so carried.

Suspected to be unlawfully shipped, how searched for, penalty.

VII. AND be it further enacted, that it shall and may be lawful for any sworn officer to go on board any ships or vessels in the day time, and search for any flour or bread on board intended for exportation without being marked and branded according to the directions of this act; and if any such shall be found, the owner thereof shall forfeit and pay five shillings for every cask, and the master of the said ship or vessel twenty shillings for every cask; and in case the master of any ship or vessel shall not permit or suffer such search to be made, he shall forfeit and pay ten pounds for every offence.

Weights and measures to be annually adjusted.

VIII. AND be it further enacted, that the weights and measures used at merchant mills shall once in every year be, by some person to be appointed by the court of the county in which such mill is erected, examined, and made agreeable to the standard of the county.

Owners, &c. of merchant-mills not to be inspectors; penalty.

Inspectors not to deal in flour.

IX. AND be it further enacted, that no owner of a merchant-mill, or any person employed in such mill, shall be appointed an inspector of flour; and if any such person shall take and execute the said office, he shall forfeit and pay fifty pounds. And it shall not be lawful for any inspector of flour to trade or deal therein; and if any such inspector shall presume so to do, he shall forfeit and pay fifty pounds for every offence. And if any person or persons shall alter or counterfeit the brand of any manufacturer or inspector of flour, the offender shall for the first offence forfeit five pounds, for the second offence ten pounds, and for the third offence shall stand in the pillory for such time as the court before whom he is convicted shall direct.

Contents, quality, stamps, of pork, beef, tar, pitch, turpentine.

X. AND be it further enacted, that every barrel of pork or beef packed within this commonwealth for sale or exportation, or imported here, shall contain at least two hundred and twenty pounds nett of good, clean, fat, found, merchantable meat, well salted between each layer, well pickled, nailed, and pegged, and no more than two heads of pork in one barrel; and no inspector shall pass or stamp any barrel of pork or beef that does not appear to such inspector to be well salted and cured before the same is packed, and after the same has been inspected, weighed, found merchantable, and passed by the inspector or inspectors residing in the county where the same shall be packed or imported, every such barrel shall be by him or them stamped or branded as aforesaid, and certificate thereof given to the owner. And every barrel of tar, pitch, and turpentine, shall contain thirty one gallons and a half wine measure at the least, and after the same shall be inspected, gauged, found clean, well and truly made merchantable, and passed by the inspector or inspectors of the county where the same shall be inspected, shall be by him or them stamped or branded, and certificate thereof given to the owners as aforesaid. And that every person making or causing to be made, wheat flour intended for exportation, shall make oath before a Justice of the Peace that the flour by him intended to be exported, or sold for exportation, is clean and pure, not mixed with meal or *Indian* corn, pease, or any other grain or pulse, to the best of his knowledge; which oath every Justice of Peace is hereby empowered, upon the request of the owner of such flower, to administer, and shall grant a certificate of such oath before him made, and such certificate being produced to the inspector, he shall diligently view and examine the flour therein mentioned; and if by him found clean, pure, unmixed, and merchantable, shall see the same packed in casks or barrels well secured for exportation, and shall stamp or brand the same in the manner herein before directed.

XI. *AND be it further enacted*, that all pork or beef exposed to sale or barter within this commonwealth in barrels, whether the same be packed here or imported from *Carolina*, or any other place, shall contain at least two hundred and twenty pounds nett meat, allowing only two and a half *per centum* for shrinkage or loss of weight; and every barrel of tar, pitch, or turpentine, exposed to sale or barter, whether made here or imported from any other place, shall contain at least thirty one gallons and a half wine measure, and be stamped or branded as this act directs. And if any person shall presume to sell, or expose to sale or barter, any barrel of pork, beef, tar, pitch, or turpentine, of less weight or gauge, he or she shall forfeit and pay to the informer twenty four shillings current money for every such barrel of pork or beef, and five shillings for every such barrel of tar, pitch, or turpentine, sold or exposed to sale or barter within this commonwealth, recoverable, with costs, by the informer, before any Justice of the county where such offence shall be committed, although the penalty shall exceed twenty five shillings current money; and every Justice of the Peace, upon such complaint before him made, and due proof of such offence, shall and may, by virtue of this act, give judgment for the whole penalty, and award execution thereupon, any law to the contrary thereof notwithstanding.

Penalties in this clause, how recoverable.

XII. *PROVIDED nevertheless*, that from such judgment, for more than twenty five shillings current money, the party grieved may appeal to the next court to be held for the county wherein such complaint was made, the appellant entering into bond, with sufficient security, before the Justice by whom the judgment shall be given, that he will prosecute his appeal with effect, and pay the same judgment, and all costs awarded by the court, if the judgment shall be affirmed; and the Justice of Peace taking such bond shall return the same, together with the whole record of his proceedings in the cause, to the same court to which such appeal shall be, which court shall and may receive, hear, and finally determine the same.

Judgments for, may be appealed from.

XIII. *AND be it further enacted*, that every seller or exporter of beef, pork, flour, tar, pitch, or turpentine, packed or filled in this commonwealth, and stamped or branded, shall make oath before a Justice of Peace, at the time of delivery of the goods sold or exported, that the several barrels by him then sold or exported are the same that were inspected and passed, and do contain the full quantity, without embezzlement or alteration to his knowledge; and every person taking a false oath, and being lawfully convicted thereof, shall suffer the pains and penalties inflicted on persons guilty of wilful and corrupt perjury, and moreover shall forfeit and pay the sum of fifty pounds, to be recovered by any person or persons that will sue for the same, to his or their own use. And that every master of a vessel, wherein pork, beef, flour, tar, pitch, or turpentine, shall be exported, shall, at the time of entry, make oath that he will not knowingly take, or suffer to be taken, on board his ship or vessel, any pork, beef, tar, pitch, turpentine, or flour, contrary to law, which oath the respective Naval Officers of this commonwealth are hereby required to administer, and such master shall also produce a certificate from the the inspectors of such commodities at the time of clearing out his vessel; and if any Naval Officer shall clear out any ship or vessel wherein pork, beef, flour, tar, pitch, or turpentine, shall be shipped, without first administering to the master of such ship or vessel the oath required by this act, or without such certificate being produced and lodged in his office, or endorsed, as the case may require, every Naval Officer so neglecting shall for every neglect forfeit and pay the sum of fifty pounds. And if any pork, beef, tar, pitch, or turpentine, packed or filled in barrels or casks for exportation, are not stamped or branded, as aforesaid, or any parcels of pork or beef unpacked, except for necessary provisions only, shall be put on board any ship or vessel to be exported as merchandise, every such cask, barrel, or parcel, may be seized by any sworn officer, and brought on shore, and the same, or the value thereof, shall be forfeited to the informer, recoverable before a Justice of Peace, and the officer seizing the same may demand and take the like fees as for serving an execution, to be paid by the party from whom such seizure shall be; and if such officer shall be sued for any thing by him done in pursuance of this act, he may plead the general issue, and give this act in evidence, and upon nonsuit or verdict for the defendant, he shall have double costs; and the master of such ship or vessel shall forfeit and pay twenty shillings for every barrel or cask of pork or beef, and five shillings for every barrel of tar, pitch or turpentine, so taken on board.

Oath of seller or exporter of beef, &c. penalty for a false oath; master of vessel's oath; penalty on Naval Officer omitting to require it; pork, &c. shipped without being branded, may be seized.

XIV. *AND be it further enacted*, that every cooper, and the master or owner of every servant or slave, who shall set up barrels for pork, beef, tar, pitch, or turpentine, shall make the same in the following manner, to wit: Barrels for pork and beef shall be made with good strong well seasoned white oak timber, clear of sap, and not less than five eighths of an inch thick, tight, and well hooped with twelve hoops at least; and in the barrels for turpentine there shall be no sap pine timber, and they shall be hooped two thirds of their length; every barrel for pork or beef to contain from twenty nine to thirty one gallons each, and every barrel for tar, pitch, or turpentine, thirty one gallons and a half at least, with his name or the name of the master of such servant or slave, at length, stamped or branded upon every barrel, under the penalty of two shillings and sixpence for every barrel set up for sale or exportation, and not so stamped or branded, or of less contents, than aforesaid.

Cooper's duty in setting up barrels for pork, &c. penalty on him.

XV. *AND be it further enacted*, that the several fines and forfeitures imposed by this act (except such as are otherwise recoverable) shall and may be recovered to the use of the informer, where the same shall not exceed twenty five shillings, before any Justice of the Peace, and for any sum above twenty five, and not exceeding five pounds, by petition, in any county court, and for all sums above five pounds, in any court of record in this commonwealth, by action of debt or information, with costs of suit.

Penalties, how recovered, and appropriated.

XVI. *PROVIDED nevertheless*, that where any officer shall discover flour to have been shipped contrary to the directions of this act, the penalty in such case inflicted on the offender, if recovered on a suit brought, shall be one moiety to such officer, and the other moiety to the person who will inform or sue for the same.

XVII. *AND be it further enacted*, that all and every other act and acts, clause and clauses, heretofore made for or concerning any matter or thing within the purview or meaning of this act, shall be, and are hereby repealed.

Repealing clause.

XVIII. *AND be it further enacted*, that this act shall continue and be in force, from and after the end of the present session of Assembly, for and during the term of two years, and from thence to the end of the next session of Assembly.

Continuance of the act.

C H A P.   XLIV.

An act for dividing the county of Fincastle *into three distinct counties, and the parish of* Botetourt *into four distinct parishes.*

Private.

C H A P.   XLV.

An act for ascertaining the boundary between the county of Augusta, *and the district of* West Augusta, *and for dividing the said district into three distinct counties.*

Private.

N

A. D. 1777.

At a GENERAL ASSEMBLY begun and held at the Capitol in the City of *Williamsburg*, on *Monday* the 5th day of *May*, in the Year of our Lord 1777.

C H A P. IV.

An act for establishing a Loan Office for the purpose of borrowing money for the use of the United States, and appointing a Commissioner for superintending the same. (a)

Preamble.

I. WHEREAS the General Congress, on the third day of *October* last, did resolve that five millions, of continental dollars should be immediately borrowed for the use of the United States of *America*, for the re-payment of which money lent at the end of three years, with the interest annually, at the place where the same is lent, the faith of the United States should be pledged, and that for the convenience of the lenders a Loan Office should be established in each of the United States, and a Commissioner appointed to superintend the same, subject to the regulations therein and herein mentioned.

II. AND whereas, on the 14th of *January* 1777, they did resolve that the further sum of two millions of dollars should be borrowed on certificates of two hundred dollars each, and that the Commissioners of the Loan Office should be directed to receive the bills of credit heretofore emitted by the states in which they respectively hold their offices for such sums as they shall be ordered by the continental Treasurer from time to time, to pay for continental purposes within such states respectively, for which monies, so borrowed upon either of the resolutions aforesaid, the lender is to receive the annual interest of six *per centum*: For carrying into execution the said resolutions of Congress in this commonwealth,

Loan Office, commissioner of, appointed,

III. BE it enacted by the General Assembly, that *William Armistead*, gentleman, be, and he is hereby constituted, a Commissioner to superintend and manage a Loan Office to be kept at the city of *Williamsburg* for the purpose of borrowing; who shall enter into bond, with good security, to be approved by the Governor and Council, in the sum of fifty thousand dollars, payable to the Hon. *John Hancock*, President of the Congress, and his successors, for the faithful discharge of the duties of his office. And the said Commissioner is empowered and required to receive from any person whatever sum of specie, continental paper dollars, or bills of credit heretofore emitted by this commonwealth, he or she shall be willing to lend for the use of the United States of *America*, upon the terms and in the proportions before recited, so as such sum be not less than two hundred dollars lent by any one person, and to give the lender a receipt for the money lent, in the form following, that is to say: *The United States of* America *acknowledge the receipt of   dollars from   which they promise to pay to the said   .   or bearer, on the day of   with interest, at the rate of six per centum per annum, agreeable to the resolutions of the United States passed the third day of* October 1776, *and the fourteenth day of* January 1777. Witness the hand of the Treasurer, this   day of   anno dom. 177   ; which shall be signed by the continental Treasurer, and transmitted to the Commissioner aforesaid in a book containing a counterpart thereof, out of which the said Commissioner shall, as often as he receives money lent, cut a certificate indentwise, fill up, countersign, and deliver the same to the lender, keeping the book as a check in his office. The said Commissioner shall, moreover, keep regular books, in which due entries shall be made of the sums borrowed, of the time when, and of the names of the persons by whom the said sums of money were lent; shall once a month transmit to the continental Treasurer an account of the cash in his office, and answer all draughts of the said Treasurer to the amount of the cash which he at any time shall have in his hands, allowing him to retain one eighth *per centum* on all monies received into his office in lieu of all claims he may have for transacting the business thereof.

for borrowing money, on certain terms, for the United States.

Certificates form of.

Commissioners duty,

and reward.

To be governed by the continental Treasurer, when to stop receiving.

IV. PROVIDED always, that when the said continental Treasurer shall order and direct the said Commissioner to forbear receiving any more money upon such loan, he shall conform to such directions, and not thereafter receive any money into his office, or issue certificates for the same, as aforesaid, but shall return all certificates remaining in his hands to the continental Treasurer.

Certificates forged, punishment for.

V. AND be it further enacted, that if any person within this commonwealth shall forge or counterfeit, alter or erase, any certificate of money lent as aforesaid, or transfer any certificate to another, or demand payment at the office of principal or interest thereupon, knowing the same to be forged or counterfeited, altered or erased, every person so offending, and being lawfully convicted, shall suffer death without benefit of clergy.

(a) *See* May 1780, *chap.* 33; November 1781, *chap.* 26.

CHAP. V.

An act for establishing an office for the purpose of borrowing money for the use of the commonwealth.

A. D 1777.

I. WHEREAS it is expedient that one million of dollars, or the value thereof in other money, should be immediately borrowed, to prevent, as far as may be, the further emission of large sums of paper money: Be it therefore enacted by the General Assembly, that George Webb, Esq; or the Treasurer for the time being, shall open an office for that purpose in the city of *Williamsburg*, previous to which, as well for the faithful discharge of the duties thereof as what may be further required of him by this act, he shall give bond, with good security, in the sum of two hundred thousand pounds, payable to the Governor and his successors, for the use of the commonwealth. And the said *George Webb*, or the Treasurer for the time being, is empowered and directed to receive from any person whatever sum of specie, continental paper dollars, or bills of credit issued by authority of this commonwealth, he or she shall be willing to lend, for any term not exceeding three years, so as such sum be not less than three hundred dollars, or the value thereof in other money, lent by any one person, and to give the lender a receipt for the money lent in the form following, that is to say: *The Treasurer of the commonwealth of Virginia acknowledgeth the receipt of* dollars from which he promises to pay to the said or bearer, on the day of with interest, at the rate of six per centum per annum, agreeable to an act passed at a General Assembly begun and held at the capitol, in the city of Williamsburg, on Monday the fifth day of May, in the year of our Lord one thousand seven hundred and seventy seven. Witness the hand of the Treasurer, this day of Which receipt shall be signed by the Treasurer, who shall keep a book containing a counterpart thereof, out of which, so often as he receives money lent, he shall cut a certificate indentwise, fill up and deliver the same to the lender, keeping the book as a check in his office. He shall, moreover, keep regular books, in which due entries shall be made of the sums borrowed, of the time when, and of the names of the persons by whom, the said sums were lent, for which services he shall be allowed to retain one eighth *per centum* on all monies received into his office, in lieu of all claims he may have for transacting the business thereof.

Preamble.

Treasurer to open a loan office,

directions to, about borrowing;

form of his certificates;

guards against counterfeits.

II. PROVIDED *always*, that when the said sum of one million of dollars, or the value thereof in other money, is borrowed, the said *George Webb*, Esq; or the Treasurer for the time being, shall forbear receiving any more money upon such loans.

Limitation of sum to be borrowed.

III. AND be it further enacted, that the Treasurer shall pay the interest of the money due upon such certificates annually, and take in and discharge the principal thereof at the time or times therein limited for that purpose; or should the lender or bearer of such certificates desire to have the same paid and discharged before the time limited for that purpose, the Treasurer is hereby authorised to comply therewith, provided the state of the treasury will admit of the same, without prejudice of the public.

Interest of money borrowed to be paid annually, the principal at the time therein limited.

IV. AND be it further enacted, that if any person within this commonwealth shall forge or counterfeit, alter or erase, any certificate of money lent as aforesaid, or transfer any certificate to another, or demand payment at the office of principal or interest thereupon, knowing the same to be forged or counterfeited, altered or erased, every person so offending, and being lawfully convicted, shall forfeit his whole estate, real and personal, receive on his bare back, at the public whipping post, thirty nine lashes, and shall be obliged to serve on board some armed vessel in the service of this state, without wages, not exceeding seven years.

For forging, &c. any certificate,

the punishment.

V. PROVIDED that the Governor and Council, for the time being, out of the offender's estate, may make such allowance to his wife and children as to them shall seem just and reasonable.

Wife, &c of the offender provided for.

VI. AND whereas it is altogether uncertain whether the above mentioned sum of money can be borrowed so soon as the exigencies of government may require: Be it further enacted, that the said *George Webb*, Esq; or the Treasurer for the time being, shall be, and he is hereby empowered, to issue treasury notes, in dollars and parts of dollars, for any sum or sums which may be requisite for the purposes of government, and which he may not be able to borrow as aforesaid, so that the money so emitted, with what is borrowed does not exceed one million of dollars, each dollar to be of the value of a *Spanish* milled dollar, and the parts of a dollar of the same proportionate value And the said Treasurer for the time being, may, and he is hereby authorised, to appoint proper persons to overlook the press, to number and sign the said notes, and to cause the said notes to be printed and engraved in such manner as he shall judge most likely to secure the same against counterfeits and forgeries.

Relating to paper money.

VII. AND be it further enacted, that all such notes to be issued shall be received and pass as a lawful tender in payment of any debt, tax, or duty whatsoever, at the same value of the other notes of credit issued by the authority of this commonwealth. And all and every person or persons who shall demand or ask more in the said notes for any gold or silver coins, or any other species of money whatsoever, than the nominal sum or amount thereof in *Spanish* milled dollars, or more for any lands, goods, or commodities, than the same could be purchased at from the same person or persons in gold or silver, or any other species of money, and refuse to sell the same for the said notes, or if any person or persons shall refuse to take the same notes in payment of any debt or demand, he, she, or they, so demanding or refusing, shall be subject to and incur the same penalties and forfeitures, to be recovered in the same manner, as are for the like offences inflicted and directed by an act of the present General Assembly entitled *An act to support the credit of the money issued by authority of Congress, and by the authority of this commonwealth, and to make the former current within this commonwealth.*

VIII. AND be it further enacted, that all the notes issued in pursuance of this act shall be redeemable on the first day of *December*, in the year of our Lord one thousand seven hundred and eighty four, shall then be taken in and discharged by the Treasurer for the time being, and shall be burnt and destroyed by a Committee to be appointed for that purpose by the General Assembly, and to enable the said Treasurer to pay and discharge the same, together with the interest of all such sums of money as may be borrowed in consequence of this act, a tax or duty shall be paid yearly upon all property, real and personal, within this commonwealth, in such manner, and in such proportions, as the General Assembly shall direct. And the person or persons appointed to overlook the press shall receive for his or their trouble fifteen pounds for every one hundred thousand pounds printed, the numberers each seven shillings and sixpence for every thousand notes by them numbered, and the signers each, for their trouble, ten shillings for every thousand notes by them signed.

IX. AND be it further enacted, that if any person or persons shall forge or counterfeit, alter or erase, any such treasury note, or tender in payment any such, or demand a redemption thereof, knowing the same to be forged or counterfeited, altered or erased, every person so offending, and being thereof lawfully convicted, shall incur the same forfeitures, and suffer the same punishment, as is herein before directed for the like offence in the case of certificates for money borrowed.

C H A P. VI.
An act to discourage desertion, and to punish persons harbouring or entertaining deserters.

C H A P. VII.
An act for providing against invasions and insurrections.   (a)

Preamble.

Decimal division of the militia, how to be completed and kept up;

to be made by the Captain, and returned to the commanding officer, under penalty; method of proceeding in case of invasion, &c.

I FOR making provision against invasions and insurrections, and laying the burthen thereof equally on all: *Be it enacted by the General Assembly,* that the division of the militia of each county into ten parts, directed by an ordinance of General Convention, shall be completed and kept up in the following manner: The commanding officer of every county, within one month after every general muster, shall enrol under some Captain such persons, not before enrolled, as ought to make a part of the militia, who, together with those before enrolled, and not yet formed into tenths, shall by such Captain, at his first muster after receiving the same, be divided into ten equal parts as nearly as may be, each part to be distinguished by fair and equal lot, by numbers from one to ten, and when so distinguished to be added to and make part of the division of the militia of such county already distinguished by the same number. And where any person subject to such allotment shall not attend, or shall refuse to draw for himself, the Captain shall cause his lot to be drawn for him by some other, in presence of the company; and as soon as such division shall be made, the Captain shall make return thereof to the commanding officer of the county. For failing to make such division, or to return the same, the Captain shall forfeit ten pounds, to be assessed by the court martial of his county. When any officer of the militia shall receive notice of any invasion or insurrection within his own county, he shall immediately give intelligence thereof to the commanding officer of the county, and if the urgency of the case requires it, he shall forthwith raise the militia under his special command, and proceed to oppose the enemy or insurgents. The commanding officer of the county, on receiving notice thereof, shall immediately, if the case will admit delay, or the danger be greater than the force of his own militia may be able to encounter, communicate the same to the Governor by express, for which purpose he may impress boats, men, and horses, and may also notify it to any militia officer of the adjacent counties, to be by him forwarded to his commanding officer; and in the mean time, if it be urgent, shall raise such part of his own militia as the case shall require and admit. The commanding officer of any adjacent county, receiving the notice so forwarded, shall immediately raise such part of his militia as the circumstances of the case may require, and order them to the assistance of such adjacent county; but any officer thinking the case of too small consequence to require these proceedings, may call a council of war, to consist of a majority of his field officers and Captains, or of a field officer and of five Captains at the least, and take their advice whether any and what force shall be raised or sent, or whether they may await the Governor's orders. The Governor, on receiving such intelligence, may, with the advice of the Council of State, cause to be embodied and marched, to oppose such invasion or insurrection, such numbers of the militia as may be needful, and from such counties as will suit the exigence of the case, and if the corps consist of three or more battalions, may appoint a general officer or officers, as the case may require, to take command thereof.

Divisions to do duty in rotation; punishment of one failing to attend, &c. when call'd on; what substitutes may be accepted; if case be urgent, nearest militia may be called on, though not in turn; arms &c directions about, for not delivering up, when required, the punishment; officers, to be appointed by commanding officer, in proportion to the number called into duty;

pay of, and of soldiers, provided for.

II. THE several divisions of the militia of any county shall be called into duty by regular rotation, from the first to the tenth; and every person failing to attend when called on, or to send an able bodied man in his room, shall, unless there be good excuse, be considered as a deserter, and suffer accordingly. Any able bodied volunteers who will enter into the service shall be accepted instead of so many of the divisions of the militia called for, or of the particular person in whose room they may offer to serve; but if the invasion or insurrection be so near and pressing as not to allow the delay of calling the division or divisions next in turn, the commanding officer may call on such part of the militia as shall be most convenient to continue in duty till such division or divisions can come in to supply their places. The soldiers of such militia, if not well armed and provided with ammunition, shall be furnished with the arms and ammunition of the country, and any deficiency in these may be supplied from the public magazines, or it the case admit not that delay, by impressing arms and ammunition of private property, which ammunition, so far as not used, and arms, shall be duly returned, as soon as they may be spared. And any person embezzling any such public or private arms, or not delivering them up when required by his commanding officer, shall, on his warrant, be committed to prison, without bail or mainprize, there to remain till he deliver or make full satisfaction for the same, unless he be sooner discharged by the court of his county. The commanding officer shall appoint such officers of the militia as he shall think most proper to command the men called out by divisions, in the following proportions: If there be called into duty not more than twenty, nor less than fifteen, he shall appoint one Ensign and one Serjeant to command them. If not more than thirty, or under twenty men, a Lieutenant, an Ensign, and two Serjeants. If not more than fifty men, a Captain, Lieutenant, an Ensign, and three Serjeants. If sixty-eight men, a Captain, two Lieutenants, an Ensign, and four Serjeants. And if not more than one hundred and fifty, nor less than one hundred, a Major shall command. If more than one hundred and fifty, and not exceeding two hundred and fifty, a Lieutenant Colonel shall command, and have under him a Major, with the proper number of Captains and other officers. A Colonel to command any number of men not exceeding five hundred, nor under two hundred and fifty. A County Lieutenant to command any number of men above five hundred, and not exceeding a battalion. A distinct list of the names and numbers of officers and soldiers sent on duty, and of all persons impressed, with the time they served, attested, on oath, by the officer commanding such party, shall be certified by the commanding officer of the county to the Auditors of Public Accounts, to be by them examined and certified to the Treasurer, for payment of what may be justly due.

Resigning, when called into duty, how to be treated.

III. ANY officer resigning his commission on being called into duty by the Governor, or his commanding officer, shall be sent on the same duty as a private, and shall, moreover, suffer punishment as for disobedience of command.

Commanding officer, &c. may impress; things impressed, to be appraised,

their value, certificate of to be delivered, and audited, &c.

IV. THE commanding officer of the corps marching to oppose any invasion or insurrection, or any commissioned officer, by warrant under the hand of such commander, may, for the necessary use of such corps, or for the transportation of them across waters, or of their baggage by land or water, impress provisions, vessels with their furniture, hands, waggons, carts, horses, oxen, utensils for intrenching, smiths, wheelwrights, carpenters, or other artificers, and arms in the case before directed. Such necessaries, or the use of them by the day, shall be previously appraised by two persons chosen, the one by such officer, and the other by the person interested, or both by the officer, if the person interested shall refuse to name one, or cannot readily be called upon, and duly sworn by the said officer, who is hereby empowered to administer the oath. Such officer shall give a receipt or certificate of every particular impressed, of its appraised value, and of the purpose for which it was impressed. And if any article impressed shall be lost, or receive damage, while in public service, such loss and damage shall be

(a) See May 1778, *chap.* 6.

inquired of, and eftimated by two men chofen and fworn in the fame manner. The faid certificates fhall be tranfmitted to the Auditors, to be by them certified and paid in manner herein before directed.

V. ALL perfons drawn into actual fervice, or impreffed by virtue of this act, fhall be exempted in their perfons and property from civil procefs, and all proceedings againft them in civil fuits fhall be ftayed during their continuance in fervice.

Privilege of thofe called into fervice.

VI. WHEN any corps or detachment of militia fhall be on duty with any corps or detachment of regulars belonging to the continent or this commonwealth, or both of them, the continental officers fhall take command of officers of the commonwealth of the fame rank, and thefe again of militia officers of the fame rank, and all militia officers of the fame rank fhall take command according to feniority, and if their commiffions be of equal date, then their rank fhall be decided by lot; a County Lieutenant, when acting in concert with regulars, taking rank as a Colonel. The commanding officer of each of the counties of *Elizabeth City, Princefs Anne, Norfolk, Northampton,* and *Accomack,* with permiffion from the Governor, may appoint any number of men, not exceeding fix, in each of the three former counties, and in the two latter not more than ten men, to keep a conftant look out to feaward, by night and by day, who, difcovering any veffels appearing to belong to an enemy, or to purpofe landing or hoftility, fhall immediately give notice thereof to fome militia officer of the county. And the Lieutenant, or next commanding officer of the feveral counties on the weftern frontier, with the like permiffion, fhall be empowered to appoint any number of proper perfons, not exceeding ten, in any one county, to act as fcouts for difcovering the approach of the *Indians,* or any other enemy on the frontiers, who, on fuch difcovery, fhall immediately give notice thereof to fome militia officer of the county, whereon fuch courfe fhall be purfued, as is before directed in cafe of an invafion or infurrection. The pay of all officers and foldiers of the militia, from the time they leave their homes by order of their commanding officer, till they return to them again, and of all look-outs or fcouts, fhall be the fame as fhall have been allowed by the laft regulations of General Affembly to regulars of the fame rank or degree. Meffengers fhall be allowed, by the Auditors of Public Accounts, according to the nature of their fervice.

Officers on duty, their rank adjufted.

Look-outs, provifion for, and duty of; fcouts on weftern frontier, provifion for, duty of. Militia &c. in fervice, pay of, the fame as of regulars. See May 1780, ch. p. 19; October 1781, chap. 47.

Meffengers, provifion for.

VII. ANY militia officer receiving notice of an invafion or infurrection, or of the approach of any veffel with hoftile purpofe, and not forwarding the fame to his commanding officer, fhall forfeit, if a field officer, one hundred pounds; if a Captain or fubaltern, fifty pounds; any commanding officer of a county, receiving fuch notice, and not raifing part of his militia, nor taking the advice of his Council of War, two hundred pounds. Such forfeitures to be recovered, with cofts, by action of debt, in the name of the other members of the faid court martial, or the furvivors of them, before any court of record, and appropriated to the fame ufes as the fines impofed by the court martial of his county.

Penalties on officers neglecting to forward to their commanding officer notice of an invafion, &c.

VIII. ANY officer or foldier guilty of mutiny, defertion, difobedience of command, abfence from duty or quarters, neglect of guard, or cowardice, fhall be punifhed at the difcretion of a court martial, by degrading, cafhiering, drumming out of the army, fine not exceeding two months pay, imprifonment not exceeding one month.

Court martial, how to punifh officers and foldiers mifbehaving;

IX. SUCH court martial, which the commanding officer is hereby empowered to order, fhall be conftituted of militia officers only, of the rank of Captains or higher, and fhall confift of feven members at the leaft, whereof one fhall be a County Lieutenant, or field officer. Provided two or more companies, without a field officer, fhould be called out to duty, the fenior officer may appoint a court martial, to confift of one Captain, and three or more commiffioned officers, whofe fentence, not extending to amercement or imprifonment, being confirmed by the commanding officer, not being a member of the court, fhall be put in execution, each of whom fhall take the following oath: *I do fwear, that I will well and truly try, and impartially determine, the caufe of the prifoner now to be tried, according to the act of Affembly for providing againft invafions and infurrections. So help me God.* Which oath fhall be adminiftered to the prefiding officer by the next in command, and then by fuch prefiding officer to the other members. The faid court fhall alfo appoint a clerk to enter and preferve their proceedings, to whom the prefident fhall adminifter an oath, truly and faithfully to execute the duties of his office. And fuch clerk fhall be paid fuch compenfation for his fervices as fhall be judged reafonable by the court martial, out of the fines impofed by this act; the fines to be collected by the fheriff, as ordered in the militia law, except fuch as can be retained out of the pay of the delinquent.

how conftituted in different cafes;

members of, their oath;

fhall appoint a clerk and pay him out of the fines

Fines, how to be collected.

X. ALL perfons called to give evidence fhall take the ufual oath or affirmation, to be adminiftered by the clerk of the court. If in any cafe the offender be not arrefted before the corps of militia on duty be difcharged, or cannot be tried for want of members fufficient to make a court, he fhall be fubject to be tried afterwards by the court martial of his county. The Governor, with the advice of the Council of State, may, and he is hereby authorifed and defired, to appoint one or more fit and able perfons to act as quartermafters to the militia drawn into actual fervice, whofe duty it fhall be to provide, in due time, all things neceffary for their accommodation. And fuch quartermafters fhall have power, and they are hereby ftrictly enjoined, to infpect and examine all provifions dealt out by any commiffary or contractor to fuch militia, and make report to the Governor, from time to time, of the quality thereof. And the faid quartermafters fhall, for their fervices, receive fuch allowance as to the Governor and Council may appear reafonable. The commanding officer of any detachment of militia drawn out into actual fervice fhall, if neceffary, appoint a commiffary or contractor to procure provifions for the faid detachment. Such commiffary, upon complaint to a court martial, to be compofed of the officers of the corps, may, by judgment of fuch court martial, be removed for mifconduct. Every commiffary or contractor appointed by virtue of this act fhall obtain a certificate of his fervice from the commanding officer of the detachment for which he ferved: on producing which to the Governor and Council he fhall be entitled to fuch reward as they think fit.

Witneffes to be fworn. Offender, how to be tried, if not tried before corps difcharged. Quartermafter, how appointed, his duty, and reward.

Commiffary, &c. may be appointed by the commanding officer; but removable for mifconduct; how rewarded.

XI. ALL other acts and ordinances, fo far as they make provifion againft invafions and infurrections, are hereby repealed.

Repealing claufe, with an exception.

XII. *PROVIDED,* that nothing in this act fhall be conftrued to alter or change any thing contained in the general form or conftitution of this government.

XIII. THIS act fhall be read to every company of the militia, by order of the Captain or next commanding officer, twice in every year, on penalty of five pounds for every omiffion.

Notification of the act, and penalty for omiffion.

A. D. 1777.

A. D. 1777.

CHAP. VIII.

An act to support the credit of the money issued by the authority of Congress and by the authority of this Commonwealth, and to make the former current within this commonwealth.   (a)

I. WHEREAS the continental money, and the money of this commonwealth, ought to be supported at the full value expressed in the respective bills, and the pernicious artifices of the enemies of *American* liberty, to impair the credit of the said bills, by raising the nominal value of gold and silver, or any other species of money whatsoever, ought to be guarded against and prevented:

II. BE it enacted, *by the General Assembly*, that all bills of credit emitted by authority of Congress shall pass current in all payments, trade, and dealings within this commonwealth, and be deemed equal to the same nominal sum in *Spanish* milled dollars; and that whosoever shall offer, ask, or receive more in the said bills, or in the bills of credit emitted by authority of this commonwealth, for any gold or silver coins, or any other species of money whatsoever, than the nominal sum or amount thereof in *Spanish* milled dollars, or more in either of the said kinds of money for any lands, goods, or commodities whatsoever, than the same could be purchased at of the same person or persons in gold or silver, or any other species of money whatsoever, or shall offer to sell any goods or commodities for gold or silver coins, or any other species of money whatsoever, and refuse to sell the same for either the said continental bills, or bills of this commonwealth, every such person shall forfeit the value of the money so exchanged, or of the house, land, or commodity, so sold or offered for sale, to be recovered with costs, by action of debt, in any court of record; the one moiety to the use of the person suing for the same, and the other moiety to the use of this commonwealth.

Bills of credit, issued by Congress, made a lawful tender, at 6s. per dollar.

III. AND be it further enacted, that the bills of credit issued by Congress shall be a lawful tender in payment of all public and private debts within this commonwealth, and a tender and refusal thereof, or of the bills of credit issued by authority of this commonwealth, shall operate as an extinguishment of interest from the time of such tender; and that debts payable in sterling shall be discharged with either of the above kinds of money, at the rate of thirty three and one third *per centum* exchange; and that the continental dollars, and dollars issued by this commonwealth, shall pass in discharge of all debts and contracts at the rate of six shillings currency *per* dollar.

How tender might be made of, in particular cases.

IV AND whereas many sums of money are now due and owing upon bills, bonds, and protested bills of exchange, to many persons, who, to avoid the force of a tender, and avail themselves of the interest, do put or place the said specialties into the hands of the persons not authorised to receive the same; For remedy whereof, *Be it enacted*, that a tender in any money made current here to any person holding, or being possessed of any bill, bond, or protested bill of exchange, of the principal and all interest due thereon by the person or persons owing the same, shall be a legal tender, and upon a refusal shall be an extinguishment of the interest; or where the debtor cannot discover who hath the possession of the specialty, by which he or she stands indebted, a tender of the principal and interest to the factor with whom the debt was contracted, shall in like manner avail such debtor, and extinguish the interest.

CHAP. IX.

An act limiting the time for continuing the Delegates to General Congress in office, and making provision for their support, and for other purposes.

Repealed.

CHAP. X.

An act to establish a mode for the speedy and summary recovery of such sums of money as are or may become due to the public, and for enforcing all contracts entered into with government.   (b)

Preamble.

I. WHEREAS divers persons, receiving money at the treasury of this commonwealth for public uses, have applied it to different purposes, and when called on refused or neglected to repay the same, for which evil no adequate remedy hath yet been provided:

II. BE it therefore enacted, *by the General Assembly*, that every officer, paymaster, commissary, victualler, contractor, agent, or other person, who hath, or hereafter may receive, any sum or sums of money at the treasury of this commonwealth for recruiting or paying the army, building, rigging, or furnishing vessels or ships of war, erecting fortifications, purchasing clothes, provisions, arms, or ammunition, erecting or carrying on the public manufactories, or for any other public use, and hath not, or shall not properly apply the same, or repay whatever sum remains unapplied into the public treasury, that then it shall and may be lawful for the Treasurer for the time being, upon a motion to be made in any court of record, to demand judgment, in the name of the Governor for the time being, against such person and his securities, for whatever sum of money remains in his hands unapplied, with interest and costs; and such court is hereby authorized and required to give judgment accordingly, and to award execution thereupon, provided such person and his securities have ten days previous notice, in writing, of such motion.

Defaulters, summary remedy against.

III. AND whereas, in the course of the present war, several persons have entered into contracts with government for supplying the army and navy with provisions and other necessaries, and failed or refused to comply therewith, and many others may hereafter occasion the like disappointments to the great prejudice of the service: For remedy whereof, BE it further enacted, that when any suit shall be brought on behalf of the commonwealth against any person whatsoever for failure of contract, or breach of covenant, the Attorney prosecuting the same shall file the declaration, and assign breaches where such are necessary, at the time the writ issues, a copy of which shall go out and be served on the defendant or defendants with the same; and when the writ, with a copy of the declaration and breaches, are served ten days before the return day of such writ, the defendant or defendants shall give special bail, if ruled thereto, and plead to issue immediately, which issue shall be tried by a jury, and judgment given for the

Contracts for provisions, &c. short remedy for inforcing, in the name of the commonwealth,

(a) See May 1780, Chap. 10; October 1780, Chap. 1; May 1781, Chap. 6; November 1781, Chap. 13, 26; October 1782, Chap. 13; May 1783, Chap. 4.

(b) See May 1778, Chap. 11; May 1782, Chap. 15.

debt, or damages and cofts, according to the very right of the caufe, any errour or mifprifion in the proceedings notwithftanding, and thereupon execution may be awarded. And when the writ, with a copy of the declaration and breaches, fhall not be ferved ten days before the return day of fuch writ, the defendant or defendants fhall plead, and the proceedings fhall be the fame at the next fucceeding court as is herein before directed to be had at the firft court, when the fervice of the writ fhall be in time. *A. D. 1777.*

IV. *PROVIDED nevertheless,* that in either cafe the court fhall have power to continue the fuit over to the fucceeding court, for good caufe to them fhewn.

V. AND whereas divers perfons have, and hereafter may enter into contracts with the agents or contractors for victualling and clothing the army and navy, and have or may fail or refufe to comply therewith: *Be it further enacted,* that upon any fuit brought by any victualler, agent, or contractor, *and in the name* against any perfon or perfons fo failing or refufing, the proceedings therein fhall be the fame, and the *of any victualler,* plaintiff fhall have the fame remedy and redrefs, as is herein before directed in fuits which may be brought *&c.* on behalf of the commonwealth.

C H A P. XI.

An act for preventing the forgery of certain warrants and certificates, and other purposes.

I. WHEREAS the crime of forgery, at all times pernicious in its nature, but particularly flagitious as committed in fome late inftances, hath not a punifhment fufficiently exemplary annexed *Preamble.* thereto: *Be it therefore enacted by the General Assembly,* that if any perfon, from and after the twenty-ninth day of *June,* in the year of our Lord one thoufand feven hundred and feventy-feven, fhall falfely make, forge, or counterfeit, or caufe or procure to be falfely made, forged, or counterfeited, *Offences declared* or willingly aid or affift in falfely making, forging, or counterfeiting, any warrant or draught of the *to be felony;* Governor or Chief Magiftrate, or of the Prefident or other member of the Privy Council acting as Lieutenant Governor, or of the Navy Board, directed to the Treafurer for the payment of public money, or any certificate of the Commiffioners or Auditors of Public Accounts directed to the Treafurer for payment of public money, or fhall prefent for payment, at the public treafury, any falfe, forged, or counterfeited warrant or draught of the Governor or Chief Magiftrate, or of the Prefident or other member of the Privy Council, acting as Lieutenant Governor, or of the Navy Board, or any falfe, forged, or counterfeited certificate of the Commiffioners or Auditors of Public Accounts, as aforefaid, knowing the fame to be falfe, forged, or counterfeited, or fhall offer to the Commiffioners or Auditors of Public Accounts, for the purpofe of obtaining their certificate directed to the Treafurer for the payment of public money, any falfe, forged, or counterfeited voucher or exhibit, knowing the fame to be falfe, forged, or counterfeited, or fhall forge and pafs any fuch voucher or exhibit, then every fuch perfon, being thereof convicted according to the due courfe of law, fhall be deemed and holden guilty of *the punishment for* felony, fhall forfeit his whole eftate, real and perfonal, fhall receive on his bare back, at the public *offender, provision* whipping poft, thirty nine lafhes, and fhall ferve on board fome armed veffel in the fervice of this com- *out of, the estate of,* monwealth, without wages, for a term not exceeding feven years; provided that the Governor and *for his wife and* Council may make out of the offender's eftate fuch an allowance as they fhall think neceffary for the *children.* maintenance of his wife and children.

II. AND whereas it hath been doubted whether it is felony to fteal continental bills of credit, treafury notes of this commonwealth, or paper money of any of the other United States;

III. BE it therefore enacted by the authority aforefaid, that if any perfon from and after the faid twenty ninth day of *June,* fhall fteal, or take by robbery, any continental bill of credit, any treafury note of this commonwealth, or any fum of the paper money of any other of the United States, fuch offender fhall be deemed guilty of felony, and fhall be obliged to reftore four times the value of the money fo ftolen, and in default thereof fhall be fold as a fervant for fuch a term, not exceeding feven years, as fhall raife the fame, and fhall further receive fuch other punifhment, not extending to life or member, as the court before whom the offender fhall be convicted fhall think adequate to his offence.

IV. *PROVIDED always, and it is hereby enacted by the authority aforefaid,* that no attainder for any *Attainder of, to* offence hereby made felony fhall work any corruption of blood, or difherifon of heirs. *work no corruption* *of blood.*

C H A P. XII.

An act for the encouragement of iron works.

I. WHEREAS the difcovery and manufacturing of iron ore, requifite for the fabricating the various implements of hufbandry, fmall arms, intrenching tools, anchors, and other things neceffary for the army and navy, is at this time effential to the welfare and exiftence of this ftate, as the ufual fupplies of pig and bar iron from foreign ftates is rendered difficult and uncertain, and *James Hunter,* near *Fredericksburg,* hath erected, and is now carrying on, at confiderable expence and labour, many extenfive factories, flitting, plating, and wire mills, and is greatly retarded through the want of pig and bar iron; and whereas there is a certain tract of land in the county of *Stafford,* called and known by the name of *Accakeek* furnace tract on which a furnace for the making of pig iron was formerly erected and carried on, which has been fince difcontinued: Therefore, for encouraging the faid *James Hunter,* and the better to enable him to profecute his works with efficacy and vigour, *Be it enacted, by the General Assembly,* that if the proprietors of the faid *Accakeek* furnace tract, or their agent after previous notice hereof, do not within one month begin, and within fix months erect thereon, a furnace and other neceffary works on a fcale equal to or larger than the former one, and profecute the fame for making pig iron and other caftings, that then it fhall and may be lawful to and for the faid *James Hunter,* after the expiration of either of the terms aforefaid, to enter upon and locate two hundred acres of the faid tract, including the old furnace feat and dam, within fuch bounds as fhall be laid off by the commiffioners herein after appointed: and the faid *James Hunter* fhall pay to the proprietors, or their agents, fuch valuation for the fame as may be made by a jury of twelve good and lawful freeholders, upon oath, who fhall be fummoned by the fheriff of the faid county of *Stafford* for that purpofe. And if a fufficient body of iron ore is not difcovered on the faid two hundred acres of land, the faid *James Hunter* fhall and may explore and open any other unimproved lands belonging to the faid *Accakeek* furnace tract, and upon difcovering a body of iron ore locate ten acres thereof, including fuch body of ore (in cafe the proprietors, or their agents, fhall not within three months open the fame) paying to the faid proprietors or their agents fuch valuation for the fame as may be made by a jury in manner aforefaid; and thereafter the fame fhall be, and is hereby vefted in the faid *James Hunter* in fee fimple.

Iron, or other ore, how they may be explored, and the land opened.

II. *AND be it further enacted,* that it shall and may be lawful for any person or persons, in company with a Justice of the Peace of any county, to explore and open, for the purpose of discovering iron or any other sort of ore, any unimproved land within this commonwealth, paying to the proprietors of such lands any and all such damages as are by them sustained thereby, to be awarded by a jury summoned and sworn in the manner aforesaid.

III. *AND be it further enacted,* that half an acre of ground for a landing, situate at some convenient place on *Aquia* or *Potowmack* creek, within such bounds as may be allotted by the commissioners as aforesaid, so that it does not deprive any person of houses or other immediate conveniences, shall be, and the same is hereby assigned to the said *James Hunter,* who shall pay such valuation for the same as may be made by a jury in manner herein before directed, and thereafter the same shall be vested in the said *James Hunter* in fee simple, so long as the said *James Hunter,* his heirs and assigns, shall continue to keep up and carry on his furnace and works aforesaid as herein before directed, otherwise such half acre of land shall revert to the former proprietor from whom the same was taken, his or her heirs, upon repaying to the said *Hunter,* or his heirs, the valuation made as aforesaid.

IV. *AND be it further enacted,* that *William Fitzhugh, Thomas Ludwell Lee, Robert Brent, Samuel Selden,* and *Charles Carter,* Esquires, or any three of them, be, and they are hereby appointed commissioners for the several purposes herein before recited, who shall make report of their proceedings and discoveries to the next session of Assembly.

V. *AND be it further enacted,* that no recruiting officer, or other person whatever, shall impress or take any horses, waggons, or waggoners, employed at any lead, copper, or iron works.

VI. *PROVIDED always,* that this act shall not be construed so as to exempt any unnecessary number of waggons or horses from being subject to the militia law, or service of the state.

VII. AND whereas it is represented that the said *James Hunter* cannot erect his dam and slitting mill at his aforesaid works without a small quantity of land adjoining thereto, the property of *John Richards,* Gentleman, be set apart for that purpose:

VIII. *BE it therefore enacted,* that the Commissioners aforesaid, if he shall refuse to sell the same for a reasonable price, having caused a jury to set a value thereon in manner herein before directed, may and shall assign to the said *James Hunter* any quantity, not exceeding half an acre, of the land belonging to the said *John Richards,* in the most convenient part for the purpose aforesaid, and the same shall be vested in the said *James Hunter* in fee simple, upon his paying the value thereof to the said *John Richards;* provided that the said *James Hunter,* his heirs and assigns, shall within six months afterwards erect and finish a slitting mill at his works aforesaid, and continue to keep the same in good repair, allowing a reasonable time for so doing in case of accident or decay, otherwise the said land shall revert to the said *John Richards,* or his heirs, he or they repaying to the said *James Hunter,* or his heirs, the valuation made as aforesaid.

C H A P. XIII.

Executed.

An act to appoint Commissioners of Oyer and Terminer for the trial of the criminals now in the public jail, and for other purposes.

C H A P. XIV.

Expired.

An act for further continuing an act entitled An act for the further continuance of certain powers given to the Governor and Council by an ordinance of the last Convention, and for other purposes.

C H A P. XV.

Supposed to be no longer in force.

An act for encouraging the making of salt.

C H A P. XVI.

Expired.

An act for further suspending the payment of the salaries heretofore given to the Clergy of the Church of England.   *(a)*

C H A P. XVII.

An act for regulating and disciplining the militia of the city of Williamsburg *and borough of* Norfolk.

Professors, &c. of the College how to be enrolled.
Companies, of what number to consist, what officers of.
The field officers, and their qualifications;
their oath.

I. FOR forming the citizens of *Williamsburg,* borough of *Norfolk,* and the professors and students of *William* and *Mary* college, into a militia, and better disciplining them: *Be it enacted by the General Assembly,* that all male persons between the ages of sixteen and fifty years, within the limits of the said city or borough, except the persons exempted by an act passed this present General Assembly, entitled *An act for regulating and disciplining the militia,* and such of the professors and students of *William* and *Mary* college as would otherwise be part of the militia of *James City* county, in which the college is situate, shall, by the commanding officers of the said city and borough, be enrolled and formed into companies of not less than thirty two, nor more than sixty eight, rank and file; and each company shall be commanded by a Captain, two Lieutenants, and an Ensign, and the whole by a Colonel and Major, who shall reside within the said city, or shall be a freeholder of the said borough, and before they enter upon the execution of their office shall take the following oath: I   *do swear, that I will be faithful and true to the commonwealth of Virginia, of which I profess myself to be a citizen, and that I will faithfully and justly execute the office of*   *in the militia of*   *according to the best of my skill and judgment. So help me God.*

County militia, the several regulations of, adopted.

II. AND the militia of the said city and borough, with the professors and students of the said college, shall be mustered, trained, and employed, at the same times, and in the same manner, and the officers

(a) See October 1779, chap. 37.

and privates thereof respectively shall be armed with the same weapons, and be subject to the same orders, regulations, and penalties, as the militia of a county, and the officers and privates thereof are, and ought to be, by the before mentioned act, and by another act also, passed this present General Assembly, entitled *An act for providing against invasions and insurrections*. And all former acts and ordinances relating to the militia of the said city and borough are declared to be repealed.

Repealing clause.

C H A P.   XVIII.

An act for the more regular laying off the borough of Norfolk.

Private.

C H A P.   XIX.

An act to confirm the Kentucky *election.*

Private.

C H A P.   XX.

An act for dissolving the vestries of several parishes.

Private.

C H A P.   XXI.

An act to empower the vestry of the parish of Botetourt *to dispose of their glebe, for dissolving the said vestry, and for other purposes therein mentioned.*

Private.

C H A P.   XXII.

An act for confirming a codicil annexed to the last will and testament of John Barr, *deceased, respecting certain slaves.*

Private.

C H A P.   XXIII.

An act to permit the trustees of the academy of Hampden Sidney, *in the county of* Prince Edward, *to raise a sum of money by lottery, for certain purposes.*

Private.

C H A P.   XXIV.

An act for dividing the county of Cumberland.

Private.

C H A P.   XXV.

An act for dividing the county of Albemarle *and parish of* Saint Anne.

Private.

C H A P.   XXVI.

An act for adding part of the county of Charlotte, *and parish of* Cornwall, *to the county of* Lunenburg *and parish of* Cumberland.

Private.

C H A P.   XXVII.

An act for appointing commissioners to inquire into and ascertain the losses sustained by the late inhabitants of the borough of Norfolk.

Private.

C H A P.   XXVIII.

An act for altering the bounds of the counties of Montgomery *and* Washington.

.Private.

C H A P.   XXIX.

An act to amend an act entitled An act for reviving several public warehouses for the reception of tobacco, and other purposes.

Repealed.

C H A P.   XXX.

An act to establish several new ferries, and for discontinuing others.

Preamble.

WHEREAS it is represented to this present General Assembly, that public ferries at the places hereafter mentioned will be of great advantage to travellers, and others: *Be it therefore enacted by the General Assembly*, that public ferries be constantly kept at the following places, and the rates for passing the same shall be as follows, that is to say: From the land of *William Howard*, in the county of *Amherst*, over *Rockfish* river, at or near the mouth thereof, to the land of the said *William Howard* on the opposite shore, in the county of *Albemarle*, the price for a man two pence, and for a horse the same; from the lands of the said *William Howard*, on each side of *Rockfish* river, in the said counties of *Amherst* and *Albemarle*, across the *Fluvanna* river, to the lands of *Thomas Anderson*, in the county of *Buckingham*, and from the said *Anderson*'s to the said *Howard*'s as aforesaid, the price for a man three pence, and for a horse the same; from the lands of *John Dix*, in the county of *Pittsylvania*, across *Dan* river, to his land on the opposite shore, the price for a man three pence, and for a horse the same; and from the land of *George Watkins*, in the county of *Halifax*, on the north side of *Banister* river, to the land of *John Murphy*, on the opposite shore, the price for a man two pence, and for a horse the same; and for the transportation of wheel carriages, tobacco, cattle, and other beasts, at any of the places aforesaid, the ferry keeper may demand and take the following rates, that is to say: For every coach, chariot, or waggon, and the driver thereof, the same as for six horses; for every cart or four

New ferries, several established, and rates of:

keeper of, demanding, &c more than the legal rates, pe-

A. D. 1777.

nalty on, and how recoverable.

wheeled chaife, and the driver thereof, the fame as for four horfes: for every two wheeled chaife or chair, the fame as for two horfes; and for every hogfhead of tobacco, as for one horfe; for every head of neat cattle, as for one horfe; for every fheep, goat or lamb, one fifth part of the ferriage for one horfe; and for every hog, one fourth part of the ferriage for one horfe, according to the prices herein before fettled at fuch ferries refpectively, and no more And if any ferry keeper fhall prefume to demand or receive, from any perfon or perfons whatfoever, any greater rates than are hereby allowed for the carriage or ferriage of any thing whatfoever, he or they, for every fuch offence, fhall forfeit and pay to the party grieved the ferriages demanded or received, and ten fhillings, to be recovered with cofts before any Juftice of the Peace, of the county where fuch offence fhall be committed.

Two ferries difcontinued.

  II. AND whereas the public ferries from the land of *Benjamin Howard*, acrofs *Fluvanra* river, to the land of *Neil Campbell*, in the county of *Albemarle*, and from the land of *John Dix*, acrofs *Dan* river, to the land of *Robert Payne*, in the county of *Pittfylvania*, have been found inconvenient: *Be it therefore further enacted*, that the faid ferries fhall henceforth be difcontinued.

At a GENERAL ASSEMBLY begun and held at the Capitol in the City of *Williamsburg*, on *Monday* the 20th day of *October*, in the Year of our Lord 1777.

Executed.

CHAP. I.

An act for fpeedily recruiting the Virginia *regiments on the continental eftablifhment, and for raifing additional troops of volunteers.*

CHAP. II.

An act for raifing a fupply of money for public exigencies.   *(a)*

Preamble.

I. WHEREAS the United *American* States in general, as well as this commonwealth in particular, in the profecution of the prefent juft and neceffary war for the defence of our lives, liberties, and property, have been compelled to iffue bills of credit for large fums of money, the quantity whereof now in circulation, greatly exceeding the medium of commerce, may occafion a depreciation of its value, to the injury of individuals, and great danger of this and the other United States, which nothing will fo effectually prevent as reducing the quantity, by eftablifhing ample funds for redeeming proportions of it annually, until the whole fhall be thereby called in an : funk: It is alfo neceffary that permanent funds fhould be eftablifhed to provide for the repayment of the money borrowed or to be borrowed by the United States, as well as by this commonwealth, for carrying on the war, and the intereft growing due upon fuch loans. For making fuch provifion for the juft proportion which this commonwealth ought to bear of finking the faid bills of credit of the United States, and of the money borrowed by them, and the intereft thereof, as well as to effect the redemption of its own particular bills of credit, and payment of the money borrowed, and intereft, in a mode which it is judged will be leaft burthen-

Taxes on various articles,.

fome to the people of any which can be adopted ; *Be it enacted by the General Affembly*, that a tax or rate of ten fhillings for every hundred pounds value, to be afcertained in manner herein after mentioned, fhall be paid for all manors, meffuages, lands, and tenements, flaves, mulatto fervants to thirty one years of age, horfes, mules, and plate, on the firft day of *Auguft* one thoufand feven hundred and feventy eight; and the like tax or rate fhall be paid on the faid firft day of *Auguft* in each of the fix next fucceeding years, by the owner or proprietor of fuch eftates refpectively. That the like rate of ten fhillings for every hundred pounds fhall be paid for all money exceeding five pounds in the poffeffion of one perfon, by the poffeffor thereof, on the faid firft day of *Auguft*, in each of the faid feven years. That a rate of two fhillings for every pound be paid for the amount of the annual intereft received upon all debts bearing intereft, alfo for the amount of all annuities, including the quitrents payable to the proprietor of the *Northern Neck*, except fuch as have been or fhall be fettled by the General Congrefs, or the Affembly or Convention of this commonwealth, as a provifion for wounded foldiers or their families, to be paid by the creditor or annuitant refpectively on the faid firft day of *Auguft*, in each of the faid feven years. That a tax or duty of ten fhillings a wheel upon all riding carriages, four pence *per* head on all neat cattle, and five fhillings *per* poll upon all tithables above the age of twenty one years (except fo diers, failors, parifh poor, and fuch as receive an annual allowance in confideration of wounds or injuries received in the public fervice, except alfo flaves and mulatto fervants to thirty one years of age, who, being property, are rated *ad valorem* as aforefaid) fhall be paid by the owner or perfon enlifting fuch carriages and tithables refpectively, on the faid firft day of *Auguft*, in each of the faid feven years. That a tax of three pounds for every ordinary licenfe, and twenty fhillings for every marriage licenfe, fhall be paid down to the clerk of the county or corporation court at the time of granting fuch licenfe, from the time of paffing this act until the firft day of *December* one thoufand feven hundred and eighty four. That a tax or rate of ten fhillings for every hundred pounds of the amount of all falaries, and of the nett income of all offices of profit (thofe of the military and fea officers in the fervice of the United States of *America*, or either of them, in refpect of their employments, only excepted) on the faid firft day of *Auguft* one thoufand feven hundred and feventy eight, and each of the fix next fucceeding years. That a tax or duty of ten fhillings be paid for every hogfhead of tobacco exported out of this commonwealth by land or water, by the exporter thereof, from the time of paffing this act until the faid firft day of *December* one thoufand feven hundred and eighty four. That a tax or duty of fix pence *per* gallon be paid for all fpirituous liquors hereafter to be diftilled in this commonwealth, to be paid by the diftiller, or diftilled in any other of the United *American* States and imported into this by land or water, at any time before the faid

doubled in certain cafes.

firft day of *December* one thoufand feven hundred and eighty four And that every perfon who hath not taken the oath or affirmation of allegiance to this ftate required to be taken by an act of the laft feffion of Affembly, and fhall not take the fame before the firft day of *May* next, and who fhall fail to produce to the affeffors in his hundred a certificate of his having taken fuch oath or affirmation, fhall pay double of the feveral rates and taxes aforefaid for fuch property and tithables hereby fubject to taxation as he fhall be owner of, or fhall be in his family.

  (a) See May 1780, *chap.* 10. *The greateft part of this act is not in force, and it is printed only becaufe referred to by feveral fubfequent acts.*

A. D. 1777.

II. PROVIDED always, that nothing herein contained shall be construed so as to charge any lands, slaves, stocks, servants, plate, money, debts, or annuities, which shall belong to the United states of America or this commonwealth, or to any county, corporation, parish, town, college, school, or religious society, with any rate or duty hereby imposed, nor to subject to the duty aforesaid any goods, wares, or merchandises, taken from the enemy, brought into this commonwealth, and condemned as lawful prize in the Court of Admiralty, in the hands of the captors.

Certain property exempted from.

III. AND for ascertaining the value of the several articles herein before taxed according to such value, It is further enacted, that the freeholders and house-keepers of each county or corporation within this commonwealth shall meet at the court-house of their respective county, city, or town, on the second Tuesday in March yearly, during the said term of six years, and they, or such of them as shall appear, shall then and there freely elect three able and discreet men of their county or coporation, being land-holders, having a right to vote for representatives in General Assembly, and having visible property therein to the value of eight hundred pounds each, and who is not a member of any of the public Boards, an officer in the navy or army, naval officer, a manager of any public works, an owner or manager of iron works or manufactory of fire arms, a master or professor in any college or school, a clergyman, sheriff, inspector, or ordinary keeper, to be commissioners of the tax for such county or corporation for the year. The sheriff of the county, and the returning officer of any city or borough, shall cause previous notice of such election to be published in each church and meeting-house in his county or corporation, at least twenty days before each annual election; and such sheriff or returning officer, together with the two senior Justices who shall be present at the election, shall proceed to take the poll fairly and impartially, and shall be the final judges of the qualifications of the voters who offer to poll, as well as of the circumstances of the persons voted for, and shall have power to set aside such person who may be voted for as in their judgment hath not visible property to the amount of the sum hereby required, and on the close of the poll shall certify the names of the three persons who have the greatest number of votes, and are so qualified, to the court of their county or corporation, there to be recorded, determining the preference by their own votes, where the number of votes for any two or more persons are equal, and the persons so returned shall be the commissioners of the tax for that year. Each commissioner, before he enters upon the execution of the trust, shall take the following oath (or, being a Quaker or Menonist, shall solemnly affirm and declare to the same effect) before some justice or the Peace, to wit: I A. B. do swear, that as a commissioner of the tax for   county, I will, to the best of my skill and judgment, execute the duties of the said office diligently and faithfully, and do equal right and justice to all men in every case wherein I shall act as a commissioner, according to the act of Assembly under which I am appointed, to the best of my knowledge, without prejudice, favour, or partiality So help me God. And shall thereupon meet from time to time, at such place or places as to them shall seem most convenient, and appoint a clerk, at ten shillings per day, to attend them for entering their proceedings, and shall, without delay, proceed to lay off the county, city or borough, into so many districts or hundreds as to them shall seem most convenient for making the assessments, bounding the same by water courses, roads, or other limits of public notoriety, and having so done, shall choose two discreet men in each hundred to be assessors or appraisers of such estate lying therein as is hereby subjected to taxation, each of whom shall be a land-holder, having a right to vote for representatives in the General Assembly, which choice shall be certified under the hands of the commissioners, and delivered to the person first named in each hundred within twenty days thereafter, together with transcripts of such parts of this act as are necessary for the direction of the assessors, and such instructions as to the form of their proceedings and return as the commissioners may think proper to give them for complying with the true intention of this act; and the commissioners in such appointment shall also limit a time, not less than four weeks, or more than six weeks, for the assessors to perform their duty in, and to make return of their proceedings to the commissioners, and shall cause a description of the several hundreds to be entered on their book, with a list of the names of the persons appointed assessors in each, and a copy of the instructions given them as aforesaid. The several persons so named assessors in each district shall, within five days after receiving notice of their appointment and instructions as aforesaid, go together to one of the said commissioners, or to a Justice of the Peace, and there take the following oath (or, being a Quaker or Menonist, shall affirm and declare to the same effect) to wit: I A. B. do swear, that I will well and truly execute the duty of an assessor, and faithfully, justly, and impartially assess the pound rate imposed by the act of Assembly for that purpose upon all property within my hundred liable thereto, according to the best of my skill and judgment, and the directions of the said act, and therein will spare none for favour or affection, nor any person aggrieve for hatred, malice, or ill-will So help me God. A certificate of which oath shall be endorsed on the appointment of each set of assessors, and returned therewith to the commissioners, to be entered on their books. And after being so sworn, the said assessors shall personally apply to every person within their district or hundred and require them respectively to give an account upon oath, which either of the assessors may administer, of all lands, slaves, mulatto servants to thirty one years of age, horses, mules, money, silver plate, and interest received which shall become due after the passing of this act on debts bearing interest, all annuities (except a public provision for wounded soldiers and their families) all riding carriages, neat cattle, and tithable persons above the age of twenty one years, not being soldiers, sailors, or parish poor, or persons receiving allowances for wounds received in the public service, slaves, or servants to thirty one years of age, of which each such person is the owner, or who belong to or reside in his or her family, or which he or she is in possession of as guardian to any orphan, or as executor or administrator of the estate of any person deceased, and also an account of all spirituous liquors distilled or imported by land or by water by any such person from and after the passing of this act for the first year, and afterwards annually from the time of rendering their last preceding account thereof; and every such person shall farther make oath, that he or she hath not shifted or changed the possession of any of the said taxable articles, or used any fraud, covin, or device, in order to evade the assessment thereof. The assessors shall also require all persons in their hundred having public salaries, to render an account of the amount thereof, and all persons holding offices of profit (except military and sea officers, in respect of their employments) and residing in their hundred, to render an account upon oath, to the best of their knowledge, of the nett annual income of such office, all and every species of which property so given in, or which the assessors shall by any other ways or means discover, they shall cause to be distinctly entered against the name of the owner or person chargeable with the tax thereon, and proceed to value the lands, slaves, horses, mules, and plate, so given in and discovered, as the same would in their judgment sell for in ready money, having regard to the local situation of lands and other circumstances, taking for such value the middle rate between them, in case the two assessors differ in opinion on the value of any article, extending the value against each species of property, and setting down in a distinct column the amount of the pound rate hereby imposed upon the whole of such property belonging to each person, as well as of the taxes of another nature imposed hereby upon such person, and giving such person a memorandum in writing of such pound rate, to enable him or her to provide for payment thereof. And where a tract of land belonging to any person residing or having a plantation with slaves thereon shall lie in two or more hundreds, the same shall be valued by the assessors of that hundred wherein the proprietor lives or hath a plantation, and if the owner doth not reside, or there be no plantation thereon, then the lands shall be assessed in that hundred wherein the greatest quantity thereof shall lie, and in such case the assessors shall

Taxable property, how value of to be ascertained; with rules for electing commissioners of the tax, their oath or affirmation, and duty.

Assessors, their oath and duty.

A. D. 1777.

enter the county in which the proprietor lives, if they are informed thereof; and when the affeffors fhall have thus valued all the faid taxable property in their hundred, they fhall make a fair return of their proceedings to the commiffioners, entering the names of the perfons affeffed in alphabetical order, with the fpecies and value of their property, and the pound rate thereon as aforefaid, and fhall therein enter their own names, with each diftinct fpecies of taxable property they feverally own or poffefs as aforefaid; and upon fuch return the commiffioners fhall examine them feverally upon oath, and thereupon extend the value of fuch property as to the commiffioners fhall feem juft, and the pound rate thereon as aforefaid, and then fhall caufe all fuch returns to be entered in their books, to which all perfons may have recourfe at any feafonable times.

Silver plate, reftraint in the valuation of.

IV. AND it is further enacted, that where any perfon refiding within this commonwealth fhall receive intereft for money from any perfon refiding in any other of the United States, and there fhall be a deduction made from the intereft due in confequence of a tax impofed in the ftate where the debtor refides, in fuch cafe the creditor, upon producing to the affeffors a certificate of fuch deduction, fhall be allowed the amount thereof out of the pound rate hereby impofed on fuch intereft; but no filver plate fhall be valued at more then ten fhillings *per* ounce *Troy* weight. Which refpective rates, or fuch as fhall be hereafter eftablifhed by the General Affembly (as the value of the money may rife or fall, or as the neceffity of the times require) fhall be obferved by the feveral commiffioners and affeffors as the rule of their conduct in the refpective valuations of fuch property.

Settlements on the Weftern Waters, fubject to taxation, and quantity of each afcertained.

V. AND whereas great numbers of people have fettled on wafte and ungranted lands fituate on the *Weftern Waters*, to which they have not been able to procure legal titles, and the General Convention of *Virginia*, on the twenty fourth day of *June* one thoufand feven hundred and feventy fix, did "refolve "that all fuch fettlers upon unappropriated lands, to which there was no prior juft claim, fhould have "the pre-emption or preference to a grant of fuch lands," and it is juft and reafonable that the lands in their poffeffion thus fecured to them fhould contribute by tax to the common charge, and a mode eftablifhed for fixing the quantity of their claims, where the fame hath not been afcertained, by regular furvey; *It is therefore further enacted*, that all perfons who, on or before the faid twenty fourth day of *June* one thoufand feven hundred and feventy fix, had *bona fide* fettled themfelves, or at his or her charge had fettled others, upon any wafte and ungranted lands on the faid *Weftern Waters*, and had not by regular entry, furvey, or contract, afcertained the quantity of their claim, fhall be allowed for every family fo fettled four hundred acres of land, to include fuch fettlement, or fuch leffer quantity as the perfon entitled thereto refpectively fhall, at the time of the firft affeffment, declare to the affeffors he or fhe defires to hold; and the affeffors of the hundred fhall proceed to affefs the pound rate upon the proprietor for fuch lands in manner herein before mentioned, entering in their return the name of every fuch perfon, and the quantity of land allotted for or chofen by him or her as aforefaid, and the affeffment fhall continue to be made from year to year, according to the quantity fo fixed, during the term of fix years, or until regular furveys fhall be made, and grants obtained for the fame. But where any fuch fettlers fhall have afcertained the quantity of their land by regular furvey or contract, in fuch cafe, upon their producing the fame to the affeffors, they fhall be affeffed for fuch quantity in the fame manner as if a patent had been obtained for the fame. But nothing in this act fhall be conftrued in any manner to affect or prejudice the prior claim or title of any perfon whatfoever in or to any fuch lands, nor to affect any perfon refiding within the territory northward of the latitude of the line ufually called *Mafon* and *Dixon*'s line, and in difpute between this commonwealth and that of *Pennfylvania*, unlefs the Legiflature of the faid commonwealth of *Pennfylvania* fhall have impofed taxes on their citizens within the faid difputed territory, and then only to fuch amount as fhall have been by them impofed on fuch their citizens.

Land-tax, proportioned between landlord and tenant

VI. AND for fettling juft proportions of the faid land tax between landlords and their tenants, to whom the lands were let for terms yet to come, at a time when the value of money was greater, and the price of lands lefs than at prefent, *It is further enacted*, that all lands under leafe for an annual rent, and fubject to the tax, fhall be valued without regard to fuch rent; but where fuch valuation fhall exceed twenty years purchafe, computed upon the annual rent, to be afcertained by the affeffors, they fhall proceed to affefs the landlord the faid pound rate upon the amount of twenty years purchafe of the rent, and fhall affefs the tenant the pound rate upon the refidue of the value of the land, and diftinguifh fuch proportions in their returns; and where fuch rent fhall be referved in tobacco, or other commodity, the affeffors fhall value the fame in money, in order to adjuft fuch proportion between landlords and tenants. Where any tenant at an annual rent fhall be willing to pay the pound rate affeffed on his landlord for the lands held by fuch tenant, it fhall be lawful for him or her fo to do, and the collector's

if paid wholly by the tenant, he may deduct his landlords proportion out of the rent.

Appeals to commiffioners againft exceffive affeffments; time of hearing.

receipt for the fame fhall entitle him or her to a deduction for the amount thereof out of the rent; and where the landlord fhall refide out of this commonwealth, or have no vifible eftate whereon to levy the pound rate for the value of his land, in fuch cafe the faid pound rate fhall be paid by or levied upon the tenant or tenants on the faid land, not exceeding the annual amount of the rents, and allowed to him or them as aforefaid. If any perfon fhall think him or herfelf aggrieved by the judgment of the affeffors of the hundred, he or fhe may appeal to the commiffioners of the tax in the county or corporation, who fhall meet annually on the fecond *Tuefday* in *July*, if fair, if not, the next fair day, at their court-houfe, for hearing fuch appeals, and may adjourn from day to day, or to any other place, until they fhall have determined all appeals made to them, and upon fuch hearing may either increafe or diminifh the affeffment made on fuch perfon or perfons, or let the fame remain unaltered, as to them fhall feem juft, and according to the fpirit and intention of this act.

Sheriff, to give bond, &c. for collecting, &c. the taxes; failing, &c. to do fo, court to appoint a collector, an attefted copy of, bond admitted as evidence.

VII. It is further enacted, that the court of each county fhall, at their court to be held in the months or *April* or *May* one thoufand feven hundred and feventy eight, and in each of the fix following years, take bond, with fufficient fecurity, of the fheriff, in the penalty of three thoufand pounds, payable to the Treafurer of this commonwealth for the time being and his fucceffors, for the ufe of the commonwealth, with condition for the true and faithful collection and accounting for all the duties and taxes hereby impofed within his county. and paying the money for which he fhall be accountable according to this act. And if any fheriff fhall refufe or fail to give fuch fecurity, the court fhall appoint fome other perfon or perfons to collect the faid taxes, and take the like bond and fecurity of him or them, which bonds fhall be recorded in the courts where they fhall refpectively be taken, and an attefted copy thereof tranfmitted by the clerk, without delay, to the public Treafurer, which fhall be admitted as evidence in any fuit or proceeding founded thereon.

Lifts in order to collection.

VIII. AND it is further enacted, that the commiffioners of the tax in each county or corporation fhall, on or before the firft day of *Auguft* annually, deliver to the fheriff of the county, or to the collector or collectors appointed as aforefaid, a full and perfect lift, formed from the returns of the feveral affeffors, of all the perfons, in alphabetical order, who refide in the county, and are to pay any rate or tax purfuant to this act, with the amount of what each perfon is to pay, collecting together what the fame perfon fhall be affeffed in different hundreds, and diftinguifhing in what hundred the perfon chargeable resides or hath effects, taking a receipt from the sheriff or collector for the same, and thereupon such sheriff or collector shall proceed to collect and receive the several taxes and rates according to such list, and to levy the same by distress and sale of the slaves, goods, and chattels, of such persons who shall fail to pay what he or she shall be so assessed on or before the first day of *September* in any year, the sale of which estate shall be made not less than five days after the distress, for ready money, and notice thereof shall be published at the parish church or most convenient meeting-house, and no security shall be taken, or writ of replevin sued out thereupon; but no sheriff or collector shall seize any slave for such taxes where other sufficient distress shall be shewn him, nor make any unreasonable distress, on pain of being liable to the action of the party grieved, wherein the plaintiff shall recover his full costs, although the damages shall be under forty shillings. And where any lands shall be assessed in a county wherein the proprietor doth not reside, nor hath any effects whereon to levy the said pound rate, and the commissioners shall discover in what other county the proprietor lives or hath effects, they shall transmit the assessment to the commissioners of such other county, to be delivered to the sheriff or collector thereof, and collected, levied, and accounted for, in like manner as the other assessments of such county.

IX. AND that lands may not be granted on, or subject to any feudal tenure, and to prevent the danger to a free state from perpetual revenue, Be it enacted, that all lands within this commonwealth shall henceforward be exempted and discharged from the payment of all quitrents, except only the lands in that tract of country or territory between *Rappahannock* and *Potowmack* rivers commonly called the *Northern Neck;* and that the abolition of quitrents may operate to the equal benefit of all the citizens of the commonwealth, the owners of all lands within the said territory, subject to the payment of an annual quitrent of two shillings sterling *per* hundred acres to the proprietor of the said *Northern Neck,* shall be allowed the sum of two shillings and sixpence current money for every hundred acres, and so in proportion for a greater or lesser quantity, out of the sum which shall be respectively assessed on such lands so long as their payment of quitrents thereon shall continue, which allowance and discount the commissioners and assessors of the tax are hereby empowered and required to make accordingly, and the commissioners of the tax in each county within the said territory shall make out a list of all such deductions made in their county, and transmit the same to the commissioners of the county of *Frederick* annually, to be by them delivered to the sheriff of the said county, and such sheriff is hereby required to collect and levy of and upon the proprietor of the said territory for the time being the said pound rate of two shillings for every pound of the amount of the said deductions, and account for and pay the same to Treasurer, in like manner, and subject to the same penalty and proceedings, as is herein before directed for accounting for and paying the other taxes.

X. AND be it further enacted, that the late Auditor, or deputy Auditor General in this commonwealth, shall, on or before the twentieth day of *March* next, transmit to the commissioners of each county, not being within the said territory of the *Northern Neck,* a certificate at what time the last quitrents were accounted for in such county by the sheriff; and the late Receiver or deputy Receiver General, shall within the same time transmit to such commissioners a true copy from his book of the account with each sheriff who hath not fully paid, and a certificate to what time the quitrents have been so fully paid in each county, and upon receiving such accounts and certificates the commissioners in each county shall proceed to call the respective persons who have been sheriffs thereof, within the time the quitrents are unaccounted for, to an account for what they have received thereof in each year, and to move for judgment in the General Court or county court against such sheriff, or his deputy or deputies, and his or their securities, or their respective executors or administrators, for the penalty of their respective bonds where they shall fail to account, or for what shall appear due on such account, if they respectively fail to pay the same, and such court shall give judgment accordingly; provided, that ten days previous notice be given of such motion. And having adjusted such accounts with the sheriffs, the commissioners of each county shall make out a list of all arrears of quitrents due from any persons for lands therein to the twenty ninth day of *September* one thousand seven hundred and seventy four, and deliver the same to the sheriff or collector, to be collected, levied, accounted for, and paid in like manner, and subject to the same penalty and proceedings for neglect, as are provided in the case of the taxes hereby imposed. And the Treasurer shall pay to the Auditor and Receiver General what the Auditors of Public Accounts shall certify to be a reasonable satisfaction for such copies and certificates.

XI. PROVIDED always, that no lands situate on the *Western Waters* shall be subject to the payment of such arrears. And where any quitrents have been paid for such lands, or for other lands to a later period than the said twenty ninth day of *September,* the sheriff receiving the same shall refund the amount thereof to the person who paid it, his or her executors or administrators; or where the money shall have been paid to the Receiver General or Treasurer, the amount thereof shall be repaid by the sheriff or collector of the county where the person entitled thereto resides, and be allowed to such sheriff or collector in his account. The said Receiver General shall also render an account upon oath of all money now in his hands received for quitrents, or upon the fund formerly appropriated to defray the contingent charges of government, and pay such balance to the Treasurer, for the use of this commonwealth, or be compelled thereto by the General Court, upon such proceedings as are herein directed for recovering money from the sheriffs or collectors received for taxes. The said Receiver shall also render an account of any arrears which may be due to the said contingent fund, which the Treasurer shall proceed to receive or recover as aforesaid. The Right Honourable *Thomas* Lord *Fairfax,* or the agent or manager of his office, shall also, on or before the said twentieth day of *March* next, transmit to the commissioners of each county within the territory of the *Northern Neck* a rent roll of all the lands paying quitrents to the said proprietor in such county, and receive from the Treasurer the sum of twenty shillings for each rent roll; and the respective commissioners shall deliver extracts therefrom to the assessors of the several hundreds, for their direction. Every sheriff or collector of the taxes hereby imposed shall, on or before the first day of *November* yearly, account with the commissioners of the taxes in his county for all the rates, taxes, and duties, put into his hands to collect for such year; and the commissioners shall adjust the said account, allowing for such only as in their judgment could not have been received by a vigilant and faithful collector, and allowing a commission of three *per centum* for collecting the residue, striking the balance due from such sheriff or collector, and certifying their having examined and passed the account. They shall also at the foot thereof state an account of what shall be due to themselves, their clerk, and the several assessors in the county, for the year's service, and deduct the same from the balance in the hands of the sheriff or collector, who shall pay the amount of such expences to the commissioners, for the use of themselves and the others; and the account so settled the commissioners shall deliver to the sheriff or collector, after having entered an exact copy thereof in their book, and they shall immediately transmit a copy from their book to the Treasurer, to enable him to call upon the sheriff or collector for the money so stated to be due.

XII. AND it is further enacted, that every person who shall carry any tobacco out of this commonwealth, by land, shall before he removes the same from the county where it is made, or from whence it is carried out of this commonwealth, apply to the clerk of the county court, and make oath what number of hogsheads or casks of tobacco he intends to carry out of the commonwealth, and pay the duty of ten

*Naval Officers,
&c how to account,
and penalty for de-
fault; accounting
but not paying, how
to be proceeded a-
gainst.*

shillings *per* hogshead or cask for the same, taking a certificate of such oath, with the marks and numbers of such hogsheads or casks, and a receipt for the tax, and of which an entry shall be made by the clerk in his books. The master or mate of every ship or vessel, in which tobacco shall be laded or put on board for exportation, shall, at the time of clearing out his ship or vessel, make a true report upon oath of all the tobacco loaden therein, with the marks and numbers of each hogshead thereof, and by whom shipped, and pay down the duty of ten shillings *per* hogshead for the same to the Naval Officer, before he is admitted to a clearance. Every Naval Officer shall half yearly, on the twenty fifth day of *April* and twenty fifth day of *October*, render an account upon oath to the public Treasurer of all duties by him received pursuant to this act in the preceding half year, and pay the money for such duties, deducting five *per centum* for receiving the same. And the clerk of each county or corporation court shall on the same days, half yearly, render an account upon oath to the said Treasurer of all the taxes by him received for marriage and ordinary licenses, and for the duty upon tobacco exported by land in the preceding half year, and pay the money for such taxes, deducting five *per centum* for receiving the same. And every Naval Officer, or clerk of a court, failing to render such account, shall forfeit and pay the sum of five hundred pounds for every offence: and every Naval Officer or clerk having accounted, and failing to pay the money stated to be due within one month, shall be proceeded against by the Treasurer for the recovery thereof, in manner herein after directed against sheriffs or collectors making default in payment. And every sheriff or other county collector, who shall fail to settle his account with the commissioners of the taxes in his county annually, on or before the said first day of *November*, shall forfeit and pay the sum of one hundred pounds for every neglect; and in such case the Treasurer may and shall proceed against such sheriff or collector and his securities, his or their heirs, executors, or administrators, as hereafter mentioned, and obtain judgment for the penalty of the bond and costs, to be discharged, except as to the costs, by the payment of what shall be found due for the taxes in such county, in case the sheriff or collector shall, before the levying of the execution, make up an account of the taxes with the commissioners, and obtain their certificate of the just balance. And if any sheriff or collector of the taxes in any county, having accounted with the commissioners as herein before is directed, shall fail to produce his account so certified to the Treasurer of this commonwealth, and pay the balance stated to be due from him on or before the first day of *December* in any year, the Treasurer is hereby empowered and directed, under pain of forfeiting five hundred pounds, to move in the General Court, on the tenth day of the next succeeding court, for judgment against such sheriff or collector and his securities, his or their executors or administrators; and the said court, on that day, or so soon afterwards as counsel can be heard, shall proceed to take trial therein by jury, if either party shall desire it, without delay, admitting the certificate of the commissioners for proof of the balance found to be due on the account, and such other legal testimony as either party may offer, and to enter judgment for what shall be found due, and costs, and thereon to award execution, upon which the clerk shall endorse that no security of any kind is to be taken, and the officer to whom the same is directed and delivered shall proceed to levy the same by distress and sale of the estate of the defendants, for ready money, taking no security either for replevying of the estate or having the same forthcoming at the day of sale. If any sheriff, or usual returning officer of a county or corporation, shall fail to give notice of the time appointed for the annual election of the commissioners of the tax, or fail to attend at such election (not being hindered by sickness, in which case the under sheriff of the county, or one of the aldermen of the corporation, shall act in his stead) every person so neglecting or failing shall forfeit five hundred pounds. If any person elected a commissioner shall refuse to serve (not having a sufficient excuse, to be judged of by his county or corporation court) he shall forfeit and pay the sum of one hundred pounds, and in case of such refusal, whether the reasons offered be adjudged a good excuse or not, or if any commissioner who undertakes the trust shall die or be disabled to act within the year, the county or corporation court shall appoint another commissioner in the room of him so refusing, dead, or disabled, to act until the next annual election, and so as often as such vacancy shall happen. And if there be no election made of commissioners for any county or corporation, as herein before directed, in such case the court of such county or corporation shall, at their next court, proceed to the choice of commissioners; and if there shall happen, from bad weather or other accident, to be no court held for any county or corporation on the court day next after the said second *Tuesday* in *March* in any year, in that case the Magistrates of such court shall, under the penalty of fifty pounds on each Magistrate failing, meet at their court-house on the next fair day, and then and there judge of the excuses of commissioners elected, and proceed to election of such as may be necessary, either by their having been none elected, or those elected refusing to act as aforesaid. Each commissioner accepting the trust shall be allowed for each day he shall act therein the sum of ten shillings. If any person appointed an assessor shall refuse to serve (not having a sufficient excuse, to be judged of by the commissioners) he shall forfeit and pay the sum of fifty pounds, and all vacancies occasioned by such refusals, or by the death or inability to act of any assessor, shall be supplied, as often as they happen, by the appointment of the commissioners; and each assessor, for performing his duty, shall be allowed what the commissioners shall judge reasonable, not exceeding ten pounds *per annum*. If any person shall refuse to give an account upon oath or affirmation, as herein before directed, of all the articles in his or her possession liable to a pound rate or tax by this act, every person so refusing shall forfeit and pay the sum of one hundred pounds; and the assessors shall proceed to inquire by other means into his or her property, and assess the same according to the best information they can procure. If any person shall carry any tobacco out of this commonwealth by land without paying the duty aforesaid, and obtaining such certificate from the clerk of the county court, as is herein before required, every person so offending shall forfeit ten pounds for every hogshead or cask of tobacco so carried out. And every master or mate of a ship or vessel, on board of which any tobacco shall be loaden for exportation, failing to make a true report of the marks and numbers of such tobacco to the naval officer at the time of clearance, shall forfeit and pay the sum of ten pounds for every hogshead of tobacco exported in such ship or vessel, and not so reported. And if any Naval Officer shall clear out any ship or vessel, in which tobacco shall be reported to be loaden, without receiving the duty hereby imposed on such tobacco, the Naval Officer shall be answerable for the duty. All the penalties and forfeitures hereby inflicted shall be recoverable with costs, by action of debt or information, in any court of record, and be appropriated, two thirds to the use of the commonwealth, and paid to the public Treasurer, to assist the purposes of this act, and the other third to the informer, or the whole to the commonwealth, in case a suit for the same shall be first instituted for the commonwealth.

*Penalty on sheriff,
failing in his duty
respecting the elec-
tion of commission-
ers; and on com-
missioner refusing to
serve.*

*Commissioners and
assessors, vacancies
in the offices of, how
to be supplied.*

*Penalty on an as-
sessor refusing to act,
and his reward for
acting.*

*Penalties for va-
rious offences;*

*how to be recovered,
and appropriated.*

*Waste lands, when
liable to assessment.*

XIII. AND *it is further enacted,* that all waste and unappropriated lands within this commonwealth, as soon as the same shall be granted pursuant to an act of the General Assembly, shall be subject to assessment of the said pound rate, in like manner as the lands already granted.

*Repeal of former
taxes.*

XIV. AND *it is further enacted,* that the land and poll tax, and all other taxes and duties imposed by any former act of Assembly or ordinance of Convention, and which were payable at any time before the first day of *January* one thousand seven hundred and eighty four, shall cease: and the said acts and ordinances, so far as they relate to the imposition, collection, and payment of the said taxes or duties, are hereby repealed, except so far as may enforce the collectors of any of the said taxes heretofore due to account for and pay the same.

XV. AND it is further enacted, that the Treasurer of this commonwealth for the time being shall apply the money which shall come to his hands by virtue of this act, in the first place for and towards the annual payment of the quota of this commonwealth of the principal and interest of money borrowed on treasury notes issued on account of the United American States, supposed by the General Congress to be two hundred and forty thousand pounds, for the present year, deducting thereout what is or shall from time to time become due from them to this commonwealth, and the residue for and towards the payment of the interest due or to become due for money borrowed or to be borrowed for the use of this commonwealth, and of the principal money, when due, for the redemption of the treasury notes issued by order of the Convention of this commonwealth, redeemable on the first day of January, one thousand seven hundred and eighty four, and by virtue of this act, or any former act of General Assembly, redeemable on the first day of December, one thousand seven hundred and eighty four, and for the annual contingent expences of this state, and to no other use whatsoever. And the said Treasurer shall keep clear and distinct accounts of the said taxes and duties hereby imposed, shewing the nett annual income of each, and lay the same before the General Assembly when required; and if there shall be any deficiency in the said taxes and duties to answer the full purposes of this act, the same shall be made good by a farther and adequate tax.

A. D 1777.
Appropriation of these.

Treasurer to keep distinct accounts of the several taxes, &c.

XVI. AND whereas it may be necessary to make some farther provision for answering such demands as may be made on the treasury before the said taxes can be collected: Be it further enacted, that George Webb, Esquire, or the Treasurer for the time being, shall, and he is hereby empowered and directed to receive from any person whatever any sum of specie, continental paper dollars, or bills of credit issued by authority of this commonwealth, he or she shall be willing to lend, for any term not exceeding three years, so as such sum be not less than three hundred dollars, or the value thereof in other money lent by any one person, and doth not exceed in the whole five hundred thousand pounds, and to give the lender a receipt for the money lent in the form prescribed in the act of Assembly establishing a Loan Office for the purpose of borrowing money for the use of the commonwealth; and the said Treasurer shall keep accounts of the money so borrowed, and conform to all regulations prescribed by the said act.

Empowered to borrow on certain terms.

XVII. AND be it further enacted, that the Treasurer shall pay the interest of the money due on such certificates annually, and take in and discharge the principal thereof at the time or times therein limited for that purpose; or should the lender or bearer of such certificates desire to have the same sooner paid and discharged, the Treasurer is hereby authorised to comply therewith, provided that the state of the treasury will admit of the same, without prejudice to the public.

Repayment, when.

XVIII. AND be it it further enacted, that if any person within this commonwealth shall forge or counterfeit, alter or erase, any certificate of money lent as aforesaid, or transfer any forged or altered certificate to another, or demand payment at the office of principal or interest thereupon, knowing the same to be forged or counterfeited, altered or erased, every person so offending, being lawfully convicted, shall forfeit his whole estate real and personal, receive on his bare back at the public whipping post thirty nine lashes, and shall be obliged to serve on board some armed vessel in the service of this state, without wages, not exceeding seven years; provided that the Governor and Council for the time being, out of the offender's estate may make such allowance to his wife and children as to them shall seem just and reasonable.

For forging, &c. any certificate of money lent, the penalty.

XIX. AND whereas it is altogether uncertain whether the above mentioned sum of money can be borrowed so soon as the exigencies of Government may require: Be it further enacted, that the said George Webb, Esquire, or the Treasurer for the time being, shall be, and he is hereby empowered to issue treasury notes, in dollars or parts of dollars, for any sum or sums which may be requisite for the purposes of government, and which he may not be able to borrow as aforesaid, so that the money so emitted, with what shall be borrowed by virtue of this act, doth not exceed seventeen hundred thousand dollars; each dollar to be of the value of a Spanish milled dollar, and the parts of a dollar of the same proportionate value. And the said Treasurer for the time being may, and he is hereby authorised to cause the said notes to be engraved and printed in such manner as he shall judge most likely to secure the same against counterfeits and forgeries, to appoint proper persons to overlook the press, to number and sign the said notes, upon the best terms on which he can procure them.

Treasury notes may be emitted, within certain limits.

XX. AND be it further enacted, that all such notes so to be issued shall pass as a lawful tender: and any person attempting to depreciate the value of the same, by any such means or device whatsoever, as is described in several acts of Assembly, shall incur the same penalties and forfeitures as are thereby imposed, to be recovered as therein directed. The said notes so to be issued shall be redeemable on the first day of December one thousand seven hundred and eighty four.

Time of redemption.

XXI. AND be it further enacted, that if any person or persons shall forge or counterfeit, alter or erase, any such treasury note, or tender in payment any such, or demand a redemption thereof, knowing the same to be forged or counterfeited, altered or erased, every person so offending, and being thereof lawfully convicted, shall incur the same forfeitures, and suffer the same punishment, as is herein before directed in the case of certificates for money borrowed.

Punishment for counterfeiting.

CHAP. III.

An act to open the Courts of Justice, and to revive and amend an act entitled An act for the better regulating and collecting certain officers fees, and other purposes therein mentioned.

Expired.

CHAP. IV.

An act for laying a public levy.

Executed.

CHAP. V.

An act to amend an act entitled An act to regulate the inoculation of the small-pox within this colony.

I. WHEREAS the small-pox, at this time in many parts of the commonwealth, is likely to spread and become general, and it hath been proved, by incontestible experience, that the late discoveries and improvements therein have produced great benefits to mankind, by rendering a distemper which taken in the common way is always dangerous and often fatal comparatively mild and

Preamble.

A. D. 1777.

Licence to inoculate, farther mode of obtaining.

Regulations for confining the infection, and penalties for transgressing them.

safe by inoculation, and the act for regulating the inoculation of the smallpox having been found in many instances inconvenient and injurious, makes it necessary that the same should be amended:

II *BE it therefore enacted by the General Assembly,* that any person, having first obtained, in writing, to be attested by two witnesses, the consent of a majority of the house-keepers residing within two miles, and not separated by a river, creek, or marsh, a quarter of a mile wide, and conforming to the following rules and regulations, may inoculate, or be inoculated for the smallpox, either in his or her own house, or at any other place. No patient in the smallpox shall remove from the house where he or she shall have the distemper, or shall go abroad into the company of any person who hath not before had the smallpox or been inoculated, or go into any public road where travellers usually pass, without retiring out of the same, or giving notice upon the approach of any passenger, until such patient hath recovered from the distemper, and hath been so well cleansed, in his or her person and clothes, as to be perfectly free from infection, under the penalty of forty shillings for every offence, to be recovered, if committed by a married woman, from her husband, if an infant, from the parent or guardian, and if by a servant or slave, from the master or mistress.

III. EVERY physician, doctor, or other person undertaking inoculation at any house, shall cause a written advertisement to be put up at the nearest public road, or other most notorious adjacent place, giving information that the smallpox is at such house, and shall continue to keep the same set up so long as the distemper or any danger of infection remains there, under the penalty of forty shillings for every day that the same shall be omitted or neglected, to be paid by the physician or doctor if the offence shall be committed when he is present, or by the master, mistress, manager, or principal person of the family respectively, if the offence is committed in the absence of the physician or doctor. Every physician, doctor, or other person, undertaking inoculation at any public place or hospital for the reception of patients, shall, before he discharges the patients, or suffers them to be removed from thence, take due care that their persons and clothes are sufficiently cleansed, and shall give such patients respectively a certificate under his hand that in his opinion they are free from all danger of spreading the infection, under the penalty of three pounds for every offence; and every person wilfully giving a false certificate shall be subject to the penalty of ten pounds.

IV. IF any person who hath not had the smallpox, other than those who have been or intend to be inoculated, shall go into any house where the smallpox then is, or intermix with the patients, and return from thence, any Justice of the Peace of the county, on due proof thereof, may, by warrant, cause such person to be conveyed to the next hospital where the smallpox is, there to remain until he or she shall have gone through the distemper, or until the physician or manager of the hospital shall certify that in his opinion such person cannot take the same; and if such person shall not be able to pay the necessary expences, the same shall be paid by the county.

V. EVERY person wilfully endeavouring to spread or propagate the smallpox without inoculation, or by inoculation in any other manner than is allowed by this act, or by the said recited act, in special cases, shall be subject to the penalty of five hundred pounds, or suffer six months imprisonment, without bail or mainprize.

The penalties, how recoverable, and appropriated.

VI. ALL the penalties inflicted by this act may be recovered with costs, by action of debt or information, in any court of record, where the sum exceeds five pounds, and where it is under, or amounts to that sum only, by petition in the court of the county where the offence shall be committed, and shall be one half to the informer, and the other half to the commonwealth; or the whole to the commonwealth, where prosecution shall be first instituted on the public behalf alone.

VII. SO much of the act of General Assembly entitled *An act to regulate the inoculation of the smallpox within this colony,* as contains any thing contrary to this act, is hereby repealed.

CHAP. VI.

Private.

An act for indemnifying the Governor and Council, and others, for removing and confining suspected persons during the late public danger.

CHAP. VII.

Had its effect.

An act for better securing the commonwealth, and for the further protection and defence thereof.

CHAP. VIII.

Had its effect.

An act for speedily clothing the troops raised by this Commonwealth now in continental service.

CHAP. IX.

An act for sequestering British property, enabling those indebted to British subjects to pay off such debts, and directing the proceedings in suits where such subjects are parties.

Preamble.

I. WHEREAS divers persons subjects of *Great Britain,* had, during our connexion with that kingdom, acquired estates, real and personal, within this commonwealth, and had also become entitled to debts to a considerable amount, and some of them had commenced suits for the recovery of such debts before the present troubles had interrupted the administration of justice, which suits were at that time depending and undetermined, and such estates being acquired, and debts incurred, under the sanction of the laws and of the connexion then subsisting, and it not being known that their sovereign hath as yet set the example of confiscating debts and estates under the like circumstances, the public faith, and the law and usages of nations, require that they should not be confiscated on our part, but the safety of the United States demands, and the same law and usages of nations, will justify that we should not strengthen the hands of our enemies during the continuance of the present war, by remitting to them the profits or proceeds of such estates, or the interest or principal of such debts:

II. *BE it therefore enacted by the General Assembly*, that the lands, slaves, stocks, and implements thereunto belonging, within this commonwealth, together with the crops now on hand, or hereafter to accrue, and all other estate, of whatever nature, not herein otherwise provided for, of the property of any *British* subject, shall be sequestered into the hands of commissioners to be appointed from time to time by the Governor and Council for each particular estate, which commissioners shall have power, by suits or actions to be brought in the names of the proprietors, to receive and recover all sums of money hereafter to become due to the said proprietors of such estates, to direct by agents, stewards, or overseers, the management of the said estates to the best advantage, to provide out of the monies so received and recovered, and the crops and profits now on hand, or hereafter accruing, for the maintenance, charges, taxes, and other current expenses of such estates, in the first place, and the residue to carry into the loan office of this commonwealth, and to take out certificates for the same from the said office in the name of the proprietor of such estate, which certificates shall be delivered in to the Governor and Council, before whom also a fair account, on oath, of the receipts and disbursements for the said estate, shall be annually laid, and if wrong, shall be subject at their instance to be revised and adjusted, in the name of the proprietors; and all balances due thereon from the said commissioners to be recovered in a court of justice, according to the ordinary forms of the law; and such balances, so recovered, to be placed in like manner in the said loan office. And the Governor and Council shall once in every year lay before the General Assembly an account of the said certificates put into their hands, specifying the names of the owners, and shall see to the safe keeping of the same, subject to the future direction of the Legislature. And where any such estate is holden in joint tenancy, tenancy in common, or of any other undivided interest with any citizen of this commonwealth, it shall be lawful for such citizen to proceed to obtain partition by such action, suit, or process, to be instituted in the General Court or High Court of Chancery, as is allowed to be had against a citizen in the like case; and service of process in any such suit on the commissioners appointed for such estate, and orders, judgments, and decrees thereon, to be rendered, shall be, to all intents and purposes, as valid and effectual as if the party himself had appeared in defence: Saving nevertheless to such defendant, if the partition be unequal, such redress as shall be hereafter allowed him by the Legislature against the party plaintiff, his heirs, executors, or administrators, and against the lands themselves allotted to the plaintiff on such unequal partition, and not sold to any person for valuable consideration actually and *bona fide* paid or agreed to be paid; but all lands so sold after partition shall be absolutely confirmed to the purchaser and all claiming under him, according to the terms of his purchase, in like manner as if the vendor had held an indefeasible estate therein. And the said commissioners shall use their best skill and endeavours to obtain a fair and equal partition for their principal, for which purpose they may employ necessary agents and counsel at his expence; and for this, and all other their trouble and expences, such allowance shall be made them out of the profits of the estate as to the Governor and Council shall seem reasonable.

III. *AND be it further enacted*, that it shall and may be lawful for any citizen of this commonwealth owing money to a subject of *Great Britain* to pay the same, or any part thereof, from time to time, as he shall think fit, into the said loan office, taking thereout a certificate for the same in the name of the creditor, with an endorsement under the hand of the commissioners of the said office expressing the name of the payer, and shall deliver such certificate to the Governor and Council, whose receipt shall discharge him from so much of the debt. And the Governor and Council shall in like manner lay before the General Assembly once in every year, an account of these certificates, specifying the names of the persons by and for whom they were paid, and shall see to the safe keeping of the same, subject to the future direction of the Legislature.

IV. *PROVIDED*, that the Governor and Council may make such allowance as they shall think reasonable, out of the said profits and interest arising on money so paid into the loan office, to the wives and children residing in this state, of such proprietors or creditors.

V. *AND be it further enacted*, that all suits which were depending in any court of law or equity within this commonwealth on the twelfth day of *April* in the year of our Lord one thousand seven hundred and seventy four, wherein *British* subjects alone are plaintiffs, and any citizen of this commonwealth is a defendant, shall stand continued (unless abated by the death of either party) in the same state in which they were at that time; and where citizens and *British* subjects are joint plaintiffs against a citizen, the court may proceed to trial and judgment, but execution as to so much of any debt sued for and recovered in such action, as will accrue to such *British* subject, shall be suspended till further direction of the Legislature. And in all such suits wherein any citizen of this commonwealth is a plaintiff, and any subject of *Great Britain* is a defendant, the court may proceed to trial, judgment, and execution, saving to the defendant such benefit of re-hearing, or new trial, as shall be hereafter allowed by the Legislature.

Marginal notes:

A. D. 1777.

Commissioners of sequestration, how to be appointed; their power and duty.

Accounts to be laid before the Assembly.

A citizen and British subject being joint tenants, &c. how process for partition may be served.

Saving in case of unequal partition.

Further duty of commissioners, and their reward.

See May 1780 chap. 3.

Provision for wives, &c. of British proprietors.

Suits by British subjects to stand continued.

What proceedings to be had in suits by such subjects jointly with a citizen, or by a citizen against such subject.

CHAP. X.

An act for authorising the seizure of salt, in the same manner as provisions for the use of the army. *Expired.*

CHAP. XI.

An act to prevent forestalling, regrating, engrossing, and public vendues.

I. *BE it enacted by the General Assembly*, that if any person shall buy, or cause to be bought, any goods, wares, merchandise, or victual, which at the time of purchase shall be under carriage or transportation to any market or fair within this commonwealth, to be sold therein, or to any city or town wherein there is no public market established, or to any port or harbour of this commonwealth for sale, or shall make any bargain, contract, or promise, for the buying or having such goods, or the pre-emption thereof, before the same shall be in or at the market, fair, city, town, port, or harbour, ready to be there sold, or shall persuade any person coming to this commonwealth, or any market therein, to forbear bringing any goods, wares, or merchandise thereto, or use any means or device for the enhancing of the price of any such goods in this commonwealth, or any market therein, every such person offending in either of the said particulars is declared a forestaller. But this shall not extend to any person living more than four miles from any town within this commonwealth, and purchasing any victual, goods, or commodities, necessary for the use and consumption of himself and his family, or those in his employ, for one year.

II. *IF* any person shall, by any means, buy, obtain, or get into his possession, in any fair or market, any victual that shall have been brought to the said fair or market to be sold, and shall make sale thereof again in the same place, or in any other place, within four miles thereof, he is declared a regrater.

Who shall be accounted a forestaller.

Who a regrater.

R

A. D. 1777.

Who an engroffer.

III. IF any perfon fhall buy within this commonwealth to fell again, in this or any of the United States, any goods, wares, merchandife, or victual, which fhall have been imported or brought into this ftate from any other ftate or place whatfoever, or any victual, commodities, manufactures, or materials for manufacture, raifed or wrought within this ftate, except fuch purchafe be made from the original importer, owner, maker, or manufacturer of fuch goods, wares, merchandife, victual, commodities, manufactures, or materials for manufacture, refpectively, every perfon fo offending is declared an engroffer. But this act fhall not extend to any perfon purchafing fuch articles from one who purchafed from the importer and retailing the fame more than twenty five miles from any tide water, nor to any agent of this commonwealth or of the United States, or any of them, purchafing neceffaries really and *bona fide* for the ufe of the army or navy, and not dealing in fuch articles on the account of himfelf or any other private perfons (fuch agent for the United States, or any of them, producing, whenfoever called on, fufficient proof of his acting under authority from the United States, or fome one of them) nor to the managers of any iron works purchafing neceffaries for the ufe of thofe employed about fuch iron works and felling them to fuch perfons, nor to the purchafers of materials for manufacture which fhall be really applied to that ufe in the family of the purchafer, or fome manufactory wherein he is interefted, nor to ordinary keepers purchafing victual to be retailed in their ordinaries, or perfons keeping private houfes for lodging or entertainment who may buy any kind of victual and retail the fame in their refpective houfes after it is prepared and dreffed for the table, nor to the owners of any imported goods fold as being damaged for the benefit of the enfurers, or condemned in the admiralty and purchafed by the faid owners.

*Foreftaller, &c.
how punifhable.*

IV. EVERY perfon becoming a foreftaller, regrater, or engroffer, as before defcribed, fhall, on conviction for the firft offence, fuffer imprifonment for the fpace of one month without bail or mainprize, and forfeit the value of the things fo by him bought or fold, and for the fecond offence fhall be imprifoned two months without bail or mainprize, and fhall forfeit the double value of the things fo by him bought or fold, and for any fuch offence afterwards committed fhall ftand in the pillory for fuch time as the court fhall direct, not exceeding two hours, fhall forfeit treble the value of the things by him bought or fold, and be imprifoned at the difcretion of the jury convicting him of the faid offence, provided fuch imprifonment doth not exceed three months.

*Public vendues
prohibited, except
in certain cafes.*

V. NO goods, wares, merchandife, victual, commodities, manufactures, or materials for manufacture, imported into this commonwealth, or raifed or manufactured within the fame (except flaves, ftocks, and houfehold furniture, goods condemned in the admiralty court, or goods which being damaged are by the law and the cuftom of merchants to be fold for the benefit of enfurers, victual, or goods fold on account and for the benefit of the United *American* States, or fome one of them, goods taken in execution or upon attachment, or diftrained for rent or public taxes, or fold by executors or adminiftrators) fhall be expofed to fale at public vendue, under penalty on each perfon felling or buying at fuch vendue, for each article fo fold, of double the value thereof.

*Appropriation of
the penalties, and
mode of recovery.*

VI. ALL the penalties hereby inflicted fhall be one half to the ufe of the commonwealth and the other to the informer, and where the fum doth not exceed twenty five fhillings, fhall be recoverable with cofts before any Juftice of the Peace, and where it fhall exceed that fum by action of debt or information, in any court of record; and in fuch action of debt the clerk fhall endorfe on the writ, that bail is to be required, whereupon the fheriff fhall take fufficient bail for the appearance of the defendant, or be anfwerable himfelf, as in other like cafes; and the court may either rule the defendant to give fpecial bail, or admit an appearance without, as to them fhall appear juft.

Repealing claufe.

VII. ALL acts of Parliament and of General Affembly, relating to any thing within the purview of this act, are hereby repealed.

C H A P. XII.

Expired.

An act for enabling the public contractors to procure ftores of provifions neceffary for the enfuing campaign, and to prohibit the exportation of beef, pork, and bacon, for a limited time.

C H A P. XIII.

Expired.

An act for further fufpending the payment of the falaries heretofore given to the Clergy of the Church of England.

C H A P. XIV.

Repealed.

An act to amend an act entitled An act limiting the time for continuing the Delegates to General Congrefs in office, and making provifion for their fupport, and for other purpofes.

C H A P. XV.

An act for eftablifhing a High Court of Chancery.   (a)

*High Court of
Chancery, to confift
of three Judges;
how chofen and
commiffioned; tenure of their office;
how many may hold
court; and how to
qualify.*

I. FOR eftablifhing a court of general jurifdiction in chancery, *Be it enacted by the General Affembly,* that at fome certain place to be appointed by act of General Affembly, and at the times herein after directed, fhall be held a principal court of judicature for this commonwealth, which fhall be called the High Court of Chancery, and fhall confift of three Judges, to be chofen from time to time by the joint ballot of both Houfes of Affembly, and commiffioned by the Governor, to hold their offices fo long as they fhall refpectively demean themfelves well therein, any two of whom may hold a court. Every perfon fo commiffioned, before he enters upon the duties of his office, fhall in open court take and fubfcribe the oath of fidelity to this commonwealth, and take the following oath of office: *You fhall fwear, that well and truly you will ferve this commonwealth in the office of a Judge of the High Court of Chancery, and that you will do equal right to all manner of people, great and fmall, high and low, rich and poor, according to equity and good confcience, and the laws and ufages of Virginia, without refpect of perfons. You fhall not take by yourfelf, or by any other, any gift, fee, or reward, of gold, filver, or any other thing, directly or indirectly, of any perfon or perfons, great or fmall, for any matter done or to be done by virtue of your*

(a) See the acts referred to in chap. 17, except the two firft;—alfo fee May 1778, chap. 7; May 1779, chap. 18.

office, except such fees or salary as shall be by law appointed. You shall not maintain by yourself, or by any other, privily or openly, any plea or quarrel depending in the courts of this commonwealth. You shall not delay any person of right for the letters or request of any person, nor for any other cause; and if any letter or request come to you contrary to law, you shall nothing do for such letter or request, but you shall proceed to do the law, any such letter or request notwithstanding. And finally, in all things belonging to your said office, during your continuance therein, you shall faithfully, justly, and truly, according to the best of your skill and judgment, do equal and impartial justice, without fraud, favour, affection, or partiality. So help you God.

II. AND if any person shall presume to execute the said office without having taken the said oaths, he shall forfeit and pay the sum of five hundred pounds for his said offence. The said court shall have general jurisdiction over all persons and in all causes in chancery, whether brought before them by original process, appeal from any inferiour court, *certiorari*, or other legal means; but no person shall commence an original suit in the said court in any matter of less value than ten pounds, except it be against the Justices of any county or other inferiour court, or the vestry of any parish, on pain of having the same dismissed with costs. There shall be two sessions of the said court in every year, to wit, one to begin on the fifth day of *April*, or if that be *Sunday*, then on the next day; the other on the fifth day of *September*, or if that be *Sunday*, then on the next day; to continue each of them eighteen days, Sundays excluded, if they shall so long have business to require their attendance. If not, they may, when the business is dispatched, adjourn to the next court. The said court shall however be considered as always open, so as to grant injunctions, writs of *ne exeat*, or other process heretofore allowed by the laws to be issued in time of vacation by the clerk of the General Court in chancery. The said court shall have power from time to time to appoint a clerk, who shall hold his office during good behaviour, and be entitled to such fees or salary as shall be established by the Legislature. All original process to bring any person to answer any bill, petition, or information in the said court, and all subsequent process thereupon, shall be issued and signed by the clerk in the name of the commonwealth, and bear teste by the first Judge of the said court, shall be returnable to the first or seventeenth days of the term, which shall be next after the suing out such process, and may be executed at any time before the return day thereof. And if any process shall be executed so late that the sheriff hath not reasonable time to return the same before the day of appearance, and thereupon any subsequent process shall be awarded, the sheriff shall not execute such subsequent process, but shall return the first process by him executed, on which there shall be the same proceedings as if it had been returned in due time. And all appeals from decrees in chancery, obtained in any inferiour court, shall be made to the third day of the next term.

Penalty for acting before taking the oaths; their jurisdiction.

Two sessions every year. and when; but the times altered since.

Length of the terms; but the court to be always open for certain purposes. The Clerk, &c. Process, directions concerning.

Appeals, to what day.

III. IN all suits in the said court the following rules and methods shall be observed: The complainant shall file his bill within one calendar month after the day of appearance, or may be ruled on the requisition of the defendant to file such bill, and if he fails so to do within one calendar month after such rule, the suit shall be dismissed with costs;

Rules to be observed.

IV. AND upon the complainants dismissing his bill, or the defendant's dismissing the same for want of prosecution, the complainant shall pay costs, to be taxed by the clerk of the court, for which costs an attachment, or other process of contempt, may issue, returnable on any return day.

V. THE complainant may amend his bill before the defendant or his attorney hath taken out a copy thereof, or in a small matter afterwards, without paying costs; but if he amend in a material point after such copy obtained, he shall pay the defendant all costs occasioned thereby.

VI. IF the defendant shall not appear on the day of appearance (which in all cases shall be the second day after the term to which the *subpœna* is returnable) an attachment shall be awarded and issued against him, returnable to the next term, which being returned executed, if the defendant doth not appear, or being brought into court upon any such process shall obstinately refuse to answer, the complainant's bill shall be taken as confessed, and the matter thereof decreed accordingly.

VII. THE defendant, within three calendar months after his appearance and bill filed, shall put in his answer to be filed with the clerk in the office, at the expiration of which time, if no answer be filed, the clerk, upon request, shall issue an attachment, returnable to the next court; and if no answer be filed upon the return of such attachment executed, the complainant's bill shall be taken as confessed, and the matter thereof decreed; and if the attachment be returned not executed, an attachment with proclamations, and such subsequent process of contempt may issue as was heretofore issuable out of the General Court sitting in chancery in like cases.

VIII. NO process of contempt shall issue unless the *subpœna* be returned served by a sworn officer, or affidavit be made of the service thereof.

IX. EVERY defendant may swear to his answer before any Judge of this or of the General Court, or any Justice of the Peace.

X. WHEN a cross bill shall be exhibited, the defendant or defendants to the first bill shall answer thereto before the defendant or defendants to the cross bill shall be compelled to answer such cross bill.

XI. THE complainant shall reply, or file exceptions, within two calendar months after the answer shall have been put in. If he fails so to do, the defendant may give a rule to reply with the clerk of the court, which being expired, and no replication or exceptions filed, the suit shall be dismissed with costs; but the court may order the same to be retained if they see cause, on payment of costs.

XII. IF the complainants attorney shall except against any answer as insufficient, he may file his exceptions, and give a rule with the clerk to make a better answer within two calendar months, and if within that time the defendant shall put in a sufficient answer, the same shall be received without costs; but if any defendant insist on the sufficiency of his answer, or neglect or refuse to put in a sufficient answer, or shall put in another insufficient answer, the plaintiff may set down his exceptions to be argued the next term in court, and after the expiration of such rule, or any second insufficient answer put in, no farther or other answer shall be received but upon payment of costs.

XIII. IF upon argument the complainant's exceptions shall be over-ruled, or the defendant's answer adjudged insufficient, the complainant shall pay to the defendant, or the defendant to the complainant, such costs as shall be allowed by the court.

XIV. UPON a second answer adjudged insufficient, costs shall be doubled.

XV. IF a defendant shall put in a third insufficient answer, which shall be so adjudged, he or she may be examined upon interrogatories, and committed until he or she shall answer them, and pay costs.

XVI. IF the defendant, after procefs of contempt, put in an infufficient anfwer, which fhall be fo adjudged, the complainant may go on with the fubfequent procefs of contempt, as if no anfwer had been put in.

XVII. RULES to plead, anfwer, reply, rejoin, or other proceedings not before particularly mentioned, when neceffary, fhall be given from month to month with the clerk in his office, and fhall be entered in a rule book for the information of all parties, attornies, or folicitors, concerned therein.

XVIII. NO defendant fhall be admitted to put in a rejoinder unlefs it be filed on or before the expiration of the rule to rejoin, but the complainant may proceed to fet his caufe down for hearing.

XIX. AFTER an attachment with proclamation returned, no plea or demurrer fhall be received unlefs by an order of court, upon motion.

XX. IF the complainant conceives any plea or demurrer to be naught, either for the matter or manner of it, he may fet it down with the clerk to be argued; or if he thinks the plea good, but not true, he may take iffue upon it, and proceed to trial by jury, as hath been heretofore ufed in other caufes in chancery where trial hath been by jury; and if thereupon the plea fhall be found falfe, the complainant fhall have the fame advantages as if it had been fo found by verdict at common law.

XXI IF a plea or demurrer be over-ruled, no other plea or demurrer fhall be thereafter received, but the defendant fhall anfwer the allegations of the bill.

XXII. IF the complainant fhall not proceed to reply to, or fet for hearing, as before mentioned, any plea or demurrer before the fecond court after filing the fame, the bill may be difmiffed of courfe with cofts.

XXIII. UPON a plea or demurrer argued and over-ruled, cofts fhall be paid as where an anfwer is judged infufficient, and the defendant fhall anfwer within two calendar months after; but if adjudged good, the defendant fhall have his cofts.

XXIV. IF any defendant, after a demurrer fhall have been over-ruled, fhall refufe to anfwer, the bill fhall be taken as confeffed, and the matter thereof decreed.

When plaintiff may have commiffion to examine witneffes before anfwer

XXV. AFTER any bill filed, and before the defendant hath anfwered, upon oath made that any of the complainant's witneffes are aged or infirm, or going out of the country, the clerk may iffue a commiffion for taking the examination of fuch witneffes *de bene effe*, the party praying fuch commiffion giving reafonable notice to the adverfe party of the time and place of taking the depofitions.

Matters of fact, how triable See October 1783, *chap.* 26.

XXVI. ALL matters of fact, material to the determination of the caufe, which in the courfe of the proceedings fhall be affirmed by the one party and denied by the other, fhall be tried by a jury upon evidence given *viva voce* in the faid court; and where witneffes are abfent through ficknefs, or other unavoidable caufe, upon their depofitions taken as the law directs, for which purpofe an iffue or iffues fhall be made up by declaration and plea, as hath been heretofore ufed in chancery, when iffues have been fpecially directed to be made up and tried by jury; for trial of which iffues, the fheriff of the county in which the court fhall fit fhall, every day of its feffion, fummon a fufficient number of jurymen of the bye-ftanders, or others found within half a mile of the courthoufe, who fhall be qualified as jurors attending the General Court, and fhall be fubject to the fame penalties for failing to attend; faving to the defendant the fame benefit of evidence, by his own anfwer, as hath been heretofore allowed in trials before the Court of Chancery.

Who may fet caufe for hearing.

XXVII. PROVIDED, that where the parties fhall wave the trial of any fuch iffue by jury, and fubmit the whole to the judgment of the court, or fhall agree that the depofitions of witneffes fhall be taken, and the caufe tried thereon, inftead of their being examined *viva voce* in court, fuch waver or agreement being figned by the parties or their council, the clerk fhall iffue commiffions for the examination of the witneffes, and ten days previous notice of the time and place of executing the fame fhall be given by the party taking out fuch commiffion to the adverfe party; and when the depofitions fhall be taken and returned, if the complainant fhall not within one calendar month thereafter fet down the caufe for hearing with the clerk, the defendant may have the fame fet down as aforefaid.

Proceedings in the office fubject to regulation by the court.
Proceedings in court to be read before figning.

XXVIII. THE court in their fittings may regulate all proceedings in the office, and for good caufe fhewn may fet afide any difmiffions, and reinftate the fuits on fuch terms as fhall appear equitable.

XXIX. FOR prevention of errors in entering up the decrees and orders of the court, the proceedings of every day fhall be drawn up at large by the clerk, and read in open court the next day, except thofe the laft day of each term, which fhall be drawn up, read, and corrected, the fame day, and any neceffary corrections made therein, when they fhall be figned by the prefiding Judge of the court, and preferved among the records.

Compleat record to be made in fuits ended.

XXX. AND for the more entire and better prefervation of the records of the court, when any caufe fhall be finally determined, the clerk fhall enter all the pleadings therein, and other matters relating thereto together, in a book to be kept for that purpofe, fo that an entire and perfect record may be made thereof, and thofe wherein the title to lands is determined fhall be entered in feparate books to be kept for that purpofe only.

Writs of certiorari, ne exeat, and injunction, how granted.

XXXI. THE court in their feffions, or any two of the Judges in vacation, may grant writs of *certiorari* for removing before them the proceedings in any fuit in chancery depending in any county or other inferiour court, writs of *ne exeat* to prevent the departure of any defendant out of the country until fecurity be given for performing the decree, and writs of injunction to ftay execution of judgments obtained in any of the courts of common law, fubject neverthelefs to the rules following:

Rules, as to writs of certiorari.

XXXII. NO writ of *certiorari* fhall be granted to remove any fuit unlefs the matter in difpute be of value fufficient to entitle the High Court of Chancery to original jurifdiction therein, nor unlefs ten days notice of the motion be given in writing to the adverfe party, in vacation but upon fuch petition and affidavit as are by law directed for writs of *certiorari* to be granted by the General Court; and, in all cafes, bond and fecurity fhall be given for performing the decree of the faid High Court of Chancery, before the iffuing of the *certiorari*.

As to writs of ne exeat, and how they may be difcharged.

XXXIII. Writs of *ne exeat* fhall not be granted but upon a bill filed and affidavits made to the truth of its allegations, which being produced to the court in term time, or to two Judges in vacation, they may grant or refuse such writ as to them shall seem just; and if granted, they shall direct to be endorsed thereon in what penalty bond and security shall be required of the defendant.

XXXIV. IF the defendant shall by answer satisfy the court that there is no reason for his restraint, or give sufficient security to perform the decree, the writ may be discharged.

XXXV. NO injunction shall be granted to stay proceedings in any suit at law unless the matter in dispute be of value sufficient to admit of original jurisdiction in the said High Court of Chancery, nor unless the court in term time, or two Judges thereof in vacation, shall be satisfied of the plaintiff's equity, either by affidavit, certified at the foot of the bill, that the allegations thereof are true, or by other means, and shall order the same; in which case the complainant shall enter into bond with sufficient security, to be approved of by the said court or Judges, for paying all money and tobacco, and costs due, or to become due, to the plaintiff in the action at law, and also all such costs as shall be awarded against him or her in case the injunction shall be dissolved. *As to injunctions.*

XXXVI. THE said High Court of Chancery shall take cognizance of and hear and determine all suits in chancery which were depending in the General Court at its last adjournment, or have been commenced therein since such adjournment, in the same manner as if the said suits had been originally instituted, or appeals entered to the said High Court of Chancery. If any suit shall be depending, or hereafter commenced, against any defendant or defendants who are out of this country, and others within the same, having in their hands effects of, or otherwise indebted to, such absent defendant or defendants, and the appearances of such absentees be not entered, and security given to the satisfaction of the court for performing the decrees, upon affidavit that such defendant or defendants are out of the country, or that upon inquiry at his, her, or their, usual places of abode, he, she, or they, could not be found, so as to be served with process, in all such cases the said High Court of Chancery may make any order, and require surety if it shall appear necessary, to restrain the defendants in this country from paying, conveying away or secreting the debts by them owing to, or the effects in their hands of such absent defendant or defendants, and for that purpose may order such debts to be paid and effects delivered to the said plaintiff or plaintiffs, upon their giving sufficient security for the return thereof to such persons, and in such manner as the court shall direct. *This court to have cognizance of suits in chancery depending in the former General Court. Absent defendants, how to be proceeded against.*

XXXVII. THE court shall also appoint some day in the succeeding term for the absent defendant or defendants to enter his or their appearance to the suit and give security for performing the decree, a copy of which order shall be forthwith published in the *Virginia* Gazette, and continued for two months successively, and shall also be published on some *Sunday* immediately after divine service in such parish church or churches as the court shall direct, and another copy shall be posted at the front door of the said court. If such absent defendant or defendants shall not appear and give such security within the time limited, or such farther time as the court may allow them for good cause shewn, the court may proceed to take such proof as the complainant shall offer; and if they shall thereupon be satisfied of the justice of the demand, they may order the bill to be taken as confessed, and make such order and decree therein as shall appear just, and may enforce due performance and execution thereof by such ways and means as hath heretofore been used for enforcing other decrees, requiring the plaintiff or plaintiffs to give security as the court shall approve for abiding such future order as may be made for restoring the estate or effects to the absent defendant or defendants, upon his or their appearance and answering the bill; and if the plaintiff or plaintiffs shall refuse to give or not be able to procure such security, the effects shall remain, under the direction of the court, in the hands of a receiver, or otherwise for so long time, and shall then be finally disposed of in such manner, as to the court shall seem just.

XXXVIII. IF any defendant or defendants shall be in custody upon any process of contempt, and be brought into court by virtue of a writ of *habeas corpus* or other process, and shall refuse or neglect to enter his or her appearance according to the rules of the court, or appoint an attorney of the court to do the same for him, the court in such case may direct an attorney to enter an appearance for the defendant or defendants, and thereupon such proceedings may be had as if he or they had actually entered an appearance; but if such defendant or defendants shall be in custody at the time a decree shall be made upon refusal or neglect to enter an appearance or to appoint an attorney as aforesaid, or shall be forthcoming so as to be served with a copy of the decree, then such defendant or defendants shall be served with such copy before any process shall be taken out to compel the performance thereof, and if such defendant or defendants shall die in custody before such service, then his heir, if any real estate be sequestered or affected by such decree, or if only personal estate, his executor or administrator shall be served with a copy in a reasonable time after such death shall be known to the plaintiff, and who is such heir, executor, or administrator.

XXXIX. IF any person or persons, who shall be out of the commonwealth at the time any decree is pronounced as aforesaid, shall within seven years from the passing such decree return and appear openly, or, in case of his or her death, if his or her heir, executor, or administrator, shall within the said seven years be and appear openly within this commonwealth, the plaintiff or plaintiffs, their executors or administrators, shall serve such person or persons so returning or appearing with a copy of the decree within a reasonable time after such return or appearance shall be known to the plaintiff or plaintiffs, and thereupon such defendants or their representatives may within twelve months after such service, or those defendants not served with a copy, or their representatives, may within seven years after the decree pronounced, appear in court and petition to have the cause re-heard, and upon their paying down or giving security for payment of such costs as the court shall think reasonable, they shall be admitted to answer the bill, and issue may be joined and witnesses on both sides examined, and such other proceedings, decree, and execution had, as if there had been no former decree in the cause; but if the several defendants, or their representatives, upon whom the decree shall be so served, shall not within twelve months after such service, and the other defendants, or their representatives, upon whom no such service is made, shall not within seven years from the time of the decree pronounced, appear and petition to have the cause re-heard as aforesaid, and pay, or secure to be paid, such costs as the court may think reasonable, all and every decree to be made in pursuance of this act, against any defendant or defendants so failing, shall stand absolutely confirmed against him, her, or them, his, her, or their heirs, executors, or administrators, and all persons claiming under him, her, or them, by virtue of any act or conveyance done or made, subsequent to the commencement of the suit, and at the end of such term the court may make such farther order for quieting the plaintiff or plaintiffs in any such suits, in their possession of and title to the estate and effects so sequestered or made liable, as to them shall seem reasonable.

XL. *AND it is further enacted,* that each of the said Judges shall receive an annual salary of five hundred pounds, to be paid by the Treasurer out of any public money in his hands; and that instead of the tax formerly imposed upon chancery process issued from the General Court, which shall henceforth cease, *Salary to the Judges. See November 1781, chap. 33.*

R

A. D. 1777.

Tax on process, what. See May 1780, chap. 10; May 1784, ch. 16.

a tax or duty of five shillings shall be paid for every original *subpœna* writ of *certiorari*, *ne exeat*, or injunction sued out of the said High Court of Chancery, by the party suing out the same, before the writ shall be issued to the clerk of the said court, and by him accounted for upon oath and paid to the Treasurer of this commonwealth half yearly, in the months of *March* and *September*, or, on his neglect, may be recovered by the said Treasurer upon a motion in the General Court, and ten days previous notice of such motion; provided, that no more than one tax shall be paid for process in any suit.

Repealed.

C H A P.　XVI.

An act for the establishing a warehouse for the reception of tobacco at South Quay *in* Nansemond *county and* Hobb's Hole *in* Essex *county*.

C H A P.　XVII.

An act for establishing a General Court.　　(a)

Preamble.

I. FOR establishing a court of common law of general jurisdiction, for the more easy and speedy administration of justice in this commonwealth, and for regulating the proceedings therein:

General Court; to consist of five Judges, how chosen and commissioned; tenure of their office; their precedence; three to be a court.

Chief Justice, the title of the first named; how the Judges to qualify.

II. BE it enacted, that at some certain place to be appointed by act of General Assembly, and at the times herein after directed, there shall be held one principal court of judicature for this commonwealth, which shall be styled the General Court of *Virginia*, and shall consist of five Judges, to be chosen by joint ballot of both Houses of the General Assembly, and commissioned by the Governor for the time being, to hold their offices so long as they shall respectively demean themselves well therein, any three of them to be a court; and the said Judges shall have precedence in court as they may stand in nomination on the ballot, and the person first named shall be called Chief Justice of such court. Every person so commissioned, before he enters upon the duties of his office, shall in open court take and subscribe the oath of fidelity to the commonwealth, and take the following oath of office, to wit: *You shall swear that well and truly you will serve this commonwealth in the office of a Judge of the General Court, and that you will do equal right to all manner of people, great and small, high and low; rich and poor, according to law, without respect of persons You shall not take by yourself, or by any other, privily or openly, any gift, fee, or reward, of gold, silver, or any other thing, directly or indirectly, of any person or persons, great or small, for any matter done or to be done by virtue of your office, except such fees or salary as shall be by law appointed. You shall not maintain by yourself, or other, privily or openly, any plea or quarrel depending in the courts of this commonwealth. You shall not deny or delay any person of common right for the letters or request of any person, nor for any other cause; and if any letter or request come to you contrary to the law, you shall nothing do for such letter or request, but you shall proceed to do the law, any such letter or request notwithstanding. And finally, in all things belonging to your said office, during your continuance therein, you shall faithfully, justly, and truly, according to the best of your skill and judgment, do equal and impartial justice, without fraud, favour, affection, or partiality. So help you God.* Which oath shall be administered by the Governor, or other presiding Chief Magistrate, in presence of the Council of State; and if any person shall presume to sit in court, or execute the said office without having taken the said oaths, he shall for such offence forfeit the sum of five hundred pounds. The jurisdiction of the said court shall be general over all persons, and in all causes, matters, or things at common law, whether brought before them by original process, by appeal from any inferior court, *habeas corpus, certiorari,* writ of error, *supersedeas, mandamus,* or by any other legal ways or means.

By whom the oath to be administered. See May 1778, ch. 9. Penalty for acting without oath. Jurisdiction of causes, of what nature;

Of what value, with exceptions.

III. PROVIDED always, that no person shall sue out original process for the trial of any matter or thing in the General Court of less value than ten pounds, or two thousand pounds of tobacco, except it be against the Justices of a county, or other inferior court, or the vestry of a parish, on penalty of being nonsuited, and having his suit dismissed with costs.

Further description of jurisdiction.

IV. THE said court shall take cognizance of, and hear and determine, all actions and suits at common law, whether real, personal, or mixed, petitions for lapsed lands, and all appeals at common law which were depending in the General Court at its last adjournment, or which have been since commenced therein, in the same manner as if the said suits had been originally instituted, or appeals entered in the said court.

Two sessions every year (two more added since)

when a single Judge may adjourn.

V. THERE shall be two sessions of the said court in every year, to wit, one to begin on the first day of *March*, if not *Sunday*, and then on the *Monday* thereafter, and the other to begin on the tenth day of *October*, if not *Sunday*, and then on the *Monday* following, to continue each of them twenty four natural days, *Sundays* exclusive, unless the business depending before them shall be finished in less time, in which case the Judges may adjourn to the next succeeding court; and if it should so happen that a sufficient number of Judges should not attend on the day appointed, any one of the said Judges may adjourn the court from day to day for six days successively, and if a sufficient number should not be able to attend at the end of such adjournment, all suits depending in such court shall stand continued over to the next succeeding court.

Clerk, &c. to be appointed during good behaviour; sheriff to attend.

VI. THE said court shall have power from time to time to appoint a clerk, one or more assistant clerks, a crier and tipstaff, who shall hold their office respectively during good behaviour, and be entitled to such fees or salaries as shall be established by law; and the sheriff, or so many of the under sheriffs as shall be thought necessary, of the county where such court may be held, shall attend the said court during their sessions.

Process, in what name, by whom to be signed, and bear teste, when returnable, and when to be executed.

VII. ALL original process to bring any person or persons to answer in any action or suit, information, bill, or plaint, in the said court, and all subsequent process thereon, all attachments, or other writs of what nature so ever, awarded by the said court, shall be issued and signed by the clerk of the said court in the name of the commonwealth, shall bear teste by the Chief Justice of the court, and be returnable on the respective days of the next succeeding court, as followeth, that is to say: All process for the commonwealth on criminal prosecutions to the sixth day, all appeals, writs of error, *supersedeas, certiorari, mandamus,* prohibition, and all other writs and process, except *subpœnas* for witnesses, to the eighth or twenty third day of the said court; and all such process may be executed at any time before the return day, except in such cases wherein it is otherwise directed by law.

(a) See May 1778, chap 9; October 1778, chap. 2; October 1780, chap. 30; May 1781, chap. 1, 9; November 1781, chap. 12; May 1783, chap. 40; October 1783, chap. 26; May 1784, chap. 35, and 27 of his session.

A. D. 1777.

VIII. AND if any writ or proceſs ſhall be executed ſo late that the ſheriff or other officer hath not reaſonable time to return the ſame before the day of appearance thereto, and an *alias*, *pluries*, attachment, or other proceſs, be awarded thereupon, the ſheriff ſhall not execute ſuch ſubſequent proceſs, but ſhall return the firſt proceſs by him executed, on which there ſhall be the ſame proceedings as if it had been returned in due time.

Executed in time, may be returned after day of appearance.

IX. IN all actions or ſuits which may be commenced againſt the Governor of this commonwealth, any member of the Privy Council, or the ſheriff of any county during his continuance in office, inſtead of the ordinary proceſs, a ſummons ſhall iſſue to the ſheriff, or other proper officer, reciting the cauſe of action, and ſummoning ſuch defendant to appear and anſwer the ſame on the proper return day in the next General Court; and if ſuch defendant, being ſummoned, or a copy left at his houſe ten days before the return day, ſhall not appear to anſwer the ſame, an attachment ſhall be awarded againſt his eſtate, and thereafter the proceedings in the ſuit ſhall be in like manner as is directed in caſe of an attachment awarded upon the ſheriffs returning *non eſt inventus* on ordinary proceſs.

In ſuits againſt Governor, &c what.

X. IN all actions to recover the penalty for breach of any penal law, not particularly directing ſpecial bail to be given, in actions of ſlander, treſpaſs, aſſault and battery, actions on the caſe for trover or other wrongs, and all other perſonal actions, except ſuch as ſhall be herein after particularly mentioned, the plaintiff, or his attorney, ſhall, on pain of having his ſuit diſmiſſed with coſts, endorſe on the original writ or ſubſequent proceſs the true ſpecies of action, that the ſheriff to whom the ſame is directed may be thereby informed whether bail is to be demanded on the execution thereof; and in the caſes before mentioned, the ſheriff may take the engagement of an attorney practiſing in the General Court, endorſed upon the writ, that he will appear for the defendant or defendants, and ſuch appearance ſhall be entered with the clerk in the office on the ſecond day after the end of the court to which ſuch proceſs is returnable, which is hereby declared to be the appearance day in all proceſs returnable to any day of the court next preceding.

In certain actions plaintiff muſt endorſe on the writ the true ſpecies, and how ſheriff may then act. Day of appearance.

XI. AND every attorney failing to enter an appearance according to ſuch engagement ſhall forfeit to the plaintiff fifty ſhillings, for which judgment ſhall be immediately entered, and execution may iſſue thereupon.

Penalty on Attorney engaging, and failing to appear.

XII. PROVIDED always, that any Judge of the the ſaid court, in actions of treſpaſs, aſſault and battery, trover and converſion, and in actions on the caſe, where upon proper affidavit or affirmation, as the caſe may be, it ſhall appear to him proper that the defendant or defendants ſhould give appearance bail, may, and he is hereby authoriſed to direct ſuch bail to be taken, by endorſement on the original writ or ſubſequent proceſs; and every ſheriff ſhall govern himſelf accordingly.

In certain caſes a Judge may direct an appearance bail.

XIII. IN all actions of debt founded on any writing obligatory, bill, or note in writing for the payment of money or tobacco, all actions of covenant or detinue, in which caſes the true ſpecies of action ſhall be endorſed on the writ as before directed, and that appearance bail is to be required, the ſheriff ſhall return on the writ the name of the bail by him taken, and a copy of the bail bond to the clerk's office before the day of appearance; and if the defendant ſhall fail to appear accordingly, or ſhall not give ſpecial bail, being ruled thereto by the court, the bail for appearance may defend the ſuit, and ſhall be ſubject to the ſame judgment and recovery as the defendant might or would be ſubject to if he had appeared and given ſpecial bail.

Directions to ſheriff where bail is required. Bail, not diſcharged, may defend, &c.

XIV. AND if the ſheriff ſhall not return bail, and a copy of the bail bond, or the bail returned, ſhall be judged inſufficient by the court, and the defendant ſhall fail to appear or give ſpecial bail, if ruled thereto, in ſuch caſe the ſheriff may have the like liberty of defence, and ſhall be ſubject to the ſame recovery, as is provided in the caſe of appearance bail. And if the ſheriff depart this life before judgment be confirmed againſt him, in ſuch caſe the judgment may be confirmed againſt his executors or adminiſtrators; or if there ſhall not be a certificate of probate or adminiſtration granted, then it may be confirmed againſt his eſtate, and a writ of *fieri facias* may in either caſe be iſſued, but the plaintiff ſhall object to the ſufficiency of the bail during the ſitting of the court to which the writ is returnable, or in the office at the firſt or ſecond rule day after that court, and at no time thereafter.

Remedy againſt ſheriff, &c neglecting to return ſufficient bail. Exceptions to bail, when to be made,

XV. AND all queſtions concerning the ſufficiency of bail, ſo objected to in the office, ſhall be determined by the court on the eighth day of the ſucceeding court; and in all cauſes where the bail ſhall be adjudged inſufficient, and judgment entered againſt the ſheriff, he ſhall have the ſame remedy againſt the eſtate of the bail as againſt the eſtate of the defendant.

and how determined; remedy for ſheriffs againſt bail adjudged inſufficient

XVI. ALSO, that every judgment entered in the office againſt a defendant and bail, or againſt a defendant and ſheriff, ſhall be ſet aſide, if the defendant, upon the eighth day of the ſucceeding court, ſhall be allowed to appear without bail, put in good bail, being ruled ſo to do, or ſurrender himſelf in cuſtody, and ſhall plead to iſſue immediately, on which eighth day the court ſhall alſo regulate all other proceedings in the office during the preceding vacation, and rectify any miſtakes or errors which may have happened therein.

Office, judgments, when ſet aſide; and errors in the office, how rectified.

XVII. IN every caſe where judgment ſhall be confirmed againſt any defendant or defendants and his bail, or the ſheriff, his executors, adminiſtrators, or eſtate, as aforeſaid, the court, upon a motion of ſuch bail, or of ſuch ſheriff, his executors or adminiſtrators, or any other perſon on behalf of his eſtate, may order an attachment againſt the eſtate of ſuch defendant or defendants, returnable to the next ſucceeding court; and upon the execution and return of ſuch attachment the court ſhall order the eſtate ſeized, or ſo much thereof as will be ſufficient to ſatisfy the judgment and coſts, and all coſts accruing on the attachment, to be ſold as goods taken in execution upon a *fieri facias*, and out of the money, ſuch judgment, and all coſts, ſhall be ſatisfied, and the ſurplus, if any, reſtored to the defendant or defendants when required.

Remedy to the bail and ſheriff againſt defendant's eſtate.

XVIII. ANY Judge of the ſaid court, when the court is not ſitting, or any Juſtice of the Peace authorized for that purpoſe by the ſaid court, may take recognizance of ſpecial bail in any action therein depending, which ſhall be taken *de bene eſſe*, and ſhall be tranſmitted by the perſon taking the ſame, before the next ſucceeding General Court, to the clerk of the ſaid court, to be filed with the papers in ſuch action; and if the plaintiff or his attorney ſhall except to the ſufficiency of bail ſo taken, notice of ſuch exception ſhall be given to the defendant or his attorney, at leaſt ten days previous to the day on which ſuch exception ſhall be taken. And if ſuch bail ſhall be judged inſufficient by the court, the recognizance thereof ſhall be diſcharged, and ſuch proceedings ſhall be had as if no ſuch bail had been taken.

How ſpecial bail may be taken in the country, and excepted to.

XIX. EVERY ſpecial bail may ſurrender the principal, before the court where the ſuit hath been or ſhall be depending, at any time either before or after judgment ſhall be given, and thereupon the bail

Surrender of principal, and proceedings thereupon.

shall be difcharged, and the defendant or defendants fhall be committed to the cuftody of the fheriff or jailer attending fuch court, if the plaintiff or his attorney fhall defire the fame; or fuch fpecial bail may difcharge himfelf or herfelf by furrendering the principal or principals to the fheriff of the county where the original writ was ferved, and fuch fheriff fhall receive fuch defendant or defendants, and commit him, her, or them, to the jail of his county, and fhall give a receipt for the body or bodies of fuch defendant or defendants, which fhall be by the bail forthwith tranfmitted to the clerk of the court where the fuit is or was depending.

XX. WHEN fuch render, after judgment, fhall be to the fheriff, he fhall keep fuch defendant or defendants in his cuftody, in the fame manner, and fubject to the like rules, as are provided for debtors committed in execution during the fpace of twenty days, unlefs the creditor, his attorney or agent, fhall fooner confent to his, her, or their difcharge. The bail fhall give immediate notice of fuch render to the creditor, his attorney or agent, and if, within the faid twenty days, fuch creditor, his attorney or agent, fhall not in writing charge the debtor or debtors in execution, he, fhe, or they, fhall be forthwith difcharged out of cuftody; but the plaintiff or plaintiffs may, neverthelefs, afterwards fue out any legal execution againft fuch debtor or debtors.

How to proceed
againft, or in be-
half of, a defendant
in prifon.

XXI. WHEN the fheriff, or other proper officer, fhall return on any original or mefne procefs, that he hath taken the body of any defendant, and committed him to prifon for want of appearance bail, the plaintiff may proceed, and the defendant make his defence, in like manner as if his appearance had been entered and accepted; but fuch defendant fhall not be difcharged out of cuftody until he fhall put in good bail, or the plaintiff fhall be ruled by the court to accept an appearance without bail; and where any defendant, after appearance entered, fhall be confined in prifon, the plaintiff may file his declaration, give a rule to plead, and deliver copies of fuch declaration and rule to the defendant or his attorney, and if the defendant fhall fail to enter his plea within two months after receiving fuch declaration and notice, the plaintiff may have judgment by default, as in other cafes.

Capias returned
‘ not found,’ what
further procefs.

Proceedings, on
attachment return-
ed ‘executed.’

XXII. WHERE the fheriff, or other proper officer, fhall return on any writ of *capias* to anfwer in any civil action, that the defendant is not found within his bailiwick, the plaintiff may either fue out an *alias*, or a *pluries capias*, until the defendant fhall be arrefted, or a *teftatum capias*, where he fhall be removed into another county, or may, at his election, fue out an attachment againft the eftate of the defendant to force an appearance; and if the fheriff, or other officer, fhall return that he hath attached any goods, and the defendant fhall not appear and replevy the fame, by entering his appearance and giving fpecial bail, in cafe he fhall be ruled fo to do, the plaintiff fhall file his declaration, and be entitled to a judgment for his debt, or damages and cofts, which judgment fhall be final in all actions of debt founded on any fpecialty, bill, or note in writing afcertaining the demand; and in other cafes, the damages fhall be fettled by a jury fworn to inquire thereof. The goods attached fhall remain in the hands of the officer till fuch final judgment be entered, and then be fold in the fame manner as goods taken upon a *fieri facias*; and if the judgment fhall not be thereby fatisfied, the plaintiff may fue out execution for the refidue, and in cafe more goods be attached than will fatisfy the judgment, the furplus fhall be returned to the defendant.

On pluries returned
‘not to be found.’

XXIII. ON the return of the *pluries*, that the defendant is not to be found, the court, inftead of the procefs to outlawry formerly ufed, may order a proclamation to be iffued, warning the defendant to appear at a certain day therein to be named, or that judgment will be rendered againft him, which proclamation fhall be publifhed on three fucceffive court days at the door of the court-houfe of the county to which the laft procefs was directed, and alfo three times in the *Virginia* Gazette; and if the defendant fails to appear purfuant to fuch proclamation, the fame proceedings fhall be had, and the fame judgment given, as in other cafes of default.

Rules to be obferv-
ed in the profecution
of fuits.

XXIV. IN the profecution of all fuits in the General Court, the following rules fhall be obferved: The plaintiff fhall file his declaration in the clerk's office at the fucceeding rule day after the defendant fhall have entered his appearance, or the defendant may then enter a rule for the plaintiff to declare, and if he fhall fail or neglect fo to do at the fucceeding rule day, or fhall at any time fail to profecute his fuit, he fhall be nonfuited, and pay to the defendant or tenant, befides his cofts, one hundred and fifty pounds of tobacco, where his place of abode is at the diftance of twenty miles or under from the place of holding the General Court, and where it is more, five pounds of tobacco for every mile above twenty. One month after the plaintiff hath filed his declaration, he may give a rule to plead with the clerk, and if the defendant fhall not plead accordingly at the expiration of fuch rule, the plaintiff may enter judgment by default for his debt, or damages and cofts.

XXV. ALL rules to declare, plead, reply, rejoin, or for other proceedings, fhall be given regularly from month to month, fhall be entered in a book to be kept by the clerk for that purpofe, and fhall be out on the fucceeding rule day.

XXVI. ALL judgments by default for want of an appearance, fpecial bail, or pleas as aforefaid, and nonfuits or difmiffions obtained in the office, and not fet afide on the eighth day of the fucceeding General Court, fhall be entered by the clerk as of that day, which judgment fhall be final in actions of debt founded on any fpecialty, bill, or note in writing afcertaining the demand; and in all other cafes, the damages fhall be afcertained by a jury to be empannelled and fworn to inquire thereof, as is herein after directed.

XXVII. IN all fuch cafes, and other judgments for plaintiff or defendant, the clerk fhall allow a lawyer's fee in the bill of cofts, if the party employed one; which fee, in real, perfonal or mixed actions, where the title or bounds of land fhall or may come in queftion, fhall be five pounds, or one thoufand pounds of tobacco, and in all other cafes fifty fhillings, or five hundred pounds of tobacco, at the election of the party paying.

XXVIII. NO plea in abatement, or of *non eft factum*, fhall be admitted or received unlefs the party offering the fame fhall prove the truth thereof by affidavit or affirmation, as the cafe may be; and where a plea in abatement fhall upon argument be judged infufficient, the plaintiff fhall recover full cofts to the time of over-ruling fuch plea, a lawyer's fee only excepted.

XXIX. THE plaintiff in replevin, and the defendant in all other actions, may plead as many feveral matters, whether of law or fact, as he fhall think neceffary for his defence.

Juftices, &c. may
be fued jointly for
fines.

XXX. IN all cafes where a fine is laid on the Juftices of any county court, or the veftry of a parifh, one action may be brought againft all the members jointly.

A. D. 1777.

XXXI. BEFORE every General Court the clerk shall enter in a particular docket all such causes, and those only in which an issue is to be tried or inquiry of damages to be made, or a special verdict, case agreed, demurrer, appeal, or other matter of law to be argued, in the same order as they stand in the course of proceeding, setting, as near as may be, an equal number of causes to each day.

Rules for docketing causes.

XXXII. WHEN any cause shall be finally determined, the clerk of the General Court shall enter all the pleadings and papers filed as evidence therein, and the judgment thereupon, so as to make a complete record thereof; and those wherein the title to lands is determined shall be entered in separate books to be kept for that purpose.

Complea record to be made of causes determined.*

XXXIII. FOR prevention of errors in entering up the judgments of the said court, the proceedings of every day shall be drawn at large by the clerk against the next sitting of the court, when the same shall be read in open court, and such corrections as are necessary being made therein, they shall be signed by the presiding Judge, and carefully preserved among the records.

Proceedings to be read and signed.

XXXIV. IN all cases where witnesses are required to attend the General Court, a summons shall be issued by the clerk, expressing the day and place where they are to appear, the names of the party to the suit, and in whose behalf summoned.

Witnesses, how to be summoned.

XXXV. WHEN any witness shall be about to depart the country, or by age, sickness, or otherwise, shall be unable to attend the court, upon affidavit thereof, or on a certificate from any Justice of the Peace, the court, when they are sitting, or any Judge thereof in vacation, may, on request of either party, award a commission for taking the deposition of such witness *de bene esse*, to be read as evidence at the trial, in case the witness shall then be unable to attend; but the party obtaining such commission shall give reasonable notice to the other party of the time and place of taking the deposition, otherwise the same shall be void.

Depositions, commission for taking, in certain cases.

XXXVI. IF any party in a suit at common law shall make oath that he verily believes his claim, or defence, as the case may be, or a material point thereof, depends on a single witness, the court or any Judge thereof, may award a commission to take the deposition of such witness *de bene esse*, although he or she be not about to depart the country, nor under any disability, the party in such case giving reasonable notice of the time and place of taking such deposition to the adverse party.

XXXVII. IF any person summoned as a witness, and attending the court, or the commissioners appointed to take his or her deposition as aforesaid, shall refuse to give evidence upon oath or affirmation, as the case may be, to the best of his or her knowledge, every person so refusing shall be committed to prison, either by the court or commissioners, there to remain, without bail or mainprise, until he or she shall give such evidence.

Witness refusing to testify, how to be dealt with.

XXXVIII. NO person convicted of perjury shall be capable of being a witness in any case, nor shall any negro, mulatto, or *Indian*, be admitted to give evidence but against or between negroes, mulattoes, or *Indians*.

Incapacities to testify.

XXXIX. IF any person summoned as a witness to attend the General Court shall fail to attend accordingly, they shall fine such person five pounds, or one thousand pounds of tobacco, at the option of the payer, to the use of the party for whom such witness was summoned, and the witness so failing shall farther be liable to the action of the party for all damages sustained by the non-attendance of such witness; but if sufficient cause of his or her inability to attend be shewn to the court at the time he or she ought to have appeared, or at the next succeeding court, then no fine or action shall be incurred by such failure.

Witnesses failing to attend, how liable;

XL. WITNESSES shall be privileged from arrests in civil cases during their attendance at the General Court, coming to and returning from thence, allowing one day for every twenty miles from their places of abode; and all such arrests shall be void. Every witness summoned, and attending the General Court, shall be paid, by the party at whose suit the summons issues two pounds of tobacco, or four pence *per* mile for travelling to the place of attendance, and the same for returning, besides ferriages, and sixty pounds of tobacco, or ten shillings *per* day for his attendance, which allowance shall be entered by the clerk of course, except where disputes arise concerning the same, and then such disputes shall be determined by the General Court. And the said court shall have power to try all issues, and inquire of damages by a jury in all causes before them, and to determine all questions concerning the legality of evidence, and other matters of law which may arise, for which trials the court shall cause the sheriff attending them to empannel and return jurors of the byestanders, qualified as the law directs, to be sworn well and truly to try the issue joined, or to inquire of damages, as the case may be, according to evidence.

Privilege of, and allowance.

How issues to be tried.

XLI. THERE shall not be allowed in the bill of costs the charge of more than three witnesses for the proof of any one particular fact.

Charge allowed of only three witnesses to one fact.

XLII. WHERE any person or persons, body politic or corporate, shall think themselves aggrieved by the judgment or sentence of any county court or court of *Hustings*, in any action, suit, or contest whatever where the debt or damages, or other thing recovered or claimed in such suit, exclusive of the costs, shall be of the value of ten pounds, or two thousand pounds of tobacco, or where the title or bounds of land shall be drawn in question, or the contest shall be concerning mills, roads, the probate of wills, or certificates for obtaining administration, such person or persons, body politic or corporate, may enter an appeal to the General Court from such judgment or sentence.

Appeals to General Court in certain cases.

XLIII. WHERE the defendant in any personal action appeals, if the judgment be affirmed, the damages, besides costs, shall be ten *per centum per annum* upon the principal sum, and costs recovered in the inferior court, in satisfaction of all damages or interest.

Damages upon affirmance.

XLIV. IN real or mixed actions, the damages shall be ten pounds, or two thousand pounds of tobacco, besides costs; and where the plaintiff appeals in any action, if the judgment be affirmed, and in all controversies about mills, roads, probate of wills, or certificates for administration, if the sentence of the inferior court be affirmed, the party appealing shall pay to the other five pounds, or one thousand pounds of tobacco, besides all costs.

XLV. NO appeal, writ of error, or *supersedeas*, shall be granted in any cause until a final judgment shall be given in the county or other inferior court.

No appeal, &c. before final judgment.

A. D. 1777.

Superfedeas, how to be obtained.

XLVI. THE party paying a writ of *superfedeas* fhall petition the Judges of the General Court for the fame, pointing out the error he means to affign in the proceedings, and procure fome attorney practifing in the General Court to certify that in his opinion there is fufficient matter of error for reverfing the judgment, whereupon the court in their feffion, or any two Judges in vacation, may order fuch writ to be iffued, or reject the petition, as to them fhall feem juft; but no *superfedeas* fhall be iffued in any cafe, except fuch as, in refpect to its value or nature, would have admitted of an appeal.

Writs of error, how to be fued out.

XLVII. WRITS of error fhall not be fued out of the General Court, to judgments of inferior courts, but with leave of the court, upon the motion of the party defiring the fame, and ten days previous notice thereof given in writing to the adverfe party.

XLVIII. BEFORE granting any appeal, or iffuing a writ of error or *superfedeas*, the party praying the fame fhall enter into bond with fufficient fecurity, in a reafonable penalty, with condition to fatisfy and pay the amount of the recovery in the county or other inferior court, and all cofts and damages awarded by the General Court, in cafe the judgment or fentence be affirmed

Judgment on re-verfal.

XLIX. IF upon hearing any appeal, writ of error, or *superfedeas*, the judgment of the inferior court fhall be reverfed, the General Court fhall enter fuch judgment thereupon as ought to have been entered in the inferior court.

Certiorari, how to be obtained.

L. IF any perfon or perfons fhall defire to remove any fuit depending in any inferior court into the General Court, provided the fame be originally cognizable therein, a *certiorari* for fuch removal may be granted by the General Court for good caufe fhewn, upon motion, and ten days notice thereof given in writing to the adverfe party; or in vacation, the party defiring fuch writ fhall, by petition to the Judges of the General Court, fet forth his or her reafons, and make oath before a Magiftrate to the truth of the allegations of fuch petition, whereupon any two Judges of the faid court may, under their hands, order the *certiorari* to iffue, and direct the penalty of the bond to be taken previous thereto, or may reject fuch petition, as to them fhall feem juft, provided that ten days previous notice of the time and place of applying for fuch writ be given in writing to the adverfe party, upon which order of the Judges the clerk fhall iffue the *certiorari*.

Rule in cafe the fuit be remanded.

LI. *PROVIDED*, that the party fhall enter into bond with fufficient fecurity, in the penalty fo directed, with condition for fatisfying all money or tobacco, and cofts, which fhall be recovered againft the party in fuch fuit; but if any fuit fo removed by writ of *certiorari* fhall be remanded to the inferior court by writ of *procedendo* or otherwife, fuch caufe fhall not afterwards be removed to the General Court before judgment fhall be given therein in the inferior court.

Punifhment of falfe fwearers.

LII. THE clerk of the General Court fhall carefully preferve all fuch petitions for writs of *certiorari*, with the affidavits thereto, in the office; and if any perfon in fuch affidavit fhall take a falfe oath, and be thereof convicted, upon a profecution commenced within twelve months after the offence committed, fuch offender fhall fuffer the pains and penalties directed for wilful and corrupt perjury.

Habeas corpus cum caufa directed in certain cafes.

LIII. WHERE any perfon fhall be committed, in any civil action, to the jail of any county or corporation, for a caufe or matter cognizable in the General Court, it fhall be lawful for the clerk of the General Court, and he is hereby required, upon the application of fuch perfon, and a certificate of his or her being actually in jail, to iffue a writ of *habeas corpus cum caufa* to remove the body of fuch prifoner into the public prifon for debtors, and the caufe of his commitment into the General Court, returnable on the firft day of the fucceeding General Court, if iffued in vacation; on the laft day of the term, if fued out whilft the court is fitting.

How prifoners in certain cafes may, for want of trial, be fet at liberty on bail.

LIV. IF any perfon committed for treafon or felony, fpecially expreffed in the warrant of commitment, fhall apply to the General Court the firft week of the term and defire to be brought to trial, and fhall not be indicted and tried fome time in that term or feffion, the Judges fhall fet fuch prifoner at liberty, upon bail for his appearance to anfwer the offence at the next fucceeding term or feffion, unlefs it appears by affidavit that the witneffes for the commonwealth could not be produced at fuch term or feffion; and if any fuch prifoner fhall not be indicted and tried the fecond term or feffion after commitment, he fhall be difcharged from his imprifonment, in manner aforefaid.

LV. *PROVIDED*, that this fhall not extend to difcharge any perfon in cuftody of the fheriff for any other caufe.

Criminal jurif-diction of the court.

LVI. The General Court to be held as aforefaid fhall have full power to hear and determine all treafons, murders, felonies, and other crimes and mifdemeanors which fhall be brought before them.

Examining court, how fummoned, and what it's power.

LVII. When any perfon, not being a flave, fhall be charged before a Juftice of the Peace with any criminal offence, which in the opinion of fuch Juftice ought to be examined into by the county court, the faid Juftice fhall take the recognizance of all material witneffes to appear before fuch court, and immediately by his warrant commit the perfon fo charged to the county jail, and moreover fhall iffue his warrant to the fheriff of the county requiring him to fummon the Juftices of the county to meet at their courthoufe on a certain day, not lefs than five or more than ten days after the date thereof, to hold a court for examination of the fact, which court fhall confider whether, as the cafe may appear to them, the prifoner may be difcharged from further profecution, may be tried in the county, or muft be tried in the General Court, and if they fhall be of opinion that the fact may be tried in the county, the prifoner fhall be bound over to the next grand jury to be held for that county for trial, or upon refufing to give fufficient bail fhall be remanded to the county jail, there to remain until fuch court, or until he or fhe fhall be bailed; but if they fhall be of opinion that the prifoner ought to be tried in the General Court, they fhall take the depofitions of the witneffes, and bind fuch as they fhall think proper recognizances to appear and give evidence againft fuch criminal at his trial, and having remanded the prifoner to jail, any two of the juftices, one being of the quorum, by warrant under their hands and feals, fhall direct the fheriff or his deputy to remove the prifoner and commit him to the public jail, there to be fafely kept until he or fhe be difcharged by due courfe of law, by virtue of which warrant, the fheriff, as foon as may be, fhall remove the prifoner, and deliver him or her with the warrant to the keeper of the public jail, who fhall receive and fafely keep him or her accordingly And for enabling the fheriff fafely to convey and deliver fuch prifoner, the faid two Juftices, by their warrant, fhall empower him, as well within his county as without, to imprefs fuch and fo many men, horfes, and boats, as fhall be neceffary for the guard and fafe conveyance of the prifoner, proceeding therein as the law may direct in cafes of impreffing on other occafions; and all perfons are to pay due obedience to fuch warrant.

LVIII. *PROVIDED*, that if fuch perfon fhall, in the opinion of the court, be bailable by law, he or fhe fhall not be removed in twenty days after the examining court, but fhall and may be admitted to bail before any Juftice of the fame county within that time, or at any time afterwards before any Judge of the General Court.

LIX. WHEN any perſon ſhall be ſo removed to be tried for treaſon or felony, the clerk of the county from whence the priſoner is removed ſhall, immediately after the court held for his or her examination, iſſue a writ of *venire facias* to the ſheriff of the county, commanding him to ſummon twelve good
and lawful men, being freeholders of the county reſiding as near as may be to the place where the fact is
alledged to have been committed, to come before the General Court on the ſixth day of its next ſeſſion
and return a pannel of their names, which freeholders, or ſo many of them as ſhall appear, not being
challenged, together with ſo many other good and lawful freeholders of the bye-ſtanders as will make
up the number twelve, ſhall be a lawful jury for the trial of ſuch priſoner.

*Juries, how
formed.
The day altered
ſince to the firſt.*

LX. EVERY *venire* man ſummoned, and attending the General Court, ſhall have the ſame allowance
for travelling and attendance as is herein before provided for witneſſes, to be paid by the public.

*Allowance to ve-
nire men.*

LXI. IF any perſon ſummoned as a *venire* man ſhall fail to attend accordingly, not having a reaſonable
excuſe, to be made at the time he ſhould have appeared, or at the next General Court, they may fine
every ſuch perſon, not exceeding forty ſhillings, or four hundred pounds of tobacco, for the uſe of the
commonwealth.

*Their fine for
non attendance.*

LXII. IF a priſoner ſhall deſire any witneſſes to be ſummoned for him or her to appear either at the
examining court or on the trial at the General Court, the clerk of the ſaid court, or of the county court,
as the caſe may be, ſhall iſſue *ſubpœnas* for ſuch witneſſes, who being ſummoned, and attending, ſhall
have the like allowance for travelling and attendance, and be ſubject to the ſame penalty for failing to
attend, as is provided for witneſſes in civil cauſes.

*Subpœnas for
priſoner's witneſ-
ſes, their allowance
&c.*

LXIII. THE keeper of the public jail, by order of any two Juſtices of his county, may impreſs guards
for the ſafe keeping of all priſoners in his cuſtody, to be paid by the public.

*Guards to the
public jail.*

LXIV. THE fee to the ſheriff of the county, and to the public jailer, for the keeping and dieting any
ſuch priſoner, ſhall be one ſhilling *per* day, and no more.

*Fees to Sheriff
&c.*

LXV. WHERE the criminal ſhall be convicted, and hath eſtate ſufficient to pay the charges of pro-
ſecution, the whole ſhall be paid out of ſuch eſtate, and the public only made chargeable where there is
no ſuch eſtate, or not ſufficient to be found.

*Charges of pro-
ſecution.*

LXVI. THE ſheriff, for the time being, of the county in which the General Court is held ſhall, before every meeting of the General Court, ſummon twenty four freeholders of this commonwealth, qualified as the laws require, for grand jurors, to appear at the ſucceeding General Court on the ſixth day
thereof, which the ſaid ſheriff is hereby empowered to do, as well without his county as within the
ſame; and the ſaid twenty four men, or any ſixteen of them, ſhall be a grand jury, and ſhall inquire of
and preſent all treaſons, murders, felonies, or other miſdemeanors whatever, which ſhall have been
committed or done within this commonwealth, and upon any indictment for a capital offence, being
found by a grand jury to be true, againſt any perſon or perſons, the Judges ſhall cauſe ſuch perſon or
perſons to be immediately arraigned and tried by a petit jury ſummoned as herein before directed, and,
he or they being found guilty, paſs ſuch judgment as the laws direct, and thereupon award execution,
and if the priſoner ſhall be found not guilty, to acquit him or her of the charge.

*Grand juries.
Altered ſince to the
firſt day.
Priſoners, how
arraigned and tri-
ed.*

LXVII. *PROVIDED*, that in all trials the defendant ſhall on petition be allowed counſel, and that
when ſentence of death ſhall be paſſed upon any priſoner there ſhall be one calendar month at leaſt between the judgment and execution.

*Allowed counſel,
and ſuſpenſion of
execution.*

LXVIII. NO grand jury ſhall make any preſentments of their own knowledge upon the information
of fewer than two of their own body, nor where the penalty inflicted by law is leſs than twenty ſhillings,
or two hundred pounds of tobacco.

*Preſentments on
grand jury's know-
ledge.*

LXIX. EVERY perſon ſummoned to appear on a grand jury, and failing to attend, not having a reaſonable excuſe, ſhall be fined by the court, not exceeding four hundred pounds of tobacco, to the uſe
of the commonwealth.

*Fine on grand
juror not attending.*

LXX. UPON preſentment made by the grand jury of an offence not capital, the court ſhall order the
clerk to iſſue a ſummons, or other proper proceſs, againſt the perſon or perſons preſented, to appear
and anſwer ſuch preſentment at the next court, and thereupon hear and determine the ſame according
to law.

*Proceſs againſt
perſons preſented for
offences not capital.*

LXXI. THE clerk of the General Court ſhall, in a book by him kept for that purpoſe, enter the
names of all *venire* men and witneſſes who attend for the trial of criminals at ſuch court, the number of
days each ſhall attend, the ferries they ſhall have croſſed, and the diſtances they ſhall have travelled on
that occaſion, and ſhall, before every ſeſſion of General Aſſembly, deliver all ſuch books to the clerk of
the Houſe of Delegates, that the allowance may be made to ſuch *venire* men and witneſſes.

*Attendance, &c.
of veniremen, &c.
to be entered.*

LXXII. THE keeper of the public jail ſhall conſtantly attend the General Court and execute the command of the court from time to time, and take or receive into his cuſtody all perſons by the court to
him committed on original or meſne proceſs, or in execution in any civil ſuit, or for any contempt of
the court, and him or them ſafely keep until thence diſcharged by due courſe of law, and may demand
and receive of every ſuch priſoner the legal fees for diet and care; but where ſuch priſoner is ſo poor as
not to be able to ſubſiſt him or herſelf in priſon, the jailer ſhall be allowed by the public one ſhilling *per*
day for the maintenance of every ſuch poor priſoner, and no ſecurity ſhall be demanded of him or her,
nor ſhall he or ſhe be detained for ſuch priſon fees. And the ſaid jailer, during his continuance in office,
ſhall be exempted from ſerving in the militia and on juries, and ſhall have ſuch allowance, over and
above the fees, as by the General Aſſembly ſhall be thought reaſonable.

*Keeper of public
jail, his duty, al-
lowance, and pri-
vilege.*

LXXIII. EACH Judge of the General Court, for performing the whole duty of his office, ſhall receive an annual ſalary of five hundred pounds, which ſhall be paid by the Treaſurer out of the public
money in his hands.

*Salary of the
Judges. See* Nov.
1781, *chap.* 33.

LXXIV. *AND it is further enacted*, that inſtead of the tax formerly impoſed on proceſs ſued out of
the General Court, which ſhall henceforth ceaſe, a duty or tax of five ſhillings for every original writ or
proceſs ſued out of the General Court, for every ejectment returnable thereto, and for every writ of
error, *certiorari*, and *ſuperſedas*, iſſued from the clerk's office of the ſaid court, ſhall be paid by the
party ſuing out ſuch writ or proceſs, before the ſame ſhall be iſſued, and by the plaintiff in ſuch ejectment before any proceeding ſhall be allowed thereon, and taxed in the bill of coſts, if the party reco-

Tax on proceſs. See
May 1780, *ch.* 10.

A. D. 1777.

vers cofts; which taxes fhall be accounted for half yearly, in the months of *March* and *September*, by the clerk of the General Court, upon oath, and paid to the Treafurer of this commonwealth, the clerk deducting five *per centum* for receiving and paying the fame, and in cafe of failure, may be recovered with cofts upon motion of the Treafurer in the General Court, and ten days previous notice given of fuch motion.

Penalties appro-
priated; duty of
clerk in tranfmiting
annual lifts of fines,
and of fheriff in
collecting them.

LXXV. ALL the penalties hereby inflicted, and not otherwife appropriated, fhall be one moiety to the ufe of the commonwealth, and difpofed of as the General Affembly fhall direct, and the other moiety to the informer, and be recovered by action of debt or information in any court of record where the fame is cognizable; and where fines fhall be laid by the General Court on any perfon or perfons for not attending as jurymen, the clerk fhall annually, before the laft day of *January*, tranfmit to the fheriff of each county a lift of all fuch fines, and all others impofed to the ufe of the commonwealth by the Ge- neral Court on perfons refiding in the county; and fuch fheriff fhall collect and levy the fame in like manner as is provided for county levies, and account for and pay the money, deducting five *per centum* for commiffion, and alfo infolvents, to the Treafurer of this commonwealth, on or before the firft day of *September*; or the faid Treafurer may recover the fame with cofts by motion in the General Court, on ten days previous notice given in writing of fuch motion; and the clerk of the General Court fhall de- liver copies of all lifts fo fent to the fheriffs to the Treafurer, to enable him to call fuch fheriffs to account.

Commencement of
this, and repeal of
former acts.

LXXVI. THIS act fhall commence and be in force from and after the firft day of *February* next; and all other acts, fo far as they relate to any matter or thing contained or within the purview of this act, are hereby repealed.

CHAP. XVIII.

Private.

An act for forming feveral new counties, and reforming the boundaries of two others.

CHAP. XIX.

Private.

An act for eftablifhing the town of Moorfield, *in the county of* Hampfhire.

CHAP. XX.

Had its effect.

An act to empower the commiffioners of the gun manufactory at Frederickfburg, *to take apprentices therein.*

CHAP. XXI.

Private.

An act for continuing an act entitled An act for the more regular laying off the borough of Norfolk, *and an act entitled An act for appointing commiffioners to inquire into and afcertain the loffes fuftained by the late inhabitants of the borough of* Norfolk, *and for other purpofes.*

CHAP. XXII.

Expired.

An act for giving certain powers to the Governor and Council.

CHAP. XXIII.

An act to amend an act entitled An act to reftrain the operations of the acts for limitation of actions and recording deeds in certain cafes.

Preamble.

I. WHEREAS during the confufions in this commonwealth, occafioned firft by the expiration of the fee bill on the twelfth day of *April* one thoufand feven hundred and feventy four, and the fufpenfion of government fubfequent thereto, the Juftices in many places omitted to hold their courts, and it would be unreafonable that perfons fhould be barred of their juft rights by acts of limitation in refpect to the time incurred during the faid confufion and omiffion to hold courts, and the portion of time withdrawn from the operation of the faid acts by one other act paffed in the year one thoufand feven hundred and feventy fix, entitled *An act to reftrain the operations of the acts for limitation of actions and recording deeds in certain cafes,* is not fufficiently extended to relieve all thofe who may juftly claim relief:

Time taken out of
the act of limita-
tions.

II. BE it therefore enacted by the General Affembly, that in all queftions which may arife in any court of record upon any act for limitation of actions, making entries into lands, or limitation of evidence in the computation of time, the period between the faid twelfth day of *April* one thoufand feven hundred and feventy four, and the twelfth day of *April* next, fhall not be accounted any part thereof, fo as to bar fuch action, entry, or evidence; but in all fuch computations, the progreffion fhall be from the faid twelfth day of *April* one thoufand feven hundred and feventy four, to the twelfth day of *April* next, as one day.

CHAP. XXIV.

An act to prevent private perfons from iffuing bills of credit in the nature of paper currency.

Preamble.

I. WHEREAS divers perfons have prefumed, upon their own private fecurity, to iffue bills of credit. or notes payable to the bearer, in the nature of paper currency, which may tend to the deception and lofs of individuals, as well as to the great injury of the public, by increaf- ing the quantity of money in circulation, already exceeding the prefent medium of commerce:

Iffuing, &c. bills
of credit payable to
bearer, reftrained
under penalty.

II. BE it therefore enacted by the General Affembly, that every perfon who, from and after the paffing of this act, fhall, without authority from the Legiflature of this commonwealth, iffue, or offer in pay- ment, any bill of credit, or note for any fum of money payable to the bearer, fhall forfeit and pay ten times the fum of every fuch bill of credit, or note payable to the bearer, fo iffued or offered in payment to be recovered with cofts, by warrant from any Juftice of the Peace where the penalty fhall not exceed the fum of twenty five fhillings, by petition in the county court where the penalty fhall be more than twenty five fhillings and fhall not exceed the fum of five pounds, or by action of debt or information in any court of record where the penalty fhall be above the fum of five pounds; one moiety whereof to the informer, and the other moiety to the ufe of the county where the offence fhall be committed, towards leffening the county levy, or the whole to the ufe of the county where the profecution fhall be firft inftituted, on behalf of the county only.

Penalty, how re-coverable, and ap-propriated.

III. AND be it further enacted, that any Juftice of the Peace for the county where fuch offence fhall be committed may, and he is hereby empowered and required, either upon his own knowledge or information, and due proof thereof made, to require any perfon iffuing or offering in payment any fuch bill of credit, or note payable to the bearer, to give bond with fufficient fecurity, in the fum of five hundred pounds, for his good behaviour, and upon refufal or neglect, to commit fuch offender to prifon, there to remain until he fhall give fecurity accordingly; and if the offender fhall thereafter iffue or offer in payment any fuch bill of credit, or note payable to the bearer, the fame fhall be adjudged a breach of the good behaviour, and forfeiture of the bond.

Power and duty of a Juftice of Peace in relation to fuch offences.

CHAP. XXV.

An act for adding part of the county of Weftmoreland to King George, and part of the county of King George to Weftmoreland.

Private.

CHAP. XXVI.

An act to enlarge the time for making draughts of the militia to recruit the Virginia regiments in the continental fervice.

Expired.

CHAP. XXVII.

An act appointing the place for holding the High Court of Chancery and General Court, and empowering the faid High Court of Chancery to appoint their own Serjeant at Arms.

I. WHEREAS by the acts conftituting the High Court of Chancery and General Court the faid courts are to be holden at fuch place as the Legiflature fhall direct, and no place hath as yet been appointed for that purpofe;

Preamble.

II. BE it therefore enacted by the General Affembly, that for the term of one year after the end of this prefent feffion of Affembly, and from thence until the end of the feffion then next enfuing, the faid courts fhall be holden in the capitol in the city of *Williamfburg*.

Now held in Rich-mond, by the act for the removal of the feat of govern-ment.

III. AND be it further enacted, that it fhall be lawful for the faid High Court of Chancery to appoint from time to time their own Serjeant at Arms, who fhall be attendant on the faid court to perform the duties of his office, for which he fhall receive fuch fees as fhall be allowed by law.

Serjeant at Arms, his duty and re-ward.

CHAP. XXVIII.

An act for giving proper falaries to certain officers of government.

Repealed.

CHAP. XXIX.

An act for appointing a Naval Officer on Nottoway and Blackwater.

Repealed.

CHAP. XXX.

An act to revive and amend an act appointing Commiffioners to afcertain the value of certain Churches and Chapels in the parifhes of Frederick, Norborne, and Beckford, and for other purpofes therein mentioned.

Private.

CHAP. XXXI.

An act to empower the Juftices of Cumberland and Fluvanna counties refpectively to appoint new places for holding their courts, and to repeal the act for laying off a town in the county of Cumberland.

Private.

CHAP. XXXII.

An act for diffolving the veftry of the parifh of Chrift Church, in the county of Lancafter.

Private.

CHAP. XXXIII.

An act for altering the court day of the county of Wafhington.

Private.

CHAP. XXXIV.

An act to empower the veftry of St. Patrick's parifh in the county of Prince Edward, to fell the glebe of the faid parifh, and to lay out the money in purchafing a more convenient glebe.

Private.

CHAP. XXXV.

An act to empower the truftees and feoffees of the town of Frederickfburg to affefs the expence of keeping the ftreets of the faid town in repair, on the inhabitants thereof.

Private.

CHAP. XXXVI.

An act for diffolving the veftries of the parifhes of Meherrin and St. Anne.

Private

CHAP. XXXVII.

An act to empower the veftry of the parifh of St. Paul, in the county of Hanover, to fell the glebe of the faid parifh, and to lay out the money in the purchafe of a more convenient glebe.

Private

A.D. 1778.

At a GENERAL ASSEMBLY begun and held at the Capitol in the City of *Williamsburg,* on *Monday* the 4th day of *May,* in the Year of our Lord 1778.

C H A P. I.

Executed.

An act for raising volunteers to join the grand army.

C H A P. II.

Executed.

An act for raising a regiment of horse.

[C H A P. III.

Executed.

An act for raising a battalion of infantry for garrison duty, and for other purposes.

C H A P. IV.

Determined.

An act for recruiting the continental army, and other purposes therein mentioned.

C H A P. V.

Executed.

An act providing a supply for the public exigencies.

C H A P. VI.

See May 1777, chap. 7. Preamble.

An act to amend an act for providing against invasions and insurrections.

I. WHEREAS by an act of General Assembly, entitled *An act for providing against invasions and insurrections,* it has been found by experience that the fine to be inflicted on any officer or soldier guilty of mutiny, desertion, disobedience of command, absence from duty or quarters, neglect of guard, or cowardice, is by no means sufficient to deter defaulters from committing all or any of the said offences:

Fines for certain offences not to exceed 6 months pay.

II. BE it therefore enacted by the General Assembly, that it shall and may be lawful for a court martial to inflict any fine upon such delinquent as they shall determine reasonable, so as such fine do not exceed six months pay.

III. AND be it further enacted, that so much of the said act as relates to the fine aforesaid shall be and the same is hereby repealed.

C H A P. VII.

See Oct. 1777, ch. 15.

An act empowering the Judges of the High Court of Chancery to supply certain vacant offices, making a temporary provision for the clerk thereof, and establishing a method of appealing to that court in particular cases.

The Judges, or any two, may appoint the clerk and serjeant, when their offices become vacant between terms.

I. BE it enacted by the General Assembly, that the Judges of the High Court of Chancery, or any two of them, may before the next term appoint a clerk thereof, in the room of him who lately died, by writing under their hands and seals, and at any time hereafter, when that office, or the office of Serjeant at Arms, shall by any means become vacant, may in like manner appoint a successor; and such succeeding clerk or serjeant, having in any court of record taken the oaths required by law, shall exercise the same power, perform the same duty, and be entitled to the same fees and profits, as he might have exercised, performed, and been entitled to, if he had been appointed in term time.

Clerk's salary till further provision by General Assembly.

II. THE clerk of the High Court of Chancery shall be paid by the Treasurer out of any public money that may be in his hands, a salary at the rate of one hundred and fifty pounds by the year, until the General Assembly shall make such other provision for him as will encourage a man of sufficient ability to accept the office.

Institution of appeal to this court, by petition.

III. ANY party thinking himself aggrieved by a decree of the court of a county, city, or borough, in chancery, and not having entered an appeal from the decree at the time it was pronounced, may appeal from such decree at any time within three months after passing this act, or within one month after the decree pronounced, lodging for that purpose with the clerk of the High Court of Chancery a copy of the proceedings in the suit, and a petition suggesting error in the decree signed by some council attending the High Court of Chancery, and also lodging with the petition a bond executed by the appellant or his agent, and a surety or sureties with the like condition as is annexed to other appeal bonds and affidavits, or solemn affirmations, verifying the sufficiency of the sureties; and the clerk shall thereupon issue a summons against the appellee, requiring him to appear and answer the said petition and appeal, and shall also issue a *supersedeas,* if necessary, to enjoin from proceeding in execution of the decree, and the court shall and may hear and determine the appeal in the same manner as if the appeal had been entered at the time the decree was pronounced.

CHAP. VIII.

An act for giving a further time to the purchasers of lots in the town of Bath to build thereon.

CHAP. IX.

An act to enable the Judges of the General Court to hold two additional sessions.

I. WHEREAS there are only two sessions of the General Court held in the year, to wit, one in the month of *March*, the other in the month of *October*, so that persons committed to the public jail for criminal offences are obliged to undergo a long and painful confinement before they can be brought to trial, which is contrary to justice, and the principles of the constitution:

II. BE *it therefore enacted*, that henceforth there shall be two other sessions of the General Court held in every year, to wit; one on the second *Tuesday* of *June*, and one other on the second *Tuesday* of *December*, at which sessions they shall hear and determine of all treasons, felonies, misdemeanors, and other pleas of the commonwealth cognizable before the said court at their sessions heretofore established, as well against those who shall be then in the public jail as others, and of no other matter or causes whatsoever; and against such as shall be found guilty by the verdict of the petit jury, the said court shall proceed to judgment according to law, and award execution thereupon, saving to the Governor his right of granting pardons to capital offenders, according to the laws or constitution of government, and shall discharge all others not so found guilty.

III. AND *be it further enacted*, that it shall and may be lawful for the sheriff of the county of *York*, and for the sheriff of the county of *James City*, for the time being, upon writs to them directed by the clerk of the General Court, which writs the said clerk is hereby empowered and required to issue six days at least before the holding such sessions, to summon each of them twelve good and lawful men, being freeholders of this commonwealth, to appear and attend at such sessions, which twenty four freeholders, or any sixteen thereof, shall be a grand jury to inquire of and present all treasons, felonies, and other criminal offences cognizable by the said court which have been committed or done in any county or counties within this commonwealth; and the said court, at their sessions aforesaid, shall have power to adjourn from day to day until all such criminals shall be tried, and shall in all cases, except in such as are herein otherwise directed, observe the same rules and regulations, in the trial of all such criminals, as are directed by an act entitled *An act for establishing a General Court*.

IV. AND whereas it is required by the above recited act, that every Judge, before he enters upon the duties of his office, shall in open court take and subscribe the oath of fidelity to the commonwealth, and also the oath of office: *Be it enacted*, that any Judge may take the aforesaid oaths at either of the sessions by this act established, to be administered by the first Justice who may be present, and may thereafter enter upon the duties of his office, in the same manner as if he had taken the said oaths at the session in *March* or *October*.

CHAP. X.

An act for continuing an act for giving certain powers to the Governor and Council.

CHAP. XI.

An act giving speedy remedy to the United States against defaulters.   (a)

I. WHEREAS divers persons receiving money of the United States of *America* for public uses apply it to different purposes, and when called on refuse or neglect to repay the same, others enter into contracts for supplying the army and navy of the United States with provisions and other necessaries, and fail or refuse to comply therewith; and whereas, in like cases respecting this commonwealth in particular, speedy remedy was given by an act of General Assembly passed in the year one thousand seven hundred and seventy seven, entitled *An act to establish a mode for the speedy and summary recovery of such sums of money as are or may become due to the public, and for enforcing all contracts entered into with government*, and it is expedient that the same speedy remedy be given in like cases respecting the United States:

II. BE *it therefore enacted by the General Assembly*, that where, in any case, a remedy is by the said act given to this commonwealth or any of its agents or contractors, in a like case, the same remedy shall be given to the United States, their agents and contractors; and where, by the said act, such proceedings are directed to be instituted by the Treasurer, in the name of the Governor for the time being, in a like case respecting the United States, the proceeding shall be instituted by their Deputy Paymaster General within this commonwealth, and in the name of the President of Congress for the time being.

CHAP. XII.

An act to attaint Josiah Philips and others, unless they render themselves to justice within a certain time.

CHAP. XIII.

An act to amend an act entitled An act for forming several new counties, and reforming the boundaries of two others.

CHAP. XIV.

An act for appointing Commissioners to ascertain the value of sundry houses the property of Robert Tucker, and for other purposes.

(a) See May 1777, chap. 10; May 1782, chap. 15.

A. D. 1778.

Expired.

CHAP. XV.

An act to increase the allowance to the members of the General Assembly.

CHAP. XVI.

An act establishing a clerkship of foreign correspondence.

Preamble.

I. WHEREAS it is neceffary for the Governor and Council to be provided with a perfon learned in the modern languages for affifting them in a communication with foreign ftates, and that a competent falary for fuch perfon fhould be provided by law:

The Governor and Council may appoint and remove the clerk.

His falary.

II. BE it therefore enacted, that a clerkfhip of foreign correfpondence be henceforth eftablifhed, under the direction and controul of the Governor and Council, who fhall from time to time, at their will, appoint fuch perfon to the faid office as they fhall find worthy of confidence, and qualified to perform the duties thereof, and remove him in like manner at their will. Such clerk having taken before them an oath of fidelity to the commonwealth, and of fecrecy in all cafes where he fhall be fpecially charged with fecrecy, may enter on the exercife of his office, and fhall receive for his trouble a yearly falary of two hundred pounds, to be paid by the Treafurer in quarterly payments, on warrant from the Auditors, who are hereby required to enter fuch warrants in account againft fuch perfon.

CHAP. XVII.

Expired.

An act to amend an act entitled An act for raifing a fupply of money for public exigencies.

CHAP. XVIII.

Expired.

An act for further fufpending the payment of the falaries heretofore given to the Clergy of the Church of England.

CHAP. XIX.

Repealed.

An act vefting powers in the Commiffioners of the navy for varying the rates of pilotage according to the exigencies of times.

At a GENERAL ASSEMBLY begun and held at the Capitol in the City of *Williamsburg*, on *Monday* the 5th day of *October*, in the Year of our Lord 1778.

CHAP. I.

An act for preventing the farther importation of flaves.

Importation of flaves hereafter, and fales of fuch prohibited.

I. FOR preventing the farther importation of flaves into this commonwealth, Be it enacted by the General Affembly, that from and after the paffing of this act no flave or flaves fhall hereafter be imported into this commonwealth by fea or land, nor fhall any flaves fo imported be fold or bought by any perfon whatfoever.

Under penalties upon importer, buyer, and feller,

II. EVERY perfon hereafter importing flaves into this commonwealth contrary to this act fhall forfeit and pay the fum of one thoufand pounds for every flave fo imported, and every perfon felling or buying any fuch flaves fhall in like manner forfeit and pay the fum of five hundred pounds for every flave fo fold or bought, one moiety of which forfeitures fhall be to the ufe of the commonwealth, and the other moiety to him or them that will fue for the fame, to be recovered by action of debt or information in any court of record.

befides emancipation of the flaves.

III. AND be it further enacted, that every flave imported into this commonwealth, contrary to the true intent and meaning of this act, fhall, upon fuch importation become free.

Except fuch flaves as belong to emigrants from the United States, taking a certain oath, or to travellers, carrying them out again.

IV. PROVIDED always, that this act fhall not be conftrued to extend to thofe who may incline to remove from any of the United States, and become citizens of this, provided, that within ten days after their removal into the fame they take the following oath before fome Magiftrate of this commonwealth: I A.B. do fwear, that my removal to the ftate of Virginia was with no intention to evade the act for preventing the farther importation of flaves within this commonwealth, nor have I brought with me, or will caufe to be brought, any flaves, with an intent of felling them, nor have any of the flaves now in my poffeffion been imported from Africa, or any of the Weft India iflands, fince the firft day of November 1778. So help me God. Or to travellers and others, making a tranfient ftay in this commonwealth, bringing flaves with them for neceffary attendance, and carrying them out again.

or come by defcent, devife, or marriage to citizens, owners of flaves refiding in the United States. 27 Geo. II. ch. 2.

V. PROVIDED alfo, and be it further enacted, that this act fhall not be conftrued to extend to perfons claiming flaves by defcent, devife, or marriage, or to any citizens of this commonwealth being now the actual owners and proprietors of flaves refiding or being in any of the United States and removing fuch flaves into this commonwealth.

VI. AND it is further enacted, that fo much of an act of Affembly made in the year one thoufand feven hundred and fifty three, entitled An act for the better government of fervants and flaves, as comes within the purview of this act, fhall be and the fame is hereby repealed.

C H A P. II.

An act to amend an act entitled An act for establishing a General Court, and other purposes.

See Oct. 1777, chap. 17.

I. BE it enacted, that instead of the days heretofore set apart for the trial of criminal causes in the General Courts held in the months of *March* and *October*, the said court shall, at the commencement of the said terms, enter upon the trial thereof, as well those for capital offences as others, setting apart the four first days for that purpose; but the Judges may direct the clerk, at any time before his docket be made out, and *subpœnas* issued for witnesses, to appropriate a longer or shorter time to such business, and to those days to set a part no other causes shall be docketed, and all process issued either from the county courts or the General Court in those causes shall be returnable to the first day of the next succeeding session.

First four days, or more or fewer, as the court shall direct, of March and October terms (See Nov. 1781, chap. 12) assigned for trials of criminal causes; process wherein shall be returnable to the first day.

II. THAT all indictments, presentments, informations, actions, and suits, which now are, or which were on the twelfth day of *April* one thousand seven hundred and seventy four, depending in any court within this commonwealth, in the name or on behalf of *George* III. King of *Great Britain*, or in the name of any persons on behalf of themselves and the said King, shall, where trials have not been already had, be carried on in the name of the commonwealth, or in the names of such persons and the commonwealth, instead of the said King, in the same manner as if they had been found, made, entered, or commenced, since the establishment of the said commonwealth.

In the name of the commonwealth may be prosecuted causes commenced before April 1774, in that of the King; appeals, and actions for breaches of recognizances, payable to him; and judgments on his behalf carried into execution, which no time shall bar.

III. THAT all appeals depending against the said King shall be carried on against the commonwealth, instead of the said King; and all bonds and recognizances entered into, to the said King, shall operate as if given to the commonwealth; and in cases of breaches thereof, suits or prosecutions may be carried on in the name of the commonwealth.

IV. THAT where trials have been had, and judgments given in the name or on behalf of the said King, or in the names of any other persons on behalf of themselves and the said King, and not satisfied, the same shall enure to the commonwealth, instead of the said King; and executions may thereupon issue accordingly, but no time shall bar the commonwealth of execution.

V. THAT all indictments, presentments, informations, actions, and suits, in the name or on behalf of the said King, or in the name of any persons on behalf of themselves and the said King, and all appeals against the said King which may have been discontinued or abated in any court within this commonwealth on account of the abolition of regal government, shall be forthwith revived, re-docketed, and carried on in the manner before directed. And all judgments for or against the commonwealth shall be the same as would have been entered for or against the said King, had no revolution in government taken place.

Criminal prosecutions, discontinued by abolition of regal government, shall be revived.

VI. THAT any persons who shall be charged with a capital offence, and not tried at the second session after their examination in the county court, and after petition to the General Court for trial, shall be acquitted and discharged of such offence, unless good cause be shewn for postponing their trial; but if they be not tried at the third session, they shall be for ever acquitted and discharged of such offence.

One accused of a capital offence, if not tried within a certain time, shall be discharged.

C H A P. III.

An act for the more effectual execution of an act entitled An act to empower the Governor and Council to lay an embargo for a limited time.

Expired.

C H A P. IV.

An act to prohibit the distillation of spirits from corn, wheat, rye, and other grain, for a limited time.

Expired.

C H A P. V.

An act to extend the powers of the Governor and Council.

I. WHEREAS the act of General Assembly entitled *An act for giving certain powers to the Governor and Council*, passed in the year of our Lord one thousand seven hundred and seventy seven, which has been continued by one other act, passed the last session of Assembly, entitled *An act for continuing an act for giving certain powers to the Governor and Council*, which will expire at the end of this session of Assembly, ought to be farther continued: *Be it therefore enacted*, that the same be continued and be in force, from and after the expiration thereof, until the end of the next session of Assembly, and no longer.

Expired.

II. AND whereas there is some reason to apprehend that the enemy are meditating an attack on our sister state of *South Carolina*, and it may be attended with bad consequences if she should not be assisted till actually invaded: *Be it further enacted*, that during the continuance of the said recited act, the Governor, with the advice of the Council, may, if he shall receive certain information that such an invasion is intended against that or any other sister state, march any number of the militia of this state, not exceeding three thousand men, to assist in repelling such invasion.

Expired.

III. AND whereas no power is given to the Governor and Council, by the act of government, to appoint Justices where so many may refuse to act, die, or remove out of any county, as not to have a sufficient number to constitute a court: *Be it enacted*, that in future, in any such case, the Governor for the time being, with the advice of the Privy Council, shall have full power to issue a commission or commissions of the peace for the appointment of any number of Magistrates, in such county so circumstanced, as shall be judged necessary for the carrying on the business of the same.

Governor, with advice of Council, may appoint Justices of Peace in certain cases; and

IV. AND there being no mode pointed out by which Justices of the Peace, who may be guilty of misconduct, can be removed from their offices, *Be it further enacted*, that upon any charge being made against a Justice of the Peace for misconduct, neglect of duty, or mal-practices, it shall and may be lawful for the Governor, with the advice of the Council, to enquire into the charge, and if the facts alledged be proved, he in that case may, with the advice aforesaid, remove such Justice from the execution of his office.

may remove any such Magistarte for malversation, or neglect.

V

A.D. 1778.

Repealed.

C H A P.   VI.

An act to empower the Governor and Council to superintend and regulate the public jail.

C H A P.   VII.

An act to revive and amend an act entitled An act to make provision for the support and maintenance of ideots lunaticks, and persons of unsound minds.   *(a)*

Continuance.

I. WHEREAS the act of Assembly entitled *An act to make provision for the support and maintenance of ideots, lunaticks, and other persons of unsound minds,* hath lately expired, and it is necessary that the same should be revived and amended: *Be it therefore enacted by the General Assembly,* that the said recited act shall be, and the same is hereby revived, and shall continue and be in force, from and after the passing of this act, for and during the term of one year, and from thence to the end of the next session of Assembly.

Further allowance to patients.

II. PROVIDED always, and it is hereby enacted, that a farther sum of twenty five pounds shall be allowed and paid for the maintenance and support of each person in the public hospital.

Directors proceedings since expiration confirmed.

III. AND whereas the Court of Directors (notwithstanding the expiration of the said act) judged it expedient and proper to proceed on the business of the hospital, trusting that the same would be approved and confirmed by the General Assembly: *Be it therefore enacted,* that all orders and rules by them made since the expiration of the said act, are hereby confirmed, and shall be as valid and effectual, to all intents and purposes, as if the said act had not expired.

C H A P.   VIII.

An act for providing a supply in aid of the Loan Office.   *(b)*

Notes, not exceeding a certain sum, how issuable and redeemable.

I. WHEREAS in aid of the loan to be procured by the Treasurer, agreeable to an act of Assembly entitled *An act to empower the Treasurer to borrow a farther sum of money,* passed this session, it may be necessary for answering the public exigencies to make a farther emission of Treasury notes: *Be it enacted by the General Assembly,* that it may and shall be lawful for the Treasurer of this commonwealth to issue treasury notes in dollars, and parts of a dollar, for any sum which may be required to answer the demands on the treasury, in addition to the sums issuable by former acts of Assembly, so as the said sum to be issued by authority hereof do not exceed one million seven hundred thousand dollars. And he shall cause the said notes to be engraved and printed in such manner, and on such paper, as he shall judge most likely to secure the same from being counterfeited, and shall appoint proper persons to overlook the press, and to number and sign the said notes upon the best terms he can procure them. And if the taxes imposed by the several acts now in force, shall be insufficient to answer the purposes for which the said taxes were laid, and also for the redemption of the notes to be issued by authority of this present act, farther provision shall be made by law for making good the deficiency, and redeeming the whole before the first day of *December,* which shall be in the year of our Lord one thousand seven hundred and eighty five.

C H A P.   IX.

An act to empower the Treasurer to borrow a farther sum of money.   *(c)*

Preamble.

I. WHEREAS it has been proved by experience that it is more beneficial to this commonwealth to borrow money on interest, than to make large emissions of paper money : *Be it therefore enacted, by the General Assembly,* that *George Webb,* Esq; or the Treasurer for the time being, shall open an office for that purpose at the treasury, previous to which, for the faithful discharge of the duties thereof, he shall give bond with sufficient security in the sum of two hundred thousand pounds, payable to the Governor and his successors, for the use of the commonwealth. And the said *George*

Treasurer required to open an office, empowered to borrow money, and give certificates, promising repayment, with interest.

Webb, or the Treasurer for the time being, is hereby empowered to receive from any person whatever sum in specie, continental paper dollars, or bills of credit, issued by authority of this commonwealth, he shall be willing to lend, so as such sum lent by any one person be not less than three hundred dollars, and to certify the receipt, and promise repayment thereof with interest, within any term not less than one nor exceeding three years from the date thereof, in the following form: The Treasurer of the commonwealth of *Virginia* acknowledgeth the receipt of   dollars from   which he promises to repay to the said   on the   day of   and to pay interest thereon annually in the meantime, at the rate of   per centum by the year, according to an act of Assembly passed in the year one thousand seven hundred and seventy eight entitled *An act to empower the Treasurer to borrow a farther sum of money.* Witness the hand of the Treasurer, this   day of   . Which certificate shall be signed by the Treasurer, who shall keep a book containing a counterpart thereof as a check, and be delivered to the lender; the said lender having carried the said certificate to the Auditors, there to be entered in account, and having obtained on the back thereof their counter-certificate of such entry, it shall be lawful for the Treasurer, and he is hereby required, to make annual payments of the interest accruing thereon, and at the term of payment, or sooner, if the lender shall so desire, and the state of the treasury will conveniently admit, repay the principal, and take in the said certificate ; such certificates, or the debts thereby attested, shall not be assignable or transferrable in law or equity by the lender, except to his representatives, in case of his death.

Certificates not assignable.

Certain Loan Office certificates to be called in, and discharged or exchanged.

II. AND the Treasurer, so soon as the state of the treasury will conveniently admit, shall call in all Loan Office certificates heretofore issued, other than those issued for the monies of *British* subjects, and shall pay off the principal and interest due thereon in money, or shall give other certificates, according to this act, in exchange for the same, at the election of the holder.

Treasurer's commission.

III. THE Treasurer shall be allowed to retain one eighth *per centum* on all monies which he shall receive in loan under this act.

(a) See October 1776, *chap.* 7; May 1781, *chap.* 11; October 1782, *chap.* 39.
(b) See May 1777, *chap.* 4; May 1780, *chap.* 33; November 1781 *chap.* 28.
(c) See October 1777, *chap.* 2; May 1780, *chap.* 10; October 1780, *chap.* 1; May 1781, *chap.* 6
November 1781, *chap.* 13, 26; October 1782, *chap.* 13; May 1783, *chap.* 4.

C H A P. X.

An act for reviving several public warehouses for the inspection of tobacco.

Expired.

C H A P. XI.

An act to increase the salaries of certain officers of government.

Expired.

C H A P. XII.

An act for establishing a Court of Appeals. (a)

C H A P. XIII.

An act for dissolving several vestries, and for other purposes.

This act would have been omitted, if the last section had been, like all the preceding, private.

I. BE it enacted by the General Assembly, that the vestries of the parishes of *Manchester*, in the county of *Chesterfield*; of *St. Paul*, in the county of *Hanover*; of *North Farnham*, in the county of *Richmond*; of *Elizabeth* river, and *Portsmouth*, in the county of *Norfolk*; of *Beckford*, in the county of *Shenandoah*; of *Nottoway* in the county of *Southampton*; of *Hanover*, and *Washington*, in the counties of *King George* and *Westmoreland*; of *St. Stephen*, in the county of *Northumberland*; and of *Blisland*, in the counties of *New Kent* and *James City*, shall be, and the same are hereby respectively dissolved.

II. *AND be it further enacted*, that the inhabitants of every of the said parishes of *Manchester, St. Paul's, North Farnham, Elizabeth* river, *Portsmouth, Beckford, Nottoway, Hanover, Washington, St. Stephen*, and *Blisland*, respectively, shall meet at some convenient time and place to be appointed and publicly advertised by the sheriffs of each of the said counties before the first day of *April* next, and then and there elect twelve able and discreet persons, who shall be a vestry for the said parishes respectively.

III. AND whereas it is represented to this General Assembly that the situation of the said parishes of *Hanover* and *Washington* is rendered inconvenient to the inhabitants thereof by a late alteration in the boundary lines of the said counties of *King George* and *Westmoreland*:

IV. FOR remedy whereof, *Be it enacted*, that all that part of the said parish of *Hanover*, lying in the said county of *Westmoreland*, be added to and made part of the said parish of *Washington*; and that all that part of the said parish of *Washington*, lying in the county of *King George*, be added to and made part of the said parish of *Hanover*.

V. AND whereas by the addition of the said parish of *Washington* to the parish of *Hanover* the present glebe of the said parish of *Washington* will be in the said parish of *Hanover*, and it is just and right that the inhabitants of the said parish of *Washington* should receive the benefit thereof: *Be it therefore enacted*, that the said glebe land, with the appurtenances, be, and the same are hereby vested in *John Martin, John Washington, Thomas Turner*, and *Beckwith Butler*, gentlemen, commissioners in trust, that they, or any three of them, shall, by deeds, of bargain and sale, sell and convey the said glebe, with the appurtenances, for the best price that can be got for the same, to any person or persons who shall be willing to purchase the said lands, to hold to such purchaser or purchasers, his or their heirs and assigns, for ever.

VI. *AND be it further enacted*, that the money arising from the sale of the said glebe shall be by the said commissioners paid to the vestry of the said parish of *Washington*, to be by them laid out in the purchase of a more convenient glebe for the use and benefit of the minister of the said parish of *Washington* for the time being.

VII. *PROVIDED always*, that the collectors of the parishes of *Hanover* and *Washington* respectively, shall have power to collect and distrain for any dues which shall remain unpaid by the inhabitants of the said parishes of *Hanover* and *Washington* at the time of the divisions taking place, and shall be answerable for the same in like manner as if this act had never been made.

VIII. *AND be it further enacted*, that the vestry of the upper parish, in the county of *Nansemond*, shall and they are hereby empowered and required to sell the workhouse and lands thereto belonging in the town of *Suffolk* for the best price that can be had, and upon receipt of the consideration money to convey the same to the purchaser or purchasers in fee simple; that the money arising from such sale shall be by the said vestry applyed for and towards lessening their parish levy.

IX. AND whereas for the want of a vestry in the parish of *Botetourt* in the county of *Botetourt*, the poor of the said parish are likely to suffer for want of proper support and maintenance: *Be it therefore enacted*, that the commissioners of the tax in the county of *Botetourt* shall, and they are hereby empowered and required to make the like provision for the poor thereof, and levy the expence in the same manner as the vestries of the several parishes within this commonwealth can or may do; and the said commissioners are hereby authorised to settle and recover all debts due to the said parish of *Botetourt*, and liquidate all demands against the same.

X. *AND be it further enacted*, that every sheriff, when required by the churchwardens of any parish within his county, shall collect the parish levy becoming due within the same, for the performance of which he shall enter into bond with sufficient security in a sum equal to the whole collection, and payable to the churchwardens and their successors; and if such sheriff shall fail to account for and pay his said collection on or before the first day of *August*, reserving a commission of six *per cent.* for his trouble in collecting, the same proceedings shall be had for the recovery thereof in the court of the county wherein the parish is situate, at the instance of the churchwardens for the time being, as is by law directed in the case of county levies.

Sheriffs required by churchwardens, shall collect, and account for, parish levies, and may be prosecuted for them, as for county levies.

C H A P. XIV.

An act to amend an act entitled An act for the better regulating and collecting certain officers fees, and other purposes. (b)

I. WHEREAS the act of Assembly entitled *An act to open the Courts of Justice, and to revive and amend an act entitled An act for the better regulating and collecting certain officers fees and other purposes therein mentioned*, will, so far as the same relates to reviving and amending the said act, shortly expire, and it is necessary the same should be farther continued and amended:

Preamble.

(a) Omitted, because the whole of it seems comprehended in chap. 22, of May 1779.
(b) See Nov. 1781, ch. 31; Oct. 1782, ch. 37, 49; May 1783, ch. 10; Oct. 1785, ch. 32.

A. D. 1778.
See subsequent acts.

II. BE *it therefore enacted,* that the act entitled *An act for the better regulating and collecting certain officers fees, and other purposes therein mentioned* (except the fifteenth section thereof) shall continue and be in force, from and after the end of this present session of Assembly, for one year, and from thence to the end of the next session of Assembly.

Tobacco fees, at what rates discchargable in money and when and how to be accounted for.

III. PROVIDED *always, and it is further enacted,* that it shall be lawful for any person or persons chargeable with any of the tobacco fees mentioned in the said act, to pay the same in money at the rate of thirty three shillings and fourpence *per hundred* of gross tobacco, for services to be performed after the passing of this act; and the clerk's of the respective county courts, of the Hustings court in the city of *Williamsburg,* and of the General Court, shall annually on or before the first day of *March,* deliver, or cause to be delivered to the sheriff of every county in this commonwealth respectively, and to the serjeant of the said city, their accounts of fees due from any person or persons residing therein, which shall be signed by the said clerk's respectively; and the said sheriff and serjeant is hereby empowered and required to receive, levy, and account for the same accordingly, on or before the first day of *August,* pursuant to the directions of the before recited act.

See some of the acts before referred to

IV. AND *be it further enacted,* that the allowances to sheriffs, jurors, and witnesses, attending the trials of criminals, shall be settled and paid in money at the rate of forty one shillings and eight-pence by the hundred.

What lawyer's fees shall be taxed in bills of costs.

V. AND whereas the lawyers fees allowed to be taxed in the bill of costs by an act entitled *An act for allowing the full fees to which the lawyers practising in the several courts of this commonwealth are entitled,* in particular cases therein mentioned, to be taxed on recovery in the bills of costs, are found insufficient, and it is, unreasonable that the party who prevails and recovers in any such action or suit should be subject to the payment of a greater fee to his lawyer than he can recover from the adverse party : *Be it therefore enacted, by the General Assembly,* that from and after the passing of this act, the clerk of the High Court in Chancery shall, and he is hereby required to tax in the bill of costs on all decrees obtained in the said court a fee of ten pounds, and the clerk of the General Court shall, and he is hereby required to tax in the bill of costs on all judgments obtained in the said court in any real, mixed, or personal action, where the title or bounds of land shall or may come in question, a fee of ten pounds, and the clerk of the said General Court shall, and he is hereby required to tax in the bill of costs on all judgments obtained in the said court in any personal action (except as before excepted) or on any petition for lapsed land, a fee of five pounds, where the party obtaining such decree or judgment employed a lawyer, except against executors or administrators, or where the plaintiff may not recover more costs than damages; and the clerk's of the respective county courts, or other inferior courts of this commonwealth, shall, and they are hereby required to tax in the bill of costs in all decrees, and every judgment obtained on real or mixed actions, where the title or bounds of land shall and may come in question, either where the plaintiff may recover or be non-suited, or where his suit shall be dismissed, four pounds; and in all other actions, except by petitions, forty shillings for an attorney's fee, if the party employed one, except against executors or administrators, or where the plaintiff may not recover more costs than damages; and in all suits by petition the clerk of the said county court, or other inferior courts, shall tax in the bill of costs the sum of fifteen shillings as an attorney's fee, against the party who shall be cast, where an attorney shall be employed, except against executors or administrators.

Repealing clause.

VI. AND *be it further enacted,* that so much of the said recited acts as is contrary to any thing contained within the purview of this act, shall be, and the same is hereby repealed.

C H A P.   XV.

Expired.

An act to empower the Governor and Council to lay an embargo for a limited time.

C H A P.   XVI.

Executed.

An act to supply the inhabitants of this commonwealth with salt upon reasonable terms.

C H A P.   XVII.

An act for establishing a board of Auditors for Public Accounts.

Auditors, how appointed, qualified and removeable.

I. BE *it enacted by the General Assembly,* that there shall be a standing board of auditors for public accounts, to consist of three persons, to be chosen from time to time as vacancies shall happen, by joint ballot of both Houses of Assembly, and to continue in office until removed by the joint vote of both the said houses; and where any person so appointed shall refuse to act, resign, or die, during the recess of Assembly, it shall be lawful for the Governor, with the advice of the Council of State, to appoint some other fit and able person to act in his stead until the next meeting of the General Assembly. The auditors so appointed shall not be capable of acting until they shall have taken the oath of fidelity to the commonwealth, and also an oath impartially and honestly to execute the duties of their office; which oaths during the sessions of the High Court of Chancery shall be taken before the said court, and during their vacation shall be taken before some Judge thereof, and by him shall be certified to his next succeeding court and entered of record; and two of the said auditors so qualified shall have power to proceed to business. The auditors now in office by virtue of former appointments shall continue to act and be considered to all future intents and purposes as if they had been appointed by virtue of this act.

Their power, duty, and subjects of examination.

II. THE said board of auditors are authorised and enquired to state and keep an exact account of all articles of debit or credit hereafter to arise between this commonwealth and the United States of *America,* or any of them, or any other state; to raise and keep accounts with all officers of civil government who are entitled to receive from the public treasury salaries or wages fixed by law; to inquire into all legal expenditures for the army, navy, or militia, of this commonwealth (including in respect to the last, those expenditures which ought to be paid by the United States, to adjust which no immediate provision shall have been made by Congress) and on requisition from the Governor and Council to give their warrant to the Treasurer for the allowance of monies for such purposes, debiting therewith the person to whom it is confided, and calling him in due time to render account of the application thereof; to examine all demands for the hire of horses, waggons, or other things employed or impressed by authority of law for the public service, or for the worth thereof, or injury done thereto, where the thing impressed has been consumed, lost, destroyed, or damaged, in such service; to make just allowances to expresses

A. D. 1778.

employed by the Governor and Council, the Navy Board, or our Delegates in Congress, or sent on the public service to the Governor and Council, or to any *Indian* nation, the Governor and Council certifying there was good reason for sending such express; or to scouts and look-outs, or any others doing services to the public for which they are entitled in law to receive payment, and no person particularly authorized to ascertain the *quantum* of such payment; to allow annual pensions to officers and soldiers of the army or navy raised by any act of General Assembly, and disabled in the service, and to the widows of those slain or dying therein, as also sums in gross for their immediate relief, proportioning the same with impartiality and discretion to the nature of every case, such sums in gross, however, to be given but once to any one person, and not to exceed one year's pay, and such annual pension not to exceed full pay; to enter in account all draughts on the Treasurer for money by the Governor and Council, or by the Navy Board, for the public service, to certify such entry to the Treasurer for payment, and to audit in due time the expenditure thereof; to give warrants on the Treasurer for the payment or advance of wages to our Delegates in Congress, debiting each Delegate respectively with the warrant given in his name; and requiring account thereof to be rendered within three months after the expiration of his appointment; to audit all accounts for wages due to the members of the General Assembly for service therein or for their travelling allowances, such attendance and allowances being previously entered with the clerk of the House of which such member is, in separate books to be kept for that purpose, and to lie during the session on the table of the House, and being certified by the said clerk to be so entered; and to audit accounts for salaries or wages to the officers and attendants of the two Houses; to settle the expences of sending for the members of either House by special messengers; of providing robes for the Speakers and Clerks of both Houses, maces, lights, fuel, blank books, parchment, paper, and other articles necessary for the use of either House, or of the Governor and Council, or Navy Board, or the superior courts of justice while on duty in the capitol; to audit all accounts for building or repairing houses or other articles of public property, such buildings or repairs being authorized by act of Assembly, or the previous vote of the two Houses of Assembly; to examine all claims for the support of prisoners where the public is chargeable with such support, or for the removal of any such to the prison of the General Court, or for the guard of criminals, or for jurors or witnesses attending their trials, or witnesses for the commonwealth attending a court of justice, or judicial officer in any other case, or for slaves executed by judgment of common law for any crime, or legally put to death under process of outlawry; to examine all claims, petitions, and applications, for money, which at the end of this present session of Assembly shall be depending and undetermined before the Assembly; and which are of a like nature with any of those submitted by this act to the examination of the said Auditors; to call for annually and to examine the accounts of expenditures for the public trade, the public hospital, and for all works undertaken and carried on at the public expence by authority from the Legislature, and to enter the same in separate accounts; to inquire into all demands for bounties or premiums payable by law out of the public treasury for the encouragement of particular manufactures, of bringing to justice public offenders, of destroying noxious animals, or of any other matter; to examine and enter in account all other demands for money on the Treasurer made under authority of any law heretofore passed, or hereafter to be passed; to settle the accounts of all public debtors, and of all collectors of any revenue, or tax, levied by act of General Assembly, and payable to the Treasurer, or of any monies due to the public, to call upon such debtors or collectors to render account at proper times; and on their failure so to do to instruct the Attorney General to institute proceedings at law for compelling them to justice, and though it should appear on trial that the defendant oweth no balance to the public, yet his having failed to render account to the Auditors, and to take from them his *quietus*, shall subject him to the payment of all costs incurred by such proceedings, as well to himself as to the commonwealth; to require information on oath from any person, party or privy, of matters relative to any account under their examination and material for their information, to administer such oath where the party is attending, and, where absent, to take out a commission from the High Court of Chancery, directed to any Justice of the Peace to take his examination on interrogatories to be stated by them; where on any such settlement a balance shall appear due to the public to certify the same under their own hands to the Treasurer, and hold the party charged therewith till he shall produce to them the Treasurer's receipt for the same, on which they shall give him a *quietus*, debit the Treasurer therewith, and certify such debits to the next committee of Assembly appointed to settle the Treasurer's accounts, and where such balance is due from the public to certify it in like manner to the Treasurer, and debit the party with such certificate; to enter in proper accounts all Loan Office certificates hereafter to be given, and endorse on such certificates that they are entered in the said Auditors office, without which endorsement no such certificates shall be valid; to require counsel of the Attorney General on all doubts in matters of law relative to the duties of their office; to state and keep all the accounts coming under their examination specially against each person, so as to shew amount of all warrants and certificates given on the Treasurer, for what service or article of public expence they were given, or where they have been for money advanced, to whom it was advanced, and for what purpose, and to preserve the vouchers in due order; and also to raise general accounts shewing the amount of the expenditures for the army, the navy, the militia, the public trade, the public works, and manufactories of every kind, of pensions, claims, and all other expences of government, each stated in a collective view under its separate and proper head, and to lay before the Assembly annually the said general accounts, together with an account of all balances due to and from the public as nearly as they shall be able.

III. *AND it is further enacted*, that it shall not be lawful for the Treasurer to pay or receive any money on account of the public but on warrant or certificate from the Board of Auditors, unless in cases where any future act of Assembly shall in express words, and not by inference or implication only, declare that in that particular case it is to be understood as the intention that the claim specified by such act shall not be audited in the regular course, save only that the salaries of the said Auditors, together with the accounts for the expences of their office for fuel, blank books, paper, presses for the preservation of their books and papers, and other implements necessary for the use of their office, shall be examined and certified for payment to the Treasurer by the Governor and Council.

By their warrant only, unless expressly directed otherwise by future act of Assembly money to be paid or received by Treasurer, except for their own salaries, &c. accounts whereof shall be examined by Governor and Council.

IV. THE said Auditors shall be allowed a clerk of accounts, and an assistant clerk, to be appointed by themselves from time to time at their will, who, before entering on the exercise of their offices shall take the like oath, and in like manner as is before directed for the said Auditors to take, and shall receive annual salaries, to wit, the said clerk of accounts four hundred pounds, and the said assistant clerk two hundred and fifty pounds by the year.

Allowed clerks, with salaries.

V. WHERE the Auditors, acting according to their discretion and judgment, shall disallow or abate any article of demand against the commonwealth, and any person shall think himself aggrieved thereby, he shall be at liberty to petition the High Court of Chancery or the General Court, according to the nature of his case, for redress, and such court shall proceed to do right thereon; and a like petition shall be allowed in all other cases to any other person who is entitled to demand against the commonwealth any right in law or equity.

Persons aggrieved by their disallowances or defalcations how redressed.

VI. THE act of General Assembly passed in the year one thousand seven hundred and seventy six, and entitled *An act to establish Auditors of public accounts*, is hereby repealed.

Repealing clause.

W

A.D. 1778.
Expired.

C H A P.   XVIII.

An act for more effectually guarding against counterfeiting of the bills of credit, treasury notes, and loan office certificates.

C H A P.   XIX.

An act for establishing several new ferries, and other purposes.

Public ferries over Potowmack and Monongalia appointed; and fares at them rated; and penalty for exceeding them.

I. WHEREAS it is represented to this present General Assembly, that public ferries at the places hereafter mentioned will be of great advantage to travellers and others, *Be it therefore enacted by the General Assembly,* that public ferries be constantly kept at the following places, and the rates for passing the same shall be as follows, that is to say: From the land of *Abraham Shepherd,* in the county of *Berkeley,* over *Potowmack* river, to the land of *Thomas Swearingen* in the state of *Maryland,* the price for a man six pence, and the price for a horse the same; from the land of *James Devore,* in the county of *Yohogania,* over *Monongalia* river, to the land of *Joseph Parkerson,* the price for a man six pence, and for a horse the same; and for the transportation of wheel carriages, tobacco, cattle, and other beasts, at any of the ferries aforesaid, the ferry keepers may demand and take the following rates, that is to say: For every coach, chariot, or waggon, and the driver thereof, the same as for six horses; for every cart, or four wheeled chaise or chair, the same as for two horses; for every hogshead of tobacco as for one horse; for every head of neat cattle as for one horse; for every sheep, goat or lamb, one fifth part of the ferriage of one horse; and for every hog one fourth part of the ferriage of one horse, according to the prices herein before settled at such ferries respectively. And if any of the said ferry keepers shall presume to demand or receive from any person whatsoever any greater rates than is hereby allowed, he, she, or they, for such offence, shall forfeit and pay to the party grieved the ferriage demanded or received, and ten shillings, to be recovered with costs before any Justice of the Peace where the offence shall be committed.

County courts impowered to make certain regulations concerning ferries.

II. AND whereas the rates for passing the several public ferries, as by law established, are found insufficient to enable the ferry keepers to provide proper boats and hands for the immediate passage of public expresses and others, *Be it therefore enacted by the General Assembly,* that the court of every county wherein any ferries have been either established by law or appointed by the courts, shall, and they are hereby directed and empowered, at their respective courts to be held in the month of *March* annually, or at their next succeeding court, to set and fix the rates for passing such ferries, and moreover to order and direct what boat or boats, and the number of hands, which shall be kept at each ferry. And the keeper thereof shall within one month after the rates shall be fixed as aforesaid, give bond with one security in the court of the county in such penalty as the court shall direct, with condition that he will duly keep such ferry, or cause the same to be kept, and will give immediate passage to all public messengers and expresses when required. Every ferry keeper neglecting or refusing to give such bond, or to cause the same to be given in his behalf, shall forfeit and pay ten pounds for every months refusal or neglect, to the use of the commonwealth, recoverable with costs by action of debt or information in any court of record.

III. AND *be it further enacted,* that so much of an act entitled *An act for the settlement and regulation of ferries, and for dispatch of public expresses,* and all and every other act or acts as comes within the meaning of this act, shall be, and the same are hereby repealed.

Supposed to be virtually repealed by subsequent revenue acts.

C H A P.   XX.

An act to amend an act entitled an act for raising a supply of money for public exigencies.

Private.

C H A P.   XXI.

An act for establishing the county of Illinois, *and for the more effectual protection and defence thereof.*

Private.

C H A P.   XXII.

An act for establishing a town at the courthouse of the county of Washington.

Expired.

C H A P.   XXIII.

An act appointing the place for holding the Court of Appeals.

Repealed.

C H A P.   XXIV.

An act to increase the allowance of the Delegates of this commonwealth in Congress.

Private.

C H A P.   XXV.

An act for altering the place of holding courts in the county of Spotsylvania.

Private.

C H A P.   XXVI.

An act for adding part of the county of Buckingham *to the county of* Cumberland, *and other purposes.*

Private.

C H A P.   XXVII.

An act to prevent swine going at large in the town of Mecklenburg, *in the county of* Berkeley.

C H A P. XXVIII.

An act to empower the freeholders of the several towns not incorporated to supply the vacancies of the trustees and directors thereof.

I. BE it enacted by the General Assembly, that upon the death, removal out of the country, or other legal disability of any one or more of the trustees and directors of the several towns within this state not incorporated, such vacancy, so often as the same shall happen, shall hereafter be supplied in manner following, that it to say: The surviving trustees and directors, or one of them, shall give immediate notice of such vacancy to the sheriff of the county wherein such town may be, who within twenty days thereafter shall notify the same to the freeholders of the said town in such manner as he may think best, requiring them to appear at a certain place therein, and on a certain day, not less than ten days thence next following, then and there to elect a trustee in the room of the one so dying, removing, or disabled. The sheriff shall attend and take the poll at such election, entering the names of the persons voted for in a distinct column, and the name of every freeholder giving his vote under the name of the person he votes for; and when no freeholders appear to vote the sheriff shall close the poll, and return the same to the next court to be held for his county upon oath, certifying the name of the person elected, to be by the clerk recorded.

II. EVERY person elected in manner directed by this act, shall to all intents and purposes, be a trustee of the town for which he was chosen.

III. SO much or all acts of Assembly as are contrary to the purview and meaning of this act, are hereby repealed.

C H A P. XXIX.

An act for extending the boundary line between Virginia *and* North Carolina.

Executed.

C H A P. XXX.

An act to enable the officers of the Virginia *line, and to encourage the soldiers of the same line, to continue in the continental service.*

Expired.

C H A P. XXXI.

An act for dividing the parishes of Camden *and* Amherst, *and for other purposes.*

Private.

C H A P. XXXII.

An act for establishing the town of Martinsburg, *in the county of* Berkeley, *and for other purposes.*

Private.

C H A P. XXXIII.

An act to vest certain lands on the Ohio *and* Green *rivers in fee simple in* Richard Henderson, *and company, and their heirs.*

Private.

C H A P. XXXIV.

An act to direct the sale of certain lands late the property of John Thornton, *Esq; deceased, and for purchasing other lands in lieu thereof, and for other purposes.*

Private.

C H A P. XXXV.

An act for vesting certain escheatable lands in trustees, and for other purposes.

Private.

C H A P. XXXVI.

An act for altering the place of holding courts in the county of Princess Anne.

Private.

C H A P. XXXVII.

An act to enlarge the powers of the trustees of the town of Manchester.

Private.

C H A P. XXXVIII.

An act for further suspending the payment of the salaries heretofore given to the clergy of the church of England.

Expired.

C H A P. XXXIX.

An act to repeal the act entitled an act to oblige the owners of mills on the river Rappidan *to make openings or slopes in their mill dams for the passage of fish.*

Expired.

C H A P. XL.

An act for altering the court days of the counties of Pittsylvania, Botetourt, *and* Henry.

Private.

C H A P. XLI.

An act to amend an act entitled an act to enable the officers of the Virginia *line, and to encourage the soldiers of the same line, to continue in the continental service.*

Expired.

A. D. 1778.

Expired.

An act to amend the act for preventing forestalling, regrating, engrossing, and public vendues.

CHAP. XLIII.

Expired.

An act to enable the Governor and Council to supply the armies and navies of the United States, and of their allies, with grain and flour.

CHAP. XLIV.

An act for establishing several new ferries, discontinuing a former one, and for other purposes.

Public ferries over Potowmack, Staunton, Fluvanna, and Dan appointed, and fares rated, with penalty for exceeding them.

I. WHEREAS it is represented to this present General Assembly, that public ferries at the places hereafter mentioned will be of advantage to travellers and others: *Be it therefore enacted by the General Assembly,* that public ferries be constantly kept at the following places, and the rates for passing the same shall be as follows, that is to say: From the land of the Earl of *Tankerville* in the county of *Loudoun* (at present in the tenure of *Christian Slimmer*) across *Potowmack* river to the opposite shore in the state of *Maryland,* the price for a man eight pence, and for a horse the same; from the land of *Thomas Noland,* in the county of *Loudoun,* across *Potowmack* river to the land of *Arthur Nelson,* in the state of *Maryland,* the price for a man eight pence, and for a horse the same; from the land of *John Ward,* in the county of *Bedford,* over *Staunton* river, to the land of the said *Ward* on the opposite shore, the price for a man six pence, and for a horse the same; from the land of *Nicholas Davis,* near the mouth of *Battery* creek, in the county of *Bedford,* over the *Fluvanna* river, to the land of the said *Davis* on the opposite shore, the price for a man six pence, and for a horse the same; from the land of *John Owens,* in the county of *Pittsylvania,* over *Dan* river, to the land of *Silvester Adams* on the opposite shore, the price for a man six pence and for a horse the same; and for the transportation of wheel carriages, tobacco, cattle, and other beasts, at any of the places aforesaid, the ferry keeper may demand and take the following rates, that is to say: For every coach, chariot, or waggon, and the driver thereof, the same as for six horses; for every cart or four wheeled chaise, and the driver thereof, the same as for four horses; for every two wheeled chaise or chair, the same as for two horses; for every hogshead of tobacco as for one horse; for every head of neat cattle as for one horse; for every sheep, goat, or lamb, one fifth part of the ferriage for one horse; and for every hog one fourth part of the ferriage for one horse, according to the prices herein before settled at such ferries respectively, and no more. And if any ferry keeper shall presume to demand or receive from any person or persons whatsoever, any greater rates than is hereby allowed for the carriage or ferriage of any thing whatsoever, he or they for every such offence shall forfeit and pay to the party grieved the ferriages demanded or received, and ten shillings, to be recovered with costs before any Justice of the Peace of the county where such offence shall be committed.

One over Potowmack discontinued.

II. AND whereas the public ferry from the land of *Josias Clapham,* in the county of *Loudoun,* across *Potowmack* river to the opposite shore in the state of *Maryland,* hath been found inconvenient: *Be it therefore enacted,* that the said ferry shall henceforth be discontinued.

Trustees for erecting a turnpike at the bridge over Nottoway appointed, toll for passing it, and penalty for taking more.

III. AND whereas it is represented to this present General Assembly, that from the many rivers and creeks making into and running through the county of *Southampton,* the inhabitants thereof are obliged to erect and support such a great number of bridges, and the expence thereof is become so burthensome that they cannot longer support and keep the same in repair by the ordinary course provided by the laws, unless some provision be made for raising money to be applied for that purpose, and the said inhabitants have petitioned this Assembly that a turnpike or toll gate may be erected on the bridge (so soon as the same shall be finished) now builing over *Nottoway* river near the court-house of the said county: *Be it therefore enacted by the General Assembly,* that the Justices of the court of the said county of *Southampton,* and their successors for ever, shall be, and they are hereby nominated and appointed trustees for the purposes following, that is to say: That they and their successors, or any four or more of them, or such person or persons as they or any four or more of them shall authorize and appoint for that purpose, shall and may build, erect, or cause to be built or erected, a turnpike or gate across any part of the bridge so to be built over the said river *Nottoway,* and also a toll house at or as near the same as may be, and shall and may demand and take the following tolls or duties before any person or persons shall be admitted to pass through the said gate, that is to say: For a man six pence, and for a horse the same; and for the passage of wheel carriages, tobacco, cattle, and other beasts, through the said gate, there shall be paid the following tolls or duties, that is to say; for every coach, chariot, or waggon, and the driver thereof, the same as for six horses; for every cart or four wheeled chaise the same as for four horses; for every two wheeled chaise or chair the same as for two horses; for every hogshead of tobacco as for one horse; for every head of neat cattle as for one horse; for every sheep, goat, or lamb, one fifth part of the toll for one horse, and for every hog one fourth part of the toll for one horse, and no more. If any person or persons appointed to receive the said tolls or duties shall presume to demand or receive from any person whatsoever, any greater tolls or duties than is hereby allowed for the passage of any thing whatsoever, he or they for every such offence shall forfeit and pay to the party grieved the tolls demanded or received, and twenty shillings, to be recovered with costs before any Justice of the Peace of the county of *Southampton.*

Duty and power of trustees in applying the tolls, and appointing the receiver.

IV. AND be it further enacted, that the money arising from the said tolls or duties shall be applied by the said trustees, or any four of them, towards paying the expence of erecting, building, amending, and keeping in repair, a bridge over the said river, a turnpike, toll-house, paying the wages of such person as they or any four of them shall from time to time under their hands and seals nominate and appoint to receive the said tolls or duties, and the residue thereof shall be applied towards lessening their county levy. And the said trustees or any four or more of them, at their first or any succeeding court after the said bridge shall be built, shall choose and appoint a fit person to be receiver of the tolls and duties aforesaid, who shall before he undertakes the execution thereof, enter into bond and security, payable to the said trustees, or any four or more of them, in the penalty of one hundred pounds with condition that he will duly attend at such turnpike, and faithfully account for and pay half yearly all tolls or duties which he may have received. And if any receiver shall neglect or refuse to render such account upon oath, and pay the money, it shall and may be lawful for the court of the said county of *Southampton* to give judgment against him for the penalty of his bond, provided such receiver have ten days previous notice thereof; which judgment may be difcharged by the receiver's accounting for and paying all the money arifing from the tolls and duties to the time of entering fuch judgment. The faid truftees or any four or more of them, fhall have power from time to time to remove any receiver of the tolls and appoint others in their ftead.

A.D. 1778.

C H A P. XLV.

An act for fpeedily recruiting the Virginia *regiments on continental eftablifhment.*

Expired.

***

At a GENERAL ASSEMBLY begun and held at the Capitol in the City of *Williamsburg*, on *Monday* the 3d day of *May*, in the Year of our Lord 1779.

***

C H A P. I.

An act to explain and amend the acts of General Affembly, providing a fupply of money for public exigencies.

Expired.

C H A P. II.

An act eftablifhing a Board of Trade.

Repealed.

C H A P. III.

An act eftablifhing a Board of War.

Repealed.

C H A P. IV.

An act for raifing a body of volunteers for the defence of the commonwealth.

Executed.

C H A P. V.

An act prefcribing the oath of fidelity, and the oaths of certain public officers.

I. **B**E it enacted by the General Affembly, that every perfon by law required to give affurance of fidelity, fhall, for that purpofe, take an oath in this form. I   *do declare myfelf a citizen of the commonwealth of* Virginia; *I relinquifh and renounce the character of fubject or citizen of any prince or other ftate whatfoever, and abjure all allegiance which may be claimed by fuch prince or other ftate: And I do fwear to be faithful and true to the faid commonwealth of* Virginia, *fo long as I continue a citizen thereof.* So help me God. And no perfon fhall have power to act in any office, legiflative, executive, or judiciary, before he fhall have given fuch affurance, and fhall moreover have taken fuch of the following oaths, if another be not fpecially prefcribed, as is adapted to his cafe. The oath of a Governor. I   *elected Governor of* Virginia, *by the reprefentatives thereof, do folemnly promife and fwear, that I will to the beft of my fkill and judgment, execute the faid office, diligently and faithfully, according to law, without favour, affection, or partiality; that I will to the utmoft of my power, protect the citizens of the commonwealth in the fecure enjoyment of all their rights, franchifes, and privileges; and will conftantly endeavour that the laws and ordinances of the commonwealth be duly obferved; and that law and juftice, in mercy, be executed in all judgments; and laftly, that I will peaceably and quietly refign the government to which I have been elected, at the feveral periods to which my continuance in the faid office is or fhall be limited by law and the conftitution.* So help me God. The oath of a Privy Counfellor. I   *elected one of the Privy Council of* Virginia *by the reprefentatives thereof, do folemnly promife and fwear, that I will, to the beft of my fkill and judgment, execute the faid office diligently and faithfully, according to law, without favour, affection, or partiality; and that I will keep fecret fuch proceedings and orders of the Privy Council, as the board fhall direct to be concealed, unlefs the fame be called for by either Houfe of General Affembly.* So help me God. The oath of one not fpecially directed to take any other. I   *do folemnly promife and fwear, that I will faithfully, impartially, and juftly perform the duty of my office of*   *according to the beft of my fkill and judgment.* So help me God. The faid oaths to be taken by a member or officer of either Houfe of General Affembly, fhall be adminiftered by any member of the Privy Council, and the taking thereof fhall be certified to the clerk of fuch Houfe; and the faid oaths to be taken by any other perfon if it be not otherwife directed, fhall be adminiftered in fome court of record or by any Judge or Juftice thereof, and the taking thereof fhall be recorded in the faid court.

Oath of fidelity.

Official of the Governor;

of a Privy Counfellor,

of any other.

C H A P. VI.

An act concerning officers, foldiers, failors, and marines.

Executed.

C H A P. VII.

An act permitting thofe who will not take oaths to be otherwife qualified.

I. **B**E it enacted by the General Affembly, that any perfon refufing to take an oath, and declaring religious fcruples to be the true and only reafon of fuch refufal, if he will ufe the folemnity and ceremony, and repeat the formulary obferved on fimilar occafions, by thofe of the church or religious focieties he profeffeth himfelf to be a member of, or to join in communion with, fhall thereupon be deemed as competent a witnefs, or to be as duly qualified to execute an office, or perform any other act, to the

Solemnities and forms inftead of oaths.

A. D. 1779.

fanction whereof an oath is or shall be required by law, and shall be subject to the same rules, derive the same advantages, or incur the same penalties or forfeitures, as if he had been sworn. In presentments, indictments, inquisitions, verdicts, examinations, or other forms, the words "upon their oath" or "sworn" may be left out, and instead of them "in solemn form" or "charged" whichever may be adapted to the case, may be inserted; but if the ancient form be adhered to, it shall not be adjudged errour.

C H A P.   VIII.

Executed.

An act for raising a body of cavalry.

C H A P.   IX.

An act for fixing the allowance of the members of the General Assembly.

Preamble.

I. WHEREAS it is just that the members of General Assembly, delegated by the people to transact for them the legislative business, should, while attending that business, have their reasonable sustenance defrayed, dedicating to the public service their time and labours, freely and without account; and it is also expedient that the public Councils should not be deprived of the aid of good and able men, who might be deterred from entering into them, by the insufficiency of their private fortunes to bear the extraordinary expences they must necessarily incur, and it being inconsistent with the principles of civil liberty, and contrary to the natural rights of the other members of the society, that any body of men therein should have authority to enlarge their own powers, prerogatives or emoluments, without restraint; the said General Assembly cannot at their own will increase the allowance which their members are to draw from the public treasury for their expences while in Assembly, but to enable them so to do, an application to the body of the people has become necessary, and such application having been accordingly made to the several counties, and a majority of them having thereupon consented that the said allowance shall be enlarged, and authorized their members to enlarge the same for themselves and the members of all future Assemblies, to fifty pounds of nett tobacco by the day for attendance on Assembly, and two pounds of like tobacco for every mile they must necessarily travel going to or from the same, together with their ferriages, to be paid in money out of the public treasury, at such rate as shall be estimated by the grand-jury at the session of the General Court next before the meeting of every session of Assembly, governing themselves in the said estimate by the worth of the said tobacco, and the competence of the same to defray the necessary expences of travelling and attendance: *Be it therefore enacted by the General Assembly,* by express authority from the body of the people, that the allowance to the several members of the present, and of all future General Assemblies, shall be of fifty pounds of tobacco by the day for attendance on the said Assemblies, two pounds of the like tobacco for every mile they must necessarily travel going to or from the same, together with their ferriages, to be paid to them in money out of the public treasury, at such rate as shall be estimated by the grand-jury at the session of the General Court next before the meeting of each respective session of Assembly, governing themselves in the said estimate by the worth of the said tobacco, and the competence of the same to defray the necessary expences of travelling and attendance.

See May 1780, chap. 5. Allowance in tobacco what and how estimated and paid.

C H A P.   X.

Executed.

An act for enabling the Treasurer to emit a sum of money for supplying the public exigencies.

C H A P.   XI.

Executed.

An act for raising a body of troops for the defence of the commonwealth.

C H A P.   XII.

An act for adjusting and settling the titles of claimers to unpatented lands under the present and former government, previous to the establishment of the commonwealth's land office.

Preamble. See Oct. 1779, ch 2, 21, 27; May, 1780, ch. 2, 7; May 1781, ch. 22; Nov. 1781, ch. 5, 29; May 1782, ch. 7, 49; Octo. 1782, ch. 25, 46; May 1783, ch 39; Oct. 1783, ch. 29.

I. WHEREAS the various and vague claims to unpatented lands under the former and present government, previous to the establishment of the commonwealth's Land Office, may produce tedious and infinite litigation and disputes, and in the mean time purchasers would be discouraged from taking up lands upon the terms lately prescribed by law, whereby the fund to be raised in aid of the taxes for discharging the public debt, would be in a great measure frustrated; and it is just and necessary, as well for the peace of individuals as for the public weal, that some certain rules should be established for settling and determining the rights to such lands, and fixing the principles upon which legal and just claimers shall be entitled to sue out grants; to the end that subsequent purchasers and adventurers may be enabled to proceed with greater certainty and safety, *Be it enacted by the General Assembly,* that all surveys of waste and unappropriated land made upon any of the western waters before the first day of *January,* in the year 1778, and upon any of the eastern waters at any time before the end of this present session of Assembly, by any county surveyor commissioned by the masters of *William* and *Mary* college, acting in conformity to the laws and rules of government then in force, and founded either upon charter, importation rights duly proved and certified according to ancient usage, as far as relates to indented servants, and other persons not being convicts, upon treasury rights for money paid the Receiver General duly authenticated upon entries on the western waters, regularly made before the 26th day of *October,* in the year 1763, or on the eastern waters at any time before the end of this present session of Assembly, with the surveyor of the county for tracts of land not exceeding four hundred acres, according to act of Assembly upon any order of Council, or entry in the Council books, and made during the time in which it shall appear either from the original or any subsequent order, entry, or proceedings in the Council books, that such order or entry remained in force, the terms of which have been complied with, or the time for performing the same unexpired, or upon any warrant from the Governor for the time being for military service, in virtue of any proclamation either from the King of *Great Britain* or any former Governor of *Virginia,* shall be, and are hereby declared good and valid; but that all surveys of waste and unpatented lands made by any other person, or upon any other pretence whatsoever, shall be, and are hereby declared null and void, provided that all officers or soldiers, their heirs or assigns, claiming under the late Governor *Dinwiddie's* proclamation of a bounty in lands to the first *Virginia* regiment, and having returned to the Secretary's office, surveys made by virtue of a special commission from the President and Masters of *William* and *Mary* college, shall be entitled to grants

Surveys what declared valid.

A. D. 1779.

thereupon on payment of the common office fees; that all officers and soldiers, their heirs or assigns under proclamation warrants for military service, having located lands by actual surveys made under any such special commission, shall have the benefit of their said locations, by taking out warrants upon such rights, resurveying such lands according to law, and thereafter proceeding according to the rules and regulations of the Land Office. All and every person or persons, his, her, or their heirs or assigns, claiming lands upon any of the before recited rights, and under surveys made as herein before mentioned, against which no caveat shall have been legally entered, shall upon the plats and certificates of such surveys being returned into the Land Office, together with the rights, entry, order, warrant, or authentic copy thereof upon which they were respectively founded, be entitled to a grant or grants for the same in manner and form herein after directed.

Proviso.

Under what rights and in what manner grants shall be made.

II. *PROVIDED*, that such surveys and rights be returned to the said office within twelve months next after the end of this present session of Assembly, otherwise they shall be, and are hereby declared forfeited and void. All persons, their heirs or assigns, claiming lands under the charter and ancient custom of *Virginia*, upon importation rights as before limited, duly proved, and certified in any court of record before the passing of this act; those claiming under treasury rights for money paid the Receiver General duly authenticated, or under proclamation warrants for military service, and not having located and fixed such lands by actual surveys as herein before mentioned, shall be admitted to warrants, entries, and grants for the same, in manner directed by the act of Assembly entitled *An act for establishing a Land Office, and ascertaining the terms and manner of granting waste and unappropriated lands*, upon producing to the Register of the Land Office the proper certificates, proofs, or warrants, as the case may be, for their respective rights within the like space of twelve months after the end of this present session of Assembly, and not afterwards. All certificates of importation rights proved before any court of record according to the ancient custom, and before the end of this present session of Assembly, are hereby declared good and valid: And all other claims for importation rights not so proved, shall be null and void; and where any person before the end of this present session of Assembly, hath made a regular entry according to act of Assembly, with the county surveyor for any tract of land not exceeding four hundred acres, upon any of the eastern waters, which hath not been surveyed or forfeited, according to the laws and rules of government in force at the time of making such entry, the surveyor of the county where such land lies, shall after advertising legal notice thereof, proceed to survey the same accordingly, and shall deliver to the proprietor a plat and certificate of survey thereof within three months; and if such person shall fail to attend at the time and place so appointed for making such survey, with chain carriers and a person to mark the lines, or shall fail to deliver such plat and certificate into the Land Office, according to the rules and regulations of the same, together with the Auditors certificate of the Treasurer's receipt for the composition money herein after mentioned, and pay the office fees, he or she shall forfeit his or her right and title; but upon performance of these requisitions, shall be entitled to a grant for such tract of land as in other cases.

Rights claimed under certain orders of Council, and a royal proclamation, declared void.

III. *AND be it enacted*, that all orders of Council or entries for land in the Council books, except so far as such orders or entries respectively have been carried into execution by actual surveys in manner herein before mentioned, shall be, and they are hereby declared void and of no effect; and except also a certain order of Council for a tract of sunken grounds, commonly called the *Dismal Swamp*, in the south eastern part of this commonwealth, contiguous to the *North Carolina* line, which said order of Council with the proceedings thereon and the claim derived from it, shall hereafter be laid before the General Assembly for their further order therein. No claim to land within this commonwealth for military service founded upon the King of *Great Britain*'s proclamation, shall hereafter be allowed, except a warrant for the same shall have been obtained from the Governor of *Virginia*, during the former government as before mentioned; or where such service was performed by an inhabitant of *Virginia*, or in some regiment or corps actually raised in the same; in either of which cases the claimant making due proof in any court of record, and producing a certificate thereof to the Register of the Land Office within the said time of twelve months, shall be admitted to a warrant, entry, and grant for the same, in the manner herein before mentioned; but nothing herein contained shall be construed or extend to give any person a title to land for service performed in any company or detachment of militia.

Provision for settlers upon the Western Waters;

IV. AND whereas great numbers of people have settled in the country upon the western waters, upon waste and unappropriated lands, for which they have been hitherto prevented from suing out patents or obtaining legal titles by the King of *Great Britain*'s proclamations or instructions to his Governors, or by the late change of government, and the present war having delayed until now, the opening of a Land Office, and the establishment of any certain terms for granting lands, and it is just that those settling under such circumstances should have some reasonable allowance for the charge and risk they have incurred, and that the property so acquired should be secured to them : *Be it therefore enacted*, that all persons who, at any time before the first day of *January*, in the year one thousand seven hundred and seventy eight, have really and *bona fide* settled themselves or their families, or at his, her, or their charge, have settled others upon any waste or unappropriated lands on the said western waters, to which no other person hath any legal right or claim, shall be allowed for every family so settled, four hundred acres of land, or such smaller quantity as the party chooses, to include such settlement. And where any such settler hath had any survey made for him or her, under any order of the former government, since the twenty sixth day of *October*, in the year one thousand seven hundred and sixty three, in consideration of such settlement for less than four hundred acres of land, such settler, his or her heirs, may claim and be allowed as much adjoining waste and unappropriated land, as together with the land so surveyed will make up the quantity of four hundred acres.

and for families settled in villages or townships.

V. AND whereas several families for their greater safety have settled themselves in villages or townships, under some agreement between the inhabitants of laying off the same into town lots, to be divided among them, and have, from present necessity, cultivated a piece of ground adjoining thereto in common: *Be it enacted*, that six hundred and forty acres of land whereon such villages and towns are situate, and to which no other person hath a previous legal claim, shall not be entered for or surveyed; but shall be reserved for the use and benefit of the said inhabitants until a true representation of their case can be made to the General Assembly, that right and justice may be done therein; and in the mean time there shall be allowed to every such family, in consideration of their settlement, the like quantity of land as is herein allowed to other settlers adjacent or convenient to their respective village or town, and to which no other person hath, by this act, the right of preemption, for which said quantities to be adjusted, ascertained, and certified by the Commissioners to be appointed by virtue of this act, in manner herein after directed. The proper claimants shall be respectively entitled to entries with the surveyor of the county wherein the land lies, upon producing to him certificates of their rights from the said Commissioners of the county, duly attested, within twelve months next after the end of this present session of Assembly, and not afterwards; which certificate the said surveyor shall record in his books, and then return them to the parties, and shall proceed to survey the lands so entered, according to law. And upon due return to the Land Office of the plats and certificates of survey, together with the certificates

A. D. 1779.

from the said Commissioners of the rights by settlement, upon which the entries were founded, grants may and shall issue to them and their heirs or assigns, in manner before directed. And if any such settlers shall desire to take up a greater quantity of land than is herein allowed them, they shall, on payment to the Treasurer of the consideration money, required from other purchasers, be entitled to the preemption of any greater quantity of land adjoining to that allowed them in consideration of settlement, not exceeding one thousand acres, and to which no other person hath any legal right or claim. And to prevent doubts concerning settlements, *It is hereby declared*, that no family shall be entitled to the allowance granted to settlers by this act, unless they have made a crop of corn in that country, or resided their at least one year since the time of their settlement. All persons who, since the said first day of *January*, in the year one thousand seven hundred and seventy eight, have actually settled on any waste or unappropriated lands on the said western waters, to which no other person hath a just or legal right or claim, shall be entitled to the preemption of any quantity of land, not exceeding four hundred acres, to include such settlement, at the state price to other purchasers. And all those who, before the said first day of *January*, in the year one thousand seven hundred and seventy eight, had marked out or chosen for themselves, any waste or unappropriated lands, and built any house or hut, or made other improvements thereon, shall also be entitled to the preemption, upon the like terms, of any quantity of land, to include such improvements, not exceeding one thousand acres, and to which no other person hath any legal right or claim; but no person shall have the right of preemption for more than one such improvement; provided they respectively demand and prove their right to such preemption, before the Commissioners for the county, to be appointed by virtue of this act within eight months, pay the consideration money, produce the Auditor's certificate for the Treasurer's receipt for the same, take out their warrants from the Register of the Land Office within ten months, and enter the same with the surveyor of the county, within twelve months next after the end of this present session of Assembly; and thereafter duly comply with the rules and regulations of the Land Office. All locations made by officers and soldiers upon the lands of actual settlers, shall be void, but the said officers, soldiers, or their assignees, may obtain warrants on producing the Commissioners certificate of their several rights, and locate their claims on other waste and unappropriated lands. To prevent the locations of those claiming under warrants for preemption, from interfering with such as claim under certificates for settlements, and to give due preference to the latter, so far as respects their rights to tracts of land not exceeding four hundred acres, the Register of the Land Office shall particularly distinguish all preemption warrants by him issued, and no county surveyor shall admit any such warrant to be entered or located in his books, before the expiration of ten months as aforesaid. And where any such warrant shall not be entered and located with the county surveyor, within the before mentioned space of twelve months, the right of preemption shall be forfeited, and the lands therein mentioned may be entered for by any other person holding another land warrant; but such preemption warrant may, nevertheless, be located upon any other waste or unappropriated lands, or upon the same lands where they have not in the mean time been entered for by some other.

Composition money in what cases to be paid.

VI. AND *be it further enacted*, that all persons claiming lands, and suing out grants upon any such surveys heretofore made, either under entries with the surveyor of any county, or under any order of Council, or entry in the Council books, for which rights have not formerly been lodged in the Secretary's office, and also those suing out grants for tracts of lands upon the western waters, not exceeding four hundred acres herein allowed them in consideration of their settlements, or under former entries with the county surveyor, for lands upon the eastern waters, shall be subject to the payment of the usual composition money under the former government, at the rate of ten shillings sterling for every hundred acres, to be discharged in current money, at the rate of thirty three and one third *per centum* exchange, before the grant issues, and to no other charge or imposition whatsoever, save the common office fees. And to all such persons, their heirs or assigns, who having title to land under the former government, had not only surveyed the same, but had lodged their certificates of survey, together with their rights, in the Secretary's office, and although no caveat hath been entered, have not obtained patents, grants shall issue in consideration thereof, upon the payment of the office fees only.

Agreements between companies claiming under orders of Council, and purchasers from them, regulated.

VII. AND whereas it hath been represented to the General Assembly, that upon lands surveyed for sundry companies by virtue of orders of Council, many people have settled without specific agreement, but yet under the faith of the terms of sale publicly offered by the said companies or their agents at the time of such settlements, who have made valuable improvements thereon: *Be it enacted and declared*, that all persons so settled upon any unpatented lands, surveyed as before mentioned, except only such lands as before the settlement of the same, were notoriously reserved by the respective companies for their own use, shall have their titles confirmed to them by the members of such companies, or their agents, upon payment of the price at which such lands were offered for sale when they were settled, together with interest thereon from the time of the respective settlements, provided they compromise their claims with the said companies, or lay them before the commissioners for their respective counties, to be appointed by virtue of this act, and have the same tried and determined by them, in manner herein after directed: And provided also, that where any such survey contains more than four hundred acres, no one settler shall be entitled to a greater quantity than three hundred acres, unless he takes the whole survey, to include his settlement, and leave the remainder in one entire and convenient piece where the same is practicable.

Commissioners for adjusting and determining claims to lands on the western waters, how appointed, their oath, duty, power, and modes and rules of proceeding.

VIII. AND whereas the claims of various persons to the lands herein allowed to the inhabitants, in consideration of their settlements, and of those who, by this act, are entitled to preemption at the state price, as well as of the settlers on the lands surveyed for sundry companies by orders of Council as aforesaid, may occasion numerous disputes, the determination of which depending upon evidence, which cannot, without great charge and trouble, be collected, but in the neighbourhood of such lands, will be most speedily and properly made by commissioners in the respective counties: *Be it enacted*, that the counties on the western waters shall be allotted into districts, to wit: The counties of *Monongalia, Yohogania*, and *Ohio*, into one district; the counties of *Augusta, Botetourt*, and *Greenbrier*, into one district; the counties of *Washington* and *Montgomery*, into one other district; and the county of *Kentucky*, shall be another district; for each of which districts, the Governor, with the advice of the Council, shall appoint four commissioners under the seal of the commonwealth, not being inhabitants of such district (any three of whom may act) to continue in office eight months from the end of this present session of Assembly, for the purpose of collecting, adjusting, and determining such claims, and four months thereafter for the purpose of adjusting the claims of settlers on land surveyed for the aforesaid companies. Every such commissioner, before he enters on the duties of his office, shall take the following oath of office: I. *A. B. do swear that I will well and truly serve this commonwealth in the office of a commissioner for the district of*   *for collecting, adjusting, and settling the claims, and determining the titles of such persons as claim lands in the said district, in consideration of their settlements; of such as claim preemption to any lands therein, and also of such settlers as claim any lands surveyed by order of Council, for sundry companies, according to an act of General Assembly, entitled "An act for adjusting and settling the titles of claimers to*

A.D. 1779.

unpatented lands, under the former and present government, previous to the establishment of the commonwealth's Land Office;" and that I will do equal right to all manner of people, without respect of persons; I will not take by myself, nor by any other person, any gift, fee, or reward for any matter done, or to be done by virtue of my office, except such fees or salary as the law shall allow me; and finally in all things belonging to my said office, I will faithfully, justly, and truly, according to the best of my skill and judgment, do equal and impartial justice, without fraud, favour, affection, or partiality. So help me God. Which oath shall be administered by any of the said commissioners, to the first of them in nomination, who shall be present, and then by him to the others. The said commissioners shall have power to hear and determine all titles claimed in consideration of settlements to lands, to which no person hath any other legal title, and the rights of all persons claiming preemption to any lands within their respective districts, as also the rights of all persons claiming any unpatented lands, surveyed by order of Council for sundry companies, by having settled thereon under the faith of the terms of sale publicly offered by such companies or their agents, and shall immediately upon receipt of their commissions, give at least twenty days previous notice by advertisements, at the forts, churches, meeting-houses, and other public places in their district, of the time and place at which they intend to meet, for the purpose of collecting hearing, and determining the said claims and titles, requiring all persons interested therein, to attend and put in their claims, and may adjourn from place to place, and time to time, as their business may require; but if they should fail to meet at any time to which they shall have adjourned, neither their commission nor any matter depending before them shall be thereby discontinued, but they shall proceed to business when they do meet, as if no such failure had happened. They shall appoint and administer an oath of office to their clerk; be attended by the sheriff, or one of the under sheriffs of the county; be empowered to administer oaths to witnesses or others, necessary for the discharge of their office; to punish contempts, enforce good behaviour in their presence, and award costs, in the same manner with the county courts; they shall have free access to the county surveyor's books, and may order the same to be laid before them, at any time or place of their sitting, and shall pay to such surveyor, out of the fees received by them for certificates, the sum of three pounds for every day he shall attend, and to the sheriff for the like attendance, two pounds for each days attendance. In all cases of disputes upon claims for settlement, the person who made the first actual settlement, his or her heirs or assigns, shall have the preference. In all disputes for the right of preemptions for improvements made on the land, the persons, their heirs or assigns respectively, who made the first improvement, and the persons to whom any right of preemption on account of settlement or improvements shall be adjudged, shall fix the quantity at their own option at the time of the judgment, so as not to exceed the number of acres respectively allowed by this act, or to interfere with the just rights of others. The clerk shall keep exact minutes of all the proceedings of the commissioners, and enter the names of all the persons to whom either lands for settlement or the right of preemption as the case is, shall be adjudged with their respective quantities and locations, and also the names of all such persons to whom titles shall be adjudged for lands within the surveys made by order of Council for any company with the quantity of acres adjudged, and in what survey; and if the same is only part of such survey, in what manner it shall be located therein, the name or style of the company, and the price to be paid them, with the time from which the same is to bear interest. Upon application of any person claiming a right to any lands in virtue of this act, and complaining that another pretends a right in opposition thereto, the said clerk shall issue a summons, stating the nature of the plaintiffs claim, and calling on the party opposing the same, to appear at a time and place certain therein to be named; and shew cause why a grant of the said lands may not issue, or a title be made to the said plaintiff: The said summons shall be served on the party by the sheriff of the county where he resides, or wherein he may be found, and such service being returned thereon, and the party appearing or failing to appear, the commissioners may proceed to trial, or for good cause shewn, may refer such trial to a further day. The clerk shall also have power at the request of either party, to issue subpœnas for witnesses to appear at the time and place of trial, which shall be had in a summary way without pleadings in writing, and the court in conducting the said trial, in all matters of evidence relative thereto, and in giving judgment, shall govern themselves by such rules and principles of law or equity, as are applicable to the case, or would be the rule of evidence or of decision, were the same before the ordinary courts of law or equity; save only as far as this act shall otherwise have specially directed. Judgment when rendered shall be final, except as herein after excepted, and shall give to the party in whose favour it is, a title against all others who were parties to the trial; and if after such judgment rendered, the party against whom it is, shall enter the said lands forcibly, or forcibly detain the same, it shall be lawful for the said commissioners or any one of them, or any justice of peace for the county, to remove such force, in like manner as if it were committed on lands holden by grant actually issued. The said commissioners shall deliver to every person to whom they shall adjudge lands for settlement, a certificate thereof under their hands, and attested by the clerk, mentioning the number of acres, and the time of settlement, and describing as near as may be, the particular location, noting also therein the quantity of adjacent land to which such person shall have the right of preemption. And to every other person to whom they shall adjudge the right of preemption to any lands, they shall in like manner deliver a certificate, specifying the quantity and location of such land, with the cause for preemption, with a memorandum for the information of the party in each certificate of the last day on which the lands therein respectively mentioned can be entered with the county surveyor: For every hundred acres of land contained within the said certificates, the party receiving the same, shall pay down to the commissioners the sum of ten shillings, besides a fee of ten shillings to the clerk for each certificate so granted; and the said certificates produced within the times herein before respectively limited to the surveyor of the county, or to the Register of the Land Office, with the Auditor's certificate of the Treasurer's receipt for the payment due on the preemption, as the nature of the case may require, shall entitle the person respectively receiving them, to an entry and survey, or a warrant for the said lands, in such way, and on such terms as are herein before prescribed. And to prevent frauds or mistakes, the said commissioners immediately upon having completed the business in their district, shall transmit to the Register of the Land Office, under their hands, and attested by the clerk, an exact list or schedule in alphabetical order, of all such certificates by them granted, and a duplicate so signed and attested to the county surveyor for their information. They shall in like manner, and upon payment of the same fees, deliver to every person to whom they shall adjudge, a title to any unpatented land, surveyed for any company by order of Council, a certificate mentioning the number of acres to which they have adjudged the title, what particular survey the same is in, and for what company made, the price to be paid such company, and the date from which the same is to bear interest, and where there is a greater quantity of land contained in the survey, describe as near as may be, the manner the land to which they have adjudged title, shall be laid off and bounded; and shall also immediately upon having completed the business in their district, transmit to the clerk of the General Court, under their hands, and attested by their clerk, a list or schedule in alphabetical order, containing exact copies of all such certificates by them granted, to remain in the said clerk's office for the information of the said companies, and as evidence and proof of the respective titles.

Y

A.D. 1779.

In what cases rights adjudged to certain claimants forfeited.

Allowances to commissioners, clerk and sheriff, what judgments may be reversed by the General Court, and how.

IX. *PROVIDED nevertheless,* that if the parties, their heirs or assigns, to whom such titles shall have been adjudged, shall not within six months at farthest, from the time of their respective judgments in their favour, pay or tender to the company to whom the same is due, or their agent, the price and interest so fixed by the said commissioners, the title of every person so failing, shall be forfeited, and shall be from thence forward, to all intents and purposes, null and void; any thing herein to the contrary thereof notwithstanding. The said commissioners for every day they shall be actually employed in the execution of their office, shall be allowed the sum of eight pounds each; they shall be accountable for all the money they shall have received upon issuing certificates as aforesaid, except the fee to the clerk, and shall settle a fair account upon oath, with the Auditors, and receive from the Treasurer whatever balance may appear due to them thereon, or pay to him any balance which shall be by them due to the commonwealth. The clerk and sheriff shall receive for their services, the fees heretofore allowed by law for the like services in the county court, and the witnesses the same allowance for their attendance, to be paid by the party, and collected in like manner as is directed in the ordinary cases of the same nature, and the clerk shall have the same power of issuing executions as the clerks of the county courts; provided that the clerk shall not be allowed any farther or other fee for entering and issuing a certificate than is herein before mentioned. But as by this summary mode of proceeding, some persons at a great distance may not have timely notice, and may be unable to appear in support of their claims: For remedy whereof, *Be it enacted,* that no grant shall issue upon any of the claims determined by the said commissioners until the first day of *December* 1780, and in the mean time, any such person injured by their determination, his or her heirs or assigns, may enter a caveat against a grant thereupon, until the matter shall be heard before the General Court, and may petition the said General Court to have his or her claim considered; and upon its being proved to the court that he or she laboured under such a disability at the time of the meeting of the commissioners thereupon, the court shall grant him or her a hearing in a summary way, and if it shall appear upon trial, that the petitioners claim is just, such court may reverse the former determination, and order a grant to issue for such land or any part thereof, on the terms herein before mentioned, to the person to whom they shall adjudge the same.

Certain land claims to be laid before the Court of Appeals, and there decided.

X. *AND be it further enacted,* that all claims for lands upon surveys under any order of Council or entry in the Council books, shall by the respective claimers be laid before the Court of Appeals; which shall meet for that purpose on the sixteenth day of *December* next, and shall adjourn from day to day until the business be finished; or if it be proved to the court that any such claimer is unable to attend and prosecute his claim, or for other just cause to them shewn, they may order such claim to be tried before them on some future day. All such claims shall be heard and determined in a summary way, without pleadings in writing, upon such evidence as in the opinion of the court, the nature of the case may require; and no such claim shall be valid, but such only as shall be so heard and established by the said Court of Appeals, and on their certificate that any such claim hath been by them established, the Register is hereby required to issue a warrant or grant thereupon, according to the nature of the case, and the rules and regulations of the Land Office; and the Attorney General is hereby required to attend the said court on behalf of the commonwealth.

Proviso for officers, &c. Registers duty in recording land warrants, and making out the grants.

XI. *PROVIDED always,* that nothing herein contained shall extend to officers, soldiers, or their assignees, claiming lands for military service. The Register of the Land Office shall regularly record all land warrants issued by virtue of this act; they may be executed in one or more surveys, and may be exchanged or divided so as best to suit the purposes of the party, and shall remain in force until lands shall have been actually obtained for them, in the same manner with the warrants to be issued by virtue of the before recited act for establishing a Land Office. And when the said Register shall make out a grant to any person or persons for lands due to him, her, or them, by virtue of this act, he shall recite therein as the consideration, the rights and cause for which the same became due, according to an act of General Assembly, passed in the year of our Lord one thousand seven hundred and seventy nine, entitled *An act for adjusting and settling the titles of claimers to unpatented lands under the former and present government, previous to the establishment of the commonwealth's Land Office;* and if any part thereof is due in consideration of the ancient composition money, or the new purchase money paid to the commonwealth, the same shall be properly distinguished, and in every other respect the grant shall be drawn and pass in the form and manner prescribed by law for future grants of lands from the commonwealth.

Proceedings upon caveats depending at the revolution.

XII. AND whereas at the time of the late change of government, many caveats against patents for lands which have been entered in the Council office, were depending and undetermined: *Be it enacted,* that all such caveats, with the papers relating thereto, shall be removed into the clerks office of the General Court, there to be proceeded on and tried in the manner directed by law for future caveats; but the same shall be determined according to the laws in force at the time they were entered; and upon the determination of any such caveat, a grant shall issue in the name of the person to whom such land shall be adjudged, his or her heirs or assigns, upon producing to the Register of the Land Office, within three months at farthest from the time of such judgment, an authentic copy thereof, together with the Auditors certificate of the Treasurer's receipt for the ancient composition money due thereon, at the rate of exchange herein before mentioned; but where the person recovering had before paid rights into the Secretary's office, a grant shall issue in consideration thereof upon payment of the office fees only.

CHAP. XIII.

An act for establishing a Land Office, and ascertaining the terms and manner of granting waste and unappropriated lands.

Preamble.
Land Office constituted.

I. WHEREAS there are large quantities of waste and unappropriated lands within the territory of this commonwealth, the granting of which will encourage the migration of foreigners hither, promote population, increase the annual revenue, and create a fund for discharging the public debt: *Be it enacted by the General Assembly,* that an office shall be, and is hereby constituted for the purpose of granting lands within this commonwealth, into which all the records now in the Secretary's office, of patents or grants for lands heretofore issued, with all papers and documents relating thereto, and all certificates of surveys of lands now in the said office, and not patented, shall be removed and lodged for their safe keeping: and all future grants of lands shall issue from the said office in manner and form herein after mentioned. A Register of the said Land Office shall be appointed, from time to time, by joint ballot of both Houses of Assembly, who shall give bond with sufficient security, to the Governor or first Magistrate of this commonwealth, in the penalty of fifty thousand pounds current money; shall hold his office during good behaviour, be entitled to receive such fees as shall hereafter be allowed by law, and shall have power to appoint a deputy and clerks to assist in executing the business of the said office, but shall nevertheless reside there himself. If any vacancy shall happen by the death, resignation, or removal of a Register during the recess of the General Assembly, the Governor or first Magistrate of the commonwealth, by and with the advice of the Council, may appoint some other person, giving bond and security in like manner, to act as Register of the said Office until the end of the next session of As-

Register of, how appointed and qualified;

fembly. All copies of the records and other papers of the said office, or of the records and papers hereby directed to be removed from the Secretary's office and lodged therein, duly attested by such Register, shall be as good evidence as the originals would be.

copies attested by him, equivolent evidence with originals

II. AND whereas a certain bounty in lands hath been engaged to the troops on continental establishment raised by the ordinances of Convention or the laws of this commonwealth, and to the troops upon *Virginia* establishment: Be it enacted, that the officers and soldiers of the said troops, as well as the officers and soldiers to whom a bounty in lands may, or shall be hereafter allowed by any law of this commonwealth, shall be entitled to the quantity of waste or unappropriated lands respectively engaged to them by such laws, a commissioned officer or his heirs, upon certificate from any general officer of the *Virginia* line, or the commanding officer of the troops on the *Virginia* establishment, as the case may be, and a non-commissioned officer or soldier, or his heirs, upon certificate from the Colonel or commanding officer of the regiment or corps to which they respectively belonged, that such officer or soldier hath served the time required by law, or hath been slain or died in the service, distinguishing particularly the time such officer or soldier hath served, and in what regiment or corps such service hath been performed, or death happened; and upon making proof before any court of record within this commonwealth by the persons own oath, or other satisfactory evidence of the truth and authenticity of the said certificate, and that the party had never before proved or claimed his right to land for the service therein mentioned, which proof the clerk of the court before whom it shall be made, is hereby empowered and required to endorse and certify upon the original certificate, making an entry or minute thereof in his order book and recording the same; and every county court shall annually, in the month of *October*, send to the Register's office, a list of all certificates granted by their respective county courts upon any of the before mentioned rights, there to be recorded. And for creating a sinking fund in aid of the annual taxes to discharge the public debt, Be it enacted, that any person may acquire title to so much waste and unappropriated lands as he or she shall desire to purchase, on paying the consideration of forty pounds for every hundred acres, and so in proportion for a greater or smaller quantity, and obtaining certificate from the public Auditors in the following manner: The consideration money shall be paid into the hands of the Treasurer, who shall thereupon give to the purchaser a receipt for the payment, specifying the purpose it was made for; which being delivered to the Auditors, they shall give to such person a certificate thereof, with the quantity of land he or she is thereby entitled to.

Rights to lands offered as bounties to officers and soldiers how to be authenticated.

For creating a sinking fund; how title to unappropriated lands acquirable.

III. AND be it enacted, that upon application of any person or persons, their heirs or assigns, having title to waste or unappropriated lands, either by military rights or treasury rights, and lodging in the Land Office a certificate thereof, the Register of the said office shall grant to such person or persons a printed warrant under his hand and the seal of his office, specifying the quantity of land and the rights upon which it is due, authorising any surveyor duly qualified according to law, to lay off and survey the same, and shall regularly enter and record in the books of his office, all such certificates and the warrants issued thereupon, which warrants shall be always good and valid until executed by actual survey, or exchanged in the manner herein after directed; provided that no warrant on treasury rights, other than preemption warrants, to be obtained by virtue of this act, shall be granted or issued before the fifteenth day of *October* next; nor shall the surveyor of any county admit the entry or location of any warrant on treasury rights, except preemption warrants, in his books, before the first day of *May* next. Any person holding a land warrant upon any of the before mentioned rights, may have the same executed in one or more surveys, and in such case, or where the lands on which any warrant is located shall be insufficient to satisfy such warrant, the party may have the said warrant exchanged by the Register of the Land Office for others of the same amount in the whole, but divided as best may answer the purposes of the party, or entitle him to so much land elsewhere as will make good the deficiency. A surveyor shall be appointed in every county, to be nominated, examined, and certified able by the President and professors of *William & Mary* college, and if of good character, commissioned by the Governor, with a reservation in such commission to the said professors, for the use of the college, of one sixth part of the legal fees which shall be received by such surveyor, for the yearly payment of which, he shall give bond with sufficient security to the President and masters of the said college. He shall hold his office during good behaviour; shall reside within his county; and before he shall be capable of entering upon the execution of his office, shall before the court of the same county, take an oath and give bond with two sufficient sureties, to the Governor and his successors, in such sum as he, with advice of his Council, shall have directed for the faithful execution of his office. All deputy surveyors shall be nominated by their principals, who shall be answerable for them, examined and certified able by the President and masters of the said college, and if of good character, commissioned by the Governor, and shall thereupon be entitled to one half of all fees received for services performed by them respectively, after deducting the proportion thereof due to the college. If any principal surveyor shall fail to nominate a sufficient number of deputies to perform the services of his office in due time, the court of the county shall direct what number he shall nominate, and in case of failure, shall nominate for him. And if any deputy surveyor, or any other on his behalf, and with his privity, shall pay or agree to pay any greater part of the profits of his office, sum of money in gross, or other valuable consideration to his principal for his recommendation or interest in procuring the deputation, such deputy and principal shall be thereby rendered for ever incapable of serving in such office; it shall not be necessary for the present chief or deputy surveyors of the several counties duly examined, commissioned, and qualified according to the laws heretofore in force, to be again commissioned and qualified under the directions of this act, nor in cases now depending before any court within this commonwealth. Every person having a land warrant founded on any of the before mentioned rights, and being desirous of locating the same on any particular waste and unappropriated lands, shall lodge such warrant with the chief surveyor of the county wherein the said lands or the greater part of them lie, who shall give a receipt for the same if required. The party shall direct the location thereof so specially and precisely, as that others may be enabled with certainty, to locate other warrants on the adjacent residuum; which location shall bear date the day on which it shall be made, and shall be entered by the surveyor in a book to be kept for that purpose, in which there shall be left no blank leaves or spaces between the different entries. And if several persons shall apply with their warrants at the office of any surveyor at the same time to make entries, they shall be preferred according to the priority of the dates of their warrants, but if such warrants be dated on the same day, the surveyor shall settle the right of priority between such persons by lot. And every surveyor shall, at the time of making entries for persons not being inhabitants of his county, appoint a time for surveying their land, and give notice thereof in writing to the persons making the same. And if on such application at his office, the surveyor shall refuse to enter such location, under pretence of a prior entry for the same lands made by some other persons, he shall have a right to demand of the said surveyor a view of the original of such prior entry in his book, and also an attested copy of it. But it shall not be lawful for any surveyor to admit an entry for any land without a warrant from the Register of the Land Office, except in the particular case of certificates from the Commissioners of the county for tracts of land, not exceeding four hundred acres, allowed in consideration of settlements, according to an act of Assembly, entitled *An act for adjusting and settling the titles of claimers to unpatented lands, under the present and former government, previous to the establishment of the commonwealth's Land Office*. No entry or

Warrants for surveys, how to be obtained, located, and executed.

Surveyor for every county and his deputy, how to be appointed and qualified; penalty upon, for sale of the office; his own warrants how to be located; duty of, in several instances.

A. D. 1779.

location of land shall be admitted within the county and limits of the *Cherokee Indians*, or on the north west side of the *Ohio* river, or on the lands reserved by act of Assembly for any particular nation or tribe of *Indians*, or on the lands granted by law to *Richard Henderson* and company, or in that tract of country reserved by resolution of the General Assembly for the benefit of the troops serving in the present war, and bounded by the *Green* river and a south east course from the head thereof to the *Cumberland* mountains, with the said mountains to the *Carolina* line, with the *Carolina* line to the *Cherokee* or *Tenesee* river, with the said river to the *Ohio* river, and with the *Ohio* to the said *Green* river, until the further order of the General Assembly. Any chief surveyor having warrant for lands, and desirous to locate the same on lands within his own county, shall enter such location before the clerk of the county, who shall return the same to his next court, there to be recorded, and the said surveyor shall proceed to have the survey made as soon as may be, and within six months at farthest, by some one of his deputies, or if he hath no deputy, then by any surveyor or deputy surveyor of an adjacent county, or his entry shall be void, and the land liable to the entry of any other person. Every chief surveyor shall proceed with all practicable dispatch, to survey all lands entered for in his office, and shall, if the party live within his county, either give him personal notice of the time at which he will attend to make such survey, or shall publish such notice by fixing an advertisement thereof on the door of the court-house of the county, on two several court days, which time so appointed shall be at least one month after personal notice given, or after the second advertisement so published; and if the surveyor shall accordingly attend, and the party, or some one for him, shall fail to appear at the time with proper chain carriers, and a person to mark the lines, if necessary, his entry shall become void, the land thereafter subject to the entry of any other person, and the surveyor shall return him the warrant, which may, notwithstanding, be located anew, upon any other waste or unappropriated lands, or again upon the same lands where it hath not, in the mean time, been entered for by another person. Where the chief surveyor doth not mean to survey himself, he shall immediately after the entry made, direct a deputy surveyor to perform the duty, who shall proceed as is before directed in the case of the chief surveyor. The persons employed to carry the chain on any survey, shall be sworn by the surveyor, whether principal or deputy, to measure justly and exactly to the best of their abilities, and to deliver a true account thereof to such surveyor, and shall be paid for their trouble by the party for whom the survey is made. The surveyor at the time of making the survey, shall see the same bounded plainly by marked trees, except where a water course or ancient marked line shall be the boundary, and shall make the breadth of each survey at least one third of its length in every part, unless where such breadth shall be restrained on both sides by mountains unfit for cultivation, by water courses, or the bounds of lands before appropriated. He shall as soon as it can conveniently be done, and within three months at farthest after making the survey, deliver to his employer, or his order, a fair and true plat and certificate of such survey, the quantity contained, the hundred (where hundreds are established in the county wherein it lies) the courses and descriptions of the several boundaries, natural and artificial, ancient and new, expressing the proper names of such natural boundaries, where they have any, and the name of every person whose former line is made a boundary; and also the nature of the warrant and rights on which such survey was made, and shall at the same time redeliver the said warrant to the party. The said surveyor may, nevertheless, detain the said certificates and warrants until the payment of his fees. The said plats and certificates shall be examined and tried by the said principal surveyor, whether truly made and legally proportioned as to length and breadth, and shall be entered within three months at farthest after the survey is made, in a book well bound, to be provided by the court of his county, at the county charge. And he shall in the month of *July* every year, return to the President and professors of *William* and *Mary* college, and also to the clerk's office of his county court, a true list of all surveys made by him, or his deputies, in the preceding twelve months, with the names of the persons for whom they were respectively made, and the quantities contained in each, there to be recorded by such clerk; and no person after the first day of *May* next, shall hold the offices of clerk of a county court and surveyor of a county, nor shall a deputy in either office act as deputy or chief in the other. Any surveyor, whether principal or deputy, failing in any of the duties aforesaid, shall be liable to be indicted in the General Court, and punished by amercement or deprivation of his office and incapacity to take it again, at the discretion of a jury; and shall moreover be liable to any party injured, for all damages he may sustain by such failure. Every county court shall once in every year, and oftener if they see cause, appoint two or more capable persons to examine the books of entries and surveys in possession of their chief surveyor, and to report in what condition and order the same are kept; and on his death or removal, shall have power to take the same into their possession, and deliver them to the succeeding chief surveyor. Every person for whom any waste or unappropriated lands shall be so located and laid off, shall within twelve months at farthest after the survey made, return the plat and certificate of the said survey into the Land Office, together with the warrant on which the lands were surveyed, and may demand of the Register a receipt for the same; and on failing to make such return within twelve months as aforesaid, or if the breadth of his plat be not one third of its length as before directed, it shall be lawful for any other person to enter a caveat in the said Land Office against the issuing of any grant to him, expressing therein for what cause the grant should not issue; or if any person shall obtain a survey of lands to which another hath by law a better right, the person having such better right, may in like manner enter a caveat to prevent his obtaining a grant until the title can be determined; such caveat also expressing the nature of

*Proceedings upon
caveats.*

the right on which the plaintiff therein claims the said land. The person entering any caveat, shall take from the Register a certified copy thereof, which, within three days thereafter, he shall deliver to the clerk of the General Court, or such caveat shall become void; the said clerk on receiving the same, shall enter it in a book, and thereupon issue a summons, reciting the cause for which such caveat is entered, and requiring the defendant to appear on the seventh day of the succeeding court, and defend his right; and on such process being returned executed, the court shall proceed to determine the right of the cause in a summary way, without pleadings in writing, empanneling and swearing a jury for the finding of such facts as are material to the cause, and are not agreed by the parties; and shall thereupon give judgment, on which no appeal or writ of error shall be allowed; a copy of such judgment, if in favour of the defendant, being delivered into the Land Office, shall vacate the said caveat; and if not delivered within three months, a new caveat may for that cause be entered against the grant; and if the said judgment be in favour of the plaintiff, upon delivering the same into the Land Office, together with a plat and certificate of the survey, and also producing a legal certificate of new rights on his own account, he shall be entitled to a grant thereof; but on failing to make such return and produce such certificates within six months after judgment so rendered, it shall be lawful for any other person to enter a caveat for that cause against issuing the grant; upon which subsequent caveats, such proceedings shall be had as are before directed in the case of an original caveat; and in any caveat where judgment shall be given for the defendant, the court shall award him his costs, and may compel the plaintiff in any caveat, if they think fit, to give security for costs, or on failure thereof, may dismiss his suit; and in case the plaintiff in any such caveat shall recover, the court may, if they think it reasonable, award costs against the defendant; provided that where any lands surveyed upon a land warrant as aforesaid, shall, in consequence of any judgment upon a caveat, be granted to any other person than the party claiming under such warrant, such party shall be entitled to a new warrant from the Register for the quantity of

A. D. 1779.

land so granted to another, reciting the original warrant and rights, and the particular cause of granting the new warrant. And to prevent confusion and mistakes in the application, exchange, or renewal of warrants, the Register of the Land Office is hereby directed and required to leave a sufficient margin in the record books of his office, and whenever any warrant shall be exchanged, renewed, or finally carried into execution by a grant, to note the same in the margin opposite to such warrant, with folio references to the grant, or other mode of application; and also to note in the margin opposite to each grant, the warrant or warrants and survey on which such grant is founded, with proper folio references to the books in which the same are recorded. All persons, as well foreigners as others, shall have right to assign or transfer warrants or certificates of survey for lands; and any foreigner purchasing warrants for lands, may locate and have the same surveyed, and after returning a certificate of survey to the Land Office, shall be allowed the term of eighteen months, either to become a citizen, or to transfer his right in such certificate of survey to some citizen of this, or any other of the United States of *America*. When any grant shall have been finally completed, the Register shall cause the plat and certificate of survey on which such grant is founded, to be exactly entered and recorded in well bound books, to be provided for that purpose at the public charge. Due returns of the several articles herein before required being made into the Land Office, the Register, within not less than six, nor more than nine months, shall make out a grant by way of deed poll to the party having right, in the following form: *A. B. Esq; Governor of the commonwealth of Virginia, to all to whom these presents shall come greeting: Know ye that in consideration of military service performed by C. D. to this commonwealth, &c. (or in consideration of military service performed by C. D. to the United American States, or in consideration of the sum of current money, paid by C. D. into the treasury of this commonwealth, &c) there is granted by the said commonwealth unto the said C. D. a certain tract or parcel of land containing   acres, lying in the county of   and hundred of   &c. (describing the particular bounds of the land and the date of the survey upon which the grant issues) with its appurtenances, to have and to hold the said tract or parcel of land with its appurtenances to the said C. D and his heirs for ever. In witness whereof the said A. B. Governor of the commonwealth of Virginia, hath hereunto set his hand, and caused the seal of the said commonwealth to be affixed at   on the   day of   in the year of our Lord   and of the commonwealth.   A. B.*

Warrants and certificates of surveys transferable.

Form of the grant; to be signed, sealed, and recorded:

Upon which grant the said Register shall endorse that the party hath title to the same; whereupon it shall be signed by the Governor, sealed with the seal of the commonwealth, and then entered of record at full length in good and well bound books to be provided for that purpose at the public expence and kept by the Register, and being so entered, shall be certified to have been registered and then be delivered, together with the original certificate of survey to the party or his order. Where a grant shall be made to the heir or assignee of a person claiming under any of the before mentioned rights, the material circumstances of the title shall be recited in such grant: And for preventing hasty and surreptitious grants and avoiding controversies and expensive law suits, *Be it enacted,* that no surveyor shall at any time within twelve months after the survey made, issue or deliver any certificate, copy or plat of land by him surveyed, except only to the person or persons for whom the same was surveyed; or to his, her, or their order, unless a caveat shall have been entered against a grant to the person claiming under such survey, to be proved by an authentic certificate of such caveat from the clerk of the General Court produced to the surveyor; and if any surveyor shall presume to issue any certificate, copy, or plat as aforesaid, to any other than the person or persons entitled thereto, every surveyor so offending shall forfeit and pay to the party injured, his or her legal representatives or assigns, fifty pounds current money for every hundred acres of land contained in the survey, whereof a certificate, copy, or plat shall be so issued, or shall be liable to the action of the party injured at the common law for his or her damages at the election of the party. Any person possessing high lands, to which any swamp, marshes, or sunken grounds are contiguous, shall have the preemption of such swamps, marshes or sunken grounds for one year, from and after the passing of this act, and if such person shall not obtain a grant for such swamps, marshes, or sunken grounds, within the said year, then any other person may enter on and obtain a grant for the same in the like manner as is directed in the case of other unappropriated lands. But nothing herein contained shall be construed or extend to give liberty to any person to survey, take up, or obtain a grant for any swamps, marshes, or sunken grounds lying contiguous to the high lands of any *feme covert,* infant under the age of twenty one years, person not being *compos mentis,* or person out of the commonwealth, according to the regulations of an act entitled *An act declaring who shall be deemed citizens of this commonwealth,* but all such persons shall be allowed one year after the removal of their several disabilities for the preemption of such lands.

Method to obtain grants of vacant swamps, &c. contiguous to patented high lands;

IV. AND whereas, through the ignorance, negligence, or fraud of surveyors, it may happen that divers persons now do or may hereafter hold within the bounds expressed in their patents or grants, greater quantities of land than are therein mentioned; for quieting such possessions, preventing controversies, and doing equal justice to the commonwealth and its citizens, *Be it enacted,* that it shall not be lawful for any person to enter for, survey, or take up, any parcel of land held as surplus in any patent or grant, except during the lifetime of the patentee or grantee, and before any transference, conveyance, or other alienation shall have been made of the lands contained in such patent or grant, and until the party intending to enter and take up the same, shall have given one full years notice to such patentee or grantee of such his intentions, and in case such patentee or grantee shall not within the year, obtain rights and sue forth a patent for the surplus land by him held, it shall be lawful for the person who gave notice as aforesaid, upon producing a certificate from the clerk of due proof of such notice before the court of the county wherein such patentee or grantee resides, to demand from the Register of the Land Office, a warrant to the surveyor of the county wherein such lands lie, to resurvey at the proper charge of the person obtaining such warrant, the whole tract within the bounds of the patent or grant, and upon such persons returning into the Land Office a plat and certificate of such resurvey, together with the warrant on which it is founded, and obtaining and producing new rights for all the surplus land found within the said bounds, he may sue forth and obtain a new grant for such surplus, which shall be granted to him in the same manner as waste or unappropriated lands; but the former patentee or grantee may assign such surplus land in any part of his tract as he shall think fit in one entire piece, the breadth of which shall be at least one third of the length; and in such new grant there shall be a recital of the original patent or grant, the resurvey of which the surplus was ascertained, and of other material circumstances.

and of surplus lands within the bounds of patents.

V. *PROVIDED always,* that if upon notice given as aforesaid, the original patentee or grantee shall within the year resurvey his tract, and it be thereupon found that he hath no more than the quantity of land expressed in his patent or grant, with the allowance herein after mentioned, the party giving such notice shall be liable to pay all charges of such resurvey, for which he shall give sufficient security to the said patentee or grantee at the time of the notice, otherwise such notice shall be void and of no effect; and moreover for his unjust vexation, shall be liable to an action upon the case at the suit of the party grieved, and that in all such new surveys, the patentee or grantee shall have an allowance at the rate of five acres in every hundred, for the variation of instruments.

Proviso for relief of landholders unjustly vexed.

VI. *AND be it enacted,* that where any person shall find any mistake or uncertainty in the courses or description of the bounds of his land, and desires to rectify the same, or shall hold two or more tracts of

Method of rectifying mistakes in

Z

A. D. 1779.

bounds, and obtaining inclusive patents.

land adjoining to each other, and is desirous to include them in one grant, he may in either case, having previously advertised his intentions and the time of application, at the door of the court-house on two several court days, and also having given notice to the owners of the adjoining lands, present a petition to the court of the county wherein such lands lie, reciting the nature and truth of the case, and such court may, and is hereby empowered to order the surveyor of their county to resurvey such lands at the charge of the party, according to his directions and the original or authentic title papers, taking care not to intrude upon the possessions of any other person, and to return a fair plat and certificate of such resurvey into the said court, to be examined and compared with the title papers; and if such court shall certify that in their opinion such resurvey is just and reasonable, the party may return the same, together with his material title papers in the Land Office, and demand the Register's receipt for them; and in case any caveat shall be entered against his obtaining a new grant upon such resurvey, the same proceedings shall be had therein as is directed in the case of other caveats, and the General Court upon hearing the same, may either prohibit such new grant, or vacate the caveat, as to them shall seem just; but if no caveat shall be entered within six months after such return, or if a caveat shall be entered and vacated as aforesaid, the party upon producing new rights for whatever surplus land appears to be within the bounds, more than the before mentioned allowance of five acres for every hundred, may sue out and obtain a new grant for such lands thereupon, in which shall be recited the dates and other material circumstances of the former title, and the title papers shall be delivered by the Register to the new owner.

The General Court shall yearly once at least cause the Land Office to be examined, and certain warrants &c. to be cancelled.
The Treasurer shall give bond, with surety, to account for money coming to his hands by virtue of this act.
Reservations and tenures in the royal grants abolished.

The Judges of the General Court shall once in every year and oftener if they see cause, appoint two or more capable persons to examine the record books and papers in the Land Office, and report in what condition and order they are kept, who shall compare all warrants of survey returned to the said office executed, with the list of those issued therefrom, and cancel all such as shall appear to have been properly executed or exchanged, an account of which shall be kept by the Register, charging therein those issued, and giving credit for those cancelled as aforesaid. The Treasurer for the time being shall annually enter into bond, with sufficient security to the Governor, in the sum of one hundred thousand pounds, for the just and faithful accounting for according to law, all money which shall come to his hands by virtue of this act. And that the proprietors of lands within this commonwealth may no longer be subject to any servile, feudal, or precarious tenure; and to prevent the danger to a free state from perpetual revenue, *Be it enacted,* that the reservation of royal mines of quitrents, and all other reservations and conditions in the patents or grants of land from the crown of *England* or of *Great Britain,* under the former government, shall be, and are hereby declared null and void; and that all lands thereby respectively granted, shall be held in absolute and unconditional property to all intents and purposes whatsoever, in the same manner with the lands hereafter to be granted by the commonwealth by virtue of this act; and no petition for lapsed land shall be admitted or received for or on account of any failure or forfeiture whatsoever, alledged to have been made or incurred after the twenty ninth day of *September,* in the year of our Lord one thousand seven hundred and seventy five. *And be it further enacted,* that

Stealing or forging a land warrant &c. or keeping an instrument for counterfeiting the Register's official seal, declared felony, without clergy.

he or she be adjudged a felon and not have the benefit of clergy, who shall steal, or by other means take from the possession or custody of another, any warrant from the Register of the Land Office of this commonwealth, to authorize a survey of waste and unappropriated lands; or who shall alter, erase, or aid or assist in, the alteration or erasement of any such warrant; or forge or counterfeit, or aid, abet, or assist in forging or counterfeiting any written or printed paper, purporting to be such warrant; or who shall transfer to the use of another, or for his or her own use, present or cause to be presented to the Register for the exchange thereof, or to a surveyor for the execution thereof, any such warrant or paper purporting to be such warrant, knowing the same so transferred or presented for the exchange or the execution thereof, to be stolen, or by other means taken from the possession or custody of another, or altered or erased, or forged or counterfeited; and he or she shall be adjudged a felon and not have the benefit of clergy, who shall falsely make or counterfeit, or aid, abet, or assist, in safely keeping or counterfeiting any instrument stamping an impression in the figure and likeness of the seal officially used by the Register of the Land Office, or who shall have in his or her possession or custody such instrument, and shall wilfully conceal the same, knowing it to be falsely made or counterfeited. So much of all former acts of Assembly as concern or relate to the entering, taking up, or seating lands, or direct the mode of proceeding in any case provided for by this act, shall be, and are hereby repealed.

See Oct. 1779, ch. 18, 40; Nov. 1781, ch. 19; May 1782, ch. 47.
Preamble.

CHAP. XIV.

An act concerning escheats and forfeitures from British subjects.

I. WHEREAS during the connection which subsisted between the now United States of *America* and the other parts of the *British* empire, and their subjection to one common Prince, the inhabitants of either part had all the rights of natural born subjects in the other, and so might lawfully take and hold real property, and transmit the same by descent to their heirs in *fee simple,* which could not be done by mere aliens; and the inhabitants on each part had accordingly acquired real property in the other, and in like manner had acquired personal property, which by their common laws might be possessed by any other than an alien enemy and transmitted to executors and administrators; but when by the tyrannies of that Prince, and the open hostilities committed by his armies and subjects inhabitants of the other parts of his dominions, on the good people of the said United States, they were obliged to wage war in defence of their rights, and finally to separate themselves from the rest of the *British* empire, to renounce all subjection to their common Prince, and to become sovereign and independent states; the said inhabitants of the other parts of the *British* empire, became aliens and enemies to the said states, and, as such, incapable of holding the property, real or personal, so acquired therein, and so much thereof as was within this commonwealth became by the laws vested in the commonwealth. Nevertheless the General Assembly, though provoked by the example of their enemies to a departure from that generosity which so honourably distinguishes the civilized nations of the present age, yet desirous to conduct themselves with moderation and temper, by an act passed at their session in the year one thousand seven hundred and seventy seven, took measures for preventing what had been the property of *British* subjects, within this commonwealth, from waste and destruction, by putting the same into the hands and under the management of commissioners appointed for that purpose, that so it might be in their power if reasonable, at a future day, to restore to the former proprietors the full value thereof.

In what manner the property of British subjects, now declared to be vested in the commonwealth, shall be sold and secured to the purchasers; allow-

II. AND whereas it is found that the said property is liable to be lost, wasted, and impaired without greater attention in the officers of civil government, than is consistent with the discharge of their public duties; and that from the advanced price at which the same would now sell, it may be most for the benefit of the former owners, if the same should be restored to them hereafter, or to the public if not so restored, that the sale thereof should take place at this time, and the proceeds be lodged in the public treasury, subject to the future direction of the Legislature: *Be it therefore enacted by the General Assembly,* that so much of the act before mentioned as may be supposed to have suspended the operation of the laws of escheat and forfeiture, shall be hereby repealed, and that all the property real and personal within

A. D. 1779.

this commonwealth, belonging at this time to any *British* subject, or which did belong to any *British* subject at the time such escheat or forfeiture may have taken place, shall be deemed to be vested in the commonwealth; the lands, slaves, and other real estate by way of escheat, and the personal estate by forfeiture. The Governor with the advice of Council so far as their information will enable them, and the commissioners of the tax within their several counties aided by their assessors, shall forwith institute proper proceedings of escheat and forfeiture for all such property real and personal, in which they shall be advised and assisted by the several Attornies for the commonwealth. Where any office in the cases before mentioned, shall be found for the commonwealth and returned to the General Court, it shall remain there but one month for the claim of any pretending right to the estate; and if within that time no such claim be made, or being made, if it be found and discussed for the commonwealth, the title of the owner to such estate real or personal, shall be for ever barred, but may be afterwards asserted as to the money proceeding from the sale thereof, with equal force and advantage as might have been to the thing itself; and such further proceedings shall be had for making sale of the right, title, claim, and interest, legal and equitable, of any *British* subject in and to the lands so found, in parcels not greater than four hundred acres (to be described by the commissioners hereafter mentioned, and measured and marked by metes and bounds by a surveyor where they shall think it necessary) and in and to the other party as in other cases of escheat and forfeiture, save only that the Governor with advice of Council, for every such sale, shall appoint two commissioners to superintend and controul the proceedings of the said escheator, which commissioners shall be sworn to use their best endeavours to have the estate to which their trust extends, sold to the best advantage.

ance to the escheator; and proceedings against him for delinquency.

Directions to the commissioners of sale.

The said sales shall be for ready money to be paid to the escheator, who shall retain thereof three *per ceutum* on the first thousand pounds arising from the sale of any such estate, and one and a half *per centum* on the remainder for his trouble. His certificate of such payment in the case of lands, and of the person purchasing, to the Register of the Land Office, shall entitle the purchaser to a grant of the said lands, free and fully exonerated from all the rights, title, claim, and interest, legal and equitable, of any *British* subject thereto; and also from the right, title, claim and interest of all and every person whatsoever, by or under any deed of mortage, the equity of redemption whereof had not been foreclosed at the time of the sale, but such mortgagees, their heirs or assigns, may nevertheless afterwards assert their claim and title to the money proceeding from the sale thereof, with equal force and advantage as they might have done to the land itself before such sale. If the said escheator shall fail to pay the said money into the hands of the Treasurer within a reasonable time after any such sale (which reasonable time shall be accounted one day for every twenty miles such sale was distant from the publick Treasury, and twenty days of grace in addition thereto) he shall pay interest thereon from the time of the said sale, at the rate of twenty *per centum per annum*; and moreover it shall be lawful for the Auditors on the last day but one of any General Court, or at any court to be held for the county wherein such property was sold, after the expiration of the time allowed for payment, to obtain judgment on motion against such escheator, his heirs, executors, and administrators, for the principal sum and such interest, together with costs. And for the information of the Auditors, the commissioners of the sale shall immediately on such sale, certify to whom and for how much such sale was made and transmit such certificate by some safe and early conveyance to the Auditors, which certificate shall be legal evidence against such escheator. The Auditors shall allow the commissioners so appointed, the expences of the surveys by them directed and made, and other their reasonable expences; and such compensation for their trouble as to them shall seem proper. Where the commissioners shall be of opinion that it will be more to the interest of the owner or public, that possession of such property, real or personal, should be retained for finishing and removing a crop, or other purpose, it shall be lawful for them to stay the possession as it now is until the sixth day of *December* next, and in such cases postpone the sale of the slaves, tools, and other personal property, necessary for their subsistence and making the said crop, until the said sixth day of *December*.

Nett proceeds to be extended in tobacco, how estimated.

The money for which such property was sold being paid into the public treasury, and all expences allowed and deductions made, the balance thereof shall be extended in nett tobacco, at the market price, as the same shall be estimated on oath by the grand jury of the succeeding General Court, and such balance of tobacco shall be considered in future as the true measure of retribution to be made to the individuals interested, if retribution be made, and in such case shall be repaid to them by the public in quantity and kind. The duties which, under this act, are to be performed by an escheator in the several counties of this commonwealth, not being within the territory commonly called the *Northern Neck*, shall in the counties within that territory be performed by the sheriff of such counties respectively, which sheriff shall have the same powers, be entitled to the same allowances, and subject to the same penalties, conditions, and legal proceedings as escheators are in the other counties.

Duty of escheators to be performed in the Northern Neck, by sheriffs.

III. AND for preventing doubts who shall be deemed *British* subjects within the meaning of this act, It is *hereby declared and enacted*, that (first) all persons subjects of his *Britannick* Majesty, who, on the nineteenth day of *April*, in the year one thousand seven hundred and seventy five, when hostilities were commenced at *Lexington*, between the United States of *America* and the other parts of the *British* empire, were resident or following their vocations in any part of the world, other than the said United States, and have not since, either entered into public employment of the said states or joined the same, and by overt act adhered to them; and (secondly) all such subjects, inhabitants of any of the said United States, as were out of the said states on the same day, and have since by overt act adhered to the enemies of the said states; and (thirdly) all inhabitants of the said states, who, after the same day and before the commencement of the act of General Assembly, entitled *An act declaring what shall be treason*, departed from the said states and joined the subjects of his *Britannick* Majesty, of their own free will, or who, by any county court within this commonwealth, were declared to be *British* subjects, within the meaning and operation of the resolution of the General Assembly of the nineteenth day of *December* 1776, for enforcing the statute staple, shall be deemed *British* subjects within the intention of this act. But this act shall not extend to debts due to *British* subjects, and payable into the loan office according to the act of General Assembly for sequestering *British* property; nor take effect on any lots of land within the town of *Richmond*, as the limits of the said town now are, or shall be at the time of the inquest found, which by the directors of the public buildings shall be included within the squares appropriated for such buildings, further than that an office shall be found as to such lots of land, and the estimated value thereof be disposed of hereafter as the price would have been by this act, had they been exposed to public sale; nor on any other such lots within the same town, whether held in severalty by any *British* subject or subjects, or by a citizen or citizens and a *British* subject or subjects, as joint tenants or tenants in common, which shall by the said directors be declared proper for the public use, until buildings be erected on the squares before mentioned, except that an office shall be found as to the interest of any *British* subject in such lots, and such interest estimated by the same jury which found the office, and at the same time, as also the interest therein of any citizen who is joint tenant or tenant in common with such *British* subject, and the value of the interest of such citizen shall be paid to him, in like manner as is directed in the case of squares of ground appropriated to the public buildings by an act passed at this present session of Assembly, entitled *An act for the removal of the seat of government*, and the value of the interest of any such *British* subject shall be disposed of hereafter as the price would have been by this act had they been exposed to public sale, and the property in such lots shall be vested in the commonwealth; provided that

British subjects described.

Property in particular instances excepted out of this act.

the eftates real and perfonal of fuch *Britifh* fubjects who have wives, widows, or children, refiding within this ftate, fhall be appropriated as follows : Such eftates where there is a widow and no children,
fhall be fubject to the widows dower; where a wife and no child, to the like claim; but where a wife
and child, or child and no wife, the whole of the eftate belonging to fuch *Britifh* fubject fhall be without
the purview of this act. The refidue of any eftate not appropriated as hereby directed, fhall be fubject
to the difpofitions of this act.

C H A P. XV.

An act for more effectually fupplying the officers, foldiers, and failors of the commonwealth with the articles
neceffary for their comfortable accommodation.

C H A P. XVI.

An act for the annual appointment of Delegates to Congrefs.

I. BE it enacted by the General Affembly, that at the firft feffion of every General Affembly, there fhall
be chofen by joint ballot of both Houfes, feven perfons to act as Delegates for this commonwealth in General Congrefs, from the firft *Monday* in *November* next enfuing the faid election
for the term of one year. Four of the faid Delegates at the leaft fhall be always at Congrefs during its
feffions; the majority of thofe prefent fhall give the vote of this commonwealth, provided there be prefent three at the leaft, otherwife they fhall give no vote; if they fhall not by agreement among themfelves, to be ftated in writing, otherwife fettle the portions of the year during which each member fhall
attend, fo as to keep up a conftant attendance of four at the leaft, then they fhall ferve as follows, to
wit: The firft member in the nomination fhall ferve during the months of *November, December, Janu-*
ary, February, June, July, and *Auguft.* The fecond, during the months of *January, February, March,*
April, May, September, and *October.* The third, during the months of *November, December, March,*
April, May, September, and *October.* The fourth, during the months of *November, December, January,*
February, June, July, and *Auguft.* The fifth, during the months of *February, March, April, July,*
Auguft, September, and *October.* The fixth, during the months of *November, December, January, May,*
June, July, and *Auguft.* And the feventh, during the months of *March, April, May, June, September,*
and *October.* No member fhall be capable of being a Delegate for more than three years in any term of
fix years, taking into account as well the paft as future time. Any of the faid Delegates fhall be fubject
to be removed at any time within the year, by the joint vote of both Houfes, and thereon, or in cafe
of the death, refignation, or refufal to act, of any fuch Delegate, they fhall proceed to choofe another,
to ferve in his ftead, and during his term: and each of the faid Delegates fhall receive from the Treafurer the fum of forty dollars for every day he fhall be at Congrefs, or for attending the Committee of
the States, and a dollar for every mile travelling to, or returning from either, with his ferriages. If
any perfon holding any office under the laws of this commonwealth, legiflative, executive, or judiciary,
be appointed a Delegate to Congrefs, fuch office fhall not thereby be vacated. The Delegates to Congrefs to be chofen during this prefent feffion of Affembly, in lieu of thofe who have refigned, or fhall
refign, together with thofe remaining in office, fhall be continued until the firft *Monday* in *November*
next, and fhall be fubject to the fame rules of voting, and entitled to the fame allowances, as are before
ftated in cafe of the members to be annually chofen.

C H A P. XVII.

An act to amend an act entitled An act for reviving feveral public warehoufes for the infpection of tobacco.

C H A P. XVIII.

An act for laying a tax, payable in certain enumerated commodities.

C H A P. XIX.

An act for obliging the feveral delinquent counties and divifions of militia in this commonwealth, to furnifh one
twenty fifth man.

C H A P. XX.

An act for the better regulation and difcipline of the militia.

C H A P. XXI.

An act for the removal of the feat of government.

I. WHEREAS great numbers of the inhabitants of this commonwealth muft frequently and of
neceffity refort to the feat of government where General Affemblies are convened, fuperior
courts are held, and the Governor and Council ufually tranfact the executive bufinefs of
government; and the equal rights of all the faid inhabitants require that fuch feat of government fhould
be as nearly central to all as may be, having regard only to navigation, the benefits of which are neceffary for promoting the growth of a town fufficient for the accommodation of thofe who refort thereto,
and able to aid the operations of government: And it has been alfo found inconvenient in the courfe
of the prefent war, where feats of government have been fo fituated as to be expofed to the infults and
injuries of the public enemy, which dangers may be avoided and equal juftice done to all the citizens of
this commonwealth by removing the feat of government to the town of *Richmond,* in the county of *Hen-*
rico, which is more fafe and central than any other town fituated on navigable water : Be it therefore
enacted by the General Affembly, that fix whole fquares of ground furrounded each of them by four ftreets,
and containing all the ground within fuch ftreets, fituate in the faid town of *Richmond,* and on an open
and airy part thereof, fhall be appropriated to the ufe and purpofe of public buildings: On one of the
faid fquares fhall be erected, one houfe for the ufe of the General Affembly, to be called the capitol,

which said capitol shall contain two apartments for the use of the Senate and their clerk, two others for the use of the House of Delegates and their clerk, and others for the purposes of conferences, committees and a lobby, of such forms and dimensions as shall be adopted to their respective purposes: On one other of the said squares shall be erected, another building to be called the halls of justice, which shall contain two apartments for the use of the Court of Appeals and its clerk, two others for the use of the High Court of Chancery and its clerk, two others for the use of the General Court and its clerk, two others for the use of the Court of Admiralty and its clerk, and others for the uses of grand and petty juries, of such forms and dimensions as shall be adopted to their respective purposes; and on the same square last mentioned shall be built a public jail: One other of the said squares shall be reserved for the purpose of building thereon hereafter, a house for the several executive boards and offices to be held in: Two others with the intervening street, shall be reserved for the use of the Governor of this commonwealth for the time being, and the remaining square shall be appropriated to the use of the public market. The said houses shall be built in a handsome manner with walls of brick or stone, and porticoes where the same may be convenient or ornamental, and with pillars and pavements of stone. There shall be appointed by joint ballot of both Houses of Assembly, five persons to be called the directors of the public buildings, who, or any three of them shall have power to make choice of such squares of ground, situate as before directed, as shall be most proper and convenient for the said public purposes, to agree on plans for the said buildings, to employ proper workmen to erect the same, to superintend them, to procure necessary materials by themselves or by the Board of Trade, and to draw on the Treasurer of this commonwealth, from time to time, for such sums of money as shall be wanting; the plans and estimates of which shall be submitted to the two Houses of Assembly whensoever called for by their joint vote, and shall be subjected to their controul. And that reasonable satisfaction may be paid and allowed for all such lots of ground as by virtue of this act may be taken and appropriated to the uses aforesaid, the clerk of the county of *Henrico*, is hereby empowered and required on requisition from the said directors, to issue a writ in nature of a writ of *ad quod damnum*, to be directed to the sheriff of the said county, commanding him to summon and empannel twelve able discreet freeholders of the vicinage no ways concerned in interest in the said lots of land, nor related to the owners or proprietors thereof, to meet on the said lots on a certain day to be named in the said writ, not under five nor more than ten days from the date thereof, of which notice shall be given by the sheriff to the proprietors and tenants of the said lots of land if they be to be found within the county, and if not, then to their agents therein if any they have, which freeholders, taking nothing on pain of being discharged from the inquest and immediately imprisoned by the sheriff, either of meat or drink from any person whatever from the time they came to the said place until their inquest sealed shall be charged by the said sheriff impartially, and to the best of their skill and judgment to value the said lots of ground in so many several and distinct parcels as shall be owned and held by several and distinct owners and tenants, and according to their respective interest and estates therein; and if the said valuation cannot be completed in one day, then the said sheriff shall adjourn the said jurors from day to day until the same be completed; and after such valuation made, the said sheriff shall forthwith return the same under the hands and seals of the said jurors to the clerk's office of the said county, and the right and property of the said owners and tenants in the said lots of land, shall be immediately devested and be transferred to this commonwealth in the full and absolute dominion, any want of consent or disability to consent in the said owners and tenants notwithstanding. The costs of the said inquest and the several sums at which the rights of the owners and tenants are valued, shall be paid by the Treasurer to the said owners, tenants, and others entitled respectively, on warrant from the Auditors.

II. AND whereas it may be expedient to enlarge the said town of *Richmond*, by laying off a number of lots to be added thereto, and it may also happen that some of the lands adjacent to the said town may be more convenient for the public uses: *Be it therefore enacted*, that the said directors cause two hundred additional lots or half acres, with necessary streets to be laid off adjacent to such parts of the said town as to them shall seem most convenient, and they shall also be at liberty to appropriate the six squares aforesaid, or any part of them, either from among the lots now in the said town, or those to be laid off as before directed, or of the lands adjacent to the said former or latter lots, and the said six squares and two hundred lots shall thenceforth be a part of the said town. And the said directors shall return into the clerk's office of the said county of *Henrico*, there to be recorded a full and distinct report under their hands and seals of the lots and squares of land added by them to the said town, or appropriated to the public uses, together with the plan thereof. The rights of the several owners and tenants of the lots of land so to be added to the town and not appropriated to the public uses, are nevertheless saved to them.

III. BUT whereas from the great expence attending the just and necessary war this commonwealth is at present engaged in, the difficulties of procuring the materials for building, and the high price for labour, it will be burthensome to the inhabitants if the said public buildings be immediately erected: *Be it therefore enacted*, that the directors aforesaid shall, with all convenient speed, cause to be erected or otherwise provide some proper and temporary buildings for the sitting of the General Assembly, the Courts of Justice, and the several boards before described.

IV. AND whereas the present jail of the county of *Henrico*, now within the said town of *Richmond*, if enlarged may be made sufficient for a public jail until a more commodious one can be built; the said directors are hereby empowered to enlarge the same. Provided nevertheless, there shall not be drawn out of the public treasury for any or all the said purposes a sum exceeding twenty thousand pounds; and the directors aforesaid are hereby prohibited from making any contracts for erecting any of the public buildings described by this act to be built on any of the squares appropriated for public use, fixing on the squares or laying off the additional lots until further provision shall be made for the same by the General Assembly. *And be it further enacted*, that from and after the last day of *April* which shall be in the year of our Lord one thousand seven hundred and eighty, the said Court of Appeals, High Court of Chancery, General Court, and Court of Admiralty shall hold their sessions in the apartments prepared for them by the said directors; that the first meeting of the General Assembly after the same day shall be in such house or houses as shall be provided by the said directors; that the clerks of the two houses of Assembly and of the several courts before mentioned, shall previously cause to be removed thither at the public expence, the records, papers, and other things belonging to their respective offices; and that the keeper of the public jail shall in like manner cause all prisoners in his custody to be removed to the public jail so to be built as before directed, which shall thenceforward be deemed and used as the public jail spoken of by the laws whether heretofore or hereafter passed.

A.D. 1779.

See May 1781,
ch. 1, 8; Nov.
1781, ch. 12.

C H A P. XXII.

An act constituting the Court of Appeals.

The court shall consist of what Judges, and how qualified; sit when and how long;

I. BE it enacted by the General Assembly, that a Court of Appeals for hearing and determining suits which ought to be instituted there, and for finally deciding those which are herein after referred to that tribunal, shall be holden twice in every year, namely, on the twenty ninth, or when that shall happen to be *Sunday*, on the thirtieth day of *March* and *August*, and shall sit in the whole, six juridical days successively each time (unless the business depending before them be sooner dispatched) at the capitol in *Williamsburg*, or at such other place as shall be appointed by the General Assembly, or in their recess, by the Governor, with advice of the Privy Council, in any such emergency as will make the adjournment of any other court by his writ lawful. The Judges of the High Court of Chancery, General Court, and Court of Admiralty, shall be Judges of the Court of Appeals, of whom the first shall take precedence, and the second be next in rank, and five of them shall be a sufficient number to constitute the court. Every Judge before he exercise this office, shall in that court openly give assurance of fidelity to the commonwealth, and take this oath: *You shall swear that you will well and truly serve this commonwealth in the office of a Judge of the Court of Appeals, and that you will do equal right to all manner of people, great and small, high and low, rich and poor, without respect of persons. You shall not take by yourself, or by any other, any gift, fee, or reward of gold, silver, or any other thing, directly or indirectly, of any person or persons great or small, for any matter done or to be done by virtue of your office, except such fees or salary as shall be by law appointed. You shall not maintain by yourself or any other, privily or openly, any plea or quarrel depending in the courts of this commonwealth. You shall not delay any person of right for the letters or request of any person, nor for any other cause; and if any letter or request come to you, contrary to the law, you shall nothing do for such letter or request, but you shall proceed to do the law, any such letter or request notwithstanding. And finally, in all things belonging to your said office, during your continuance therein, you shall faithfully, justly, and truly, according to the best of your skill and judgment, do equal and impartial justice, without fraud, favour, or affection.* This court shall have jurisdiction, not only in suits originating there and adjourned thither for trials by virtue of any statute, which trials shall be by juries according to the course of law, but also in such as shall be brought before them by appeals and writs of error to reverse decrees of the High Court of Chancery, judgments of the General Court, and sentences of the Court of Admiralty; after those decisions shall be final there, if the matter in controversy be equal in value, exclusive of costs, to fifty pounds, or be a freehold or franchise; and also in such cases as shall be removed before them by adjournment from the other courts before mentioned, when questions, in their opinion, new and difficult occur; and moreover in such, wherein appeals to reverse decrees and judgments of the former General Court, and sentences of the Court of Vice Admiralty, as had not been determined, the one by the King of *Great Britain* in his Privy Council, the other by the High Court of Admiralty of *Great Britain*, before the fifteenth day of *April*, one thousand seven hundred and seventy six. The court shall appoint a clerk, tipstaff, and crier, the first removeable for misbehaviour, the two others at pleasure, and shall be attended by the sheriff of the county in which they sit, as their officer. The party desiring to prosecute such appeal or writ of error, shall proceed in like manner, and shall be liable to like damages if the decree, judgment, or sentence be affirmed; and the said clerk shall issue the like process for summoning the adverse party, removing the records, suspending execution, and for every other requisite purpose, making those alterations in the form which are necessary to adapt it to the case, as are prescribed and ascertained in case of an appeal or writ of error to reverse the decree, sentence, or judgment of a county, city, or borough court; and such prosecution shall be commenced within the time limited in the case last mentioned, unless it be such appeal to the said King or High Court of Admiralty, in which instance the prosecution shall be commenced within twelve months after the first session of the said Court of Appeals shall be ended. The said clerk shall carefully preserve the transcripts of records certified to his court, with the bonds for prosecution, and all papers relative to them, and other suits depending therein, docketing them in the order he shall receive them, that they may be heard in the same course, unless the court for good cause to them shewn, direct any to be heard out of its turn; and shall faithfully record their proceedings and decisions, and certify such as shall be given upon appeals, writs of error, and matters removed by adjournment to the proper courts. A clear and concise state of the case of each party in such appeal, writ of error, or controversy adjourned by reason of novelty and difficulty, with the points intended to be insisted upon, signed by his counsel and printed, the expence whereof shall be taxed in the bill of costs, shall be delivered to every Judge time enough before the hearing for his consideration; but the court, if this be neglected, may nevertheless hear and determine the matter, and may take into their consideration any thing apparent in the manuscript record, although it be omitted in such printed case, and may give such decree, judgment, or sentence, if it be not affirmed or reversed in the whole, as the court whose error is sought to be corrected, ought to have given (affirming in those cases where the voices on both sides shall be equal, with an allowance of the costs of appeal) to the party prevailing, to be certified as well as their opinion upon any adjourned question to the court, from which the matter was removed, who shall enter it as their own, and award execution thereupon accordingly. So much of a former act of Assembly constituting a Court of Appeals, as comes within the purview of this act, is hereby repealed.

have jurisdiction in what cases, and how brought before them; and

appoint their officers.

Duty of their clerk.

Cases to be stated for them.

Their opinions upon adjourned questions, how certified.

C H A P. XXIII.

An act to secure the moveable property of those who have joined, or hereafter may join the enemy.

Executed.

C H A P. XXIV.

See Oct. 1780.
ch. 30.

An act for punishing persons guilty of certain thefts and forgeries, and fixing the allowance to sheriffs, veniremen and witnesses, in certain cases.

Stealing or counterfeiting certain warrants, &c. made felony without Clergy.

I. BE it enacted by the General Assembly, that he or she shall be adjudged a felon and not have the benefit of clergy, who shall steal, or by robbery take from the possession or custody of another, any bill of credit or treasury note, or Loan Office certificate of the United States, or any of them, or any warrant of the Governor or other person exercising that function, or any certificate of the Auditors for public accounts to the Treasurer, authorising the payment of money, or shall present, or cause to be presented such Loan Office certificate at a Loan Office of the United States, or any of them, for the discharge of the whole or any part thereof, or such warrant or Auditors certificate at the public treasury for the payment thereof, knowing such Loan Office certificate or warrant, or Auditors certificate, to have been stolen, or by robbery taken from the possession or custody of another. And he or she shall be adjudged a felon and not have the benefit of clergy, who shall falsely make, forge, or counterfeit, or aid or assist

A. D. 1779.

m falfely making, forging, or counterfeiting a writing, figned and directed, or certified to the public Treafurer, purporting to be a warrant of the Governor or other perfon exercifing that function, or a certificate of the Auditors for public accounts to authorize the payment of money; or caufe or procure fuch writing to be falfely made, forged, or counterfeited; or prefent fuch writing, or caufe or procure it to be prefented at the public treafury, knowing it to have been falfely made, forged, or counterfeited; in order to receive the money, or any part of the money therein mentioned; or fhall falfely make, forge, or counterfeit, or aid or affift in falfely making, forging, or counterfeiting, a writing to be offered to the Auditors for public accounts as a voucher, in order to obtain their allowance of a demand, and certificate of fuch allowance; or caufe or procure fuch writing to be falfely made, forged, or counterfeited, or offer fuch writing, or caufe or procure it to be offered to the faid Auditors, knowing it to have been falfely made, forged, or counterfeited, in order to obtain their allowance and certificate aforefaid. And he or fhe fhall be adjudged a felon and not have the benefit of clergy, who fhall forge or counterfeit, alter or erafe, any bill of credit or treafury note, or Loan Office certificate of the United States of *America*, or any or either of them; or fhall caufe or procure fuch bill of credit or treafury note or Loan Office certificate to be forged or counterfeited, altered or erafed, or fhall aid or affift in forging or counterfeiting, altering or erafing fuch bill of credit or treafury note, or Loan Office certificate; or fhall pafs or tender, or fhall caufe or procure to be paffed or tendered, any fuch bill of credit or treafury note, or Loan Office certificate, in payment or exchange, knowing the fame to have been forged or counterfeited, altered or erafed; or fhall have in his or her cuftody or poffeffion, any prefs, types, ftamp, plate, or other inftrument neceffary to be ufed in the fabrication of fuch bill of credit or treafury note, or Loan Office certificate, and not actually ufed in fome public printing office; or any paper with or without fignature, on which the characters, words, and numerical figures, contained in a genuine bill of credit or treafury note, or Loan Office certificate, are or fhall be impreffed or infcribed in like order as they are in fuch bill of credit or treafury note, or Loan Office certificate, or any fuch bill of credit, treafury note, or Loan Office certificate, which hath been altered or erafed, knowing the fame to have been altered or erafed, and fhall not difcover fuch prefs, types, ftamp, plate, inftrument, paper, or altered or erafed bill of credit or treafury note, or Loan Office certificate, to two Juftices of the Peace before the laft day of *June*, in this prefent year, one thoufand feven hundred and feventy nine, or within five days after they fhall have come to his poffeffion. When the Juftices of a county in which any fuch felony as is before defcribed fhall be fuppofed to have been done, fhall have determined upon examination, that the perfon charged therewith ought to be tried before the General Court, the High Sheriff, or if he be not able to attend, the Coroner fhall deliver to them a lift of the names of thirty fix good and lawful men, out of which twenty four fhall be ftricken, one after another, the Juftices and the prifoner ftriking alternately, or if the prifoner refufe to ftrike, the Juftices ftriking only, and the remaining twelve men fhall be fummoned by the writ of *venire facias* for trial of the prifoner. When a Juftice of Peace,

Method of proceeding againft fuch offenders.

before whom a perfon charged upon oath with any fuch felony as aforefaid, fhall inform the Governor that he hath caufe to fufpect that the offender, if he or fhe fhould be committed to the jail of the county in which the felony was done, would be refcued (which information the Juftice is required to give in writing, with fecrecy and defpatch) or when a perfon fhall be charged upon oath made before the Governor with fuch felony, in either cafe, the Governor, with advice of the Council of State, may by his warrant, empower and order fo many men as fhall be judged fufficient to apprehend the perfon accufed, and convey and commit him or her to any other jail, in which he or fhe fhall be detained, and fhall by another warrant direct the fheriff of that county in which the laft mentioned jail is, to fummon the Juftices thereof to meet at the court-houfe before the end of twenty days afterwards; and thereupon the faid Juftices fhall proceed in the fame manner as they might have proceeded if the fact alledged againft the prifoner had been done in their own county. And if he or fhe be remanded, the clerk of the peace attending the faid Juftices, fhall, within twenty days afterwards, certify the fame to the fheriff of the county in which the fact was done, or failing to do fo, fhall forfeit one hundred pounds; and the fame fheriff fhall fummon the Juftices of his county to meet at the court-houfe thereof, within ten days after receipt of fuch certificate, and then deliver to them fuch lift as aforefaid, out of which twenty four fhall be ftricken, in manner before directed, any agent authorized by the prifoner, ftriking for him or her, or if no fuch appear, the Juftices ftriking only; and the remaining twelve fhall be fummoned as jurors for trial of the prifoner, by writ of *venire facias*, to be iffued by the clerk of the laft mentioned county. Every juror fummoned by virtue of any fuch writ of *venire facias*, who fhall fail at the return thereof, and from that time until he be difcharged, to attend the General Court, fhall forfeit one hundred pounds, unlefs the defaulter fhew good caufe to the contrary, having been fummoned for that purpofe. Any Juftice of the Peace may, by his warrant, caufe to be apprehended and brought before him, every fuch perfon travelling in the county of the faid Juftice, as he fhall fufpect to carry forged bills of credit or treafury notes, or Loan Office certificates, and fearch to be made in the wearing apparel and baggage of the faid traveller by force, if he or fhe expofe them not voluntarily. The Governor, with advice of the Council of State, may offer rewards for apprehending thofe who, having been charged upon oath with any of the felonies before prefcribed, fhall have fled from juftice, and may draw warrants for fuch rewards not exceeding one thoufand pounds for any one fugitive, which fhall be paid out of the public treafury. The Auditors fhall grant certificates to all witneffes, veniremen, and fheriffs, for their attendance in criminal cafes, and fhall allow them, in fuch certificates, two fhillings *per* mile for travelling, and four pounds *per* day for their attendance, befides ferriages (inftead of the allowances heretofore eftablifhed by law) which the Treafurer is directed to pay, for their attendance at the General Court, held in this prefent month, and to all others who may attend at future General Courts after the paffing this act. The certificate from the Auditors to be granted upon teftimonial from the clerk of the court at which the witneffes, veniremen, or fheriffs fhall have attended. This act fhall be in force until the firft day of *January*, one thoufand feven hundred and eighty one; and fo much of the act of laft feffion *For more effectually guarding againft counterfeiting of the bills of credit, treafury notes, and Loan Office certificates*, and of every other act as is within the purview of, and inconfiftent with this, is repealed.

Allowance to witneffes, veniremen, and fheriffs, what, and how to be paid.

CHAP. XXV.

An act for declaring and afferting the rights of this commonwealth, concerning purchafing lands from Indian natives.

I. TO remove and prevent all doubt concerning purchafes of land from the *Indian* natives, Be it declared by the General *Affembly*, that this commonwealth hath the exclufive right of preemption from the *Indians* of all lands within the limits of its own chartered territory, as defcribed by the act and conftitution of government in the year one thoufand feven hundred and feventy fix; that no perfon or perfons whatfoever have, or ever had, a right to purchafe any lands within the fame from any *Indian* nation, except only perfons duly authorized to make fuch purchafes on the public account, formerly for the ufe and benefit of the colony, and lately of the commonwealth; and that fuch exclufive right of preemption will, and ought to be maintained by this commonwealth to the utmoft of its power.

Commonwealth's exclufive right of preemption from Indians of lands within its chartered limits afcertained

A.D. 1779.

Purchases for-
merly made from
Indians shall inure
to the common-
wealth.

II. AND *be it further declared and enacted*, that every purchase of lands heretofore made by, or on behalf of the crown of *England* or of *Great Britain*, from any *Indian* nation or nations within the before mentioned limits, doth and ought to enure for ever to and for the use and benefit of this commonwealth, and to and for no other use or purpose whatsoever; and that all sales and deeds which have been or shall be made by any *Indian* or *Indians*, or by any *Indian* nation or nations, for lands within the said limits, to or for the separate use of any person or persons whatsoever, shall be, and the same are hereby declared utterly void and of no effect.

CHAP. XXVI.

An act constituting the Court of Admiralty.

See May 1780,
ch. 7, 30.

Judges of this
court shall consist of
what number;
have jurisdiction of
what causes;
shall be governed in
their decisions by
what rules;

how appointed and
qualified;

I. BE *it enacted by the General Assembly*, that the Court of Admiralty to consist of three Judges, any two of whom are declared to be a sufficient number to constitute a court, shall have jurisdiction in all maritime causes, except those wherein any parties may be accused of capital offences now depending and hereafter to be brought before them, shall take precedence in court according to the order in time of their appointments, and shall be governed in their proceedings and decisions by the regulations of the Congress of the United States of *America*, by the acts of the General Assembly, by the laws of *Oleron*, and the *Rhodian* and *Imperial* laws, so far as they have been heretofore observed in the *English* Courts of Admiralty, and by the laws of nature and nations. If the regulations of Congress happen to differ from those of General Assembly, the latter are declared to be supreme in cases wherein citizens only are litigants, and the former in all other cases: Every future Judge of this court shall be chosen by joint ballot of both Houses of Assembly; and before he enters on the duties of his office, besides taking the oath of fidelity, he shall take the following oath, to be administered by the Governor in Council: *You shall swear that well and truly you will serve this commonwealth in the office of a Judge of the Court of Admiralty; that you will do equal right to all manner of people, great and small, high and low, rich and poor, of what country or nation soever they be, without respect of persons. You shall not take by yourself, or by any other, any gift, fee, or reward, of gold, silver, or any other thing, directly or indirectly, of any person or per-sons, great or small, for any matter done or to be done by virtue of your office, except such fees or salary as shall be by law appointed. You shall not maintain by yourself, or by any other, privily or openly, any plea or quarrel depending in the said court: You shall not delay any person of right for the letters or request of any one, nor for any other cause; and if any letter or request come to you contrary to the law, you shall nothing do for such letter or request, but you shall proceed to do the law; any such letter or request not-withstanding. And finally in all things belonging to your said office, during your continuance therein, you shall faithfully, justly, and truly, ac-cording to the best of your skill and judgment, do equal and impartial justice, without fraud, favour, affection, or partiality.* The taking of which oath, or the certificate thereof, shall be registered in the said court. Any Judge executing his office before he shall have taken the said oath, or given assurance of fidelity to the commonwealth, shall forfeit five hundred pounds of current money, to the use of the common-*may appoint certain officers;* wealth. This court or any two Judges thereof, when it is not sitting, shall appoint a Register, an Ad-vocate, and a Marshal, when those offices shall become vacant, who shall take the oath of office, and of whom the Register and Marshal shall moreover give bonds, the former in one thousand pounds, and the other in ten thousand pounds, payable to the Governor or his successors, with sureties, to be approved by the court or two Judges, with condition that they will faithfully and impartially perform their re-spective offices, and account for and pay all money which may come to their hands by virtue thereof; upon which bonds, suits may be severally brought for the benefit and at the costs of any persons grieved by breach of the conditions until the damages to be recovered shall be equal to the penalties. The *shall sit where, and when.* Judges, Register, Advocate, and Marshal, shall continue in office so long as they respectively demean themselves well therein. The court shall sit so often as there shall be occasion, at the capitol in *Wil-liamsburg*, until the General Assembly shall appoint another place, or at, or in such house or place as the Governor, with advice of the Council, shall by writ of adjournment direct, in case an accident by *Their process, com-manders of vessels shall assist in execut-ing;* fire or tempest, or a pestilential disease, or an enemy, shall make it necessary. This court shall have power to order sale of perishable goods to be made at any time, taking sufficient caution for securing the proceeds of the sale to him who shall be entitled to them by the final sentence. Every commander of a ship of war or other vessel belonging to the commonwealth, or to any citizen thereof, when he shall be required, shall assist the Marshal of the said court acting by virtue of the process thereof, to seize and secure any vessel or goods subject to such process, so as not to violate the right of any other of the United *in what mode shall proceed.* States, or of any State, or Prince in amity with them. When a citation shall have been served upon the owner or master of a vessel therein mentioned, if no person appear at the return day, or at such further time as the court for peculiar reasons shall appoint, and enter into the litigation, the libel shall be taken for confessed; and if return be made that the master or owner was not found, and no person appear and claim, the court shall make an order, to be published three times in the *Virginia* gazette, that the libel be taken for confessed, unless the party interested shall appear and shew cause to the contrary at a certain day to be limited in the order, not being less than three nor more than six weeks after the making thereof; and the said order being to published, if there be no such appearance before expiration of the time limited, the libel shall be taken for confessed accordingly, caution being given to secure the effects so that they may be subject to the future order of the court; and the sentence given thereupon shall be published in manner aforesaid; and if the master, owner, or other person interested at any time within one year after such last mentioned publication, or that being omitted within seven years after sentence, by petition desire that the cause be reheard, and give security for payment of such costs as may be award-ed against him, the court shall admit such party to make his defence or claim, in the same manner as if he had appeared at the return of the citation and give such sentence as they think just and agreeable with the laws prescribed for the rules of their decisions. Commissions for taking the examinations of *Examinations of witnesses when al-lowed as evidence.* witnesses may be awarded, and such examinations may be read in like cases as they may be in an action at common law. In a case where both parties are citizens of the commonwealth, every matter of fact affirmed by the one and denied by the other, shall be stated as a formal issue and tried by the same court by a jury in like manner as such issue ought to be tried in an action at common law. The court may at any time after, but not before an interlocutory sentence, if they see good cause, require a person pretending a claim to any vessel or goods mentioned in the libel to give security for the costs which may be occasion-ed by discussion of the claim, and may refuse to admit him until such security be given, and may award any party to pay costs when they judge it reasonable, unless he be the master or owner appearing and making a defence or a claim at the return of a citation; and the like execution for such costs may issue, and there shall be like proceedings thereupon as for costs recovered by judgment in an action of common law, otherwise than that the execution shall bear teste the day of emanation, and may be made return-able to any day not less than one month thereafter. In case of a capture from an enemy, if there be a *Appeals from their sentences, to whom to be made.* condemnation, and neither of the United States in general, nor the commonwealth in particular be in-terested therein, the court shall order the sales to be made, and accounts thereof to be returned by the libellant or his agent, if it be his desire. A party thinking himself aggrieved may appeal from the final sentence of the court, to such court and in such manner as is or shall be appointed by Congress; except in cases between the citizens of this commonwealth; which shall be to the Court of Appeals, giving bond with surety, in the latter to prosecute the appeal and perform the sentence, if it be affirmed. If the seizure of any vessel has been or hereafter shall be made by an officer of this commonwealth, and a prosecution instituted thereon, in which the respondent or respondents shall have prevailed or hereafter may prevail, one moiety of the costs of such prosecution after having been audited by the Auditors of public accounts, shall be paid by the Treasurer, provided the court have certified or shall certify that there was probable cause for such seizure. The Judges of the present Court of Admiralty, to wit: *Benjamin Waller, Richard Cary,* and *William Roscow Wilson Curle,* Esquires, are hereby confirmed in their office, and shall take precedence as they are here named.

A. D. 1779.

C H A P. XXVII.

An act to sever certain lots from the town of Dumfries, *held by* William Grayson, *Gentleman.*

Private.

C H A P. XXVIII.

An act to authorize certain trustees to pay to William Todd, *Gentleman, the money arising from the sale of lands, and for other purposes.*

Private.

C H A P. XXIX.

An act for paying the wages of the members of this present session of Assembly.

Executed.

C H A P. XXX.

An act for continuing an act entitled An act to empower the Governor and Council to lay an embargo for a limited time.

Expired.

C H A P. XXXI.

An act for continuing an act entitled An act for giving certain powers to the Governor and Council.

Expired.

C H A P. XXXII.

An act for continuing an act entitled An act to empower the Governor and Council to superintend and regulate the public jail.

Expired.

C H A P. XXXIII.

An act for continuing an act entitled An act to enable the Governor and Council to supply the armies and navies of the United States, and of their allies, with grain and flour.

Executed.

C H A P. XXXIV.

An act to increase the salaries of the clerks to the Auditors of public accounts.

Repealed.

C H A P. XXXV.

An act to empower the Justices of Stafford *county to fix on a proper place for erecting their court-house.*

Private.

C H A P. XXXVI.

An act for giving a further time to the purchasers of lots in the town of Bath *to build thereon.*

Private.

C H A P. XXXVII.

An act for disposing of the glebe of Russell *parish, and for other purposes.*

Private.

C H A P. XXXVIII.

An act to empower the Justices of Nansemond *county to hold courts at such place as they shall appoint, and for other purposes.*

Private

C H A P. XXXIX.

An act for further suspending the payment of the salaries heretofore given the clergy of the church of England.

Expired.

C H A P. XL.

An act to repeal an act entitled An act to prohibit the distillation of spirits from corn, wheat, rye, and other grain, for a limited time.

Executed.

C H A P. XLI.

An act for disposing of the glebe in the parish of Saint Anne, *in the county of* Albemarle, *and for other purposes.*

Private.

A. D. 1779.

CHAP. XLII.

An act to restrict the Delegates of this commonwealth in Congress from engaging in any trade, either foreign or domestic.

Oath to be taken by Delegates before one of the Privy Council:

I. BE it enacted by the General Assembly, that every Delegate hereafter to be chosen to represent this commonwealth in Congress, shall before he departs this state, take the following oath or affirmation, to be administered by any member of the Privy Council, or Justice of the Peace within this commonwealth, to wit: I A. B. *do solemnly swear (or affirm) that I am not directly or indirectly engaged in any merchandize, either foreign or domestic, except for commodities of my own growth or manufacture; and that I will not engage in any such merchandize so long as I continue a Delegate in Congress.* So help me God.

Before one of themselves.

II. AND be it farther enacted, that each of the Delegates heretofore chosen, and now representing this state in Congress, shall take the said oath or affirmation, which shall be administered to them by any one of the Delegates hereafter to be chosen, he having previously taken the said oath or affirmation.

CHAP. XLIII.

An act for adding part of the county of Augusta to the county of Monongalia, and for other purposes.

Private.

CHAP. XLIV.

An act for the manumission of a certain slave.

Private.

CHAP. XLV.

An act concerning Escheators.

One escheator for every county, except in the Northern Neck, shall execute his office in person;
how appointed and qualified;
shall sit where, and take inquests by whom, and in what manner.
Inquests whether to be returned.
Proceedings upon traverse monstrans de droit, or petition of right, or where no claim shall be made.

I. BE it enacted by the General Assembly, that there shall be one Escheator commissioned in every county by the Governor, on recommendation from the court of the same county, except the counties in the *Northern Neck*, who shall execute his office in proper person, and not by deputy, and shall before the court of the county be bound in the penalty of two thousand pounds, with security, to be approved by the same court, duly to perform the duties of his said office. The said Escheator shall sit in convenient and open places, and shall take his inquests of fit persons, who shall be returned and empannelled by the sheriff of the county, and shall suffer every person to give evidence openly in their presence to such inquest; and the said inquisition so taken, shall be by indentures, to be made between the said Escheator and them of the inquest, whereof the counterpart, sealed by the Escheator, shall remain in the possession of the first person that shall be sworn in the said jury, and by him shall be returned to the court of the same county, there to be recorded; and the other part, sealed by the jurors, shall by the Escheator be sent into the General Court within two months after the inquest taken; and if it be found for the commonwealth, and there be any man that will make claim to the lands, he shall there be heard without delay on a traverse to the office, *monstrans de droit*, or petition of right; and the said lands or tenements shall be committed to him if he shew good evidence of his right and title, to hold until the right shall be found and discussed for the commonwealth, or for the party finding sufficient surety to prosecute his suit with effect, and to render and pay to the commonwealth the yearly value of the lands, if the right be discussed for the commonwealth. No lands or tenements seized into the hands of the commonwealth, upon such inquests taken before Escheators, shall be in any wise granted, nor to farm let to any if it be not to him or them which claim as is aforesaid, till the same inquests and verdicts be fully returned into the General Court, nor within twelve months after the same return, but shall entirely and continually remain in the hands of the Escheators, who shall answer to the commonwealth the issues and profits yearly coming of the said lands and tenements, without doing waste or destruction. If no person within the twelve months before mentioned make claim to the lands or tenements so seized, or claim being so made, if it be found and discussed for the commonwealth, the clerk of the General Court shall, within two months thereafter, certify to the Escheator of the county wherein the lands lie, that no claim hath been made, or that being made, it hath been discussed for the commonwealth; which Escheator shall thereupon proceed to make sale of the land for the benefit of the commonwealth, to him who will give the most, after one month's public notice of the time and place of doing the same; and shall certify the purchaser and price to the Register of the Land Office, who on receiving a certificate that such price hath been paid into the treasury, shall have a grant executed to the purchaser in such manner as by law directed in the case of unappropriated lands. Where any person holds lands or tenements for term of years, or hath any rent, common office fee, or other profit, apprehender of any estate of freehold, or for years, or otherwise out of such lands or tenements, which shall not be found in such office or inquisition, such person shall hold and enjoy his lease, interest, rent, common office fee, and profit, apprehender in manner as if no such office or inquisition had been found, or as if such lease, interest, rent, common office, or profit, apprehender hath been found in such inquisition. Also if one person or more be found heir by office or inquisition in one county, and another person be found heir to the same person in another county; or if any person be untruly found lunatic, ideot, or dead; or where it shall be untruly found that any person attainted of treason or felony is seized of any lands, tenements, or hereditaments, at the time of such treason or felony committed, or any time after, whereunto any other person hath any just title or interest of any estate of freehold, the person grieved by such office or inquisition, may have his traverse or *monstrans de droit* to the same, without being driven to any petition of right, and proceed to trial therein, and have like remedy and restitution upon his title found or judged for him therein, as in other cases of traverse upon untrue inquisition found.

Particular interests in land seized shall be secured.

Remedy in cases of inconsistent or untrue inquests.

CHAP. XLVI.

An act giving salaries to certain officers of government.

Repealed.

CHAP. XLVII.

An act to displace the trustees of the town of Stanton, and for other purposes therein mentioned.

Private.

CHAP. XLVIII.

An act empowering certain persons to convey the land whereof Sarah the wife of John Rootes was seized, to the purchaser in fee simple.

Private.

C H A P. XLIX.

An act for continuing an act entitled an act for appointing Naval Officers, and ascertaining their fees.

Repealed.

C H A P. L.

An act for discontinuing the Navy Board.

Executed.

C H A P. LI.

An act for establishing several new ferries, and for other purposes.

BE it enacted by the General Assembly, that public ferries shall be constantly kept at the following places, and the rates for passing the same shall be as follows, that is to say: From the lands of James Wilkins in the county of Mecklenburg across Roanoke river to the lands of Robert Munford on the opposite shore, the price for a man two shilings, and for a horse the same; from the lands of Thomas Bryan Martin where John Nicholas lately lived, in the county of Frederick, across Shenandoah river to the lands of the honourable Thomas Lord Fairfax on the opposite shore, the price for a man two shillings, and for a horse the same; from the lands of Thomas Williamson in the county of Southampton, across Blackwater river to the lands of George Fearn, in the county of Isle of Wight, on the opposite shore, the price for a man six pence, and for a horse the same; from the lands of Elias Herring, in the county of Southampton, to the lands of Hancock Barret, in the county of Isle of Wight on the opposite shore, the price for a man six pence, and for a horse the same; from the lands of Thomas Peirce, adjoining the town of Smithfield, in the county of Isle of Wight, across Pagan creek to the lands of William Hodsden on the opposite shore, the price for a man one shilling, and for a horse the same; and for the transportation of wheel carriages, tobacco, cattle, and other beasts, at either of the ferries aforesaid, the ferry keepers may demand and take the following rates, that is to say: For every coach, chariot, or waggon, and the driver thereof, the same as for six horses; for every cart or four wheeled chaise or chair, the same as for two horses; for every hogshead of tobacco, as for one horse; for every head of neat cattle, as for one horse; for every sheep or goat one fifth part of the ferriage of one horse; and for every hog, one fourth part of the ferriage of one horse, according to the prices herein before settled at such ferries respectively. And if any ferry keeper shall presume to demand or receive from any person whatsoever, any greater rates than is hereby allowed, he, she, or they, for every such offence, shall forfeit and pay to the party grieved, treble the ferriages demanded, and five pounds; to be recovered before any Justice of the Peace where the offence shall be committed; and in the stern of every ferry-boat, shall be affixed by the keeper thereof, an attested copy of the rates of such ferriages as shall be established by the court of the county in which such ferry shall be, under the penalty of five pounds for every such neglect, to be recovered as aforesaid.

Public ferries established over Roanoke, Shenandoah, Blackwater, and Pagan creek, with fares for passing them.

C H A P. LII.

An act concerning Gold and Silver Coin.

Had its effect.

C H A P. LIII.

An act for regulating certain tobacco fees, and for other purposes.

Repealed.

C H A P. LIV.

An act for continuing an act entitled An act appointing the place for holding the High Court of Chancery and General Court, and empowering the said High Court of Chancery to appoint their own Serjeant at Arms.

Expired.

C H A P. LV.

An act declaring who shall be deemed citizens of this commonwealth.

Repealed.

At a GENERAL ASSEMBLY begun and held at the Capitol in the City of *Williamsburg*, on *Monday* the 4th day of *October*, in the Year of our Lord 1779.

C H A P. I.

An act for providing a great seal for the commonwealth, and directing the lesser seal of the commonwealth to be affixed to all grants for land, and to commissions, civil and military.

BE it enacted by the General Assembly, that the Governor, with the advice of the Council, be empowered, and he is hereby required, to provide, at the public charge, a great seal for the commonwealth, and to procure the same to be engraved, either in America or Europe, with the same device as was directed by the resolution of Convention, in the year one thousand seven hundred and seventy six; save only that the motto on the reverse be changed to the word PERSEVERANDO.

Great seal to be provided by Executive; device and motto of.

II. AND be it further enacted, that the seal which hath been already provided by virtue of the said resolution of Convention, be henceforward called the lesser seal of the commonwealth, and that the said lesser seal be affixed to all grants for lands, and to all commissions, civil and military, signed by the Governor: Provided nevertheless, that all such commissions heretofore signed and issued, without affixing the seal, shall be good and valid.

Lesser seal, to what acts affixed.

A.D. 1779.
Expired.

CHAP. II.

An act for giving further time to officers and soldiers to ascertain their claims to lands.

CHAP. III.

An act for discouraging extensive credits, and repealing the act prescribing the method of proving book debts

Preamble.
22 Geo. II. ch.
19, repealed.

I. WHEREAS the method of proving book debts, and the long and extensive credits formerly given by merchants and traders, hath been found by experience injurious to the people of this commonwealth: *Be it enacted by the General Assembly,* that from and after the first day of *May* next, the act entitled *An act prescribing the method of proving book debts,* shall be, and the same is hereby repealed; except only so far as relates to goods, wares, and merchandize, sold and delivered, or debts contracted before the said first day of *May.*

Time for com-
mencing certain ac-
tions limited.

II. AND *be it further enacted,* that all actions or suits founded upon account for goods, wares, and merchandize, sold and delivered, or for any articles charged in any store account, after the said first day of *May,* shall be commenced and sued within six months next, after the cause of such action or suit, or the delivery of such goods, wares and merchandize, and not after; except that in case of the death of the creditors or debtors, before the expiration of the said term of six months, the further time of twelve months from the death of such creditor or debtor, shall be allowed for the commencement of any such action or suit. And to prevent imposition or deception herein, the respective time or date of the delivery of the several articles charged in any such account, or of any receipt taken for the delivery of them, shall be particularly specified. And if any merchant or trader shall wilfully post-date, any article or articles in such account, or the receipt taken for the delivery of them, he shall forfeit and pay tenfold the amount of the article or articles, or of the receipt taken for the delivery of them, so post-dated, to be recovered with costs in any court of record, by petition where the penalty incurred shall be under five pounds, or amounts to that sum only, and by action of debt or information, where the penalty shall be more than five pounds, to the informer, where the informer prosecutes, or to the commonwealth, where the prosecution shall be first instituted on the public behalf. And to prevent any doubt in the construction hereof, it is hereby declared, that the before mentioned limitation of six months, shall take place and be computed from the respective dates or times of delivery of the several articles entered or charged in any such account, and that all such articles as shall have been of more than six months standing when the action or suit was commenced, shall be disallowed and rejected, and verdict shall be given or judgment rendered for no more than the amount of such articles as appear to have been actually charged or delivered, within six months next before the commencement of the suit, as aforesaid.

Courts and juries
ex officio to take
notice of the act.

III. AND *be it further enacted,* that every court and jury, by or before whom, any such action or suit shall be tried, shall, and they are hereby required, *ex officio,* to take notice of this act, and determine accordingly, although the defendant shall not have pleaded it, in the same manner as if the same had been specially pleaded; any law, custom, or usage to the contrary notwithstanding.

CHAP. IV.

Private.

An act for establishing the town of Boonsborough, *in the county of* Kentucky.

CHAP. V.

See Nov. 1781,
ch. 1.

An act for continuing the Court of Admiralty in the city of Williamsburg.

I. WHEREAS many inconveniences may attend the removal of the Court of Admiralty at a distance from the sea: *Be it enacted by the General Assembly,* that the said Court of Admiralty shall continue to sit so often as there shall be occasion, at the capitol, in *Williamsburg,* unless the same shall at any time be lawfully adjourned, until the General Assembly shall hereafter otherwise direct and appoint; any thing in the act of General Assembly, entitled *An act for the removal of the seat of government,* to the contrary notwithstanding.

CHAP. VI.

Omitted because sup-
posed to be repealed,
by May 1780, ch. 5.

An act to explain and amend two several acts of the last session of General Assembly for fixing the allowance of the members thereof.

CHAP. VII.

Private.

An act for granting warrants to Charles Simms, *Gentleman, to survey certain lands.*

CHAP. VIII.

Expired.

An act for further continuing an act entitled An act to empower the Governor and Council to lay an embargo for a limited time.

CHAP. IX.

Had its effect.

An act for giving a bounty of lands to the chaplains, surgeons, and surgeon's mates of regiments or brigades raised by this state, and upon continental establishment.

CHAP. X.

Expired.

An act for further continuing an act entitled An act for giving certain powers to the Governor and Council.

CHAP. XI.

An act for further continuing an act entitled An act to enable the Governor and Council to supply the armies and navies of the United States, and of their allies, with grain and flour.

Expired.

CHAP. XII.

An act for marking and opening a road over the Cumberland mountains into the county of Kentucky.

Private.

CHAP. XIII.

An act to amend an act entitled An act for regulating ordinaries and restraint of tippling-houses.

See Geo. II. ch.

I. WHEREAS the number of tippling houses is become a public nusance, encouraging idleness, drunkenness, and all manner of vice and immorality, and the laws heretofore made have proved insufficient to restrain so growing and dangerous an evil: *Be it therefore enacted by the General assembly,* that every person keeping a tippling house, or retailing liquors, contrary to the act entitled *An act for regulating ordinaries and restraint of tippling-houses,* shall over and above the penalties inflicted by the said act, forfeit and pay the sum of fifty pounds for each and every offence, to be recovered with costs by action of debt or information in any court of record; one half to the informer, and the other half to the commonwealth, or the whole to the commonwealth, where prosecution shall be first instituted on the public behalf alone; and shall moreover be subject to the proceedings and punishment herein after directed.

Preamble.

Further penalty for keeping ordinary contrary to law.

II. EVERY person having been convicted of keeping a tippling house, or retailing liquors as aforesaid, who shall afterwards be guilty of the same offence, and be thereof again convicted, shall by the court before whom such conviction shall be had, be committed to prison, there to remain for, and during the term of six months, without bail or mainprize. The presiding Justice present shall give this and the before recited act, in special charge to the grand jury of the county at every grand jury court; and whenever any prosecution or suit shall be instituted thereupon, the court before whom the same shall be depending, shall proceed to speedy trial thereof, out of course and without delay. And every Justice of the Peace is hereby required and strictly enjoined to cause this and the before recited act to be put into due execution within his county; and if any Justice, either from information, his own knowledge, or other just cause, shall suspect any person of keeping a tippling house, or retailing liquors as aforesaid, he is hereby empowered and required to summon such person to appear before him, together with such witnesses as he may judge necessary, and upon the person's appearing, or failing to appear, if the justice, upon examining the witnesses on oath shall find sufficient cause, he may, and is hereby required to direct the Attorney for the commonwealth in such county to institute a prosecution against such person on the public behalf, which such Attorney is hereby required to institute accordingly. And such Justice may also cause the person so suspected, to give bond, with two sufficient securities, for his or her good behaviour for the term of one year, the principal in the sum of fifty pounds, and the securities in the sum of twenty five pounds each; and upon failing to give such bond and security within three days after being thereunto required, such person may be committed to the jail of the county, there to remain, until he or she shall give bond and security accordingly; and if such person shall afterwards, during the said term, keep a tippling house, or retail liquors as aforesaid, the same shall be, and is hereby declared a breach of the good behaviour, and of the condition of such bond.

Offenders twice convicted, may be committed; concerning them, grand juries to be charged; against them, prosecutions to be tried speedily; and may be ordered by Justices;

may be bound to the behaviour, or committed.

III. PROVIDED always, that nothing in this, or the before recited act contained, shall extend, or be construed to prohibit any person or persons from retailing such liquors as shall actually have been made from the produce of such person's own estate, or brewed or distilled by him, her, or them, or those in his, her, or their employ; so as such liquors be not drank, or intended to be drank at the house or plantation where the same shall be sold; but where any dispute shall arise concerning the making such liquors, the burthen of proof shall be on the defendant.

Proviso in favour of brewers and distillers.

IV. AND whereas by the before recited act, the courts of the respective counties are vested with the power of settling the rates and prices to be paid at ordinaries for liquors, diet, lodging, provender, stablage, fodder, and pasturage, only at their court in the month of *March;* therefore, *Be it further enacted,* that each county court shall have full power to set the rates and prices to be paid at all ordinaries within their respective counties, for liquors, diet, lodging, provender, stablage, fodder, and pasturage, as well in any other month as in the month of *March,* and may increase or lessen the rates as often as they shall see cause, but shall not fail to fix the rates at least twice in a year, under penalty of one hundred pounds on every member of such court so failing. And every ordinary keeper shall, within one month after the rates so set, obtain of the county court clerk, a fair table of such rates, which shall be openly set up in the public entertaining room of every ordinary, and there kept until the rates shall be again set by the court, and then a copy thereof shall be again so obtained and kept, from time to time, under penalty of fifty pounds on every ordinary keeper failing so to do; and if any ordinary keeper shall demand and take any greater price for any drink, diet, lodging, provender, stablage, fodder, or pasturage, than by such rates shall be allowed, he or she so offending, shall forfeit and pay one hundred pounds for every such offence; which penalty, as well as the penalty of fifty pounds for failing to set up the table of rates as above directed, and that on the members of a court failing to fix the rates, shall be recoverable by action of debt or information, by any person that shall sue for the same, in any court of record within this commonwealth.

Liquors, &c. may be rated twice yearly.

Tables of them to be set up in ordinaries;

penalty for omitting this, or exceeding the rates.

V. AND be it further enacted, that so much of an act entitled *An act for regulating ordinaries and restraint of tippling houses,* as is contrary to this act, is hereby repealed; and this act shall commence and be in force, from and after the last day of *February* next.

CHAP. XIV.

An act to empower the Treasurer to receive certain certificates.

I. WHEREAS it hath been represented to this present General Assembly, that many of the inhabitants of this state are possessed of certificates, payable on the first day of *March* next, given in exchange for the emissions of *May* the twentieth, one thousand seven hundred and seventy seven, and *April* the eleventh, one thousand seven hundred and seventy eight, which were taken out of circulation by a resolution of Congress; and that many of the holders of such certificates are en-

Preamble.

Certain certificates receivable in payment for treasury land warrants.

C c

A. D. 1779.

titled to the preemption of unappropriated lands, and others incline to purchase lands, which they cannot, unless such certificates are received in payment at the treasury: *Be it therefore enacted*, that the Treasurer shall, and he is hereby directed to receive from all persons inhabitants of this state, such of the said certificates as have been issued therein, and shall be offered in payment for treasury warrants for waste or unappropriated lands.

Loan office certificates, with interest, receivable for waste lands.

II. *AND be it further enacted*, that from and after the first day of *March* next, the Treasurer be also directed to receive the loan office certificates of this state, and to allow the interest due thereon to the day of receiving the same, for treasury warrants for any waste or unappropriated lands within this commonwealth.

C H A P. XV.

Expired.

An act for laying an embargo on salt, and for other purposes.

C H A P. XVI.

Supposed to be repealed.

An act to encourage the importation of salt.

C H A P. XVII.

An act for amending an act entitled An act for appointing the place for holding the High Court of Chancery and. General Court, and empowering the said High Court of Chancery to appoint their own Serjeant at Arms.

Preamble.

I. WHEREAS an act, entitled *An act appointing the place for holding the High Court of Chancery and General Court, and empowering the said High Court of Chancery to appoint their own Serjeant at Arms*, was continued by an act of the last session of Assembly for and during the term of one year, and from thence to the end of the next session of Assembly.

Courts to be held at Richmond.

II. AND whereas so much of the said act as fixes the place for holding the said courts, is contradictory to the act for the removal of the seat of government: *Be it therefore enacted*, that so much of the said act as directs the place for holding the said Courts of Chancery and General Court, shall be and the same is hereby repealed; and that the first meeting of the Court of Appeals, High Court of Chancery, and General Court, in the year one thousand seven hundred and eighty, shall be at the town of *Richmond*, in the county of *Henrico*, at the apartments to be provided for that purpose. And any act within the purview of this act, shall be and the same is hereby repealed.

C H A P. XVIII.

An act to amend the act entitled An act concerning escheats and forfeitures from British subjects.

Preamble.

I. WHEREAS some doubts have arisen respecting the construction of the act of Assembly entitled *An act concerning escheats and forfeitures from British subjects*, by which unnecessary delays may be occasioned, and the purposes of the said recited act altogether defeated: *It is hereby declared and enacted by the General Assembly*, that an office found for the commonwealth, and returned to the General Court, shall remain there but thirty days, to be computed from the day of the return for the claim of any one. Where a traverse hath been filed by a *British* subject, or other person for him, such traverse shall be withdrawn, and any *British* subject, or other person on his behalf, shall be heard before the General Court, by a *monstrans de droit*, and any person, other than a *British* subject, on a traverse to the office or *monstrans de droit*. Where a *monstrans de droit* hath been filed by or in behalf of any *British* subject, the court shall direct an issue to be made up without delay, to try whether such claimant be a *British* subject within the meaning of the said recited act. Where a *monstrans de droit* hath been filed in the name of any person for, and in behalf of a *British* subject, or where a traverse to the office, or *monstrans de droit*, by any person other than a *British* subject, pretending a right to the estate, before replication made for the commonwealth, the party shall, in the first case, shew to the court probable reason why such *British* subject is not within the said recited act; and in the latter case give evidence of some title in him or her to the estate, or failing so to do, such traverse or *monstrans de droit*, shall be quashed. No exception for that the proceedings of escheat and forfeiture were not instituted by the Governor and Council, or by the Commissioners of the tax, aided by their assessors within their several counties, or for want of form in the inquisition, shall at any time be admitted, and the trial of every issue shall be in the session at which it is made up, on which the *onus probandi* shall lie on the person making claim to the estate. Where an estate is held by a citizen or citizens of this commonwealth, and a *British* subject or subjects, as tenants in common, or joint tenants, the proportion to the whole estate of the interest of such citizen therein, shall be ascertained by the jury summoned to find the inquisition, who shall find an office as to the whole of the estate; and if it be for the commonwealth, such citizen or citizens may retain his or their interest in the estate, and only the interest of such *British* subject or subjects therein, be sold, or the whole of the estate sold, and the value of his or their interest paid to such citizen or citizens, at his or their option, to be made before the General Court.

Mode and rules of proceeding on traverse of office, and monstrans de droit.

II. *AND be it further enacted*, that the General Court, during their session in the month of *December* in the present year one thousand seven hundred and seventy nine, shall determine all matters brought before the General Court at any time by the operation of the said recited act: *Provided*, that they may, on good cause shewn, delay the discussion of the right in any case to the next term, and no longer. Where the certificate of the clerk of the General Court, that no claim hath been made, or that being made, it hath been discussed for the commonwealth, shall come to the Escheator, or in the *Northern Neck* to the sheriff of the county where the estate lies, he shall proceed to sell the estate, and shall retain the same compensation, and be subject to the same penalties and legal proceedings as if such sale had been within the time limited by the said recited act. All actual and *bona fide* sales made by *British* subjects of their estates by deed duly executed and recorded, before the passing of the said recited act, shall be, and they are hereby confirmed. All sales made by collusion of the estates real or personal which come within the intent and meaning of this act, and according thereto, are subject to forfeiture under the said recited act, shall be, and the same are hereby declared to be void; and for discovery of any such collusive sales, it shall and may be lawful for the Escheator or sheriff, as the case may be, at the time of taking his inquest, to examine on oath, the party claiming such estate, and the General Court afterwards, when it comes before them, shall have the same power.

Collusive sales declared void; how to be detected.

III. *AND be it further enacted*, that whenever the mortgagees of any estate shall be found to come within the purview of this act, as *British* subjects, and the mortgaged premises are included within the

Mortgagees of, and those who claim

A.D. 1779.

inquifition; or where any citizen or citizens of this ftate may have an equitable intereft in any eftate as to which an inquifition hath been found for the commonwealth, any one Judge of the High Court of Chancery may award an injunction to ftay the fale of fuch eftate, unlefs the contract fhall have been made fince the paffing of the before recited act, of which the Efcheator or fheriff fhall take notice, until the faid equitable claim fhall be determined: And the faid Court of Chancery fhall, at their next feffion, proceed to hear and determine fuch equitable claims, in preference to all other matters whatfoever, and may either make the injunction perpetual, or take fuch other order therein as to them fhall feem juft; faving to the wives, widows, or children of *Britifh* fubjects, refiding within this ftate, the benefit of exception to them extended by the faid recited act; any thing in this act to the contrary notwithftanding.

equitable interefts in lands found to be efcheated, how relievable.

IV. AND whereas it hath been reprefented to this General Affembly, that many perfons natives of this ftate who are entitled to property therein, have at divers periods before and foon after the prefent war between *Great Britain* and *America*, removed themfelves to fome parts of the *Britifh* dominions, or have been induced to go thither by their hufbands, parents, or guardians.

V. BE it therefore enacted by the General Affembly, that all *femes coverts*, widows, and infants, natives of this ftate, now or lately refident in *Great Britain*, or other parts beyond the feas; all widows natives of this ftate, or widows of natives of this ftate, or infants the iffue of natives of this ftate, and all other perfons either natives of this ftate or who were actually married to natives of this ftate, and *bona fide* inhabitants thereof for at leaft one year at any time within four years next before the commencement of hoftilities, on the nineteenth day of *April* one thoufand feven hundred and feventy five, and who have left *North America* at any time before the paffing of the act *Declaring what fhall be treafon*, and have not been guilty of any overt act injurious to the rights or liberties of *America*; and alfo all perfons who left this ftate in their nonage, and have during their abfence arrived to full age within four years laft paft; and alfo the barons of *feme coverts* natives of this ftate as aforefaid, as far as relates to any property which they held in right of fuch *feme coverts*, fhall and they are hereby declared to be excepted out of the faid recited act; provided they have already returned, or fhall return to this commonwealth, and become citizens thereof in two years, to be computed in the cafe of infants from the time they arrive to the age of twenty one years, and in all other cafes from the end of this prefent feffion of Affembly: *Provided alfo,* that fuch claim be made before the General Court, and that where before claim made a fale of fuch eftate may have been, or notice fent by the clerk of the General Court that no claim hath been made, that then the purchafer fhall hold the eftate free and exonerated from fuch claim, but the owner may affert his or her right to the money arifing from the fale with the fame force he or fhe might have done to the thing itfelf. So much of the before recited act as comes within the purview of and is inconfiftent with this act, fhall be and is hereby repealed.

Who are excepted out of the former act; and how relievable.

C H A P. XIX.

An act to empower the Judges of the General Court to fuperintend and regulate the public jail.

See Oct. 1782, ch. 3.
Preamble.

I. WHEREAS the act of Affembly paffed in the year one thoufand feven hundred and feventy eight, entitled *An act to empower the Governor and Council to fuperintend and regulate the public jail*, has been found inconvenient by placing that bufinefs in the hands of the Governor and Council, and it is judged proper to put the direction of the faid jail into the hands of the Judges of the General Court:

II. BE it therefore enacted, that from and after the end of this feffion of Affembly, the Judges of the General Court fhall have the direction of the public jail; and they are hereby empowered and required, from time to time, to order and direct fuch allowance to be made for the maintenance of the prifoners confined there, and to fix what fhall be paid to the keeper thereof for his trouble, as the faid Judges, or a majority of them, fhall think reafonable; and the faid Judges are hereby empowered to certify fuch allowance, from time to time, to the Board of Auditors, who are hereby directed to debit the fame, and to give a warrant upon the Treafurer for the payment thereof.

General Court fhall have direction of the public jail; and make allowances to the keeper.

III. THIS act fhall continue and be in force until the firft day of *January* one thoufand feven hundred and eighty three, and no longer.

C H A P. XX.

An act to revive an act entitled An act to amend an act for preventing forestalling, regrating, engroffing, and public vendues.

Partly expired, and partly repealed as is fuppofed, by the duty lacus.

C H A P. XXI.

An act for more effectually fecuring to the officers and foldiers of the Virginia *line, the lands referved to them, for difcouraging prefent fettlements on the north weft fide of the* Ohio *river, and for punifhing perfons attempting to prevent the execution of Land Office warrants.*

Preamble.

WHEREAS all the lands lying between the *Green* river and the *Teniffee* river, from the *Alleghany* mountains to the *Ohio* river, except the tract granted unto *Richard Henderfon*, Efq; and company, have been referved for the officers and foldiers of the *Virginia* line, on continental and ftate eftablifhment, to give them choice of good lands, not only for the public bounty due to them for military fervice, but alfo in their private adventures as citizens; and no perfon was allowed by law to enter any of the faid lands, until they fhall have been firft fatisfied, and it is now reprefented to the General Affembly, that feveral perfons are, notwithftanding, fettling upon the lands fo referved; whereby the faid officers and foldiers may be in danger of lofing the preference and benefit intended for them by the Legiflature: Be it enacted by the General Affembly, that every perfon hereafter fettling upon the lands referved for the officers and foldiers as aforefaid, or who having already fettled thereon, fhall not remove from the faid lands within fix months next after the end of this prefent feffion of Affembly, fhall forfeit all his or her goods and chattels to the commonwealth; for the recovery of which, the Attorney for the ftate in the county of *Kentucky* for the time being, is hereby required immediately after the expiration of the faid term, to enter profecution by way of information in the court of the faid county on behalf of the commonwealth, and on judgment being obtained, immediately to iffue execution and proceed to the fale of fuch goods and chattels; and if the perfon or perfons fo profecuted fhall not remove from off the faid lands in three months after profecution fo entered, the faid Attorney fhall certify

Penalty on fettlers who fhall not evacuate the referved lands; and how recoverable.

A.D. 1779.

to the Governor the name or names of the person or persons so refusing to remove, who, with the advice of the Council may, and he is hereby required, to issue orders to the commanding officer of the said county, or to any other officer in the pay of this state, to remove such person or persons, or any others that may be settled thereon, from off the said lands, by force of arms, except such as were actually settled prior to the first day of *January*, one thousand seven hundred and seventy eight.

Proportions of officers, soldiers, and sailors ascertained.

II. AND whereas no law of this commonwealth hath yet ascertained the proportions or quantity of land to be granted, at the end of the present war, to the officers of the *Virginia* line on continental or state establishment, or to the officers of the *Virginia* navy, and doubts may arise respecting the particular quantity of land due to the soldiers and sailors from the different terms of their enlistments: *Be it enacted*, that the officers who shall have served in the *Virginia* line on continental establishment, or in the army or navy upon state establishment to the end of the present war, and the non commissioned officers, soldiers, and sailors, upon either of the said establishments, their heirs or legal representatives, shall respectively be entitled to and receive the proportion and quantities of land following, that is to say: Every Colonel, five thousand acres; every Lieutenant Colonel, four thousand five hundred acres, every Major, four thousand acres; every Captain, three thousand acres; every subaltern, two thousand acres; every non-commissioned officer who having enlisted for the war, shall have served to the end thereof, four hundred acres; and every soldier and sailor under the like circumstances, two hundred acres; every non-commissioned officer, who having enlisted for the term of three years, shall have served out the

Rights of descendents shall devolve on their heirs, &c

same, or to the end of the present war, two hundred acres; and every soldier and sailor under the like circumstances, one hundred acres; every officer of the navy the same quantity of land as an officer of equal rank in the army. And where any officer, soldier, or sailor, shall have fallen or died in the service, his heirs or legal representatives shall be entitled to and receive the same quantity of land as would have been due to such officer, soldier, or sailor respectively, had he been living.

Settlements on the north-west side of Ohio reprobated and prohibited, with an exception.

III. AND whereas, although no lands were allowed by law to be entered or warrants to be located on the north-west side of the *Ohio* river, until the farther order of the General Assembly, several persons are notwithstanding removing themselves to and making new settlements on the lands upon the north-west side of the said river, which will probably bring on an *Indian* war with some tribes still in amity with the United *American* States, and thereby involve the commonwealth in great expence and bring distress on the inhabitants of our western frontier: *Be it declared and enacted*, that no person so removing to and settling on the said lands on the north-west side of the *Ohio* river, shall be entitled to or allowed any right of preemption or other benefit whatever, from such settlement or occupancy; and the Governor is hereby desired to issue a proclamation, requiring all persons settled on the said lands immediately to remove therefrom, and forbidding others to settle in future, and moreover, with the advice of the Council, from time to time, to order such armed force as shall be thought necessary to remove from the said lands such person or persons as shall remain on or settle contrary to the said proclamation: *Provided*, that nothing herein contained shall be construed in any manner to injure or affect any *French, Canadian*, or other families, or persons heretofore actually settled in or about the villages near or adjacent to the posts reduced by the forces of this state.

Penalty for violent opposition to the execution of certain land warrants.

IV. AND whereas various reports have been industriously circulated by evil minded and designing men, of a combination to hinder by force and violence, the execution and survey of legal land warrants, whereby many people have been deterred from purchasing unappropriated lands upon the south-east side of the *Ohio* river within this commonwealth, and the receipt of considerable sums of money at the treasury thereby prevented to the injury of the public credit, and tending to destroy all confidence in the laws of the land: *Be it further enacted*, that all and every person or persons who shall by force or violence, or by threats of force or violence, attempt to hinder or prevent the execution of any warrant from the Register of the Land Office upon waste and unappropriated lands, or who shall by force or violence, or by threats of force or violence, attempt to hinder, restrain, or prevent any surveyor, chain carriers, markers, or other persons necessarily employed therein, from laying off, marking, or bounding any waste or unappropriated land according to law, by virtue of such warrant; and also all and every person or persons, aiding, abetting, or assisting in, or accessary to such force or violence, shall upon conviction thereof, forfeit and loose his, her, or their title to all ungranted land which he, she, or they, may or shall have acquired by settlement, preemption right, Land Office warrant, or any other means whatsoever, and shall moreover suffer twelve months imprisonment without bail or mainprize, and be rendered ineligible and incapable of being appointed to, or holding any office of trust or profit, civil or military, within this commonwealth, for the space of seven years. And all Justices of the Peace,

Civil officers to suppress force.

and other civil officers, are hereby strictly enjoined and required to suppress all such force or violence, and to cause the offenders to be apprehended and brought to justice; and all and every person or persons rescuing or attempting to rescue any such offender, shall be deemed and are hereby declared accessaries, and subject to the same penalties and punishment as the principal.

C H A P.   XXII.

An act for the better support of the Delegates to Congress, and for other purposes.

Preamble.

I. WHEREAS the act of the last session of Assembly, entitled *An act for the annual appointment of Delegates to Congress*, hath been found inconvenient, and not to answer the end proposed; and whereas the allowance heretofore given to the Delegates of this state attending in Congress, has been found insufficient for their support, and it is judged expedient, for the ease of the people, to lessen the number of our said Delegates, to the intent that their allowance may be increased without greatly adding to the annual expence: *Be it therefore enacted by the General Assembly*, that from

Members how many may represent the commonwealth and vote. Allowance.

and after the passing of this act, five shall be the number of persons to represent this commonwealth in General Congress, any one of which, or a majority of those present, if more than one, to give the vote of the commonwealth. The said Delegates for the time being, shall be allowed the expence for such part of their families as they may severally incline to keep with them, provisions for necessary servants and horses, not exceeding three servants and four horses for each; pay for house-rent and fuel, and also the further sum of twenty dollars to each of the said Delegates for every day they shall be in Congress, or attending a Committee of the States, and two dollars for every mile travelling to or returning from either, and their ferriages, to be paid them by the Treasurer.

Accounts, how discharged.

II. AND that the said Delegates may always keep in remembrance that œconomy is expected from them by their country, *Be it further enacted*, that a general account of all their disbursements for house-keeping as aforesaid, shall by the said Delegates be transmitted quarterly to the Auditors of public accounts, shall by them be passed, and an order given on the Treasurer, who is hereby directed to pay the same out of the public money in his hands.

III. AND whereas by the said recited act, *It is further enacted*, that if any person holding any office under the laws of this commonwealth, legislative, executive, or judiciary, be appointed a Delegate to Congress, such office thereby shall not be vacated, which may tend greatly to the prejudice of suitors in the supreme courts, and to the injury of the commonwealth, or innocent persons under prosecution, by the delay of justice in criminal cases, and otherwise to the great detriment of the public, by the absence from this state of those holding offices in the judiciary or executive departments: *Be it enacted*, that from and after the passing of this act, no person appointed a Delegate to Congress, shall exercise any office, judiciary or executive, under the laws of this commonwealth, during the term of acting under such appointment; and so much of the said recited act as comes within the meaning of this act is hereby repealed.

A.D. 1779.

Not capable of certain offices.

CHAP. XXIII.

An act to amend an act entitled An act concerning highways, mill dams, and bridges.

1. **B**E *it enacted*, that all male labouring persons, being tithable, shall when required, attend the surveyor and assist him in laying out, clearing, and repairing the roads in his precinct, except such who are masters of two or more tithable male labouring servants or slaves, who are hereby declared exempted from personal service or attendance; but every other tithable free male labouring person failing to attend with proper tools when required by the surveyor, or refusing to work when there, or not providing and sending another person to work in his room, for every such failure shall forfeit and pay three pounds, and the master or owner of tithable male labouring servants or slaves, shall be liable to the like penalty of three pounds for every such tithable he or she shall fail to send; and if any surveyor shall fail to send his own male labouring tithables, he shall forfeit and pay three pounds for every tithable he fails to send, which said penalties shall be to the informer, and recoverable with costs before a Justice of Peace of the county where such offence shall be committed. If any surveyor shall fail to perform his duty as required by the act of Assembly, entitled *An act concerning highways, mill-dams, and bridges*, he shall forfeit and pay ten pounds on the presentment of the grand jury of the county wherein he shall be surveyor, for the use of the said county, to be applied towards lessening the county levy, and where the information shall be made before a Justice, the same shall be to the informer, recoverable with costs before a Justice as aforesaid. So much of the said recited act as comes within the purview and meaning of this act, is hereby repealed.

Who shall attend surveyors of roads.

Penalties on delinquents.

II. *PROVIDED always*, that nothing herein contained shall be deemed or taken to compel those persons to attend and work on the highways, who are exempted by law.

Persons exempt by former act remain so.

CHAP. XXIV.

An act for raising a supply of money for the service of the United States.

Repealed.

CHAP. XXV.

An act for incorporating the town of Alexandria *in the county of* Fairfax, *and the town of* Winchester *in the county of* Frederick.

Private.

CHAP. XXVI.

An act to exempt the drivers of waggons in the continental service from militia duty.

Expired.

CHAP. XXVII.

An act for explaining and amending an act entitled An act for adjusting and settling the titles of claimers to unpatented lands, under the present and former governments, previous to the establishment of the commonwealth's Land Office.

1. **B**E *it enacted by the General Assembly*, that whereas doubts have arisen concerning the manner of proving rights for military service, under the proclamation of the King of *Great Britain*, in the year one thousand seven hundred and sixty three, whereby great frauds may be committed: *Be it declared and enacted*, that no person, his heirs or assigns, other than those who had obtained warrants under the former government, shall hereafter be admitted to any warrant for such military service, unless he, she, or they, produce to the Register of the Land Office, within eight months after the passing of this act, a proper certificate of proof made before some court of record within the commonwealth, by the oath of the party claiming, or other satisfactory evidence that such party was *bona fide* an inhabitant of this commonwealth, at the time of passing the said recited act, or that the person having performed such military service, was an officer or soldier in some regiment or corps (other than militia) actually raised in *Virginia* before the date of the said proclamation, and had continued to serve until the same was disbanded, had been discharged on account of wounds, or bodily infirmity, or had died in the service, distinguishing particularly in what regiment or corps such service had been performed, discharge granted, or death happened, and that the party had never before obtained a warrant or certificate for such military service: Provided, that nothing in this act shall be construed in any manner to affect, change, or alter the title of any person under a warrant heretofore issued.

Preamble.

Rights for military service how to be authenticated.

II. AND whereas the time limited in the before recited act to the commissioners for adjusting and settling the claims to unpatented lands within their respective districts may be too short for that purpose: *Be it further enacted*, that all the powers given to the said commissioners by the said recited act, shall be continued and remain in force, for and during the further term of two months, from and after the expiration of the time prescribed by the said act, and no longer. And where it shall appear to the said commissioners that any person, being an inhabitant of their respective districts, and entitled to the preemption of certain lands, in consideration of an actual settlement, is unable to advance the sum required for the payment of the state price, previous to the issuing of a warrant for surveying such land, the said commissioners shall certify the same to the Register of the Land Office, who shall thereupon issue such preemption warrant to the party entitled thereto, upon twelve months credit for the purchase money, at the state price, from the date of the warrant. The said Register shall keep an exact account of all such warrants issued upon credit, and shall not issue grants upon surveys made thereupon, until certifi-

Commissioners for adjusting claims to unpatented lands, their power prorogued, with directions to them and the register concerning warrants to be issued on credit.

A. D. 1779.

cates are produced to him from the Auditors of public accounts of the payment of the purchase money respectively due thereon into the treasury; and if the same shall not be paid within the said term, the warrant, survey, and title found thereon, shall be void, and thereafter any other person may obtain a warrant, entry, and grant, for such land, in the same manner as for any other waste and unappropriated land: *Provided,* that nothing herein contained shall be construed to extend to any person claiming right to the preemption of any land for having built an house or hut, or made any improvements thereon, other than an actual settlement as described in the said recited act. No certificate of right to land for actual settlement or of preemption right shall hereafter be granted by the said commissioners, unless the person entitled thereto hath taken the oath of fidelity to this commonwealth, or shall take such oath before the said commissioners, which they are hereby empowered and directed to tender and administer; except only in the particular case of the inhabitants of the territory in dispute between this commonwealth and that of *Pennsylvania,* who shall be entitled to certificates upon taking the oath of fidelity to the United States of *America.*

Upon what certificates and terms grants of lands surveyed by orders of Council may be obtained.

III. *AND be it further enacted,* that all persons, their heirs or assigns, claiming lands by virtue of any order of Council, upon any of the eastern waters, under actual surveys made by the surveyor of the county in which the land lay, may upon the plats and certificates of such surveyors being returned into the Land Office, together with the Auditors certificate of the Treasurer's receipt for the composition money of thirteen shillings and four pence *per* hundred acres due thereon, obtain grants for the same according to the rules and regulations of the said office; notwithstanding such surveys or claims have not been laid before the Court of Appeals. And all other claims for lands upon surveys made by a county surveyor duly qualified, under any order of Council, shall by the respective claimers be laid before the Court of Appeals, at their next sitting, which shall proceed thereupon in the manner directed by the before recited act. Any person claiming right to land surveyed for another before the establishment of the commonwealth's Land Office, may enter a caveat and proceed thereupon in the same manner as is directed by the act of Assembly for establishing the said office, and upon recovering judgment, shall be entitled to a grant upon the same terms, and under the same conditions, rules, and regulations, as are prescribed by the said act in the case of judgments upon other caveats, upon producing to the Register a certificate from the Auditors of the Treasurer's receipt for the composition money of thirteen shillings and four pence *per* hundred acres due thereon.

CHAP. XXVIII.

Repealed.

An act to repeal and amend part of an act entitled An act to amend an act entitled An act for reviving several public warehouses for the inspection of tobacco, and for other purposes.

CHAP. XXIX.

An act for establishing a fund to borrow money for the use of the United States, and for other purposes.

See may 1780, *chap.* 7.
Five eighths of a tax in tobacco appropriated as a fund for borrowing 5,000,000l. *upon interest.*

I. FOR establishing a fund whereon to borrow a sum of money for the use of the United States, and to give the lenders the fullest assurance of being paid the interest thereof annually, and for making provision for repaying the principal money so to be borrowed at the appointed time, *Be it enacted by the General Assembly,* that a tax of thirty pounds of inspected tobacco in transfer notes, shall be paid on or before the first day of *August* next, and at the same time in each of the next succeeding eleven years, by every tithable person in this commonwealth, except free white tithables between the age of fifteen and twenty one years, and those who shall have been discharged by the county courts from the payment of levies, and except also such slaves as have been or shall be exempted from taxation by the commissioners of the tax on account of old age or bodily infirmity. Five eighths of the nett produce of the said tax shall be appropriated as a fund, whereon the Treasurer of this commonwealth for the time being may,–and he is hereby empowered and required to borrow a sum of money not exceeding five millions of pounds, current money, from any person or persons willing to lend, in sums not less than one thousand pounds from any person, at an interest of five *per centum per annum.* The interest to grow due on all sums so borrowed shall be regularly paid to the lenders respectively, or to their order as hereafter limited, at the treasury annually as it shall become due, and the surplus remaining after all such interest shall be paid, arising from the said five eighths of this tax, the Treasurer may, and he is hereby empowered and required to pay to such of the said public creditors as may be willing to receive their principal, giving preference in such payments to each creditor as he or they may make application for the same in priority of time, until the surplusage shall be paid away in each of the said years.

Standard for adjusting value of principal and interest.

II. AND for fixing the nominal sum of money, which every such creditor shall receive as interest and principal agreeable to the directions of this act, so as to secure the creditors on the one hand from being losers by receiving less than the real value of the sum lent at the time of the loan, and to guard the state on the other hand from paying a greater sum either as interest or principal, than the real value of such interest at the time it shall become due, or the principal was worth at the time of the loan: *Be it further enacted,* that the rule and standard for fixing the value of all the money to be borrowed, and of all interest and principal to be thereafter paid in consequence of this act, shall be as followeth: For all monies to be borrowed upon this fund between the first day of *January* next, and the sixth day of the next General Court, one hundred pounds of inspected nett crop tobacco shall be held, deemed, and taken as the standard and true value of thirty pounds current money, and so in proportion for any greater or lesser sum which may be borrowed by that time, and for all money to be borrowed after that day upon this fund. And for fixing the value of all interest accruing on all the money to be borrowed, in consequence of this act, the following rules shall be observed. The Judges of the General Court, at some day during the first six days of their session in the month of *March* next, and at every succeeding session of that court during the continuance of this act, shall and they are hereby empowered and required to administer an oath to the grand jury attending every session of that court, well and truly to estimate the true market price of inspected crop tobacco, according to the best of their skill and judgment at the time, taking for their guide neither the greatest nor smallest, but the average market price, at the time of making the estimate, which estimate shall be entered upon record, from time to time, by the clerk of the said court, and every such estimate respectively, shall be held, deemed, and taken as the true and only standard and measure thereafter to fix as well the value of the money to be borrowed under this act, as of the interest accruing or principal paid between that and the next succeeding estimate. The Treasurer for the time being, shall make out and deliver to every lender of money upon this fund, one or more indented certificates, signed by him, and countersigned by some one of the Auditors' of public accounts, or of their clerks, to be appointed for this special purpose, in the left hand corner

Forms and marks of Treasurer's certificates; and mode of assigning them.

thereof, and entered in their office to the debit of the Treasurer, expressing the sum so borrowed, the rate of interest, payable annually therefor, and day of payment; and also the last estimate of money compared with tobacco agreeable to the directions of this act; and every such creditor shall be entitled to demand and receive so much money for interest, upon the money lent, as will purchase the same quantity of tobacco, at the time such interest shall become due, that the nominal sum then due for interest on the principal borrowed would have purchased at the time the money was lent, to be fixed by the certificate in the former, and by the estimate of the grand jury as aforesaid, for that period of time in which such interest shall become due in the latter instance. In the payment of all sums to any creditor for principal money borrowed, the same rule, standard, and only measure shall be observed between the state and the creditor as is above directed for the payment of interest. All certificates to be issued for money borrowed by virtue of this act, shall be made payable to the lender, his executors and administrators; but such lender, or his executors or administrators, may by writing under his, her, or their hand and seal, and attested by two Magistrates of this commonwealth, or of any other of the United States, or by any officer of public notoriety in any other country, assign and transfer any such certificate; and an assignment made agreeable to the directions of this act shall entitle every such assignee, his executors and administrators, and every subsequent assignee of any assignee, and the executors and administrators of every such assignee, to receive at the treasury the interest and principal money due on every such certificate, in the same manner, and at such time, as the lender would have been entitled to receive the same by virtue of this act.

III. EVERY person who shall counterfeit, alter or erase, any certificate to be issued by virtue of this act, or shall demand payment of any money on any such certificate, knowing the same to be counterfeited, altered, or erased, or shall be aiding, assisting, or abetting, in such forging or counterfeiting, altering, or erasing, shall be deemed and judged guilty of felony, and on being thereof legally convicted, shall suffer death without benefit of clergy. And that the lenders of money, upon the faith of this act, may have the fullest assurance of receiving the interest and principal of their respective debts on the terms of this act, and at the appointed times, *Be it further enacted*, and it is hereby declared, that the General Assembly will make good all deficiencies which may happen in this fund, by either increasing the present tax, or substituting some other in aid thereof, that the public faith hereby pledged may be preserved inviolate. The remaining three eighths of the amount of all the taxes to be collected by virtue of this act, shall be reserved for the purpose of purchasing military stores, clothing, and other necessaries for the use of the army and navy, as the Executive of this state may from time to time direct, but subject to the future direction and controul of the General Assembly. The clerk of the General Court, when any new estimate shall be made of tobacco agreeable to the directions of this act, shall cause an attested copy thereof to be published for two months successively, in each of the gazettes of this state, and the Treasurer moreover immediately after every *June* court, shall cause a copy of the last estimate so as aforesaid to be made, to be transmitted forthwith to every sheriff and other collector of the tax hereby imposed in this commonwealth. And for the better collection of the said taxes, *Be it further enacted*, that the sheriff or collector of every county and corporation in this state, at the court to be held for their respective counties or corporations in the month of *April* in each year during the continuance of this act, or at the next succeeding court, in case no court shall be held in that month, shall give bond with good security, to be approved by such court, in the sum of thirty thousand pounds, payable to the Governor for the time being, and his successors, for the use of the commonwealth, conditioned for the diligent and faithful collection and payment of this tax, to be levied, collected, accounted for, and settled with the commissioners of the tax, and paid into the treasury in the same manner, at the same time, and under the like forfeitures, as are appointed, prescribed, and inflicted, in the case of collecting the taxes upon assessments by one act of Assembly, entitled *An act for raising a supply of money for public exigencies*; and the sheriffs and other collectors shall be allowed a commission of three *per centum* upon all sums of money and quantities of tobacco by them to be collected by virtue of this act, and a credit for all real insolvencies, to be settled by the commissioners of the tax in each county and corporation respectively.

IV. AND for the ease and conveniency of the people in paying the said tax, *Be it further enacted*, that the sheriffs and other collectors of this tax, shall cause a copy of the estimate to be made by the grand jury as aforesaid, at every *June* court, to be set up at the doors of their respective court-houses, two several court days, in the months of *August* and *September*, and also at the door of every church, chapel, and meeting-house, in every such county and corporation, two several *Sunday's* in the said two months, during the continuance of this act; and all persons liable to this tax, may either pay the same in money at the price fixed by the grand jury in the preceding *June* court, or in tobacco agreeable to the directions of this act, and the law which shall be then in force for regulating the inspection of tobacco, deducting six *per centum* for such price for the difference between crop and transfer tobacco, where the payment shall be made in money. All persons neglecting or refusing to pay the tax hereby imposed agreeable to the directions of this act, may be proceeded against, and the sheriff or other collector may proceed against the said delinquent, and shall be entitled to the same commission in case of distress as is provided in case of failing to pay county and parish levies. And for preventing sheriffs and other collectors from withholding from the public the tobacco which shall actually be collected, *It is further enacted*, that the several collectors shall annually, during the continuance of this act, account and settle with the commissioners of the taxes upon oath, which the said commissioners are hereby empowered and required to administer, for all the tobacco and money severally and actually by them received in discharge of this tax; every such sheriff or collector previous to their making such settlement, shall cause all the transfer tobacco by them so collected, to be prized and cropped agreeable to the direction of the laws which may be at such time in force for regulating the inspection of tobacco, and the commissioners shall allow them a credit in their accounts of six *per centum* for shrinkage, prizing, and nails, and thirty pounds of tobacco for each cask; and where any balance of tobacco not sufficient to make a hogshead shall remain in the hands of any collector, such balance or fraction shall be accounted for by every such collector in his account for the succeeding year, or shall be by them respectively paid to the succeeding collectors; and the commissioners having allowed every collector credit for his commissions on collection for all sums paid or due to them, their clerk, and to the assessors for their respective services, and for all real insolvencies, shall together with their account of the other annual taxes, transmit a duplicate of every such account to the Auditors of public accounts, noting the numbers, weights, and marks, of all crop tobacco in such collections.

V. THE assessors of every hundred or district, shall in every year during the continuance of this act, at the time of making their assessment, demand an account upon oath or affirmation, which they are hereby empowered and required to administer, of all persons liable to this tax, an account of all his, her, or their tithables subject thereto, or which are then resident in his, her, or their family; and the assessors at the time of returning the accounts of their assessments, shall also return lists of the tithables so by them to be taken; and the commissioners of the taxes shall cause copies of the said lists of tithables

Counterfeiting certificates, punishable with death.

Deficiency, if any, to be made good, and how.

Appropriation of the other 3 eighths.

Estimates of tobacco to be published, and transmitted to collectors; and how they shall be appointed, and accountable.

The tax payable in money instead of tobacco, according to what estimate;

may be distrained for, if witheld.

Collectors shall settle their accounts with commissioners of the taxes; when and how.

Duty of Assessors.

A. D. 1779.

Remedy against delinquents.

to be delivered to the several sheriffs or collectors at the time of delivering them the accounts of the affessments, to enable them to collect the tax. Every person refusing to give in to the affessors, an account of his, her, or their tithables, as aforesaid, shall forfeit and pay treble the value of the tax upon every such tithable not given in, to be recovered by action of debt in any court of record, in the name of the commissioners of the taxes for such county or corporation. Every person knowingly taking a false oath, or making a false affirmation in the premises, shall be subject to the like pains and penalties as are inflicted in the case of wilful and corrupt perjury.

Application of the money borrowed. Continuance of the act.

VI. ALL the money to be borrowed upon this fund shall be applied to the payment of the money required by Congress from this state, to such persons only as shall be authorized by Congress to receive the same, and upon warrant from the Governor; and the accounts of the receipts and payments in consequence of this act, shall be kept distinct and separate from all other accounts whatsoever. This act shall continue and remain in force for and during the term of twelve years, and no longer.

Owners of certificates not to be of the grand jury for estimating tobacco.

VII. AND be it further enacted, that no person interested by having money in, or interest due upon the said fund, or possessing any certificate for money advanced on the said loan, shall at any time be capable of serving on any grand jury for estimating the price of tobacco; and for discovery thereof, the Judges of the General Court are hereby empowered and required to examine upon oath any person who shall be summoned, or called upon such grand jury, concerning his interest in the same.

Operation of the act, partly suspended.

VIII. PROVIDED, that the operation of so much of this act as relates to the time of the payment of the first year's tax, of thirty pounds of tobacco for every tithable, shall be, and the same is hereby declared to be suspended until the first day of *December*, in the year one thousand seven hundred and eighty, when the several sheriffs or collectors, having previously given bond and security, as herein before directed, shall proceed to collect, levy, and account for the said first year's tax, and pay the same into the treasury, on or before the first day of *March* next following, in the same manner, and under the same rules, regulations, and penalties, as are herein before prescribed.

C H A P. XXX.

Repealed.

An act for providing a further supply for the exigencies of government.

C H A P. XXXI.

Private.

An act to confirm certain sales and leases made by the trustees of the town of Alexandria, *and to enlarge the said town.*

C H A P. XXXII.

Private.

An act concerning a lead mine the property of John *and* Mead Anderson.

C H A P. XXXIII.

Had its effect.

An act concerning nonjurors.

C H A P. XXXIV.

Private.

An act to indemnify William Campbell, Walter Crockett, *and others, concerned in suppressing a late conspiracy.*

C H A P. XXXV.

An act for establishing several new ferries, and for other purposes.

New ferries over the Rappahannock *and* Kentucky *established; and the fares.*

I. WHEREAS it is represented to this present General Assembly, that public ferries at the places hereafter mentioned will be of great advantage to travellers and others: Be it therefore enacted, that public ferries be constantly kept at the following places, and the rates for passing the same shall be as follows, that is to say: From the land of *Edward West*, in the county of *Stafford*, across the north fork of *Rappahannock* river, to the land of *Simon Miller*, in the county of *Culpeper*, the price for a man one shilling, and for a horse the same. From the land of *Gawin Lawson*, in the county of *Stafford*, across *Rappahannock* river, to the land of *Fielding Lewis*, in the county of *Spotsylvania*, the price for a man one shilling and six pence, and for a horse the same. At the town of *Boonsborough*, in the county of *Kentucky*, across *Kentucky* river to the land on the opposite shore, the price for a man three shillings, and for a horse the same; the keeping of which last mentioned ferry and emoluments arising therefrom, are hereby given and granted to *Richard Callaway*, his heirs or assigns, so long as he or they shall well and faithfully keep the same according to the directions of this act. And for the transportation of wheel carriages, tobacco, cattle, and other beasts, at the places aforesaid, the ferry-keeper may demand and take the following rates, that is to say: For every coach, chariot, or waggon, and the driver thereof, the same as for six horses; for every cart, or four wheel chaise, and the driver thereof, the same as for four horses; for every two wheel chaise, or chair, the same as for two horses; for every hogshead of tobacco, as for one horse; for every head of neat cattle, as for one horse; for every sheep, goat, or lamb, one fifth part of the ferriage for one horse; and for every hog, one fourth part of the ferriage for one horse, and no more. And if any ferry-keeper shall presume to demand or receive, from any person or persons whatsoever, any greater rates than is hereby allowed for the carriage or ferriage of any thing whatsoever, he shall, for every such offence, forfeit and pay to the party grieved, the ferriages demanded or received, and ten shillings, to be recovered with costs before a Justice of Peace of the county where such offence shall be committed.

Privilege of foot passengers at the

II. AND be it further enacted, that so much of an act of Assembly passed in the year one thousand seven hundred and seventy six, as compels *James Bowie* the younger, his heirs or assigns, to set over the ferry from the public landing at the town of *Port Royal*, in the county of *Caroline*, acrofs *Rappahannock* river to the land of *Francis Conway*, all fuch foot paffengers as may incline to crofs without demanding or re- ceiving any ferriage for the fame, fhall be, and the fame is hereby repealed.

III. *AND be it further enacted*, that fo much of an act of Affembly paffed in the year one thoufand feven hundred and feventy eight, as eftablifhes a ferry from the land of *Abraham Shepherd*, in the county of *Berkeley*, over *Potowmack* river to the land of *Thomas Swearingen*, in the ftate of *Maryland*, fhall be, and the fame is hereby repealed.

C H A P. XXXVI.

An act to repeal fo much of the act for the fupport of the clergy, and for the regular collecting and paying the parifh levies, as relates to the payment of the falaries heretofore given to the clergy of the church of England.

I. **B**E it enacted by the General Affembly, that fo much of the act entitled *An act for the fupport of the cler- gy, and for the regular collecting and paying the parifh levies*, and of all and every other act or acts providing falaries for the Minifters, and authorifing the veftries to levy the fame, fhall be, and the fame is hereby repealed.

II. *PROVIDED neverthelefs*, that the veftries of the feveral parifhes, where the fame hath not been already done, may, and they are hereby authorized and required, at fuch time as they fhall appoint, to levy and affefs on all tithables within their refpective parifhes, all fuch falaries and arrears of falaries as were due to the Minifters or incumbents of their parifhes for fervices to the firft day of *January*, in the year one thoufand feven hundred and feventy feven; moreover to make fuch affefments on all titha- bles as will enable the faid veftries to comply with their legal engagements entered into before the fame day; and laftly, to continue fuch future provifion for the poor in their refpective parifhes as they have hitherto by law been accuftomed to make, and levy the fame in the manner heretofore directed by law, any thing in this act to the contrary, or feeming to the contrary, notwithftanding.

C H A P. XXXVII.

An act to amend an act entitled An act eftablifhing a Board of War.

C H A P. XXXVIII.

An act to prevent the mifapplication of the money collected for taxes.

I. **W**HEREAS great inconveniences have arifen to the public from the mifapplication of the taxes collected by the fheriffs in feveral counties of this ftate, fome of whom have applied the fame to private purpofes in fpeculative bargains for the emolument of themfelves or their friends, thereby contributing to raife the prices of the neceffaries of life, and to depreciate the paper currency in circulation, defeating the purpofes of taxation, and hazarding the ruin of public credit; and experi- ence hath proved that the laws heretofore made, are infufficient to prevent or reftrain fo growing and dangerous an evil: *Be it therefore enacted by the General Affembly*, that if any fheriff or collector fhall hereafter appropriate to his own ufe, or otherwife mifapply any public money which fhall be by him collected for taxes, he fhall forfeit and pay double the fum fo appropriated or mifapplied, to be recover- ed with cofts, on bill, plaint, or information, in any court of record within this commonwealth, one half to the informer, and the other half to the commonwealth; or the whole to the commonwealth if in- formation is made by a public officer; and every perfon receiving fuch public money, knowing it to be fuch, and applying it to private purpofes, fhall in like manner forfeit double the fum fo received, to be recovered as before directed. And for the more effectually preventing fuch pernicious practices in fu- ture, the commiffioners of the taxes in their refpective counties, or a majority of them, fhall, upon in- formation or fufpicion of any fuch mifapplication, call upon the fheriff or collector to make up an ac- count of the money which he fhall have collected, upon oath, and to demand of him that the money collected fhall be produced and compared with the accounts fo made up; and if any fheriff or collector of taxes fhall fail to make up his accounts, or to produce to the commiffioners when required, the taxes collected as aforefaid, within the fpace of one week after fuch demand, he fhall forfeit and pay the fum of one hundred pounds for every week thereafter, until he fhall comply with the demand of the faid commiffioners, who fhall give information, either to the Attorney General, or to the Attorney for the commonwealth in the county, either of whom as the cafe may be, fhall lodge a bill, plaint, or infor- mation, againft fuch fheriff or collector, at the next court having cognizance of the faid offence, which he fhall renew fo often as the faid fheriff or collector fhall continue his faid offence: And no commiffioner of the tax fhall hereafter be admitted as fecurity for any fheriff or collector, nor fhall any perfon who is or fhall be fecurity for a fheriff be eligible as a commiffioner of the tax. Whenever a bill, plaint, or information, fhall be lodged in any county court, under this act, the faid court fhall compel the defendant to plead immediately to iffue, which iffue they fhall proceed to try at the very next court thereafter, before any other matter or thing whatfoever: And if the faid bill, plaint, or information, is made in the General Court, they fhall caufe the iffue to be made up and tried at the fame time. And fhould any fheriff or collector, after fuch procefs hath been legally ferved on him, fail to appear and plead at the next court or term as the cafe may be, fuch court fhall order the clerk to make an iffue for him, and proceed to trial in like manner as herein above directed. And for the more effectually fecuring the payment of all taxes now due, or which fhall hereafter be collected, and not accounted for and paid as the law directs, the Auditors of public accounts fhall have power to move for judgments againft all fheriffs and collectors of taxes, without any farther notice than this act, on the firft days of the *June* and *December* General Courts, and on the firft *Saturday* in the *March* and *October* General Courts; and the faid courts fhall take cognizance thereof at all or any of the faid feffions, and give judgments accordingly, or for good caufe may poftpone the proceedings upon any fuch motion till a future day; and any judgment given on fuch motion fhall carry twenty *per centum* intereft, until the fame fhall be levied or difcharged.

Failing to make up an account and produce the money collected when re- quired by the Com- miffioners, incur a weekly forfeiture; how recoverable.

Commiffioners fhall not be fureties for collectors.

Proceedings in profecutions under this act.

CHAP. XXXIX.

An act for confirming the titles of purchasers of escheated and forfeited estates.

Preamble.
Titles to estates found to have been escheated or forfeited, to which a claim either had not been made, or had been discussed for the commonwealth, confirmed to the purchasers; saving the rights of all persons to the purchase money.

I. WHEREAS some sales have been already made, and many others will soon be made under the *Act concerning escheats and forfeitures from British subjects,* upon certificates from the clerk of the General Court, that no claim had been filed in due time; and it hath been apprehended that should the inquisitions prove defective in substance, or the particular requisitions of the law not to be complied with, the former owners may at a future day reclaim their estates, and expel the purchasers from the possession; and such apprehensions and doubts may deter many persons from purchasing, and cause such estates to sell at an under value: *Be it therefore enacted by the General Assembly,* that in every case where any estate shall have been found to belong to a *British* subject, in which the clerk of the General Court hath certified, or shall certify, that no claim hath been filed to any such estate; or where any claim shall have been filed and discussed for the commonwealth, the title of the purchaser or purchasers thereto, shall be, and is hereby confirmed to him, her, or them, and his, her, or their heirs and assigns for ever, upon due payment of the purchase money; notwithstanding any defect in the inquisition, or that the requisitions of the above recited act may not have been complied with; saving the right of all persons to assert their claim to the money arising from such sales, as by the said act, and one other act passed at the present session of Assembly entitled *An act to amend the act concerning escheats and forfeitures from British subjects* is directed.

CHAP. XL.

An act for the protection and encouragement of the commerce of nations acknowledging the independence of the United States of America.

Consuls from such states as acknowledge the independence of America, how received; deemed subjects or citizens of the states by whom appointed; guilty of crimes against this state, shall be remanded to their sovereigns for punishment;

I. FOR preserving friendship and harmony with those nations who have, or shall hereafter acknowledge the independence of the United States of *America;* speedily determining disputes wherein their subjects or citizens are parties; protecting and encouraging their commerce within this commonwealth; *Be it enacted by the General Assembly,* that it shall be lawful for the Governor, with the advice of the Council of State, to receive and admit, from time to time, a consul or consuls appointed by any such state to be resident within this commonwealth; such consul if he were not a citizen of this commonwealth at the time of receiving his appointment, shall be deemed a subject or citizen of the state from which he was appointed, and shall be exempted from all personal services required by the laws of this commonwealth from its own citizens; and if he shall do any act which by the laws of this commonwealth would subject him to criminal prosecution, it shall be lawful for the Governor, with the advice of the Council of State, in their discretion, either before the prosecution instituted, or in any stage thereof, to remand such consul to his own sovereign or state for punishment, and for that purpose to command him to be delivered by any civil officer in whose custody he may be. It shall be lawful for the said consul to take cognizance of all differences, controversies, and litigations arising between subjects or citizens of his own state only, and finally to determine and compose them according to such rules or laws as he shall

power; in execution thereof, how to be aided.

think fit, and such determinations to carry into execution. And where he shall require aid for executing the same, it shall be lawful for the Governor, with the advice of the Council of State, using their discretion therein, to order any sheriff within his own county, or any military officer whatsoever, to execute or to aid and assist in executing any such determination; provided the same does not extend to life or limb of the offender. Where any sailor, seaman, or marine belonging to any vessel of such state within this commonwealth shall desert, or be found wandering from his vessel, it shall be lawful for the master of such vessel to reclaim such sailor, seaman or marine, notwithstanding such sailor, seaman, or marine may in the meantime have been naturalized in this commonwealth. And any Justice of the Peace to whom the master shall apply, shall grant his warrant for taking and conveying such sailor, seaman, or marine from constable to constable to the said vessel, or on application from the Consul, the Governor, with the advice of the Council of State, may issue such orders to any sheriff, constable, or military officer, who shall yield due obedience thereto. *And be it farther enacted,* that any suit commenced in the High

Mode of proceeding in suits, wherein 'foreigners' are parties.

Court of Chancery, or General Court, by or against any subject or citizen of such state, shall be heard or tried in the term to which the process shall be returned regularly executed or so soon afterwards as may be, and to this end, subsequent process to compel appearance may be returnable to any day of a term, and rules to bring the matter in dispute to speedy issue may be given to expire at any shorter time than what is prescribed in ordinary cases. If such suit be commenced in the court of a county, city, or borough, it may, without any other reason, on the motion or petition of either party, be removed by writ of *certiorari,* and the hearing or trial thereof shall be accelerated by like means as if it had originated in the court to which it shall be removed. And the Court of Appeals, High Court of Chancery, or General Court, shall determine every such suit brought before them, by writ of error or appeal, with all the expedition which the necessary forms of their proceedings will allow.

CHAP. XLI.

An act for continuing an act entitled An act to revive and amend an act entitled An act to make provision for the support and maintenance of ideots, lunatics, and persons of unsound minds.

The former act continued.

I. WHEREAS the act of Assembly, passed in the year one thousand seven hundred and seventy eight, entitled *An act to revive and amend an act entitled An act to make provision for the support and maintenance of ideots, lunatics, and persons of unsound minds,* will expire at the end of this present session of Assembly, and it is necessary the same should be continued: *Be it therefore enacted by the General Assembly,* that the act entitled *An act to revive and amend an act entitled An act to make provision for the support and maintenance of ideots, lunatics, and persons of unsound minds,* shall continue and be in force, from and after the expiration thereof, for and during the term of one year, and from thence to the end of the next session of Assembly.

Further allowance for support of patients.

II. AND be it further enacted, that the further sum of fifty pounds shall be allowed and paid for the maintenance and support of each person in the public hospital.

CHAP. XLII.

An act to suppress excessive gaming.

A. D. 1779.

BE it enacted by the General Assembly, that every promise, agreement, note, bill, bond, or other contract, to pay, deliver, or secure money or other thing won, or obtained by playing at cards, dice, tables, tennis, bowles, or other games, or by betting or laying on the hands or sides of any person who shall play at such games, or won or obtained by betting or laying on any horse-race, or cock-fighting, or at any other sport or pastime, or on any wager whatsoever, or to repay or secure money or other thing lent or advanced for that purpose, or lent or advanced at the time of such gaming, sporting, or wager, to a person then actually playing, betting, laying, or adventuring, shall be void. Any conveyance or lease of lands, tenements or hereditaments, sold, demised, or mortgaged, and any sale, mortgage, or other transfer of slaves, or other personal estate, to any person, or for his use, to satisfy or secure money or other thing by him won of, or lent, or advanced to the seller, lessor, or mortgager, or whereof money or other thing so won, or lent, or advanced, shall be part or all of the consideration money, shall inure to the use of the heir of such mortgager, lessor, bargainer, or vender, and shall vest the whole estate and interest of such person in the lands, tenements, or hereditaments, so leased, mortgaged, bargained, or sold, and in the slaves or other personal estate so sold, mortgaged, or otherwise transferred, to all intents and purposes in the heir of such lessor, bargainer, mortgager, or vender, as if such lessor, bargainer, mortgager, or vender, had died intestate.

Contracts for paying money &c. won by gaming, void. Conveyances to secure money, &c. so won, enure to the benefit of the loser's heir.

II. IF any person by playing or betting at any game or wager whatsoever at any time within the space of twenty four hours shall lose or win, to or from another, a greater sum or any thing of greater value than five pounds, the loser and winner shall be rendered incapable of holding any office, civil or military, within the state, during the space of two years, and moreover shall be liable to pay ten shillings in the pound for every pound over and above the said sum of five pounds, which he shall so win or lose; and upon information thereof made to any county court, and due proof thereof had, such county court shall levy upon the goods and chattels of the offenders the full penalty incurred, to be applied to lessening the levy of the county wherein such offence shall be committed; and upon conviction before such county court, shall incur the forfeiture hereby inflicted, and be ipso facto deprived of his office aforesaid. Any person who shall bet or play for money or other goods, or who shall bet on the hands or sides of those who play at any game in a tavern, race-field, or other place of public resort, shall be deemed an infamous gambler, and shall not be eligible to any office of trust or honour within this state.

Penalties upon those who play or bet;

III. ANY tavern-keeper who shall permit cards, dice, billiards, or any instrument of gaming to be made use of in his house, or shall permit any person to bet or play for money or other goods, in any out-house, or under any booth, arbour, or other place, upon the messuage or tenement he possesses, and shall not make information thereof, and give in the names of the offenders to the next court which may be held for the county, city, or borough wherein he resides, shall be deprived of his license, and moreover shall pay to the informer, one hundred pounds, to be recovered by action of debt, in any court of record.

and upon tavern-keepers permitting it in their houses.

IV. TWO Justices of the Peace may cause any person not possessing a visible estate, nor exercising some lawful trade or profession, who shall be suspected by them to support himself, for the most part, by gaming, to come or be brought before them, and if the suspicion shall appear upon examination to be well founded, may require security of him for his good behaviour, during the term of twelve months, and if before the expiration thereof, he shall play for or bet any money or other thing, at any game whatsoever, he shall be adjudged to have broken the condition of his recognizance.

Power of Justices of Peace to bind gamesters to their behaviour.

V. NO person, in order to raise money for himself or another, shall publicly or privately put up a lottery of blanks and prizes, to be drawn or adventured for, or any prize or thing to be raffled or played for; and whoever shall offend herein, shall forfeit the whole sum of money proposed to be raised by such lottery, raffling, or playing, to the use of the commonwealth. The presiding Justice, as well in the General, as in all the inferior courts of law in this commonwealth, shall constantly give this act in charge to the grand juries of their courts at the times when such grand juries shall be sworn. This act shall commence and be in force, from and after the first day of *March* next.

Lotteries, &c. prohibited. This act to be given in charge to grand juries.]

CHAP. XLIII.

An act for the relief of Christopher Godwin.

Private.

CHAP. XLIV.

An act to amend an act entitled An act to increase the salaries of the clerks to the Auditors of Public Accounts.

Repealed.

CHAP. XLV.

An act concerning the Naval Office of the district of South Potowmack.

Repealed.

CHAP. XLVI.

An act for dividing the parish of Drysdale, in the counties of Caroline and King and Queen.

Private.

CHAP. XLVII.

An act for the manumission of certain slaves.

Private.

CHAP. XLVIII.

An act to repeal so much of the several acts of Assembly which empower the county courts to make provision for the support of the wives, parents, and families of the soldiers of this state in the service of this commonwealth, or in the service of the United States and for other purposes.

Had its effect.

C H A P. LIII.

An act for the recovery of arms, cattle, horses, and other property belonging to the commonwealth, or to the United States.

Preamble.

I. WHEREAS it is represented to the General Assembly, that divers persons within this commonwealth are in possession of arms, cattle, horses, or other property belonging to this state, or the United States, and it is expedient that such persons should be compelled to deliver such articles to some officer of the line, or of the staff, in the service of this state, or of the United States: *Be it therefore enacted,* that where any person shall be found not legally possessed of any bullock or other cattle, or any horse or horses, or arms, belonging to this state, or to the United States, any officer of the line, or of the staff, in the service of this state, or of the United States, shall be entitled to commence his action or petition in his own name against the delinquent for the recovery thereof, with full costs of suit, to the use of the United States, or of the commonwealth, as the case may be. The county courts are hereby empowered and required to proceed to the trial of any suit or petition commenced as aforesaid, in preference to all private suits, and to award execution for restitution of the effects and costs of suit, and shall transmit to the Governor and Council copies of their proceedings in such suits, that the plaintiff may be amenable to their order as to the disposition of any property so recovered.

Articles belonging to this state or the United States, recoverable from the unlawful possessor by officers.

- -

At a GENERAL ASSEMBLY begun and held at the Public Buildings in the Town of *Richmond,* on *Monday* the 1st day of *May,* in the Year of our Lord 1780.

C H A P. II.

An act to secure to the public certain lands heretofore held as common.

Preamble.

(a) May 1779, chap. 13.

Reserved lands described.

I. WHEREAS certain unappropriated lands on the bay, sea, and river shores, in the eastern parts of this commonwealth, have been heretofore reserved as common to all the citizens thereof; and whereas by the act of General Assembly entitled *An act for establishing a Land Office, and ascertaining the terms and manner of granting waste and unappropriated lands (a)* no reservation thereof is made, but the same is now subject to be entered for and appropriated by any person or persons, whereby the benefits formerly derived to the public therefrom, will be monopolized by a few individuals, and the poor laid under contribution for exercising the accustomed privilege of fishing: *Be it therefore enacted by the General Assembly,* that all unappropriated lands on the bay of *Chesapeake,* on the sea shore, or on the shores of any river or creek in the eastern parts of this commonwealth, which have remained ungranted by the former government, and which have been used as common to all the good people thereof, shall be, and the same are hereby excepted out of the said recited act, and no grant issued by the Register of the Land Office for the same, either in consequence of any survey already made, or which may hereafter be made, shall be valid or effectual in law, to pass any estate or interest therein.

CHAP. III.

An act repealing part of the act entitled An act for sequestering British property, enabling those indebted to British subjects to pay off such debts, and directing the proceedings in suits, where such subjects are parties.

A. D. 1780.

See Oct. 1777, chap. 9.

Act allowing debtors to British subjects to pay the debts into the treasury, repealed as to so much.

I. BE it enacted by the General Assembly, that so much of the act passed in the year one thousand seven hundred and seventy seven, entitled *An act for sequestering British property, enabling those indebted to British subjects to pay off such debts, and direct the proceedings in suits where such subjects are parties,* as enables persons owing money to a subject of *Great Britain* to pay the same, or any part thereof into the public Loan Office, and obtain certificate of such payment in the name of the creditor, shall be, and the same is hereby repealed.

CHAP. IV.

An act to empower the Justices of Spotsylvania *county, to hold courts in the house of* John Holladay.

Private.

CHAP. V.

An act to empower the sheriff of Henrico *to summon a grand jury, and for explaining the several acts of Assembly respecting the wages of the members of the General Assembly.*

See may 1779, ch. 9.

Sheriff of Henrico empowered to summon a grand jury to attend the General Court.

I. BE it enacted by the General Assembly, that the sheriff of *Henrico* county shall before every session of the General Court, so long as the same may continue to be held in the said county, summon a grand jury of twenty four freeholders, either within or without his county to attend the said court, any sixteen of whom appearing, shall be a sufficient number. And the said sheriff or his deputies, shall also perform the same services to the several superior courts to be held in the said county, as the sheriffs of the counties of *York* and *James City* have heretofore discharged.

Price of tobacco due to members of Assembly to be settled by grand jury at each of the quarterly sessions of the General Court.

II. AND whereas doubts have arisen upon the construction of the several acts of Assembly, for fixing and paying the allowance of the members of the General Assembly, and inconveniencies have also been occasioned from the fluctuating price of tobacco, and of the rates of the necessary expences of the said members: To remedy which, *Be it enacted,* that the grand jury at each and every of the four annual sessions of the General Court, shall upon oath, estimate in money the value of the tobacco then due, or to become due to the members of the General Assembly, according to the worth thereof at the time of such valuation, and the competence of the same to defray the necessary and reasonable expences of travelling and attendance; and the last valuation of such tobacco shall always be the rule by which the said allowance shall be settled, and paid to the several members, in the manner and under the regulations prescribed by law; provided that nothing contained in this act, shall affect the wages of the members of this present General Assembly, until the 13th instant, *June.*

CHAP. VI.

An act to amend an act entitled An act to embody militia for the relief of South Carolina, *and for other purposes.*

Executed.

CHAP. VII.

An act for regulating the fees of the Register of the Land Office, and for other purposes.

See Nov. 1781, ch. 31.

Preamble.

I. WHEREAS the fees allowed by law to the Register of the Land Office are very inadequate to the trouble and expence of conducting the business thereof: *Be it therefore enacted,* that the Register of the Land Office shall be entitled to the fees herein after mentioned, to be paid by the party at whose instance any such service shall be performed, at the time of his or her requiring the same, that is to say: For issuing a warrant of survey, and recording the same, thirty pounds of tobacco; for recording the rights or certificates upon which such warrant of survey is founded, ten pounds of tobacco; for every warrant issued in exchange of another warrant, or where lands claimed under a former warrant shall be recovered upon a caveat, and recording the same, thirty pounds of tobacco; for receiving a plat and certificate, and giving a receipt for the same, five pounds of tobacco; for issuing and recording a grant thereupon, if the quantity therein contained exceed not four hundred acres, sixty pounds of tobacco; for every hundred acres exceeding that of four hundred, five pounds of tobacco; for recording a plat and certificate of survey, if the quantity does not exceed four hundred acres, twenty pounds of tobacco; for every hundred acres exceeding that quantity, five pounds of tobacco; for entering a caveat, or for a copy thereof, twenty pounds of tobacco; for a copy of any grant or patent of land, thirty pounds of tobacco; for a search for any thing, or for reading the same, if a copy be not required, ten pounds of tobacco; for recording a list of certificates proved in any county court, or allowed by the commissioners of any district, or for keeping a regular account of warrants, examined and cancelled, to be paid by the Treasurer, on the Auditors warrant, for each certificate or warrant contained in such list, three pounds of tobacco.

Fees for various services.

For public services.

Surveyors, their fees. See Oct. 1783, ch. 32.

II. *AND be it further enacted,* that every surveyor, instead of the former allowance given by law, shall be entitled to receive the following fees for the services herein after mentioned, to be paid by the person employing him: For every survey by him plainly bounded as the law directs, and for a plat of such survey, after the delivery of such plat, where the survey shall not exceed four hundred acres of land, two hundred and fifty pounds of tobacco; for every hundred acres contained in one survey above four hundred, fifteen pounds of tobacco; for surveying a lot in a town, twenty pounds of tobacco; and where the surveyor shall be stopped or hindered from finishing a survey by him begun, to be paid by the party who required the survey to be made, one hundred and twenty five pounds of tobacco; for running a dividing line, one hundred and twenty five pounds of tobacco; for surveying an acre of land for a mill, fifty pounds of tobacco; for every survey of land formerly patented, and which shall be required to be surveyed, and for a plat thereof delivered as aforesaid, the same fee as for land not before surveyed; and where a survey shall be made of any lands which are to be added to other lands, in an inclusive patent, the surveyor shall not be paid a second fee for the land first surveyed, but shall only receive what the survey of the additional land shall amount to; and where any surveys have been actually made of several parcels of land adjoining, and several plats delivered, if the party shall desire one inclusive plat thereof, the surveyor shall make out such plat for fifty pounds of tobacco; for running

A. D. 1780.

a dividing line between any county or parish, to be paid by such respective counties or parishes in proportion to the number of tithables, if ten miles or under, five hundred pounds of tobacco; and for every mile above ten, fifteen pounds of tobacco; for receiving a warrant of survey, and giving a receipt therefor, ten pounds of tobacco; for recording a certificate from the commissioners of any district of a claim to land allowed by them, to be paid by the claimant, ten pounds of tobacco; for making an entry for land, or for a copy thereof, ten pounds of tobacco; for a copy of a plat of land, or of a certificate of survey, fifteen pounds of tobacco.

Witnesses, their allowance.

III. AND be it further enacted, that every witness attending upon summons the High Court of Chancery, General Court, or Court of Admiralty; and every witness, venire-man, or sheriff, attending the General Court in criminal cases, shall be paid sixty pounds of tobacco for each day's attendance, and two pounds of tobacco *per* mile for travelling, and their ferriages; and every witness attending upon summons in any county, or other inferiour court, or upon a survey of lands, shall be paid twenty five pounds of tobacco for each days attendance; and if residing in and summoned out of another county, the same allowance for travelling and ferriages as witnesses in the superior courts. And that all persons who shall hereafter become chargeable with tobacco for any of the services mentioned in this, or the act entitled *An act to amend an act for the better regulating and collecting certain officers fees, and for other purposes,* shall at their election discharge the same, either in transfer tobacco notes, or money in lieu thereof, at such rate as shall be estimated by the Grand Jury, at each of the sessions of the General Court, in the months of *June* and *October* in every year, confining themselves in making such estimate, to fix the same at one half of the average price of crop tobacco, which shall, and is hereby declared to be the rate at which the said tobacco fees due, or becoming due between every estimate, shall be paid in money. *(a)* The clerk of the General Court shall, as soon as may be after every estimate, furnish the Register of the Land Office, and the clerks of the county courts each, with a copy of such estimate; that to the Register to be by him constantly kept in his office, and those to the clerks to be by them recorded.

(a) Altered by Oct. 1781, ch. 31.

Marshal of the admiralty, his commissions.

IV. AND whereas the allowance heretofore made to the Marshal of the Court of Admiralty is very inadequate to his risk and trouble: Be it therefore enacted, that the Marshal of the Court of Admiralty, for taking charge of and selling any vessel or cargo, the tackle, apparel, or furniture of any vessel, agreeable to the sentence of the said court, shall be entitled to receive, instead of the allowance heretofore made him by law, two *per centum* commission upon the amount of every such sale. So much of an act entitled *An act for regulating tobacco fees, and for other purposes;* and of an act entitled *An act for punishing persons guilty of certain thefts and forgeries, and fixing the allowance to sheriffs, venire-men, and witnesses, in certain cases,* as comes within the purview of this act, is hereby repealed.

C H A P.　VIII.

Executed.

An act for procuring a supply of provisions and other necessaries for the use of the army.

C H A P.　IX.

See May 1779, ch. 12.

An Act for giving further time to obtain warrants upon certificates for preemption rights, and returning certain surveys to the Land Office, and for other purposes.

Preamble.

WHEREAS the time fixed by an act entitled *An act for adjusting and settling the titles of claimers to unpatented lands under the present and former governments, previous to the establishment of the commonwealth's Land Office,* for surveying and returning surveys to the Land Office upon entries made with the surveyor of a county, before the twenty sixth day of *June* one thousand seven hundred and seventy nine, for lands lying upon the eastern waters, and for returning the plats of legal surveys made upon the western waters under the former government, and exchanging military warrants granted under the royal proclamation of one thousand seven hundred and sixty three, and not yet executed, will shortly expire, and many persons be thereby deprived of the benefit of such warrants and surveys: Be it therefore enacted, that all persons having such warrants, shall be allowed until the first day of *July* one thousand seven hundred and eighty one, to exchange such warrants; that the like time shall be allowed for returning such surveys to the Land Office, to such who were entitled to land for military service, for which certificates have not yet been obtained.

Time allowed for returning surveys.

Further time allowed to the western commissioners.

II. AND whereas the time limited in the act for explaining and amending the said recited act, to the commissioners for adjusting and settling the claims to unpatented lands within their respective districts, has been found too short for that purpose: Be it therefore enacted, that all the powers given to the said commissioners, except the commissioners for the county of *Kentucky,* by any act or acts of Assembly, shall be continued and remain in force for and during the farther term of twelve months.

Further allowance to them and their officers.

Tax upon litigants increased.

III. AND whereas the allowance made to the said commissioners, surveyors, and sheriffs, by the first recited act, is inadequate to their services; Be it enacted, that each commissioner for every day he hath or shall be necessarily employed, in going to, attending on, and returning from the business of his office, shall receive sixteen pounds, the surveyor six pounds, and the sheriff four pounds, instead of and in lieu of the former allowances given by the said recited act; and that all necessary expences for expresses and paper, shall be allowed the said commissioners in settling their accounts. And whereas the expence of carrying the said act into execution, will be greatly increased, and it is reasonable and just that the greatest part of such expence should be defrayed by the persons who are to be benefited by the same: Be it enacted, that every person who shall institute any suit for the title of lands before the said commissioners, shall pay down the sum of ten pounds, which shall be taxed in the bill of costs against the defendant, if he shall be cast in the said suit and credited by the said commissioners in their account against the public, in the same manner as the tax of ten shillings *per* hundred is accounted fo—

Further time to enter warrants on preemption certificates, with the surveyor.

IV. AND be it further enacted, that the further time of eighteen months be given to all persons who may obtain certificates from the said commissioners for preemptions on their obtaining warrants from the Register of the Land Office to enter the same with the surveyor of the respective counties in which their claims were adjusted: Provided that the court of commissioners for the district of the counties of *Monongalia, Yohogania,* and *Ohio,* do not use or exercise any jurisdiction respecting claims to lands within the territory in dispute between the states of *Virginia* and *Pennsylvania* north of *Mason's* and *Dixon's* line, until such dispute shall be finally adjusted and settled.

V. *AND be it further enacted,* that all surveys upon entries, the execution of all warrants, and the iſſuing of patents for lands within the ſaid territory ſhall alſo be ſuſpended until the ſaid diſpute ſhall have been finally adjuſted and ſettled; but that ſuch ſuſpenſion ſhall not be conſtrued in any manner to injure or affect the title of any perſon claiming ſuch lands. And whereas the buſineſs of the commiſſioners for ſettling the claims to unpatented lands, will be much leſſened in the counties of *Monongalia, Yoho-gania,* and *Ohio: Be it therefore enacted,* that the Governor, with the advice of Council, be empowered to appoint commiſſioners within or without the ſaid diſtrict as he may think reaſonable. And to the end that preemption certificates heretofore granted by the commiſſioners of any diſtrict, and not returned to the Regiſter's office for want of time, or other impracticability, may not be loſt to the holders thereof, *Be it enacted,* that where ſuch preemption certificates may have been, or may hereafter be loſt out of the owners poſſeſſion; he or ſhe upon a certificate from a court of record of ſuch loſs, which ſhall be granted upon ſatisfactory proof being made to ſuch court, ſhall be entitled to receive from the Regiſter a warrant thereupon, in the ſame manner as he or ſhe might have done upon the original certificate; that the further time of twelve months after the paſſing of this act, ſhall be allowed to ſuch perſons to return the ſaid certificates to the Regiſter's office for obtaining a warrant, and four months thereafter to enter the ſame with the ſurveyor of the county, which entries ſhall be good and valid as though they had been entered within the time heretofore preſcribed by the ſaid recited act.

VI. *AND* whereas many warrants from the Regiſter, may have been, or may hereafter be caſually loſt: *Be it enacted,* that upon ſatisfactory proof thereof being made before any court of record, the owner ſhall obtain from ſuch court a certificate, which ſhall authoriſe the Regiſter to iſſue a duplicate of ſuch warrant, which ſhall have the ſame force as the original would have had; but ſuch original ſhall be void, unleſs a grant ſhall be actually iſſued upon ſuch original before application for the duplicate.

VII. *AND* whereas ſome doubts have ariſen upon the conſtruction of the acts, directing the granting warrants for land due for military ſervice under the King of *Great Britain's* proclamation in the year one thouſand ſeven hundred and ſixty three: It is hereby declared that no officer, his heirs, executors, adminiſtrators, or aſſigns, ſhall be entitled to a warrant of ſurvey for any other or greater quantity of land than was due to him, her, or them, in virtue of the higheſt commiſſion or rank in which ſuch officer had ſerved, nor in virtue of more than one ſuch commiſſion for ſervices in different regiments or corps, nor ſhall any non-commiſſioned officer or ſoldier be entitled to a bounty for land under the ſaid proclamation, for his ſervice in more than one regiment or corps.

VIII. *AND it is further declared,* that the Regiſter ſhall not iſſue to any perſon or perſons whatever, his or their heirs or aſſigns, a grant for land for more than one ſervice, as above deſcribed, nor to thoſe who have received warrants for ſervices ſince *October* one thouſand ſeven hundred and ſixty three, not-withſtanding a warrant or warrants may have been heretofore iſſued, and the land ſurveyed, unleſs the claimant ſhall within ſix months from the end of this preſent ſeſſion of Aſſembly, produce to the ſaid Regiſter the Auditors certificate for the payment of the ſtate price of forty pounds *per* hundred, for the quantity of land in ſuch warrant or warrants; and if ſuch money is not ſo paid, that then the ſaid warrants or ſurveys ſhall be to all intents and purpoſes void; and that the Regiſter may be able to com-ply with this law, he is hereby directed to make out, and keep an alphabetical liſt of all military war-rants iſſued under the former as well as the preſent government; in caſe of any aſſignment, making therein the name of every aſſignor; and the ſeveral ſurveyors with whom military warrants obtained under the former government, have been lodged or located, are directed to tranſmit to the Regiſter in the month of *November* next, or before that time, a liſt of all ſuch warrants.

C H A P. X.

An act for calling in and redeeming the money now in circulation, and for emitting and funding new bills of credit, according to the reſolutions of Congreſs of the 18th of March *laſt.*

I. **W**HEREAS the juſt and neceſſary war into which the United States have been driven, obliged Congreſs to emit bills of credit before the ſeveral ſtates were ſufficiently organized to enforce the collection of taxes, or funds could be eſtabliſhed to ſupport the credit of ſuch bills; by which means the bills ſo emitted ſoon exceeded the ſum neceſſary for a circulating medium, and conſe-quently depreciated ſo as to create an alarming redundancy of money, whereby it is become neceſſary to reduce the quantity of ſuch bills, to call in and deſtroy the exceſſive maſs of money now in circulation, and to utter other bills, on funds which ſhall enſure the redemption thereof. And whereas the certain conſequences of not calling in and redeeming the money now in circulation in the depreciated value at which it hath been generally received would be to increaſe the national debt thirty nine times greater than it really is, and conſequently to ſubject the good people of this commonwealth to many years of grievous and unneceſſary taxation: And ſince Congreſs by their reſolution of the eighteenth of *March* laſt have called upon the ſeveral ſtates to make proper proviſion for the purpoſes aforeſaid: *Be it there-fore enacted by the General Aſſembly,* that for the purpoſes of calling in and deſtroying this ſtate's quota of the two hundred millions of dollars of continental money heretofore iſſued by Congreſs; and alſo for calling in and deſtroying in like manner the money of this ſtate now in circulation, whether emitted by the Convention, or by the General Aſſembly, either before or ſince the revolution, the following fund ſhall be appropriated, and the following taxes impoſed: The product of the ſeveral taxes which are re-ceivable in the months of *Auguſt* and *September* of the preſent year, in virtue of the act paſſed in the year one thouſand ſeven hundred and ſeventy ſeven, entitled *An act for raiſing a ſupply of money for the public exigencies (a)* and of the ſeveral ſubſequent acts amendatory thereof, ſhall be applied to the ſaid purpoſe of calling in and deſtroying the ſaid money as before deſcribed: And in aid thereof, *Be it further enacted,* that a new tax be levied and collected by a general aſſeſſment of all and every article or articles of pro-perty directed to be valued and aſſeſſed by the act of one thouſand ſeven hundred and ſeventy ſeven; and alſo on all plate, according to its real value, except only that the ſaid valuations and aſſeſſment ſhall be in ſpecie, as the ſame or the like property would have ſold in the year one thouſand ſeven hundred and ſeventy four, for ready money. And that an average price may be affixed to landed property within the reſpective counties, the commiſſioners of the tax ſhall, on or before the firſt day of *October* next, call together their ſeveral aſſeſſors, to meet at ſuch place as they ſhall appoint, and ſhall then and there ad-miniſter to them the following oath: *I do ſwear, or affirm, that I will, when called on by the com-miſſioners of the tax for my county, truly, candidly, and without reſerve, declare the worth of the ſeveral kinds of lands within my county as they would have ſold for in ready money in the year one thouſand ſeven hundred and ſeventy four, for ſpecie, had the ſame been ſold ſeparately from other lands.* So help me God. The ſaid commiſſioners ſhall then proceed to deſcribe the lands of their county (except lots in towns, which ſhall be ſeparately valued by the aſſeſſors of the hundred in which ſuch lots ſhall be) in ſo many general claſſes, not exceeding ſix, as their different natures or kinds may require; and ſhall call on each aſſeſſor

Preamble.

The ſtate's quota of continental money and all ſtate papers to be called in and deſtroyed.

The taxes payable in Auguſt and Sep-tember of this year applied thereto. (a) See Oct. 1777. *ch. 2, and notes. Further taxes.*

Commiſſioners and aſſeſſors to meet and claſs the lands.

Their oath on that occaſion.

A. D. 1780.

singly to declare, under the obligation of his oath or affirmation, what he thinks each several kind of the said land would have sold for by the acre for ready money in the year one thousand seven hundred and seventy four, which several opinions they shall state in writing for each kind of land separately, and shall add together the sums at which the same kind of land is rated by the several assessors, and then divide the aggregate sum by the number of persons whose opinions were stated, and shall take the quotient or the sum nearest thereto, so as to avoid the difficulty of fractions, which may be thus approved by a majority of the said assessors, as the average price of such kind of land, and so shall proceed to deduce an average price for every other kind into which they shall have classed the land of their county as before directed; but lots of land in towns, ferry landings, mines of coal or metal, mills, and all other buildings, shall not be included within any class, but shall be valued by the assessors within whose bounds they are, as the same or the like would now sell for in specie. One of the said commissioners shall then

General oath of assessors.

administer to the said assessors, the following oath or affirmation: *I   do swear, or affirm, that I will, to the best of my skill and judgment, value and assess the several parcels of land within the bounds of my assessment as now classed and described, that I will faithfully, justly, and impartially value all other property to be assessed under this act, in gold or silver, as the same or the like property would have sold in the year one thousand seven hundred and seventy four, had the same been sold separately from other property of the same kind; that I will spare none for favour or affection, and none aggrieve for hatred, malice, or ill-will, but in all things do my duty of an assessor honestly, impartially, and to the best of my abilities. So help me God.* And

Rule if a difference in opinion between them.

if any assessor was not present at the meeting, the said last mentioned oath shall be administered to him by a commissioner or magistrate, before he shall proceed to assess. And if in the course of the said assessment the assessors shall differ in opinion, the medium between the two sums shall be taken as the true value of any kind of property.

New taxes.

II. AND be it further enacted, that in lieu of the present tax imposed on the said property, there shall be collected, paid, and distrained for, the assessment or pound rate of thirty pounds of the money now in circulation, for every hundred pounds of such valuation of property, as the same would have sold for in ready money in one thousand seven hundred and seventy four, which said thirty pounds shall be paid at each of the three following periods: The first payment shall be on or before the first of *January* next; the second, on or before the fifteenth day of *April* next, and the third, on or before the fifteenth day of *September*, which shall be in the year one thousand seven hundred and eighty one.

III. AND be it further enacted, that at each of the said three last mentioned periods, the following further taxes shall be paid in the paper money of this state, or of the continent, now in circulation, at the rates following: For every hundred pounds of the said money which any person shall have in his possession, either on the first day of *October* next, on the first day of *March* next, or on the first day of *August*, in the year one thousand seven hundred and eighty one, at sun-rise of the said respective days, of which he shall render an account on oath as heretofore, he shall pay fifteen shillings; for every white male tithable above the age of twenty one years, shall be paid three pounds six shillings and eight pence (except the officers of the line or navy, soldiers or sailors in the service of this commonwealth or of the United States, or persons disabled in such service; except also such of the militia who may be in actual service at the time when the said taxes shall respectively become due, and those who have been or shall be exempted from the payment of levies by the county court;) for every white servant whatsoever, except apprentices under the age of twenty one years, shall be paid the like tax; for every head of neat cattle, six shillings; for every coach or chariot, twenty six pounds, six shillings, and eight pence; for four wheeled chaise, and stage waggon used for riding carriages, twenty pounds; for every two wheeled chaise and chair, six pounds six shillings and eight pence; for every gallon of brandy distilled within this state, ten shillings; and for every gallon of spirits in like manner distilled from grain and not before taxed, eight shillings; for each marriage licence, ten pounds; and for every ordinary license, two hundred pounds; the said tax on marriage and ordinary licences to be received and accounted for on oath by the clerk of the court. The same rules and regulations both in the assessments of the taxes for calling in the money now in circulation, and for redeeming the money herein after directed to be emitted, shall be observed with respect to and between landlords and tenants (unless the contract between them shall be specially otherwise) and the same discount for quitrents on the lands in the *Northern Neck*, as are directed by the said first recited act of one thousand seven hundred and seventy seven. And in order to fix the price of unappropriated lands belonging to this commonwealth at a rate to make up the depreciation of the money, *Be it enacted*, that the sum of one hundred and sixty pounds

The price of waste lands raised; that and taxes in what money to be paid.

for every one hundred acres, shall hereafter be paid for all treasury land warrants, except preemption. All which said several taxes together with the consideration money for unappropriated lands shall be payable in the bills of credit of the United States or of this state, now in circulation, or in *Spanish* milled dollars at the rate of six shillings each, and so in other lawful gold and silver coin at a proportionate value, or the bills of credit to be emitted upon the security of this commonwealth, according to the said resolutions of Congress of the eighteenth of *March* last. *Provided*, that the said specie and the said bills of credit so to be emitted, shall be received at the rate of one dollar for forty dollars of the said bills of credit of the United States or of this commonwealth, now in circulation.

Tobacco, hemp, flax, and flour, to be received, and at what rates.

IV. AND whereas the speedily calling in such large sums, may occasion difficulty in the payment of the said taxes for sinking the money now in circulation: *Be it further enacted*, that good merchantable crop tobacco, not inspected more than one year, when offered in payment, be received in discharge of such taxes, at the rate of forty five pounds *per* hundred, with an allowance of twelve pounds for cask and inspection; good merchantable hemp, at the rate of ninety pounds *per* hundred; good swingled flax at one pound four shillings *per* pound; and good merchantable fine inspected flour, at the rate of thirty

If taxes deficient, Assembly will provide other adequate funds.

eight pounds *per* hundred: All of the said prices to be of the money now in circulation, to be delivered at the charge of the payer at such places, and to such commissioners, as the Governor with the advice of the Council shall appoint, whose certificates of receipt delivered to the sheriff, shall be equal to the payment of so much money; and the Governor with the advice of his Council shall take proper measures for selling the same, for the best price which can be had, and shall cause the product thereof to be paid into the treasury, to be applied to the foregoing purposes. And if the taxes herein directed to be paid, and the fund appropriated for the purpose of redeeming this state's quota of the two hundred millions of dollars heretofore issued by Congress, and also of the state money now in circulation, shall prove insufficient for the said purpose, the General Assembly will hereafter provide and establish adequate funds for

Assessors their duty.

calling in, or redeeming, at the same rate, so much thereof as shall then remain outstanding. And for determining the duty of, and making an adequate allowance to the commissioners and assessors for services herein, *It is further enacted*, that the said assessors shall immediately after their meeting for ascer-

Commissioners their duty.

taining an average price of lands on the said first day of *October* next, proceed to assess and value all property of whatever kind which is directed to be assessed herein, or which is directed to be valued under the said law of one thousand seven hundred and seventy seven, before recited, according to the principle and under the rules prescribed by this act, upon which said valuation, an account of which shall be

A. D. 1780.

returned to the commissioners by the first day of *November* following, the said three payments of the tax called for by this act, shall be regulated and assessed, and by the said commissioners of the tax ordered to be collected. *Provided*, that the said assessors shall, in the months of *March* and *August* immediately preceding the second and third payment of the said tax, call on each person within their district for an account of brandy and spirits distilled since the last account thereof rendered; and also for a distinct account of the specie and of the paper money as before directed to be accounted for, which accounts together with any change of property, by transfer, by accident, by increase or decrease, or by the alteration in the number of free taxables, shall by the persons to whom they may respectively happen, be rendered to the said assessors on oath, who shall make application for that purpose, which accounts shall be returned to the commissioners, in the second instance, by the first day of *April*, and in the third, by the first day of *September*. And from the returns so made by the said assessors, the com- missioners shall adjust the accounts and orders for collecting the said three payments respectively, and shall make out for the sheriff or collector, a list formed from such returns as a direction for his collection according to the said act of one thousand seven hundred and seventy seven, who shall and may distrain for all taxes imposed by this act, both for sinking the old money and for establishing funds on which to emit the new within twenty days after the same shall become due and payable, and shall, within twenty days thereafter, make up and render to the said commissioners an account of his said collection, who shall, within thirty days after receiving the said account so made up and rendered, return to the Auditors an account of the said settlement, to enable them to adjust the dues and balances of the said sheriffs or collectors. And the said several sheriffs and collectors shall also be called to account for the said taxes according to the laws now in force to enforce the payment of the present taxes. If the said commissioners, or any of them shall refuse to act, the county courts shall fill up vacancies as directed by the laws now in force, who, thus chosen or appointed, shall, with their clerk, have and be allowed twenty pounds per day each for every day they shall be imployed in the said business, of the money now in circulation, for their trouble and expences; and may also at their discretion, make an allowance unto each of the said assessors, a sum not exceeding two hundred pounds, and not less than one hundred pounds of the like money, as a recompence for making the said general assessment in the month of *October* next; and may also make to the said assessors an allowance not exceeding eight pounds *per day* of the like money each, for every day which it shall appear to the said commissioners by the oath of the said assessor or otherwise, that he was actually employed in the months preceding the said second and third payments, in collecting returns and affidavits of the several alterations which may have happened in his district.

V. AND be it further enacted, that the money, both state and continental, called in by all and every of the funds and taxes above established shall not be reissued, but shall remain in the treasury to be burnt and destroyed; and that whatever sums of the like money shall by any other means be paid into the treasury, after the money hereafter to be issued under the resolutions of Congress shall be ready for the purpose, the same shall remain in the treasury to be also burnt and destroyed. And in order to establish a means of defraying the expenditure of government, and also to furnish a circulating medium in lieu of the bills so called in to be destroyed; Be it further enacted, that there be emitted on the funds herein after provided, and the faith of the United States as pledged by their said resolutions of the said 18th day of *March* last, a sum not exceeding the sum of one million six hundred and sixty six thousand six hundred and sixty six and two thirds dollars, in bills of credit, bearing an annual interest of five *per centum* upon the funds of this commonwealth, the same being one twentieth part of thirty three millions three hundred and thirty three thousand three hundred and thirty three and one third dollars, hereby to be redeemed and destroyed as this commonwealth's quota of the said two hundred millions of dollars heretofore issued by Congress. The face of the said bills, and the endorsement thereon shall be in the manner and words as is directed by the said resolutions. The said new bills thus to be issued shall be redeemable in specie by the said thirty first day of *December* one thousand seven hundred and eighty six, and the interest thereon shall be paid, either on the redemption of the said bills, or annually, at the election of the holder, according to the said resolutions of Congress, and the promises in the face of the said bills. The said bills to be emitted shall be completed no faster than in the proportion of one to twenty of the present circulating continental money brought in to be destroyed, in lieu of every twenty dollars of which money so destroyed, shall issue one dollar according to the said resolutions; for the preparing and signing of which the Governor shall, with the advice of his Council, appoint proper persons in conjunction with com- missioners to be appointed by Congress to attend the completing the same, and to superintend the burning and destroying of the old money hereby called in and redeemed. As fast as the said new bills to be emitted shall be completed, six tenths of the same in value shall be received into the treasury of this commonwealth, to be thence issued as before directed to support the expences of the war and defray other public charges; the other four tenths shall be subject to the orders of Congress and carried to the credit of this commonwealth, in proper accounts to be opened and stated in the Auditors books. And whenever interest on the said bills to be emitted shall be paid prior to the time of their final redemption, such bills shall be thereupon exchanged for other bills of the like tenor, to bear date from the expiration of the year for which such interest is paid, and then burnt and destroyed; and the commissioners to be appointed on the part of this state, are hereby authorized to join with the said commissioners of Congress in completing such other bills for that purpose. And for effectually sinking or redeeming the said new bills of credit, and paying the interest thereon, which may be due from this commonwealth at the period prefixed for their redemption, It is further enacted, that a tax of one hundred and seven thousand pounds (exclusive of all charges of collection and losses by insolvency or otherwise) shall be annually paid and collected from the last day of *December* in the year one thousand seven hundred and eighty one, for and during the term of five years. And that the sum of seven thousand pounds thereof shall be annually retained and preserved in the treasury in specie, if so much specie shall be received in each year, or otherwise in the said bills of credit, or in the said hereafter enumerated commodities, to be exchanged for specie, or for the said new money, which shall be received in any of the said years, and shall be applied to the payment of the interest due from this commonwealth on the said money so to be emitted. *Provided*, that if any of the said bills shall be retained in the treasury for the payment of the said interest, over and above what are annually to be destroyed, the same shall, on being replaced by specie, be re- issued. The remaining one hundred thousand pounds of the annual product of the said tax shall, if paid in the said bills so to be emitted, be annually cancelled and destroyed, or if paid in whole or in part in specie, the said specie shall be retained in the treasury for the final redemption of such of the said bills of credit as may remain outstanding at the period of redemption, and if paid in the commodities hereafter to be enumerated, the Governor with the advice of his Council, shall take proper measures for selling the same, either for the said new bills of credit, or for specie, at the best price which can be obtained, and shall take care to pay the product thereof into the treasury, to be applied to the foregoing purposes, in the same manner as if the said tax had been paid therein. And in order to raise the said sum of one hundred and seven thousand pounds, It is further enacted, that a tax or pound rate of one *per centum*, according to the value, or twenty shillings in every hundred pounds, be laid and levied upon all articles of property before directed to be valued and assessed for the redemption of the money now in circulation; and also the like tax on every hundred pounds of specie, and so in propor-

A. D. 1780.

Payable a moiety half yearly,

and other taxes.

tion for a greater or leffer fum, to be levied and paid at the rate of one half *per centum*, or ten fhillings for every hundred pounds of fuch property, twice in each and every of the faid five years, to wit: On or before the laft days of *May* and *September*; and that at each and every of the faid periods there be alfo paid for the fame purpofe, a tax of two fhillings for all free male perfons above the age of twenty one years, and the fame fum for all white fervants (except as before excepted in the poll tax herein impofed for calling in the old money) a tax of three pence *per* head for neat cattle; a tax of twenty five fhillings for all coaches and chariots; of twenty fhillings for all phætons, four wheeled chaifes, and ftage waggons ufed for riding carriages; and of five fhillings for all chairs and two wheeled chaifes : Alfo a tax at the rate of ten fhillings in the hundred pounds upon every merchant's or factor's worth or ftock in trade; and a tax of one fhilling in the pound upon the annual profits of all public offices not fixed by certain falaries, All the faid taxes to be rated by the affeffors, with the right of appeal to the commiffioners of the tax if the party fhall be aggrieved or over rated, whereupon the commiffioners, upon the oath of the party or other fatisfactory evidence, may alter the rate according to their beft judgment and difcretion. A like tax of two fhillings in the pound fhall be gathered and paid upon all annuities, including the quitrents payable to the proprietor of the *Northern Neck*, other than annuities arifing out of property, for which the owner is fubject to affeffment, and penfions given by the General Affembly. A tax fhall alfo be paid of three pence *per* gallon on all brandy; and of two pence halfpenny upon all fpirits diftilled from grain within this commonwealth. Alfo a tax of five fhillings upon all marriage licenfes; and of fifty fhillings upon all ordinary licences; the faid tax on marriage and ordinary licences to be received and accounted for on oath by the clerk of the county. All which faid taxes hereby impofed

In what payable.

for eftablifhing a fund for thus redeeming and finking the money fo to be iffued under the refolutions of Congrefs, fhall be payable in *Spanifh* milled dollars, at the rate of fix fhillings, and other lawful gold and filver coin at a proportionable value in the faid new bills of credit to be emitted upon the funds and fecurity of this commonwealth, according to the refolutions of Congrefs of the eighteenth of *March* laft, or during the war, in good merchantable crop tobacco, not infpected more than one year when offered in payment, at the rate of twenty two fhillings and fixpence *per* hundred, with an allowance of fix fhillings for cafk and infpection; in good merchantable hemp, at the rate of forty five fhillings *per* hundred; or in good fwingled flax, at the rate of feven pence *per* pound, to be delivered at the charge of the payer, at fuch places, and to fuch commiffioners as the Governor, with the advice of the Council fhall appoint, whofe certificates of

Difpofition of any furplus.

receipt, delivered to the fheriff, fhall be equal to the payment of fo much money. And as it is probable a large furplus may arife, after paying the principal and intereft of the faid fum of one hundred and

Providing for deficiency.

feven thoufand pounds, It is further enacted, that the fame, if any, fhall be annually applied to the ufe of this commonwealth towards fupporting the expences of the war and defraying other public charges; but if the faid taxes fhould prove infufficient for raifing the faid fum of one hundred and feven thoufand pounds annually as aforefaid, fuch deficiency fhall be made good, and fhall be provided for by the General Affembly, by increafing the faid taxes.

All other taxes, except fpecific, to ceafe in Dec. 1781.

VI. AND be it further enacted, that all taxes heretofore impofed fhall ceafe and be difcontinued on the faid laft day of *December* one thoufand feven hundred and eighty one, except the fpecific taxes heretofore eftablifhed, whether the fame be payable with or without an alternative, the laws relative to which fhall ftill continue in force as if this law had never been made.

Commiffioners to act two years.

VII. AND be it further enacted, that the commiffioners of the tax fhall hereafter be chofen for and act two years inftead of one; and together with their clerk fhall, after the faid laft day of *December* one

Affeffors to be annually chofen, but affefs once in two years.

thoufand feven hundred and eighty one, take and be allowed fifteen fhillings *per* day each for their fervices. The affeffors fhall be annually appointed by the faid commiffioners, but fhall make their valuations under which thefe taxes are to be collected only every other year, to wit: In the years one thoufand feven hundred and eighty two, one thoufand feven hundred and eighty four, and one thoufand feven hundred and eighty fix, between the firft and laft days of *March* in each year; but fhall neverthelefs obferve the fame method in afcertaining the transference, increafe, or decreafe of property in the intervals between the different affeffments immediately preceding each affeffment, as is herein before

Their allowance.

prefcribed to be obferved in afcertaining the taxes to be gathered for calling in and finking the old money. The faid feveral affeffors fhall be allowed not more than fifteen pounds, and not lefs than feven pounds ten fhillings, at the difcretion of the commiffioners annually, for affefing in the faid three years of one thoufand feven hundred and eighty two, one thoufand feven hundred and eighty four, and one thoufand feven hundred and eighty fix, and the fum of fix fhillings each *per* day, for every day it fhall appear to the commiffioners, by oath or otherwife, that they were refpectively employed in rendering the fervices to be performed in the faid intermediate terms between the different affeffments.

Penalty on commiffioners, affeffors and fheriffs.

VIII. AND be it further enacted, that the faid commiffioners fhall refpectively, either for refufing to ferve in the faid office when chofen thereto, or for any neglect of duty in the execution thereof, forfeit and pay one hundred pounds. The faid affeffors fhall each for any of the like offences, forfeit and pay fifty pounds; and every fheriff and collector who fhall fail to comply with the injunctions hereby laid upon him, fhall forfeit and pay one hundred pounds. All the faid forfeitures to be recovered by bill, plaint, or information, in any court of record within this commonwealth, one half to the informer, and the other to the leffening the levy of the county in which the offender fhall refide, and if there fhall be no information, then the whole to the laft mentioned purpofe. The faid commiffioners, affeffors, and fheriffs, fhall alfo over and above the faid penalties, be liable to an action on the cafe for damages in the name of the Attorney General, for the time being, on behalf of the commonwealth, for all loffes and injuries which fhall accrue to the ftate by any offence aforefaid, wherein the damages fhall be affeffed by a jury, which fhall after judgment and execution therefor, be paid into the public treafury for the purpofes of government.

Bonds to be annually taken of the fheriffs by the courts

IX. AND it is further enacted, that the faid fheriffs, commiffioners, and affeffors, fhall in all things not herein fpecially directed, govern themfelves according to the rules and regulations laid down and prefcribed in the faid act of one thoufand feven hundred and feventy feven, entitled An act for raifing a fupply of money for public exigencies. The court of the county fhall in the months of *October* and *March* next, and in the month of *July* in the year one thoufand feven hundred and eighty one, take bond of the fheriff with fufficient fecurity, in the penalty of one hundred thoufand pounds, payable to the Treafurer of this commonwealth for the time being, and his fucceffors, for the ufe of this commonwealth, and conditioned for the true and faithful collecting, paying, and accounting for all duties and taxes within his county hereby impofed, for calling in and finking the money now in circulation; the faid court fhall likewife annually, after the firft day of *December* one thoufand feven hundred and eighty one, in the month of *March* in each year, for the five fucceeding years, take a like bond of the fheriff in the penalty of four thoufand pounds, conditioned for the difcharge of his duty with refpect to the taxes hereby impofed, for eftablifhing a fund for the new money to be iffued under the faid refolutions of Congrefs; the faid bonds fhall be recorded in the courts were they are taken, and an attefted copy thereof fhall be tranfmitted by the refpective clerks without delay to the public Treafurer, which fhall be admitted as evidence in any suit or proceeding founded thereon. If any person shall make, counterseit, alter, or erase, any of the said bills of credit to be emitted under the said resolutions, or shall be concerned in aiding or abetting any person or persons in such making, counterfeiting, altering, or erasing, or shall be possessed of any plate or plates for the purpose of such counterfeiting, such person shall be adjudged guilty of the same crime, as if he had so made, altered, counterfeited, or erased, the money now in circulation, or had been possessed of a plate or plates for that purpose; and such person shall be tried under the laws now in force, for punishing the said offences, which are hereby declared to be extended to any of the like offences committed with respect to the said bills of credit hereby to be issued.

X. *PROVIDED nevertheless*, that the execution of this act shall be suspended until his Excellency the Governor shall have received authentic advices that a majority of the United States of America (except *Georgia* and *South Carolina*, whose determination thereupon will probably be suspended until the enemy shall be expelled therefrom) have actually or conditionally approved of and acceded to the said resolutions of Congress of the eighteenth of *March* last; and upon receiving such information, he shall with the advice of his Council, immediately take care to carry this act into full execution, of which he shall apprise the good people of this commonwealth, by a proclamation to be issued for that purpose.

CHAP. XI.

An act to empower the High Sheriffs to proceed in a summary way against their deputies, and for other purposes.

I. BE it enacted, that where the sheriff of any county heretofore hath, or shall hereafter appoint any person to be his under sheriff, to collect the taxes required by law in his county, and such under sheriff shall neglect or refuse to account for and pay such taxes to the sheriff under whom he hath been or shall be appointed, or to the Treasurer at the time appointed for paying the same, it shall and may be lawful for the General Court, or court of the county whereof he hath been, now is, or shall be sheriff, upon motion to them made, by such sheriff, to give judgment against such under sheriff and his securities, their heirs, executors, and administrators, for all the money wherewith he shall be chargeable, and twenty *per centum* interest thereon, and to award execution for the same, provided that such under sheriff and his securities have ten days previous notice of such motion.

II. *PROVIDED also*, that no execution shall be issued against an under sheriff and his securities, for the twenty *per centum*, unless judgment shall have been obtained against the sheriff for the same.

III. *AND be it further enacted*, that every sheriff, under sheriff, or collector of taxes, now in office, shall in the court of his county, in one of the two succeeding courts after the passing of this act, take the following oath or affirmation, to wit: I A. B. *do swear, or affirm, that all and every sum or sums of money that I may collect or receive by virtue of my office of sheriff, or collector, shall not directly or indirectly by me or by my procurement, be disposed of to any other purpose than as directed by law.* And every sheriff or collector of taxes hereafter to come into office before he shall enter into the duties thereof, shall take the like oath or affirmation; and every sheriff or collector of taxes shall once at least in every month, under penalty of five thousand weight of tobacco for every failure, to be recovered with costs, at the suit of the commissioners, in any court of record, by bill, plaint, or information, one moiety whereof to the use of the commissioners, and the other for lessening the levy of the county, apply to one of the commissioners of the taxes of his county, with all the collections of taxes he shall have made, and before him, the said sheriff, under sheriff, or collector, shall count the said money, and the said commissioners shall take an exact list of the bills so counted, and their respective denominations, with the amount of the whole, and transmit the account and list so taken, to the Treasurer of the commonwealth, signed by himself, and a copy of such list shall, together with the money so counted, be sealed up by the said commissioners and returned to the said sheriff or collector, who shall not again open the same until he pays the money to the public Treasurer; and the commissioner for his trouble and expence herein, shall receive one fifth *per centum* on all the money so counted and sealed up. Any sheriff or collector of taxes misapplying any part of the money by him collected and received, to private purposes, and being thereof convicted, shall forfeit and pay treble the sum of the money so misapplied, for the use of the commonwealth, and suffer as in case of wilful perjury.

IV. *AND be it further enacted*, that every quarter-master and commissary, or their deputies, now employed in the staff department, in the service of this commonwealth, shall in the court of his county, on one of the two succeeding courts after the passing this act, take the following oath or affirmation, to wit: I A. B. *do swear, or affirm, that all and every sum or sums of money that I shall receive by virtue of my office, for public uses (as commissary, quarter-master, or deputies of either) shall be by me said out to the best advantage for the public, in such articles as I may be directed from time to time to purchase, and that I will not, directly or indirectly, by myself, or any person or persons whatsoever, dispose or make use of such money, or any part thereof, for my own emolument, or the emolument of any other person, for private purposes, other than my legal commission.* And every person who shall hereafter be appointed to either of the offices aforementioned, shall before he shall proceed to execute his office, take the like oath or affirmation, or failing so to do, he shall forfeit and pay five thousand pounds of crop tobacco, to be recovered with costs, by bill, plaint, or information, in any court of record, by any person that will sue for the same. Any quarter-master, commissary, or the deputies of either, misapplying any part of the money by him received as aforesaid, to private purposes, and being thereof convicted, shall forfeit and pay treble the sum of the money so misapplied, for the use of the commonwealth, and suffer as in case of wilful perjury.

V. *AND be it enacted*, that instead of the former allowance made to the sheriffs for collection, they shall hereafter receive a commission of five *per centum* on all public monies by them to be collected.

CHAP. XII.

An act for speedily recruiting the quota of this state for the continental army.

CHAP. XIII.

An act the more effectually to prevent and punish desertion.

A. D 1780.

Expired.

CHAP. XVI.

An act affixing penalties to certain crimes injurious to the independence of America, but less than treason, and repealing the act for the punishment of certain offences

---

Had its effect.

CHAP. XV.

An act to amend an act for raising a supply of money for the use of the United States, and for other purposes.

Repealed. May 1783, ch. 10.

CHAP. XVI.

An act to amend the several acts of Assembly respecting the inspection of tobacco.

Temporary. See Oct. 1777, ch. 15, 17; May 1783, ch. 33.

CHAP. XVII.

An act for altering the salaries heretofore given to the Judges of the superior courts.

Repealed. May 1783, ch. 33.

CHAP. XVIII.

An act for giving more permanent salaries to the Governor, the Council, and to the other officers of state.

Had its effect.

CHAP. XIX.

An act for emitting and funding a sum of money for supplying the present urgent necessities of this commonwealth

---

See May 1777, ch. 73; and May 1779, ch. 20.

CHAP. XX.

An act for giving more adequate wages to scouts.

Future allowance.

I. WHEREAS the wages allowed to scouts for discovering the approach of the *Indians* or any other enemy on the frontiers, as by an act of Assembly entitled *An act for providing against invasions and insurrections,* is inadequate to their fatigue and trouble: *Be it enacted,* that every scout appointed as by the before recited act is directed, shall, in lieu of the former allowance, be entitled to, and receive, for every day he shall be employed in such service, seventeen and an half pounds of tobacco, to be paid in money, according to the valuation of the grand jury made immediately preceding the service of such scout.

Private.

CHAP. XXI.

An act to vest certain escheated lands in the county of Kentucky in trustees for a public school.

CHAP. XXII.

An act for dissolving several vestries, and electing overseers of the poor.

See May 1782, ch. 36.

Preamble.

I. WHEREAS great inconveniences have arisen from the mode prescribed for making provision for the poor and other duties of the vestries, as by law now directed in the counties of *Rockbridge, Botetourt, Montgomery, Washington, Greenbrier, Augusta,* and *Frederick:* *Be it enacted by the General Assembly,* that where any of the above enumerated counties have vestries, or other bodies vested with powers to provide for the poor, the same are hereby dissolved. And for providing for the poor, and such other parochial duties as have heretofore been exercised by the vestries, church-wardens, or other bodies of the respective parishes, *Be it enacted,* that the sheriffs of the said counties shall, at their respective courts to be held in the month of *October* next (first giving twenty days previous notice thereof) proceed to elect five freeholders, resident in their said counties, to serve for three years, and be known by the name of Overseers of the Poor; in which election the said sheriffs shall observe the same rules, regulations, and rights of suffrage, as were formerly used in the election of vestry-men, saving and reserving to the church now, and at all times hereafter, every right, title, or claim, appertained thereto, as formerly reserved by an act entitled *An act for exempting the different societies of dissenters from contributing to the support and maintenance of the church of England, as by law established, and its ministers, and for other purposes therein mentioned.*

Their power and duty.

How vacancies are to be filled up.

II. AND be it further enacted, that the Overseers of the Poor, so to be chosen, or a majority of them having first taken an oath in their respective counties, well and truly to execute the duties of their office, as well as the oath of fidelity to the state, shall be deemed a body politic and corporate, to sue and be sued, and be invested with all the powers, and subject to the same penalties, that the vestries or church-wardens formerly were liable to and vested with, before the passing of this act. And in case of the death, resignation, removal, or refusal to act of any such overseer or overseers, the court of the county shall appoint some other person or persons in the room of such who shall so die, resign, remove, or refuse to act, who having taken the oaths as before directed, shall continue in office until the next general election of overseers. Twenty days before the *October* court, triennially, the sheriffs of the said counties respectively, shall in like manner give notice to the freeholders and house-keepers of each county, to meet at the court-house, on the first day of the succeeding court, for the election of Overseers of the Poor, to act for other three years, and so from time to time, that a perpetual succession of such overseers may be kept up by triennial elections.

Vestries in several counties dissolved.

Overseers to be elected for 3 years.

III. *AND be it further enacted*, that the courts of the aforesaid counties shall direct their orders to the Overseers of the Poor, to be elected by this act, in the same manner as they were formerly directed to the different vestries and churchwardens.

IV. *AND be it further enacted*, that if any sheriff shall fail or neglect to discharge his duty as is herein before directed, he shall forfeit and pay five hundred pounds, to be recovered by action of debt, bill, plaint, or information, in any court of record in this commonwealth, one half to the informer, and the other half to the use of the poor of the county in which such failure or neglect shall happen.

Penalty on sheriff n glecting to have elections triennially.

V. *AND be it further enacted*, that the present vestries of the counties aforesaid shall, on or before the first day of *February* next, make up and settle their accounts with the Overseers of the Poor of their respective counties, of all monies or tobacco by them levied or disbursed in virtue of the said office.

Former vestries to account with overseers.

C H A P. XXIII.

An act to revive and amend an act entitled An act for the inspection of pork, beef, flour, tar, pitch, and turpentine.

See Oct. 1776, ch 43; Nov. 1781, ch. 37; May 1782, ch. 40, 52; May 1783, ch 7.
Preamble.
Revival and continuance of former act.
Fees altered.

I. WHEREAS the act of Assembly passed in the year one thousand seven hundred and seventy six, entitled *An act for the inspection of pork, beef, flour, tar, pitch, and turpentine*, expired on the twenty sixth day of *June* last; and it is expedient and necessary that the same should be revived and amended; *Be it therefore enacted*, that the act entitled *An act for the inspection of pork, beef, flour, tar, pitch, and turpentine*, be revived and shall continue and be in force from and after the end of the present session of Assembly, for and during the term of two years, and from thence to the end of the next session of Assembly. And the several inspectors to be appointed in virtue of the said recited act, shall receive the following fees instead of those established by the same, to wit: For every barrel of pork or beef inspected and stamped, twenty shillings; for every barrel of tar, pitch, or turpentine, one dollar; for every barrel of flour containing two hundred and twenty pounds nett, or less, five shillings, and in proportion for every cask of greater weight, and no more, to be paid down by the owner.

II. *AND be it further enacted*, that all the penalties and forfeitures to be incurred by the said recited act for failure or neglect of duty, shall be forty times as much as the respective sums of money specified in the said act, and shall be sued for and recovered in the same manner and applied to the same uses as therein directed.

Penalties altered.

C H A P. XXIV.

An act to repeal an act establishing a Board of War, and one other act establishing a Board of Trade, and authorizing the Governor and Council to appoint a Commissioner of the Navy, a Commissioner of the War office, and a Commercial Agent.

Had its effect.

C H A P. XXV.

An act to give further time to delinquent counties to pay their specific tax, and for other purposes.

Expired.

C H A P. XXVI.

An act for establishing the town of Louisville at the falls of Ohio, and one other town in the county of Rockingham.

Private.

C H A P. XXVII.

An act for putting the eastern frontier of this commonwealth into a posture of defence.

Had its effect.

C H A P. XXVIII.

An act to suspend in part the operation of the act concerning escheats and forfeitures from British subjects, and for other purposes.

Private.

C H A P. XXIX.

An act to enable the Governor to provide a laboratory and proper magazines for the reception of arms, ammunition, and other public stores.

Preamble.
Power to Governor with advice of Council, to erect buildings.
Method of acquiring lands to build on.

I. WHEREAS it is expedient that proper magazines for the reception of the arms, ammunition, and other public stores, and a laboratory be speedily provided, *Be it enacted by the General Assembly*, that the Governor with the advice of his Council may, and he is hereby empowered and required to cause such and so many magazines as shall be judged necessary, and a laboratory to be immediately erected at the public expence, at such place or places as they shall think proper; and that reasonable satisfaction may be made to the proprietors of all lands which by virtue of this act may be taken and appropriated to the uses aforesaid, the clerk of the county wherein any such land shall lie, is hereby empowered and required, on requisition from the Governor for the time being, to issue a writ *ad quod damnum*, to be directed to the sheriff of the said county, commanding him to summon and empannel twelve able discreet freeholders of the viciage, no ways concerned in interest in the said lands, nor related to the owners or proprietors thereof, to meet on the said lands respectively on a certain day to be mentioned in the said writ, not under five, nor more than ten days from the date thereof, of which notice shall be given to the respective proprietors of the said lands, if they be to be found within the county, and if not, then to their respective agents if any there be; which freeholders taking nothing on pain of being discharged from the inquest and immediately imprisoned by the sheriff, either of meat or drink from any person whatever, from the time they came to the said place until their inquest sealed, shall be charged by the said sheriff impartially, and to the best of their skill and judgment to value the lands on which the said magazines and laboratory are to be erected, to be laid off by order of the Governor, and not exceeding three acres for each of the said buildings; and after such valuation made, the

A. D. 1780.

said sheriff shall forthwith return the same under the hands and seals of the said jurors, to the clerk's office of the said county; and the right and property of the said lands so laid off and valued, shall be immediately devested and be transferred to this commonwealth in fee simple; any want of consent or disability to consent in the said owners notwithstanding. The cost of building such magazines and labora-

Expence to be paid.

tory, the cost of the said inquest, and the several sums at which the rights of the owners are valued, shall be paid by the Treasurer, out of the public money in his hands, to the undertakers of the said magazines and laboratory, to the said proprietors and others respectively entitled, on warrants from the Auditors, countersigned by the Governor.

CHAP. XXX.

Private.

An act to continue and amend the act entitled An act for establishing the county of Ilinois, and for the more effectual protection and defence of the same, and for other purposes.

CHAP. XXXI.

Repealed. May 1783, ch. 21.

An act for further continuing and amending an act entitled An act for appointing Naval Officers and ascertaining their fees.

CHAP. XXXII.

Expired.

An act for further continuing an act entitled An act to empower the Governor and Council to lay an embargo for a limited time.

CHAP. XXXIII.

Expired.

An act to authorize the citizens of South Carolina and Georgia to remove their slaves into this state.

CHAP. XXXIV.

See May 1777, ch 4.

An act to amend the act entitled an act establishing a Loan Office for the purpose of borrowing money for the use of the United States and appointing a Commissioner for superintending the same.

Removing the office to Richmond.

Supplying vacancies in the Commissioner.

I. BE it enacted by the General Assembly, that so much of an act entitled An act for establishing a Loan Office for the purpose of borrowing money for the use of the United States, and appointing a Commissioner for superintending the same, as directs the Loan Office thereby established, to be kept in the city of *Williamsburg,* shall be and the same are hereby repealed; and that from and after the passing of this act the Commissioner of Loans for the time being, shall keep his said office at the town of *Richmond,* or such other place as the Governor with the advice of Council shall and may direct. And be it further enacted, that in case of the death or resignation of any such Commissioner during the recess of the General Assembly, the Governor and Council shall and may appoint some other proper person to supply the vacancy thereby occasioned, to be approved of by the General Assembly.

CHAP. XXXV.

Expired.

An act for giving further powers to the Governor and Council, and for other purposes.

CHAP. XXXVI.

Private.

An act for establishing three new counties upon the western waters.

CHAP. XXXVII.

Private.

An act for locating the public squares, to enlarge the town of Richmond, and for other purposes.

At a GENERAL ASSEMBLY begun and held at the Public Buildings in the Town of *Richmond,* on *Monday* the 16th day of *October,* in the Year of our Lord 1780.

CHAP. I.

See May 1780, ch 10.

Preamble.

An act to explain and amend the act for calling in and redeeming the money now in circulation, and for emitting and funding new bills of credit according to the resolutions of Congress of the 18th of March last.

Treasurer to exchange this for other paper.

I. WHEREAS various constructions have been made, and doubts have arisen, on several parts of the act entitled An act for calling in and redeeming the money now in circulation, and for emitting and funding new bills of credit according to the resolutions of Congress of the eighteenth of March last; and it is necessary that the same should be explained and amended: Be it therefore enacted, that the Treasurer of this commonwealth shall, and he is hereby empowered and required, to give in change the money to be emitted by virtue of the said recited act for the money now current; except the money emitted by virtue of an act of the last session, entitled *An act for emitting and funding a sum of money for supplying the present urgent necessities of this commonwealth*, at the rate of one dollar of the former for forty of the latter, to any person willing to change the same.

A. D. 1780.

II. *AND be it further enacted*, that there shall be collected, paid, and distrained for, the pound rate of ninety pounds of the money now in circulation for every hundred pounds value of property assessed by virtue of the said act, to be paid at three equal payments, that is to say: The sum of thirty pounds on the first day of *January* next, and the like sum at each of the periods of the fifteenth day of *April* and the fifteenth day of *September* then next following, and no more. That every gallon of brandy or other spirits distilled from grain, and every marriage and ordinary licence, shall and they are hereby declared to be only once subject to the payment of the tax imposed thereon, instead of paying the same at each of the periods before mentioned. And that all taxes imposed prior to the passing of the above recited act, except the specific taxes heretofore established shall cease and be discontinued on the last day of *December* one thousand seven hundred and eighty.

The tax on assessed property what it is.

All other taxes to cease except specific.

III. *AND whereas* the money emitted by an act of the last session of Assembly, agreeable to the resolutions of Congress of the eighteenth of *March* last, hath not been declared a legal tender, and it is politic and expedient that the money so emitted should receive all due credit among the good people of this commonwealth: *Be it therefore enacted*, that the money emitted by virtue of the said act, shall be received and passed as a legal tender in discharge of all debts and contracts whatsoever, so long as the same shall continue in circulation, except specific contracts expressing the contrary: *Provided always*, that the said money shall be passed and received, in all cases, at the rate of one dollar thereof for forty dollars of the money now in circulation, agreeable to the said resolutions of Congress of the eighteenth of *March* last.

This money declared a tender at one for forty.

IV. *AND be it further enacted*, that the money emitted by virtue of another act of the same session, entitled *An act for emitting and funding a sum of money for supplying the present urgent necessities of this commonwealth*, shall be receivable in discharge of any tax or duty whatsoever, and shall in like manner be received and passed as a legal tender in discharge of all debts and contracts, so long as it shall continue in circulation (except as before excepted) and the Treasurer is hereby empowered to exchange the money emitted by the said act, and so received in taxes, for the continental money now in circulation emitted prior to the passing of the said act.

Also the money issued by another act of May 1780.

V. *AND be it further enacted*, that four tenths of the money emitted, agreeable to the said resolutions of Congress of the eighteenth of *March* last, be retained in the office of the commissioner of continental loans within this state, to be by him applied agreeable to the directions of the act adopting the said resolutions; and the said commissioner is directed to certify to the Auditors of public accounts, all drafts or requisitions which may be made upon him by any order or resolution of Congress, to be by them stated in account with the United States.

Appropriation of this money.

VI. *AND be it further enacted*, that the proprietors of the lots in the towns of *Norfolk*, *Portsmouth*, and *Suffolk*, the houses and improvements thereon, being destroyed either by the act of Convention in one thousand seven hundred and seventy six, or by the *British* army since that time, shall, and are hereby declared to be exempt from the payment of the taxes imposed by the said first recited act. *Provided*, that the lots in the said towns, the property whereof hath been since transferred or new improvements made thereon, shall, notwithstanding the above exemption, be still subject to the payment of the said taxes.

Certain lots in Norfolk Portsmouth, and Suffolk, exempted from taxes.

VII. *AND whereas*, since the assessment directed to be made by the said first recited act hath been complicated, some of the good people inhabiting the counties on the eastern frontier of this commonwealth, have been deprived by the *British* army of many assessed articles of their property: *Be it therefore enacted*, that the commissioners of the tax in each of the counties, which have been thus distressed, may, and they are hereby empowered, upon satisfactory testimony being produced to them, that any person within their respective counties hath been deprived as aforesaid, of any assessed article of his property, grant a certificate thereof to such person, directed to the collector of their county, who upon receipt of such certificate shall refund the amount of such persons tax upon such article or articles of property as shall be contained in the commissioners certificate, if such tax hath been collected, or if it hath not been collected, then the said collector shall cease to make any collection for such assessed articles of property.

Also certain persons on the eastern frontier.

CHAP. II

An act for granting pardon to certain offenders.

Private.

CHAP. III.

An act for recruiting this state's quota of troops to serve in the continental army.

Had its effect.

CHAP. IV.

An act for supplying the army with clothes, provisions, and waggons.

Had its effect.

CHAP. V.

An act to revive and amend the act entitled An act for procuring a supply of provisions and other necessaries for the use of the army.

Had its effect.

CHAP. VI.

An act to establish a corps of invalids to serve as guards and on garrison duty.

Had its effect.

CHAP. VII.

An act for procuring a supply of money for the exigencies of the war.

Had its effect.

A. D. 1780.

Private.

CHAP. VIII.

An act directing the money arising from the sales of the estate of John Meacom, deceased, to be paid to his widow and children.

CHAP. IX.

Private.

An act for adding part of the county of Augusta to the county of Monongalia.

CHAP. X.

Expired.

An act to extend the jurisdiction of a single Magistrate in certain cases.

CHAP. XI.

Repealed. Oct.
1783, ch. 32.

An act to amend the act for establishing a Land Office, and for ascertaining the terms and manner of granting waste and unappropriated lands.

CHAP. XII.

See May 1779, ch. 12.

An act to amend an act entitled An act for adjusting and settling the titles of claimers to unpatented lands under the present and former government, previous to the establishment of the commonwealth's Land Office.

Preamble.

I. WHEREAS it is represented to this present General Assembly, that from the inclemency of the weather during the sitting of the commissioners appointed to adjust and settle the titles of claimers to unpatented lands, many witnesses were prevented from attending the said commissioners and the parties at whose instance they were summoned, lost the benefit of their testimony, and thereby failed to support their claims: For remedy whereof, *Be it enacted*, that it shall and may be lawful for any *Caveats allowed against the judgment of the Commissioners.* person, his or her heirs or assigns, aggrieved or injured by the determination of the said commissioners, to enter a caveat against a grant thereupon, until the matter shall be heard before the General Court; and that any person or persons who may hereafter in like manner be aggrieved by the determination of any commissioners who shall sit for the purpose aforesaid, shall be entitled to the same mode of redress as above mentioned, and may petition the said court to have his or her claim considered, and upon its being proved that he or she laboured under such disability at the time of the meeting of the said commissioners thereupon, the court shall grant him or her a hearing in a summary way, and if it shall appear that the petitioners claim is just, the court may reverse the former determination and order a grant to issue for such land, or any part thereof, to the person to whom they shall adjudge the same, on the terms prescribed by an act entitled *An act for adjusting and settling the titles of claimers to unpatented lands under the present and former governments, previous to the establishment of the commonwealth's Land Office.*

Further allowance to Commissioners and attendants.

II. AND whereas the allowance made to commissioners who are appointed to carry into execution the above mentioned act, and to the surveyors, sheriffs, and clerks attending the same, are now insufficient: For remedy whereof, *Be it enacted*, that each commissioner for every day he shall be necessarily employed in going to, attending on, and returning from the business of his office, shall receive thirty pounds; the surveyor twelve pounds, and the sheriff eight pounds, in lieu of the allowance formerly provided.

Tax on litigants raised.

III. AND whereas the expence of carrying the said act into execution will be greatly increased, and it is reasonable and just that the greatest part of such expence should be defrayed by the persons who are to be benefited by the same: *Be it further enacted*, that for every hundred acres of land contained within the certificates to be granted by the commissioners, the party receiving the same shall pay five dollars to the commissioners, besides a fee of twenty shillings for each certificate to the clerk.

CHAP. XIII.

Repealed. May
1783, ch. 10.

An act to amend an act entitled an act to amend the several acts of Assembly respecting the inspection of tobacco.

CHAP. XIV.

Had its effect.

An act to amend the act for giving farther time to delinquent counties to pay their specific tax.

CHAP. XV.

An act for the more effectual collection of taxes and public dues.

Preamble.

I. WHEREAS it hath been found by experience that an alteration is necessary to be made in the Auditors office, and that a Solicitor or superintendant of accounts should be appointed, for the more fully calling to account all persons indebted to the public: *Be it therefore enacted*, that a person be chosen by joint ballot of both Houses of Assembly, to act as Solicitor General, and to *Solicitor General appointed.* be exempt from militia duty, and to continue in office until removed by the Governor, with advice of Council, or by joint vote of both Houses, and in case of death or resignation, that the Governor and Council during the recess of the Assembly be empowered to appoint some other fit and able person to act in his stead until the end of the next General Assembly. The Solicitor so appointed shall not be able to act or perform any of the duties of his office until he shall have taken the oath of fidelity to the com- *His oath;* monwealth, and also an oath impartially and honestly to execute his duty, which oaths shall be taken during the sitting of the Honourable General Court before the said court, and during their vacation before some Judge thereof, or before any county court within this commonwealth, and be entered of record; any Judge of the General Court administering such oath to certify the same to his next court, in

A. D. 1780.
and duty.

order that the fame may be recorded, and a certificate fhall be given to the perfon fo qualified by the Judge or the clerk of fuch court before whom the faid oaths may be taken. The faid Solicitor, immediately on his qualifying as aforefaid, is hereby authorized and empowered to examine from time to time the books of accounts kept by the Board of Auditors, and to compare the fame with their vouchers, to fee that all monies to be paid by their warrants are entered and charged to the proper accounts therefor, or to the perfons properly chargeable therewith, and that the taxes levied be alfo credited to their refpective and proper accounts, keeping all taxes raifed under any one law feparate and apart from the other. To caufe a correct lift of all balances due either to or from the public to be ftated together with the amount of the feveral taxes, and lay the fame before the General Affembly at the firft meeting of every feffion. To ftate and prepare in a regular manner accounts againft all and every perfons indebted to the public, on monies advanced them for any purpofe, and failing to account with the Auditors therefor in due and reafonable time and attend the Attorney General therewith and with fuch vouchers as the faid Attorney may think neceffary. Alfo to ftate accounts for money or other public property againft all public officers of every denomination indebted to the public, efpecially againft fheriffs, efcheators, clerks, infpectors, commiffaries, quartermafters, keepers of public ftores, paymafters, naval officers, county lieutenants, or recruiting officers, either in the land or fea fervice, to collect the vouchers likewife neceffary to prove their accounts, and attend the Attorney for the purpofe of obtaining judgments thereon at fuch times as are already or may hereafter be directed by law for the more fpeedy recovery of money in their hands due to the public.

II. AND for the more effectually obtaining that end, *Be it enacted*, that it may and fhall be lawful for the Attorney General to move for judgments on any day during the fitting of the General or Oyer Courts againft any perfon or perfons indebted to the public. The Solicitor hereby appointed is alfo further authorized and required to ftate and enter into the Auditors books the amount of all judgments that may be obtained, together with the damages and cofts, that the fame may be charged to the proper account of the perfon againft whom a judgment has been entered, and thereupon to iffue executions and fend the fame by exprefs to the fheriff or coroner, the charge of which exprefs, as well as of giving notice being firft paid by the public, to be recovered of the perfon againft whom fuch execution iffued, by motion in the General or county Court. The Solicitor is alfo directed to attend to the ftating and adjufting in a proper book or books for that purpofe to be provided at public expence, all accounts for monies heretofore advanced to fundry perfons before the eftablifhment of the Auditors Board, and ftill remaining unfettled and unaccounted for, and to charge on all fuch debts that may appear due, depreciation, regulating himfelf by the price of tobacco at the time of advance, from the beft information he can procure, and the price of tobacco at the time of payment agreeable to the valuation of the grand jury. And for the more effectually fettling the accounts of the public, prior to the eftablifhment of the Auditors Board, the faid Solicitor is empowered to infpect the books and papers of the Committee of Safety, the Council of State, the Treafury Office and the Navy Board, and to collect all papers and vouchers neceffary for the recovery of the faid money, and alfo to fuperintend the ftating of the continental account both paft and future, the collection of the vouchers neceffary for the fupport thereof, and direct the mode moft proper for the adjufting the fame. And the faid Solicitor is directed in all doubtful matters of law, to require counfel of the Attorney General, and when further affiftance in the profecution of his duty is neceffary, to employ one or more clerks, who fhall be allowed for their fervices what the Solicitor and any two of the Auditors fhall think proper, fo that the fame fhall not exceed the falaries given by law to the clerks of the Auditors, to be paid by the Treafurer on warrant from the Auditors. And for the fervices of the Solicitor, he fhall be allowed and paid out of the public treafury in quarterly payments on warrant from the Auditors, thirty thoufand pounds of tobacco, to be eftimated in the fame manner as directed by the act of Affembly for giving more permanent falaries to the Governor, the Council, and the other officers of ftate.

To take advice of the Attorney General.
To appoint a clerk.
Solicitor's allowance.

III. AND whereas great delays in collecting the money, arife from the commiffioners failing to return the county affeffments to the Auditors office in due time, and by the remiffnefs of county courts and affeffors in the difcharge of their duties refpectively: *Be it enacted*, that the Juftices of every county failing either to appoint commiffioners in cafes directed by law, or neglecting their duty in any other refpect as directed by the feveral acts of Affembly for appointing commiffioners and preferibing their duty, fhall forfeit and pay five thoufand pounds of tobacco each. The commiffioners failing in their duty as required by the faid acts, fhall forfeit and pay ten thoufand pounds of tobacco each, and the affeffors failing or refufing to perform their duty as required by the faid acts, fhall each of them forfeit and pay five thoufand pounds of tobacco.

Penalty on county courts, commiffioners, and affeffors, increafed.

CHAP. XVI.

An act declaring what fhall be a lawful marriage.

I. FOR encouraging marriages and for removing doubts concerning the validity of marriages celebrated by Minifters, other than the church of *England*, *Be it enacted by the General Affembly*, that it fhall and may be lawful for any Minifter of any fociety or congregation of chriftians, and for the fociety of chriftians called Quakers and Menonifts, to celebrate the rights of matrimony, and to join together as man and wife, thofe who may apply to them, agreeable to the rules and ufage of the refpective focieties to which the parties to be married refpectively belong, and fuch marriage, as well as thofe heretofore celebrated by diffenting Minifters, fhall be, and they are hereby declared good and valid in law.

See May 1783, ch. 35.
Preamble.
Who may marry.

Former marriages by diffenting minifters confirmed.

II. *PROVIDED always*, and it is the true intent and meaning of this act, that nothing herein before contained fhall extend or be conftrued to extend to confirm any marriages heretofore celebrated, or hereafter to be celebrated, between parties within the degrees of affinity or confanguinity forbidden by law. *Provided alfo*, that no perfons except the people called Quakers and Menonifts, fhall hereafter be joined together as man and wife, without lawful licenfe firft had, or thrice publication of banns in the refpective parifhes or congregations where the parties to be married may feverally refide, agreeable to the directions of an act of Affembly paffed in the year one thoufand feven hundred and forty eight, entitled *An act concerning marriages*; provided, that the licenfe fo obtained may be directed to any regular Minifter that the parties to be married may require. Every Minifter of any fociety or congregation, not of the church of *England*, offending againft the directions of the faid act concerning marriages, fhall be fubject to the fame pains and penalties in cafes of omiffion or neglect as by the faid recited act are impofed upon Minifters of the church of *England*.

Exception to cafes of inceft.

No marriage (except between Quakers and Menonifts) but on licence or publication of banns.
Penalty.

III. AND be it further enacted, that inftead of the fees preferibed by the faid recited act, the feveral Minifters may demand and receive for the celebration of every marriage, twenty five pounds of tobacco, and no more, to be paid in current money at the rate which fhall be fettled by the grand jury at the term of the General Court next preceding fuch marriage.

Fees.

A. D. 1780.

Certificates of marriages to be returned to the clerk of the court and recorded

IV. AND that a regifter of all marriages may be preferved, *Be it enacted*, that a certificate of every marriage hereafter to be folemnized figned by the Minifter celebrating the fame, or in the cafe of Quakers, by the clerk of the meeting, fhall be by fuch Minifter or clerk, as the cafe may be, tranfmitted to the clerk of the county wherein the marriage is folemnized, within three months thereafter, to be entered upon record by fuch clerk, in a book to be by him kept for that purpofe, which fhall be evidence of fuch marriage. The clerk fhall be entitled to receive and demand of the party fo married, ten pounds of tobacco for recording fuch certificate. *And be it further enacted*, that every Minifter or clerk of a Quaker's or Menonift's meeting, as the cafe may be, failing to tranfmit fuch certificate to the clerk of the court in due time, fhall forfeit and pay the fum of five hundred pounds, to be recovered with cofts of fuit by the informer in any court of record. This act fhall commence and be in force from and after the firft day of *January* in the year of our Lord one thoufand feven hundred and eighty one.

Penalty on Minifter or clerk of Quaker fociety failing to tranfmit certificates.

County courts to licence diffenting Minifters to marry, not exceeding four of one fect.

V. FOR carrying this act into execution, *Be it further enacted*, that the courts of the different counties fhall and are hereby authorized on recommendation from the elders of the feveral religious fects, to grant licenfe to diffenting Minifters of the gofpel, not exceeding the number of four of each fect in any one county, to join together in holy matrimony, any perfons within their counties only; which licenfe fhall be figned by the Judge or elder Magiftrate under his hand and feal.

CHAP. XVII.

Private.

An act for dividing the county of Brunfwick into two diftinct counties.

CHAP. XVIII.

An act for eftablifhing feveral public ferries and difcontinuing a former one.

See 1769, ch. 25, and notes.

Batte's ferry difcontinued.

Several new ferries, and the rates of ferriage.

I. BE it enacted by the General Affembly, that the ferry eftablifhed from the land of the late *Henry Batte*, in the county of *Henrico* to the land of the late *Alexander Bolling*, in the county of *Prince George*, be difcontinued, and that public ferries be conftantly kept at the following places, and the rates for paffing the fame fhall be as follows, that is to fay: From the land of *John Fox* in the county of *Gloucefter*, acrofs *York* river to the land formerly the property of *John Tabb*, on the oppofite fhore, the price for a man feven dollars, and for a horfe the fame; from the upper end of the land of *Thomas Batte*, the younger, in the county of *Chefterfield*, acrofs *Appamattox* river, to the lot of land the property of *William Gilliam*, in the town of *Broadway* and county of *Prince George*, and from the lot of land of the faid *William Gilliam* to the lands of the faid *Thomas Batte*, the price for a man two dollars, and for a horfe the fame; from the lands of *Landon Carter*, in the county of *Culpeper*, acrofs *Rappahannock* river, at *Norman's* ford, the price for a man two dollars, and for a horfe the fame; and from the lands of *David Rofs*, in the county of *Bedford*, acrofs *James* river at the mouth of *Archer's* creek, to the lands of *Robert Bolling*, deceafed, the price for a man one dollar, and for a horfe the fame: And for the tranfportation of wheel carriages, tobacco, cattle, and other beafts, at the ferries aforefaid, the ferry keeper may demand and take the following rates, that is to fay: For every coach, chariot, or waggon, and the driver thereof, the fame as for fix horfes; for every cart, or four wheel chaife, or chair, the fame as for two horfes; for every hogfhead of tobacco as for one horfe; for every head of neat cattle as for one horfe; for every fheep, goat, or lamb, one fifth part of the ferriage of one horfe; and for every hog, one fourth part of the ferriage for a horfe, according to the prices herein before fettled at fuch ferries; and if any ferry keeper fhall prefume to demand and receive from any perfon whatfoever, any greater rates than is hereby allowed, he fhall for every fuch offence forfeit and pay the party grieved the ferriage demanded or received and ten fhillings, to be recovered with cofts before a Juftice of the Peace where the offence fhall be committed.

Penalty for over charging.

CHAP. XIX.

Private.

An act for diffolving the veftry of the parifh of Albemarle in the county of Suffex.

CHAP. XX.

Private.

An act to empower the court of Greenbrier county to have a waggon road opened from their courthoufe to the eaftern waters.

CHAP. XXI.

See Oct. 1779, ch. 23.

An act to amend an act entitled an act to amend an act entitled an act concerning high-ways, mill dams, and bridges.

Preamble.

Penalty in tobacco on overfeer.

On mafters or overfeers failing to fend; and on others compelled to work on roads.

I. WHEREAS the penalties impofed by an act of Affembly entitled *An act to amend an act entitled an act concerning high-ways, mill dams, and bridges*, have been found infufficient to compel the due execution thereof: *Be it therefore enacted*, that inftead of the penalty inflicted by the faid act upon every furveyor of a road for neglect of duty, he fhall forfeit and pay two hundred and fifty pounds of tobacco; and that for every male labouring fervant or flave the owner thereof, or overfeer, as the cafe may be, fhall fail to fend when required by a furveyor, he or fhe fhall forfeit and pay fifty pounds of tobacco, and all other perfons who are by the faid recited act compelled to labour on roads, failing to attend and labour when required by the furveyor, with fuch tools as he fhall direct them to bring, fhall alfo forfeit and pay fifty pounds of tobacco; which faid penalties fhall be to the informer, and recoverable before a Juftice of the Peace of the county where fuch offence fhall be committed.

Penalty for felling a tree into a road and not removing it, or killing trees near the road; or making a fence acrofs; or to cut, pull up, deftroy or deface a direction ftone or poft.

II. AND be it enacted, that if any perfon fhall fell any tree or trees into fuch high way, or caufe the fame to be felled, and not cut and carried away immediately, or fhall kill any tree or trees within the diftance of fixty feet from fuch high-way, or caufe the fame to be killed and not felled, or fhall make any fence into fuch high-way, fuch perfon fhall for every fuch offence forfeit and pay one hundred weight of tobacco, recoverable as aforefaid. And that if any perfon fhall prefume to cut, pull up, deftroy, or deface, any ftone or poft, or the infcriptions thereon, and be thereof convicted by confeffion or the oath of one or more creditable witneffes before a Juftice of the Peace of the county where fuch offence fhall be committed, he or fhe fhall forfeit and pay two hundred weight of tobacco, recoverable as aforefaid.

III. *AND be it further enacted,* that all overseers of high-ways shall be personally exempted from working on any other high-way beside the road he is appointed overseer of. And where any presentment shall be made by a grand jury against any surveyor, the penalty shall be applied towards lessening the county levy. So much of the said recited act as comes within the purview of this act, is hereby repealed.

Overseers exempt from working on other roads.
On presentments, the fines to the use of the county.

C H A P. XXII.

An act for the more equal division of the parishes of Amherst *and* Lexington, *in the county of* Amherst.

Private.

C H A P. XXIII.

An act for ascertaining the center of the county of Stafford.

Private.

C H A P. XXIV.

An act for restoring certain slaves to George Harmer.

Private.

C H A P. XXXV.

An act for the manumission of certain slaves.

Private.

C H A P. XXVI.

An act to vest certain houses and tenements in the town of Alexandria *in* John Sutton *and his heirs in fee simple.*

Private.

C H A P. XXVII.

An act for making good the future pay of the army, and for other purposes.

See Oct. 1781, ch. 19; May 1, 82, ch. 47; Oct. 1782, ch. 1; May 1783, ch. 8; Oct. 1783, ch. 4;

I. BE it enacted by the General Assembly, that the commander in chief and commanding officer in the southern department, be desired to cause the officers belonging to this state, to meet and agree upon the officers to command the regiments raised by this state for continental service, out of those who incline to continue in service, and in case they cannot agree among themselves about their rank, the same shall be determined and settled by the commander in chief; that from and after the passing of this act, the said officers shall supply themselves with clothing; and the better to enable them so to do, they shall be entitled to and receive the pay and rations as stated and allowed before the first day of *January* one thousand seven hundred and seventy seven, in specie, or the value thereof in paper money, to be ascertained by the Auditors agreeable to the table of depreciation fixed by Congress, or which shall he hereafter fixed by them; and the soldiers both in continental and state service, shall be also entitled to their pay in specie, or the value thereof in paper money, to be settled and discharged in like manner as directed in the case of officers; that the public store be henceforth discontinued, and the Governor with advice of Council, is hereby required and empowered to appoint a clothier general or some person to supply the *Virginia* troops with necessary clothes and blankets, the person so appointed to give bond and good security for the due and faithful discharge of his office, and the clothes so supplied and furnished the said troops, shall be paid for by stopping so much of their pay as may be necessary for that purpose.

Method of reducing continental officers of this state.
Officers to supply themselves with cloathing.
Their pay and rations to be made equal to specie. Also the soldiers pay.
Public stores discontinued and Governor to appoint a Clothier General.

II. *AND be it further enacted,* that any officer of this state on continental establishment, who hath died or shall hereafter die in the service, and leave a widow, she shall receive annually for the space of seven years, half pay of such officer in specie, or the value thereof in paper money, from the public treasury, and in case there be no widow, or there being a widow, she dies or intermarries within the said term of seven years, the orphan children of such officer shall then be entitled to receive the said pay for the term aforesaid, or so much thereof as shall be unexpired at the death or intermarriage of such widow.

Provision for widows and children of officers dying in the services.

III. *AND be it enacted,* that all allowances of half pay given by this state under any act or resolution of Assembly to the widow of any officer who hath died in the service, shall hereafter be paid agreeable to the table of depreciation aforesaid; that the officers of this state in continental service who shall continue therein to the end of the present war, shall receive half pay during life, or until they shall again be called into service.

to be paid according to the Congress scale of depreciation.
Officers to have half pay for life.

IV. AND whereas no provision has been made in land for the general officers of this state in continental service; therefore, *Be it enacted,* that there shall be allowed to a Major General fifteen thousand acres of land, and to a Brigadier General ten thousand acres of land, to be reserved to them and their heirs, in the same manner and on the same conditions as is by law heretofore directed for the officers and soldiers of the *Virginia* line in continental service, and there shall be moreover allowed to all the officers of this state on continental or state establishments, or to the legal representatives of such officers according to their respective ranks, an additional bounty in lands, in the proportion of one third of any former bounty heretofore granted them.

Land given to the General officers.

Bounty in lands increased to other officers.

V. *AND be it further enacted,* that the legal representative of any officer on continental or state establishments, who may have died in the service before the bounty of lands granted by this or any former law, shall be entitled to demand and receive the same in like manner as the officer himself might have done when living, agreeable to his rank. And as a testimony of the high sense the General Assembly of *Virginia* entertain of the important services rendered the United States by the Honourable Major General Baron *Steuben, It is further enacted,* that fifteen thousand acres of land be granted to the said Major General Baron *Steuben,* in like manner as is herein before granted to other Major Generals.

Land given to Baron Steuben.

A. D. 1780.

Expired.

CHAP. XXVIII.

An act for further continuing an act entitled An act to empower the Governor and Council to lay an embargo for a limited time.

Had its effect.

CHAP. XXIX.

An act for the more effectual and speedy clothing of the army.

CHAP. XXX.

See May 1779, ch. 24.

An act for further continuing part of an act entitled An act for punishing persons guilty of certain thefts and forgeries, and fixing the allowance to sheriffs, venire-men, and witnesses, in certain cases, and for fixing the allowance to the clerk of the General Court for ex officio and public services.

Preamble.

So much as respects the punishment of persons guilty of thefts and forgeries, made perpetual.

I. WHEREAS so much of the act of Assembly passed in the year one thousand seven hundred and seventy nine, entitled *An act for punishing persons guilty of certain thefts and forgeries, and fixing the allowance to sheriffs, venire-men, and witnesses, in certain cases,* as respects the punishment of persons guilty of certain thefts and forgeries, will expire on the first day of *January* next, and it is expedient that the same should be further continued: *Be it therefore enacted by the General Assembly,* that so much of the act entitled *An act for punishing persons guilty of certain thefts and forgeries, and fixing the allowance to sheriffs, venire-men, and witnesses, in certain cases,* as respects the punishment of persons guilty of certain thefts and forgeries, shall be and is hereby continued and made perpetual.

Allowance to the clerk for ex officio services.

II. AND whereas there is no provision made by law for paying the clerk of the General Court, for *ex officio* and public services, and those services have become very considerable: *Be it therefore enacted,* that the clerk of the said court be allowed eight thousand pounds of tobacco annually, for all his *ex officio* and public services, to commence from the tenth day of *December,* one thousand seven hundred and seventy nine, to which period allowance hath been made for the same, and that the Auditors of public accounts be authorized and required to issue their warrant upon the public Treasurer for payment of the same quarterly, according to the estimated price of crop tobacco made by the grand jury next preceding the time of issuing such warrant.

CHAP. XXXI.

An act for the defence of the eastern frontier of this commonwealth.

Preamble.

These regulations at an end.

I. WHEREAS the trade of this commonwealth hath of late been greatly obstructed, and the citizens of the same inhabiting the shores of the navigable rivers and bays, greatly distressed by means of small cruisers belonging to the enemies of *America,* which might be effectually prevented by a small force provided for that purpose: *Be it therefore enacted by the General Assembly,* that the brig *Jefferson,* with the armed boats *Liberty* and *Patriot,* be forthwith manned and fitted out for the purpose of suppressing the cruisers belonging to the enemy, and affording protection and safety to the good citizens inhabiting the shores of the bay and rivers, exposed to the ravages of such cruisers. The *Thetis* and the *Lewis* galley shall also be forthwith and without delay, made ready and compleated for the same service. That the armed vessels aforesaid, as well as others hereafter to be fitted for the service of the commonwealth, may with the greater ease and expedition be manned, the Governor with the advice of Council may, and he is hereby authorized and empowered, if the exigencies of the service aforesaid should render it necessary, to issue his warrant to any officer commanding an armed vessel in the service of this state, authorizing and directing such officer to impress into the service of this commonwealth any seamen or mariners, under the following restrictions and limitations: The seamen on board any vessel belonging to the inhabitants of either sister state, and those on board any vessel belonging to foreigners, and in no part owned by any inhabitant or inhabitants of this commonwealth, shall be and the same are hereby exempt from impressment. The seamen on board any vessel to whomsoever belonging, loaded and outward bound, shall also be exempt from impressment. The seamen or mariners on board any other ship or vessel, except as before is excepted, shall and may be impressed into the service of the state, by warrant from the Governor as aforesaid; provided that not more than one fifth man be taken from on board any such ship or vessel. The seamen or mariners so as aforesaid impressed into the service of the commonwealth, shall not be compelled to serve at any one time more than nine months; and when their time of service shall be ended, such men as shall faithfully continue to serve during the said term of nine months, shall be exempt from any future impress for twelve months thereafter; and to ascertain such faithful service, the officer discharging any seaman after the said term of nine months service, shall give a certificate to such seaman, stating the time of his service and when it ended or expired.

II. IN order to render the naval service more agreeable, and to enable the seamen and mariners who may by virtue hereof be impressed into the service, or those who may voluntarily enlist or have already voluntarily enlisted into the same, to provide themselves with the necessaries of life, the pay of all such able seamen and mariners shall henceforward in lieu of the pay heretofore allowed, be two shillings *per* day, and the pay of ordinary seamen or landsmen shall be one shilling and six pence *per* day, and the pay of boys one shilling *per* day, in specie; and if it should so happen that the specie cannot be procured for the purpose of paying the same, then such seamen and boys shall receive in lieu thereof as much paper money as will be equivalent to the pay aforesaid, at the time the same is received by them, the difference between which, from time to time, shall be ascertained by the Governor with the advice of Council. The officers and men on board any armed vessel in the service of this commonwealth, shall henceforward be entitled to the whole of any prize by them taken, to be distributed among them according to the continental regulations in such cases made and provided, saving nevertheless the right to all and every person or persons claiming such prize as a recapture or otherwise, according to the Admiralty regulations established by the Continental Congress or by this commonwealth.

III. FOR more effectually clothing and providing necessaries for the seamen in the service of this state, and discharging with punctuality their pay, the Governor shall and he is hereby directed from time to time to issue his warrant to the paymaster of the navy, for as much money as may be necessary to purchase canvass for hammocks, clothing, and slops, for the seamen and mariners, and also for their pay; the purchases of such canvass, clothing, and slops, shall from time to time be made, with advice of the commissioner of the navy, and when made, distributed by the said commissioner among the seamen and mariners, as he shall judge proper and necessary for the good of the service. The pay-master shall once in six weeks settle his accounts with the Auditors of public accounts, and in case of failure, the Auditors shall and they are hereby directed to proceed against such pay-master as they are directed to do against delinquent sheriffs and collectors. The Captains of each and every armed vessel in the service of this state, shall carefully attend to the issuing the clothing and slops to the seamen and mariners on board their respective vessels, and keep an exact account thereof against each seaman and mariner for what he receives, and the amount thereof shall from time to time be deducted from each seaman's pay, a copy of which amount shall in due time, before the day of payment, be by every Captain returned upon oath to the pay-master, that he may ascertain the sum due to each seaman; a like copy shall also by each Captain be returned to the commissioner of the navy once in every six months, who is hereby directed to lodge the same in the Auditors office as a check upon such pay-master. Henceforward in lieu of the pay and clothing heretofore allowed to the officers of the navy, they and each of them shall receive the following allowances, to wit: A Commodore fourteen shillings, a Captain eight shillings and three pence, a Lieutenant six shillings, a Master five shillings, a Mate four shillings, a Midshipman two shillings and nine pence, a Quartermaster two shillings and nine pence, a Boatswain four shillings, a Boatswain's mate two shillings and nine pence, a Sail-maker two shillings and nine pence, a Gunner four shillings, a Gunner's mate two shillings and nine pence, a Quarter-Gunner two shillings and six pence, an Armourer two shillings and six pence, a Carpenter four shillings, a Carpenter's mate two shillings and six pence, Carpenter's crew two shillings each, a Surgeon six shillings, Surgeon's mate three shillings, and Master at Arms two shillings and six pence *per* day, in specie, and in case specie cannot be procured, then as much paper money as will be equivalent to each officers pay as above, to be ascertained in the same manner as the pay of the seamen and mariners, shall be received by each officer.

A. D. 1780.

IV. THAT vessels of war in the service of this commonwealth may be properly supported for the purpose of protecting the trade of *Chesapeake* bay, the following duties shall be paid by the owner or master of every merchant vessel to the Naval Officer of the port where such merchant vessel enters, to wit: A duty of fifteen pence in specie, shall be paid by the owners of each merchant vessel upon every ton such vessel will carry, which shall be ascertained by the register of such merchant vessel; upon every gallon of rum, gin, brandy, and other spirits imported into this commonwealth by water, a duty of one penny in specie shall be paid; upon *Madeira* wine four pence *per* gallon; upon all other wines two pence *per* gallon in specie; upon molasses and other syrups a duty of one penny *per* gallon; upon coffee a duty of one shilling *per* hundred weight shall be paid; upon loaf sugar one shilling and six pence for every hundred weight shall be paid; upon clayed sugar one shilling and three pence shall be paid for every hundred weight; upon *Muscovado* sugar there shall be paid a duty of one shilling for every hundred weight; upon all imported dry goods, except salt, munitions for war, and iron from *Maryland*, there shall be paid one *per centum* upon the value, to be ascertained by the costs thereof, at the port where laden or put on board, by the Captain or owner of the vessel importing the same. The duties hereby imposed shall be paid in specie or current money of this commonwealth equivalent thereto (the ratio whereof shall from time to time be fixed by the Governor and Council and transmitted to the respective Naval Officers) by the Captain or owners of all and every vessel or vessels, at the port of importation, to the Naval Officer of the district with whom such vessel or vessels shall be entered; for the true and due collection whereof, every Captain of a vessel shall at the time of entering the same, give bond and approved security to the Naval Officer, well and truly to pay the same within one month after such importation, the penalty of which bond shall be two thousand pounds specie for a vessel of one hundred tons burthen, and one thousand pounds like money for a vessel of fifty tons burthen, and so in proportion for a larger or smaller vessel trading to this state; and where any vessel importing any of the dutiable articles aforesaid shall arrive in this state, the Captain of which shall fail to give such bond as aforesaid, to the Naval Officer with whom his vessel shall be entered, at the time of entering the same, such vessel, with her tackle, apparel, and furniture, shall be subject to seizure by the Naval Officer or his deputy for the district wherein such vessel lies, and shall be forfeited, one half to the use of the commonwealth, the other half to the use and benefit of the Naval Officer or other person prosecuting for the same. And where any Captain or commander of a vessel trading to this commonwealth, shall after having entered into bond as aforesaid, secrete or conceal, or where the owner or owners of such vessel shall secrete or conceal any of the dutiable articles aforesaid, to avoid the payment of the duty imposed upon the same, the vessel, with her tackle, apparel, rigging, and furniture, shall be forfeited therefor, one half of which forfeiture shall be to the use of the commonwealth, the other half to the person or persons who shall inform and prosecute for the same. To prevent delays in the payment of the duties hereby imposed, it shall and may be lawful for the General Court, or court of the county wherein the Naval Office is kept, for the district within which any failure may happen, upon motion made by such Naval Officer, to give judgment against the person making default, and his securities, their heirs, executors, and administrators, for the sum remaining due, with costs, and to award execution for the same, the parties having ten days notice of such motion. Each and every Naval Officer, before he enters upon the duties of this act, shall give bond with approved security, payable to the Governor of the commonwealth for the time being, in the penalty of ten thousand pounds specie, conditioned for the true and faithful performance of the duties hereby required of such Naval Officer, and in case of refusal, shall forfeit his office. Each and every Naval Officer after having entered into bond as aforesaid, which bond shall be lodged in the Auditors office, shall once in every six months, settle his accounts with the said Auditors of public accounts, and after deducting five *per centum* for his commissions, shall pay the balance due from him for the duties hereby imposed, into the treasury, stating in each account by him rendered, from whom and for what the duties by him to be collected were paid. As an encouragement to Captains and masters of vessels to make a true and faithful return of dutied goods, they shall be allowed to import in any vessel of one hundred tons burthen, two hundred pounds worth at first cost of goods duty free, and to Captains of any vessel of fifty tons burthen, there shall be allowed the privilege of importing one hundred pounds worth of goods at first cost, duty free, and so in proportion for larger or smaller vessels; but this privilege shall nevertheless be forfeited upon discovery of wilful concealment or an untrue report made by any such Captain or commander to the Naval Officer.

Repealed by Nov 1781, *ch.* 40.

These regulations altered by subsequent laws.

Encouragement to masters of vessels to make a true report.

V. THE rules and regulations established by Congress, shall in future be observed in this state, for the trial and punishment of all offenders in the navy of this commonwealth, and the workmen employed in the public ship yard, foundery, rope walks, and other publick works, shall be and they are hereby declared to be exempt from military duty of every kind, if engaged to serve for six months. The duties hereby to be collected, shall be appropriated solely to the purposes of the navy of this commonwealth, and a distinct and seperate account thereof shall be kept by the treasurer, stating the monies received upon these funds and the expenditure thereof. The pay-master, for his services herein, shall be allowed two and a half per centum upon all the money by him expended in discharge of the duties hereby imposed upon him, in lieu of all former pay by him heretofore received.

At an end.

And this also.

A. D. 1735.

VI. FOR the more effectual future protection of the trade of *Chesopeake* bay, the commissioner of the navy shall, and he is hereby required, to obtain as speedily as possible a true and exact plan of the gallies built by order of Congress, at *Philadelphia*, in the year of our Lord one thousand seven hundred and seventy six, and as soon thereafter as may be, to cause two galleys of the same size and on the same construction, to be built and equipt to carry two thirty two pounders in the bow, and the like number in the stern, with six pounders at the sides; the said galleys shall be rigged as the commissioner of the navy shall direct, and the rigging, sails, guns, and other materials, shall be provided while the said galleys are on the stocks, to the end that no time may be lost in equipping them for a cruise after they shall be launched.

Courts shall bind out at least half their male orphans to the sea.

VII. AND whereas by an act of Assembly passed in the year of our Lord one thousand seven hundred and forty eight, entitled *An act for the better management and security of orphans and their estates*, the county courts are directed to cause such orphans coming under certain descriptions therein mentioned, to be bound out: *Be it enacted*, that the same shall be and is hereby amended, so far as that the said county courts, instead of binding out all such orphans as shall come within the description in the said act contained, they shall, and are hereby empowered and required, to cause one half of such male orphans, at least, who may live below the falls of the respective rivers in the eastern parts of this commonwealth, to be bound to the sea, under the most prudent Captains that can be procured to take them.

Duty on seamen for an hospital.

VIII. TO the end that an hospital for the relief of sick and disabled seamen may be established, the several and respective Naval Officers within this commonwealth shall receive from each Captain or commander of any vessel belonging to the same, at the time of their entrance or clearance, nine pence a month in specie, or an equivalent in current money as aforesaid, out of the wages due to the seamen on board his vessel, an account of which each and every Captain is hereby required to render upon oath, and pay to such Naval Officer, before he shall be permitted to clear or enter his vessel. And the pay-master of the navy shall deduct out of the wages due to the seamen and mariners in the service of the state, the like sum from their monthly pay, which sums, when collected, shall be paid by the Naval Officers and pay-master respectively, into the hands of such person as the Governor, with the advice of Council, shall appoint, the Naval Officer deducting therefrom five *per cent.* for his trouble of collection; and the hospital shall also be established at such convenient place as the Governor, with the advice of Council, shall fix upon, and be under the management of some proper person by him to be appointed for that purpose. All the other vessels belonging to this commonwealth, not herein before mentioned, shall immediately be sold, under the direction of the commissioner of the navy, for the most that can be got for the same, in such manner as shall be most conducive to the public interest; and the money arising from such sale shall be applied to the purposes of the navy.

C H A P. XXXII.

Expired.

An act to revive and amend an act entitled An act for giving further powers to the Governor and Council.

At a GENERAL ASSEMBLY begun and held at the Public Buildings in the Town of *Richmond*, on *Thursday* the 1st day of *March*, in the Year of our Lord 1781.

C H A P. I.

Executed.

An act to raise two legions for the defence of the state.

C H A P. II.

Executed.

An act to remedy the inconveniencies arising from the interruption given to the execution of two acts passed at the last session of Assembly, for recruiting this state's quota of troops to serve in the continental army, and for supplying the army with clothes, provisions, and waggons.

C H A P. III.

Executed.

An act for ascertaining the number of militia in this state.

C H A P. IV.

Expired.

An act to exempt artificers employed at iron works from militia duty.

C H A P. V.

Repealed.

An act for punishing the counterfeiters of the paper money of this state or of the United States, and for making the same a legal tender.

C H A P. VI.

Executed.

An act for emitting a sum of money for public exigencies.

C H A P. VII.

Executed.

An act for burning the paper bills of credit of this state.

CHAP. VIII.

An act to continue the several acts of Assembly which would otherwise have expired at the end or during the present session.

CHAP. IX.

An act to amend the act entitled An act for establishing a General Court.

I. WHEREAS by the act of Assembly establishing the General Court, no provision is made in case a grand jury-man should be sick or die after being empannelled and sworn, by which means it has happened and may again happen that one or more of the jury may fall sick or die, and of consequence all the powers with which they are invested by the laws and constitutions are unexecuted; and whereas no power is given to a single member of the court, after a sufficient number has once met, to adjourn in case one or more of the said members should be sick or die during the term; for remedy whereof, *Be it enacted,* that whenever it shall so happen that one or more of the jury should be sick or die after being sworn, that the Judges, if it be necessary, shall cause to be summoned, empannelled, and sworn, any by-standers, being qualified according to law; and all the proceedings of such grand jury shall be binding in the same manner as in any other case.

The place of a grand jury-man, dying or taken sick, so that he cannot attend, may be supplied by a by-stander.

II. *AND be it enacted,* that if any member of the court shall be sick or die, or by any other unavoidable accident, should be prevented from attending at any time after a sufficient number hath met to constitute the same, it shall and may be lawful for any one or more of the remaining Judges to adjourn from day to day throughout the term, until a court can be had.

One Judge, or two, if the attendance of more be prevented, may adjourn the court.

III. AND whereas by the sickness and non-attendance of a jury-man during the present setting of the General Court, the grand jury was dissolved by means of there not being members sufficient to proceed on business, in consequence whereof the price of tobacco could not be settled as by law directed, and the officers of government and others will be unpaid for their services : *Be it therefore enacted,* that immediately after the passing of this act, and during the present session of the General Court the Judges thereof shall cause to be summoned a grand jury for the purpose aforesaid, any law to the contrary notwithstanding.

Executed.

IV. AND whereas the prison in the town of *Richmond,* is too small to contain the prisoners committed thereto, and from their being crowded together, there will be danger of infectious disorders : *It is further enacted,* that the Governor with advice of Council may, and he is hereby desired to rent a temporary building, most proper for the business, in or near the said town of *Richmond,* which shall be under the direction of the Judges in the same manner as the prison now is, and which shall be applied to the purpose of confining such prisoners as the Judges of the General Court shall particularly order thither and no other.

The Governor empowered to rent a house for confining certain prisoners.

V. AND whereas great inconveniences have arisen from the law now in force, empowering the Judges of the High Court of Chancery alone to qualify Auditors of public accounts: *Be it therefore enacted,* that either of the Judges of the General Court shall have full power to qualify all Auditors of public accounts that shall hereafter be appointed.

One Judge of the General Court may qualify the Auditors of public accounts.

CHAP. X.

An act to amend an act entitled An act for giving further time to obtain warrants upon certificates for pre-emption rights, and returning certain surveys to the Land Office, and for other purposes.

CHAP. XI.

An act to amend the act entitled an An act for laying a tax payable in certain enumerated commodities.

At a GENERAL ASSEMBLY begun and held at the Public Buildings in the town of *Richmond,* on *Monday* the 7th day of *May,* in the Year of our Lord 1781, and from thence continued by adjournment to the town of *Staunton,* in the county of *Augusta.*

CHAP. I.

An act concerning the adjournment of the Supreme Courts.

I. WHEREAS upon the punctual administration of justice, criminal as well as civil, the public peace and well being depend for support, and it may be often interrupted by hostile alarms and other obstacles, if the courts be stationary at particular places: *Be it enacted by the General Assembly,* that so often as it shall appear necessary, it shall be lawful for the Governor, with the advice of the Council of State, by a proclamation, bearing date one month at least before the first day of meeting, and dispersed throughout the several counties (that of *Illinois* excepted) to cause the Court of Appeals, the High Court of Chancery, and the General Court, to meet at any convenient place within the commonwealth, there to hold their respective sessions immediately succeeding each proclamation. If it shall so happen that the cause of adjournment shall occur within the space of a month next preceding the day of meeting, it shall be lawful for the Governor, with the advice of the Council of State, by a proclamation dispersed as aforesaid, to postpone the time of meeting beyond the day, taking care that

Preamble.

Governor and Council may by proclamation change the place of holding courts; and the time.

A D. 1781.

Judges may adjourn if they think they cannot sit with safety.
Court of Admiralty may sit any where on proper occasions.
Courts held under proclamation not one of the two for trial or discharge of criminals.
No discontinuance if courts not held in usual terms.

one month at least shall intervene between the date thereof and such new day, and that the new day does not fall within the month next preceding a stated term, except that in the case of postponing the *March* and *October* sessions of the General Court, no regard need be had to the *June* and *December* terms. If after a session begun, a majority of the Judges of the aforesaid courts who are present, shall be of opinion and so record, that they cannot sit with safety at the place fixed by law, or the proclamation aforesaid, it shall be lawful for them to adjourn to the succeeding term; and thereupon all business shall stand continued over. A majority of the Judges of the Court of Admiralty may, on any necessary occasion, sit at places other than that appointed by law, but reasonable notice shall be given by the Marshal or his deputy, to all parties to suits depending therein, of such adjournment, if to be found, or to their proctor if absent; and if neither they nor their proctor be found, three weeks publication in the *Virginia* gazette shall be adjudged sufficient notice of the adjournment. Copies of any proclamation of adjournment shall be sent, under signature of the Governor and seal of the commonwealth, to each of the Judges aforesaid, whose court may be so adjourned. No court, thus holden under a proclamation, shall be adjudged one of those, at which a criminal, petitioning to be tried, and not being tried, shall be discharged and acquitted; nor shall there be a discontinuance in any proceeding whatsoever, if the courts aforesaid, or either of them, should not be holden in their usual terms.

Suspended Nov. 1781, ch 9. Repealed Oct. 1782, ch. 42.

CHAP. II.

An act to enable the Congress of the United States to levy a duty on certain goods and merchandizes, and also on all prizes.

Repealed Oct. 1782, ch. 16.

CHAP. III.

An act to amend the act for raising two legions for the defence of the state.

Expired.

CHAP. IV.

An act for establishing martial law within twenty miles of the American army, or the enemy's camp.

Expired.

CHAP. V.

An act to empower the sheriffs to hold elections, in certain cases, at other places than those appointed by law.

CHAP. VI.

An act for calling in and exchanging this state's quota of continental money.

See May 1780, ch. 10.
This money not to be exchanged.

I. BE it enacted by the General Assembly, that so much of the act of Assembly, entitled *An act to explain and amend the act for calling in and redeeming the money now in circulation, and for emitting and funding new bills of credit according to the resolutions of Congress of the eighteenth of* March last, *as* directs the Treasurer to exchange the old continental bills in the manner as by the said act is directed, shall be, and the same is hereby repealed.

Old money not to be a tender.
But receivable for taxes and public debts.

II. AND be it further enacted, that from and after the first day of *July* next, the said old money shall cease to be a legal tender in discharge of any debt or contract whatsoever: *Provided*, that the sheriffs and other public collectors shall continue to receive the same in payment of all public debts and taxes, and upon the settlement of their several collections to pay the same into the public treasury in discharge thereof.

No more of this money to be issued.

III. AND be it further enacted, that the Treasurer of this commonwealth shall not pay out of the treasury, for any cause whatsoever, any part of the said money to be issued in virtue of the resolutions of Congress of the eighteenth day of *March*, one thousand seven hundred and eighty, except by the directions of the Executive or the Legislature.

Expired.

CHAP. VII.

An act for giving certain powers to the Governor and Council, and for punishing those who shall oppose the execution of laws.

Repealed by the act of Oct. 1784.

CHAP. VIII.

An act to amend the act for regulating and disciplining the militia, and for other purposes.

CHAP. IX.

An act preventing a discontinuance of the General Court, and suspending the proceedings of certain courts in particular cases.

Preamble.

I. WHEREAS the additional session of the General Court which ought by law to have been holden on the second *Tuesday* in the month of *June*, in the present year of our Lord one thousand seven hundred and eighty one, was omitted to be so holden from an invasion of this commonwealth, and without some legislative provision a discontinuance of the said court may thereby be produced: And whereas amidst those distractions and exertions which are caused and called for by a state of war, no leisure is left for questions of a nature merely private: *Be it enacted*, that no discontinuance shall take place in the General Court, or in any proceeding depending therein or belonging thereto, by the failure to hold the additional session aforesaid at the time aforesaid, but in every construction or adjudication in the said court or elsewhere, the adjournment from the session of the said court which was in the month of *March* in the present year of our Lord one thousand seven hundred

No discontinuance of court or proceedings.

and eighty one, to the said additional session, shall be taken and deemed as if it had been an adjournment to the session to be holden in the month of *October* in the same year, or to a session holden under a proclamation by the Governor pursuant to an act of General Assembly entitled *An act for giving certain powers to the Governor and Council, and for punishing those who shall oppose the execution of laws,* according as the one or the other shall be first holden.

II. *AND be it further enacted,* that until a declaration shall be made by the General Assembly to the contrary, neither the Court of Appeals, the High Court of Chancery, the General Court, nor any county court, shall hear or determine any matter, cause, or thing, except mere pleas of the commonwealth, private questions brought on by consent, suits instituted for the division of estates, contestations of wills, and such other cases in which the law requires not a declaration or bill in equity to be filed; but the said courts shall still be open for the issuing of dedimuses, for the examination of witnesses, writs of *ne exeat republica,* injunction, and *habeas corpus, de homine replegiando,* for the institution of suits in *perpetuam rei memoriam,* and for no other purpose whatsoever. And as the issuing of patents whilst there is so great difficulty in entering caveats may produce much injustice, *It is further enacted,* that the Register shall not issue any patent until the term of six months shall have elapsed after such declaration as aforesaid shall take place; and any patent so issued shall be void. Any caveat may be entered aginst the issuing a patent at any time within the said six months. Of the time between the first day of *January,* in the year aforesaid, to the last day of that session of the General Assembly, at which the foregoing suspension of judiciary proceedings shall be removed, no account shall be made in any computation upon the act of limitations.

C H A P. X.

An act for further continuing an act entitled An act to empower the Governor and Council to lay an embargo for a limited time.

C H A P. XI.

An act for further continuing an act entitled An act to revive and amend an act to make provision for the support and maintenance of Ideots, Lunatics, and persons of unsound minds.

I. WHEREAS the act of Assembly passed in the year one thousand seven hundred and seventy eight, entitled, *An act to revive and amend an act to make provision for the support and maintenance of ideots, lunatics, and persons of unsound minds,* will expire at the end of this present session of Assembly, and it is necessary that the same should be further continued; *Be it therefore enacted by the General Assembly,* that the act entitled *An act to revive and amend an act to make provision for the support and maintenance of ideots, lunatics, and persons of unsound minds,* shall continue and be in force from and after the expiration thereof, for and during the term of one year, and from thence to the end of the next session of Assembly, and no longer.

C H A P. XII.

An act for continuing an act entitled An act to exempt artificers employed at iron works from militia duty.

I. WHEREAS the act of Assembly passed at the last session, entitled *An act to exempt artificers employed at iron works from militia duty,* will expire at the end of this present session of Assembly, and it is expedient that the same should be continued; *Be it therefore enacted by the General Assembly,* that the act entitled *An act to exempt artificers employed at iron works from militia duty,* shall continue and be in force from and after the expiration thereof until the end of the next session of Assembly, and no longer.

C H A P. XIII.

An act for further continuing an act entitled An act to amend an act for preventing forestalling, regrating, engrossing, and public vendues.

C H A P. XIV.

An act to revive an act entitled An act to enable the Governor and Council to supply the armies and navies of the United States and of their allies with grain and flour.

C H A P. XV.

An act to regulate the department of the war office.

C H A P. XVI.

An act for making the money emitted at this session of Assembly a legal tender, and for punishing the counterfeiters of the same.

C H A P. XVII.

An act to empower the Treasurer to emit a further sum of money.

C H A P. XVIII.

An act for the relief of certain persons now resident on the western frontier.

C H A P. XIX.

An act for making provision for the payment of the salaries of the officers of government.

A. D. 1781.

Had its effect.

CHAP. XX.

An act for enlisting soldiers to serve in the continental army.

Expired.

CHAP. XXI.

An act for giving further time to delinquent counties to pay their specific tax.

CHAP. XXII.

See May 1779, ch. 12.

An act to amend the act entitled An act for adjusting and settling the titles of claimers to unpatented lands under the present and former government, previous to the establishment of the commonwealth's land office.

Preamble.

Allowance to commissioners and attendants.

I. WHEREAS the allowance heretofore made to the commissioners appointed to carry into execution an act entitled *An act for adjusting and settling the title of claimers to unpatented lands,* and to the sheriffs, surveyors and clerks attending the same, is inadequate to their trouble and expences; *Be it enacted,* that each commissioner for every day he shall necessarily be employed in going to, attending on and returning from the business of his office, shall receive sixty pounds, the sheriff thirty pounds for every day he shall attend, and the surveyor thirty pounds for every day he shall attend, in lieu of the former allowance made by the said recited act.

Increased tax on litigants.

II. AND whereas the expence of carrying the said act into execution will be greatly increased, and it is reasonable and just that such expence should be defrayed by the persons to be benefited thereby: *Be it further enacted,* that for every hundred acres of land contained within the certificates to be granted by the commissioners, the party receiving the same shall pay twenty dollars to the commissioners, besides a fee of ten dollars for each certificate to the clerk.

County courts in Kentucky settlement to hear and determine disputes unfinished.

III. AND whereas the commissioners appointed for the purpose of carrying into execution the before recited act, were discontinued in the district of *Kentucky,* whereby many good people of this commonwealth were prevented from proving their rights of settlement and preemption in due time, owing to their being engaged in the public service of this country: *Be it therefore enacted,* that the county courts in which such lands may lie, are hereby empowered and required to hear and determine such disputes as have not heretofore been determined by commissioners acting in that country under the act of Assembly, taking for their guide and direction the acts of Assembly whereby the commissioners were governed: And the Register of the Land Office is hereby empowered and directed to grant titles on the determination of such courts in the same manner as if the commissioners had determined the same.

CHAP. XXIII.

Had its effect.

An act to empower the Governor and Council to fix the value of provisions impressed for the use of the army.

At a GENERAL ASSEMBLY begun and held at the Public Buildings in the Town of *Richmond,* on *Monday* the 5th day of *November,* in the Year of our Lord 1781.

CHAP. I.

Private.

An act for incorporating the town of Fredericksburg, in the county of Spotsylvania.

CHAP. II.

Had its effect.

An act to repeal an act entitled An act for further continuing an act entitled an act to empower the Governor and Council to lay an embargo for a limited time.

CHAP. III.

See March 1781, ch. 4.

An act for further continuing an act entitled An act to exempt artificers employed at iron works from militia duty.

Preamble.

I. WHEREAS the act of Assembly passed at the last *March* session, entitled *An act to exempt artificers employed at iron works from militia duty,* which was continued by an act passed at the last session, will expire at the end of this present session of Assembly; and it is expedient and necessary that the same should be further continued.

Continuance.

II. BE it therefore enacted by the General Assembly, that the act entitled *An act to exempt artificers employed at iron works from militia duty,* shall continue and be in force from and after the expiration thereof until the end of the next session of Assembly, and no longer.

CHAP. IV.

Private.

An act to suspend the execution of an act entitled An act to empower the court of Green Brier county to have a waggon road opened from their courthouse to the eastern waters.

CHAP. V.

An act to empower the Register of the Land Office to appoint a deputy on the western waters.

I. WHEREAS under the prefent mode eftablifhed by law for obtaining grants for wafte and unappropriated lands within this commonwealth, many of the good citizens thereof are fubject to great inconvenience and expence in travelling to the Land Office in order to produce the necefiary title papers for obtaining grants on the fame. For remedy whereof, *Be it enacted by the General Affembly*, that the Regifter of the Land Office fhall, and he is hereby empowered to appoint a deputy, for whofe good conduct he fhall be accountable, to refide in fome convenient part of the *Kentucky* country, whofe bufinefs it fhall be to receive the plats and certificates of all furveys made within the counties of *Lincoln, Jefferfon,* and *Fayette,* together with the title papers upon which they are founded, to be by him regiftered in a book to be kept for that purpofe; all which plats and certificates of furvey, as well as all fuch title papers, the faid Deputy Regifter fhall once in every fix months, or oftener if convenient, tranfmit to the principal Land Office, to be proceeded on in the fame manner as if the entry had been there firft made. And when titles are compleated upon the faid plats and certificates of furvey, the Regifter fhall forward the fame to his deputy, who fhall, after making a proper entry thereof in his office, deliver them out to the proprietors.

CHAP. VI.

An act to fecure to perfons who derive titles to lots, lands or tenements under the lottery, or under a deed of truft of the late William Byrd, *Efquire, a fee fimple eftate therein.*

CHAP. VII.

An act for dividing the county of Bedford.

CHAP. VIII.

An act for regulating the military and naval arrangements of this ftate.

CHAP. IX.

An act to fufpend the operation of an act to enable the Congrefs of the United States to levy a duty on certain goods and merchandizes, and alfo on all prizes.

CHAP. X.

An act for reftoring to Robert Baine *his former eftate.*

CHAP. XI.

An act for the relief of perfons who have been or may be injured by the deftruction of the records of county courts.

I. WHEREAS during the late invafion, the records of feveral county courts within this commonwealth, with other papers of confequence, were burnt or otherwife deftroyed by the enemy, and this Affembly being willing to afford all poffible relief to the perfons concerned in the faid misfortune, whofe eftates, titles, and intereft, may be affected thereby: *Be it therefore enacted by the General Affembly*, that the courts of the counties where any fuch deftruction may have happened, when any original deeds with the endorfement of the acknowledgment or proof thereof, and order for recording the fame, attefted by the clerk of the court, or the copies of any deeds with the endorfements fo attefted, or of any wills with the endorfement of the proof and order for recording the fame fo attefted, or of any judgment, decree, or order of court, in like manner attefted, the original records of which deeds, wills, judgments, decrees, or orders, are loft (fhall be produced to them for that purpofe) fhall order the clerk to again record all fuch original deeds, copies of deeds, or wills, with the faid endorfements refpectively, and all fuch copies of judgments, decrees, and orders of the court of their county; and the faid clerk, when he fhall have recorded any thing in purfuance of this act, fhall endorfe on the fame that the original hath been deftroyed by the enemy, to which he fhall fubfcribe his name, and likewife enter the fame endorfement upon record with the thing recorded, which fhall have the fame operation and effect in law, to all intents and purpofes, as if the faid original records had not been loft.

II. *AND be it further enacted*, that the clerks of the feveral courts fhall do and perform the fervices in this act mentioned for the fame fee that is or fhall be allowed by law in other cafes for a copy of any thing herein before mentioned; and in like manner fhall take no other or greater fee for the recording any deed which hath been already made and recorded, or fhall be made by occafion only of the misfortune aforefaid, for the fettling the right or title of any perfon or perfons whatfoever to lands and tenements, flaves, or goods and chattels, than in other cafes is or fhall be allowed by law for a copy of any fuch deed, any law, cuftom, or ufage, to the contrary notwithftanding.

III. AND for perpetuating the teftimony of witneffes in relation to any deed, will, inventory, or other writing recorded in the county courts where the original is loft and no attefted copy thereof can be produced, *Be it further enacted*, that it fhall and may be lawful for the Governor, with the advice of Council, to iffue one or more commiffions (as the cafe may require) under the feal of the commonwealth, to nine able and difcreet perfons directed, giving them, or any three or more of them, full power and authority to meet at fome convenient place by them to be appointed, and to adjourn from time to time as they fhall think fit, and to fummon, hear, and examine, all witneffes at the inftance of any perfon whatfoever touching the premifes, and to take their depofitions in writing, and to return the fame, with fuch commiffion or commiffions, to the Executive, which depofitions fhall be by them laid before the General Affembly at the next feffion, to the end they may be enabled to give fuch effectual relief to the fufferers, by the lofs of the faid records, as to them fhall feem moft juft and reafonable. And the faid commiffioners fhall have power to appoint fome fit perfon fkilled in clerkfhip to attend them for keeping a journal of their proceedings, and drawing the depofitions aforefaid, which perfon fhall be paid for his fervices by each county refpectively.

For perpetuating teftimony on fuch occafions.
Commiffions to iffue to 9 or any 3.
How to be executed and returned
Commiffioners to appoint a clerk.

A. D. 1781.

See May 1781,
ch 9.
Preamble.

CHAP. XII.

An act to remove the suspension of the superior courts, and to alter the terms of holding the same.

Courts to proceed
as before.
Future terms of
the superior courts.

I. WHEREAS by an act passed the last session of Assembly, the county, as well as other courts, were suspended under certain exceptions; and such suspension being now unnecessary and improper: Be it therefore enacted, that the said courts shall hear and determine any matter, cause, or thing, in like manner as they could or might have done before the passing of the said act. That the sessions of the General Court shall hereafter begin on the first day of *April* and *October* in every year, if not *Sunday*, and then on the *Monday* thereafter. That a Court of Appeals shall hereafter be holden on the twenty ninth, or when that shall happen to be *Sunday*, on the thirtieth day of *April* and *October* in every year. That the two sessions of the Court of Chancery shall hereafter begin on the fifth day of *May* and *November* in every year, if not *Sunday*, and then on the *Monday* following.

Court of Appeals
may sit beyond their
term.
In that case the
Chancery term
when to commence.

II. PROVIDED always, and be it further enacted, that the Court of Appeals shall have power to hold their court any number of days exceeding the term now fixed by law, as they may think necessary to go through the business depending before them, in which case the Court of Chancery shall stand adjourned to, and commence on, the day next succeeding the rising of the said court, if not *Sunday*, and then the day following.

CHAP. XIII.

An act for calling in and funding the paper money of this state.

See Oct. 1782,
ch. 13.

State paper not a
tender except for
arrears of taxes.
To be returned to
the Treasurer by
October 1782.
To be destroyed.
Not returned to be
forfeited.

I. BE it enacted by the General Assembly, that from and after the passing of this act, the paper money heretofore issued by this state shall cease to be a tender in payment of any debt or contract whatsoever, except in payment of taxes due to the several collectors thereof for the year one thousand seven hundred and eighty one; and that on or before the first day of *October*, in the year one thousand seven hundred and eighty two, the proprietors or holders of the said paper money shall deliver or cause the same to be delivered to the Treasurer for the time being, at his office, where the said paper money so received shall be destroyed and not re-issued; and if any proprietor or holder of the said paper money shall refuse or neglect to deliver the same to the Treasurer, at his office, as aforesaid, such proprietor or holder shall forfeit his, her, or their interest in the same, and the said paper money so withheld or neglected to be delivered, shall not, from and after the said first day of *October*, in the year one thousand seven hundred and eighty two, be redeemable.

To ascertain the
public debt on this
occasion.
Treasurer to de-
liver a Loan Office
certificate in specie,
at the rate of one
for a thousand.
Redeemable prin-
cipal in 1790, and
interest annually at
6 per cent.

II. AND whereas it is necessary that the just value of the public debt in specie, arising from the emissions of the paper money aforesaid, should be ascertained, and that equitable compensation should be made to the proprietors or holders of the said money: Be it further enacted by the authority aforesaid, that the Treasurer for the time being, upon the receipt of the paper money as aforesaid, shall deliver to the proprietors or holders thereof, a loan office certificate, of the value of the said paper money received from such proprietors or holders, in specie, at the rate or difference of one thousand for one in specie, to be entered with the Auditors of public accounts, which said certificates shall be redeemable, and paid in specie, by the Treasurer for the time being, that is to say, the principal for which such certificate shall be granted, on or before the first day of *December*, in the year one thousand seven hundred and ninety, and the interest, at the rate of six *per centum*, as the same shall become due thereon, annually, from the date of the said certificates; and for the punctual payment of the interest aforesaid, as the same shall become due, the Treasurer for the time being, shall annually set apart so much of the revenue arising from taxes upon lands, and paid into the treasury, as shall be sufficient to discharge the same, which money so set apart as aforesaid, shall be applied to the payment of the interest aforesaid, and to no other use or purpose whatsoever.

Partial payments
to be endorsed;
also assignments,
or forfeited to the
commonwealth.
State or continen-
tal money may be
received for land.

III. AND be it further enacted, that the Treasurer for the time being, shall preserve a check or counterpart to all certificates granted by virtue of this act, and shall compare the same upon any demand for payment of interest or principal thereof, before the same shall be paid; and when any payment shall be made by virtue of this act, the Treasurer shall specify the same in his hand writing, together with the date thereof, upon the back of the said certificate; and where any of the said certificates shall be transferred by the proprietor thereof, the same shall be done by assignment in writing on the back thereof, declaring the day when, and the person to whom, the same shall have been assigned; and where any certificate shall be transferred contrary to this act, the same shall be forfeited to the commonwealth, and be cancelled whenever the same shall be presented to the treasury for payment thereof: Provided nevertheless, that any person possessed of, or holding any money emitted by Congress, or by this state, shall be at liberty to lay out the same in the purchase of warrants for unappropriated lands, at the price now established by law, at any time before the said first day of *October* next.

Former acts re-
pealed.

IV. AND be it further enacted by the authority aforesaid, that so much of all and every other act or acts providing for the redemption of the bills of credit emitted by this commonwealth, as is within the purview of this act, be, and the same is hereby repealed.

CHAP. XIV.

Private.

An act to empower the Justices of James City county to hold their courts at any other place within the same than Williamsburg, during the continuance of the small-pox there.

CHAP. XV.

Had its effect.

An act to empower the Executive to fit out a certain naval force.

CHAP. XVI.

An act for establishing a new ferry.

A. D. 1781.
See 1769, ch. 25, and notes.
A new ferry.

I. BE it enacted by the General Assembly, that a public ferry be constantly kept at the following place, and the rates for passing the same shall be as follows, that is to say: From the land of *William Black*, in the county of *Chesterfield*, across *James* river, to the public landing at *Rocket*'s, in the county of *Henrico*, the price for a man four pence, and for a horse the same. And for the transportation of wheel carriages, tobacco, cattle, and other beasts, at the place aforesaid, the ferry keeper may demand and take the following rates, that is to say: For every coach, chariot, or waggon, and the driver thereof, the same as for six horses; for every cart or four wheel chaise and the driver thereof, the same as for four horses; for every two wheel chaise or chair, the same as for two horses; for every hogshead of tobacco as for one horse; for every head of neat cattle as for one horse; for every sheep, goat, or lamb, one fifth part of the ferriage for one horse; and for every hog, one fourth part of the ferriage for one horse, and no more. If the ferry keeper shall presume to demand or receive from any person or persons whatsoever, any greater rates than is hereby allowed for the carriage or ferriage of any thing, he shall, for every such offence, forfeit and pay to the party grieved, the ferriages demanded or received, and ten shillings; to be recovered with costs before a justice of Peace of the county where such offence shall be committed.

Ferriage. Regulations.

Penalty for over-charging.

II. AND be it further enacted, that from and after the first day of *August* next, the ferry heretofore kept from the lands of *John Lynch*, in *Bedford* county, across the *Fluvanna* to the opposite shore in *Amherst*, shall be discontinued: and that instead thereof, a ferry shall be kept from the lands of the said *John Lynch*, lately purchased of *Edmund Winston*, Esquire, across the said river to the opposite shore in *Amherst*, for transportation, over which the same rates of ferriages shall be demandable in specie, as were before the year one thousand seven hundred and seventy seven, and the courts shall have the same powers, and the keepers be subject to the same penalties at the new ferry, as they had or were subject to, at the present one, before the said term.

Lynch's ferry discontinued. Repealed May 1782, ch. 20. Another appointed.

CHAP. XVII.

An act giving powers to the Governor, with the advice of Council, to appoint a special court for the trial of certain offenders.

Expired.

CHAP. XVIII.

An act for the relief of military pensioners.

Private.

CHAP. XIX.

An act to adjust and regulate the pay and accounts of the officers and soldiers of the Virginia *line* on continental establishment, and also of the officers, soldiers, sailors, and marines, in the service of this state, and for other purposes.

I. WHEREAS from the depreciation of the paper money and other concurring circumstances, the pay of the officers and soldiers of the *Virginia* line on continental establishment hath been altogether inadequate to their services: To the end therefore, that justice may be done and redress afforded as far as the present circumstances of the state will admit, Be it enacted by the General Assembly, that the whole pay and subsistence of the officers and soldiers of the *Virginia* line in continental service shall be made equal to specie from the first day of *January*, one thousand seven hundred and seventy seven; that the Auditors of public accounts do settle and adjust the pay and accounts of the said officers and soldiers from the said first day of *January*, one thousand seven hundred and seventy seven, to the last day of *December*, one thousand seven hundred and eighty one. And the said Auditors are hereby authorized and directed to estimate in specie all sums of continental and state money received by the said officers and soldiers on account of their pay within the period aforesaid, agreeable to the dates of their receipts respectively, and according to a scale of depreciation hereafter mentioned and contained. And printed certificates (payable on or before the first day of *January*, one thousand seven hundred and eighty five, with interest at the rate of six *per centum per annum*) expressing the sum in specie, shall, by the said Auditors, be individually given to the said officers and soldiers for the respective balances that may appear to be due them by the public. And the said Auditors shall, in like manner, settle and adjust the accounts of all officers and soldiers of the said line who have fallen or died in the service during the said period; and their lawful representatives shall be entitled to such certificates, and all other benefits and advantages hereby granted to the officers and soldiers now in the line.

Preamble.

For what time pay shall be made equal to specie.

Auditors to adjust accounts according to scale of depreciation; and give printed certificates payable with interest.

Also, of officers and soldiers dead,

II. AND whereas a number of officers and soldiers, who are now out of the service by the resignation of the officers and expiration of the term of the soldiers, received no pay for some space of time before their leaving the service, by which the public is considerably in arrears to them: Be it therefore enacted, that the said Auditors shall in like manner settle the accounts of the said officers and soldiers to the time of their leaving the service, and grant them certificates for the sums that may be found due them in manner as herein before directed for the officers and private men now in the line. And the said Auditors shall, after having adjusted and settled the accounts aforesaid, return an exact list to the Treasurer for the time being of the sums due and certificates granted therefor, of which a correct account shall be kept by the Treasurer for his government at the time the said certificate shall be redeemable. And in the mean time, for the immediate relief of the officers of the line aforesaid, the Auditors of public accounts are hereby directed to issue immediately after the passing this act, to all such of the said officers who shall have been in the said line prior to the first day of *May*, one thousand seven hundred and seventy seven, and still belonging thereto, like certificates for the amount of two years pay in specie, agreeable to the allowances made by a resolution of Congress of the twelfth day of *August*, one thousand seven hundred and eighty, payable as aforesaid, with interest at the rate of six *per centum per annum*; and to all such of the said officers who shall have come into the service since that period, similar certificates for the amount of one year's pay, provided they shall have been in the service one year.

or out of the service, for the time they served.

Auditors to return a list of certificates to Treasurer.

Advance to officers.

III. AND be it further enacted, that the wages of the said officers and soldiers shall, in future, be regularly paid in specie, or the value thereof, once in every quarter of a year at least.

Future pay in specie.

Officers to account for money advanced; in what manner;

IV. AND be it further enacted, that the said Auditors be, and they are hereby authorized, to call on all officers of the said line who have drawn, from the continent or state, monies for public purposes, and have not accounted for the same, to settle their accounts thereon, according to the table of depreciation by this act established; and where it shall appear to the Auditors aforesaid, that from captivity or other circumstances, officers have sufficient reasons for not having had their accounts settled in due time, or where it shall be manifested that there has been no misapplication of the said monies on the part of the said officers, that in such cases no depreciation shall be charged thereon; and that where it shall be made appear that officers have advanced of their own monies for the public service, they shall be allowed the

and for cloathing.

full depreciation thereon. And all officers who have received cloathing from the state at stated prices, are to account for the same.

Certificates to be received on sale of forfeited estates.

V. AND be it further enacted, that the sales of all forfeited and escheated estates which shall hereafter be sold, shall be made in specie or tobacco, at a price to be fixed by the Auditors of public accounts, and the persons employed in selling the same are hereby authorized and directed to receive the certificates to be given to the officers and soldiers of the *Virginia* line by virtue of this act, as equal to specie; and in all cases where monies are payable to the public for the sales of forfeited estates, the said certificates are to be considered as a lawful tender for the like sums of gold and silver.

If sales paid for in specie, that to be reserved for redeeming certificates.

VI. AND be it further enacted, that in case any of the above-mentioned forfeited estates shall be sold, and paid for in specie, the persons receiving the same shall pay the said money to the Treasurer for the time being, which he is hereby directed to reserve for redeeming the certificates aforesaid which shall remain unpaid, in such manner as the General Assembly shall order and direct; And the certificates for the sales of the said forfeited estates, and in other cases where the same may have been paid to the public in lieu of specie, shall be, by the persons so receiving them, delivered to the Treasurer aforesaid, who is hereby directed to keep them to be cancelled and destroyed in such manner as the General Assembly shall order and direct.

Scale of depreciation,

VII. AND be it further enacted, that the following scale of depreciation shall be the rule by which the said Auditors shall be governed in the settlement aforesaid, to wit:

In the year one thousand seven hundred and seventy seven.

January one and a half, *February* one and a half, *March* two, *April* two and a half, *May* two and a half, *June* two and a half, *July* three, *August* three, *September* three, *October* three, *November* three, *December* four.

In the year one thousand seven hundred and seventy eight.

January four, *February* five, *March* five, *April* five, *May* five, *June* five, *July* five, *August* five, *September* five, *October* five, *November* six, *December* six.

In the year one thousand seven hundred and seventy nine.

January eight, *February* ten, *March* ten, *April* sixteen, *May* twenty, *June* twenty, *July* twenty one, *August* twenty two, *September* twenty four, *October* twenty eight, *November* thirty six, *December* forty.

In the year one thousand seven hundred and eighty.

January forty two, *February* forty five, *March* fifty, *April* sixty, *May* sixty, *June* sixty five, *July* sixty five, *August* seventy, *September* seventy two, *October* seventy three, *November* seventy four, *December* seventy five.

In the year one thousand seven hundred and eighty one.

January seventy five, *February* eighty, *March* ninety, *April* one hundred, *May* one hundred and fifty, *June* two hundred and fifty, *July* four hundred, *August* five hundred, *September* six hundred, *October* seven hundred, *November* eight hundred, *December* one thousand.

Further tract of territory allotted for the officers and soldiers.

VIII. AND whereas a considerable part of the tract of country allotted for the officers and soldiers by an act of Assembly entitled *An act for establishing a Land Office, and ascertaining the terms and manner of granting waste and unappropriated lands,* hath, upon the extention of the boundary line between this state and *North Carolina,* fallen into that state, and the intentions of the said act are so far frustrated: Be it therefore enacted, that all that tract of land included within the rivers *Mississippi, Ohio,* and *Tenissee,* and the *Carolina* boundary line, shall be, and the same is hereby substituted in lieu of such lands so fallen into the said state of *North Carolina,* to be in the same manner subject to be claimed by the said officers and soldiers.

When and how their lands may be surveyed.

IX. AND be it further enacted, that the Governor, with the advice of the Council, shall as soon as the circumstances of affairs will admit, appoint surveyors, to be nominated, examined, and commissioned in the usual form, for the purpose of surveying and apportioning the said lands and the tract heretofore reserved for the said purpose to the said officers and soldiers agreeable to their ranks respectively, in such manner and in such proportions as are allowed by act of Assembly as a bounty for military services. And it shall be lawful for the said officers to depute and appoint as many of their number as they may think proper to superintend the laying off the said lands, who shall have power to choose the best of the same thus to be allotted, and point the same out to the said surveyors, who shall proceed to survey the same in the proportion as they shall be directed by the said superintendants, and shall in the same manner be subject to their orders throughout the survey, which said surveys shall be at the expence of the officers and soldiers, and after such survey, the portions of each rank shall be numbered, and the said officers and soldiers shall, according to their ranks respectively, proceed to draw lots for the numbers, which they shall have power to locate as soon as they shall think proper; which said lands shall be free from taxation during the continuance of the present war. *Provided nevertheless,* that if at any time after the said location and allotment shall have taken place, any officer shall resign, or by his misconduct forfeit his commission, the lot by him so located shall revert to the state: *And provided also,* that nothing contained in this act shall be construed to debar the officers of the artillery and cavalry, citizens of this state who received their appointments originally in the same, and have by a regular line of succession been, or shall be, promoted to a corpse raised in another state, from any of the benefits hereby granted, or intended to be granted, to the officers of the *Virginia* line.

Return to be made of state officers and their merits.

X. AND whereas by the reduction of the battalions and corps in the state service, a considerable number of officers have become supernumerary; Be it enacted, that a return of all the state officers shall be made to the next Assembly, wherein the corps, the rank of each officer, the date of his commission, the number of men at first raised in each corps, number of men when reduced and time when reduced, shall be particularly specified by the Executive; and the Executive are hereby empowered and required to set on foot proper enquiries to discriminate such officers as by unworthy conduct, or by any means whatever, be thought unfit to be considered as entitled to half pay.

A. D. 1781.

XI. *AND be it enacted*, that the whole pay and subsistence of the state troops be made good from the first day of *January* one thousand seven hundred and seventy seven, according to their times of service; and that the Auditors of public accounts shall immediately liquidate and adjust the accounts of the officers and soldiers of the state battalions and corps, on the same principles and agreeable to the same scale of depreciation as is above directed in the case of the continental officers, and give certificates equal to specie individually for the respective balances; and that the state officers who now are in actual service shall have the same advances of pay, and in the same manner, for their present relief, as the officers in continental service.

Their pay and subsistence to be made good.

XII. *AND be it enacted*, that the bounties of land given to the officers of the *Virginia* line in continental service, and the regulations for the surveying and appropriating the same, shall be extended to the state officers.

Also their bounty in land, to be surveyed as the regulars.

XIII. *AND be it also enacted*, that the same indulgencies and advantages given to the state infantry shall be, and are hereby given to the officers and soldiers of the state cavalry, and on the same terms.

Cavalry the same advantages as infantry.

XIV. *AND be it further enacted*, that the officers and seamen of the navy of this state, as they stand arranged by a late regulation, shall be entitled to the same advantages as the officers belonging to this state in the land service, agreeable to their respective ranks.

Officers and seamen of the navy same as land service.

XV. *AND be it further enacted*, that all tobacco arising from the sale of confiscated estates shall be appropriated to the redemption and payment of the said certificates, and to no other intent or purpose whatsoever; and the Treasurer is hereby directed and required to take speedy and effectual measures for the sale of all such tobacco for specie or the said certificates, and shall appropriate all the specie arising from such sales to the payment and redemption of such certificates as shall remain unpaid, and to no other purpose whatsoever.

Tobacco received for confiscated estates to be sold and the money to redeem certificates.

CHAP. XX.

An act for adjusting claims for property impressed or taken for public service.

Had its effect.

CHAP. XXI.

An act to vest certain lands whereof Burgess Ball is seised as tenant for life, in trustees, and for other purposes.

Private.

CHAP. XXII.

An act directing the mode of adjusting and settling the payment of certain debts and contracts, and for other purposes.

I. WHEREAS the paper currency of this state hath, from various causes, greatly depreciated in its value, insomuch that it is neither a proper medium of circulation nor a just standard whereby to settle and adjust debts and contracts, and it hath therefore become absolutely necessary to declare that the same should no longer pass current, except in payment of certain taxes calculated for the express purpose of calling in and redeeming the same.

Preamble.

II. AND whereas the good people of this state will labour under many inconveniencies for want of some rule, whereby to settle and adjust the payment of debts and contracts entered into and made between the first day of *January*, one thousand seven hundred and seventy seven, and the first day of *January*, one thousand seven hundred and eighty two, unless some rule shall be by law established for liquidating and adjusting the same, so as to do justice as well to the debtors as creditors: *Be it therefore enacted by the General Assembly*, that from and after the passing of this act, all debts and contracts entered into or made in the current money of this state or of the United States, excepting at all times contracts entered into for gold and silver coin, tobacco, or any other specific property, within the period aforesaid, now remaining due and unfulfilled, or which may become due at any future day or days, for the payment of any sum or sums of money, shall be liquidated, settled and adjusted, agreeable to a scale of depreciation herein after mentioned and contained, that is to say, by reducing the amount of all such debts and contracts to the true value in specie at the days or times the same were incurred or entered into; and upon payment of said value so found in specie, or other money equivalent thereto, the debtors or contractors shall be for ever discharged of and from the said debts or contracts, any law custom or usage to the contrary in any wise notwithstanding: *Provided always nevertheless*, that in all cases where actual payments have been made, by any person or persons, of any sum or sums of the aforesaid paper currency, at any time or times, either to the full amount or in part payment of any debt, contract or obligation whatsoever, the party paying the same, or upon whose account such sum or sums have been actually paid, shall have full credit for the nominal amount of such payments, and such payments shall not be reduced, any thing in this act, or in any other act or acts, to the contrary in any manner notwithstanding.

Contracts described.

How to be settled.

Actual payments full or partial, to stand for nominal amount.

III. AND whereas many of the inhabitants of this state have been exposed to the ravages of the enemy, and other distresses incident to a state of war, by means whereof they have been by violence deprived of the fruits of their labour and industry, and thereby rendered for the present incapable of paying many of their just debts: *Be it therefore enacted*, that in all cases, except such as are hereafter excepted, where judgment has been or may hereafter be obtained for the payment of any sum or sums of money, execution shall not issue thereupon before the first day of *December*, one thousand seven hundred and eighty three, except when judgment has been or may be obtained for any sum or sums of money due to the commonwealth, for taxes or otherwise, against any public collector, or any other person or persons whatsoever; and also in all cases where any such judgment hath been or may hereafter be obtained for monies due for the rent or use of any lands, plantations, houses, ferries, or fisheries, or for the hire of any slave or slaves, or of any servant or servants: *Provided*, that all judgments so staid shall carry interest at the rate of five *per centum per annum* until paid.

Executions suspended, except for debts due to the commonwealth. See May 1782, ch. 44; Oct. 1782, ch 46; Oct. 1783, ch. 30. Except also for rents, and hire of slaves or servants.

IV. AND be it further *enacted*, that the following scale of depreciation shall be the rule to determine the value of the several debts, contracts, and demands in this act mentioned, compared with silver and gold:

Scale of depreciation.

In the year one thousand seven hundred and seventy seven.

January one and a half, *February* one and a half, *March* two, *April* two and a half, *May* two and a half, *June* two and a half, *July* three, *August* three, *September* three, *October* three, *November* three, *December* four.

A D. 1781.

In the year one thousand seven hundred and seventy eight.

January four, *February* five, *March* five, *April* five, *May* five, *June* five, *July* five, *August* five, *September* five, *October* five, *November* six, *December* six.

In the year one thousand seven hundred and seventy nine.

January eight, *February* ten, *March* ten, *April* sixteen, *May* twenty, *June* twenty, *July* twenty one, *August* twenty two, *September* twenty four, *October* twenty eight, *November* thirty six, *December* forty.

In the year one thousand seven hundred and eighty.

January forty two, *February* forty five, *March* fifty, *April* sixty, *May* sixty, *June* sixty five, *July* sixty five, *August* seventy, *September* seventy two, *October* seventy three, *November* seventy four, *December* seventy five.

In the year one thousand seven hundred and eighty one.

January seventy five, *February* eighty, *March* ninety, *April* one hundred, *May* one hundred and fifty, *June* two hundred and fifty, *July* four hundred, *August* five hundred, *September* six hundred, *October* seven hundred, *November* eight hundred, *December* one thousand.

Courts may determine disputes according to equity.

Rule for settling intermediate judgments.

V. *AND be it enacted*, that where a suit shall be brought for the recovery of a debt, and it shall appear that the value thereof hath been tendered and refused; or where it shall appear that the non-payment thereof is owing to the creditor; or where other circumstances arise which, in the opinion of the court before whom the cause is brought to issue, would render a determination agreeable to the above table unjust; in either case it shall and may be lawful for the court to award such judgment as to them shall appear just and equitable. And where any verdict hath been given for damages between the first day of *January* one thousand seven hundred and seventy seven, and the first day of *January*, one thousand seven hundred and eighty two, and the judgment remains unsatisfied, it shall be lawful for the several courts within this commonwealth, in a summary way, by motion to them made, either before any execution issues or at the return day of such execution, to fix, settle, and direct, at what depreciation the said damages shall be discharged, having regard to the original injury or contract on which the damages are founded, and any other proof or circumstances that the nature of the case will admit.

C H A P. XXIII.

Repealed, May 1783, ch. 10.

An act to continue and amend the several acts of Assembly respecting the inspection of tobacco, and for other purposes

C H A P. XXIV.

Private

An act to indemnify Thomas Nelson, *jun. Esq. late Governor of this commonwealth, and to legalize certain acts of his administration.*

C H A P. XXV.

Repealed, May 1783, ch. 21.

An act to amend an act entitled An act for further continuing and amending an act for appointing Naval Officers, and ascertaining their fees, and for other purposes.

C H A P. XXVI.

See Oct. 1777, ch. 2, and notes.

An act to empower the Treasurer to borrow money, tobacco, hemp, or flour, for the immediate support of government.

Preamble.

Treasurer empowered to borrow.

Limitation.

Interest at 6 per cent. on commodities, and 100 for 90 on money.

Receivable in taxes as their denomination represents.

I. WHEREAS it is impracticable to collect any of the taxes for the ensuing year, soon enough to answer the many pressing and immediate demands of government, whereby great inconveniencies and much mischief may arise to the commonwealth: For remedy whereof, Be it enacted by the General Assembly, that the Treasurer be, and he is hereby empowered and directed forthwith to borrow such sum or sums of specie, or such quantity of tobacco, hemp, or flour, as he may find necessary to answer the demands which may be made on the treasury till the end of the next session of Assembly, or till the collection of taxes may render such loan unnecessary; Provided, that such sums of money or quantities of tobacco, hemp, or flour, shall not exceed one half of the probable nett produce of the taxes on each of the said articles respectively so borrowed, allowing an interest of six per centum on the tobacco, hemp, or flour, and one hundred pounds specie for every ninety pounds of such money payable at the end of twelve months from the receipt of the same; and the Treasurer's receipts given for such quantities of tobacco, hemp, or flour, or for any sum or sums of money, shall be payable at the treasury, the tobacco, hemp, or flour, at the current prices of those articles when delivered, and the specie as before directed, to the first holder or assignee of such receipts, and shall also be received in payment of all such taxes as they shall, by their denominations, respectively represent; and the Treasurer is also hereby empowered and directed to prepare and give the said receipts, guarded against counterfeits by such precautions and devices as he may think proper.

C H A P. XXVII.

Had its effect.

An act for supplying the southern army with waggons and horses.

C H A P. XXVIII.

Had its effect.

An act to regulate and affix the pay of the militia heretofore called into service.

CHAP. XXIX.

An act to amend an act entitled An act for giving further time to obtain warrants upon certificates for pre-emption rights, and returning certain surveys to the Land Office, and for other purposes.

A. D. 1781.
See May 1779,
ch. 12, and notes.

I. WHEREAS the time limited in the act entitled *An act for giving further time to obtain warrants upon certificates for preemption rights, and returning certain surveys to the Land Office, and for other purposes*, to the commissioners for adjusting and settling the claims to unpatented lands within their respective districts, has been found to be too short for that purpose: Be it therefore enacted, that all the powers given to the said commissioners by any act or acts of Assembly, shall be and continue in force during the farther term of six months; and that the farther time of three months be allowed for obtaining warrants upon certificates of preemption rights, and entering the same with the surveyor of the county.

Preamble. Continuance of the commissioners power.

Further time to obtain warrants, and enter them with the surveyor.

II. AND whereas the allowance heretofore made to the commissioners appointed to carry into execution the said act, and to sheriffs, surveyors and clerks attending the same, is inadequate to their trouble and expence: Be it enacted, that each commissioner for every day he shall necessarily be employed going to, attending on, and returning from the business of his office, shall receive twelve shillings and six pence in specie, the sheriff six shillings in specie, and the surveyor eight shillings in specie.

Allowance to commissioners and attending officers.

III. AND whereas the expence of carrying the said act into execution hath been greatly increased, and it is reasonable and just that such expence should be defrayed by the persons to be benefited thereby, Be it further enacted, that for every hundred acres of land contained in the certificates to be granted by the commissioners, the party receiving the same shall pay one shilling and six pence in specie, besides a fee of six pence in specie to the clerk for every certificate.

Tax on litigants,

IV. AND whereas many disputes may arise between settlers in the several districts who have obtained settlement and preemption rights from the commissioners appointed to settle the claims of unpatented land: Be it therefore enacted, that the county courts shall and are hereby authorized to hear and determine all such disputes as may arise in surveying or laying off settlement or preemption rights; and where any such disputes shall arise, it shall be lawful for either party to petition the court and set forth the nature of their claim, and if the court shall be of an opinion that the claim of the petitioner is just, they shall order a summons to issue for the other party, who shall appear at the next court; and the said court shall then proceed to hear and determine the right and to settle the boundary lines between the claimants, in a summary way, without the usual formality of a suit of law; or may appoint a jury of twelve men to attend the surveyor at a certain day on the land in dispute, which jury shall on oath, hear and determine the right of the claimants and settle the boundary lines; and the said jury shall return their proceedings to the next county court for their confirmation.

County courts to hear and determine disputes in surveying preemption certificates.

V. AND be it further enacted, that where warrants have been obtained for military service, and surveys have not yet been made, it shall be lawful for the persons having such warrants to lay the same within the like time as is allowed to persons claiming lands upon preemption right.

Within what time military warrants to be located.

VI. AND be it further enacted, that all persons who had, during the former government, made locations of land under military warrants, according to the laws and rules then in force, shall have the benefit of their said locations, provided they do not interfere with actual settlements made on such lands before the first day of January, one thousand seven hundred and seventy eight, and shall be admitted to surveys and grants therefor, upon re-entering their lands and hereafter complying with the rules and regulations of the Land Office: Provided, that all lands claimed by virtue of such former locations shall be re-entered with the county surveyors within twelve months after the end of this present session of Assembly.

Military warrants under former government.

VII. AND whereas by the act of General Assembly for adjusting and settling the titles of claimers to unpatented lands, a certain time was limited within which the surveyors of the counties on the eastern waters should survey all lands within their counties regularly entered for before the end of the session of Assembly in which the said act was passed, which time was, by subsequent acts, extended to other definitive periods, and it not being in the power of the party claiming such entries to compel the surveyor to a performance of his duty, or to controul those accidents which may some times render such performance impracticable, it is therefore unjust that he should lose his rights on any failure of duty in the surveyor, whether wilful or involuntary: Be it therefore enacted, that the surveyors of the several counties on the said eastern waters shall proceed, with all practicable dispatch, to survey the said entries before described, and for this purpose shall proceed in notifying the party, making the survey, delivering a plat and certificate, and in all other circumstances as by the act for establishing the Land Office is directed in the case of surveys to be made on entries subsequent to the end of the said session of Assembly; and the party interested shall be subject also to the same forfeitures of right if he fail in any thing prescribed by the same act last mentioned, to be done on his part.

When surveys shall be made of entries on the eastern waters.

VIII. AND whereas by the said law for establishing the Land Office, all orders of Council or entries in the Council-books for lands not carried into execution by actual survey, were made void, which, so far as it respected lands on the eastern waters, produced much injury to individuals and no utility to the public: Be it therefore enacted, that all orders of Council and entries in the Council-books for lands on the eastern waters, which were in force at the passing of the said act, and which have been precluded from revival by entries or surveys regularly made for the same lands since the passing of the said act, shall stand revived and re-established, and the rights accruing thereon be vested in the persons then owning the same, their heirs or other representatives: And that the said orders of Council or entries in the Council-books shall stand on the footing of entries in the surveyors books, and as such be considered to every intent and purpose, save only that where they exceed the quantity of four hundred acres, they shall be good for their whole quantity, so far as they would have been good by authority of the said orders of Council or entries in the Council-books before the passing of the said act.

Orders of Council for land on the eastern waters to be valid.

IX. AND whereas many persons have obtained certificates for surveys of lands and returned the same to the Land Office, and patents cannot issue for the same until six months after opening the Courts of Justice, whereby a great proportion of landed property will be covered from taxation, and unjust inequality in the public burdens upon the good people of this commonwealth be produced: For remedy whereof, Be it enacted, that patents shall issue agreeable to all certificates for surveys of land at the times respectively and in the manner practised under the laws preceding the act of the last session, entitled *An act preventing a discontinuance of the General Court, and suspending the proceedings of certain courts in particular cases,* the said act notwithstanding. And the Register of the Land Office shall deduct out of the calculation of time for which patents have been usually detained, five months and no more for the late

Patents to issue as usual, notwithstanding the act of May 1781, ch. 9.

Register to allow 5 months for the late occlusion of the courts.

A. D. 1781.

Not neceffary to exchange warrants for military fervice laft war.

occlufion of the courts, and patents fhall forthwith iffue in all cafes in the ufual manner, the faid recited act notwithftanding.

X. AND *be it further enacted*, that it fhall not be neceffary to exchange warrants for military fervice performed laft war, but that all locations made under the fame fhall ftand upon the fame footing as thofe made under treafury warrants, and the parties fhall be entitled to furveys and grants in the fame manner.

C H A P. XXX.

An act to enable Henry M'Cabe to difpofe of certain lands.

Private.

C H A P. XXXI.

An act for regulating tobacco fees, and fixing the allowance to fheriffs, witneffes, and venire-men.

See May 1780, ch 7. Oct. 1782, ch 24, 49. May 1783 ch. 10, fect. 31. Oct. 1783, ch. 32. fect. 9.

Valuation by grand jury repealed.

How tobacco fees fhall be paid.

I. WHEREAS it has become neceffary to alter the mode for fixing the rate at which tobacco fees, fheriffs, venire-men, and witneffes attendance fhould be difcharged in money: *Be it therefore enacted*, that fo much of the act of Affembly entitled *An act for regulating the fees of the Regifter of the Land Office, and for other purpofes*, as directs the grand jury at the *October* and *June* courts to fix fuch rate in paper currency, fhall be, and the fame is hereby repealed. And that from and after the paffing of this act, all perfons who now are, or fhall hereafter become chargeable with any tobacco fees for fervices mentioned in the faid recited act, or in any other act now in force, fhall difcharge the fame in transfer tobacco notes, or in fpecie, at the rate of twelve fhillings and fix pence for every hundred pounds of grofs tobacco.

Payment of venire-men, witneffes, and fheriffs in criminal cafes.

II. AND *be it further enacted*, that venire-men, witneffes, and fheriffs attending the General Court in criminal cafes, fhall be entitled to receive for that particular fervice, from the treafury by warrant from the Auditors, the fum of feven fhillings and fix pence in fpecie for every days attendance, and four pence *per* mile for travelling and their ferriages.

C H A P. XXXII.

An act for laying taxes in certain enumerated commodities.

Executed.

C H A P. XXXIII.

An act for afcertaining the falaries to the officers of civil government.

Preamble.

Annual falaries to be paid quarterly.

Governor.
Council.
Judges.
Treafurer.
Attorney General.
Auditors.
Commercial Agent and Commiffioner of war office at an end.
Solicitor General.
Clerks.

I. WHEREAS the provifion made for the officers of government by an act of Affembly paffed in *May* laft, hath been found inadequate to their fervices, as well on account of the *quantum* as the depreciation between each quarterly payment: *Be it therefore enacted by the General Affembly*, that from and after the firft day of *January*, one thoufand feven hundred and eighty two, the feveral officers herein after mentioned fhall, for their refpective fervices, be entitled to the following annually falaries, to be paid in fpecie out of the public treafury, in quarterly payments, after the fame fhall have been audited according to law: To the Governor or Chief Magiftrate, the fum of one thoufand pounds; to the Privy Councillors, the fum of three thoufand two hundred pounds, to be divided amongft them according to their attendance; to the Judges of the High Court of Chancery, the General Court, and Court of Admiralty, each, the fum of three hundred pounds; to the Treafurer the fum of fix hundred pounds; to the Attorney General, the fum of three hundred pounds; to the Auditors of public accounts, the fum of four hundred pounds; to the Commercial Agent, the fum of four hundred pounds; to the Commiffioner of the War-Office, the fum of four hundred pounds; to the Solicitor General, the fum of three hundred pounds; to the firft clerk of the Council, the fum of one hundred and fifty pounds; to the affiftant clerk of the Council, the fum of one hundred pounds; and to each of the clerks of the Auditors, Solicitor General, Commiffioner of War, and Treafurer, the fum of one hundred and fifty pounds; to the firft clerk of the Commercial Agent, one hundred and fifty pounds; to the fecond clerk to the Commercial Agent, one hundred pounds.

Salaries from July to be made good.

II. AND *be it further enacted*, that the falaries heretofore allowed to the faid officers refpectively, fhall be made good to them in fpecie from the firft day of *July* laft, after the rate of twenty fhillings for each hundred pounds of tobacco; and the Auditors are hereby authorized to audit the fame, and to iffue their warrants on the treafury accordingly.

Former acts repealed.

III. AND *be it further enacted*, that all other act or acts coming within the purview of this act, fhall be, and the fame are hereby repealed.

C H A P. XXXIV.

An act for allowing further time to fheriffs or collectors of taxes due for the year 1781, and for other purpofes.

Had its effect.

C H A P. XXXV.

An act to empower the Juftices of Elizabeth City county to hold their courts at any other place than the court houfe in the faid county.

Private.

C H A P. XXXVI.

An act to regulate impreffes.

Preamble.

All impreffes prohibited.

I. WHEREAS many continental officers, foldiers, commiffaries, quarter-mafters, and other perfons have, upon pretence of a right to imprefs, committed great violences upon the property of the citizens of this ftate; and it being the duty of the reprefentatives of the people to protect them in the quiet poffeffion of their property: *Be it therefore enacted*, that if any officer foldier, commiffary, quarter-mafter, or other perfon fhall prefume to take from any citizen or citizens of this commonwealth, any part of their property by way of imprefs, unlefs it be by warrant from the executive, in cafe of actual invafion, or by fheriffs bringing criminals to the General Court, it fhall be lawful for any Magiftrate in the county where the offence is committed, upon information on oath, to iffue his warrant for the immediate taking and fafe keeping of fuch offender or offenders, till they are delivered by due courfe of law; and all county lieutenants and other officers of the militia are hereby enjoined to fupport the civil power in fecuring and bringing fuch offenders to juftice.

Exceptions.
Proceedings on illegal impreffes.

C H A P. XXXVII.

An act to regulate the infpection of flour.

See May 1782, ch. 52.

I. WHEREAS the law now in force for the infpection of flour, is found infufficient for giving due encouragement to fo valuable a branch of our commerce in guarding againft abufes; and as found policy requires that our flour trade fhould be put upon a refpectable footing, which can only be done by eftablifhing fuch regulations as will prevent the manufacturer from bringing to market any flour that will not pafs the public infpections with credit, or entitle the merchant to preference in every foreign market: *Be it therefore enacted by the General Affembly,* that fo much of the act paffed in May, one thoufand feven hundred and eighty, as relates to the infpection of flour, be, and the fame is hereby repealed.

Preamble.

So much of May 1780, ch. 23, as relates to flour, repealed.

II. AND *be it further enacted,* that all flour, before it fhall be exported, fhall be firft infpected and weighed at the public infpections of tax flour at *Alexandria, Fredericksburg, Richmond, Petersburg,* and *Weft Point,* by the infpectors to be appointed under an act of this prefent feffion of Affembly for afcertaining certain taxes and duties, and for eftablifhing a permanent revenue, who fhall be allowed two pence *per* barrel for their trouble, to be paid by the owner.

Flour before exported, fhall be infpected.
Places of infpection.
Fee for infpection.

III. AND for afcertaining the condition of fuch flour as ought to pafs infpection, and alfo the duty of the infpectors, *Be it enacted,* that the barrels fhall be made of found and well feafoned timber of a fufficient thicknefs, and be hooped with twelve hoops, and to contain not lefs than one hundred and ninety fix, nor more than two hundred and four pounds weight of nett flour. The infpectors fhall mark on each cafk by them infpected, the name of the miller, the name of the place where it is infpected, and the quality, whether fuperfine, fine, or feconds; and when the flour is thus marked, they fhall grant to the owner a certificate of the number of barrels fo by them infpected, diftinguifhing therein the quantities and qualities of each kind, which fhall entitle the owner to difpofe of the fame as flour fit for exportation.

How barrels to be made.
Contents.
Marks when infpected.
Certificates to be granted.

IV. AND *be it further enacted,* that for the conveniency of millers as well as fhippers of flour who live inconvenient to the public infpections, infpectors fhall be appointed at the following places, to wit: *New-Caftle, York, Falmouth, Port Royal, Hobb's Hole, Colchefter, Dumfries, Manchefter, Ofborne's Pokahuntus, Nomony, Broadway, Low Point* in Surry, *Suffolk, South Quay,* and *Norfolk;* and the county courts in which the above pofts are, are hereby directed and empowered to appoint infpectors, who fhall take an oath for the faithful performance of their duty, and fhall receive the fame allowance for infpection, and be fubject to the fame penalties for neglect, as the infpectors at *Alexandria, Fredericksburg, Weft Point, Richmond,* and *Petersburg:* Provided neverthelefs, that where any merchant mill is, or fhall be fituated on navigable water below the falls, that it fhall and may be lawful for the owner of fuch mill or mills, to call on one of the infpectors of flour in the county where fuch mill is, who is hereby directed to attend and infpect the fame, and grant certificates as in other cafes.

Other places of infpection.
Infpectors to be appointed.
Their oath.
When flour may be infpected at merchant mills;

V. AND *be it further enacted,* that all flour brought by water to the infpections aforefaid, may be infpected at the landings for the greater conveniency of the owner for exportation; and all flour that fhall be fhipped for exportation without being infpected as before directed (a certificate of which fhall be produced on oath to the Naval Officer of the diftrict) fhall be liable to be feized by the faid officer, and being profecuted before the court of the county where the feizure is made on the information of fuch officer and condemned by fuch court, fhall, by the faid officer, be fold for the benefit of the ftate, who fhall receive for his reward ten *per centum* on the fales, and after deducting his commiffions, pay the amount of fuch fales into the treafury. And all flour that fhall be found on infpection to be falfe packed, fhall be forfeited and given to the poor of the parifh; and where any fhall be refufed for the want of good cafks, the owner fhall be at liberty to repack it in good cafks before it is removed from the public infpection.

or at landing if carried by water.
Flour fhipped uninfpected, forfeited to the ftate.
How to be profecuted.
Flour found to be falfe packed, forfeited to the poor.
If refufed for want of good cafks, may be repacked in fuch.

C H A P. XXXVIII.

An act to recruit the Virginia line on the continental eftablifhment.

Had its effect.

C H A P. XXXIX.

An act to empower the Naval Officers to receive the duties in their feveral diftricts.

Provided for May 1783. ch. 21.

C H A P. XL.

An act for afcertaining certain taxes and duties, and for eftablifhing a permanent revenue.

See Oct. 1777, ch. 2, and notes.

I. BE *it enacted by the General Affembly,* that the fheriff, and in cafe there fhould be no fheriff, the firft acting Magiftrate of each county within this commonwealth, fhall annually appoint fome day in the month of *February,* or at any time before the fifteenth day of the next fucceeding month, if prevented from holding fuch courts in the faid month of *February* by any accidents, from and after the paffing of this act, on which a court fhall be held in his faid county, and the faid fheriff or Magiftrate, as the cafe may be, fhall give notice thereof to the Juftices and to the clerk of his faid county, who fhall attend at the court-houfe thereof on the day appointed, if fair, if not, on the next fair day, and the faid Juftices fhall then and there appoint three reputable freeholders refident in their faid county, to be commiffioners for afcertaining the value of all lands within the fame, except the lands belonging to the faid commiffioners, which fhall be valued by two Juftices to be appointed by the refpective courts, who

Commiffioners of the tax how to be appointed.

A.D. 1781.

Their oath.

shall proceed in the same manner, and be allowed the same pay and be liable to the same penalties, as directed in the case of commissioners by this act, which said commissioners, before they enter upon the duties of their office, shall take the following oath or affirmation, to wit: I A. B. *do solemnly swear (or affirm as the case may be) that I will truly, candidly, and impartially, ascertain and fix the value of the several kinds of land within my county, as the same shall be worth in specie, if sold for ready money, separately from other lands, after giving reasonable public notice, according to the best of my judgment: So help me God.* Which oath or affirmation shall be administered by any Magistrate within the county, and the two com-

Their duty.

missioners first named in the appointment of the court shall proceed to take an account in writing of the quantity of land belonging to all persons within their said county, except as before excepted, and also of the name of the proprietor or proprietors thereof, and shall ascertain the value of the said lands by the acre, computing the same by an average of the value of the quantity contained in each tract or parcel

Lands and lots to be valued without regard to buildings. Rules of Oct. 1777, ch. 2, to be observed.

of land separately, lots in any town excepted, which shall be valued separately from other lands, and with due regard to their situation; and where any lands or lots as aforesaid shall be valued pursuant to this act, the same shall be done without having regard to any buildings or other improvements thereon. And in all valuations of land pursuant to this act, the same rules and regulations shall be observed with respect to and between landlords and tenants (unless the contract between them shall be specially otherwise) and the same discount for quitrents on the lands in the Northern Neck as are directed by the act of one thousand seven hundred and seventy seven, entitled *An act for raising a supply of money for the public exigencies.* And in case of the death or inability of either of the two commissioners first named, the

How vacancies in the commission to be supplied.

third commissioner shall then proceed to act in his stead; and in case of the death or inability of any two or all of the said commissioners, the first Magistrate acting in the said county shall, by warrant under his hand and seal, appoint other reputable freeholders in his said county to act in their stead; which warrant shall be directed to, and executed by the sheriff of the said county, who shall return the same to the next succeeding court, there to be recorded as the act of the said court: And the persons so appointed shall take the oath as above mentioned, and shall perform the duties required of commissioners by this act, either in the whole or in part, as the case may require. And where any two commissioners acting pursuant to this act shall differ in opinion as to the value of any land or lots as aforesaid, the two sums shall be added together and one half thereof shall be taken for the value of said land or lots. And

Penalty on pro-prietors failing to give account of lands.

if any proprietor or proprietors of lands or lots as aforesaid, his, her, or their tenant, attorney, or overseer, residing upon the land or lots aforesaid, or in case of any infant, or infants, his, her, or their guardian, shall refuse or neglect to give an account of the quantity of lands or lots held by any of them or under their respective management, within the time limited for the commissioners to make return of their proceedings according to this act, such person or persons, so refusing or neglecting as aforesaid, shall forfeit and pay the sum of one hundred pounds, recoverable by information in any county courts within this commonwealth, to be applied towards lessening the county levy where the same shall be recovered; and the said land or lots shall be liable to double taxes upon the quantity when duly ascertained, or on the estimation of the said commissioners, in the list returned by them. And the said commis-

Commissioners duty in returning list of lands to the clerk. And of clerks therein.

sioners shall make out a fair list of the names of the proprietors of lands or lots, the quantity of land and lots belonging to each proprietor, and the value thereof, in separate columns, and return the same to the clerk of the court of their said county, on or before the first day of *June* annually; and the said clerk shall file the same in his office, and shall make out therefrom three fair copies, one of which shall be delivered to the Auditors of public accounts, at their office, by the said clerk, on or before the first day of *August* in each year, one other copy to be set up in the court-house of the county on the next succeeding court day, and the other to be delivered to the sheriff or collector of public taxes in the said county, on or before the tenth day of *June* annually. And each commissioner shall be allowed the sum of fifteen

Allowance to commissioners; to clerk and sheriff.

shillings *per* day for the time he shall be actually employed in performing the duties required of him by this act, the account of which shall be allowed on oath by the court of the county, and certified by the clerk thereof to the sheriff or collector of the public taxes, for payment out of the public money in his hands. And the court of each county shall make such allowance to the clerk and sheriff of their said county for the services required of them as aforesaid, as they shall think reasonable, which shall be certified and paid in manner aforesaid; and all such payments shall be allowed to the said sheriff or collector, by the Auditors of public accounts, on passing the accounts of the same. And when any sheriff, Justice,

Penalty on she-riff, Justice, clerk, and commissioner. How to be reco-vered and appro-priated.

clerk, or commissioner, shall refuse or neglect to perform the duties required of them respectively as above mentioned, such person or persons shall forfeit and pay for such refusal or neglect the sum of one hundred pounds in specie, recoverable on information in any county court within this commonwealth, who shall thereupon enter judgment and award execution for the said penalty, to be applied towards lessening the county levy where the same shall be recovered. *Provided nevertheless*, that the party shall have ten days previous notice of such information: *Provided also*, that where there shall be two or more

Two sets of com-missioners where two battalions of militia.

battalions of militia in any county, the court of the said county may, if they see cause, appoint three commissioners for the district of each battalion, who shall in all respects be governed in their respective districts by the directions of this act for the commissioners of counties.

The taxes.

II. AND be it *further enacted*, that there shall be collected, paid, and distrained for the tax of one pound for every hundred pounds, and so in proportion for every greater or lesser sum, of the valuation of all lands and lots, as the same shall be returned by the commissioners to the clerk of each county within this commonwealth; also a tax of ten shillings by every free male person above the age of twenty one years, who shall be a citizen of this commonwealth, and also upon all slaves, to be paid by the owners thereof, except such free persons and slaves as shall be exempted on applications to the respective county courts through age or infirmity; also two shillings for every horse, mare, colt, and mule; also three pence *per* head for all neat cattle; also five shillings *per* wheel for all coaches, chariots, phætons, four wheeled chaises, stage waggons for riding carriages, chairs, and two wheeled chaises; also fifty pounds for every billiard table, and five pounds for every ordinary licence; which said taxes shall be paid annually in the manner herein after directed.

Justices to be ap-pointed to take lists of taxable articles,

III. AND for the regular listing of all articles enumerated above, *Be it enacted*, that the court of every county respectively shall divide the same into convenient precincts, and annually before the tenth day of *April*, appoint one of the Justices for each precinct to take a list of the said enumerated articles therein,

and return them to the clerk.

and every such Justice shall, before that day, give public notice of his being so appointed, and at what place or places he intends to receive the list, by advertising the same at the most public places within his precinct, and shall accordingly attend on the said tenth day of *April*, if it be not *Sunday*, and then on the next day, and on or before the first day of *June* next following shall deliver to the clerk of the county court, together with the vouchers by him taken, a fair list of the names of all free male persons above the age of twenty one years as aforesaid, and resident within his said precinct, and of the names of all slaves, specifying to whom they belong; and also the number of neat cattle, horses, mares, colts, and mules; wheels for riding carriages above specified in this act, billiard tables and ordinary licences; which said enumerated articles shall be placed under the names of the persons to whom they

Clerk's duty therein.

belong, and the said clerk shall file the same in his office, and shall make out three fair copies from all the lists so taken and delivered to him, and shall dispose of the same in like manner and within the same

A. D. 1781.

time as is herein before directed in the cafe of the returns made by the commiffioners for the valuing of lands, and the said clerk shall be allowed for his fervices, and shall receive payment in the same manner as is provided therein, and he shall moreover be subject to the same penalty, which shall be recoverable and applied in the same manner therein alfo directed; and the sheriff or collector shall be allowed the same in paffing his accounts with the Auditors of public accounts. And if any Juftice fo appointed shall refufe to take, or shall fail to return such lifts and vouchers as aforefaid, he shall forfeit and pay two thousand pounds of tobacco for the ufe of the county where such failure or refufal shall be, towards leffening the county levy, to be recovered by information in any county court within this commonwealth, giving ten days notice of such information to the party. And that every master or owner of a family; or in his absence or non-refidence at the plantation, his or her agent, attorney, or overfeer, shall on the said tenth day of *April*, by a lift under his or her hand, deliver, or caufe to be delivered, to the Justice appointed for that precinct, the names and number of all tithable persons abiding in or belonging to his or her family the ninth day of *April*, alfo the number of his or her neat cattle, horfes, mares, colts, and mules, wheels for riding carriages as herein before mentioned, billiard tables, and ordinary licences; or the master or owner thereof, or in cafe of his or her absence or non-refidence upon the plantation, the overfeer, shall be adjudged a concealer of such and fo many articles above enumerated as shall not be lifted and given in, and for every article fo concealed, shall forfeit and pay five hundred pounds of tobacco, to be recovered by information in any county court within this commonwealth, for the ufe of the county where such concealment shall be, for leffening the county levy. And when any of the articles above enumerated shall not be lifted and given in as aforefaid, the master or owner shall be subject to the payment of the taxes in the same manner as if the same had been duly lifted and given in. And if any Juftice appointed to take the lift of articles above mentioned, shall not truly enter and lift all thofe which belong to himfelf in that precinct, in which the lift is taken by him, he shall be judged a concealer, and shall forfeit and pay for every article fo concealed, one thousand pounds of tobacco, to be applied and recovered as aforefaid: *Provided neverthelefs*, that if any owner, agent, attorney, or overfeer, shall happen by sickness, absence, or ignorance of the person or place, to omit delivering his or her lift on the said tenth day of *April*, to the Juftice appointed to take the same, it shall be lawful for such person to deliver or fend his or her lift to the houfe of such Juftice at any time before the last day of the said month, which shall discharge him or her from the penalty aforefaid.

his allowance and penalty.

Penalty on Juftice failing;

and on proprietors failing to give in accounts.

How this penalty may be faved.

IV. AND for the collecting and accounting for the taxes impofed by this act, *Be it enacted*, that the court of every county within this commonwealth refpectively, shall, in or before the month of *May* annually, take bond of the sheriff, with sufficient-security, in the penalty of ten thousand pounds, payable to the Treafurer of this commonwealth for the time being, and his succeffors, for the ufe of this commonwealth, and conditioned for the true and faithful collecting, paying, and accounting for, all taxes in his county hereby impofed, and the said bond shall be recorded in the court where the same is taken, and an attefted copy thereof shall be tranfmitted by the refpective clerks without delay to the Auditors of public accounts, which shall be admitted as evidence in any suit or proceeding founded thereon. And the said sheriff shall, from and after the tenth day of *June* annually, collect and receive from all and every perfon and perfons chargeable therewith, the taxes impofed by this act in his said county; and in cafe payment be not made or received on or before the first day of *July* annually, the said sheriff shall have power to diftrain the lands or flaves, goods or chattels, which shall be found upon the lands, and in the poffeffion of the perfon fo indebted or failing, notwithftanding such lands, flaves, goods, or chattels, shall be comprifed in any deed or mortgage; and if the owner thereof shall not pay the taxes due within five days after such diftrefs, such sheriff or collector shall and may lawfully fell the same, or fo much thereof as shall be sufficient to difcharge the said taxes and the charges of diftrefs and fale, giving fix days notice of the day and place of fale, by advertifing the same at the church or other public places in the parish wherein such diftrefs shall be, on the next *Sunday* after the expiration of the said five days, which fate shall be good and effectual in law, against all perfons whatfoever: *Provided*, that in all cafes where any sheriff or collector shall make seizure of any lands by virtue of this act, he shall give at least four weeks notice in the public papers before any fale shall be made of the fame; and where other sufficient effects can be had thereon, diftrefs shall not be made of such lands: *Provided always*, that where unreafonable seizures or diftreffes shall be made, the party grieved shall have an action against the sheriff or collector, and shall recover full cofts where any damages shall be given; and the said sheriff or collector shall duly account for and pay into the treafury of this commonwealth, on or before the first day of *September* annually, the full amount of all taxes impofed in his said county, deducting therefrom an allowance for infolvents, and such other allowances as this act directs to be made, and five *per centum* for his commiffions thereon; and before any allowance shall be made in the cafe of infolvents, the sheriff shall return a lift thereof to the court of his said county, and shall make oath that the same is a true lift of infolvents within his county, an attefted copy of which shall be delivered to the Auditors of public accounts by the sheriff, and the same shall by them be allowed in paffing the accounts of such sheriff. And in cafe the said sheriff shall fail to account for and pay into the treafury as aforefaid, the money or other articles in lieu thereof, impofed by this act, and received by him for taxes, every such delinquent sheriff or collector shall be liable to a judgment against him, on motion to be made by the Solicitor or other perfon appointed for that purpofe, at any time during the sitting of the General Court in the month of *October*, after such failure, for the amount of the taxes due, and ten *per centum* for intereft and damages, for the ufe of the commonwealth; and thereupon execution shall iffue. And there shall be paid by all and every perfon and perfons chargeable therewith, to the sheriff or collector of the fame, the taxes herein before enumerated; which said taxes shall be paid in *Spanish* milled dollars at the rate of fix shillings each, or in other current gold or silver coin at a proportionate value, or in the bills of credit herein after mentioned, or in such produce of this commonwealth, at such rate, and in such manner and proportion, as is herein after mentioned, to wit: One tenth part, or two shillings in the pound, of the tax on land, shall be payable, at the option of the perfons paying the said tax, in the bills of credit emitted on the funds of this commonwealth and the faith of the United States as pledged by the refolutions of Congrefs of the eighteenth of *March*, in the year on thousand seven hundred and eighty, and the intereft due on the said bills shall be computed and allowed to the payer at the time of payment thereof, for the said tax; and the said bills of credit fo received shall be paid into the treafury and not re-iffued, but shall remain in the treafury to be burnt and deftroyed. And all other taxes on articles enumerated as aforefaid, to be paid by this act (except the tax on land) shall be payable (at the option of the payer) one half thereof in fpecie, tobacco, or hemp, and the other half in fpecie, tobacco, hemp, or flour, to wit: in infpectors receipts or notes for good merchantable crop tobacco, not infpected more than one year when offered in payment, at the rate of twenty five shillings *per* hundred, with an allowance of twelve shillings and fix pence for infpection and cafk, or in transfer receipts or notes for tobacco at the rate of one hundred and fix pounds for one hundred pounds of crop tobacco, at any public infpection within this commonwealth; or in infpectors receipts or notes for found, clean, and merchantable hemp, delivered at the warehoufes provided or to be provided for the reception thereof, at the towns of *Alexandria, Frederickfburg, Richmond, Peterfburg,* and *Weft Point,* which said receipts or notes for hemp shall be received in difcharge of taxes, according to this act, at the rate of fifty shillings *per*

Bonds for collection to be annually taken of sheriffs;

a copy fent to the Auditors which shall be evidence.

When the tax to be collected.

When diftrained for

directions in cafe of lands diftrained.

Penalty for unreafonable seizures or diftreffes.

Sheriff when to account and pay taxes.

How to account.

How proceeded against for failure.

How taxes may be paid.

A. D. 1781.

hundred; or in receipts for found and merchantable flour, delivered at the warehouses, provided or to be provided by the inspectors and receivers of hemp at the aforesaid towns in casks, and not inspected more than three months, when offered in payment, at the rate of sixteen shillings and eight pence per hundred, with an allowance of two shillings and six pence for cask and inspection; and any person or persons chargeable with taxes by this act, and paying the same in the manner herein directed, shall be discharged thereof, and may demand and receive of the sheriff or collector a receipt or discharge accordingly. *Provided nevertheless*, that the Governor, with the advice of the Privy Council, may appoint such other place or places, person or persons, for the reception of flour pursuant to this act, as the exigencies of this commonwealth shall require, and the notes or receipts of such persons shall pass in payment of taxes in the manner herein before directed for paying the notes of the receivers of flour, on public account. And the Treasurer for the time being shall make out a fair list of the receipts so paid into the treasury for taxes as aforesaid, and shall deliver the same, duly certified, to the Governor of this commonwealth, who, with the advice of the Privy Council, shall direct the said tobacco, hemp, and flour, to be sold from time to time as occasion may require, for current gold or silver coin, which shall be forthwith paid into the treasury, or otherwise to dispose of the said hemp, tobacco, and flour, in payment of the debts and contracts of this commonwealth, on the best terms that can be obtained, in like manner as if the same had been current gold and silver coin actually paid into the treasury, having a due regard to the appropriations which are or shall be made of the revenue of the commonwealth, arising from this act, by the General Assembly. And the courts of the counties respectively in which the aforesaid towns of *Alexandria*, *Fredericksburg*, *Richmond*, *Petersburg*, and *West Point*, shall be, are hereby authorized and required, to provide good and sufficient warehouses for the storage of hemp and flour according to this act, and to appoint one or two reputable persons, as the case may require, within the said towns respectively, for the receiving, safe keeping, and delivering of the said hemp and flour on public account, and for inspecting the said hemp, who, in the receipts given by them, or either of them, shall specify the names of the persons or owners delivering the same, the number and quantity of each bundle of hemp, and the warehouse number and nett weight of each barrel of inspected flour received, for which the inspectors manifest shall be produced and filed at the said warehouse as a voucher, to prove the inspection thereof, before the delivery by the owner. And the said courts respectively shall make such reasonable allowance to the inspectors or receivers aforesaid, for their services, as they shall think proper, and shall certify the same to the Auditors of public accounts, and all other expences attending the said warehouses, for the receiving and delivering of the hemp and flour aforesaid, shall be allowed and certified in like manner, and shall be paid out of the money in the public treasury arising from the sale thereof. And the said inspectors or receivers of hemp and flour shall, before entering upon the duties of their office, give bond in a reasonable penalty, payable to the Treasurer for the time being, or to his successors, for the use of the commonwealth, conditioned for the due and faithful performance of the duties required of them by law, in the execution of their said office; and in case of failure in any court, inspector, or receiver, respectively as aforesaid, such court shall be liable to the same penalties as is provided in the case of courts neglecting or refusing to appoint commissioners by this act, to be recovered and applied in like manner; and such inspector or receiver shall be liable to damages, upon the action of the party grieved, and shall moreover forfeit and pay the sum of one hundred pounds, recoverable in any county court, for the use of this commonwealth.

Treasurer to deliver list of receipts to the Governor, who shall direct the sale of the commodities.

Directions for appointing inspectors of flour.

Tax on patents exceeding 1400 acres; except bounties to officers.

V. AND *be it further enacted*, that there shall be received, accounted for on oath, and paid into the treasury of this commonwealth by the Register of the Land Office for the time being, every half year, to wit: On or before the first day of *April* and the first day of *October* in every year, the tax of five shillings for every hundred acres of land exceeding fourteen hundred acres contained in any patent hereafter to be granted, except in cases of land allowed to officers as bounties, which said tax the said Register is authorised to demand and receive before granting the said patent; and the said Register shall account for and pay the money arising from the aforesaid tax, in the same manner as is directed by this act in the case of sheriffs accounting for and paying the taxes received by them, and in case of failure shall be liable to the like penalties, to be recovered in like manner.

Duty on vessels;

on spirits and wine imported;

On sugar;

On coffee;

On all other goods imported.

VI. AND *be it further enacted*, that on all vessels, at entrance or clearance from or to foreign parts, there shall be paid by the master or owner thereof, the duty of one shilling and three pence *per* ton, to the collector of duties at the port or ports established or to be established for the entrance and clearance of such vessels; and for every gallon of rum, brandy, and other distilled spirits, and for every gallon of wine which shall be imported or brought into this commonwealth either by land or water, from any port or place whatsoever, the duty or custom of four pence shall be paid by the owner or importer of the same; and for every hundred pounds of sugar which shall be imported or brought into this commonwealth as aforesaid, from any port or place whatsoever, the duty or custom of four shillings and two pence; and for every pound of coffee which shall be imported or brought into this commonwealth as aforesaid, from any port or place whatsoever, the duty of one penny; and for all other goods or merchandise which shall be imported or brought into this commonwealth as aforesaid, from any port or place whatsoever, the duty of one *per centum*, *ad valorem* on the amount *per* invoice of such goods and merchandise; all which said duties shall be paid by the owner or importer of any of the articles or merchandise above mentioned.

Masters of vessels importing goods, when and how to report.

VII. AND *be it further enacted*, that the master or purser of every ship or other vessel, importing any goods, wares, or merchandise, liable to a duty, by virtue of this act, to any port or place within this commonwealth, shall, within forty eight hours after his arrival, make a true and just report upon oath with the collector of the duties in the said port or place, of the burthen, contents, and loading of such ship or vessel, with the particular marks and numbers of every cask or package whatsoever therein laden, with spirits, wine, sugar, coffee, and other merchandise, and the quantity of such spirits, wine, sugar, and coffee, and the value of such other merchandise, and to whom consigned, to the best of his knowledge; and also where and in what port the same were laden and taken on board, upon penalty of forfeiting one hundred pounds current money.

Dutiable goods not to be landed before entry;

VIII. AND *be it further enacted*, that no spirits, wine, sugar, coffee, or other merchandise liable to the said duties, imported or brought into this commonwealth by water, by any person or persons whatsoever, shall be landed or put on shore until due entry made thereof with the collector of the duties in such port or place, and a true account of the marks and numbers of every cask and package as aforesaid at that port or place where the same was shipped or taken on board, given on oath before the said collector, who shall certify the same upon the back of the original invoice, or a true copy thereof to him produced; and thereupon such importer, paying the duties laid by this act, or securing the payment thereof within six months, shall obtain a permit under the hand of such collector for the landing and delivery of the same; and all spirits, wine, sugar, coffee, or other merchandise landed, put on shore or delivered, contrary to the true intent and meaning of this act, or the value thereof, shall be forfeited and lost, and may be seized or recovered by the said collector of the port or place where the same shall be put on shore or delivered, or by any other person or persons whatsoever. And the owner or importer of any of the aforefaid fpirits, wine, fugar, coffee, or other merchandife by land, fhall in like manner make due entry of the fame within ten days after the importation, with the collector of the duties aforefaid, and give a true account thereof upon oath, and pay the duties hereby impofed, or give bond with good fecurity for payment thereof within fix months, and thereupon obtain a permit, under the hand of the faid collector, for felling or making ufe of the fame; and all fpirits, wines, fugar, coffee and other merchandife imported by land without fuch entry made and permit obtained, or the value thereof, fhall be forfeited and may be recovered or feized by the collector of the faid duties, or any other perfons whatfoever: *Provided always*, that no perfon fhall be required to give account upon oath, of the true contents of any pipe or leffer cafk of wine, or any hogfhead or leffer cafk of fpirits imported, but fhall have liberty to enter a pipe of wine, or hogfhead of fpirits as aforefaid, at one hundred gallons, and all leffer cafks after the fame proportion, any thing in this act to the contrary notwithftanding.

nor till duty paid or bonded, and permit obtained; goods landed otherwife to be forfeited; fame regulations as to goods imported by land.

How cafks of liquors to be entered.

IX. AND be it further enacted, that if any perfon or perfons whatfoever, fhall wittingly or willingly make a falfe entry, and be thereof convicted, fuch perfon or perfons fhall forfeit and pay one hundred pounds current money.

Penalty for making a falfe entry.

X. AND be it further enacted, that the collectors of the duties aforefaid, or any perfon by them appointed, fhall have full power and authority to go and enter on board of any fhip or other veffel, and from thence to bring on fhore any articles whatfoever, liable to a duty by virtue of this act, if fuch duty be not paid or agreed for within ten days after the firft entry of fuch fhip or veffel, or bond with good and fufficient fecurity given for payment of the fame, within fix months next after fuch entry, which bond, if offered, the collector is hereby authorized and required to accept and take, and fuch articles fo brought on fhore, to fecure and detain until due payment fhall be made or fecurity given for the fame as aforefaid; and if fuch payment or fecurity be not made or given within two days from the time of fuch feizure, the collector of the duties aforefaid is hereby empowered to fell the fame, or fo much thereof as fhall be fufficient to difcharge the faid duties, and five *per centum* for the charges of fuch feizure and fale: *Provided neverthelefs*, that notice fhall be given of fuch fale, by advertifing the fame two weeks in the gazette; and they are alfo empowered to ftay and remain on board fuch fhip or veffel until all fuch wines, fpirit, fugar, coffee, and other merchandife be difcharged and delivered out of the fame. And if any collector or collectors of the faid duties, or any other perfon or perfons deputed by them or any of them, fhall directly or indirectly take or receive any bribe, recompence or reward, in any kind whatfoever, or fhall connive at any falfe entry of the articles liable to a duty or cuftom by virtue of this act, the perfon or perfons fo offending fhall forfeit and pay the fum of one hundred pounds current money, and be for ever after difabled in his faid office, and rendered incapable of holding any office or employment relating to the cuftoms within this commonwealth; and the perfon or perfons giving or offering fuch bribe, reward or recompence, fhall forfeit and pay one hundred pounds current money.

If duty not paid or bonded in ten days after entry collector may enter the veffel and feize the goods, and in two days fell as much as will pay the duty and charges.

Penalty on collector receiving a bribe or conniving at a falfe entry.

And on perfon offering a bribe.

XI. AND be it further enacted, that it fhall be lawful to and for all and every collector and collectors of the duties aforefaid, by warrant under the hand of a Juftice of Peace (which warrant fhall not be granted but upon an information made to him upon oath, and accompanied with a conftable) to break open, in the day time, any houfe, warehoufe or ftorehoufe, to fearch for, feize and carry away any wine, fpirits, fugar, coffee, and other merchandife liable to a duty by this act, and for which the faid duty fhall not have been paid or fecured to be paid as aforefaid. And if any collector or conftable fhall be fued or molefted for any thing done in execution of the powers hereby given them, fuch collector or conftable may plead the general iffue, and give this act in evidence; and if in fuch fuit, the plaintiff be non-fuit, or judgment pafs againft him, the defendant fhall recover double cofts: And in all actions, fuits, or informations to be brought, or where any feizure fhall be made purfuant to this act, if the property thereof be claimed by any perfon, as the owner or importer thereof, in fuch cafe the *onus probandi* fhall lie upon fuch owner or claimer.

Collector by warrant from a Juftice, accompanied by conftable, may break open any houfe in the day time to fearch for goods for which the duty is not paid or fecured.

In fuits and feizures the proof fhall lie upon the claimer of the goods.

XII. AND be it further enacted, that when any wine, fpirits, fugar, coffee, or other merchandife, fhall be configned to any perfon, other than the mafter or the owner of the fhip or veffel importing the fame, every fuch perfon to whom fuch articles fhall be fo configned, fhall, upon the importation thereof, pay to the mafter or owner of the fhip or veffel importing the fame, the duty payable for fuch articles by this act; and if any perfon or perfons to whom fuch articles fhall be configned as aforefaid, fhall neglect or refufe to pay the faid duty, or give bond, with fecurity, for the payment thereof to the mafter or owner of the fhip or veffel importing the fame, at fuch time as the fame fhall become payable, it fhall and may be lawful for the mafter or owner of fuch fhip or veffel to detain fuch articles until the duty fhall be paid, or fecured to be paid, as aforefaid.

Mafter may detain goods configned till duty paid or fecurity given.

XIII. AND be it further enacted, that if any importer of wines, fpirits, fugar, coffee or other merchandife, fhall defire to tranfport the fame from one diftrict to another within this commonwealth, he fhall, before he depart out of the diftrict wherein fuch articles fhall be laden or taken on board, make oath before the collector of the duties in the faid diftrict, that he hath duly entered fuch articles, and paid, or fecured to be paid, all the duties by this act impofed, and alfo deliver on oath an account of the quantity of fuch wines, fpirits, fugar, and coffee, and alfo of the value of fuch other merchandife, and that he will not take, or fuffer to be taken on board the faid fhip, boat, or other veffel, any more of the faid articles than in the faid account fhall be fpecified, and fhall likewife take a certificate from fuch collector of the account fo delivered, and that fuch oath hath been made thereto; which certificate being produced to the collector of the duties in the diftrict to which the faid articles fhall be tranfported, fhall be a fufficient warrant for the owner thereof to fell the fame, in fuch other diftrict; and all articles whatfoever, on which there is a duty, which fhall be tranfported by water from one diftrict to another, and landed or fold, without producing fuch certificate as aforefaid to the collector in whofe diftrict the fame fhall be tranfported, fhall be liable to be feized and forfeited.

Directions in cafe of tranfportation of goods imported, to another diftrict.

XIV. AND be it further enacted, that if any perfon or perfons fhall pay any of the duties accruing due by virtue of this act, at the time of making the entries hereby required with the collectors, in gold or filver coin, current in this commonwealth, of his or their own importation in the faid fhip or veffel at the time of faid entry, and fhall make oath that he or they did import the fame, and did not carry it out of this commonwealth with an intent to bring it back again and obtain a benefit thereby, fuch perfon or perfons fhall have an abatement of twenty five *per centum* on all duties fo paid and fatisfied, and every collector is hereby required to make fuch allowance for money fo imported and paid.

Bounty for paying duties in imported money.

XV. AND to prevent delays in the payment of the faid duties, Be it enacted, that where any perfon fhall become bound for the payment of the faid duties impofed by this act, and fhall not pay the fame at the time limited, whether fuch bond be payable to the commonwealth or to the collector of the faid duties, it fhall and may be lawful to and for the faid collector to fue out of the General Court, or the court of

Proceedings on bonds for duties;

A.D. 1781. the county wherein such person or his securities respectively reside, one or more writs of *scire facias* in the name of the commonwealth, returnable to the said court, against the person or persons chargeable with the said duties, and his or their securities, their executors or administrators, to shew cause why execution ought not to issue against him, them, or any of them, for the duties so unpaid, and thereupon to sue out execution accordingly; and the said collectors respectively shall be allowed for collecting, accounting for and paying the said duties imposed by this act into the treasury of this commonwealth, **allowance to collectors,** the sum of five *per centum* on the money so collected by them, or any of them; and they are hereby required to account for and pay into the treasury aforesaid every half year, to wit: on the tenth day of **who are to account and pay half yearly.** *April* and the tenth day of *October* in every year, or within ten days afterwards, all money received by them respectively on public account pursuant to this act, upon pain of forfeiting one half of their commissions, to be carried to the credit of the public treasury, and of being suspended from their said office of collector until such payment be made.

Forfeitures appropriated. XVI. AND *be it further enacted*, that the several forfeitures and penalties which shall or may arise in any wise by virtue of so much of this act as relates to the collections of duties on wine, spirits, sugar, coffee, and other merchandise, and on tunnage, shall be for and towards the erecting of public wharves, at the port of the respective districts within this commonwealth.

Lands, &c seized, to be sold on credit if they will not sell for three fourths of their value. XVII. AND *be it further enacted*, that where any distress shall be made pursuant to this act, and the lands, goods, or chattels, will not sell for three fourths of their value in the opinion of the officer making such distress, the same shall be sold for three months credit, in the same manner as goods taken by *fieri facias*.

All things in any prior act for imposing taxes, except specific, repealed. XVIII. AND *be it further enacted*, that all matters or things contained in any act or acts heretofore made for the imposing and collecting taxes and duties, except so much thereof as respects the manner of collecting, accounting for, and paying the arrears of taxes and duties now due, be, and the same are hereby repealed.

At a GENERAL ASSEMBLY begun and held at the Public Buildings in the Town of *Richmond*, on *Monday* the 6th day of *May*, in the Year of our Lord 1782.

CHAP. I.

Temporary. *An act giving further time to pay taxes in certain enumerated commodities and paying the allowances to the wives, parents, and families of soldiers.*

CHAP. II.

An act for appropriating the public revenue.

See May 1783, ch. 11.
Preamble.
I. WHEREAS in a just appropriation of the revenue of the state, the public faith will be best preserved, its credit supported, public inconvenience avoided, and the *quantum* of supplies furnished for the use of the United States more certainly ascertained: *Be it therefore enacted by* the General Assembly, that the Treasurer of this commonwealth shall raise and state an account upon his **Treasurer to keep distinct accounts of the revenue.** books for the amount of all monies received for every species or subject of taxation specified in the act for ascertaining certain taxes and duties and for establishing a permanent revenue; in which accounts, except the one for the land tax, shall be distinguished the articles commutable for the same, the amount of the receipts paid into the treasury therefor, and the places were deposited.

Appropriation. II. AND *be it enacted*, that a sufficient sum arising from the land tax, as also upon all other taxable articles except as hereafter excepted, shall be set apart and applied to the sole purpose of paying off and discharging all sums of money due to the several officers of civil government, including the members of Congress and of the General Assembly, and the officers of every denomination attending thereon; also that the sum of ten thousand pounds be applied to the use of the Executive, to enable them to defray the contingent charges of government; and the residue, if any there be, shall be appropriated to the payment of the interest which shall become due on the several emissions of paper money called in and funded under the act for calling in and funding the paper money of this state; and a further sum which may be sufficient for the payment of the interest as aforesaid, shall also be set apart and applied to the said purpose.

III. AND *be it further enacted*, that all sums of money which shall be received into the treasury for taxes upon all taxable articles, except as before directed, and as hereafter excepted, shall be appropriated to continental purposes, and shall be applied to the credit of this commonwealth, upon the requisitions of Congress of the fourth day of *October*, one thousand seven hundred and eighty one, retaining so much money or specifics only as shall be sufficient to discharge certain debts now due from the State Agent for the purposes of his department; and also the sum of fifteen thousand pounds to discharge future expenditures in the military department of the state.

IV. AND *be it further enacted*, that the money arising from the taxes payable in certain specific articles agreeable to the act for laying taxes in certain enumerated commodities, shall be appropriated by the Treasurer, in aid of the other appropriations herein before directed, towards the credit of this state upon the requisitions of Congress, retaining the sum of five thousand pounds for the payment of pensions due to wounded or disabled soldiers, agreeable to any act or resolutions of the General Assembly, or of pensions or allowances to wounded or disabled officers, or to the widows or children of any officer or soldier.

V. *AND be it further enacted,* that the duties on tonnage and on all articles of import specified by the said last recited act, shall be appropriated for and towards the naval disbursements of this common wealth as directed by law, and to no other use, intent, or purpose whatsoever.

VI. AND whereas the necessities of civil government and the arrears due thereon, require some more immediate provision than the appropriations of revenue herein directed will create: *Be it further enacted,* that warrants issued by the Auditors of public accounts for all arrears of wages, or salaries, allowed by law to the Governor, the members of the Privy Council, Judges of the High Court of Chancery, Judges of the General Court, Judges of the Court of Admiralty, the Treasurer, Attorney General, Auditors for public accounts, Commercial Agent, Commissioner of War, Solicitor General, clerks to the Council, to the Treasurer, to the Auditors, to the Commercial Agent, clerk to the Solicitor General, to the Commissioner of War, the Agent appointed to state and adjust the accounts of this commonwealth against the United States, the keeper of the public jail, the public armourer, the director of the hospital, the public printer, the door-keepers to the Council and to the Auditors, the Delegates to Congress, the Speaker of the Senate, and of the House of Delegates, the members of the General Assembly, and the officers of every denomination attending thereon, the secretary to the late Governor, and the clerks of the superior courts and other officers attending thereon, and which may be due to the time of issuing such warrants, shall be receivable in discharge of taxes imposed by the said last recited act: And the several sheriffs or collectors shall be allowed a discount with the Treasurer, in their settlements for the said taxes, for all warrants so by them received.

What civil list warrants are to be received for taxes.

VII. *AND be it further enacted,* that all matters or things contained in any act or acts heretofore made, and coming within the purview of this act, shall be, and the same are hereby repealed.

CHAP. III.

An act for recruiting this state's quota of troops to serve in the army of the United States.

Had its effect.

CHAP. IV.

An act to empower the Justices of York to hold their courts at any other place in the said county than their present courthouse.

Private.

CHAP. V.

An act for further continuing an act entitled An act to exempt artificers employed at iron works from militia duty.

See March 1781, ch. 4.

I. WHEREAS the act of Assembly passed in the year one thousand seven hundred and eighty one, entitled *An act to exempt artificers employed at iron works from militia duty,* which was continued by several subsequent acts, will expire at the end of this present session of Assembly; and it is expedient and necessary that the same should be farther continued: *Be it therefore enacted,* that the act entitled *An act to exempt artificers employed at iron works from militia duty,* shall continue and be in force from and after the expiration thereof, for and during the term of one year, and from thence until the end of the next session of Assembly, and no longer.

Preamble.

Continuance of the act.

CHAP. VI.

An act for granting pardon to James Hughes *and* Robert Smith.

Private.

CHAP. VII.

An act to authorise the Treasurer to receive certain warrants and certificates in payment for waste and unappropriated lands.

See Oct. 1780. ch 27.

I. BE it enacted by the General Assembly, that Auditors warrants and certificates for military service shall be received by the Treasurer in payment for waste and unappropriated lands, at the same scale of depreciation as is allowed by an act of Assembly entitled *An act for calling in and funding the paper money of this state.*

Warrants and certificates for military service to be received for land.

CHAP. VIII.

An act for the recovery of slaves, horses, and other property, lost during the war.

I. WHEREAS great numbers of slaves, horses, and other property belonging to the citizens of this commonwealth and of the neighbouring states, have during the war been carried off, or have gone from their owners and been concealed by wicked and evil disposed persons; and it is reasonable that the owners should be enabled to recover their property in an easy and expeditious manner: *Be it therefore enacted,* that any person or persons who have any such slave or slaves, horses, or other property in his or her possession, and who shall not before the first day of *October* next deliver such slave or slaves, horses or other property to the owner or owners thereof, if known, and if not known, publish a particular description of such slave or slaves, horses or other property three times in the *Virginia* gazette, shall forfeit and pay the sum of fifty pounds. And if any person or persons possessed of such slave or slaves, horses, or other property as aforesaid, shall delay to deliver or publish the same as above directed, within the time hereby limited, he or she shall forfeit and pay the sum of five pounds, for every month he or she shall so delay after the said first day of *October* next, and shall moreover be liable to the action of the party grieved at the common law, in which the plaintiff shall recover double damages; and if the defendant in any such action shall not immediately pay and satisfy the damages, he or she shall be imprisoned six months, without bail or mainprize, unless the damages are sooner discharged; the act of insolvency, or any other law to the contrary notwithstanding, and the act of limitation shall be no bar to such action.

Preamble.

How assessors of such property shall act.

Penalty for not publishing and delivering.

II. *AND be it further enacted,* that all and every person and persons from whom any such slave or slaves, horses, or other property have gone or been taken as aforesaid, on application to any two Justices of the Peace for the county where such slave or slaves, horses, or other property may be, and making

A D. 1782.

Proprietors may obtain warrants for taking their property; giving bond and security.

proof to the fatisfaction of fuch Juftices, of his or her right to fuch flaves, horfes or other property, and that the fame were taken or went off from him or her in confequence of the invafion of this or any of the neighbouring ftates, fhall be entitled to a warrant from fuch Juftices, under their hands and feals, directed to the fheriff or any conftable of the faid county, commanding them and each and every of them to take fuch flave or flaves, horfe or horfes, or other property, and deliver the fame to the owners thereof, *Provided*, that before granting fuch warrant, the perfon or perfons demanding the fame fhall give bond with fufficient fecurity, in fuch fum as the Juftices fhall direct, payable to the perfon or perfons in whofe poffeffion the flave or flaves, horfe or horfes, or other property claimed as aforefaid may be, to return the fame to the poffeffors in cafe he or fhe fo claiming fhall fail to prove his or her right to fuch flaves, horfes, or other property, at the trial of any fuit to be brought for the fame.

Two Juftices may fecure property fuf-pected to belong to others unknown.

Wandering flaves may be committed to prifon. Proceedings thereon

Penalties how to be recovered and appropriated.

III. *AND be it further enacted*, that where any perfon or perfons fhall be poffeffed of any flaves, horfes, or other property fufpected to have gone or to have been taken from their owners, in confequence of any invafion as aforefaid, it fhall be lawful for any two Juftices of the Peace for the county where fuch perfons refide, on information to them made, to caufe fuch perfon or perfons to come before them, and if fuch fufpicion fhall appear to them to be well founded, after hearing the parties, to caufe fuch perfon or perfons to enter into a recognizance to the Governor or Chief Magiftrate of this commonwealth, in fuch fum as the faid Juftices fhall judge reafonable, and with fufficient fecurity, on condition that he or fhe fhall not fell, difpofe of or fecrete any fuch flave or flaves, horfes, or other property, for fuch time as the faid Juftices fhall think proper, not exceeding one year. And when any flave or flaves fhall be found wandering about, it fhall be lawful for any Juftice of the Peace to commit fuch flave or flaves to the jail of his county, by warrant under his hand and feal, and the fheriff or jailer is hereby required to receive fuch flave or flaves, and to confine him, her, or them in clofe jail for three months, unlefs the owner or owners of fuch flave or flaves fhall fooner appear. And fuch fheriff or jailer fhall, within three weeks after fuch commitment, caufe fuch flave or flaves to be advertifed in the *Virginia* gazette, which advertifement fhall be inferted in three fucceffive papers, and if no owner fhall appear within the time limited for the confinement of fuch flave or flaves, the fheriff or jailer may hire out fuch flave or flaves for the payment of his prifon fees and the expences of advertifing; and if the owner fhall apply within the time aforefaid, he fhall pay the faid fees and expences of advertifing, and the further fum of twenty fhillings for each flave fo confined and advertifed as aforefaid.

Bona fide pur-chafers exempted from penalties.

Act not to ex-tend to property ta-ken by enemy and retaken in action.

IV. *AND it is further enacted*, that the penalties by this act impofed may be recovered in any court of record in this commonwealth, by action of debt, indictment, or information, and fhall be applied, the one half thereof to the ufe of the commonwealth, and the other half to the ufe of the informer. *Pro-vided always*, that this act, fo far as it refpects the penalties to be incurred for not delivering to the owner, or not publifhing any fuch flaves, horfes, or other property, fhall not extend to *bona fide* pur-chafers of fuch flaves, horfes, or other property, or to fuch as may have purfued the method directed by the laws now in force for taking up of ftrays. *Provided alfo*, that this act fhall not extend to flaves, horfes, or other property, taken by the enemy and retaken in action by any foldier or citizen of this ftate, or any of the United States, except where the fame were by capitulation or agreement to be re-turned to their owners.

Private.

CHAP. IX.

An act giving further time to the purchafers of lots in the towns of Moorefield *and* Bath *to build thereon.*

Expired. See May 1783, ch 4; Oct. 1783, ch. 10.

CHAP. X.

An act to afcertain the loffes and injuries fuftained from the depredations of the enemy within this commonwealth.

Private.

CHAP. XI.

An act to furvey certain roads.

Private.

CHAP. XII.

An act to eftablifh a town at the court-houfe in the county of Buckingham.

Private.

CHAP. XIII.

An act for altering the place of holding courts in the county of Lunenburg.

See May 1779, ch. 16, and notes.

CHAP. XIV.

An act to amend the feveral acts of Affembly for appointing and fupporting our Delegates in Congrefs.

Preamble.

I. WHEREAS by an act entitled *An act to amend an act entitled An act limiting the time for continuing the Delegates to General Congrefs in office and making provifion for their fupport, and for other pur-pofes*, it is enacted, that no perfon fhall thereafter be eligible to or capable of ferving in Congrefs for more than three years in any term of fix years; and fince the paffing the faid law the confeder-ation of the United States hath been completed, whereby it is declared that no perfon fhall be capable of fitting in Congrefs longer than three years at any one time, and thereby fo much of the faid recited act is become unneceffary. And whereas the prefent mode of fupporting the Delegates in Congrefs is inconve-nient: *Be it enacted by the General Affembly*, that fo much of the faid recited act as limits the time of continuing the Delegates in Congrefs from this commonwealth, fhall be, and the fame is hereby repealed. And for providing a more certain and adequate mode of fupporting and paying the Delegates in Con-grefs from this ftate, in lieu of the former pay and allowance heretofore made them, they, and each of them, fhall have and receive the fum of eight dollars *per* day for every day they fhall be travelling to, attending on, and returning from Congrefs, to be paid them quarterly out of fuch public money as fhall hereafter be fet apart and appropriated for that ufe. All and every act or acts that come within the purview and meaning of this act fhall be, and the fame are hereby repealed.

Limitation to 3 years fervice re-pealed.

Future provifion for Delegates. Repealing claufe.

C H A P. XV

An act for the speedy recovery of debts or effects due and belonging to the United States.

I. BE it enacted by the General Assembly, that it shall be lawful for any court within this commonwealth, and they are hereby required, upon motion and legal proof to them made, to give judgment against every person or persons for the amount of all such sums of money as he or they shall owe or be indebted to the United States; also upon motion and legal proof, to give judgment against all and every person or persons possessed of any of the effects or property belonging to the United States for such effects and property, together with costs in either case, and to award execution thereupon; *Provided* ten days previous notice be given to the defendant or defendants of every such motion, and the party making the same producing to the court a proper power and authority to receive such money, effects, or property, in behalf of the said United States.

Proceedings against debtors.

Also against those having their effects. Proviso.

C H A P. XVI.

An act giving certain powers to the commissioners appointed to settle the accounts between this state and the United States.

I. BE it enacted by the General Assembly, that the commissioners appointed or to be appointed by authority of Congress to settle the accounts between this state and the United States, as well as the accounts of the quarter-masters and commissaries, the hospital, clothier, and marine departments, shall be, and they are hereby empowered to call before them and examine, upon oath or affirmation, any witnesses they may think necessary respecting the settlement of the said accounts. Every person called upon and refusing or neglecting to appear before the said commissioners and give testimony, not shewing good cause for such refusal or neglect, shall be adjudged of by the court, shall forfeit and pay the sum of thirty pounds, to be recovered by motion in any court of record, with costs, and applied to the use of the commonwealth; *Provided* the party hath ten days previous notice of such motion. Witnesses thought necessary shall attend in consequence of a summon from the commissioners, and those residing within the same county shall be allowed the same pay as witnesses attending the county court, and such as live in other counties shall be allowed the same pay as witnesses attending the General Court.

Commissioners empowered to call witnesses before them.

Penalty on those who refuse to give evidence.

Allowance to witnesses.

C H A P. XVII.

An act to empower the Court of Hustings within the borough of Winchester *to licence and regulate ordinary keepers.*

Private.

C H A P. XVIII.

An act to amend an act entitled An act for suspending in part the operation of the act concerning escheats and forfeitures from British *subjects.*

Private.

C H A P. XIX.

An act to establish a town on the lands of William Bradley, *in the county of* Culpeper.

Private.

C H A P. XX.

An act to repeal so much of an act of the last session of Assembly as discontinued Lynch's *ferry.*

I. WHEREAS it hath been represented, that the discontinuing of the ferry from the lands of *John Lynch*, in *Bedford* county, across the *Fluvanna* to the opposite shore in the county of *Amherst*, so much of the act of Assembly passed at the last session, entitled *An act for establishing a new ferry*, as discontinues the said ferry, shall be, and the same is hereby repealed.

Preamble.

So much of former act repealed.

C H A P. XXI.

An act to authorize the manumission of slaves.

I. WHEREAS application hath been made to this present General Assembly, that those persons who are disposed to emancipate their slaves may be empowered so to do, and the same hath been judged expedient under certain restrictions: *Be it therefore enacted*, that it shall hereafter be lawful for any person, by his or her last will and testament, or by any other instrument in writing, under his or her hand and seal, attested and proved in the county court by two witnesses, or acknowledged by the party in the court of the county where he or she resides, to emancipate and set free, his or her slaves, or any of them, who shall thereupon be entirely and fully discharged from the performance of any contract entered into during servitude, and enjoy as full freedom as if they had been particularly named and freed by this act.

Preamble.

How slaves may be emancipated.

II. *PROVIDED always*, and be it further enacted, that all slaves so set free, not being in the judgment of the court, of sound mind and body, or being above the age of forty five years, or being males under the age of twenty one, or females under the age of eighteen years, shall respectively be supported and maintained by the person so liberating them, or by his or her estate; and upon neglect or refusal so to do, the court of the county where such neglect or refusal may be, is hereby empowered and required, upon application to them made, to order the sheriff to distrain and sell so much of the person's estate as shall be sufficient for that purpose. *Provided also*, that every person by written instrument in his life time, or if by last will and testament, the executors of every person freeing any slave, shall cause to be delivered to him or her, a copy of the instrument or emancipation; attested by the clerk of the court of the county, who shall be paid therefor, by the person emancipating, five shillings, to be collected in the manner of other clerks fees. Every person neglecting or refusing to deliver to any slave by him or her set free, such copy, shall forfeit and pay ten pounds, to be recovered with costs in any court of record, one half

Aged or infirm to be supported by former master; or expence levied on them by order of court.

Copy of instrument of emancipation to be delivered to the slave.

Penalty for neglect on the master;

A.D. 1782.

and on the slave travelling out of his county.

thereof to the person suing for the same, and the other to the person to whom such copy ought to have been delivered   It shall be lawful for any Justice of the Peace to commit to the jail of his county, any emancipated slave travelling out of the county of his or her residence without a copy of the instrument of his or her emancipation, there to remain till such copy is produced and the jailers fees paid.

Liberated slave neglecting to pay levies and taxes to be hired out to raise them.

Saving the titles of all but the person emancipating.

III. AND *be it further enacted*, that in case any slave so liberated shall neglect in any year to pay all taxes and levies imposed or to be imposed by law, the court of the county shall order the sheriff to hire out him or her for so long time as will raise the said taxes and levies; *Provided* sufficient distress cannot be made upon his or her estate; saving nevertheless to all and every person and persons, bodies politic or corporate, and their heirs and successors, other than the person or persons claiming under those so emancipating their slaves, all such right and title as they or any of them could or might claim if this act had never been made.

C H A P.   XXII.

Expired.   See May 1783, ch. 4.

An act to ascertain the number of people within this commonwealth.

C H A P.   XXIII.

An act for defending and protecting the trade of Chesapeake Bay.

See Oct. 1782, ch. 32.

Preamble.

Vessels to be provided.

Money to be raised and paid to commissioners.

Tonnage and import duties appropriated.

Commissioners how to be appointed.

To be under the direction of the Executive

And concert with Maryland measures for defending the bay trade.

Power to adjust disputes between the officers of the two states.

Vessels not to be sent out of the Capes.

Prizes to be divided among the captors.

Vacancies in the commission how to be filled.

I. FOR defending and protecting the trade and commerce of *Chesapeake* bay and its dependencies, in the most effectual manner possible under our present circumstances, *Be it enacted by the General Assembly, and it is hereby enacted by the authority of the same;* that the ship *Cormorant* and the boat *Liberty* be immediately and forthwith fitted out and prepared for that purpose: That two row-gallies and two barges or whale boats, upon such construction and so equipped as may render them most proper for the purpose aforesaid, be forthwith built or purchased at the public expence. In order to defray the expence of purchasing, building, or equipping the said vessels, the ship *Loyalist* with her appurtenances, shall be sold in such manner and upon such conditions as may be judged best by the commissioners herein after mentioned, and the money arising from such sale shall, by the said commissioners, be applied in such manner as they shall think best towards procuring, equipping, and manning the said vessels. There shall also be paid into the hands of the said commissioners the sum of one thousand pounds, by the Commercial Agent, out of the public monies in his hands: and the revenue arising from the duties imposed upon imports and tonnage, by an act entitled *An act for ascertaining certain taxes and duties and for establishing a permanent revenue,* shall be, and the same are hereby set apart and appropriated for the purpose of defending and protecting the trade and commerce of *Chesapeake* bay and its dependencies; and the Treasurer shall, from time to time, pay to the said commissioners or their order, the Auditors having duly authorized the same, the money he may receive for such duties, and to no other purpose whatsoever; and the Naval Officers, instead of accounting for and paying to the Treasurer the duties received by them under the said recited act once in six months, shall, and they are hereby directed to account for and pay the monies received by them for the duties aforesaid once every three months, or oftener if it may be convenient. There shall be appointed by the General Assembly three commissioners to superintend and provide for the defence and protection of our bay trade, who shall be, and they are hereby vested with full powers to employ all and every sum or sums of money hereby set apart for that purpose, towards the defence and protection of our trade and commerce in the *Chesapeake* bay. They shall be under the direction of the Executive of this commonwealth, from time to time, and under the inspection of the said Executive, shall, from time to time, correspond with the Executive of the state of *Maryland*, or other persons by the said state to be appointed, and concert, together with the state of *Maryland*, such measures for the co-operation of the marine force of each state, as may be most likely to render effectual protection to the trade and the citizens of each state on the shores of *Chesapeake* bay and its dependencies; and also consult about such other future operations as may be most likely to effect this desirable end, the plan of which future operations shall, through the hands of his Excellency the Governor, by the said commissioners be laid before the next succeeding Assembly for their approbation. The said commissioners shall have full power on the part of this commonwealth, to settle and adjust all disputes that may arise between the officers of the two states relative to command or otherwise, and to direct and controul the procuring, building, and equipping the said vessels in such manner as they shall judge most advantageous to the said service: *Provided,* that they shall in no instance order the said vessels upon any duty without the capes of *Virginia.* And in order to man effectually the said vessels when equipped, the said commissioners may, and they are hereby authorized and directed, to take such methods as they may have in their power and which the means hereby furnished them may enable them, towards accomplishing the same. They shall allow such pay, subsistence and other necessaries, to the seamen enlisted on board such ships, as may be consistent with the distressed state of our finances at present, and as is consistent with the general service hereby required. Such officers shall be appointed to command the said vessels as are at present in the navy service of this state, according to their rank or such other circumstances as the said commissioners shall judge entitles them to such command. And as an encouragement to seamen or marines on board such vessels, any prizes or booty taken by them from the enemy shall be divided among the captors in such proportion as regulated in like cases by Congress. In case of the death, resignation, or refusal to act, of any one or more of the said commissioners, his Excellency the Governor, with the advice of the Privy Council, may, and he is hereby authorized to appoint such other person or persons to fill such vacancy as he, with the advice aforesaid, may think proper to execute the duties required by this act, until the meeting of the succeeding General Assembly.

C H A P.   XXIV.

Private.

An act to empower the Mayor, Recorder, Aldermen, and Common-Council of the town of Alexandria *to lay a wharfage tax, and to extend* Water *and* Union *streets.*

C H A P.   XXV.

Private.

An act for incorporating the town of Richmond *and for other purposes.*

C H A P. XXVI.

An act concerning wrecks.

A D. 1782.

I. WHEREAS many veſſels have been and may hereafter be ſtranded on the ſea coaſt, bay or river ſhores within this commonwealth, and the goods or other property belonging to ſuch veſſels may be embezzled and ſtolen, to the great injury of the owners: For remedy whereof, *Be it enacted, by the General Aſſembly,* that it ſhall be lawful for the Governor, with advice of Council, and he is hereby required to appoint and commiſſion two diſcreet perſons in each of the counties bordering on the ſea or bay ſhores in this ſtate whoſe buſineſs and duty it ſhall be, on the earlieſt intelligence or on application to them made by or on behalf of any owner or commander of a ſhip or other veſſel being in danger of being ſtranded, or being ſtranded, to command any conſtable or conſtables, to be appointed by them for that purpoſe, neareſt the coaſt where ſuch ſhip or veſſel ſhall be in danger, to ſummon as many men as ſhall be thought neceſſary to the aſſiſtance of ſuch ſhip or veſſel; and if there ſhall be any ſhip or veſſel belonging to the ſtate riding near the place, the commiſſioner or commiſſioners ſhall have power to demand of the commanding officer of ſuch ſhip or veſſel, aſſiſtance by their boats and ſuch hands as they can conveniently ſpare; and if any commanding officer ſhall neglect to give ſuch aſſiſtance, he ſhall forfeit one hundred pounds, to be recovered by the officer or owner of the ſhip in diſtreſs, with coſts, in any court of record within this commonwealth. The commiſſioner or commiſſioners, and the commanding officer of any ſhip or veſſels, and all others who ſhall aſſiſt in preſerving any ſhip or other veſſel in diſtreſs, or their cargoes, ſhall, within forty days, be paid a reaſonable reward by the commander or owner of the ſhip or other veſſel in diſtreſs, or by the merchant whoſe veſſel or goods ſhall be ſaved, and in default thereof the veſſel or goods ſhall remain in the cuſtody of the commiſſioner or commiſſioners until all charges be paid, or ſecurity given for that purpoſe, to the ſatisfaction of the parties. And in caſe the parties ſhall diſagree touching the monies deſerved by the perſons employed, it ſhall be lawful for the commander of ſuch veſſel ſaved, or the owner of the goods or merchant intereſted, to chooſe one indifferent perſon, and alſo for the commiſſioner or commiſſioners to nominate one other indifferent perſon, who ſhall adjuſt the *quantum* of the gratuities to be paid to the ſeveral perſons, and ſuch adjuſtments ſhall be binding on all parties, and to be recoverable with coſts in any court of record within this commonwealth, by action on the caſe. If no perſon ſhall claim the goods ſaved, the commiſſioners or one of them ſhall take poſſeſſion thereof, and cauſe a true deſcription of the marks, numbers, and kinds of ſuch goods to be advertiſed four weeks in the *Virginia* gazette, and if no perſon ſhall claim the ſame within three months, public ſale ſhall be made thereof (but if periſhable the goods ſhall be forthwith ſold) and after charges deducted, the reſidue of the money, with an account of the whole, ſhall be tranſmitted to the Treaſurer, who ſhall keep an account of the ſame for the benefit of the owners, who upon proof of his property to the ſatisfaction of the Auditors, ſhall upon their warrant receive the ſame. If any perſon beſides thoſe empowered by the commiſſioners or one of them, ſhall enter or endeavour to enter on board any veſſel in diſtreſs, without the leave of the commanding officer, or in caſe any perſon ſhall moleſt them in ſaving the veſſel or goods, or ſhall endeavour to hinder the ſaving ſuch veſſel or goods, or ſhall deface the marks of any ſuch goods before they be taken down in a book by the commiſſioners or one of them, every ſuch perſon ſhall forfeit and pay the ſum of ten pounds, to be recovered with coſts by information in any court of record within this commonwealth, and applied to the uſe of the owners of the veſſel or goods as the caſe may be; and in caſe of failure to pay ſuch forfeiture immediately, or giving ſecurity to pay the ſame within one month, he, ſhe, or they ſhall receive ten laſhes on his, her, or their bare back, by order of ſuch court. It ſhall be lawful for any commanding officer of a veſſel in diſtreſs, or the commiſſioners, to repel by force any perſons as ſhall, without conſent as aforeſaid, preſs on board any veſſel in diſtreſs, and thereby moleſt them in preſerving the veſſel or goods; and in caſe any goods ſhall be found upon any perſon that were ſtolen or carried off from any veſſel in diſtreſs, the perſon on whom ſuch goods be found ſhall, upon demand, commiſſioners or owner to receive ſuch goods, or ſhall be liable to pay treble the value, to be recovered with coſts in any court of record. If any perſon ſhall make or be aſſiſting in making a hole in any veſſel in diſtreſs, or ſteal any pump, materials or goods, or ſhall be aiding in ſtealing ſuch pump, materials or goods from any veſſel, or ſhall wilfully do any thing tending to the immediate loſs of ſuch veſſel, ſuch perſon ſhall be guilty of felony, and ſuffer death without benefit of clergy; and any commiſſioner by fraud or wilful neglect, abuſing the truſt repoſed in him, ſhall, upon conviction thereof, forfeit and pay treble damages to the party aggrieved, to be recovered with coſts by action on the caſe in any court of record, and ſhall thenceforth be incapable of acting as a commiſſioner. Any conſtable, or perſon ſummoned by him, refuſing or neglecting to give the aſſiſtance required for the ſaving of any veſſel or her cargo, ſhall forfeit and pay twenty five ſhillings, to be recovered before any Juſtice by the commiſſioners ordering the duty, and ſhall be moreover ſubject to the payment of the ſame damages, and to be recovered by the party aggrieved in the ſame manner as in the caſe of a commiſſioner. The commiſſioners ſhall ſet up a copy of this act once in every year in each of the courthouſes of the counties wherein they reſpectively reſide.

II. *PROVIDED always, and be it further enacted,* that the commiſſioners appointed by virtue of this act ſhall reſpectively give bond and ſecurity in the court of the county where he reſides, in the ſum of one thouſand pounds, for the due and faithful execution of his office, and that it ſhall not be lawful for ſuch commiſſioner, or any of them, to enter upon the duties of his office before he gives bond and ſecurity as aforeſaid.

III. *AND be it further enacted,* that where any veſſel ſhall be ſtranded and totally loſt, goods ſaved from the wreck ſhall not be liable to entry and duties; but if any veſſel be drove or caſt on ſhore, and the damage ſuſtained on the goods does not appear to exceed ten *per centum* in the judgment of the commiſſioners, ſuch goods ſhall be duly entered with the Naval Officer neareſt the place where the caſe happened, according to law.

Margin notes

Preamble.

Commiſſioners to be appointed on the ſea and bay ſhores.
Their duty on intelligence of a veſſel ſtranded or in danger.

Thoſe who aſſiſt in ſaving a veſſel or cargo, to have a reward;
and may retain veſſel or goods til reward paid or ſecured.
Reward how to be aſcertained.
Proceeding if the goods ſaved be not claimed.

Penalty on thoſe who intermeddle without power from commiſſioners.
Or hinder thoſe employed in ſaving the goods.
Or deface the marks

Commiſſioners may repel force by force.
Goods carried from a veſſel in diſtreſs and found in any perſon's poſſeſſion to be reſtored.
Penalty.
Death to make a hole in a veſſel in diſtreſs.
Or ſteal pump, materials or goods;
or do any thing tending to the loſs of the veſſel.
Penalty on commiſſioner abuſing his truſt;
and on conſtable and aſſiſtants for neglect.
Act to be ſet up in each court-houſe.

Commiſſioners to give bond and ſecurity.

If veſſel totally loſt, goods ſaved to pay no duty.
If veſſel caſt on ſhore, and the damage on the goods not more than ten per cent goods to be entered and pay duty.

C H A P. XXVII.

An act to veſt the eſtate of Samuel Giſt, *in* Mary *the wife of* William Anderſon, *and her heirs and aſſigns, and for other purpoſes.*

Private.

C H A P. XXVIII.

An act to reveſt certain lands in Charles Carter, *and his heirs.*

Private.

A. D. 1782.

Private.

C H A P. XXIX.

An act to enable the court of Botetourt *to levy certain arrears due the incumbent of the parish.*

C H A P. XXX.

Private.

An act to appoint Trustees for the towns of Woodstock, Cobham, Manchester, *and* Blandford.

C H A P. XXXI.

See 1772, *ch.* 20.

An act to amend the act for erecting a light house on cape Henry.

Preamble.

I. **W**HEREAS an act of Assembly passed in the year one thousand seven hundred and seventy two, for erecting a light-house on cape *Henry* and appointing directors for building and finishing the said light-house as soon as the Assembly of *Maryland* should pass an act for the same purposes: And whereas several of the said directors are since dead, and the surviving ones cannot conveniently meet to make a settlement of the accounts and adjust the balances due to the several creditors; *Be it therefore*

New Directors.
To adjust balances.
Former duties appropriated.

enacted, that *John Hutchings, Paul Loyall, Thomas Newton,* jun. George Kelly, William White, and Lemuel Corneck, gentlemen, or any three of them be, and they are hereby appointed directors, and empowered to adjust the several claims and ascertain the balances, which they shall certify to his Excellency the Governor, and upon a warrant thereupon obtained from the Auditors, the Treasurer is hereby authorized to pay the said sum or sums out of the money which shall arise from duties and tonnage on shipping imposed by the above recited act.

Directors to be
Trustees of the
common. See May
1780, *ch.* 2.

II. *BE it further enacted,* that the said directors be, and they are hereby appointed trustees for the land heretofore and now deemed and held as common.

C H A P. XXXII.

An act concerning slaves.

Preamble.

I. **W**HEREAS great inconveniences have arisen from persons permitting their slaves to go at large and hire themselves out, under a promise of paying their masters or owners a certain sum of money in lieu of their services: For remedy whereof, *Be it enacted,* that if any person shall, after the tenth day of *August* next, permit or suffer his or her slave to go at large and hire him or herself out,

Slaves permitted
to go at large and
hire themselves out.

it shall be lawful for any person to apprehend and carry every such slave before a Justice of the Peace in the county where apprehended, and if it shall appear to the Justice that such slave comes within the purview of this act, he shall order him or her to the jail of the county, there to be safely kept until the next court, when, if it shall be made appear to the court that the slave so ordered to jail hath been per-

May be sold by
order of court.

mitted or suffered to hire him or herself out, contrary to the meaning of this act, it shall be lawful for the court, and they are hereby required to order the sheriff of the county to sell and dispose of every such slave for ready money, at the next court held for the said county, notice being given by the sheriff at the courthouse door at least twenty days before the said sale.

Allowance to coun-
ty and sheriff.

II. *AND be it further enacted,* that twenty five *per centum* upon the amount of the sale of every slave made under this act, shall be applied by the court ordering such sale, towards lessening the county levy, and the residue shall be paid by the sheriff, after deducting five *per centum* for his trouble and the jailer's fees, to the owner of such slave.

C H A P. XXXIII.

Private.

An act to repeal so much of an act of Assembly as prohibits swine going at large in the town of Staunton.

C H A P. XXXIV.

Private. See
Oct. 1778, *ch.* 35.

An act to repeal an act entitled An act to vest certain escheatable lands in trustees, and for other purposes.

C H A P. XXXV.

Private.

An act to sell the late court-house, prison, and lots, of Bedford *county.*

C H A P. XXXVI.

See May 1780,
ch. 21.

An act to amend an act for dissolving several vestries, and electing overseers of the poor.

Preamble.

I. **W**HEREAS by experience it is found that the act for dissolving several vestries and electing overseers of the poor, in the counties therein named, hath greatly removed the inconveniences for making provision for the poor in the said act recited; and the counties of *Shenandoah,* Henry, Monongalia, Ohio, and Berkeley, being subject to the same inconveniences experienced in the aforesaid counties before the said act was passed: For remedy whereof, *Be it enacted,* that where

Extended to other
parishes.

the above enumerated counties have any vestries or other bodies vested with powers to provide for the poor, the same shall, from and after the first day of *October* next, be dissolved.

II. AND for the providing for the poor, and other parochial duties as have heretofore been exercised by the vestries, church-wardens, or other bodies of the respective counties or parishes, *Be it enacted,* that the sheriffs of the said counties of Shenandoah, Henry, Monongalia, Ohio, and Berkeley, shall take

Overseers how to
be elected.

the same order in their respective counties to hold elections for overseers of the poor in all times coming as the respective sheriffs in the above recited act are directed to do; and the overseers so elected, first being qualified as the said act directs, shall, in all things, have the same powers, be incorporated in the

Their duty.

same manner, and subject to the same rules and government as the overseers are in the above recited act: And the courts of the said counties of Shenandoah, Henry, Monongalia, Ohio, and Berkeley, in case of death, refignation, removal, or refufal to act, of any overfeer, fhall fupply fuch vacancy; and alfo fhall direct their orders to the overfeers fo elected and qualified in the fame manner as the courts of the faid counties in the above recited act are directed to do. And if any fheriff or fheriffs of the faid counties of *Shenandoah, Henry, Monongalia, Ohio,* and *Berkeley,* fhall fail or neglect his or their duty as directed in the aforefaid recited act, he or they fhall be fubject to forfeit and pay the fame penalties, and in all things fubject to the fame forfeitures as the fheriffs in the faid recited act are fubject to. *Penalty on fheriff*

III. *AND be it further enacted,* that where any fuit or fuits are depending, in which the veftries or church-wardens are plaintiffs, by virtue of their office, no fuch fuit fhall be difmiffed in purfuance of this act, but the overfeers of the poor fhall be taken and efteemed plaintiffs therein, and the fuit or fuits fhall be perpetuated to a legal decifion in the name of the faid overfeers. *Provided alfo,* that where any veftry or church-wardens hath fuffered fuit to be brought againft them for breach of duty or neglect, the fame fhall be profecuted againft the faid veftry or church-wardens, in the fame manner as if this act had not been made. *Suits by and againft v-ftries or church-wardens faved.*

IV. *AND be it further enacted,* that the veftries of the aforefaid counties of *Shenandoah, Henry, Monongalia, Ohio,* and *Berkeley,* fhall, on or before the firft day of *January* next, make up and fettle their accounts with the overfeers of the poor of their refpective counties, of all monies or tobacco by them levied or difburfed in virtue of their office. *Veftries to account.*

V. *AND be it further enacted,* that all penalties, fines, and forfeitures, recovered by virtue of this act, fhall be appropriated in the fame manner as is directed in the above recited act.

CHAP. XXXVII.

An act to increafe the reward for killing wolves in certain counties.

I. WHEREAS it is reprefented to this General Affembly, that the giving further rewards in certain counties for the deftroying of wolves will be attended with very great advantage to the inhabitants thereof; *Be it enacted,* that from and after the paffing of this act, and during the continuance thereof, any perfon who fhall kill any wolf within the counties of *Henry, Pittfylvania, Bedford, Campbell, Botetourt, Montgomery, Greenbrier, Amherft, Buckingham, Louifa, Shenandoah, Frederick, Berkeley, Prince William, Fairfax, Loudoun, Hampfhire, Orange, Culpeper, Monongalia, Ohio, Rockbridge, Rockingham, Charlotte, Fauquier, Norfolk, Princefs Anne, Augufta, Wafhington,* and *Albemarle,* fhall have an additional reward of one hundred pounds of nett tobacco for every young wolf not exceeding the age of fix months, and for every wolf above that age, two hundred pounds of like tobacco, to be levied and paid in fuch counties wherein the fervices fhall be performed; and the feveral county courts before named are hereby empowered and required to levy the fame in their annual county levy to the perfons entitled thereto. This act fhall continue and be in force for and during the term of three years, and from thence to the end of the next feffion of Affembly. *Preamble. Counties named; Additional reward; to be levied in the county. Continuance of act.*

CHAP. XXXVIII.

An act to veft the eftate of Robert Williams *equally among* Mace Freeland, Spice Pendleton, *and* Elizabeth Jones, *and their heirs.* *Private.*

CHAP. XXXIX.

An act to amend the act for afcertaining certain taxes and duties, and for eftablifhing a permanent revenue. *See November 1781, ch. 40. Preamble.*

I. WHEREAS from the late cruel ravages of the enemy and deftruction of private property, together with the great burthens already borne by the good people of this ftate, it is neceffary to give them every poffible alleviation in the payment of taxes required for the fupport of the war: *Be it therefore enacted,* that one half of the taxes impofed by an act entitled *An act for afcertaining certain taxes and duties, and for eftablifhing a permanent revenue,* fhall be collected, received, or diftrained for, on the firft day of *July* next enfuing, in the manner directed by the faid act; and the other half on the firft day of *November* following. *Collection of taxes divided.*

II. *AND be it further enacted,* that fkins of deer, well dreffed and fitted for the purpofe of making breeches, be added to the fpecifics made commutable with fpecie in payment of the taxes, that on land excepted, by the faid act. That the fkins fo to be paid, fhall be received at the places appointed for the reception of other fpecifics, and at the price of eight fhillings *per* pound for every deer fkin; and that the towns of *Manchefter, Dumfries, Harrodfburg,* and of *Falmouth,* be, and the fame are hereby added to thofe appointed by the faid act for the reception of fpecific articles. *Deer fkins to be taken New places to receive fpecifics.*

III. *AND be it alfo enacted,* that where the fheriff cannot or will not give fecurity for the due collection of the taxes impofed by the faid act, as thereby required, in fuch cafe the court of the county where fuch failure may happen, fhall appoint one or more collector or collectors in due time, who fhall give the fecurity and do the duty required of the fheriff by the faid act. *Sheriff not able to give fecurity; a collector to be appointed.*

IV. *AND be it further enacted,* that where the faid act inflicts a forfeiture of one hundred pounds on any proprietor or proprietors of land, his, her or their tenant, attorney or overfeer, or in cafe of infants, his, her or their guardians refufing or neglecting to give an account of the quantity of lands or lots held by any of them, or under their refpective management, the faid forfeiture fhall be of twenty pounds only, to be recovered as the faid act directs. *Penalty on proprietors failing to account reduced.*

V. *AND be it further enacted,* that inftead of a lift of all tithable perfons, the fame fhall be given in of all perfons taxable by the faid act; and that the taxes impofed upon neat cattle, fhall be paid on cattle of all ages. *Explanation of tithables.*

VI. *AND be it further enacted,* that all duties and cuftoms which now are, or hereafter fhall become due to this commonwealth, upon fhips, goods, wares and merchandizes, or any other articles whatfoever by virtue of any law of this commonwealth, fhall be paid to the Naval Officer of the diftrict where fuch duty or cuftom is directed to be paid; and the refpective Naval Officers are hereby required to collect, account for, and pay into the public treafury, the amount of all fuch duties and cuftoms, according to the feveral acts impofing the fame, and under the pains and penalties therein contained. *Duties on fhips and goods to be paid to Naval Officers;*

A.D. 1782.

If none, or importation by land, to county court clerks.

And where there shall be no Naval Officer, or where any goods are imported by land, due entry shall be made thereof with the clerk of the county court wherein they are brought, who shall receive the taxes or duties payable thereupon, or take bond from the importer for the payment thereof, at the treasury, within the time prescribed by law.

Sheriff to give receipts for taxes. And return a distinct account.

VII. *AND be it further enacted,* that the sheriff or collector shall give a receipt to each person from whom he receives the taxes, specifying in what article such person paid his tax; and shall moreover return a list, on oath, of such payments to the clerk of his county court, immediately after his collection, copies of which list shall be fixed up in the said court-house for the inspection of the people; and the Auditors are hereby required not to settle with any sheriff for the taxes collected under the said act, except the said sheriff do produce to them a copy of such list, certified by the clerk of his court.

Allowance to commissioners.

VIII. *AND be it further enacted,* that in future the pay and allowance to the commissioners for assessing lands, shall be the sum of seven shillings and six pence each *per* day, and no more.

How lands and goods distrained shall be sold.

IX. *AND be it further enacted,* that so much of the said act as declares, that where any distress shall be made pursuant to the said act, and the lands, goods, or chattels, will not sell for three fourths of their value, in the opinion of the officer making such distress, the same shall be sold for three months credit; in the same manner as goods taken by *fieri facias,* shall be repealed: And in all such cases as aforesaid, the officer making such distress, shall sell the lands, goods, or chattels, so distrained, for one month's credit, and shall take sufficient security residing in the county, for the payment thereof; and in case the same shall not be paid within the said one month, such officer is hereby authorized and required to make immediate distress on the lands, goods, or chattels, of such purchaser or purchasers, his, her, or their security or securities, and proceed to sell the same for the best price that can be got in ready money.

Bonded duties recoverable on motion

X. AND whereas the mode prescribed by the said recited act for recovering the duties bonded with the collectors will admit of great delay in the collection: For remedy whereof, *Be it enacted,* that it shall and may be lawful to and for the said collectors to recover the said duties so bonded, by motion made in the General Court, or the county court wherein the principal or either of his securities respectively reside, and such court shall give judgment for the sum due on such bonds, with costs, and interest of five *per centum* on the same until paid. *Provided always,* ten days previous notice in writing shall be given by such collector to the person or persons so to be moved against.

Power to officers in Williamsburg.

XI. *AND be it further enacted,* that the Court of Hustings of the city of *Williamsburg,* and the serjeant for the said city, shall have the same power to proceed in the execution of the said recited act, as the county courts and the respective sheriffs.

Morris's notes to be received.

XII. AND whereas *Robert Morris,* Esquire, Superintendant of the Finances of these United States, hath by his letter bearing date the twenty ninth day of *April* last, given assurance to this state, that his notes of the following tenor, to wit: *At sight pay to the bearer . dollars, for which this shall be your sufficient warrant;* signed *Robert Morris,* and directed to *John Swanwick, Philadelphia,* shall be received at the treasury of the United States in discharge of any debt due from this state, and hath therefore requested that the same may be taken in payment of taxes; and whereas the receiving such notes in the present circumstances of the country will tend greatly to the relief of the people in the payment of their taxes: *Be it therefore enacted,* that the sheriffs and collectors shall receive all bills of the above tenor that may be offered them in discharge of taxes due, or which may become due in the year one thousand seven hundred and eighty two, by virtue of an act entitled *An act for ascertaining certain taxes and duties, and for establishing a permanent revenue;* which bills or notes the sheriffs or collectors shall account for and *bona fide* pay into the treasury. And in case any sheriff or collector shall fail to account with and pay to the Treasurer for the time being, all the notes or bills of the above description he may receive for taxes, he shall forfeit and pay double the amount of the said notes he shall have so collected, to be sued for and recovered in the manner directed by the above recited act, for the recovery of other penalties therein mentioned.

Militia or military certificates when to be received for taxes.

XIII. AND whereas the practice of granting certificates for militia service, and of issuing treasury receipts thereupon anticipating the revenue hath obtained to the great prejudice of the public and the derangement of the finances, and it is necessary and essential to the public interest that every anticipation of the public revenue should be most explicitly forbidden and prevented; *Be it therefore enacted,* that no certificates, receipts or warrants for militia or military service, except receipts given under the act for supplying the southern army with waggons and horses, and except also certificates granted for money advanced agreeable to a requisition of the Governor and Council of the twenty eighth of *February* one thousand seven hundred and eighty two, for recruiting soldiers, shall be received in discharge of the taxes imposed by the act *For ascertaining certain taxes and duties, and for establishing a permanent revenue,* and that the several sheriffs or collectors of taxes or duties in this commonwealth, shall not be allowed to discount any such certificates, receipts or warrants issued by virtue of any former law, and by them received or to be received for their respective collections; but judgment shall be given in manner directed by the said recited act against the said sheriffs or collectors respectively for the full amount of their several collections, or of the deficiency due thereon, in case of failure to account for the same in due time, without regard to any such certificates, receipts or warrants.

Tonnage of vessels explained.

XIV. AND whereas doubts have arisen in the construction of the sixth section of the said recited act, wherein it is enacted, that on all vessels at entrance or clearance from or to foreign parts there shall be paid by the master or owner thereof, certain duties in the said section enumerated; and it hath by some been supposed that the said words " foreign parts" were intended to exclude vessels and goods coming from any state in this union from paying the tonnage and other duties by the said section directed to be paid: For the removing of such doubts and misconstruction; *Be it enacted,* that all vessels coming within this state from any of the United States, or from any port or place whatsoever, vessels of war excepted, shall be liable to pay the tonnage and other duties by the said recited act directed to be paid, in the manner by law prescribed.

Sheriffs to continue collection tho' out of office.

XV. *AND be it further enacted,* that the several sheriffs throughout this commonwealth, whose appointments will terminate in the month of *October* next, shall nevertheless have full power and authority to complete the collection of the taxes aforesaid, which they are hereby required to perform, and shall have the same right and authority to collect or distrain for the payment of the said taxes, and shall be subject to account for and pay the same into the public treasury, in like manner as if their appointments had not then expired.

XVI. *AND be it further enacted*, that all and every part or parts of the act *For ascertaining certain taxes and duties, and for establishing a permanent revenue*, as shall in any manner contravene this act or any part thereof, be and is hereby repealed.

XVII. *AND be it enacted*, that the several sheriffs and collectors shall account for and pay all monies and other articles by them respectively received, in payment for, and which may exceed the amount of the first half of the said taxes, at the time, in the manner, and under the penalties contained in the said recited act: and shall also in the same manner account for and pay the money and other articles by them respectively received, for the other half of the said taxes, or for the balances due thereon, on or before the first day of *January* next, under the penalties prescribed in the said recited act, to be moved for and recovered at any session of the General Court succeeding that time.

When and how to account.

CHAP. XL.

An act to continue and amend the act entitled An act for the inspection of pork, beef, flour, tar, pitch, and turpentine.

I. WHEREAS the act of Assembly passed in the year one thousand seven hundred and sixty two, entitled *An act for the inspection of pork, beef, flour, tar, pitch, and turpentine*, which was continued and amended by several subsequent acts, will expire at the next session of Assembly, and it is expedient and necessary that the same should be farther continued and amended: *Be it therefore enacted*, that the act entitled *An act for the inspection of pork, beef, flour, tar, pitch, and turpentine*, except so much thereof as respects the article of flour, shall continue and be in force from and after the expiration thereof, for and during the term of two years, and from thence until the end of the next session of Assembly, and no longer.

See Oct. 1776, ch. 48; May 1780, ch. 22; May 1783, ch. 7.

Preamble. Should be Oct. 1776, ch. 43.

Continuance of act.

II. *AND be it further enacted*, that the several inspectors appointed, or to be appointed by virtue of the said recited act, shall receive the following fees in lieu of those heretofore established, to wit: For every barrel of pork or beef inspected and stamped, one shilling; and for every barrel of tar, pitch, and turpentine, seven pence half penny.

Inspectors fees.

III. *AND be it further enacted*, that all the penalties and forfeitures to be incurred by the said recited act, for failure or neglect of duty, shall be the same as those established and specified in the said act passed in the year one thousand seven hundred and sixty two, and recovered and applied as is directed by the said act.

Penalties and their application.

CHAP. XLI.

An act to continue and amend an act entitled An act for the relief of persons who have been or may be injured by the destruction of the records of county courts.

I. WHEREAS the powers of the commissioners appointed by the Governor, with the advice of Council, to carry into execution an act of the last session, entitled *An act for the relief of persons who have been or may be injured by the destruction of the records of county courts*, will expire at the end of this present session of Assembly, and it is expedient and necessary that the same should be further continued and amended: *Be it therefore enacted*, that the act entitled *An act for the relief of persons who have been or may be injured by the destruction of the records of county courts*, shall continue and be in force from and after the expiration thereof until the purposes for which it was enacted shall be effected.

See Nov. 1781, ch. 11.

Preamble.

Continuance of act.

II. AND whereas doubts have arisen whether the commissioners appointed or to be appointed in virtue of the said recited act can receive testimony respecting the loss of any papers other than those particularly mentioned in the aforesaid act: *Be it enacted*, that the said commissioners are hereby empowered and required to proceed in the same manner with respect to all bonds, bills, notes, and other papers necessarily filed in the office where such destruction hath happened, as if the same had been entered of record.

Extended to all papers filed in court.

CHAP. XLII.

An act for dissolving the vestries of the parishes of Antrim and Westover.

Private.

CHAP. XLIII.

An act to regulate the pay of the militia heretofore called into service.

Had its effect.

CHAP. XLIV.

An act to repeal so much of a former act as suspends the issuing of executions upon certain judgments until December 1783.

I. BE *it enacted by the General Assembly*, that so much of an act passed at the last session of Assembly entitled *An act for directing the mode of adjusting and settling the payment of certain debts and contracts, and for other purposes*, as suspends the issuing of execution on any judgment or judgments, for any sum or sums of money that have been or shall be obtained, until the first day of *December*, in the year of our Lord one thousand seven hundred and eighty three, shall, from and after the first day of *March* next ensuing, be, and the same is hereby repealed.

See Nov. 1781, ch. 22. Repealing clause.

II. *AND be it further enacted*, that no debt or demand whatsoever, originally due to a subject of *Great Britain* shall be recoverable in any court in this commonwealth, although the same may be transferred to a citizen of this state, or to any other person capable of maintaining such action, unless the assignment hath been or may be made for a valuable consideration, *bona fide* paid before the first day of *May*, in the year one thousand seven hundred and seventy seven, the proof of which consideration and

British debts assigned.

A. D. 1782.

Tobacco, hemp and flour may be tendered in execution.

At what price.

the time thereof, fhall be on the plaintiff. *Provided always,* that when any execution fhall be iffued between the firft day of *March,* one thoufand feven hundred and eighty three, and the firft day of *December,* one thoufand feven hundred and eighty three, upon a judgment for any fum of money, and actually ferved, it fhall and may be lawful for the perfon or perfons againft whom fuch execution fhall iffue, to difcharge the fame, with the cofts of fuit, in infpected crop tobacco, merchantable infpected hemp, or merchantable infpected flour upon navigation. And the county courts fhall fettle every month the then current price of the feveral alternatives, as the fame fhall be upon navigation; and the Judges of the General Court fhall do the fame at their quarterly feffions. And every fuch execution may be difcharged as aforefaid, according to the prices fettled by the court from whence it iffued, agreeable to the laft preceding valuation before the fervice of fuch execution; and the fheriff or other officer receiving the alternatives aforefaid in difcharge of any execution, may be proceeded againft for the recovery

Judgments on future contracts excepted.

of the fame. in like manner as by law fuch fheriff or other officer might have been proceeded againft upon the execution of any *fieri facias* for money. *Provided alfo,* that executions iffued upon judgments to be obtained upon contracts or debts, entered into or made after the paffing of this act, fhall not be fubject to be difcharged in any of the alternatives above mentioned, if the fame iffued for any fum or

Repeal as to lawyers fees, See Oct. 1778, ch. 14.

fums of money. So much of the act entitled *An act to amend an act entitled An act for the better regulating and collecting certain officers fees, and other purpofes,* as repeals part of the act for allowing the full fees to which the lawyers practifing in the feveral courts of this commonwealth are entitled, fhall be, and the fame is hereby repealed.

C H A P. XLV.

Had its effect.

An act to amend the act for adjufting claims for property impreffed or taken for public fervice.

C H A P. XLVI.

Had its effect.

An act for adjufting certain public claims.

C H A P. XLVII.

See Oct. 1780, ch. 27, and notes.

An act for providing more effectual funds for the redemption of certificates granted the officers and foldiers raifed by this ftate.

Preamble.

I. WHEREAS by an act of the laft feffion of Affembly certain certificates were directed to be granted the officers and foldiers raifed by this ftate, for depreciation and arrears of pay due them, which certificates, from the urgent neceffity of the faid officers and foldiers, and from the infufficiency of the funds provided for their redemption, have already depreciated in their value, and without the aid of the Legiflature, will not anfwer the equitable purpofe for which they were intended: *Be it therefore enacted,* that all perfons who have obtained or may hereafter obtained injunc-

Injunctions or pleas to ftay fale of efcheated property to be expedited.

tions in chancery to ftay the fale of any efcheated or forfeited eftates, or have filed, or may hereafter, file, a plea of *monftrans de droit or traverfe,* fhall be confidered as plaintiffs profecuting againft the commonwealth, in which the proof fhall lie upon them; and the Court of Chancery or General Court, as the cafe may be, fhall, at their fecond feffions after any injunction obtained, or plea of *monftrans de droit,* or *traverfe* filed, proceed to hear, try, and determine the fame, unlefs good caufe for a continuance be fhewn to the court, otherwife every fuch injunction fhall be confidered as diffolved, or plea of *monftrans de droit,* or *traverfe* fet afide.

Fraudulent conveyances by Britifh fubjects.

II. AND *be it further enacted,* that upon any information being given to an efcheator, that any *Britifh* fubject, or other perfon abfent, or his or their attorney, on his or their behalf, hath made a fraudulent or fictitious conveyance of the eftate of fuch *Britifh* fubject, or abfentee, fince the nineteenth day of *April,* one thoufand feven hundred and feventy five, fuch efcheator fhall, and he is hereby empowered and required to fummon, as well the truftee, or perfon to whom fuch eftate may have been conveyed, as alfo fuch other perfons as can give evidence thereon, to appear before a jury of inqueft, and if the faid jury upon examination of the witneffes, the oath of the party, or other fufficient evidence, fhall find that fuch *Britifh* fubject, or abfentee, hath any prefent or future intereft in the faid eftate, fuch intereft fhall be forfeited to the commonwealth for the purpofes aforefaid.

Payment of Britifh debts into treafury, revived. Creditors may attach.

III. AND *be it further enacted,* that fo much of the act for fequeftering *Britifh* debts as authorizes the payment thereof, be, and it is hereby revived and put in full force. And all perfons indebted to *Britifh* fubjects, and others, abfentees as aforefaid, who fhall annually in the month of *May,* pay into the public treafury, in fpecie, or in tobacco or hemp, at the price to be fixed by the Auditors, one tenth part or more of the debts they refpectively owe to fuch *Britifh* fubjects, or abfentees, fhall be fo far exonerated from the fame: Saving, however, to any *bona fide* creditors of fuch *Britifh* fubjects, or abfentees, the right which by law they may have to attach fuch debts in the General Court or court of any county where fuch debtor or debtors to any *Britifh* fubject, or abfentee, refides. And the Treafurer is hereby directed to fell at public auction, as foon as may be, for fpecie or the faid certificates, all fuch tobaccoes or hemp, and the money arifing therefrom, as alfo all fums as may be paid into the treafury by the faid debtors, fhall, in the month of *June* in every year, be applied to the difcharge of the intereft due upon the faid certificates, which faid intereft fhall be computed to commence on the firft day of *January* laft. And fhould it fo happen, that after the payment of the intereft as aforefaid, there fhall be remaining in the treafury, on the firft day of *July* for two years next to come, any monies arifing from the funds appropriated for payment of the intereft and redemption of the faid certificates, the fame fhall be paid to the holders thereof in equal proportion.

Sale of forfeited eftates.

IV. AND *be it further enacted,* that no efcheated or forfeited eftate fhall hereafter be fold without three months previous notice thereof in the gazette.

Officers and foldiers to pafs their accounts on oath.

V. AND whereas the documents required by the Auditors of public accounts as legal vouchers for the fettlement of the pay accounts of the officers and foldiers, who have ferved in the northern or fouthern armies, or in the county of *Illinois,* can never be produced, owing to the deaths of many individuals and the unavoidable feparation and other accidents which the events of war have occafioned: *Be it therefore enacted,* that the faid officers who have ferved for any term not lefs than one year prior to the year one thoufand feven hundred and eighty one, fhall be admitted to fettle their pay accounts with the public Auditors on oath: And any foldier producing the difcharge of his Captain or commanding officer, fhall be entitled to the arrears of cloathing and his pay for the time expreffed in the difcharge, or in cafe of fuch time not being afcertained, then fhall be entitled to his pay for the term of his enliftment. And the like certificates for the balances, if any fhall appear to be due, fhall be thereupon granted by the Auditors to the faid officers and foldiers.

VI. *PROVIDED always, and it is hereby further enacted,* that the more effectually to guard againſt the depreciation of the ſaid certificates, the Auditors of public accounts ſhall, for the preſent, iſſue certificates for the one third part only of the ſeveral balances which may appear due to the reſpective officers and ſoldiers, and the remainder at ſuch times, and in ſuch proportions, as hereafter may, to the Governor in Council, appear fit, upon the application of any three or more of the General and field officers heretofore appointed by the ſaid officers to act for them in this behalf.

VII. AND whereas it is neceſſary that the number of claims to any part of the lands appropriated for the benefit of the ſaid officers and ſoldiers ſhould be ſpeedily aſcertained: *Be it therefore enacted,* that all perſons having claims as aforeſaid be required, and they are hereby directed, to tranſmit authenticated vouchers of the ſame to the War Office, on or before the firſt day of *January* next; and if any perſon having ſuch claim ſhall be without the ſtate, he ſhall tranſmit the ſame on or before the firſt day of *June* next following.

VIII. AND be it further enacted, that the Regiſter of the Land Office be, and he is hereby empowered and required to grant to the ſaid officers and ſoldiers, warrants for the lands allotted them, upon producing to the Regiſter a certificate of their claims reſpectively from the Commiſſioner of War, and no otherwiſe.

IX. AND be it further enacted, that any officer or ſoldier who hath not been caſhiered or ſuperſeded, and who hath ſerved the term of three ſucceſſively, ſhall have an abſolute and unconditional title to his reſpective apportionment of the land appropriated as aforeſaid. And for every year which every officer or ſoldier may have continued, or ſhall hereafter continue in ſervice beyond the term of ſix years, to be computed from the time he laſt went into ſervice, he ſhall be entitled to one ſixth part in addition to the quantity of the land apportioned to his rank reſpectively.

X. *PROVIDED always, and it is hereby enacted,* that no ſurveyor ſhall be permitted to receive any location upon any warrant for lands within the country reſerved for the officers and ſoldiers, until the apportionment and draught for the ſame, as directed by the act entitled *An act to adjuſt and regulate the pay and accounts of the officers and ſoldiers of the* Virginia *line on continental eſtabliſhment, and alſo of the officers, ſoldiers, ſailors, and marines, in the ſervice of this ſtate, and for other purpoſes.*

XI. AND be it further enacted, that the ſaid officers and ſoldiers certificates ſhall be received in lieu of any fees or other monies which may be hereafter due to the public for patents for the lands aſſigned to the ſaid officers and ſoldiers by law.

XII. AND be it further enacted, that ſo many officers and ſoldiers in Lieutenant Colonel Lee's legion, or any other corps, as are credited to the quota of troops required from this ſtate and properly belonging to the ſame, as alſo all military ſtaff officers appointed from, and acting in, the *Virginia* continental line, upon producing to the Auditors a certificate in favour of any ſuch officer or ſoldier from the Commiſſioner of War, ſhall be allowed certificates for depreciation and arrears of pay, in like manner and upon the ſame terms as the other troops raiſed by this ſtate: And the Commiſſioner of War is hereby authorized and required to take the moſt effectual precautions which he may think proper, preciſely to aſcertain the claims of ſuch ſtaff officers.

XIII. AND be it further enacted, that the navy officers, ſailors, and marines, of this ſtate, ſhall, in all reſpects, have the ſame claims, and be ſubject to the ſame reſtrictions and regulations, in all matters coming within the purview of this act, as are allowed to the officers and ſoldiers in the land ſervice of the ſame. So much of the act entitled *An act to adjuſt and regulate the pay and accounts of the officers and ſoldiers of the* Virginia *line on continental eſtabliſhment, and alſo the officers, ſoldiers, ſailors, and marines, in the ſervice of this ſtate, and for other purpoſes,* as comes within the purview of this act, ſhall be, and is hereby repealed.

C H A P. XLVIII.

An act for eſtabliſhing a diſtrict court on the weſtern waters.

I. WHEREAS the mode of adminiſtering juſtice has become exceedingly inconvenient and burthenſome to ſuitors living weſtwardly of the *Allegany* mountains: *Be it therefore enacted,* that from and after the firſt day of *Auguſt* next, the counties of *Jefferſon, Fayette,* and *Lincoln,* ſhall be one diſtrict, and called the *Kentucky* diſtrict, for which there ſhall be a ſupreme court of judicature of original juriſdiction (ſeparate and independent of all other courts except the Court of Appeals) which ſaid court ſhall have cognizance and juriſdiction of all treaſons, murders, felonies, crimes and miſdemeanors committed in the ſaid diſtrict, except thoſe made triable by the conſtitution before the General Court; and alſo of all other crimes, matters and things at common law and in chancery ariſing therein; of which the High Court of Chancery and General Court now have cognizance; and from and after the ſaid firſt day of *Auguſt,* the ſaid High Court of Chancery and General Court ſhall ceaſe to exerciſe any original juriſdiction whatſoever within the ſaid diſtrict, except in the caſe before mentioned, and thereafter the court of the diſtrict ſhall have and exerciſe the ſame controuling power over the county and other inferiour courts within the diſtrict, which are now exerciſed over them by the High Court of Chancery and General Court, and all appeals from ſuch inferior courts ſhall be made to the court of the diſtrict There ſhall be one Judge and two aſſiſtant Judges for the ſaid court, choſen by joint ballot of both Houſes of Aſſembly and commiſſioned by the Governor, who ſhall reſide in the diſtrict, and any two of them may hold a court, and vacancies during the receſs of the Aſſembly ſhall be ſupplied in the manner pointed out by the conſtitution. The ſaid Judges ſhall, before entering upon the duties of their office, take the oaths preſcribed by law to be taken by the Judges of the High Court of Chancery and General Court, adapting them to their reſpective caſes, which oaths may be adminiſtered to any one of the ſaid Judges by one of the others, and by him to the other two. They ſhall hold four ſeſſions in every year, to commence on the firſt *Mondays* in *March, June, September,* and *November,* and continue eighteen days, excluſive of *Sundays,* unleſs the buſineſs depending before them be ſooner finiſhed; and if two of the ſaid Judges ſhall not attend on the firſt day of any term, one Judge may adjourn the court till the next day, and ſo on from day to day for ſix days, and if another Judge ſhall not then attend, the ſaid court ſhall be adjourned till the court in courſe, and thereupon all cauſes, matters and things depending before the court ſhall ſtand continued till the next court. The firſt three days of every term ſhall be ſet apart for the trial of criminal matters, the next five days for chancery matters, and the reſt of the term for the trial of other buſineſs; but the Judges for good cauſe may, before iſſuing ſubpœnas, order the clerk to regulate his docket otherwiſe ſo as not to poſtpone cri-

A.D. 1782.

minal matters which shall be first tried. The said court shall be a court of record, and shall, at any time

Power as to deeds and wills.

during the term, take cognizance of matters arising within the district respecting the probate of deeds and wills and granting letters of administration, and may admit deeds to record within the time limited by law, either upon proof or acknowledgment thereof before such court, or upon a certificate of such proof or acknowledgment before any other common law court from the clerk of such court and under

Escheats and forfeitures.
Caveats and local actions.
Process.

the seal thereof. The said court shall also have jurisdiction of all matters respecting escheats and forfeitures arising within the district, and in those cases escheators returns shall be made thereto and other proceedings had therein according to law. All caveats against grants for land lying in the said district, and all local actions accruing therein, heretofore cognizable before the said High Court of Chancery and General Court, shall be tried in the court of the district; and such caveats may, after the said first day of *August*, be entered in the office of the deputy register, and all caveats, within one month after such entries, respectively be entered in the office of the clerk of the district, and summonses issued thereupon; but after the return of the plats and certificates to the Land Office, caveats shall be entered in the Register's office, and the term of six months allowed for the entry thereof in the office of the clerk of the district.

May be sent out of the district in certain cases.

All process shall bear test in the name of, and be signed by the clerk of the said court, and may be sent into any county in the district; and where local actions shall be commenced against defendants living out of the district, or defendants in other actions shall remove therefrom after the commencement of any suits, process may in those cases be sent into the counties in which the defendants live. Executions, attachments for contempts, commissions for taking acknowledgments of *feme coverts* to deeds, for taking depositions of witnesses not living in the district, which the said court shall award, upon good cause shewn may in like manner be sent to the counties in which the parties live. All process issuing from the

Return days.

said court shall be returnable to the days herein after mentioned, to wit: Writs of *habeas corpus* issued in vocation, unless ordered to be returned before a single Judge, and process in criminal cases, to the first day of every court: Process and appeals in chancery, to the fourth or seventeenth days: *Habeas corpuses* issued in term time, in such days as the court shall direct: Appeals in other cases,

Rule proceedings when to be regulated
Grand jury.

and all other process, except subpœnas, on the ninth or seventeenth days: Subpœnas for witnesses, on such days as the suits shall stand docketed to, and the court shall, on the ninth day thereof, regulate all matters respecting the rule docket, and try all disputes respecting bail. At the commencement of every term, the sheriff of the county in which the court may be held, and as many of his deputies as are necessary, shall constantly attend, and shall summon twenty four able and discreet freeholders, or others qualified by law to serve as jurors, to appear on the first day thereof, who, or any sixteen of them appearing, may be sworn a grand jury for the district, who shall have power to present all offences committed therein, but the court shall have power to discharge such grand jury whenever it is necessary, order another to be summoned, and may proceed to the trial of criminals at any time during the term, if such

Trial of criminals.

criminals shall desire it All persons committing capital offences in the said district, shall be examined in the courts respectively of the counties in which they are apprehended, and shall be tried by juries from the counties in which the offences are committed, and may be removed to and tried in the court

Their execution respited.
Suits now in the Chancery or General Court transferred.

of the district, in the same manner as is now practised in the General Court. *Provided,* that there shall be at least six weeks between the time of passing sentence of death upon any criminal and the execution thereof; and the Judges shall have power, for good cause shewn, to respite execution of any such criminal eight months. All actions, suits, and other matters depending in the High Court of Chancery and General Court, which by this act are made cognizable in the court of the said district, shall be transferred to the docket of such court, to be proceeded on in the same manner as if they had originated therein. And all papers and pleadings filed in such suits, shall be delivered to the clerk of the said court, to be filed in his office. The clerk of the said court shall call over his appearance docket, both

Appearance day.

in common law and chancery, on the fourth *Mondays* in those months in which courts are held, which are hereby declared to be the appearance days upon process, returnable to the preceding courts, and shall call over his docket on the same day in every month between the terms, whereupon

Rule days.

such steps shall be taken as are directed in like cases in the High Court of Chancery and General Court, and the same rules of proceeding observed therein, and when issues are made up, or suits in chancery

Rules.
Docket to be regulated.

set for trial, they shall be entered on the court docket for trial at the next term, the clerk setting as nearly an equal number thereof as may be, or as the court shall direct, to the days set apart for the

Judgments to be final, except the power of Court of Appeals.

trial thereof. And the judgments and decrees of the said court when rendered, shall be final in all cases, except those in which the Court of Appeals hath a controuling power over the High Court of Chancery and General Court, in which cases the Court of Appeals shall have the like controuling power over the

To appoint clerk and jailer, and superintend the jail.

court of the district. The said district court shall have power to appoint their clerk and jailer, and to superintend and regulate all matters respecting their jail, and may also appoint persons to contract for building, repairing, or enlarging the court-house and prison; and such jailer, by warrant of a Justice of

Build court house and prison.
Jailer to impress guards.

the Peace of his county, may summon guards to attend the jail during the confinement of criminals, who shall obey such summons, or be liable to be fined by the said court, at their discretion, not exceeding twenty shillings for one offence. The said court shall also order seals to be provided for the use of

Providing for seals.
Power of one Judge out of session.

the court, and any one of the Judges thereof, out of session, shall have power to award writs of *ne exeat, injunction, supersedeas,* and *certiorari,* to award writs of *habeas corpus,* returnable before him at his chambers, to take recognizance of special bail, and to perform all other duties which a Judge of the High

Attorney for the commonwealth:
He and the Judges to hold their offices during good behaviour.

Court of Chancery or General Court can perform; and any acting Justice of the Peace may in like manner take recognizance of special bail, in suits depending in the said district court. There shall be a person appointed by joint ballot of both Houses of Assembly, to attend the said court as attorney for the commonwealth; and in case of a vacancy during the recess of the Assembly, it shall be supplied by the Governor and Council *pro tempore,* which said Attorney and Judges shall hold their offices on the same terms, and be punishable for misfeazance therein, in the same manner with the Judges of the General

General rules for court and officers.

Court and the Attorney General, and shall as well as their clerk, be exempted from military duty.

II. *AND be it further enacted,* that where it is not otherwise directed by this act, all officers of the said court shall have the same powers, perform the same duties, and be entitled to the same fees as are given to, required of, or payable to the like officers of the High Court of Chancery and General Court; and that in all cases not hereby particularly provided for, the said court shall be governed by the laws and regulations now in force in the High Court of Chancery and General Court.

Tax on suitors.
How disposed of.

III. AND whereas it is just that those who receive the benefit of the before mentioned regulations should bear the expence thereof: *Be it enacted,* that upon the commencement of any action or suit in the said court, there shall be paid to the clerk a tax of twenty shillings, to be by him accounted for and paid at the end of every term, that is to say: The sum of fifty pounds to the Judge, the sum of twenty shillings to each assistant Judge for every day they shall respectively attend, and the sum of thirty seven pounds ten shillings quarterly to the Attorney of the commonwealth, and the remainder of such tax, if any, to be applied towards defraying the expences of the public buildings, and such clerk shall be entitled to five *per centum* for his trouble in collecting and paying the same.

Present place of session.

IV. *AND be it further enacted,* that the Judges of the said court shall hold their sessions at *Harrodsburg* in the county of *Lincoln,* until proper buildings shall be erected at such place as the General Assembly shall direct, and in the mean time shall have power to adjourn the said court to such places as they may *A.D. 1782.* think proper; and shall also have power over the jailer of the county in which the courts are held, who shall receive into his custody all persons committed by the said court.

VII. AND whereas it may not be expedient to proceed immediately to the appointment of the Judges *Governor to make* and Attorney for the said district: *Be it therefore enacted*, that the Governor with the advice of the *temporary appoint-* Council, shall make temporary appointments in the mean time; the persons so appointed to have the *ments of Judges* same powers, and be entitled to the same salaries, as are by this act given or payable to the Attorney *and Attorney.* and Judges to be appointed by the General Assembly. *Provided always*, that nothing herein contained shall be construed to prevent the Solicitor General from obtaining judgments in the General Court against delinquent sheriffs and collectors in the district aforesaid.

CHAP. XLIX.

An act for further continuing an act for giving further time to obtain warrants upon certificates for preemption *See May 1779,* *rights and returning certain surveys to the Land Office, and for other purposes.* *ch. 12, and notes.*

I. WHEREAS the powers of the Commissioners for adjusting and settling the titles of claimers to un- *Preamble.* patented lands will expire before the business can be finished: *Be it therefore enacted*, that all *Powers to com-* the powers heretofore given them, except in the district of *Kentucky*, shall continue and be in force until *missioners continued.* the first day of *June* next, and that the like time be allowed for locating preemption warrants in the *Time to return* surveyors offices respectively. *warrants to sur-* *veyors;*

II. AND whereas sundry persons omitted to have their certificates recorded in the surveyor's office *and to have certifi-* and to enter their settlement rights in his books within the time prescribed by law: *Be it therefore enacted,* *cates recorded.* that such persons shall be allowed until the first day of *May* next to make such entries and record such certificates.

III. AND whereas great inconveniences have arisen from the Register's not having been furnished with a copy of the proceedings of the Commissioners for the district of *Kentucky*: *Be it therefore enacted*, that *Books and papers* the said Commissioners shall forthwith deliver to the said Register all the books and papers respecting *of commissioners to* their said business, which books, or authentic copies of any certificates, shall be sufficient authority to *be delivered to Re-* the Register to issue preemption warrants upon the claimants performing the other requisites in those *gister.* cases.

IV. AND whereas in some cases plots and certificates of survey have not been recorded in the sur- *Lands saved if* veyor's office nor returned to the Register's office within the times respectively limited by law, and it *duties performed* is doubtful whether the lands held under such surveys are not still liable to be caveated: *Be it therefore* *before caveat.* enacted, that where no caveat shall be entered before the said duties respectively shall be performed, such lands shall not thereafter be liable to forfeiture on account of such failure. Every person instituting a *Tax on litigants* suit before any court of Commissioners, shall pay down six shillings in lieu of the ten pounds heretofore *before commissioners* directed to be paid.

V. AND be it further enacted, that specie certificates, being first audited, or warrants upon the trea- *Specie certificates* sury, shall hereafter be receivable in discharge of the composition money, payable upon certificates of *or warrants to be* surveys on entries made with the surveyors before the establishment of the commonwealth's Land Office, *taken for land.* and upon certificates of survey of settlement rights; and that the deputy Register of the Land Office for the time being, shall be, and he is hereby empowered to receive such composition money or certificates, together with the plots and certificates of survey, in the *Kentucky* country.

VI. AND be it further enacted, that there shall be allowed a term of twelve months from the end of this present session of Assembly, for returning to the Land Office certificates of survey of land heretofore *Further time to* surveyed, and the Register of the Land Office is hereby empowered and required to receive the same, *return surveys.* notwithstanding the time limited for that purpose may have expired.

VII. AND be it further enacted, that the surveyor of any county within the district in which the right *Pre-emption war-* of preemption was granted, is hereby authorized and directed to locate and survey any preemption war- *rants may be locat-* rant on any waste and unappropriated lands within the district, without exchanging the same: *Provided*, *ed on any waste* they do not have any force of preemption, but shall be equal and on the same footing with treasury *lands;* warrants. *but to lose their force* *of pre-emption.*

CHAP. L.

An act for calling in and redeeming certain certificates.   *Temporary.*

CHAP. LI.

An act to continue and amend the act for reviving several public warehouses for the inspection of tobacco. *Repealed May* *1783, ch. 10.*

CHAP. LII.

An act to amend an act entitled An act to regulate the inspection of flour and for other purposes. *See Nov. 1781,*

I. WHEREAS inconveniencies may arise from allowing the millers or manufacturers of wheat at *ch 37.* their discretion to put into each barrel any indefinite quantity of flour, not less than one hun- *Preamble.* dred and ninety six pounds nor more than two hundred and four pounds; and in order that the export- ers of flour from this state may be enabled to go to market with the same conveniency as the exporter from any of our sister states: *Be it enacted by the General Assembly*, that every barrel of flour for export- *Contents of barrel.* ation shall contain one hundred and ninety six pounds, and no more.

II. AND be it further enacted, that all flour that may be paid for taxes shall be inspected at *Warwick*, *Paid for taxes* in the county of *Chesterfield*, or some one of the public inspections already established, or to be established, *what.* agreeable to the direction of an act *For ascertaining certain taxes and duties, and for establishing a permanent revenue*, under the same regulations as are provided in the aforesaid act for regulating the inspection of flour, and that each barrel shall contain one hundred and ninety six pounds, and no more.

A. D. 1782.

Tendered on ex-ecutions what.

III. AND whereas by an act of this seffion entitled *An act to repeal so much of a former act as suspends the issuing of executions upon certain judgments until* December *one thousand seven hundred and eighty three,* it is enacted, that executions may be discharged among other commutable articles in merchantable in-fpected hemp and flour : *Be it therefore enacted,* that all hemp and flour tendered in payment of any debt or execution, shall be first inspected at the aforesaid public inspections, and that the receipts of the inspectors for hemp or flour may be paid agreeable to the tenor of the said act, and no other. *Pro-vided always,* that no inspectors receipt for flour shall be offered in payment when the flour has been inspected more than three months.

Warehouses may be rented.

IV. *AND be it further enacted,* that the Governor and Council shall be empowered to rent other warehouses at the heads of navigation, if the public warehouses are not sufficient to hold all the flour and hemp to be inspected as aforesaid.

Tax for rents.

For inspection of hemp.

V. *AND be it further enacted,* that there shall be paid upon the delivery of the private hemp or flour, by the person holding the receipts for the same, three shillings for every ton of hemp per month, and four pence for every barrel of flour per month, for every month that the same may lie in the warehouse, to be applied towards paying the rent of such warehouses as the Governor may hire; and that the inspec-tors of hemp shall be allowed five shillings *per* ton for inspecting the same, to be paid by the person depositing the same at the warehouse.

Death to counter-feit receipts for hemp or flour.

VI. *AND be it further enacted,* that if any person whatsoever shall forge or counterfeit, alter or erase, the stamp or receipt of any inspector of flour or hemp, or tender in payment any such forged or coun-terfeited, altered or erased receipt, knowing it to be such, and shall thereof be convicted, he or they shall be adjudged a felon, and suffer death as in case of felony, without the benefit of clergy.

Private.

C H A P. LIII.

An act to establish a town at the courthouse in the county of Fayette.

C H A P. LIV.

Repealed May 1783, ch. 6.

An act for seizure and condemnation of British *goods found on land.*

C H A P. LV.

An act to amend the act for establishing a district court on the western waters.

See chap. 48.
Discontinuance prevented.

I. BE it enacted, that in case the Judges of the court of the district of *Kentucky* shall not attend at the place appointed for holding the first court, they shall hold a court on such court day as they may attend, in the same manner as if the court had been adjourned to such day, and if all the judges should fail to attend on any court day, the court shall stand adjourned till the court in course, and all matters depending therein shall be continued till such court.

Return of process sent out of district.

II. *AND be it further enacted,* that whenever process shall be sent out of the district, the same may be made returnable on any return day within the term of nine months from the date thereof.

Certain transitory actions provided for

III. *AND be it further enacted,* that where transitory actions shall be depending in the High Court of Chancery or the General Court on the first day of *August* next, between inhabitants of the district of *Kentucky* and inhabitants of any other part of this commonwealth, or where witnesses in any action or suit which may hereafter be depending in the said courts shall be living in the said district, the like process may in those cases issue from such courts to any county in the said district, which are directed to issue from the court of the said district to any other part of this commonwealth.

At a GENERAL ASSEMBLY begun and held at the Public Buildings in the City of *Richmond,* on *Monday* the 21st day of *October,* in the Year of our Lord 1782.

C H A P. I.

See Oct. 1780.
ch 27.
Preamble.

An act concerning the certificates issued to the officers and soldiers of the Virginia *line.*

I. WHEREAS it is just that the officers and soldiers of the *Virginia* lines on continental and state establishment should annually receive interest upon the amount of the certificates which have been or may be issued to them for pay and depreciation, until such certificates shall be fully

interest what, when and how to be paid.

paid and redeemed : *Be it therefore enacted by the General Assembly,* that the Treasurer for the time being shall, and he is hereby directed and required to pay annually, as the same shall become due, to the holder thereof, an interest of six *per centum* upon the amount of every certificate so as aforesaid issued to the said officers and soldiers, the amount of which interest shall be ascertained by the Auditors of public accounts, and commence the first day of *January,* one thousand seven hundred and eighty two, endorf-ing on every such certificate at the time of payment the sum paid for interest, and taking a receipt for the same

To pay taxes of officers and soldiers.

And as a further relief to the said officers and soldiers, it shall be lawful for them to discharge their public taxes with the said certificates in manner following, that is to say : the amount of such offi-cers or soldiers tax shall be endorsed by the sheriff or collector on the back of the said certificate, passing his receipt at the same time to the said officer or soldier for the amount thereof, expressing that the same is by endorsement on such certificate, and taking from the said officer or soldier a certificate of the same, to be transmitted by such sheriff or collector to the Auditors of public accounts, who are hereby directed to issue warrants to the amount thereof, charging the same to each respective officer or soldier to be deducted annually out of the principal due to such officer or soldier.

II. AND whereas *William Brown*, of the county of *Fairfax*, acted as surgeon to the second *Virginia* regiment raised by this state in the year one thousand seven hundred and seventy five, until some time in the year one thousand seven hundred and seventy six, when he was appointed by Congress physician to the general hospital, and acted in that capacity, as well as assistant director and physician general and surgeon general, until the year one thousand seven hundred and eighty, when he resigned the said appointments: And whereas no provision is made by law for settling the pay and depreciation of the said *William Brown*, who is moreover excluded from the bounty in lands allowed by law to surgeons and chaplains, by accepting the said appointments and not continuing regimental surgeon for the term of three years: For remedy whereof, *Be it enacted*, that the Auditors of public accounts shall settle the pay and depreciation of the said *William Brown*, for his services aforesaid, and issue certificates for the balance in the same manner and upon the like proof as is prescribed in the case of officers and soldiers.

Provision for doctor William Brown.

III. AND be it further enacted, that the said *William Brown* shall be entitled to the bounty of lands allowed by law to surgeons of regiments raised under authority of this state.

IV. AND be it further enacted, that so much of an act entitled *An act for providing more effectual funds for the redemption of certificates granted the officers and soldiers raised by this state,* as directs the Auditors of public accounts to issue for the present, certificates for the one third part only of the several balances which may appear due to the respective officers and soldiers, shall be, and the same is hereby repealed.

Restriction in issuing certificates repealed.

V. AND be it further enacted, that every officer and soldier availing or meaning to avail himself of the right hereby granted of discharging his public taxes in the said certificates, shall, at the time of giving in a list of his property or of paying his taxes for the same, make oath before any Justice of the Peace, or other proper person or persons authorized by law to administer such oath, that no part of such property has been conveyed to or received by him with a view of providing thereby for the payment of the taxes thereof in the said certificates; a copy of which said oath, attested under the hand of the person or persons who shall have administered the same, shall be produced by the said officer or soldier to the sheriff or collector, at the time of payment of his said taxes. *Provided always,* that where any officer or soldier shall be absent on actual duty, it shall be lawful for the attorney or agent of such absent officer or soldier to make oath in the manner herein before directed for his principal.

Oath to prevent paying taxes of others with certificates.

CHAP. II.

An act to continue the act entitled An act to ascertain the number of people within this commonwealth.

Expired.

CHAP. III.

An act to continue the act entitled An act to empower the Judges of the General Court to superintend and regulate the public jail.

See Oct. 1779, ch 19.

I. WHEREAS the act of Assembly passed in the year one thousand seven hundred and seventy nine, entitled *An act to empower the Judges of the General Court to superintend and regulate the public jail,* will expire on the first day of *January* next, and it is expedient and necessary that the same should be continued: *Be it therefore enacted,* that the act entitled *An act to empower the Judges of the General Court to superintend and regulate the public jail,* shall continue and be in force from and after the expiration thereof, for and during the term of two years, and from thence to the end of the next session of Assembly, and no longer.

Preamble.

Continuance of the act.

CHAP. IV.

An act to continue the act entitled An act to ascertain the losses and injuries sustained from the depredations of the enemy within this commonwealth.

Expired. See Oct. 1783, ch. 10.

CHAP. V.

An act to vest certain lands in William Robinson, *in fee.*

Private.

CHAP. VI.

An act concerning John M'Clean.

Private.

CHAP. VII.

An act for giving further time to the freeholders and house-keepers of the parishes of Antrim *and* Westover *to elect new vestries.*

Private.

CHAP. VIII.

An act to amend and reduce the several acts of Assembly for ascertaining certain taxes and duties, and for establishing a permanent revenue, into one act.

See Oct. 1777, ch. 2, and notes. Preamble.

I. FOR amending and reducing the several acts for ascertaining certain taxes and duties, and for establishing a permanent revenue, into one act: AND WHEREAS the sum produced by the land tax is disproportionate to that of other subjects of taxation; and it is just and right that property of every kind should be equally burthened for the defence and protection of the state:

II. Be it enacted, that from every owner of land or lots within this commonwealth, in addition to the tax already imposed, there shall be collected and distrained for, fifty per centum on the amount, or ten shillings on the pound of all sums payable for tax on land and lots, as the same may be charged by the examiners appointed under the act of the present session of Assembly, for equalizing the land tax; also a tax of ten shillings by every free male person above the age of twenty one years, who shall be a citizen of this commonwealth; and also upon all slaves, to be paid by the owners thereof, except such free persons and slaves as shall be exempted on applications to the county courts, through age or infirmity; also

Additional tax on land.

Tax on other articles.

A.D. 1782.

two shillings for every horse, mare, colt, and mule, except covering horses; and for every covering horse there shall be paid by the owner thereof, the sum which such horse covers one mare the season, which rate or sum the owner shall note down when he delivers in his list of property to the Justice; also three pence *per* head for cattle of all ages; also six shillings *per* wheel for all coaches, chariots, phætons, four wheeled chaises, stage waggons for riding carriages, chairs, and two wheeled chaises; also fifteen pounds for every billiard table, and five pounds for every ordinary license; which said taxes shall be paid annually in manner herein after directed. And for the regular listing of all the articles enumerated above,

Lists of taxable property how to be taken annually; and returned.

III. BE it enacted, that the court of every county shall divide the same into convenient precincts, and annually before the tenth of *March*, appoint one of the Justices for each precinct, to take a list of the said enumerated articles therein; and every Justice shall give public notice of his being so appointed, and at what times and places he intends to receive the lists, by advertising the same at the most public places within his precinct; and shall, on or before the twentieth day of *April* next following, deliver to the clerk of the county court, together with the vouchers by him taken, a fair alphabetical list of the names of all free male persons above the age of twenty one years as aforesaid, and resident within his precinct, and of the names of all slaves, specifying to whom they belong, distinguishing in a separate column, such as are above the age of sixteen, for the purpose of carrying into execution the laws concerning county and parish levies, and the *Act for calling in and redeeming certain certificates*, which distinction so made, shall, for the act last mentioned, be clearly certified in the lists, by the clerks of the several courts, to the Auditors to be delivered; and also the number of cattle, horses, mares, colts, and

Clerk's duty;

mules, wheels for riding carriages above specified in this act, billiard tables and ordinary licenses; which said enumerated articles shall be placed under the names of the persons to whom they belong; and the said clerk shall file the same in his office, and shall make out three fair copies from all the lists so taken and delivered to him, one of which shall be delivered to the Auditors of public accounts, at their office, by the said clerk, on or before the first day of *July* in each year, one other copy to be set up in the

and allowance. Penalty on clerk and Justice.

courthouse of the county at *May* court, and the other to be delivered to the sheriff or collector of public taxes in the said county, on or before the first day of *May* annually. There shall be allowed to each county court clerk, the sum of five pounds, for *extra officium* services by this act required. If any Justice or clerk shall refuse or neglect to perform the duties required of them respectively as above mentioned, such person or persons shall forfeit and pay, for such refusal or neglect, the sum of one hundred pounds, recoverable on information in any county court within this commonwealth, who shall thereupon enter judgment and award execution for the same, to be applied towards lessening the county levy where the same shall be recovered; provided the party have ten days previous notice of such information.

IV. AND to enable the Justices for each precinct to make out lists of the said enumerated articles, *Be it enacted*, that every master or owner of a family, or in his absence or non-residence at the plantation, his or her agent, attorney, or overseer, shall, between the tenth day of *March* and the tenth day of *April* annually, by a list under his or her hand, deliver or cause to be delivered to the Justice appointed for that precinct, the names of all free male persons above the age of twenty one years, and the names and number of slaves, distinguishing those that are tithables abiding in or belonging to his or her family the ninth day of *March*, also the number of his or her cattle, horses, mares, colts, and mules, wheels for riding carriages as herein before mentioned, billiard tables, and ordinary licenses; or the master or owner thereof, or in case of his or her absence or non-residence upon the plantation, the overseer, shall

On proprietor's concealing property;

be adjudged a concealer of such and so many articles above enumerated as shall not be listed and given in, and for every article so concealed, shall forfeit and pay five hundred pounds of tobacco, to be recovered by information in any county court within this commonwealth, for the use of the county where

How it may be saved.

such concealment shall be, for lessening the county levy; the master or owner shall be subject nevertheless, to the payment of the taxes, in the same manner as if the same had been duly listed and given in. If any owner, agent, attorney, or overseer, shall happen by sickness, absence, or ignorance, of the person or place, to omit delivering his or her list before the said tenth day of *April*, to the Justice appointed to take the same, and shall deliver or send his or her list to the clerk of the court before the last day of the said month, he or she shall thereupon be discharged from the penalty aforesaid; and the clerk shall add all such lists so delivered to him, to the several lists of the Justices to whom the same should have been given in, for which it shall be lawful for the clerk to charge the party fifteen pounds of tobacco for each list so added, to be paid in the same manner as other clerks fees. And the said sheriff shall, from

Sheriffs when to collect and distrain.

and after the first day of *May* annually, collect and receive from all and every person and persons chargeable therewith, the taxes imposed by this act, in his said county; and in case payment be not made or received on or before the first day of *June* annually, the said sheriff shall have power to distrain the lands or slaves, goods or chattels, which shall be found upon the lands and in the possession of the person so indebted or failing, notwithstanding such lands, slaves, goods, or chattels, shall be comprized in any deed or mortgage; and if the owner thereof shall not pay the taxes due within five days after such distress,

Manner of sale.

such sheriff or collector shall and may lawfully sell the same, or so much thereof as shall be sufficient to discharge the said taxes and the charges of distress and sale, for ready money; but if the same will not

As to lands seized.

sell, in the opinion of the officer making such distress, for three fourths of their value, then the same shall be sold for one month's credit, giving six days notice of the day and place of sale, by advertising the same at the church, or other public places in the parish wherein such distress shall be, on the next *Sunday* after the expiration of the said five days, and shall take sufficient security residing in the county, for the payment thereof; and in case the same shall not be paid within the said one month, such officer is hereby authorized and required to make immediate distress on the lands, goods or chattels, of such purchaser or purchasers, his, her, or their security or securities, and proceed to sell the same for the best price that can be got in ready money; which several sales shall be good and effectual in law against all persons whatsoever. *Provided always*, that where any sheriff or collector shall make seizure of any lands by virtue of this act, he shall sell the smallest number of acres that the lowest bidder will pay the taxes for, together with the charges of distress and sale, which shall be laid off by the surveyor of the county, and conveyed by the sheriff. The proprietor of the land, his or her agent or attorney, may appoint, on the day of sale, what part of the tract shall be sold; and in case of failure so to do, the sheriff or collector shall sell that part as in his opinion will least injure or prejudice the tract; and where other sufficient

Unreasonable distress how punished.

cient effects can be had thereon, distress shall not be made of such lands. *Provided always*, that where unreasonable seizures or distresses shall be made, the party grieved shall have an action against the sheriff or collector, and shall recover full costs where any damages shall be given; and the said sheriff or col-

Sheriffs when to account and pay.

lector shall duly account for and pay into the treasury of this commonwealth, on or before the fifteenth of *September* annually, the full amount of all taxes imposed in his said county, deducting therefrom an

How to account.

allowance for insolvents, and such other allowances as this act directs to be made, and five *per centum* for his commissions thereon; and before any allowance shall be made in the case of insolvents, the sheriff or collector shall return a list thereof to the court of his county, and shall also render an account of all monies or other articles by him received for property concealed, with the names of the concealers as well those who have, as those who have not paid taxes, and shall make oath that the said list of insol-

A. D. 1781.

vents, and the account rendered for taxes received for property concealed as aforesaid, are just and true, an attested copy of which shall be delivered to the Auditors of public accounts by the sheriff or collector, and the same shall by them be allowed in passing his accounts. And in case the said sheriff or collector shall fail to account for and pay into the treasury as aforesaid, the money or other articles in lieu thereof, imposed by this act and received by him for taxes, every such delinquent sheriff or collector shall be liable to a judgment against him, on motion, to be made by the Solicitor, or other person appointed for that purpose, at the *October* General Court, or any subsequent court after such failure, for the amount of the taxes due, and fifteen *per centum* damages, together with an interest of five *per centum* upon the whole amount, until paid, for the use of the commonwealth, and thereupon execution shall issue; provided the party has ten days previous notice of the day on which such motion is to be made. The said court, upon good cause to them shewn, are hereby empowered to remit the said damages and interest, or any part thereof, on every such judgment. There shall be paid by all and every person and persons chargeable therewith, to the sheriff or collector of the same, the taxes herein before enumerated, which said taxes shall be paid in *Spanish* milled dollars, at the rate of six shillings each, or in other current silver or gold coin, at a proportionable value, or in the bills of credit herein after mentioned, or in such produce of this commonwealth, at such rate, and in such manner and proportion as is herein after mentioned, to wit: One tenth part or two shillings in the pound of the tax on land, shall be payable at the option of the persons paying the said tax, in the bills of credit emitted on the funds of this commonwealth, and the faith of the United States, as pledged by the resolutions of Congress of the eighteenth of *March*, in the year one thousand seven hundred and eighty, and the interest due on such bills shall be computed and allowed to the payer, at the time of payment thereof, for the said tax: And the bills of credit so received, shall be paid into the treasury, and not re-issued, but shall remain in the treasury to be burnt and destroyed; and other four-tenths of the said tax on land shall be paid in commutable articles, as by this act is directed. *Provided always*, that the gold coin paid into the treasury by virtue of this act, shall be received at the following rates, to wit: The johannes, weighing eighteen pennyweight, at four pounds sixteen shillings; half johannes, weighing nine pennyweight, at two pounds eight shillings; guineas, whether *French* or *English*, weighing five pennyweight six grains, at one pound eight shillings; half guineas, weighing two pennyweight fifteen grains, at fourteen shillings; moidores, weighing six pennyweight eighteen grains, at one pound sixteen shillings; doubloons, weighing seventeen pennyweight, at four pounds ten shillings; pistoles, weighing four pennyweight six grains, at one pound two shillings and six pence. And all other taxes, on articles enumerated as aforesaid, to be paid by this act (except the tax on land) shall be payable, at the option of the payer, one half thereof in specie, tobacco, or hemp, and the other half in specie, tobacco, hemp, or flour, to wit: In inspectors receipts or notes for good merchantable crop tobacco, not less than nine hundred and fifty nett weight, and not inspected more than one year when offered in payment, at the rate of twenty shillings *per* hundred, with an allowance of twelve shillings and six pence for inspection and cask, or in transfer receipts or notes for tobacco, at the rate of one hundred and six pounds for one hundred pounds of crop tobacco, at any public inspection within this commonwealth; or inspectors receipts or notes for sound clean and merchantable hemp, delivered at the warehouses provided or to be provided for the reception thereof, at the towns of *Alexandria, Dumfries, Falmouth, Fredericksburg, Harrodsburg, Lewisburg, Abingdon, Richmond, Manchester, Petersburg*, and *West Point*; provided, that skins as herein after described, shall be the only article receivable at the towns of *Lewisburg* and *Abingdon*; which said receipts or notes for hemp, shall be received in discharge of taxes according to this act, at the rate of fifty shillings *per* hundred, or in receipts for sound and merchantable flour, in casks, delivered at the warehouses provided or to be provided by the inspectors and receivers of hemp, at the aforesaid towns, between the first day of *November* and the first day of *May* annually, preceding the collection of the said taxes, at the rate of thirteen shillings and four pence *per* hundred, with an allowance of two shillings and six pence for cask and inspection; and any person or persons chargeable with taxes by this act, and paying the same in manner herein directed, shall be discharged thereof, and may demand and receive of the sheriff or collector, a receipt specifying in what article such person paid his tax, whether it be specie, bills of credit as aforesaid, or commutables, particularising the warehouse from which the tobacco notes he may have received shall have issued; and shall, moreover, return a list on oath of such payments to the clerk of the court of his county, immediately after his collection, copies of which list shall be fixed up in the said court-house, for the inspection of the people; and the Auditors are hereby required not to settle with any sheriff for the taxes collected under this act, except the said sheriff do produce to them a copy of such list, certified by the clerk of his county; and the Auditors shall, upon settlement with the sheriff, give their order to the Treasurer to receive such specie, paper money, or commutables, from the sheriff, agreeable to the said list; and every sheriff failing to pay the same accordingly, shall forfeit and pay the sum of five hundred pounds, to be recovered in like manner as is prescribed in the case of delinquent sheriffs.

V. AND that the flour so paid in discharge of taxes may be converted to the purposes by this act intended, before the same shall be injured or lost, *Be it enacted*, that the inspectors or receivers of flour, shall once in every month, during the time herein before limited for the reception of flour, make out and transmit to the Treasurer, a fair and accurate list of the quantity of flour by him or them received, and for whom, and on failure so to do, he or they shall forfeit and pay the sum of fifty pounds, to be recovered by motion in the General Court, or the court of the county where such inspections may be, with costs, to the use of the commonwealth, and thereupon execution shall issue, provided the party has ten days previous notice of such motion. And the Treasurer for the time being, shall sell the said tobacco, hemp, skins, and flour, from time to time, as occasion may require, for current gold or silver coin, or otherwise to dispose of the said tobacco, hemp, skins, and flour, in payment of the debts and contracts of this commonwealth, on the best terms that can be obtained, in like manner as if the same had been current gold or silver coin actually paid into the treasury, having a due regard to the appropriations which are or shall be made of the revenue of the commonwealth, and shall also sell or dispose of all the commutable articles which are now on hand, or may hereafter be paid in from the collection of the present year. And the courts of the counties respectively in which the aforesaid towns of *Alexandria, Dumfries, Falmouth, Fredericksburg, Harrodsburg, Richmond, Manchester, Petersburg, Lewisburg, Abingdon*, and *West Point* are, shall be, and are hereby authorized and required, to provide good and sufficient warehouses for the storage of hemp and flour according to this act, and to appoint one or two reputable persons, as the case may require, within the said towns respectively, for the receiving, safe keeping, and delivering of the said hemp and flour on public account, and for inspecting the said hemp, who in the receipts given by them, or either of them, shall specify the names of the persons or owners delivering the same, the number and quantity of each bundle of hemp, and the warehouse, number, and nett weight, of each barrel of inspected flour received, for which the inspectors manifest shall be produced, and filed at the said warehouse, as a voucher to prove the inspection thereof, before the delivery by the owner. And the said courts respectively, shall make such reasonable allowance to the inspectors or receivers aforesaid, for their services, as they shall think proper, and shall certify the same to the Auditors of public accounts, and all other expences attending the said warehouses, for the receiving and delivering of the hemp and flour aforesaid, shall be allowed and certified in like manner, and shall

Penalty.

Power in the court to remit the damages and interest.

How taxes may be paid.

Rates of gold paid for taxes.

How certain commodities may be received.

Sheriff to return a list of payments to the clerk.

A copy to be set up in the courthouse.

Inspectors of flour to return lists monthly to Treasurer. Penalty.

Treasurer to sell commodities speedily

Courts to provide warehouses for hemp and flour;

And appoint receivers.

Their duty;

and allowance.

T t

A. D. 1782.

To give bond.

be paid out of the money in the public treasury, arising from the sale thereof: And the said inspectors or receivers of hemp and flour shall, before entering upon the duties of their office, give bond, in a reasonable penalty, payable to the Treasurer for the time being, or to his successors, for the use of the commonwealth, conditioned for the due and faithful performance of the duties required of them by law, in the execution of their said office; and in case of failure in any court, inspector, or receiver, respectively, as aforesaid, such court shall be liable to the same penalties as is provided in the case of the Justices neglecting or refusing to take and return lists of enumerated articles, by this act to be recovered, and applied in like manner: And such inspector or receiver shall be liable to damages upon the action of the party grieved, and shall moreover forfeit and pay the sum of one hundred pounds, recoverable on information in any county court, for the use of this commonwealth.

Penalties on them and courts.

Hemp and flour how to be weighed.

VI. AND be it further enacted, that hemp, flour, and all other articles directed to be paid by this act, shall be weighed by the nett or short hundred, and that the several certificates for hemp and flour shall be separate and distinct, so that the several commutable articles may appear in a clear and distinct view.

Tax on certain patents.

VII. AND be it further enacted, that there shall be received, accounted for on oath, and paid into the treasury of this commonwealth, by the Register of the Land Office for the time being, every half year to wit: on or before the first day of April and the first day of October in every year, the tax of five shillings for every hundred acres of land exceeding fourteen hundred acres, contiguous to or contained in any patent hereafter to be granted to any person or persons, except in cases of land allowed to officers as bounties; which said tax the said Register is authorized to demand and receive before granting the said patent. And for the Register's direction herein, the surveyor shall certify on every plat by him to be returned for surveys made after the first day of April next, whether the land contained in such plat is adjacent to other lands surveyed or patented for the same person or persons; and the quantity of such adjacent land, if any, according to the best of his knowledge, information and belief; and that no patent shall issue without such certificate being made by the surveyors: And the said Register shall account for and pay the money arising from the aforesaid tax, in the same manner as is directed by this act in the case of sheriffs accounting for and paying the taxes received by them; and in case of failure shall be liable to the like penalties, to be recovered in like manner.

Tonnage on vessels.

VIII. AND be it further enacted, that on all vessels, at entrance or clearance, from or to foreign parts, or from or to any of the United States, vessels of war excepted, there shall be paid, by the master or owner thereof, the duty of one shilling and three pence per ton, to the collector of duties, at the port or ports established, or to be established for the entrance and clearance of such vessels; and for every gallon of rum, brandy, and other distilled spirits, and for every gallon of wine, which shall be imported or brought into this commonwealth, either by land or water, from any port or place whatsoever, the duty or custom of four pence, which shall be paid by the owner or importer of the same; and for every hundred pounds of sugar, which shall be brought or imported into this commonwealth, as aforesaid, from any port or place whatsoever, the duty or custom of four shillings and two pence; and for every pound of coffee which shall be imported or brought into this commonwealth, as aforesaid, from any port or place whatsoever, the duty of one penny; and for all other goods or merchandize, which shall be imported or brought into this commonwealth, as aforesaid, from any port or place whatsoever, the duty of one per centum, ad valorem, on the amount, per invoice, of such goods and merchandize, all which said duties shall be paid by the owner or importer of any of the articles or merchandize above mentioned.

Duty on spirits and wine imported.

On sugar.

Coffee.

One per cent. on all other goods.

Masters of vessels when to report.

IX. AND be it further enacted, that the master or purser of every ship, or other vessel, importing any goods wares, or merchandize, liable to a duty by virtue of this act, to any port or place within this commonwealth, shall, within forty eight hours after his arrival, make a true and just report upon oath, with the collector of the duties in the said port or place, of the burthen, contents, and loading of such ship or vessel, with the particular marks and numbers of every cask or package whatsoever therein laden, with spirits, wine, sugar, coffee, and other merchandize, and the quantity of such spirits, wine, sugar, and coffee, and the value of such other merchandize, to whom consigned, to the best of his knowledge; and also where, and in what port the same were laden and taken on board, upon penalty of forfeiting three hundred pounds current money, recoverable on information, in any court within this commonwealth, who shall thereupon enter judgment, and award execution for the same, to be applied, one moiety to the use of the informer, and the other to the use of the commonwealth.

And how.

Penalty.

Dutiable goods landed before entry, forfeited.

X. AND be it further enacted, that no spirits, wine, sugar, coffee, or other merchandize, liable to the said duties, imported or brought into this commonwealth by water, by any person or persons whatsoever, shall be landed or put on shore, until due entry made thereof with the collector of the duties in such port or place and a true account of the marks and numbers of every cask and package, as aforesaid, at that port or place where the same was shipped or taken on board, given on oath before the said collector, who shall certify the same upon the back of the original invoice, or a true copy thereof, to him produced; and thereupon such importer, paying the duties laid by this act, or securing the payment thereof within six months, shall obtain a permit, under the hand of such collector, for the landing and delivery of the same; and all spirits, wine, sugar, coffee, or other merchandize, landed, put on shore, or delivered, contrary to the true intent and meaning of this act, or the value thereof, shall be forfeited and lost, and may be seized or recovered by the said collector of the port or place where the same shall be put on shore or delivered, or by any other person or persons whatsoever. And the owner or importer of any of the aforesaid spirits, wine, sugar, coffee, or other merchandize, by land, shall, in like manner, make due entry of the same within ten days after the importation, with the clerk of the county court wherein they are brought, who shall receive the taxes or duties payable thereon, or take bond with good and sufficient security from the importer, for the payment thereof within six months; and the said clerks shall, in case the owner or importer of the said articles shall fail to pay the duties imposed thereon, or give bond as aforesaid, proceed in like manner to seize and sell the same as is directed in the case of seizures made by the Collectors or Naval Officers. Provided always, that no person shall be required to give account upon oath, of the true contents of any pipe, or lesser cask of wine, or any hogshead, or lesser cask of spirits imported, but shall have liberty to enter a pipe of wine, or hogshead of spirits as aforesaid at one hundred gallons, and all lesser casks after the same proportion, any thing in this act to the contrary, notwithstanding.

Importations by land to be entered with clerk of the court.

Direction as to casks.

Penalty for a false entry.

XI. AND be it further enacted, that if any person or persons whatsoever, shall willingly make a false entry, and be thereof convicted, such person or persons shall forfeit and pay one hundred pounds current money, and also forfeit the goods, recoverable on information, in any court within this commonwealth, who shall thereupon enter judgment, and award execution for the same, to be applied one moiety to the use of the informer, and the other to the use of the commonwealth.

XII. AND be it further enacted, that the collectors of the duties aforesaid, or any person by them appointed, shall have full power and authority to go and enter on board any ship or other vessel, and from thence to bring on fhore, any articles whatfoever liable to a duty by virtue of this act, if fuch duty be not paid or agreed for within ten days after the firft entry of fuch fhip or veffel, or bond with good and fufficient fecurity given for payment of the fame within fix months next after fuch entry, which bond, if offered, the collector is hereby authorized and required to accept and take, and fuch articles fo brought on fhore to fecure and detain until due payment fhall be made, or fecurity given for the fame as aforefaid. And if fuch payment or fecurity be not made or given within two days from the time of fuch feizure, the collector of the duties aforefaid is hereby empowered to fell the fame, or fo much thereof as fhall be fufficient to difcharge the faid duties, and five *per centum* for the charges of fuch feizure and fale. *Provided neverthelefs*, that notice fhall be given of fuch fale by advertifing the fame two weeks in the *Virginia* gazette. And they are alfo empowered to ftay and remain on board fuch fhip or veffel until all fuch wines, fpirits, fugar, coffee, and other merchandize, be difcharged and delivered out of the fame. And if any collector or collectors of the faid duties, or clerks of the county courts, or any other perfon or perfons deputed by them, or any of them, fhall directly or indirectly take or receive any bribe, recompence, or reward, in any kind whatfoever, or fhall connive at any falfe entry of the articles liable to a duty or cuftom by virtue of this act, the perfon or perfons fo offending fhall forfeit and pay the fum of one hundred pounds current money, and be for ever after difabled in his faid office, and rendered incapable of holding any office or employment relating to the cuftoms within this commonwealth, and the perfon or perfons giving or offering fuch bribe, reward, or recompence, fhall forfeit and pay one hundred pounds current money.

Marginal notes:
A. D. 1782.
Collectors may feize goods on board a veffel, if duty not paid.
Proceedings thereon
Penalty on collector receiving a bribe or conniving at a falfe entry;
and on the perfon offering it.

XIII. AND *be it further enacted*, that it fhall be lawful to and for all and every collector and collectors of the duties aforefaid, or clerks of county courts, by warrant under the hand of a Juftice of the Peace (which warrant fhall not be granted but upon an information made to him upon oath, and accompanied with a conftable) to break open in the day time any houfe, warehoufe, or ftorehoufe, to fearch for, feize, and carry way, any wine, fpirits, fugar, coffee, and other merchandize, liable to a duty by this act, and for which the faid duty fhall not have been paid or fecured to be paid as aforefaid, and if any collector, clerk, or conftable fhall be fued or molefted for any thing done in execution of the powers hereby given them, fuch collector, clerk, or conftable fhall be fued or molefted for any thing done in execution of the powers hereby given them, fuch collector, clerk, or conftable fhall plead the general iffue, and give this act in evidence, and if in fuch fuit the plaintiff be non-fuited or judgment pafs againft him, the defendant fhall recover double cofts; and in all actions fuits, or informations to be brought, or where any feizure fhall be made purfuant to this act, if the property thereof be claimed by any perfon as the owner or importer thereof, in fuch cafe the *onus probandi* fhall lie upon the owner or claimer.

Marginal notes:
Collector by warrant and with a conftable in the day time may break open houfes.
Indemnified.
Proof to lie on the claimant of goods feized.

XIV. AND *be it further enacted*, that when any wine, fpirits, fugar, coffee, or other merchandize, fhall be configned to any perfon other than the mafter or owner of the fhip or veffel importing the fame, every perfon to whom fuch articles fhall be configned, fhall, upon the importation thereof, pay to the mafter or owner of the fhip or veffel importing the fame, the duty payable for fuch articles by this act, and if any perfon or perfons to whom fuch articles fhall be configned as aforefaid, fhall neglect or refufe to pay the faid duty, or give bond with fecurity for the payment thereof to the mafter or owner of the fhip or veffel importing the fame, at fuch time as the fame fhall become payable, it fhall and may be lawful for the mafter or owner of fuch fhip or veffel to detain fuch articles until the duty fhall be paid, or fecured to be paid as aforefaid.

Mafter may detain dutiable goods configned till duty paid or fecured.

XV. AND *be it further enacted*, that if any importer of wines, fpirits, fugar, coffee, or other merchandize, fhall defire to tranfport the fame from one diftrict to another, within this commonwealth, he fhall, before he depart out of the diftrict wherein fuch articles fhall be laden or taken on board, make oath before a Juftice of the Peace that the fame were legally imported, and the duties fecured according to law, and that he will not fuffer any other goods to be taken on board his veffel, and the Juftice fhall give him a certificate thereof, fpecifying the marks and numbers of the faid goods, and if any other goods fhall be found on board fuch veffel they fhall be forfeited, to be recoverable on information in any court of record, one half to the ufe of the commonwealth, and the other half to the informer.

How goods entered may be carried to another diftrict.

XVI. AND *be it further enacted*, that it fhall and may be lawful to and for the faid collectors and clerks to recover the faid duties fo bonded by motion made in the General Court, or the county court wherein the principal or either of his fecurities refpectively refide, and fuch court fhall give judgment for the fum due on fuch bonds, with cofts and intereft of five *per centum* on the fame until paid. *Provided always* ten days previous notice in writing fhall be given by fuch collector or clerk, to the perfon or perfons fo to be moved againft. And the faid collectors and clerks refpectively, fhall be allowed for collecting, accounting for, and paying the faid duties impofed by this act into the treafury of this commonwealth, the fum of five *per centum* on the money fo collected by them or any of them, and they are hereby required to account for, and pay into the treafury aforefaid, every half year, to wit: on the tenth day of *April*, and the tenth day of *October* in every year, or within ten days afterwards, all money received by them refpectively, on public account, purfuant to this act, upon pain of forfeiting one half of their commiffions, to be carried to the credit of the public treafury, and of being fufpended from their faid office of collector or clerk until fuch payment be made.

Marginal notes:
Bonded duties how to be recovered.
Allowance to collectors.
Penalty for not accounting and paying.

XVII. AND *be it further enacted*, that no certificates, receipts, or warrants for militia, or military fervice, except receipts given under the act for fupplying the fouthern army with waggons and horfes, except alfo certificates granted for money advanced, agreeable to a requifition of the Governor and Council of the twenty eighth of *February* one thoufand feven hundred and eighty two, and except alfo fo much of the certificates iffued, or to be iffued to the officers and foldiers of the *Virginia* lines, on account of pay and depreciation, as fhall pay the taxes on the property of every fuch officer and foldier, and the certificates or warrants for intereft due to the faid officers or foldiers as herein after mentioned, in manner prefcribed by an act paffed this prefent feffion of Affembly entitled *An act concerning the certificates iffued to the officers and foldiers of the* Virginia *line*, fhall be received in difcharge of the taxes impofed by this act.

Marginal note:
Certificates what not to be received for taxes.

XVIII. AND *be it further enacted*, that warrants iffued by the Auditors of public accounts for all arrears of wages, or falaries allowed by law, to the Governor, the members of the Privy Council, the Delegates to Congrefs, the Speaker of the Senate, and of the Houfe of Delegates, the members of the General Affembly, and the officers of every denomination attending thereon, Judges of the High Court of Chancery, Judges of the General Court, Judges of the Court of Admiralty, the Treafurer, Attorney General, Auditors for public accounts, Solicitor General, Commiffioners of the navy, Clerks to the Council, to the Treafurer, to the Auditors, to the Solicitor General, to the Affiftant Commiffary of Stores, the Keeper of the Public Jail, the Public Armourer, the Commiffioner of the gun manufactory at *Frederickfburg*, the Director of the hofpital, the Public Printer, the Door-Keepers to the Council, the Clerks to the Superior Courts, and other officers attending thereon, alfo all warrants iffued by the Auditors for intereft due on the certificates granted, or to be granted to the officers and folders, both

Marginal note:
What to be received.

A.D. 1782. land and naval, of the *Virginia* lines, on continental and state establishments, shall be receiveable in discharge of taxes imposed by this act, and the several sheriffs or collectors, shall be allowed a discount with the Treasurer in their settlements for the said taxes, for all warrants so by them received.

Powers in Williamsburg and Norfolk.

XIX. AND *be it further enacted*, that the Court of Hustings in the city of *Williamsburg* and borough of *Norfolk*, and the serjeants for the said city and borough, shall have the same power to proceed in the execution of this act, and be subject to the same penalties and forfeitures, and recoverable in the same manner, as the county courts and the respective sheriffs.

Tax on private acts of Assembly.

XX. AND *be it further enacted*, that on all private acts which shall hereafter pass the General Assembly, the party or parties applying for the same, and benefited thereby, shall pay down to the clerk of the House of Delegates, for the use of the public, the sum of ten pounds, before the same shall be signed by the Speaker of either House, for which the said clerk shall, at the end of each session of Assembly, account on oath and pay into the public treasury, under penalty of being incapacitated from his said office, for failure herein.

Forfeitures appropriated.

XXI. AND *be it further enacted*, that the several forfeitures and penalties which shall or may arise in any wise by virtue of so much of this act as relates to the collection of duties on wines, spirits, sugar, coffee, and other merchandize, and on tonnage, shall be one half for and towards the raising and supporting the hospital for aged and disabled seamen, and the other half to the use of the informer, to be recovered upon information in any court of record.

Deer-skins added to commutables.

XXII. AND *be it further enacted*, that skins of deer, well dressed and fitted for the purpose of making breeches, be added to the specificks made commutable with specie in payment of taxes, that on land excepted, by the said act. That the skins so to be paid, shall be received at the places appointed for the reception of other specificks, and at the price of eight shillings *per* pound for every deer skin.

This act to be given in charge to the grand jury.

XXIII. AND *be it further enacted*, that the presiding Magistrate of the respective courts to be held in the months of *May* and *November* annually, shall give this act in charge to the grand jury; and the clerk of the court shall also furnish the said jury with a list of the taxable property taken by the Justices of the county, for their inspection and information. All and every act or acts, matter or thing, contrary to and not within the purview of this act, are hereby repealed.

Northern Neck quit-rents sequestered.

XXIV. AND whereas no provision is made by this act, or by the act for equalizing the land tax, to credit the citizens in the Northern-Neck for so much of the land tax as their respective quit-rents may amount to: And whereas, since the death of the late proprietor of the Northern-Neck, there is reason to suppose that the said proprietorship hath descended upon alien enemies: *Be it therefore enacted*, that persons holding land in the Northern-Neck, shall retain sequestered in their hands, all quit-rents which are now due, until the right of descent shall be more fully ascertained, and the General Assembly shall make final provision thereon; and all quit-rents which may hereafter become due within the limits of the said Northern-Neck, shall be paid into the public treasury under the operation of the laws of this session of Assembly, for which quit-rents the inhabitants of the said Northern-Neck shall be exonerated from the future claim of the proprietor.

C H A P. IX.

An act granting a conditional pardon to certain offenders.

Private.

C H A P. X.

An act to dissolve the vestry of the parish of St. Anne, *in the county of* Essex.

Private.

C H A P. XI.

An act to empower the Justices of Greenbrier *county to clear a waggon road from the Warm Springs to* Augusta.

Private.

C H A P. XII.

An act for the recovery of arms and accoutrements belonging to the state.

Preamble.

I. WHEREAS sundry arms and accoutrements belonging to the public are in the hands of individuals, who have neglected to return them to the proper officers; and it is necessary that such arms and accoutrements should be recovered as speedily as possible: *Be it enacted*, that the Governor do, on the passing of this act, issue his proclamation, enjoining all persons having in their possession any arms or accoutrements whatsoever, belonging to the state, to deliver them without delay to the Lieutenant or commanding officer of the county for the time being; and the sheriff of each county within this commonwealth, shall cause copies of the said proclamation, which shall be transmitted to him by the Executive, to be fixed up in the most public places in his county, and if after one month from such public notice having been given, any person possessing any such public arms or accoutrements shall be convicted of having failed to deliver them up as aforesaid, such person shall, upon every such conviction, be liable to the penalty of twenty pounds, to be recovered by action of debt, bill, plaint or information, in any court of record within this commonwealth, one half of which penalty shall go to the informer, on conviction of the offender, and the other half shall be applied in aid of the county levy where such offender shall reside. And the Lieutenant, or commanding officer of each county, shall make returns from time to time, to the Executive, of all arms and accoutrements so delivered to him, and also deliver them to the order of the Executive, under the penalty, if he fail in all or any part of his duty, of fifty pounds, to be recovered as aforesaid, and applied in diminution of the county levy: *Provided always*, that where muskets and bayonets have been by order of government placed in any county on eastern or western frontier for defence against incursions of the enemy, it shall be lawful for the Lieutenant or commanding officer to return such muskets and bayonets to the militia, taking a receipt from each person for what shall be so returned.

Proclamation for return of public arms.

Penalty on those who detain them.

County Lieutenants to return account of arms received.
Penalty.
Saving as to arms placed on frontiers.

C H A P. XIII.

An act to amend the act for calling in and funding the paper money of this state.

A. D. 1782.
See Nov. 1781,
ch. 13.
Preamble.

I. WHEREAS the time limited by an act for calling in and funding the paper money of this state hath been found too short, and many of the citizens have, from their remote situation, been precluded from an opportunity of sending their money to the public treasury: For remedy whereof, *Be it enacted,* that the Treasurer shall be, and he is hereby authorized and required, to receive the paper money issued by this state, and grant certificates for the same in manner prescribed by the said recited act, until the first day of *June* next, and no longer; any law to the contrary thereof notwithstanding.

Time for returning money lengthened.

II. AND *be it further enacted,* that any person possessed of, or holding any money emitted by Congress, or by this state, shall be at liberty to lay out the same in the purchase of warrants for unappropriated lands, at the price now established by law, at any time before the said first day of *June.*

State or continental money to be received for land.

C H A P. XIV.

An act to repeal the several acts of Assembly respecting the Commissioner of the War Office, and the Commercial Agent.

Had its effect.

C H A P. XV.

An act to indemnify certain persons in suppressing a conspiracy against this state.

Private.

C H A P. XVI.

An act concerning the two legions raised by this state.

Had its effect.

C H A P. XVII.

An act to prohibit intercourse with, and the admission of British *subjects into this state.*

Supposed to be temporary and at an end.

C H A P. XVIII.

An act to establish a town at the court-house in the county of Greenbrier.

Private.

C H A P. XIX.

An act for equalizing the land tax.

I. WHEREAS the land tax, as at present charged by the commissioners of the several counties, is found to be very unequal, and from experience of the past, it is certain that future valuations or assessments (although attended with great expence and delay) will not produce that equality so essentially necessary to the happiness of all the good citizens of this commonwealth: And whereas, by arranging the several counties whose soil and situation are nearly similar, into districts, a standard value is produced, whereby the accounts of every person within the said district may be justly regulated for all charges on land hereafter to be imposed, and a rule established whereby in future the tax upon landed property may be laid with ease and certainty, and collected with all possible equality: *Be it enacted,* that the counties within this commonwealth shall be laid off into four districts in manner following, that is to say: The counties of *Accomack, Northampton, Princess Anne, Norfolk, Nansemond, Isle of Wight, Southampton, Surry, Sussex, Prince George, Dinwiddie, Greensville, Brunswick, Chesterfield, Henrico, Charles City, James City, New Kent, York, Warwick, King and Queen, Elizabeth City, Hanover, Gloucester, Middlesex, Essex, King William, Caroline, Spotsylvania, Lancaster, Northumberland, Richmond, Westmoreland, King George, Stafford, Prince William, Goochland, Powhatan, Cumberland, Amelia,* and *Fairfax,* shall compose the first class. The counties of *Loudoun, Fauquier, Culpeper, Orange, Louisa, Fluvanna, Lunenburg, Mecklenburg, Prince Edward, Charlotte, Albemarle, Buckingham, Berkeley, Amherst, Campbell, Halifax, Bedford,* and *Frederick,* shall compose the second class. The counties of *Pittsylvania, Henry, Botetourt, Shenandoah, Rockingham, Augusta, Rockbridge,* and *Hampshire,* shall compose the third class: And the counties of *Washington, Montgomery, Greenbrier, Monongalia, Ohio, Fayette, Jefferson,* and *Lincoln,* the fourth class. And *John Pendleton,* junior, and *Samuel Jones,* gentlemen, are hereby appointed to examine the returns made of the valuations of the present year, and to ascertain the average price *per* acre of all the lands in each county, within the districts aforesaid, and (carrying all fractions of a penny to the benefit of the revenue) by comparing the same with the standard or average value of each district herein after declared, shall, and they are hereby empowered, directed, and required, by a just *per centage,* to apply the difference to the account of every individual within the district, and add to or deduct from the same accordingly. And the said examiners shall, before they proceed on the business aforesaid, take the following oath, viz. I A. B. *do solemnly swear that I will to the best of my skill and judgment, ascertain the true average price* per *acre of the lands within the several counties of this commonwealth, agreeable to the returns made, and by comparing the same to the standard by law established, will make out a just account of the land tax of every person charged in the said returns agreeable to this act, and transmit the same as by law required. So help me God.* And each of the said examiners, for their services herein, shall receive from the Treasurer of this commonwealth, by warrant from the Auditors (which upon receipt of the books herein after mentioned, they are and shall be empowered to grant) the sum of three hundred pounds.

Preamble.

Lands classed by counties.

Commissioners appointed to regulate the tax by the assessments.

II. AND *be it enacted,* that the average or standard of the first district is and shall be ten shillings; the average or standard of the second district is and shall be seven shillings and six pence; the average or standard of the third district five shillings and six pence; and the average or standard of the fourth district three shillings. And that the tax upon land thus equalized may be duly collected, the examiners afore-

Standard tax of each class.
Collection by their books.

V v

A. D. 1782.

said are hereby required to make out a book of the accounts of each county, and on or before the first day of *May* next transmit the same to the commissioners of the tax for each county hereafter to be appointed, who shall grant receipts for the same, and the said county commissioners shall cause a copy of the said book to be delivered to the sheriff, on or before the fifteenth day of the said month, by which the sheriff shall proceed to collect from every person named therein, the sum charged in the said book and no more. And the said examiners are hereby required to make up a separate book, or books, for each class of counties, in which each county shall be separate and distinct, arranging in alphabetical order the charges against every individual in each county, which said books shall be kept in the Auditors office.

Commissioners of the tax to be chosen for three years.

III. AND to prevent loss and confusion in consequence of alienations of property, as well as that all lands within the several counties which now are vacant and may hereafter be taken up, or which may not have been valued by the county commissioners for the present year, may be charged with a just and proper tax; *Be it enacted*, that the court of each county within this commonwealth shall, at their sessions in the months of *March* or *April*, nominate and appoint two fit persons to execute the office of commissioners of the tax within the same, who shall remain in office three years from the time of their appointment, which said commissioners, before they enter upon the duties of their office, shall before the court of the said county, take the following oath, to wit: *I A. B. do solemnly swear (or affirm, as the*

Their oath.

case may be) that I will diligent enquiry make of all lands within the county, which have not heretofore been valued, and a just valuation thereof make, agreeable to that of other lands of equal quality and situation within the said county; also of all alienations or partitions which may be made, and in all other matters and things discharge the duties of my office agreeable to law, with diligence and impartiality, to the best of my skill and judgment. So help me God. And in case of the death, refusal, or disability to act, of the said commissioners,

Duty in case of alienations on partitions.

or either of them, the county court as aforesaid shall, at any time, appoint others in their place. That it shall be the duty of the said commissioners, in all cases of alienation or partition within their said county, from the time of delivery to the sheriff of the book for collection in any one year, to the same time in the next succeeding year, to go upon the land so alienated or divided, and valuing the same at a price equal to other lands in the said county similar in soil and situation, shall give a credit to the person disposing of the same, and charge the purchaser or receiver with the tax payable thereon, and in like manner in cases where lands have not been heretofore valued, or where lands which now are vacant and may hereafter be taken up, the said county commissioners shall, and they hereby are required to value the same, and charge the owner thereof with the tax in manner aforesaid. And the said county commissioners shall annually, within two months after delivery to the sheriff of the book or list for collection, make return to the Auditors office of all alterations in the county book by addition, alienation, or partition, as aforesaid, that corresponding entries may be made in the book for each county kept at the said office; and shall make such additions or alterations in the list or book by them to be delivered for the collection

To correct former errors.

of the current year. The said commissioners shall also, and they are hereby required upon application and full proof to them made, to correct all errors which may have been made by the former commissioners, either with respect to the quantity of land or to the ownership thereof, and charge or give credit for the same; and for every entry of alteration or alienation, the said commissioners may demand and receive the sum of five shillings.

IV. AND to enable the county commissioners to make full and just valuations and returns as aforesaid, *Be it enacted*, that the clerk of the General Court shall, on or before the first day of *May* in every year,

Lists of conveyances and partitions to be furnished;

transmit, and the clerk of the county court deliver to the said commissioners, a list of all conveyances or partitions within the preceding year in the respective courts admitted to record, certifying the quantity and situation of the land so conveyed, and if the purchaser or seller shall not before the said first day of *May*, have satisfied the said commissioners as to the just value of the land, the same shall be charged as land of the best quality in the said county; and in cases of land which may now be vacant, the Register of the Land Office shall, and he is hereby required to transmit, on or before the first day of *April*,

and of patents.

in the year one thousand seven hundred and eighty four, to the commissioners of each county, a list of all grants issued from his office, or made out for vacancies within the said county, since the first day of *January* last, and in like manner before the first day of *April* in each succeeding year, of all grants issued or made out within the year preceding, to be by them valued and charged as aforesaid, for which valuation they shall be paid by the public, at the rate of two shillings and sixpence for every hundred acres contained in the said grant; and in cases of partition, by will or inheritance, the same fee may be demanded from the person entitled to such partition as where the same is done by conveyance.

V. AND whereas alienations or partitions may have been made since the valuations of the present year, or may be made before the first day of *May* next: *Be it enacted*, that the said county commissioners shall, and they are hereby authorised and required, to value all such alienations or partitions, and charge the owner with the tax arising from the same, together with the fees, in manner as heretofore is directed; and the said commissioners shall be entitled to receive from the public, the sum of twelve pounds, for copying the book or list annually, to be delivered to the sheriff, and for delivering the same and the sum of eight pounds for the return to the Auditors office, of such alterations or additions as

Allowance to auditors.

may annually take place within the county; the fees chargeable to the public shall be paid by the Treasurer on the Auditors warrants at the time of making the annual return to the Auditors office as aforesaid. The said examiners failing to perform the services by this act required, shall forfeit and pay the sum of two thousand pounds each; the Register of the Land Office shall forfeit and pay, for every offence, the sum of fifty pounds; the county commissioners for every offence, the sum of two hundred pounds each; the clerk of the General Court, or of the county courts, the sum of fifty pounds each; and the Justices of the several counties failing to make the appointments by this act required, shall forfeit and pay the sum of fifty pounds each. All which forfeitures shall be one half to the informer, the other

Penalties.

half to the use of the county where the offences shall be committed, to be recovered by information, in any court of record, giving ten days previous notice.

VI. AND be it enacted, that the valuation of lots in the cities boroughs or towns, shall (except where manifest inequality may have taken place) stand and remain as they now are; and in cases where lots

Rule as to lots in towns.

may be added to any city, borough or town, or where new towns may be established, or where alienations or partitions may take place, or where mistakes may have been made in former valuations, the county commissioners aforesaid shall be governed by the same rules and regulations as by this act are established with regard to land in like cases.

VII. AND be it further enacted, that in case of the death, disability, or refusal to act of the examiners appointed by this act, or either of them, it shall be lawful for the Governor, with advice of Council, to fill up the vacancy occasioned thereby.

A. D. 1782.

C H A P.   XX.

An act to secure the estate of Maurice Wheeler *to* Lettice Wheeler *his widow, and four children.*

Private.

C H A P.   XXI.

An act concerning pensioners.

Private.

C H A P.   XXII.

An act to sell certain lands belonging to the estate of William Kennon, *deceased, for the benefit of his children.*

Private.

C H A P.   XXIII.

An act to vest certain escheatable property in the children of William Short, *deceased.*

Private.

C H A P.   XXIV.

An act concerning the titles of settlers on lands surveyed for sundry companies.

See May 1779, ch. 12. Preamble.

I. WHEREAS by the act of Assembly entitled *An act for adjusting and settling the titles of claimers to unpatented lands, under the present and former government, previous to the establishment of the commonwealth's Land Office,* the titles of settlers on land surveyed for sundry companies by orders of Council, were to be adjudged by certain commissioners appointed for that purpose; and that if the parties, their heirs or assigns, to whom such titles shall be adjudged, shall not, within six months at farthest, from the time of their respective judgments in their favour, pay or tender to the company to whom the same is due, or their agent, the price and interest so fixed by the commissioners, the title of every person so failing, shall be forfeited, and to all intents and purposes, null and void.

II. AND whereas it is represented to this present General Assembly, that from the great scarcity of specie, the persons to whom such titles have been adjudged, have not been able to pay the price of their lands and interest within the time limited by the said act: *Be it therefore enacted,* that so much of the said recited act, as respects the forfeiture of the titles of settlers on lands surveyed for any company, shall be, and the same is hereby repealed; and the time limited as above for the settlers to pay the price of their lands, shall be, and hereby is prolonged for twelve months, at the end of which time, the said settlers shall be liable to pay the principal and interest due for their lands, upon good and sufficient titles being tendered or made to them; and on failure of such payment, the said land shall be forfeited and revert to the grantees.

Farther time allowed to pay their money.

C H A P.   XXV.

An act to confirm the sale of certain lots and land made by Andrew Wodrow, *administrator of* Alexander Wodrow, *deceased, and for other purposes.*

Private.

C H A P.   XXVI.

An act to vest the capitol square, with the buildings thereon, in the city of Williamsburg, *in the Mayor, Recorder, Aldermen, and Common Council of the said city.*

Private.

C H A P.   XXVII.

An act granting pardon to Demsey Butler.

Private.

C H A P.   XXVIII.

An act to authorize the adjournment of the courts of Henrico *and of the city of* Richmond, *in certain cases, and for other purposes.*

Private.

C H A P.   XXIX.

An act concerning John Younghusband.

Private.

C H A P.   XXX.

An act to suspend in part the operation of the laws concerning escheats and forfeitures from British *subjects.*

Private.

C H A P.   XXXI.

An act for giving certain powers to the corporation of the city of Richmond, *and for other purposes.*

Private.

C H A P.   XXXII.

An act to appoint persons to convey certain lands to Edwin Gray, *and for other purposes.*

Private.

C H A P.   XXXIII.

An act concerning Surveyors.

See Oct. 1783, ch. 32. Preamble.

I. WHEREAS by the laws of this commonwealth, no entry for vacant and unappropriated lands can be made with any person except the principal surveyor of the county in which such vacant and unappropriated land lies, and in many of the counties on the eastern waters great inconveniencies have arisen from having no surveyor, nor any person residing within the county willing

A.D. 1782.

Surveyors on eaf-
tern waters may be
non-refidents.
Altered Oct. 1783,
ch. 32.

to undertake the said office: *Be it therefore enacted*, that where the court of any county on the eastern waters shall recommend any person, not resident in their county, to the Governor and Council, who shall be found qualified by the President and Masters of *William* and *Mary* College, to execute the office of surveyor, the Governor may, and he is hereby authorized, to commission such person in the same manner as if he was actually resident within the county from which such recommendation came; and when thus commissioned as surveyor, such person may and shall act and do in all respects as the surveyor of such county. And where any person shall hold a warrant from the Land Office, or be desirous to make an entry in any county on the said eastern waters for vacant and unappropriated land, and there shall be no surveyor qualified to act in such county, then it shall and may be lawful for such person to make such entry with the clerk of the county court, and the same surveyed by any legal surveyor of the next or neighbouring county, shall be good and sufficient to enable such person to obtain a patent or grant therefor.

Entries how to be
made when no fur-
veyor;
and how furveyed.
Principal may ap-
point one deputy.
Entries in the
Northern-Neck.

II. AND be it further enacted, that it shall and may be lawful for the principal surveyor of any county within this commonwealth, to appoint one deputy, for whose conduct the principal shall be answerable; who shall, in the absence or indisposition of such principal, keep the office, and transact the business of the same, in the same manner as such principal surveyor might have done.

III. AND whereas the death of the Right Honorable *Thomas* Lord *Fairfax*, may occasion great inconvenience to those who may incline to make entries for vacant lands in the Northern-Neck: *Be it therefore further enacted*, that all entries made with the surveyors of the counties within the Northern-Neck, and returned to the office formerly kept by the said *Thomas* Lord *Fairfax*, shall be held, deemed, and taken, as good and valid in law as those heretofore made under the direction of the said *Thomas* Lord *Fairfax*, until some mode shall be taken up and adopted by the General Assembly concerning the territory of the Northern-Neck.

C H A P. XXXIV.

An act to amend the act for defending and protecting the trade of Chesapeake *bay.*

See May 1782,
ch 23.
Sale of ship direct-
ed.

I. BE it enacted by the General Assembly, that the commissioners appointed under the act for defending and protecting the trade of *Chesapeake* bay, shall, and they are hereby empowered and required, to sell and dispose of the ship *Cormorant*, with her appurtenances, in such manner and upon such conditions, as they may judge best; and the money arising therefrom, to be by the said commissioners applied towards building and fitting out other vessels more proper for the defence of the trade of the said bay.

Tax on feamen
and mariners.

II. AND be it further enacted, that the several and respective Naval Officers within this commonwealth, shall receive from each Captain or commander of any vessel at the time of their entrance or clearance, one shilling for every seaman and mariner on board his vessel, an account of which each and every Captain is hereby required to render upon oath, and pay to such Naval Officer, before he shall be permitted to clear or enter his vessel, to be accounted for and paid by the said Naval Officers in like manner and under the same penalties and forfeitures as is directed and prescribed in the case of other duties; and that the money arising from the duty aforesaid, shall be applied towards building and supporting an hospital for disabled seamen and mariners.

For an hospital.

Wages of feamen
how to be paid.

III. AND to the end that the officers, seamen, and mariners, may be punctually paid their wages, *Be it enacted*, that the said commissioners shall fix certain days and a particular place for paying the said wages once in three months, at which time and place the same shall be paid to each respective officer, seaman, and mariner. In case any officer, seaman, or mariner, shall fail to attend as aforesaid to receive his wages, the same shall be paid whenever afterwards demanded. If any officer, seaman, or mariner, be killed in action with the enemy, his widow and children shall receive the wages due at the time of his death. And that all officers, seamen, and mariners, or their representatives, shall be entitled to the same bounty in lands and other emoluments as the officers and soldiers of the *Virginia* line on continental establishment.

Officers, feamen,
and mariners, to
have land bounty.

Their fitnefs to be
inquired into.

IV. AND be it further enacted, that the Executive shall direct a court to be held to consist of not less than three experienced officers in the naval department, for the purpose of enquiring into the abilities and fitness of the several officers belonging to the navy, and the said court shall certify their proceedings to the Executive, who are empowered and required to discharge such of the said officers as shall appear expedient to them; and the Governor with advice of Council shall have power to commission, on recommendation from the commissioners, any other officers that may be judged necessary and proper.

C H A P. XXXV.

An act to repeal part of the act for feizure and condemnation of British *goods found on land.*

Repealed, May
1783, ch. 6.

C H A P. XXXVI.

An act for the better collecting the fees due, or to become due, to the clerks of the fuperior courts.

See ch. 48.

Preamble.
When the accounts of
fees to be delivered.

When to be collected
or distrained for.

When to be ac-
counted for.

I. FOR the better collecting and paying the fees which are now due, or may hereafter become due, to the clerks of the Courts of Appeals, High Court of Chancery, and General Court, *Be it enacted*, that the clerk of each of the said courts shall annually before the first day of *May*, deliver, or cause to be delivered, to the sheriff of every county within this commonwealth, their accounts of fees due from any person residing therein, which shall be signed by the said clerks. And the sheriff is hereby empowered and required to receive such accounts, and to collect, levy, and receive, the several quantities of tobacco therein charged, of the persons chargeable therewith; and if such person or persons, after the said fees shall be demanded, shall refuse or delay to pay the same until after the first day of *July* in any year, the sheriff of that county wherein such person inhabits, shall have full power, and he is hereby required, to make distress and sale of the slaves or goods and chattels of the party so refusing or delaying payment. That the sheriff of every county shall, on or before the fifteenth day of *September* in every year, account with each of the said clerks for all fees put into his hands pursuant to this act, and pay the same to them at their offices in *Richmond*, or in such other place as the treasury may be kept in at the time of the payment, abating ten *per cent.* for collecting. And if any sheriff shall refuse or neglect to account or pay the whole account of fees put into his hands after the deduction aforesaid is made, together with an allowance of what is charged to persons not dwelling, or having no visible estate, in his county, of which insolvencies an account shall be made out upon oath; it shall and may be lawful for each of the said clerks, upon a motion made to the next succeeding General Court, on the twentieth day thereof, to demand judgment against such sheriff, for all fees wherewith he shall be chargeable by virtue of this act; and such court, without any other notice being given of such motion than is given by this act, is hereby authorized and required to give judgment accordingly, in which no attorney's fees shall be taxed, and thereupon to award execution, upon which the clerk shall endorse "that no security is to be taken;" and upon such motion, which the said court may, if they see cause, continue to any other day of the court, or until the next court, the sheriff's receipt given for the said fees shall be admitted as full and complete evidence of the amount thereof put into his hands to collect.

A. D. 1782.

Remedy against sheriffs.

II. *AND be it further enacted,* that so much of all and every act or acts of Assembly as comes within the purview of this act, be, and the same is hereby repealed.

Repealing clause

C H A P. XXXVII.

An act for incorporating the Rector and Trustees of Liberty-Hall *academy.*

Private.

C H A P. XXXVIII.

An act for further continuing and amending the act to make provision for the support and maintenance of ideots, lunatics, and persons of unsound minds.

See Oct. 1778, ch. 6, and notes.

I. WHEREAS the act of General Assembly passed in the year of our Lord one thousand seven hundred and seventy nine, entitled *An act to make provision for the support and maintenance of ideots, lunatics, and persons of unsound minds,* which hath been continued and amended by several subsequent acts, will expire at the end of the present session of Assembly, and it is expedient and necessary to continue and amend the same: *Be it therefore enacted,* that the said act shall continue and be in force from and after the present session of Assembly, for and during the term of ten years, and from thence to the end of the next session of Assembly.

Preamble.

Continuance of act.

II. AND whereas great inconveniencies have arisen from the want of proper funds to support the hospital established for the purpose of providing for such unfortunate persons: *Be it enacted,* that the Treasurer for the time being, upon the Governor's warrant to the Court of Directors, is hereby empowered and required to pay annually, out of the treasury, such sum or sums of money as shall be by law appropriated for the repairing the said hospital, the payment of salaries to the keeper and matrons, and also to the nurses, guards, physicians, or surgeons, that may be employed by the said Court of Directors, and any additional sum not exceeding twenty five pounds *per annum,* for the support and maintenance of each person that shall be confined in the said hospital. And the sheriff, or other officer, conveying such unfortunate persons to the said hospital, agreeable to the directions of the said recited act, shall receive from the Treasurer such compensation for his trouble and expences, as to the Court of Directors shall seem reasonable, to be certified by them to the Auditors of public accounts, whereupon a warrant shall issue to the Treasurer for the payment of the same, who is hereby authorized to pay the amount of such warrant to such sheriff, or other officer, out of such money as shall be by law appropriated for that purpose. All and every act or acts, coming within the purview and meaning of this act, shall be, and the same are hereby repealed.

Money to be paid by treasurer.

Allowance to sheriff for conveying

Repeal.

C H A P. XXXIX.

An act concerning the appointment of sheriffs.

See May 1783, ch. 32; Oct. 1783, ch. 2.

I. BE it enacted by the General Assembly, that the court of every county within this commonwealth, shall annually between the last day of *March* and the last day of *May,* nominate to the Governor or Chief Magistrate for the time being, two persons named in the commission of the peace for their county, one of which persons so nominated shall be commissioned by the Governor to execute the office of sheriff of that county, and shall qualify to his commission at the court to be held for the county in *November,* or if no court shall be then held, or he shall be unable to attend, at the next succeeding court. Every person accepting the commission of sheriff, shall, before his being sworn into or executing his office, enter into bond before the Justices of his county court, with good and sufficient security, in the sum of ten thousand pounds, for the true and faithful collecting, accounting for, and paying the taxes imposed by law in his county; which bond every county court is hereby empowered and required to demand, take, and cause to be acknowledged before them in open court, and recorded; and an attested copy thereof shall be transmitted by the clerk, to the Auditors of public accounts, at the same time that he delivers to the said Auditors a copy of the list of the taxable property in his said county, which shall be admitted as evidence in any suit or proceeding founded thereon. Any person recommended as aforesaid, or appointed sheriff, refusing to accept and execute such commission to him directed, shall forfeit and pay the sum of fifty pounds, for the use of the county where such refusal shall be, to be recovered with costs, by action of debt or information, in any court of record, except as is excepted in the act, entitled *An act prescribing the method of appointing sheriffs. and for limiting the time of their continuance in office, and directing their duty therein.* So much of the said recited act as comes within the purview of this act is hereby repealed.

How to be recommended and appointed.

To give bond.

Penalty for refusing office.

Repeal.

C H A P. XL.

An act to amend the act for calling in and redeeming certain certificates.

Had its effect.

C H A P. LXI.

An act concerning the legion under the command of Colonel Dabney.

Had its effect.

W w

C H A P.   XLII.

An act to repeal the act entitled An act to enable the Congress of the United States to levy a duty on certain goods and merchandizes, and also on all prizes.

C H A P.   XLIII.

Private.

An act for establishing a town in the county of Bedford.

C H A P.   XLIV.

Repealed Oct 1784.

An act to amend the act entitled An act for establishing and regulating the militia.

C H A P.   XLV.

An act to amend an act entitled An act to repeal so much of a former act as suspends the issuing of executions on certain judgments until December 1783.

See Nov. 1781, ch 22; May 1782, ch. 44.

Preamble.

British debts.

I. WHEREAS from an act entitled *An act to repeal so much of a former act as suspends the issuing executions upon certain judgments until* December *one thousand seven hundred and eighty three,* sundry great and ruinous inconveniencies and hardships will result to the good people of this commonwealth, unless a speedy remedy be applied: *Be it enacted by the General Assembly,* that no debt or demand whatsoever contracted with, or due to any *British* subject, or contracted with or due to any other person, for the use of, or in concern with, any *British* subject, and still remaining unpaid, shall be recoverable in any court of record within this commonwealth, notwithstanding the same may have been renewed, changed, altered, or acknowledged to any agent, partner, or assignee of such *British* subject, or to any other person whatsoever, either for their own use or benefit, or for the use or benefit of such *British* subject, since the nineteenth day of *April,* in the year one thousand seven hundred and seventy five, any law to the contrary in any wise notwithstanding.

II. AND whereas from the commencement of hostilities by the *British* against these United States, and the subsequent proceedings of the General Convention and General Assembly, there is reason to believe that much fraud has been used to secure the debts due to *British* subjects, their agents or factors within this commonwealth, by pretended sales, exchanges or assignments (to the citizens thereof, or other persons qualified to maintain suits for the recovery of such debts) bearing date prior to the nineteenth day of *April* one thousand seven hundred and seventy five, thereby interesting a part of the citizens in supporting the *British* interest and connection, to the injury of another part, and to the disturbance of the peace and harmony of the commonwealth: *Be it therefore enacted;* that where any debt or demand whatsoever originally due to a *British* subject, his or her agent or factor, shall have been transferred by assignment or otherwise, to any citizen of this commonwealth, or to any other person capable of maintaining a suit for the recovery of the same, before the said nineteenth day of *April* in the year one thousand seven hundred and seventy five, such debt or demand shall not be recoverable in any court within this commonwealth, unless it shall appear on the trial of any suit or suits for the recovery thereof, that the same was transferred or assigned for the full value thereof *bona fide* paid at the time of such assignment or transfer, before the said nineteenth day of *April* one thousand seven hundred and seventy five, and that notice thereof shall have been given to the debtor before the tenth day of *September,* in the year one thousand seven hundred and seventy five, the proof of the said consideration paid, the time of assignment or transfer, and the notice thereof given as aforesaid, to be on the person or persons claiming such debt or demand.

III. AND be it further enacted, that where it shall appear on the trial of any suit for the recovery of any such debt originally due to a *British* subject, that the person or persons so claiming the same, or any other person for them, hath been privy to any fraud or collusion in procuring or accepting any assignment or transfer of such debt, judgment shall be given for treble costs to the defendant: *Provided always,*

Citizens partners with British creditors.

that nothing herein contained shall be construed to prevent any citizen of this commonwealth who has been in copartnership with any *British* subject or subjects, and who was resident therein before the said nineteenth day of *April* one thousand seven hundred and seventy five, continued so since that time, and given assurance of fidelity as the law requires, from prosecuting by attachment in the High Court of Chancery, or any county court in Chancery, and recovering the just sum or balance which may be due to him for his share or proportion of the debts or effects of such copartnership.

IV. AND be it further enacted, that no such citizen who has been in partnership as aforesaid, shall be compelled to pay the debts due from such copartners to any person whatsoever, unless it shall appear that he has refused to discover other debts or effects whereof the claim of such citizen could be made.

V. AND whereas the afore recited act substitutes merchantable inspected crop tobacco, hemp, and flour, in lieu of money to discharge executions to be issued on certain judgments, but from the want of a sufficiency of specie and the great scarcity of those commutable articles, arising from the late general and deplorable drought, the ease and benefit intended by the Legislature from the said act, will not be derived to the citizens of this commonwealth, and it is reasonable that other commutables be substituted in addition to those named in the said recited act: *Be it therefore enacted,* that whenever judgments have been or shall be obtained, or *scire facias* sued out to revive a judgment for any sum or sums of money exceeding one hundred pounds current money, it shall and may be lawful for the debtor, or his attorney, to tender to the creditor, or his attorney, lands in discharge of the said judgment, and submit his title papers to the opinion of the court, and the said title being approved, execution may be then awarded; provided that the creditor shall appoint one freeholder, and the debtor another, convenient to the land; and on refusal of the debtor or his attorney, so to do, execution shall issue without such appointment. And whenever executions shall issue in manner and form aforesaid, the freeholders so elected, shall, within twenty days after notice given, under penalty of one hundred pounds each, to be recovered at the suit of the creditor, proceed on oath, which oath may be administered by any Magistrate in the county where the lands lie, to value the lands so tendered as the same would sell for in specie for ready money, according to the best of their judgments; and whenever it shall so happen that the two so elected shall disagree, then they are directed to appoint one other freeholder, who, on oath, first to be administered as aforesaid, shall affix the valuation to which-ever of the two valuations he shall think most just and reasonable. *Provided always,* that no debtor shall be admitted to tender any lands without discovering first, on oath, whether there are any prior mortgages or incumbrances thereon within his knowledge, and that the said lands be in one entire tract, or part of a larger tract, in convenient form, and situated within one hundred miles of the usual place of residence of the creditor; and where the

Lands may be tendered on a judgment above 100l.

Proceedings thereon.

A. D. 1782.

Creditor is not resident within this state, then within one hundred miles of the usual place of residence of the debtor. And that good and sufficient deeds for the same be made, executed and delivered, before the debtor shall be discharged from the execution, and then the creditor shall receive the same according to the valuation aforesaid, in discharge of the execution, or so much thereof as the said valuation may amount to. *Provided also*, that where lands shall be so tendered, and executions issue as aforesaid, then the debtor, on finding good and sufficient security for the doing and performing all things required by this act, may be discharged from close custody.

VI. AND be it further *enacted*, that whenever judgment shall be obtained, or *scire facias* to renew judgment for any sum exceeding twenty pounds current money sued out, it shall and may be lawful to discharge the same in negroes, to be tendered and valued in manner directed for the tendering and valuation of lands. *Provided always*, that whenever it shall so happen that the title to lands or negroes shall afterwards be evicted not to have been in the debtor at the time of payment to the creditor; in all such cases, it shall and may be lawful for the creditor to sue out new execution on his former judgment, and moreover shall have his action of damages against such debtor, for all damages and costs of suits which he has incurred in defending the title.

Slaves may be tendered on judgments above 20l.

VII. AND whereas by the afore recited act, no executions are permitted to be issued until the first of *March* one thousand seven hundred and eighty three, and from the construction thereof many frauds have and may arise: In remedy whereof, *Be it enacted*, that whenever any person confesses judgment in custody, where no special bail has been given, or where such person or persons have been delivered up by his or their special bail, in discharge of his or their recognizance, in all such cases it shall and may be lawful for the plaintiff to pray the defendant in execution; any thing in the said law to the contrary notwithstanding; and then and thereafter the same process may be had in such cases as has been heretofore in use within the limits of this commonwealth. *Provided always*, that any thing herein contained, shall not be construed to extend to any contract specifying in what manner the same shall be paid, unless the said contract specifies payment to be made in coin, which has been heretofore in use in this country, nor to any contract whatsoever, made or entered into since the first day of *January* one thousand seven hundred and eighty two, for all which debts or contracts, judgment may be obtained, execution issue, to be discharged in manner specified by the said contract, and no commutable article whatever be admitted to pay the same. And all and every thing in the said act or any other act whatsoever, not compatible with the above and every part thereof, is, and the same is hereby declared to be repealed. *Provided always*, that nothing in this or any other act (except for *British* debts as aforesaid) shall prevent the recovering by executions, debts under five pounds, but that the same shall be prosecuted in like manner as if this or any other act to the contrary thereof, had never been made.

New execution if creditors be evicted of lands or slaves.

Debtor may be committed on confessing judgment in custody or being surrendered.

Contracts, what kind excepted.

Debts under 5l. excepted.

VIII. AND whereas the settlers on lands surveyed for sundry companies, which settlers, by an act entitled *An act concerning the titles of settlers on lands surveyed for sundry companies*, passed this present session of Assembly, are to have the time prolonged for the term of twelve months to pay the principal and interest of the purchase money for their lands to the said grantees or agents; and it is just and reasonable that the said settlers should be benefitted in the same manner as other debtors are: *Be it enacted*, that the said settlers shall and may discharge the said principal and interest, in the commutables mentioned in this act, without any judgment or execution issuing at or before the end of the term limited for the said lands to revert to the grantees. *Provided nevertheless*, that this act shall continue and be in force from and after the passing thereof, until the first day of *December* one thousand seven hundred and eighty three.

Land purchasers of companies included.

Continuance of act.

CHAP. XLVI.

An act to regulate the pay of the militia heretofore called into service in cases not provided for by law.

I. WHEREAS no provision is made by law for the pay of the militia heretofore called into service, except such militia shall have marched out of the state, or joined the army acting within this state: For remedy whereof, *Be it enacted*, that all militia called into service since the first day of *January*, one thousand seven hundred and eighty, or who shall hereafter be called into service, whose rolls have not already been settled, shall receive the same pay and rations as the officers and soldiers of the continental army; and the Auditors of public accounts are hereby directed to grant printed certificates for the same. *Provided nevertheless*, that no militia officer or soldier shall be entitled to receive pay as aforesaid, except such officer or soldier shall have been on duty ten days:

Preamble.

Their pay.

None for less than ten days service.

II. AND whereas the allowance to scouts employed for discovering the approach of *Indian* or any other enemy, on the frontiers, is inadequate to their fatigue and trouble: *Be it enacted*, that every scout who shall hereafter be employed, as by law directed, shall be entitled to receive for every day he shall be so employed, the sum of five shillings *per* day, to be audited and paid in the same manner as the militia in this act is directed to be paid.

Pay of scouts.

CHAP. XLVII.

An act to empower the Naval officers to receive the duties in the several districts.

I. BE it enacted by the General *Assembly*, that all duties and customs which now, or shall hereafter accrue due to this commonwealth, upon ships, vessels, goods, wares, and merchandizes, or any other articles whatsoever, by virtue of any law of this commonwealth, may and shall be paid to the Naval Officer of the district where such duty or custom is directed to be paid. And the respective Naval Officers are hereby required to collect, account for, and pay into the public treasury, the amount of all such duties or customs, according to the several acts imposing the same, and under the pains and penalties therein contained.

Naval Officers appointed to be collectors of duties on ships, &c.

CHAP. XLVIII.

An act to revive and amend an act, for the better regulating and collecting certain officers fees, and for other purposes therein mentioned.

See act 1745, ch. 2; also this session, ch. 36.

Preamble.

I. WHEREAS the act of Assembly passed in the year of our Lord one thousand seven hundred and forty five, entitled *An act for the better regulating and collecting certain officers fees, and other purposes therein mentioned*, hath expired, and it is expedient and necessary that the same should be revived and amended: *Be it therefore enacted*, that the act entitled, *An act for the better regu-*

A. D. 1782.

Former act revived.

lating and collecting certain officers and fees, and other purposes therein mentioned, be revived and shall continue and be in force from and after the passing of this act, for and during the term of two years, and from thence to the end of the next session of Assembly, and no longer.

See Oct. 1781, *ch.* 31.

II. AND be it further enacted, that all persons who now are, or shall hereafter become chargeable with any tobacco fees, for services mentioned in the said recited act, shall discharge the same in manner directed by the act of Assembly passed in the year one thousand seven hundred and eighty one, entitled *An act for regulating tobacco fees, and fixing the allowance to sheriffs, witnesses, and venire-men.*

Attornies act revived. See 1761, *ch.* 3.

III. AND whereas the act of Assembly passed in the year one thousand seven hundred and sixty one, entitled *An act for regulating the practice of attornies,* hath expired, and it is necessary the same should be revived: *Be it therefore enacted by the General Assembly,* that the act entitled *An act for regulating the practice of attornies,* shall be, and the same is hereby revived.

C H A P.   XLIX.

Executed.

An act to amend the act entitled An act for adjusting certain public claims.

At a GENERAL ASSEMBLY begun and held at the Public Buildings in the City of *Richmond,* on *Monday* the 5th day of *May,* in the Year of our Lord 1783.

C H A P.   I.

An act for establishing pilots and regulating their fees.

See Oct. 1783, *ch.* 13.

Preamble.

Certain persons appointed to examine and grant them branches.

Pilots to keep sufficient boats.

Penalties.

I. WHEREAS it is necessary for the safety and preservation of vessels coming into the bay of *Chesapeake,* bound up the rivers of this commonwealth, that able and experienced pilots should be established to conduct such vessels, for reasonable fees, to their several moorings, and to prevent ignorant and unskilful persons from undertaking such pilotage: *Be it enacted,* that *Paul Loyal, Thomas Brown, James Barron, John Gwinn, Edward Cowper, Charles Bailey,* and *William Ballard,* or any three of them, be, and they are hereby appointed to examine every person that shall desire to be admitted a pilot, he first producing a certificate from the county court where he resides, of his honesty and good behaviour, paying down to the examiners the sum of thirty shillings; and if upon examination the person shall appear of sufficient skill and ability, the said examiners shall thereupon grant such person a branch, and thenceforth he shall be reputed a lawful pilot. *Provided,* that no person whatsoever, shall be permitted to execute the business of a pilot, notwithstanding he may have such branch as aforesaid, unless he or the company to which he belongs, shall keep one sufficient boat of eighteen feet keel at the least, under the penalty of fifty pounds for every vessel such pilot shall undertake to conduct; to be recovered with costs, in any court of record in this state, by the party suing for the same, to his or their own use: And if any person not having such branch, and keeping such boat as aforesaid, shall presume to take upon himself to conduct or pilot any vessel coming from sea to any place or places hereafter mentioned, every such person shall forfeit and pay the sum of fifty pounds; to be recovered with costs, in any court within this state, by the party suing for the same; and moreover such person shall be liable for all damages occasioned by his undertaking the pilotage; to be recovered by action at common law, in any court within this state, by the party grieved. *Provided,* that this act shall not be construed to extend to hinder any person or persons from assisting any vessel in distress, so as he or they shall deliver up such vessel to the pilot who shall come on board and offer to undertake the conduct of her, for which such assistant shall and may demand and receive from the said pilot, half the fees allowed for pilotage by this act.

Proviso.

No more than two pilots to be in partnership.

II. AND whereas great inconveniencies have arisen from pilots entering into combination or partnership, which has occasioned great neglect of their duty: For prevention whereof, *Be it enacted,* that no more than two pilots shall be in partnership, under the penalty of one hundred pounds each, to be recovered with costs, by any person suing for the same.

Rules for masters of ships and pilots.

III. AND for the encouragement of pilots to do their duty, and that all pilots may be induced to keep a good look-out, *Be it enacted,* that every master of a merchant's vessel coming from sea, shall be obliged to receive the first pilot who offers to conduct his vessel, or shall pay him full pilotage to the first port, and shall continue the same pilot to his first port of discharge; and every pilot cruising or standing out to sea, shall offer his services first to the vessel which may be nearest the land, or in most distress. And if any pilot, not being hindred by sickness, or other lawful cause, shall refuse to go on board any vessel, when required by the master, to execute his office, such pilot or pilots, in either case, shall, upon complaint and conviction before the examiners, or any three of them, forfeit to the party grieved, twenty pounds, and be liable to be suspended by them, for such term or time as they shall think fit.

Pilots incapacitated and liable to damages for losing ships.

IV. AND be it enacted, that if any pilot shall negligently or carelessly lose any vessel under his care, and be thereof convicted by due course of law, he shall forever after such conviction, be incapable of acting as a pilot in this state, and shall be also liable to pay all such damages any person or persons shall sustain by such negligence or carelessness, to be recovered as is before directed.

Rates of pilotage.

V. AND for preventing any exorbitant demands for pilotage, *Be it enacted,* that the following, and no greater prices, shall be taken or demanded, to wit: On *James* river, for all square rigged vessels coming from sea, from cape *Henry* or *Lynhaven* bay to *Hampton* road, forty shillings; and for going out to sea, thirty shillings; and for each foot depth of water they draw, from *Hampton* road or *Seawell's* point to *Norfolk*, two shillings *per* foot; to *Sleepy-Hole* or *Sack Point*, in *Nansemond*, three shillings *per* foot; to *Pagan* creek, two shillings and three pence *per* foot; to *Jamestown*, six shillings *per* foot; to *Martin's Brandon*, six shillings and six pence per foot; to *Flower de Hundred*, seven shillings *per* foot; to *City-Point* or *Bermuda Hundred*, nine shillings *per* foot; to *Four-Mile* creek, eleven shillings *per* foot; to *Osborne's*, twelve shillings and six pence *per* foot; to *Warwick*, fourteen shillings *per* foot; and to *Richmond*, fifteen shillings *per* foot. On *York* river, coming from sea, from the cape or *Lynhaven* to *York* town, three pounds; and for going out to sea, two pounds; from *Back* river or *Egg*-island to *York* town, thirty shillings; from *York* town to *West-Point*, four shillings *per* foot; to *Cumberland* five shillings *per* foot; to the highest landings on *Pamunkey*, six shillings and three pence *per* foot; to *Shepherd's* four shillings and six pence *per* foot; to *Meredith's*, *Moore's*, or the highest landings on *Mattapony*, six shillings *per* foot. From cape *Henry*, to any river on *Mobjack* bay, the same pilotage as to *York* town; from the cape to *Urbanna*, coming from sea, four pounds; and for going out to sea three pounds; from *Urbanna* to *Hobbs's Hole*, three shillings *per* foot; to *Naylor's Hole*, four shillings *per* foot; to *Leed's* or *Micou's*, six shillings and six pence *per* foot; to *Port Royal* nine shillings *per* foot; to *Fredericksburg*, eleven shillings and six pence *per* foot. From the cape to *Pianketank*, the same pilotage as to *Urbanna*. From the cape to *Smith's* point, on south *Potowmack*, coming from sea, six pounds; and for going out five pounds; from *Smith's* point to *Coan* ior *Yocomico*, two shillings and six pence *per* foot; to *Machodack*, three shillings, to *Upper Machodack*, four shillings *per* foot; to *Nangomy*, five shillings; to *Boyd's Hole*, five shillings and six pence *per* foot; to *Quantico* six shillings; to *Occaquan*, six shillings and six pence *per* foot; to *Piscataway*, eight shillings; to *Alexandria*, nine shillings and six pence *per* foot; to *Eastern Branch*, ten shillings *per* foot; and the same fees by the foot back again; and from the places aforesaid to the capes, and no more; and for all sloops and schooners, two thirds of the rates of pilotage. And when any master of a vessel shall give reasonable notice to the pilot he shall employ, of the time and place such master shall appoint for his attendance, and such pilot shall attend accordingly, he may demand and take the sum of ten shillings for every day he shall be detained by such master's not being ready to proceed according to his notice; and if any pilot shall demand or exact any other greater fee, he shall forfeit double the sum so demanded, recoverable before two Justices, one of them being of the quorum, with cost, by the informer.

And allowance for disappointment.

VI. AND be it enacted, that every pilot, before he obtains his branch, shall take one white apprentice at the least, and employ him constantly on board his boat, instructing him in the art of his business, which apprentice shall have the usual allowances made him at the expiration of his apprenticeship, and shall be exempt from militia duty. *Provided always;* that no masters of vessels shall be obliged to take a pilot who shall not offer himself below the *Horse-Shoe*, but every vessel having no pilot on board, and following another that has a pilot, shall pay him half fees.

Pilot to have one white apprentice at least.
Proviso.

VII. AND to the end that strangers may not be imposed on in the rates of pilotage, as settled by this act; *Be it enacted*, that every pilot appointed in pursuance of this act shall be obliged, when he is in execution of his office, to carry with him a copy thereof, and when he receives the fees for the services performed on board any vessel, he shall produce the said copy to the master of the vessel, to shew that he demands no greater fee than is allowed by this act; and if any pilot shall neglect or refuse such copy, as aforesaid, he shall forfeit and pay twenty pounds to any person who shall sue for the same, to be recovered in any court within this state.

Pilots to carry with them and produce a copy of this act
Penalty.

VIII. AND for the further encouragement of pilots to do their duty, *Be it enacted*, that every branch pilot shall, and he is hereby exempted from, militia duty, during the time he shall act as a pilot. This act shall take place from and after the first day of *July* one thousand seven hundred and eighty three.

Branch pilots exempted from militia duty.
Commencement

IX. AND be it enacted, that the public printer shall furnish the examiners, on demand, fifty copies of this act, one of which copies, signed by three of the said examiners, shall be delivered to each pilot when he obtains his branch.

of act.

CHAP. II.

An act for the relief of sheriffs.

Occasional and at an end.

CHAP. III.

An act to amend the act entitled An act to amend the act for adjusting claims for property impressed or taken for public service.

Temporary.

CHAP. IV.

An act for further continuing several acts of Assembly.

I. WHEREAS three acts of Assembly passed in the years one thousand seven hundred and eighty one, and one thousand seven hundred and eighty two, the one entitled *An act for calling in and funding the paper money of this state, (a)* one other entitled *An act to ascertain the losses and injuries sustained from the depredations of the enemy within this commonwealth, (b)* and one other entitled *An act to ascertain the number of people within this commonwealth, (c)* will expire at the end of this present session of Assembly, and it is expedient and necessary that the same should be further continued: *Be it therefore enacted*, that the said several recited acts shall continue and be in force from and after the expiration thereof until the first day of *December* next, and no longer.

(a) See Nov. 1781, ch. 13, and Oct. 1782, ch 13.
(b) See May 1782, ch 10, Oct. 1782, ch. 4, Oct. 1783, ch 10.
(c) See May 1782, ch. 22, and Oct. 1782, ch 2.

CHAP. V.

An act to suspend the operation of the act entitled An act to amend and reduce the several acts of Assembly for ascertaining certain taxes and duties, and for establishing a permanent revenue, into one act.

Temporary and expired.

CHAP. VI.

An act to repeal the several acts of Assembly for seizure and condemnation of British goods found on land.

Had its effect.

A. D. 1783.

See Oct. 1776, ch. 43, and notes.

Preamble.

CHAP. VII.

An act to amend an act entitled An act to continue and amend an act for the inspection of pork, beef, flour, tar, pitch, and turpentine.

Price for inspection of tar, pitch and turpentine reduced.

I. WHEREAS by an act of Assembly passed the sixth day of *May*, one thousand seven hundred and eighty two, entitled *An act to continue and amend the act entitled An act for the inspection of pork, beef, flour, tar, pitch, and turpentine*, amongst other rates of inspection it is enacted, that seven pence half-penny *per* barrel be paid for the inspection of tar, pitch, and turpentine, which said rate is found to be higher than the said articles of tar, pitch, and turpentine, will bear: For remedy whereof, *Be it enacted*, that three pence *per* barrel only, be paid for the inspection of tar, pitch, and turpentine, from and after the passing of this act, any law to the contrary notwithstanding.

CHAP. VIII.

See Oct. 1780, ch. 27, and notes.

An act to establish certain and adequate funds for the redemption of certificates granted to the officers and soldiers for their arrears of pay and depreciation.

Preamble.

Tax on particular goods imported, in aid of former funds.

I. WHEREAS the funds formerly appropriated by law for the redemption of the certificates granted, or to be granted, to the officers and soldiers of the *Virginia* line, on continental and state establishments, for their arrears of pay and depreciation, have hitherto proved inadequate, and the finances of the state are at present in such circumstances that the same cannot be paid within the time limited by law, without greatly distressing the citizens thereof: And whereas certain officers, deputed on behalf of the said officers and soldiers, have presented to this present General Assembly an humble and dutiful memorial, expressing their sincere desire to prevent every embarrassment to the public during the present exhausted state of the country, and declaring their voluntary consent to postpone such payment for a reasonable time, in full confidence that the Legislature will establish certain and adequate funds for the redemption of such certificates, within the time which may be now appointed for the same: *Be it therefore enacted by the General Assembly*, that in aid of the funds hitherto appropriated for the redemption of the certificates granted, or to be granted, to the said officers and soldiers for their arrears of pay and depreciation, the following duties shall be paid on the goods, wares, and merchandize, herein after enumerated, which may be imported, either by land or water, into this state; and the money arising therefrom appropriated to the sole purpose of redeeming the said certificates, and the warrants already issued, or which may hereafter issue, for the interest of the said certificates, that is to say: On every bushel of salt, the sum of nine pence; on every gallon of distilled spirits, the sum of four pence; on every gallon of wine, the sum of four pence; on every hundred pounds of hemp, the sum of two shillings; on every hundred pounds of cordage, the sum of one shilling; on every gallon of beer, ale, or porter, the sum of four pence; on every pound of snuff, the sum of one shilling.

Master of vessel importing those goods to report his vessel and cargo in 48 hours.

Penalty.

II. AND be it further enacted, that the master or purser of every ship, or other vessel, importing any goods, wares, or merchandize, liable to a duty by virtue of this act, to any port or place within this commonwealth, shall, within forty eight hours after his arrival, make a true and just report, upon oath, with the collector of the duties in the said port or place, of the burthen, contents, or loading of such ship or vessel, with the particular numbers of every cask or package therein laden, and containing any of the aforesaid goods, wares, or merchandize, and of all parcels or quantities of any such goods, wares, or merchandize, which may be laden or stowed in bulk on board such ship or vessel, and where, and in what port, the same were laden and taken on board, upon penalty of forfeiting two hundred pounds current money, recoverable on information in any court within this commonwealth, who shall thereupon enter judgment and award execution for the same, to be applied, one moiety to the use of the informer, and the other to the use of the commonwealth.

Dutiable goods not to be landed till entry, and payment or securing the duties.

Forfeiture of goods otherwise landed.

These goods imported by land how to be entered and duty paid or secured.

Contents of certain casks ascertained.

III. AND be it further enacted, that none of the goods, wares, or merchandizes, liable to the said duties, imported or brought into this commonwealth by water, by any person or persons whatsoever, shall be landed or put on shore until due entry made thereof with the collector of the duties in such port or place, and a true account of the numbers of every cask, and quantity of distilled spirits, wine, snuff, ale, beer, or porter; and also the quantity of salt, hemp, or cordage, as aforesaid, at that port or place where the same was shipped or taken on board, given on oath before the said collector, who shall certify the same upon the back of the original invoice, or a true copy thereof to him produced, and thereupon such importer paying the duties laid by this act, or securing the payment thereof within six months, shall obtain a permit under the hand of such collector, for the landing and delivery of the same. And all spirits, wine, salt, hemp, cordage, snuff, beer, ale, or porter, landed or put on shore, or delivered, contrary to the true intent and meaning of this act, or the value thereof, shall be forfeited and lost, and may be seized or recovered by the said collector of the port or place where the same shall be put on shore or delivered, or by any other person or persons whatsoever; and the owner or importer of any of the aforesaid spirits, wine, salt, hemp, cordage, snuff, ale, beer, or porter, by land, shall, in like manner, make due entry of the same, within ten days after the importation, with the clerk of the county court wherein they are brought, who shall receive the taxes or duties payable thereon, or take bond with good and sufficient security from the importer, for the payment thereof within three months; and the said clerks shall, in case the owner or importer of the said articles shall fail to pay the duties imposed thereon, or give bond as aforesaid, proceed in like manner to seize and sell the same as is directed in the case of seizures made by the collectors or Naval Officers. *Provided always*, that no person shall be required to give account upon oath of the true contents of any pipe or lesser cask of wine, or any hogshead or lesser cask of spirits imported, but shall have liberty to enter a pipe of wine or hogshead of spirits as aforesaid, at one hundred gallons, and all lesser casks after the same proportion; any thing in this act to the contrary notwithstanding.

Penalty for a false entry.

IV. AND be it further enacted, that if any person or persons whatsoever, shall willingly make a false entry, and be thereof convicted, such person or persons shall forfeit and pay two hundred pounds current money, and also forfeit the goods, recoverable on information in any Court within this commonwealth, who shall thereupon enter judgment and award execution for the same, to be applied, one moiety to the use of the informer, and the other to the use of the commonwealth.

Officers may enter vessels and bring away dutiable goods if duty not paid or agreed for in 10 days after entry.

V. AND be it further enacted, that the collectors of the duties aforesaid, or any person by them appointed, shall have full power and authority to go and enter on board any ship or other vessel, and from thence to bring on shore any articles whatsoever, liable to a duty by virtue of this act, if such duty be not paid or agreed for within ten days after the first entry of such ship or vessel, or bond with good and sufficient security given for payment of the same within three months next after such entry, which bond, if offered, the collector is hereby authorized and required to accept and take, and such articles so brought on fhore to fecure and detain until due payment fhall be made, or fecurity given as aforefaid; and if fuch payment or fecurity be not made or given within two days from the time of fuch feizure, the collector of the duties aforefaid is hereby empowered to fell the fame, or fo much thereof as fhall be fufficient to difcharge the faid duties, and five *per centum* for the charges of fuch feizure and fale. *Provided neverthelefs*, that notice fhall be given of fuch fale, by advertifing the fame two weeks in the *Virginia* gazette; and they are alfo empowered to flay and remain on board fuch fhip or veffel until all fuch wines, fpirits, falt, hemp, cordage, fnuff, beer, ale, and porter, be difcharged and delivered out of the fame; and if any collector or collectors of the faid duties, or clerks of the county courts, or any other perfon or perfons deputed by them, or any of them, fhall directly or indirectly take or receive any bribe, recompence, or reward, in any kind whatfoever, or fhall connive at any falfe entry of the articles liable to a duty or cuftom by virtue of this act, the perfon or perfons fo offending fhall forfeit and pay the fum of two hundred pounds current money, and be for ever difabled in his faid office, and rendered incapable of holding any office or employment relating to the cuftoms within this commonwealth; and the perfon or perfons giving or offering fuch bribe, reward, or recompence, fhall forfeit and pay two hundred pounds current money.

A. D. 1783.

Proceeding thereupon.

Penalty on collector receiving a bribe or conniving at a falfe entry;

and on the perfon giving or offering fuch bribe.

VI. *AND be it further enacted,* that it fhall be lawful to and for all and every collector and collectors of the duties aforefaid, or clerks of county courts, by warrant under the hand of a Juftice of the Peace, which warrant fhall not be granted but upon an information made to him upon oath, and and accompanied with a conftable, to break open, in the day time, any houfe, warehoufe, or ftorehoufe, to fearch for, feize, and carry away, any wine, fpirits, falt, hemp, cordage, fnuff, beer, ale, or porter, liable to a duty by this act, and for which the faid duty fhall not have been paid or fecured to be paid as aforefaid; and if any collector, clerk, or conftable, fhall be fued or molefted for any thing done in execution of the powers hereby given them, fuch collector, clerk, or conftable, may plead the general iffue, and give this act in evidence; and if in fuch fuit the plaintiff be non-fuited, or judgment paffed againft him, the defendant fhall recover double cofts; and in all actions, fuits, or informations to be brought, or where any feizure fhall be made purfuant to this act, if the property thereof be claimed by any perfon as the owner or importer thereof, in fuch cafe the *onus probandi* fhall lie upon the owner or claimer.

Collectors, by warrant, and with a conftable, in the day time, may break open houfes to fearch for dutiable goods not paid for.

Onus probandi on whom thrown.

VII. *AND be it further enacted,* that when any wine, fpirits, falt, hemp, cordage, fnuff, beer, ale, or porter, fhall be configned to any perfon, other than the mafter or owner of the fhip or veffel importing the fame, every perfon to whom fuch articles fhall be configned, fhall, upon the imporation thereof, pay to the mafter or owner of the fhip or veffel importing the fame, the duty payable for fuch articles by this act; and if any perfon or perfons to whom fuch articles fhall be configned as aforefaid, fhall neglect or refufe to pay the faid duties, or give bond with fecurity for the payment thereof, to the mafter or owner of the fhip or veffel importing the fame, at fuch time as the fame fhall become payable, it fhall and may be lawful for the mafter or owner of fuch fhip or veffel, to detain fuch articles until the duty fhall be paid, or fecured to be paid, as aforefaid.

How mafters of veffels may fecure the duty of goods imported by others.

VIII. *AND be it further enacted,* that if any importer of any of the goods, wares, or merchandize aforefaid, fhall defire to tranfport the fame from one diftrict to another, within this commonwealth, he fhall before he depart out of the diftrict where fuch articles fhall be laden or taken on board, make oath before a Juftice of the Peace that the fame were legally imported, and the duties fecured according to law, and that he will not fuffer any other goods to be taken on board his veffel; and the juftices fhall give him a certificate thereof, fpecifying the marks and numbers of the faid goods, and if any other goods fhall be found on board fuch veffel, they fhall be forfeited, one half thereof to the ufe of the commonwealth, and the other half to the ufe of the informer.

Proceeding where imported goods are tranfported from one diftrict to another.

IX. *AND be it further enacted,* that it fhall and may be lawful to and for the faid collectors and clerks to recover the faid duties fo bonded, by motion made in the General Court, or the county court wherein the principal or either of his fecurities refpectively refide, and fuch court fhall give judgment for the fum due on fuch bonds, with cofts, and intereft of fix *per centum* on the fame, until paid. *Provided always,* ten days previous notice in writing fhall be given by fuch collector or clerk to the perfon or perfons fo to be moved againft: And the faid collectors and clerks refpectively, fhall be allowed for collecting, accounting for, and paying the faid duties impofed by this act, into the treafury of this commonwealth, the fum of two and an half *per centum* on the money fo collected by them or any of them; and they are hereby required to account for and pay into the treafury aforefaid, every three months, to wit: on the tenth day of *January*, on the tenth day of *April*, on the tenth day of *July*, and on the tenth day of *October*, in every year, or within ten days afterwards, all money received by them refpectively, on public account, purfuant to this act, upon pain of forfeiting one half of their commiffions, to be carried to the credit of the public Treafury, and of being fufpended from their faid office of collector or clerk, until fuch payment be made.

Collectors how they may recover the bonded duties.

Their allowance for collecting.

When to account and pay.

Or forfeit one half their commiffions and be fufpended from office till payment.

X. *AND be it further enacted,* that there fhall be paid by the owner or fhipper of every hogfhead of tobacco laden on board any fhip or other veffel for exportation, to any port or place whatfoever, the fum of four fhillings, which faid duty fhall be paid to the infpectors at the time of delivery of the fame, and fhall be accounted for, and paid by them, at the fame time, in like manner, and under the fame penalties, as is prefcribed and inflicted by the act *To amend and reduce the feveral acts of Affembly concerning the infpection of tobacco, into one act.*

Duty of 4 s. a hhd. on tobacco exported.

IX. *AND be it further enacted,* that the aforefaid duties and cuftoms fhall be appropriated to the exprefs purpofe of paying the principal and intereft of the aforefaid certificates, and fhall not be applied to any other ufe or purpofe whatfoever; and if the faid duties and cuftoms fhall not be fufficient to pay the intereft becoming due annually on the faid certificates, and alfo to pay one eighth part of the principal of the fame annually, the firft payment of fuch principal to commence on the firft day of *January*, one thoufand feven hundred and eighty five, the full amount of fuch deficiences fhall be paid out of the fund arifing from the flave tax; and if the amount of fuch duties and cuftoms fhall at any time before the faid firft day of *January*, one thoufand feven hundred and eighty five, exceed the amount of intereft due on the faid certificates, all fuch overplus fhall be paid in difcharge of part of the principal in juft and equal proportion to the holders of fuch certificates.

Duties appropriated to payment of the principal and intereft due to officers and foldiers,

Deficiency to be made up out of the flave tax.

XII. *AND be it further enacted,* to afcertain and eftablifh the credit of the faid certificates on the moft certain and permanent foundation, that all warrants hereafter granted by the Auditors for intereft on the faid certificates, fhall be by them endorfed on the back of fuch certificate at the time of iffuing fuch warrants, and fhall be receivable by the feveral fheriffs or collectors of taxes within this commonwealth in payment of all taxes whatfoever, and the Treafurer fhall receive the fame of fuch fheriffs or collectors

Warrants for intereft to be receivable for taxes.

A. D. 1783.

accordingly. And in order to prevent frauds and counterfeits, the said Auditors shall make a fair and distinct entry of all such certificates and warrants by them granted, in a book to be by them kept for that purpose, and shall supply the Treasurer, from time to time, as he may require the same, with a fair and distinct account of all certificates and warrants so issued.

Proportions of the money collected to be pai

XIII. AND that equal justice may be done to the holders of all such military certificates and warrants, Be it enacted, that the Treasurer shall, once at least in every six months, and not oftener than once in every three months, proportion the money in his hands, arising from the said duties and customs, equally amongst the holders of the said certificates or warrants, and shall give notice at least two weeks successively in the public gazettes of the proportion in the public treasury, to be paid on such certificates or warrants, and appointing a particular day for such payment, before which day such proportion shall not be paid; and if any of the holders of such certificates or warrants shall fail to apply for the same on the day appointed by the Treasurer for such purpose, the full proportion of the persons failing so to apply shall be retained in the public treasury, to be paid them at any future day when application shall be made for such payment. And the Treasurer shall keep a fair and distinct account, in a book for that purpose, of every payment made of certificates or warrants, and when any payment is made in part only of such certificates or warrants, the Treasurer, at the time of such payment, shall endorse the same on the back of such certificate or warrant, as the case may be.

Death to counterfeit warrants.

XIV. AND be it further enacted, that if any person shall counterfeit, alter, or erase, any certificate or warrant issued or to be issued to the officers and soldiers of the continental or state line, or of the navy, by the Auditors of public accounts, by virtue of this or any former act of Assembly, or shall demand payment of any money on such certificate or warrant, knowing the same to be counterfeited altered or erased, or shall be aiding, assisting, or abetting, in such forging or counterfeiting, altering or erasing, he or she shall be deemed and judged guilty of felony, and on being thereof legally convicted, shall suffer death, without the benefit of clergy.

Repeal of all tobacco tax but that in tobacco law of this session.

XV. AND be it further enacted, that so much of all and every other act or acts of Assembly imposing a tax upon tobacco exported, except the tax imposed by an act of the present session, To amend and reduce the several acts of Assembly for the inspection of tobacco into one act, shall be, and the same is hereby repealed.

CHAP. IX.

An act to vest the gun factory and public lands at Fredericksburg, in trustees for the purposes of an academy.

Private.

CHAP. X.

An act to amend and reduce the several acts of Assembly for the inspection of tobacco, into one act.

Preamble.

I. WHEREAS the several acts of Assembly for the inspection of tobacco are, from the many alterations made therein, rendered difficult to be understood, whereby many penalties may be incurred; and it is necessary that the said acts should be amended and reduced into one act; and doubts have arisen whether the said acts, or any, or which of them are now in force: Be it therefore enacted by the General Assembly, that no person shall put on board, or receive into any ship or vessel, in order to be exported therein, any tobacco not packed in hogsheads or casks, upon any pretence whatsoever, nor in any hogshead or cask to be in that or any ship or other vessel exported out of this state, before the same shall have been reviewed and inspected according to the directions of this act; but that all tobacco whatsoever, to be received or taken on board any ship or other vessel, and to be therein exported, or to be carried and put on board any ship or vessel for exportation as aforesaid, shall be received and taken on board at the several warehouses for that purpose herein after mentioned, or some or one of them, and at no other place whatsoever: And every master, mate, or boatswain, of any ship or other vessel which shall arrive in this state, in order to load tobacco during the continuance of this act, shall, before the said ship or vessel be permitted to take on board any tobacco whatsoever, make oath before the Naval Officer of the district wherein such ship or vessel shall arrive, which oath the said Naval Officer is hereby empowered and required to administer, that they will not permit any tobacco whatsoever to be taken on board their respective ships or vessels, except the same be packed in hogsheads or casks stamped by some inspector legally thereunto appointed; which oath they shall subscribe in a book, to be kept by the Naval Officer for that purpose. And if any master shall cause any person who is not really and bona fide mate or boatswain, to come on shore and take such oath, he shall, for the said offence, forfeit and pay five hundred pounds: And if any master or commander of any ship or other vessel, shall take on board, or suffer to be taken on board the ship or vessel whereof he is master, any tobacco brought from any other place than some or one of the public warehouses herein after mentioned, or any hogshead or cask of tobacco, not stamped by some lawful inspector, or shall suffer to be brought on board, any tobacco, except in hogsheads or casks, stamped as aforesaid, every such master or commander shall forfeit and pay fifty pounds for every hogshead or cask of tobacco which shall not have been brought from one of the said public warehouses, or which shall not be stamped as aforesaid; and moreover, every such hogshead or cask of tobacco shall be forfeited, one moiety thereof to the use of the informer, and the other moiety to the use of the commonwealth.

No tobacco to be exported, but in casks and inspected.

The oaths of masters of vessels intending to load with tobacco.

Penalties.

No tobacco to be taken on board any vessel in bulk or parcels.

Penalties.

II. AND be it further enacted, that if any person, not being a servant or slave, taking upon himself to carry any tobacco to or from any of the said warehouses in his boat or other vessel, for hire, shall take on board, or permit or suffer to be taken on board, any tobacco whatsoever, in bulk or parcels, such tobacco shall not only be forfeited, and may be seized by any person or persons whatsoever, but the master or skipper offending herein, shall forfeit and pay two shillings for every pound weight of such tobacco; and the master or commander of any ship or vessel wherein any tobacco in bulk or parcels shall be found, shall over and above the forfeiture thereof, be subject and liable to the same penalty; to be recovered, if it doth not exceed five pounds, before any two Justices of the Peace of any county near the place where such ship, boat, or other vessel, shall lie; and if it exceeds five pounds, in any court of record; by action of debt, wherein the plaintiff shall recover his costs. And if any servant, or other person employed in navigating any such boat or other vessel, shall connive at or conceal the taking or receiving on board any tobacco, in bulk or parcel as aforesaid, he shall pay the sum of five pounds, to be recovered as aforesaid; and if such servant or other person shall be unable to pay the said sum, he or they, and every slave so employed, shall, by order of such Justice, receive on his bare back, thirty nine lashes well laid on; and if such boat or other vessel be under the care and management of a servant who cannot pay and satisfy the penalty so to be inflicted on the master or skipper offending as aforesaid, then such servant, and every other person employed under him, unable to pay the said penalty, who shall be guilty of conniving at or concealing the taking on board tobacco in bulk or parcels as aforesaid, shall, upon every complaint and proof thereof made to a Justice of the Peace, have and receive, by order of the said Justice, thirty nine lashes well laid on; and if any servant shall again be entrusted with the care and management of any boat or other vessel, and shall be convicted a second time of taking or receiving on board the same, any tobacco in bulk or parcel, contrary to the directions of this act, the owner of such servant shall forfeit and pay the like sum of two shillings *per* pound for every pound weight of such tobacco so taken or received on board in bulk or parcel, and shall also forfeit and pay ten shillings for every day such servant shall thereafter be employed as skipper or master of any boat or vessel to him belonging, to be recovered and applied as aforesaid. *Provided nevertheless,* that it shall be lawful for the proprietor or proprietors to break any hogshead of tobacco after it shall be passed and stamped, and to repack and prize the same into small casks for the convenience of stowing, provided it be done at the warehouse where the same was inspected and weighed, marked, and stamped; and the inspectors shall particularize all such casks in their manifests to be given to the masters or skippers of the vessel in which such tobacco be laden. *Provided always,* that nothing herein before contained shall be construed to prohibit any person from carrying, or causing to be carried to the said warehouses, in any boat or other vessel, any tobacco in bulk or parcels, for the payment of his or her levies, debts, or other duties, or to prohibit any person to put or take on board any boat or other vessel, any hogsheads or cask of tobacco to be waterborn to any warehouse appointed by this act, so as the same be not carried out of the Naval Officer's district wherein the said tobacco shall be made, nor to prohibit the owner of any tobacco to transport his crops, or any part thereof, in hogsheads or casks, from one plantation to another, for the better handling and managing thereof, nor any purchaser of tobacco from bringing the same by water to be repacked, sorted, stemmed, or prized, before the same be carried to the said warehouses, so as such last mentioned tobacco be packed in hogsheads or casks; but no tobacco, on any pretence whatsoever, shall be carried or transported by water to be inspected out of the district limited and appointed for the several Naval Officers of this state, wherein the same shall be made, or being so carried, shall not be inspected or passed by any inspectors knowing the same to be made out of such district, on pain of forfeiting, by the owner of such tobacco, and the inspectors who shall pass the same, fifty shillings for every hogshead to the informer. *Provided nevertheless,* that it shall and may be lawful for the inhabitants of *Fleet*'s bay, on the south side of *Indian* creek, in the county of *Lancaster,* to carry their tobacco by water to the public warehouse at *Indian* creek; and the inhabitants at *Warrasqueake* bay, and the parts adjacent, to carry their tobacco to be passed at any warehouse in the upper district of *James* river.

III. *AND be it further enacted,* that every master of a ship or vessel wherein tobacco shall be laden, shall at the time of clearing, deliver to the Naval Officer, a fair manifest of all the tobacco on board his ship or vessel, expressing the marks and numbers of every hogshead or cask, and the tare and nett weight stamped thereon, the person by whom shipped, and from what warehouse, and shall make oath thereto, and that the same is a just and true account of the marks, numbers, tare, and nett weight, of each respective hogshead or cask, as the same was taken down by the person or persons appointed by him to take the same before the said tobacco was stowed away; and no ship or vessel shall be cleared by the Naval Officer before he shall have received such list and manifest, which shall by the said Naval Officer be transmitted to the Treasurer of this commonwealth for the time being.

IV. *AND be it further enacted,* that if the skipper of any boat or vessel, or the person or persons to whom the care and management thereof shall be entrusted, shall land or put on shore any hogshead, cask, or package of tobacco, put on board the same to be carried to any public warehouse at any other place or places than the warehouses by this act appointed for the reception and inspection of tobacco, or at some or one of them, or the wharves or other landing to such warehouse or warehouses belonging, or shall put the same on board any other vessel, or suffer the same to be done, so as the same be not delivered at some of the said public warehouses, without fraud or embezzlement, or shall open any hogshead or cask of tobacco so as aforesaid waterborn and landed, and take thereout any tobacco before the same be received by the inspectors according to the directions of this act; or after the same has been viewed shall fraudulently open any hogshead or cask, and take thereout any tobacco, every such offence shall be judged felony, and the offender or offenders shall suffer as in the case of felony. *Provided always,* that nothing herein before contained shall be construed to prohibit the landing or putting on shore any hogshead, cask, or package of tobacco, out of any boat or other vessel, which by distress of weather shall be forced on ground, or become leaky, so as such landing be really and *bona fide* for the preservation of the tobacco laden in such vessel, and that the same may with all convenient speed be thereafter carried to the warehouse or ship (as the case may be) to which it was designed, without embezzlement. *Provided also,* that if by any of the accidents aforesaid, or negligence of the master or skipper of any vessel, any tobacco which hath been viewed and stamped, shall in its carriage to the ship or vessel in which it is intended to be exported, receive so much damage as that the master of such ship or vessel will not receive it on board, every hogshead or cask of tobacco so damnified shall with convenient speed be carried to some warehouse appointed by this act, and there lodged until the owner of the said tobacco, or master of the vessel in which it was damaged, shall have separated the same and repacked the good tobacco, and then the same shall be weighed and stamped with the weight by the inspector attending such warehouse without fee or reward; but if the owner of such tobacco, or the master of the vessel in which it was damaged, shall fail or delay to separate and repack the same within ten days, then the inspectors at the warehouse where such damaged tobacco shall be landed, shall, and they are hereby required to separate, repack, weigh, and stamp the same; and such inspectors shall receive of the owner ten shillings for their trouble and nails.

V. *AND be it further enacted,* that public warehouses for the reception of tobacco, pursuant to this act, shall be kept at the several places herein after mentioned, that is to say: In the county of *Accomack,* at *Pitt*'s landing, upon *Pocomoke,* at *Guilford,* and at *Pungoteague,* under one inspection; in the county of *Caroline,* at *Roy*'s in the county of *Charles City,* at *Kennon*'s; in the county of *Dinwiddie,* at *Bolling*'s point, *Bollingbrooke* and *Cedar Point;* in the county of *Essex,* at *Hobb's Hole,* at *Bowler*'s, and at *Layton*'s; in the county of *Fairfax,* at *Colchester,* at *Alexandria,* and at the falls of *Potowmack;* in the county of *Gloucester,* at *Poropotank,* and at *Deacon's Neck;* in the county of *Hanover,* at *Page*'s, and at *Meriwether*'s; in the county of *Chesterfield,* at *Rocky Ridge,* at *Warwick,* at *Osborne*'s, and at *John Bolling*'s; in the county of *Henrico,* at *Byrd*'s, at *Shockoe,* and at *Rockett*'s; in the county of *Isle of Wight,* at *Smithfield,* and at *Faigham*'s, under one inspection; in the county of *King and Queen,* at *Shepherd*'s, at *Mantapike,* and at *Frazer*'s, in *King William,* under one inspection; and at *Todd*'s, in *King and Queen,* and at *Aylett*'s, in the county of *King William,* under one inspection; in the county of *King George,* at *Boyd*'s Hole, at *Machodack,* under one inspection, and at *Gibson*'s; in the county of *Lancaster,* at *Davis*'s and *Lowry*'s, under one inspection, and at *Deep Creek* and *Glasscock*'s, under one inspection; in the county

A D. 1783.

of *Northumberland*, at *Coan* and *North Wicomico*, under one inspection; and *South Wicomico* and *Indian* creek, under one inspection; in the county of *Middlesex*, at *Urbanna*; in the county of *Nansemond*, at *Milner's*, and *Wilkinson's*; in the county of *Northampton*, at *Cherrystones* and *Nafwaddox*, under one inspection; in the county of *New Kent*, at *Littlepage's*, and at the *Brick-House*; in the county of *Prince George*, at *Boyd's*, *Davis's*, and *Blandford*; in the county of *Prince William*, at *Quantico* and at *Dumfries*; in the county of *Richmond*, at *Cat point*, and at *Totusky*; in the county of *Surry*, at *Gray's* creek, and at *Low-Point*; in the county of *Stafford*, at *Falmouth*, at *Aquia*, and at *Dixon's*; in the county of *Spotsylvania*, at *Fredericksburg*, and at *Royston's*; in the county of *Warwick*, at *Denbigh*; in the county of *Westmoreland*, at *Nomini*, at *Leed's*, and *Mattox*, under one inspection; at *Yocomico* and *Rust's*, under one inspection; at the *College Landing*, in the county of *James City*, and at *York* town, in the county of *York*, under one inspection; at *Hampton*, in the county of *Elizabeth City*.

Rents of warehouses.

VI. AND *be it further enacted*, that the rents of the several warehouses hereby established, shall be and they are hereby established at the following rates: At *Pitt's* and *Guilford's*, ten pounds; at *Pungoteague*, eight pounds; at *Cherrystone's* and *Nafwaddox*, eight pounds; at *Hampton* ten pounds; at *College* landing, ten pounds; and at all the other warehouses there shall be allowed and paid for the rents of the same, one shilling and six pence for every hogshead of tobacco that already have been or shall be received, inspected, and delivered out of such warehouses respectively. And there shall be paid to the proprietors of each warehouse, for all tobacco lying therein more than twelve months, at the rate of three pence *per* month for each hogshead, to be paid by the shipper thereof at the time of shipping the same.

Proviso as to wharves.

Provided always, that where wharves are or shall be necessary to be built or kept in repair at any of the said warehouses, and the rents hereby established are not sufficient for building and keeping in repair such wharves, or where any new warehouse shall hereafter be built in pursuance of this act, and the rent hereby established shall not be proportionable to the expence of such building, in both the said cases such further allowance shall be made by the General Assembly as shall be thought reasonable; and the rents aforesaid, together with the inspectors salaries, shall be paid and allowed by the Treasurer to the several inspectors upon the passing their accounts, and the inspectors shall pay the rents to the persons entitled to receive the same, out of the money received by them for inspecting tobacco; and if the money received by the inspectors at any warehouse shall not be sufficient to pay the salaries and rents aforesaid, and other incident charges in this act mentioned, such deficiency shall be made good out of the general fund arising by the profits of the other warehouses; and if that shall prove deficient, then the said rents and charges, together with the inspectors salaries, shall be paid and satisfied out of any other public money in the hands of the Treasurer, for the time being, not otherwise appropriated by law.

Proprietors of old warehouses to let them to inspectors.

VII. AND *be it further enacted*, that where the warehouses are already built at any of the places herein before mentioned, and appointed for keeping the same, and are now made use of for public ware houses, the proprietors and owners of such ware-houses shall be, and they are hereby obliged, to let the same to the inspectors during the continuance of this act, at the rent hereby established for such warehouses respectively; and if any proprietor or owner shall refuse so to do, he shall forfeit and pay

Courts to direct the number and kind of new warehouses and wharves.

five hundred pounds; and where warehouses are not already built at any of the places aforesaid, or where any new warehouses shall be hereafter appointed to be kept at any other place, it shall be lawful for the Justices of the court of that county, wherein such place is or shall be, and they are hereby required, at the next court to be held for their county after the commencement of this act, or after such new warehouse shall be so appointed (as the case may be) to order and direct so many strong, close, and substantial houses, secured with strong doors, hung on iron hinges, and with strong locks or bolts, as will contain sufficient room for two thirds of the number of hogsheads, which, in their opinion, will be annually brought to the same, and one brick square or funnel six feet high at least, and four feet diameter, with a proper arch at the bottom of the same, for burning tobacco refused and picked, at such warehouses, and such wharves and other conveniences as shall be necessary; and shall cause the owner or proprietor of the land where such warehouses are appointed to be kept, and if such owner or proprietor be under age, *feme covert*, or out of the country, then the guardian, husband, or known attorney, or agent (as the case may be) of such owner or proprietor, to be summoned to appear before them

And take bond with security of the proprietor if he chuse to build and let them.

at the next succeeding county court after such summons shall issue, then to declare whether they will undertake to erect and build such houses, funnel, wharves, and other conveniencies, and let the same to the inspectors appointed to attend at such warehouses, at the rent settled by this act, or which shall be hereafter settled for the same; and in case such owner, guardian, husband, known attorney, or agent, will undertake the same, then the said court shall, and they are hereby required, to take bond with sufficient security, in a reasonable penalty, payable to the Governor and his successors, to the use of the commonwealth, with condition for the due performance of such undertaking. And if such owner, guardian, husband, known attorney, or agent, shall refuse to undertake the same, or give such bond as aforesaid, then it shall be lawful for the said Justices, and they are hereby required, to value an acre of the said land, and to pay or tender to the proprietor, his or her guardian, husband, known attorney, or agent, the value thereof, which shall be repaid to the said Justices by the public; and from thenceforth

If he refuses the land paid for and houses, &c. built at expence of the public and rents paid to Treasurer.

the Justices of the county for the time being, shall be seized in fee of the said land, in trust, and for the use of the public, during the time the said place shall be made use of for a public warehouse; and the said Justices shall agree with some person or persons to erect and build thereon such houses, funnels, wharves, and other conveniencies, as is herein before directed, and shall certify the charge thereof to the Treasurer of this state for the time being, who is hereby directed and required to pay the same out of the public money in his hands arising from the inspection of tobacco, and shall take and receive of the inspectors the rent established at such warehouses for reimbursing the public the charge of such buildings, until the same shall be repaid with lawful interest. And where the Justices of any county court, or any other person or persons, have already built warehouses on lands of another person, by virtue of, or in pursuance of, the laws lately or now in force, the said Justices, or other person or persons, shall in like manner be seized in fee of the acre of land upon which such warehouses are built, so long as the said places respectively shall be made use of for public warehouses; but if any of the warehouses which are

Where warehouses are discontinued.

or shall be built by the public, the Justices, or other persons, shall hereafter be discontinued, the proprietor of the land, returning the price paid for the same, with lawful interest, shall be thenceforth seized of his former estate.

Inspectors yearly to lay before the court an account of tobacco inspected and condition of the houses.

VIII. AND *be it further enacted*, that the inspectors at the several warehouses shall, at the court to be held for their respective counties in the month of *September* yearly, or at the next succeeding court to be held for their respective counties in the month of *September* yearly, or at the next succeeding court, produce and render into court an exact account, under their hands, of the number of hogsheads of tobacco inspected at their respective warehouses the preceding year, and of the condition of the warehouses under their charge, and the quantity of tobacco they are capable of containing, and thereupon such

Court may order houses to be repaired or secured, and new houses built if necessary.

court, if they shall not be satisfied that the warehouses already built at any of the said inspections are properly secured, and contain sufficient room for two thirds of the number of hogsheads mentioned in such account to be conveniently stowed, shall enter an order that the owner or proprietor of such warehouses shall, within such reasonable time as the said court shall think fit to allow, repair and make close the warehouses already built, and secure the same with strong doors hung on iron hinges, and with strong locks or bolts; and that such owner or proprietor shall also before the first day of *April*, in the ensuing year, erect, build, and completely finish, such and so many other strong, close, and substantial houses, as with the other houses already built, shall be sufficient, in the opinion of such court, conveniently to contain two thirds of the quantity of tobacco mentioned in such inspectors account, and secure the same in manner herein before directed; a copy of which order shall be served on such owner or proprietor, or his or her guardian, husband, attorney, or agent (as the case may be) and if such owner or proprietor, his or her guardian, husband, attorney, or agent, shall fail to appear at the next succeeding court, after such notice, and enter into bond with sufficient security, in a reasonable penalty, payable to the Governor for the time being and his successors, with a condition for the due performance of the same, then it shall be lawful for the said court, and they are hereby required, to cause such repairs and houses to be made and built as aforesaid, and shall certify the charge thereof to the Treasurer of this state for the time being, who is hereby required to pay the same out of the public money in his hands arising from the inspection of tobacco, and shall take and receive from the inspectors the whole or a proportion of the rents established at such warehouses, for reimbursing the public the charge of such buildings and repairs, with interest thereon, which proportion shall be settled by the court, and by them certified to the Treasurer; but if there shall appear to be an immediate occasion to hire houses before others can be built as aforesaid, the rent of such houses shall be paid by the public, without any charge upon the landlord. *Provided*, that where two or more inspections are established in one county, within the distance of six miles, and that it shall be necessary to build more houses at any of them, the court shall direct the building such additional houses, at such of the said inspections as to them shall seem most proper, and if there shall be in the whole sufficient house room, according to the directions of this act, for two thirds of the tobacco brought to such inspection, the court shall not direct the building other houses at any of them.

By the proprietor or public.

Proviso for united inspections.

IX. *AND be it further enacted*, that if any county court shall fail or refuse to do their duty in directing such houses, funnels, and wharves, and other necessary conveniences at the places established by this act for erecting new warehouses, or such additional buildings and repairs at the places where houses are already built, and causing the same to be built or made according to the directions of this act, every Justice so failing on refusing shall forfeit and pay thirty pounds; to be recovered in the General Court with costs, by action of debt or information against such Justices jointly. *Provided always*, that nothing herein contained shall be construed to give power to the said Justices to take away the houses, orchards, or other immediate conveniencies of any proprietors of lands for the purposes aforesaid, nor to the said inspectors to keep any horses, cattle, or hogs, at any public warehouses, except their riding horses, upon the land appointed for such warehouses; and if any swine belonging to the said inspectors, or any of them, shall be found at large upon the land appropriated for such ware houses, or the lands adjoining thereto, it shall be lawful for the proprietors of the said lands to kill, or cause to be killed or destroyed, all such swine. *Provided also*, that where any ware-houses have been or shall be built by the Justices or other persons as aforesaid, and the first proprietor of the land shall desire to have the same again, such proprietor, upon payment of so much money as shall be sufficient to reimburse the said Justices or other person the principal money expended for the purchase of the land and the building such warehouses, with lawful interest, deducting the rents received by the said Justices or other person, shall be restored to his former estate in the land whereon such warehouses are built, and shall receive the rents aforesaid growing due for such warehouses. *Provided also*, that if any proprietor so as aforesaid restored to his estate, shall neglect or refuse to build and repair such houses and wharves as the court shall think necessary, the Justices shall again be seized of the fee simple estate in such land during the time such place shall be made use of for a public warehouse, and such proprietor shall not have any benefit of the rents that shall hereafter become due.

Penalty on county courts for neglect.

Conveniencies not to be taken from proprietors

Nor inspectors to keep horses, cattle, or hogs on the land.

How proprietors may be restored to the former estate,

But if he again fails to build or repair, to be revested in the public.

X. *AND be it further enacted*, that on complaint being made by the owner or owners of any of the warehouses aforesaid, to any Justice of the Peace in the county where such warehouse shall lie, against any person or persons for breaking, tearing, or committing any waste or destruction of, or in, such warehouse or warehouses, it shall be lawful for such Justice, and he is hereby empowered and required, to give judgment and award execution against the body or estate of such offender if found guilty, for all damages occasioned by such breaking, tearing, or waste or destruction, provided such damages do not exceed the sum of twenty five shillings in his opinion; and if such damages shall exceed that sum, then it shall be lawful for such owner or owners to commence and prosecute his or their action at law against any such offender, in any court of record within this state, in which the plaintiff shall recover costs, although the damage shall be under forty shillings.

Waste or destruction of warehouses, how to be punished

XI. *AND be it further enacted*, that there shall be kept at every one of the said warehouses herein before appointed, and at all others hereafter to be appointed, a good and sufficient pair of scales with weights, to weigh fifteen hundred pounds at the least, and a set of small weights the same that are or ought to be provided for the standard weights of each county; and where such scales and weights are not already provided, or now are or shall hereafter be worn out or become unfit for use, the Justices of the respective county courts wherein any of the said warehouses are or shall be, are hereby directed and required to provide the same with all convenient speed; and the Treasurer, for the time being, is hereby empowered and required to pay the purchase money out of the public money in his hands arising from the inspection of tobacco; and moreover the said Justices are hereby required and directed, twice in every year at least, to appoint one or more of their number to view the said scales, and examine and try the weights at the several warehouses by the standard weights of the county, and if the said scales and weights shall want repairing, or the weights be found deficient or differing from the lawful standard, the said Justices shall cause the same to be repaired and mended, and the weights made conformable to the standard; and if the Justice or Justices so appointed, shall refuse or neglect to do the same, the Justice or Justices so refusing, shall forfeit and pay the sum of fifty pounds; and the charge of repairing and amending the said scales and weights, and also for removing the standard to the several warehouses for trying the same, shall be paid by the inspectors respectively, and be again allowed to them in their accounts with the Treasurer.

Scales and weights to be provided,

and tried and repaired twice a year.

XII. *AND be it further enacted*, that all tobacco which shall be brought to any of the public warehouses shall be viewed, inspected, and examined, by two persons to be thereunto appointed, who shall be called inspectors, which said inspectors shall be appointed in the following manner, that is to say: The courts of the several counties within this state, wherein any of the public warehouses appointed by this act are established, shall, and they are hereby required, once in every year, and no oftener, at their respective county courts held in the months of *August* or *September*, to nominate and recommend to the Governor, for the time being, for so many offices of inspection as are or shall be in their respective counties, four fit and able persons, reputed to be skilful in tobacco, for the execution of the office of inspectors; and where two ware-houses, under one and the same inspection, happen to lie in different counties, in that case the court of each county shall nominate and recommend two for such inspection,

Manner of appointing inspectors.

which nomination the said court shall cause to be entered upon record; and the clerks of the said courts shall, and they are hereby required, forthwith to transmit a certificate of the same to the clerk of the Council; and out of the said four persons nominated and recommend for each inspection, the Governor, with advice and consent of Council, shall choose and appoint two to execute the office of inspectors at such inspection; and in default of such nomination or recommendation by the county courts as aforesaid, the Governor, with the like advice and consent, shall appoint such persons as he shall think fit to be inspectors at such inspection for which no nomination or recommendation shall be made as aforesaid; and also in case of the death, resignation, or removal of any inspector, the Governor shall and may appoint any person named in the last recommendation from the county court for that inspection where the vacancy shall happen, to succeed him until the next nomination and appointment of inspectors; but if either of the persons named in such last recommendation, will not accept the said office, in that case the Governor, with the advice and consent of the Council, may appoint any other person they shall think fit; and besides the two inspectors appointed as aforesaid, the Governor, for the time being, with the advice of the Council, shall appoint one of the persons recommended with such inspectors, to be additional inspector at the ware-house for which he shall be recommended, which additional inspector shall officiate as such only in cases of the disagreement in opinion of the other inspectors as to the quality of tobacco brought to their inspection, or where either of them shall through sickness or otherwise be absent from his duty, or shall bring his own tobacco to the ware-house whereof he is inspector, to be viewed; and the said additional inspector shall be paid for the services he shall perform, by occasion of the absence of either of the other inspectors, out of the salary of such absentee, in proportion to the time he shall officiate.

An additional inspector, and when to act.

XIII. AND be it further enacted, that if any inspector shall hereafter accept, receive, or take, directly or indirectly, any fee, gratuity, service, or reward whatsoever, of any person, for resigning or giving up his office of inspector, he shall not only be forever disabled from holding the like office, but for such offence shall forfeit and pay the sum of two hundred pounds, to be recovered with costs, by action of debt, in any court of record within this state, by any person suing for the same; and every person offering or paying, directly or indirectly, any fee, service, gratuity, or reward whatsoever, to any inspector to resign his said office, shall for the said offence, be forever disabled from holding the office of inspector within this state. Provided always, that no Justice of the Peace, being an inspector, or recommended to be an inspector, shall be allowed to vote in nomination and recommendation of persons to be inspectors as aforesaid; and where any person once recommended as aforesaid, and executing the office of inspector in pursuance of such recommendation, shall be again recommended the succeeding year, the same shall be a sufficient appointment to him to continue in the said office for another year without any new commission, and so from year to year, so long as he shall be so recommended as aforesaid.

No inspector to take a reward for resigning.

Penalty on giver and receiver.

No inspector to vote in recommendation.

Inspectors in office recommended, continue without new commissions.

XIV. AND be it further enacted, that every person appointed, or to be appointed, inspector by virtue of this act, shall, before he enters upon the execution of the said office, enter into bond with good security, in the penalty of one thousand pounds, payable to the Governor for the time being, and his successors, with condition for the true and faithful performance of his duty, according to the directions of this act, which bond shall be recorded in the county, and transmitted by the clerk of the court to the Treasurer, under the penalty of one hundred pounds, who shall move for judgment against every inspector failing to discharge the same within two months after failure, under the penalty of one hundred pounds; and every such inspector shall also take the following oath at the time he gives bond, that is to say: *You shall swear, that you will diligently and carefully view and examine all tobacco brought to the public ware-house or ware-houses where you are appointed inspector, and that not separately and apart from your fellow, but in his presence; and that you will not receive or pass any tobacco that is not, in your judgment, sound, well conditioned, merchantable, and clear of trash; nor receive, pass, or stamp, any tobacco hogshead or cask of tobacco, contrary to the act entitled* An act to amend and reduce the several acts of Assembly for the inspection of tobacco into one act, *nor refuse any tobacco that, in your judgment, is sound, well conditioned, merchantable, and clear of trash; and that you will not change, alter, or give out, any tobacco, other than such hogsheads or casks for which the receipt to be taken was given; but that you will in all things well and faithfully discharge your duty in the office of an inspector, according to the best of your skill and judgment, and according to the directions of this act, without fear, favour, affection, malice, or partiality. So help you God.* Which oath shall be taken before the Governor of this state for the time being, before the General Court, or in the court of the county wherein such inspector shall reside, or the ware-houses at which he shall be inspector shall stand. But before any inspector shall enter upon the execution of his office, he shall produce a certificate, if sworn before the Governor or General Court, as the case may be, of his having taken such oath, which certificate shall be lodged with the clerk of the county where such inspector shall be. And if any person shall presume to execute the office of inspector, before he shall have given such bond, and taken such oath as aforesaid, he shall forfeit and pay five hundred pounds.

Inspectors to give bond and take an oath.

Penalty.

XV. AND be it further enacted, that all inspectors to be appointed by virtue of this act, shall constantly attend their duty at the warehouse or warehouses under their charge, from the first day of October, to the tenth day of August, yearly, except Sundays, and the holydays observed at Christmas, Easter, and Whitsuntide, or when hindered by sickness; and afterwards they, or one of them, shall constantly attend at the same, except Sundays, to deliver out tobacco for exportation, until all the tobacco remaining there the said tenth day of August shall be delivered; but no inspector shall be obliged to view any tobacco between the said tenth day of August and the said first day of October, except such as remained in the warehouse on the said tenth day of August. And every inspector neglecting to attend as aforesaid, shall forfeit and pay to the party grieved five shillings for every neglect, or shall be liable to an action upon the case of the party grieved, to recover all such damages as he or they shall have sustained by occasion of any such neglect, together with his or their full costs, at the election of such party. And that all persons having tobacco at the public warehouses may have equal justice, the inspectors shall enter in a book, to be kept for that purpose, the marks and owners names of all tobacco brought to their respective warehouses for inspection, as the same shall be brought in, and shall view and inspect the same in due turn, as it shall be entered in such book, without favour or partiality; and shall uncase and break every hogshead or cask of tobacco brought them to be inspected as aforesaid; and if they shall agree that the same is good, sound, well conditioned, merchantable, and clear of trash, then such tobacco shall be weighed in scales with weights of the lawful standard, and the hogshead or cask shall be stamped in the presence of the said inspectors, or one of them, with the name of the warehouse at which inspected, and also the tare of the hogshead or cask, and quantity of nett tobacco therein contained. And the inspectors at such warehouses shall issue a receipt for each hogshead of tobacco they shall pass, if required by the owner, which receipt shall be in the form following, to wit:

Time inspectors are to attend.

Penalty for not attending.

Tobacco to be entered as brought in, and viewed in due turn.

Each hogshead to be uncased and viewed, and if found good, stamped and receipts given.

River:
Warehouse, the   day of   , 178
Sweet scented.   Oronoko.
Leaf.   Stemmed.   Leaf.
Marks. No. Grofs. Tare. Nett. Grofs. Tare. Nett. Grofs. Tare. Nett.

RECEIVED of hogsheads of crop tobacco, marks, numbers, weights, and species, as *per* margin; to be delivered by us to the said ___ or his order, for exportation, when demanded. Witness our hands.

A. D. 1783.

Form of the receipt, which is to be printed, for crop tobacco.

And no inspector or inspectors shall, under any pretence whatsoever, issue a receipt for any tobacco other than such as shall be printed, in which the date shall be inserted at full length. And if any inspector or inspectors shall presume to issue a receipt in any other manner than is hereby expressed, he or they, for every such offence, shall forfeit and pay the sum of one hundred pounds, to be recovered with costs, by any person who may sue for the same, in any court of record within this state; which receipts as aforesaid, shall be furnished by the public printer, and at the public expence. But if the said two inspectors shall at any time disagree concerning the quality of any tobacco brought for their inspection to any warehouse under their charge, they shall, as soon as conveniently may be, call in the additional inspector appointed to attend such warehouse, who shall determine, and pass or reject such tobacco; and if he shall pass the same, his name shall be entered in a book kept by the inspectors, opposite the mark, number, and weight, of the hogshead by him passed, together with the name of the inspector at such warehouse who shall officiate with him. And the inspectors at each of the warehouses established by this act, shall constantly keep so many able hands at their respective warehouses, not exceeding two, as the courts of the several counties wherein they live shall from time to time judge necessary and direct, for the purpose of taking care of all tobacco brought to such warehouse, and stowing it away after the same shall be inspected and stamped. And no inspector shall, by himself, his servant, or any other person, either directly or indirectly, be concerned in picking any refused tobacco, unless it be his own property, on any pretence whatsoever, under the penalty of being for ever thereafter disabled from holding the office of inspector.

Where the inspectors disagree.

What hands the inspectors shall keep

Inspectors or servants not to be concerned in picking tobacco.

XVI. AND be it further enacted, that when any tobacco shall be refused by the inspectors, the proprietor thereof shall be at liberty to separate the good from the bad; but if he refuses or neglects so to do within one month of such refusal, the inspectors shall employ one of the pickers attending the warehouse, to pick and separate such refused tobacco, and give the owner credit for so much thereof as shall be found merchantable, after paying the pickers one fifteenth part of the quantity saved; and the inspectors shall cause the tobacco which shall by them be judged unfit to pass, to be burnt in the brick funnel, erected or to be erected at such warehouse, under the penalty of forty shillings for every failure to the informer, recoverable with costs, before any Justice of the county wherein such warehouse shall lie.

Refused tobacco may be picked.

XVII. AND whereas it has been found that many persons attending the warehouses under the denomination of tobacco pickers, have been found guilty of great frauds, impositions, and abuses therein: For remedy whereof, Be it enacted, that the courts of the several counties wherein any of the public warehouses appointed by this act are established, shall, and they are hereby required, to nominate and appoint, from time to time, such and so many persons as to them shall seem necessary, who are willing to undertake the same, to attend the several warehouses within this state, to turn up, sort, separate, and pick such tobacco as shall be refused by the inspectors. And every person so appointed a picker, shall make oath before the court at the time of his appointment, or at the next succeeding court, that he will carefully and diligently, without fraud or embezzlement, sort and separate all such tobacco as shall be refused by the inspectors, and the owner or proprietor thereof, or the inspectors, shall employ him to pick. And every picker of tobacco shall be allowed to demand and receive from the respective proprietors, one shilling and three pence *per* hogshead for opening, and one fifteenth part of all the tobacco saved out of any refused hogshead by him picked, for his services in opening, sorting, and picking the same, and no more. And no picker of tobacco shall keep or employ any negro or mulatto slave at any public warehouse, on any pretence whatsoever; nor shall any picker presume to hinder any person who may choose to open their own tobacco, or to pick what may be refused by the inspectors, from the free use of the picking house and prize for the conveniency of picking and prizing the same. And if any picker shall misbehave himself in his said office, it shall and may be lawful for the court of the county where such picker shall be appointed, on complaint and motion to them made, to remove such picker from his said office, and to appoint another person to act in his room, if to them it shall seem necessary; and every picker so removed, shall for ever after be rendered incapable of serving as picker at any public warehouse, provided such picker hath ten days previous notice of such motion; and any person who shall be aggrieved by any such misbehaviour in a picker, may make complaint thereof to any Justice of the Peace, who is hereby empowered and directed to take depositions therein, provided such picker have notice thereof, and to transmit the same to the next court to be held for the county where the offence shall be committed, to be there given in evidence on the examination into such misbehaviour. And if any person, not being appointed and sworn as aforesaid, shall presume to undertake the opening, sorting, picking, or separating any such tobacco for hire or reward, every person so offending shall forfeit and pay twenty shillings for every such offence, to be recovered by the informer to his own use before any Justice of the Peace. Provided, that any proprietor of tobacco who may choose to open, pick, and prize his own tobacco, may employ his own servants or slaves, or any other person or persons, other than the hands kept by the inspectors, to assist him in opening, picking, or prizing the same; and the person or persons so employed, shall not incur or be subject to the last mentioned or any other penalty or forfeiture for so doing; and the inspectors shall issue receipts for all tobacco saved by picking to the proprietors only of such tobacco, and not to the pickers of the same. And the inspectors shall not suffer or permit any picker to prize up any tobacco, that he shall have saved by picking, for his own use. And if any tobacco packed in any hogshead or cask by an overseer, or the hands under his care, shall be burnt by the inspectors by reason of its being bad, unsound, or not in good condition, the overseer who had the care of making and packing the same shall be at the loss of the tobacco so burnt, and make satisfaction for the same out of his share of the crop, or otherwise; and the inspectors shall be obliged to keep an account of all tobacco so burnt.

Pickers, how to be appointed.

Their oath.

Allowance.

Duty.

Punishment for misbehaviour.

Penalty for picking without being so appointed; except by the proprietor, his hands, or others.

Overseers liable for tobacco refused and burnt.

XVIII. AND be it further enacted, that where any tobacco shall be brought to any of the said warehouses for the discharge of any public or private debt or contract, the said inspectors, or one of them, after they have viewed, examined, and weighed the said tobacco, according to the directions of this act,

A. D. 1783.

Form of transfer receipts.

shall be obliged to deliver to the person bringing the same, as many receipts, under the hands of the said inspectors, as shall be required for the full quantity of tobacco received by them, in which shall be expressed whether the tobacco so received be sweet scented or oronoko, stemmed or leaf; which receipt shall be in the form following, to wit: "   River, number   ,   warehouse, the   day of   , 17 . Received of   ,   pounds of transfer tobacco to be delivered on demand to him or to his order, according to the directions of the act, entitled *An act to amend and reduce the several acts of Assembly for the inspection of tobacco, into one act.*" Witness our hands."

Their date and currency.

And shall bear date the day the tobacco for which the same is given shall be received and passed, and shall be current in all tobacco payments, according to the species expressed in the receipt, within the county wherein such inspectors shall officiate, and in any other county next adjacent thereto, and not separate therefrom by any of the great rivers or bay herein after mentioned, that is to say: *James* river, below the mouth of *Appamattox*; *York*, below *West Point*; *Rappahannock*, below *Taliaferro's Mount* or by the bay of *Chesapeake*; and shall be transferrable from one to another in all such payments, except as herein is excepted, and shall be paid and satisfied by the inspector or inspectors who signed the same, upon demand.

Allowance for cask.

And for every hogshead of tobacco brought to any public warehouse and transferred, there shall be allowed by the inspectors thereof, to the person bringing the same, after the rate of four pounds of tobacco for every hundred pounds of tobacco the said hogshead shall contain, for the cask; so as such allowance do not exceed thirty pounds of tobacco, provided the cask or hogshead is good, and of such dimensions as is herein after expressed; and the said inspectors shall, and they are hereby obliged, to make every hogshead by them paid away in discharge of any receipt by them given as aforesaid, to contain one thousand pounds of nett tobacco at the least; and for every hogshead of tobacco by them paid away, well lined and nailed, fit for shipping, there shall be paid by the person shipping such hogshead, six shillings for inspection, and three shillings and six pence for prizing and nails; which said sum of three shillings and six pence the inspectors may retain in their hands for their own use, to reimburse them the expence and trouble of providing nails and prizing.

Weight of tobacco prized in discharge of notes.

6 s. inspection, and 3 s. 6 d. for prizing and nails.

Allowance to be made for cask and shrinkage.

And the person demanding or receiving tobacco in discharge of receipts as aforesaid, shall allow to the inspectors thirty pounds of tobacco for each hogshead so received for the cask, and two pounds of tobacco for every hundred pounds of tobacco contained in such receipts, and so in proportion for a greater or lesser quantity, for shrinkage and wasting, if the said tobacco be paid within two months after the date of the receipt given for the same, and one pound of tobacco for every hundred for every month the same shall be unpaid after the said allowance, so as such allowance for shrinkage and wasting do not exceed in the whole six pounds of tobacco for every hundred.

Remedy against inspectors.

And if any inspector or inspectors, by whom any such receipts for tobacco as aforesaid shall be signed, shall refuse or delay to pay and satisfy the same when demanded, every inspector so refusing or delaying, shall forfeit and pay to the party injured double the tobacco so refused or delayed to be paid, to be recovered with costs, in any court of record within this state, if the receipt or receipts so refused or delayed to be paid exceed two hundred pounds of tobacco; and if the said receipt or receipts do not exceed two hundred pounds of tobacco, the double value aforesaid shall and may be recovered before any Justice of the Peace of the county wherein the warehouse shall be at which the receipt or receipts ought to be paid.

How receipts are to be given for crop tobacco.

XIX. AND be it further enacted, that all tobacco brought to any of the said warehouses in hogsheads, to be exported on account, and for the use of the owner thereof, after the same shall have been received, examined, found to be good, and weighed, shall be stamped as herein before directed; and the said inspectors, or one of them, shall deliver to the person bringing the same, as many receipts signed as aforesaid, as shall be required for the number of hogsheads so brought and stamped, in which shall be expressed, whether the tobacco so received be sweet scented or oronoko, stemmed or leaf, and whether the same be tied up in bundles or not; and where any hogshead hath part leaf and part stemmed, shall signify the same at the bottom of the receipt, and they shall not mix stemmed and leaf tobacco in any hogshead which they shall prize, and pay away in discharge of their transfer receipts; and for every hogshead brought to any of the said warehouses, to be exported by land or by water out of this state, there shall be paid to the inspectors attending at such warehouses, by the exporter, at the time of demanding the same for exportation, the sum of six shillings; and the owners of the tobacco shall find and provide nails sufficient for securing and nailing thereof, and where they shall fail so to do, the inspectors at such warehouse shall furnish nails for the purpose aforesaid; and shall be allowed and paid by the owner eight pence for each hogshead so secured.

Six shillings inspection tax to be paid by exporter.

Penalty on inspectors changing tobacco.

And if any inspector or inspectors shall alter, change, or deliver out, any hogshead of tobacco, other than the hogshead for which the receipt for crop tobacco to be taken in, was by him or them given; or shall alter or change any such tobacco, although no such receipt shall have been given, such inspector or inspectors shall forfeit and pay fifty pounds for every hogshead so altered, changed, or delivered out.

Or failing to deliver it, when demanded.

And if any inspector shall fail or refuse to deliver any hogshead of tobacco, when the same shall be demanded for exportation, such inspectors shall forfeit and pay to the owner thereof double the value of the tobacco which they shall so refuse or fail to deliver.

To transfer crop tobacco.

And all inspectors shall, and they are hereby obliged, if required, to take in any receipt or receipts by them given for crop tobacco, and after having weighed such tobacco to give transfer receipts for the same, with an allowance of four *per centum* for the cask, so as such allowance do not exceed thirty pounds of tobacco for every cask. Provided, that such hogshead shall contain at least one thousand pounds of nett tobacco, and not mixed leaf and stemmed. Provided nevertheless, that no inspectors shall give their receipt or receipts for any transfer or crop tobacco, which shall be opened or picked, by any picker legally appointed, until the proprietor of such tobacco, or his or her agent, shall have first paid or tendered to such picker his lawful charges for opening or picking the same.

Rule as to paying pickers.

And in the absence of any such picker, a payment or tender to any of the inspectors there attending, for the use of the picker, shall be as effectual as if made to such picker in person. And if any inspectors shall deliver their receipt or receipts for any such tobacco, so opened or picked, before such payment or tender be made, they shall be liable to such picker for the amount of the same.

Stem'd tobacco to be laid straight. Size of tobacco hogsheads.

XX. AND for restraining the undue practice of mixing trash with stemmed tobacco, and preventing the packing of tobacco in unsizeable casks, Be it enacted, that all stemmed tobacco not laid straight, whether the same be packed loose or in bundles, shall be accounted unlawful tobacco; and that no tobacco packed in hogsheads which exceed forty eight inches in the length of the stave, or thirty inches at the head, within the crow, making reasonable allowance for prizing, which allowance shall not exceed two inches above the gauge, in the prizing head, shall be passed or received; but the owner of such tobacco packed in casks of greater dimensions than before expressed, shall be obliged to repack the same in sizeable casks, at his own charge, before the same shall be received or stamped by the inspectors.

Penalty for delivering tobacco without an order from the proprietor.

XXI. AND whereas many and great inconveniencies have arisen from inspectors undertaking to deliver tobacco the property of others, in their warehouses, without order from the proprietor of the same: Be it enacted, that from and after the passing of this act, if any inspector shall presume to deliver any tobacco in his warehouse, without order from the owner or proprietor of such tobacco, every in-

-fpector fo offending, and being thereof duly convicted in the court of the county wherein he officiates, is declared incapable of ferving for ever after as an infpector in this ftate, and moreover fhall be liable to the penalty of fifty pounds, for every hogfhead of tobacco fo as aforefaid delivered, without order of the owner or proprietor thereof, to be recovered by fuch owner or proprietor thereof, if he or fhe fhall profecute within four months after the offence committed; or if he or fhe decline the profecution, then after that time, by any perfon who fhall inform or fue for the fame, by action of debt or information, in any court of record within this commonwealth. And if any infpector fhall deliver any transfer re- ceipts, or notes of credit, for tobacco, to any perfon or perfons, unlefs at the time of delivering the fame, he fhall have actually and *bona fide* received and paffed tobacco the property of him, her, or them, in whofe name or names fuch receipts or notes fhall be made out to the full amount of the quantity therein fpecified, every infpector fo offending, and being duly convicted, fhall be difabled from ferving as an infpector, and moreover fhall forfeit five pounds for every hundred weight of tobacco fuch fictiti- ous note fhall exprefs, to any perfon who will fue for the fame, recoverable by action of debt in any court of record. And for every profecution againft any infpector or infpectors, for the faid offence, the proof of his or their innocence fhall lie upon the defendant.

And for iffuing fictitious transfer notes, in fuits for which the proof fhall lie on the in-fpector.

XXII. *AND be it further enacted,* that the owner of any transfer receipts may, at any time before the fale of the tobacco contained in fuch transfer receipts, as herein after is directed, receive and mark hogfheads of tobacco to fatisfy fuch receipts; and the infpectors fhall take in their former receipts and deliver crop receipts for fuch hogfheads, and fhall be anfwerable for the fafe keeping thereof in the fame manner as they are for crop tobacco; but the perfons receiving fuch hogfhead, fhall pay to the infpec- tors nine fhillings and fix pence for the infpection and nails for every hogfhead, that is to fay, three fhil- lings and fix pence down to the infpectors for their ufe, for nails and their trouble in prizing, and fix fhillings as infpection, when the tobacco is delivered. And the infpectors fhall, at the court held for their county in the month of *September* yearly, or if there be no court in that month, then at the next court held for their county, lay before the court an account, upon oath, of all transfer receipts that were not by them taken in and received before the time of fale herein before mentioned; and after fuch account exhibited, and oath made, fhall fell the tobacco in fuch receipts contained, deducting the allow- ance for fhrinkage and wafting, at public auction, at the door of the court-houfe, between the hours of twelve and two; and the infpectors fhall pay the money arifing by fuch fale in fatisfaction of their receipts, from time to time, to the proprietors thereof, making their demand, under the fame penalty as is in- flicted for not paying infpectors receipts. And all infpectors fhall keep a juft and true account of the tobacco gained or faved upon the allowance made for cafk and for fhrinkage of transfer tobacco, or otherwife; and if any tobacco fhall be fo gained or faved, fhall exhibit an account thereof, and fhall alfo fell the tobacco fo gained and faved, in the manner as is directed for the fale of transfer tobacco, and fhall account for the money arifing by fuch fale to the Treafurer of this ftate, for the time being, in their next account with him; and the faid Treafurer fhall account for the fame to the General Affem- bly; and no infpector fhall convert any tobacco fo gained to his own ufe.

Infpectors to give crop notes in ex-change for transfer.

And in September court yearly account, and fell the tobacco for all notes out-ftanding. Alfo tobacco gained by allowance for cafk and fhrinkage.

XXIII. *AND be it further enacted,* that all infpectors fhall, before the tenth day of *October* in every year, account with the Treafurer of this ftate, upon oath, for all monies received, or which ought to be received, by them by virtue of this act, except the money paid for nails and for their trouble in priz- ing, or for repacking damaged tobacco which fhall be relanded at their infpection, for every hogfhead of transfer tobacco; in which account they fhall be allowed their falaries, the rents of the warehoufes, and all other neceffary difburfements in purfuance of this act. And in order to eafe the infpectors giving their perfonal attendance at the Treafury, they are hereby required, after ftating their accounts with the Treafurer, as above directed, to take the following oath, before fome one Juftice of the Peace of the county where they officiate, to wit: *We A. B. and C. D. do fwear, that the account now produced contains an exact ftate of all the tobacco fhipped the preceding year from ————— warehoufe, all taxes received or due for the fame, alfo all tobacco gained at the faid infpection, by any means whatfoever. So help us God.* And the Juftice of the Peace, before whom they are fworn, fhall, and he is hereby required, to certify on the faid account that they have taken this oath.

To account with the Treafurer upon oath when and how

XXIV. AND for the more effectual prevention of frauds in fhipping uninfpected tobacco, and in the not regularly entering and reporting at the naval offices tobaccoes fhipped from the warehoufes; *Be it further enacted,* that the feveral infpectors of tobacco in this ftate fhall, annually, at the time of fettling their accounts with the Treafurer, deliver to him an account, upon oath, of all the tobacco fhipped from their refpective warehoufes within the year preceding, containing the number of hogfheads or cafks fent on board each fhip or veffel refpectively; and every infpector failing herein, fhall forfeit and pay the fum of fifty pounds. And that the feveral Naval Officers fhall, on or before the twenty fifth day of *Oc-tober* annually, return to the faid Treafurer an account, upon oath, of all the tobacco on board each fhip or veffel which fhall have been cleared out in fuch Naval Officer's diftrict in the preceding year, according to the manifefts thereof delivered by the mafter of fuch fhip or veffel at the time of clearing, diftinguifh- ing the number of hogfheads or cafks put on board fuch fhip or veffel from each refpective warehoufe; and every Naval Officer failing herein, fhall forfeit and pay the fum of one hundred pounds for every failure. And if any Juftice of the Peace fhall know, or be informed upon oath, of any tobacco preffed or packed, in order to be fhipped off or carried out of this ftate by water, without being infpected, fuch Juftice by himfelf, or any fheriff, or conftable, by warrant from fuch Juftice, within the limits of his county, fhall have power and authority, and is hereby required, to enter any fufpected houfes, and to break open all doors in the day time, the keys of fuch doors having been firft demanded, and refufed to be delivered, to fearch for the fame; and if any tobacco fhall be found by fuch Juftice, fheriff, or conftable, preffed in any hogfhead, cafk, barrel, or other package whatfoever, fuch Juftice, fheriff, or conftable, fhall feize the fame; and the perfon in whofe poffeffion fuch tobacco fhall be found, fhall forfeit to the informer five pounds for every hundred weight, and fo in proportion for a lefs quantity, to be recovered with cofts in any court of record, if it be twenty five fhillings or upwards. And any Juftice of the Peace of any county near the place where any fhip or other veffel fhall ride, upon infor- mation to him made upon oath, by any free man, that there is good caufe to fufpect any tobacco unin- fpected, in cafk, bulk, or parcels, to be on board fuch fhip or other veffel, fhall, and he is hereby empowered and required to iffue his warrant directed to the fheriff or any conftable of his county; and the fheriff or any conftable of his county; and the fheriff or conftable fhall have full power and authority, and he is hereby required to enter and go on board fuch fhip or other veffel, to fearch for and feize fuch tobacco, and the fame being feized, fhall be brought on fhore and carried before the fame or any other Juf- tice, who fhall caufe the faid tobacco to be carried to the neareft warehoufe and there infpected, and if paffed reftored to the owner in cafe he fhall be innocent of the fraud; but if he fhall appear to have been concerned in fuch fraud, or if no owner fhall claim within three months, the faid tobacco fhall be fold by the in- fpectors, and the money arifing from fuch fale be paid into the public treafury, and accounted for to the General Affembly. And the commanding officer or fkipper of any fhip or veffel on board which fuch tobacco is found, fhall forfeit to the informer five pounds for every hundred weight, and fo in propor-

To return an ac- count annually of all tobacco fhipped, and the penalty.

Naval officers an account of the to- bacco entered—pe- nalty.

Proceeding where tobacco is about to exported by water, uninfpected.

tion for a lefs quantity; to be recovered with cofts, in any court of record, if it be twenty five fhillings or more. And if any mafter or commanding officer or fkipper of any fhip or veffel, or any other perfon whatfoever, fhall refift the officer in the execution of any fuch warrant, every fuch mafter, commanding officer, or fkipper, fhall forfeit and pay two hundred pounds; and every failor or other perfon fo refifting, fhall forfeit and pay twenty five pounds. And if any action fhall be brought againft any Juftice of the Peace, fheriff, or conftable, for doing any thing in execution of this act, the defendant may plead the general iffue and give this act in evidence; and if the plaintiff fhall be non-fuited, or a verdict pafs againft him, or a judgment on demurrer, the defendant fhall recover double cofts.

Old tobacco to be fold.

XXV. AND be it further enacted, that where any tobacco hath remained, or fhall hereafter remain, undemanded in a public warehoufe two years, after the fame hath been or fhall be infpected, the infpectors at fuch warehoufe fhall advertife in the *Virginia* gazette, for three weeks fuccefively, a lift of the marks, numbers, and weights of fuch tobacco, with the names of the perfons for whom it was infpected; and if no owner appears to claim the fame within three months, they fhall at the next court to be held for the county in which fuch warehoufe fhall be, after the expiration thereof, and advertifing as aforefaid, deliver to the court the like lift, which court is hereby empowered and required to order the fame to be publicly fold at the court-houfe door, on a court day, to the higheft bidder; and the money arifing from the fale thereof fhall be paid by the infpectors to the Treafurer of this ftate for the time being, who fhall account for the fame, from time to time, to the General Affembly. And if any perfon having a right to any tobacco fo fold, fhall prove his property therein, the faid Treafurer fhall re-pay to fuch perfon the money for which fuch tobacco was fold.

Infpectors incapacitated for other offices.

XXVI. AND be it further enacted, that no perfon taking upon himfelf the office of infpector, fhall during his continuance in that office, or within two years after he fhall be out of his faid office, be capable of being elected a member of either Houfe of Affembly, or fhall prefume to intermeddle or concern himfelf with an election of a member or members of either of the faid Houfes, otherwife than by giving his vote, or fhall endeavour to influence any perfon or perfons in giving his or their vote, under the penalty of fifty pounds for every offence; nor fhall any infpector by himfelf, or any perfon for him, be allowed to keep an ordinary or houfe of entertainment at or near the warehoufe where he is an infpector; and every infpector herein offending fhall be incapable of ferving in that office; neither fhall any infpector during his continuance in that office, be, or undertake to be, collector of any public tax, other than what relates to fuch office, county or parifh levies, or any officer's fees; nor fhall directly or indirectly for himfelf, or for any other perfon, buy, or receive by way of barter, loan, or exchange, any tobacco whatfoever, under the penalty of fifty fhillings for every hundred pounds of tobacco fo bought or received. *Provided*, that nothing herein contained fhall be conftrued to hinder any infpector from receiving his rents in tobacco, which fhall be firft viewed, examined, and ftamped, according to the directions of this act.

Penalty on infpectors receiving other gratuity than falaries.

XXVII. AND for the further and better directions of the infpectors aforefaid in their duty; Be it enacted, that no infpectors fhall take, accept, or receive, directly or indirectly, any gratuity, fee, or reward, for any thing by him to be done in purfuance of this act, other than his falary, and the other payments and allowances herein before mentioned and expreffed; and if any infpector fhall take, accept, or receive, any fuch gratuity, fee, or reward, fuch infpector being thereof convicted, fhall forfeit and pay the fum of one hundred pounds, to be recovered with cofts, by any perfon or perfons who fhall inform and fue for the fame, by action of debt or information, in any court of record within this commonwealth, and moreover fhall be difabled from holding the office of infpector during the continuance of this act. And if any perfon fhall offer any bribe, reward, or gratuity, to any infpector for any thing

And on the perfon offering a bribe.

by him to be done in purfuance of this act, other than the fees and allowances herein before directed, every perfon fo offending, and being thereof convicted, fhall, for every fuch offence, forfeit and pay the fum of twenty pounds current money, to be recovered in any court of record within this ftate, one half of which forfeiture fhall be to and for the ufe of fuch infpector refufing fuch bribe or reward, and the other half to the perfon who will inform and fue for the fame. And there fhall be paid to the feveral infpectors, appointed to attend and attending the faid feveral warehoufes, the falaries herein after men-

Infpector's falaries.

tioned, that is to fay: At *Pitt's*, *Guildford*, and *Pungoteague*, under one infpection, thirty five pounds; at *Roy's*, fixty pounds; at *Kennon's*, thirty pounds; at *Bolling's Point*, eighty pounds; at *Bollingbrooke*, eighty pounds; at *Cedar Point*, eighty pounds, if the warehoufes fhall be rebuilt and infpectors appointed; at *Hobb's Hole*, thirty five pounds; at *Bowler's*, thirty pounds; at *Layton's*, thirty pounds; at *Colchefter*, fifty pounds; at *Alexandria*, forty pounds; at the falls of *Potowmack*, forty pounds; at *Deacon Neck*, thirty pounds; at *Page's*, eighty pounds; at *Meriwether's*, fixty pounds; at *Poropotank*, thirty pounds; at *Rocky Ridge*, eighty pounds; at *Warwick*, feventy pounds; at *Ofborne's*, fixty pounds; at *John Bolling's*, fixty pounds; at *Byrd's*, eighty pounds; at *Shockoe's*, eighty pounds; at *Rockett's* eighty pounds; at *Smithfield* and *Fulgham's*, under one infpection, thirty five pounds; at *Mantapike* and *Frazer's*, under one infpection, forty pounds; at *Shepherd's*, thirty pounds; at *Aylett's* and *Todd's*, under one infpection, forty pounds; at *Boyd's Hole* and *Machodack*, under one infpection, forty five pounds; at *Gibfon's*, thirty pounds; at *Davis's* and *Lowry's*, under one infpection, thirty pounds; at *Urbanna*, thirty pounds; at *Coan's* and *North-Wicomico*, under one infpection, forty pounds; at *Deep Creek* and *Glafcock's*, under one infpection, thirty five pounds; at *Indian Creek* and *South Wicomico*, under one infpection, forty pounds; at *Milner's* and *Wilkinfon's*, under one infpection, forty pounds; at *Cherryftone's* and *Nafwaddox*, under one infpection, thirty five pounds; at *Littlepage's*, thirty five pounds; at the *Brick-Houfe*, thirty pounds; at *Boyd's* eighty pounds; at *Davis's*, in *Blandford*, eighty pounds; at *Blandford*, eighty pounds; at *Quantico*, feventy pounds; at *Dumfries*, feventy pounds; at *Cat Point*, thirty pounds; at *Totufky*, thirty pounds; at *Gray's Creek* thirty five pounds; at *Low Point*, forty pounds; at *Falmouth*, fixty pounds; at *Acquia*, fifty pounds; at *Dixon's*, fixty pounds; at *Frederickfburg*, feventy pounds; at *Royfton's*, feventy pounds; at *D-nhigh*, twenty five pounds; at *Nominy*, thirty pounds; at *Leed's* and *Maddox*, under one infpection, fifty pounds; at *Yocomico* and *Ruff's*, under one infpection, forty pounds; at *York* town and the *College Landing*, under one infpection, forty pounds; at *Hampton*, ten pounds.

Method of detecting infpectors who fhall not do their duty.

XXVIII. AND for the better detecting infpectors who fhall not do their duty, and for the more fpeedy and eafy examination into complaints againft them; Be it enacted, that any two Juftices of the Peace, not being infpectors, fhall have power to hear all complaints againft any infpector within their county, and to take the depofitions of witneffes upon the matter of fuch complaint on both fides, which fhall be tranfmitted by them to the Governor and Council for their determination. And to the end fuch depofitions may be taken in the beft manner, the clerk of the county, or fome fufficient perfon by him to be appointed, fhall attend the faid Juftices for that purpofe, and be paid by the county the fame fees as is or fhall be by law eftablifhed for attending the examination of witneffes upon a *dedimus poteftatem*. And moreover any two Juftices fhall have power to vifit all or any of the public warehoufes within their county, and if they fhall difcover any negligence in the infpectors either in fecuring the tobacco or ftowing

A. D. 1783.

the fame away in a proper manner for faving the room in fuch houfes, or that they are guilty of any other breach or breaches of their duty, the Juftices fhall certify the Governor and Council thereof. And if any infpector fhall be adjudged guilty of a breach of his duty, he fhall be removed from his office, and be for ever after incapable of ferving as an infpector. And if any infpector fhall be removed from his office, upon a complaint and profecution againft him in the method by this act prefcribed, he fhall be liable to the action on the cafe of the profecutor for his neceffary cofts and expences in fuch profecution, in which the profecutor fhall recover his full cofts of fuit; but if the infpector or infpectors fhall be acquitted upon fuch examination, the profecutor fhall be liable to the action of fuch infpector or infpectors for the recovery of all damages and expences which he or they fhall have fuftained or been put to by fuch profecution and cofts, unlefs the Governor and Council fhall certify that there was reafonable caufe for fuch complaint; and every infpector fhall moreover be liable to the action of the party grieved for all lofs and damage that may happen or arife to any perfon by occafion of any failure of duty or neglect of any fuch infpector, in which action the plaintiff fhall recover his full cofts although the damages do not exceed forty fhillings.

XXIX. *AND be it further enacted*, that all tobacco due or to grow due and payable for public, county, and parifh levies, or for clerks, fheriffs, furveyors, or other officers fees, fhall be paid and difcharged by transfer receipts in the following manner, that is to fay: All levies fhall be paid in fome warehoufe in the county where fuch levies are laid, and all officers fees in the county where the perfon chargeable therewith lives, except fuch perfon fhall have a plantation with flaves thereon in the county where the fervice is performed, and then all fees fhall be paid in fuch county; but the faid levies and fees due and payable in any county where no public warehoufe is eftablifhed, fhall be paid at fome warehoufe in the next adjacent county. *Provided always*, that the receipts from the warehoufes hereafter mentioned fhall pafs in payment of all levies and officers fees payable in the counties following, that is to fay: In the county of *Accomack, Cherryftone's*, and *Nafwaddox*; in the county of *Albemarle, Page's, Fredericksburg, Royfton's, Meriwether's, Rocky Ridge, Byrd's, Shockoe's*, and *Rocket's*; *Amelia, Charlotte, Halifax, Henry, Lunenburg, Mecklenburg, Pittfylvania*, and *Prince Edward*, at *Blandford, Bolling's Point, Bollingbrooke, Davis's, Cedar Point, Boyd's, Rocky Ridge, Warwick*, and *Ofborne's*; *Amherft*, at *Byrd's, Shockoe's, Rockett's, Rocky Ridge, Page's*, and *Meriwether's*; *Bedford and Campbell*, at *Byrd's, Shockoe's, Recketi's, Rocky Ridge*, and *Warwick*; *Brunfwick* and *Greenfville*, at *Blandford, Bolling's Point, Bollingbrooke, John Bolling's, Boyd's, Davis's, Cedar Point, Smithfield, Fulgham's, Low Point*, and *Gray's Creek*; *Nanfemond*, at *Smithfield, Fulgham's*, and *Low Point*; *Buckingham*, at *Byrd's, Shockoe's, Rocket's, Rocky Ridge, Warwick*, and *Ofborne's*; *Caroline*, at *Todd's, Aylett's*, and *Layton's*; *Culpeper*, at *Dixon's, Quantico, Dumfries, Acquia, Falmouth, Frederickfburg*, and *Royfton's*; *Cumberland* and *Powhatan*, at *Byrd's, Shockoe's, Rockett's, Rocky Ridge, Warwick*, and *Ofborne's*; *Dinwiddie*, at *Blandford, Boya's, John Bolling's*, and *Davis's*; *Elizabeth City*, at *Hampton*; *Effex*, at *Port Royal, Todd's*, and *Mantapike*; *Fauquier*, at *Falmouth, Dixon's, Quantico, Dumfries*, and *Acquia*; *Goochland* and *Fluvanna*, at *Byrd's, Shockoe's, Rockett's, Page's Meriwether's*, and *Rocky Ridge*; *James City*, at *Littlepage's, Kennon's*, the *Brick-Houfe, York*, and *College Landing*; *King George*, at *Dixon's, Falmouth*, and *Mattox*; *Ifle of Wight*, at *Kennon's, Wilkinfon's*, and *Milner's*; *King William*, at *Meriwether's* and *Page's*; *Lancafter*, at *Indian Creek*; *Loudoun*, at any of the warehoufes in *Fairfax* and *Prince William*; *Louifa* and *Orange*, at *Frederickfburg, Royfton's, Page's, Meriwether's, Byrd's, Shockoe's*, and *Rockett's*; *Norfolk*, at any of the warehoufes in *Nanfemond* and *Elizabeth City*; *Northampton*, at *Pitt's, Guildford*, and *Pungoteague*; *New Kent*, at the *Brick Houfe, Littlepage's*, and *Kennon's*; *Northumberland*, at *Yeocomico* and *Ruffs*; *Prince George*, at *Bolling's Point, John Bolling's, Cedar Point, Bollingbrooke, Davis's, Blandford, Low Point, Gray's Creek*, and *Kennon's*; *Prince William* at *Alexandria, Acquia*, and *Colchefter*; *Fairfax*, at *Quantico* and *Dumfries*; *Gloucefter*, at *Deacon's Neck* and *Poropotank*; *Princefs Anne*, at any of the warehoufes in *Nanfemond* and *Elizabeth City*; *Southampton*, at any of the warehoufes in *Ifle* of *Wight* and at *Low Point*; *Stafford*, at *Boya's Hole, Gibfon's, Dumfries*, and *Quantico*; *Surry*, at *Kennon's, Blandford, Boyd's*, and *Davis's*; *Suffex*, at *Blandford, Bolling's Point, Bollingbrooke, John Bolling's, Davis's, Boya's, Cedar Point, Gray's Creek, Low Point*, and *Smithfield*; *Weftmoreland*, at *Machodack* and *Gibfon's*; *York*, at *College Landing, Denbigh*, and the *Brick-Houfe*.

XXX. *AND be it further enacted*, that all public, county, and parifh levies, fheriffs, clerks, furveyors, and other officers fees, payable in tobacco, fhall be paid and fatisfied, by the perfons chargeable with, and indebted for the fame, to the fheriffs or other collectors, by transfer receipts before the tenth day of *June* yearly. And if any perfon chargeable with the levies and fees aforefaid, fhall neglect or refufe to pay the fame within the time aforefaid, it fhall be lawful to and for the fheriffs and other collectors, immediately after the faid tenth day of *June*, to diftrain the goods and chattels of the perfon or perfons fo neglecting or refufing, and to fell and difpofe thereof for tobacco in the fame manner as is directed by law for goods taken in execution; and the overplus (if any be) after paying the feveral levies and fees, and the charge of diftrefs, which is hereby declared to be the fame as for ferving an execution, fhall be returned to the debtor. And the fheriffs or other collectors of the faid levies and fees, fhall, before the laft day of *July* yearly, pay and deliver to each creditor, according to their refpective debts or claims, all the infpectors receipts he or they fhall have received in fatisfaction thereof; and if any fheriff or other collector fhall refufe or delay to make payment accordingly, if required, he or they fo refufing or delaying, fhall forfeit and pay to the party grieved double the value of the tobacco fo refufed or delayed to be paid; to be recovered with cofts, in any court of record within this ftate.

XXXI. *AND be it further enacted*, that if any of the warehoufes herein before mentioned, fhall happen to be burnt, the lofs fuftained thereby fhall be made good and repaired to the feveral perfons injured, by the General Affembly; and in cafe of fuch accident, no infpector fhall be fued or molefted for or by reafon of any receipts by them given, or for any tobacco burnt in any of the faid warehoufes, but fhall be altogether acquitted and difcharged of, and from the payment of the tobacco in fuch receipts mentioned; any thing herein before contained to the contrary notwithftanding. *Provided always*, that if the receipts for tobacco fo burnt and deftroyed fhall be of an older date than twelve months, the tobacco fhall not be paid for by the public, but the owner or proprietor thereof fhall bear the lofs.

XXXII. *AND be it further enacted*, that the infpectors fhall not permit the proprietor or any other perfon to make ufe of the warehoufe at which they are infpectors. And if any warehoufe fhall hereafter happen to be burnt, and it fhall appear that fuch warehoufe was burnt by means of the infpectors permiting the proprietor or any other perfon to make ufe thereof, fuch infpectors fhall re-pay to the Treafurer for the time being, all fuch fum or fums of money as fhall have been paid to the perfon or perfons fo injured.

XXXIII. *AND be it further enacted*, that if any perfon hereafter fhall make any fire within any public warehoufe, or without doors, within one hundred yards of fuch warehoufe, other than in the infpectors

How tobacco due for levies, &c. fhall be paid.

When they may be diftrained for.

When the fheriffs are to account.

Warehoufes burnt, the public to pay for the tobacco, and infpectors indemnified.

Exception.

Warehoufes not to be ufed for private purpofes.

No fire to be kindled in or near a warehoufe.

A. D. 1783.

Nor wooden chim-
neys built near.

counting room, fquares, or funnels, fuch perfon, if a freeman, fhall, for every fuch offence, forfeit and pay ten pounds, to be recovered, with cofts, by action of debt or information, in any court of record within this ftate, by the informer to his own ufe; and if a fervant or flave, he or fhe fhall, by order of any Juftice of the Peace, receive on his or her bare back twenty lafhes for every fuch offence. And it fhall not be lawful for any perfon whatfoever to erect or build, or caufe to be erected or built, any wooden chimney or chimnies within two hundred yards of any public warehoufe; and where any fuch are already built, within the diftance aforefaid of any public warehoufe, the owner or proprietor there-of fhall pull down the fame, or on refufal or neglect fo to do in one month after the paffing of this act, it fhall be lawful for the fheriff of the county, and he is hereby required, to caufe fuch chimney or chim-nies to be pulled down and demolifhed.

Infpectors to keep
books, &c.

and deliver mani-
fefts with each load
of tobacco.

Tobacco relanded
or put on board
other fhips.

XXXIV. AND to the intent that the juft quantity of tobacco exported may be more exactly known, and evil practices to defraud the public of the duty prevented; *Be it enacted,* that all infpectors fhall carefully enter in a book, to be provided and kept for that purpofe, the marks, numbers, grofs, nett weight, and tare, of all tobacco viewed and ftamped by them as aforefaid, and in what fhip or veffel the the fame fhall be laden or put on board; and fhall alfo, with every floop or boat load of tobacco, fend a lift of the marks, numbers, grofs, nett weight, and tare, of every hogfhead or cafk of tobacco then de-livered, to be given to the mafter of the fhip or veffel in which the fame fhall be put on board; and if the tobacco delivered to the fame floop or boat is intended to be put on board feveral fhips or veffels, then they fhall deliver fo many diftinct and feveral lifts as aforefaid of the hogfheads or cafks to be put on board fuch fhip or veffel refpectively; which lifts every mafter of a fhip or veffel is required to pro-duce to and lodge with the Naval Officer of the diftrict where the fame fhip or veffel whereof he is maf-ter fhall ride, or by whom he fhall be cleared, fome time before his clearance. But whereas it may happen that the fhip in which fuch tobacco was intended to be put, may be fo full as not to be able to ftow all the tobacco contained in fuch lift, in fuch cafe it fhall be lawful to fhip the faid tobacco, or any part thereof, on board any other fhip or fhips where the owner thereof fhall think fit, the mafters of fuch fhips endorfing on the faid lifts the marks and numbers of the refpective hogfheads by them taken on board, and giving notice to the infpectors of the warehoufe from which the fame was brought; or if there be no fhip to receive the faid tobacco, then it fhall be lawful for the mafter of the firft mentioned fhip or veffel to put the faid tobacco into any warehoufe in the diftrict where fuch fhip or veffel fhall ride, giving immediate notice thereof to the infpectors who ftamped the fame. And the infpectors of that warehoufe where fuch tobacco fhall be delivered, fhall receive from the perfons re-landing fuch tobacco, one fhilling and fix pence for every hogfhead fo re-landed, and fhall give a receipt for the fame; which money fo received by the infpectors, fhall be paid by them to the perfon or perfons entitled to receive the rent of the faid warehoufe.

Death to counter-
feit notes, &c.

XXXV. AND be it further enacted, that he or fhe fhall be adjudged a felon, and not have the benefit of clergy, who fhall forge or counterfeit, alter or erafe, the ftamp or receipt of any infpector or infpec-tors; or fhall caufe or procure fuch ftamp or receipt to be forged or counterfeited, altered or erafed; or fhall aid or affift in forging or counterfeiting, altering or erafing fuch ftamp or receipt; or fhall pafs or tender, or fhall caufe or procure to be paffed or tendered, any fuch ftamp or receipt, in payment or ex-change, knowing the fame to have been forged or counterfeited, altered or erafed; or fhall have in his or her cuftody or poffeffion any infpectors ftamp or receipt, which hath been altered or erafed, knowing the fame to have been altered or erafed, and fhall not difcover fuch altered or erafed ftamp or receipt to two Juftices of the Peace before the firft day of *July,* in the prefent year, or within five days after they or either of them, fhall have come to his or her poffeffion; or fhall export, or caufe to be exported, any hogfhead or cafk of tobacco ftamped with a forged or counterfeited ftamp; or fhall receive or de-mand tobacco of an infpector upon any forged or counterfeited, altered or erafed ftamp or receipt, knowing fuch ftamp or receipt to be forged or counterfeited, altered or erafed; or fhall put or pack, or caufe or procure to be put or packed, into any hogfhead or cafk, ftamped by an infpector, any tobacco whatfoever; or fhall draw or take out, or caufe or procure to be drawn or taken out, any ftaves, plank, or heading board, of any hogfhead or cafk of tobacco, fo ftamped as aforefaid, after the fame fhall be delivered out of any of the public warehoufes aforefaid.

Or to iffue double
notes for the fame to-
bacco, or notes for
tobacco not received.

XXXVI. AND be it further enacted, that if any infpector or infpectors fhall give, deliver, or iffue, to any perfon whatfoever, his or their receipt, expreffed to be for any hogfhead or cafk of tobacco, or for any quantity of transfer tobacco, which they have not actually received into the warehoufe whereof they are infpectors, at the time of giving fuch receipt; or fhall give, deliver, iffue, or caufe or procure to be given, delivered, or iffued, more than one receipt for any hogfhead or cafk of tobacco, or quantity of transfer tobacco, by him or them received, except where authorized by law fo to do, fuch infpector or infpectors, being thereof convicted by due courfe of law, fhall be adjudged a felon, and fhall fuffer death as in cafe of felony, without benefit of clergy.

Method to be taken
where receipts are
loft.

Penalty for falfe
oath, or producing
a forged certificate.

XXXVII. AND be it further enacted, that if any infpectors receipt be cafually loft, miflaid, or deftroy-ed, the perfon or perfons entitled to receive the tobacco, by virtue of any fuch receipt, fhall make oath before any Juftice of the Peace of the county where the fame is payable, to the number and date of every fuch receipt, to whom and where payable, and for what quantity of tobacco the fame was given, and that fuch receipt is loft, miflaid, or deftroyed, and that he, fhe, or they, at the time fuch receipt was loft, miflaid, or deftroyed, was lawfully entitled to receive the tobacco therein mentioned, and fhall take a certificate thereof from fuch Juftice; and upon producing a certificate of fuch oath to the infpec-tors who figned fuch receipt, and lodging the fame with them, the infpectors fhall, and are hereby di-rected, to pay and deliver to the perfon obtaining fuch certificate, the tobacco for which any fuch receipt was given, if the fame or any part thereof fhall not have been before by them paid by virtue of the faid receipts, and fhall be thereby difcharged from all actions, fuits, and demands, on account of fuch re-ceipts. And if any perfon fhall be convicted of making a falfe oath, or producing a forged certificate in the cafe aforefaid, fuch perfon fhall fuffer as in cafe of wilful and corrupt perjury.

New infpectors to
give their predecef-
fors a receipt for the
tobacco in the ware-
houfes.

Infpectors difcharg-
ed on the delivery of
tobacco.

XXXVIII. AND be it enacted, that when any new infpectors fhall be appointed at any of the faid warehoufes, fuch infpectors fhall, and they are hereby required, to give to the perfon or perfons whom they fhall fucceed, a receipt, with his or their hands fubfcribed, containing the numbers, marks, grofs, tare, and nett weight, of all and every hogfhead or cafk of tobacco which fhall be then remaining at the warehoufe or warehoufes at which time they are appointed infpectors, with the delivery and pay-ment of which faid hogfheads or cafks of tobacco fo remaining, he or they fhall from thenceforth be chargeable and liable; but he or they fhall in no wife be accountable or anfwerable for the lofs of weight or for quality of tobacco contained in any hogfhead or cafk, for which receipt was by him or them fo as aforefaid given. And if any hogfhead or cafk of tobacco fhall hereafter be received by any perfon or perfons whatfoever, and delivered out of any of the faid warehoufes for exportation, by the infpector or infpectors attending the fame, fuch infpector or infpectors from the time of fuch delivery, fhall be

A. D. 1783.

for ever difcharged and acquitted from all actions, cofts, and charges for, or by reafon of, the tobacco contained in any fuch hogfhead or cafk being unfound and unmerchantable, or of lefs quantity than the receipts given for the fame fhall fpecify; any thing herein before contained to the contrary notwith-ftanding. And when any prized tobacco fhall be brought to any public warehoufe, in order to be fhip-ped on freight or otherwife, and the infpectors there attending fhall refufe to pafs fuch tobacco, unlefs fuch as fhall be bad and unmerchantable fhall be picked and feparated from the reft; or where any light crop tobacco fhall hereafter be brought to any of the faid warehoufes, in either cafe, the faid infpectors, if required, fhall permit the owner or other perfon bringing fuch tobacco, to make ufe of one or more of their prizes, for the re-packing, prizing, or making heavier, fuch tobacco, without fee or reward; and if there fhall be feveral hogfheads of tobacco, belonging to feveral owners, to be picked, re-packed, or prized, at any public warehoufe, the owner or other perfon bringing the fame, whofe tobacco fhall be firft viewed and refufed, or found light, fhall be firft permitted and allowed to make ufe of fuch prize or prizes, for the purpofes aforefaid; and no infpector fhall take or convert to his own ufe, or other-wife difpofe of, any draughts or famples of transfer or crop tobacco, but the fame, if fit to pafs, fhall be put into the hogfhead or bulk out of which it was drawn, under the penalty of forfeiting twenty fhillings for every draught fo taken away and not returned as aforefaid, contrary to the directions of this act, to be recovered by the informer, one moiety to his own ufe, and the other moiety to the ufe of the proprietor of fuch tobacco, before any Juftice of the Peace of the county wherein fuch offence fhall be committed. And all infpectors, if required, fhall alter the mark and number of any hogfhead of re-prized tobacco for which they have before given a receipt; and for preventing confufion and mif-takes fhall keep a wafte book, in which fhall be entered the marks and numbers of all hogfheads of to-bacco received by them, and another book, in which fhall be entered the marks, numbers, and weights thereof, when the fame fhall be delivered out by them; and all infpectors, when required, fhall be oblig-ed to prize any light hogfhead of tobacco under one thoufand pounds, fo as to make it up the weight one thoufand pounds nett, but fhall receive the fame fee upon fuch hogfhead as for transfer tobacco. And where any tobacco fhall be brought to the warehoufe by the overfeer of the owner thereof, the infpectors fhall give receipts in the name of the owner and not of the overfeer.

Prizes to be ufed in turn for prizing tobacco picked or light hogfheads.

Penalty for taking and ufing drafts.

Infpectors to prize light crop tobacco on requeft.
To give notes in the name of the owner, not the overfeer.

XXXIX. AND be it enacted, that the infpectors of tobacco at the feveral warehoufes within this ftate, fhall, immediately on the delivery of every hogfhead of tobacco at the warehoufe whereof they are infpectors, give a receipt for fuch tobacco, if required by the proprietor or perfon bringing the fame to the faid warehoufes, expreffing therein that the fame is for uninfpected tobacco; every infpector refufing fo to do, fhall forfeit and pay to the owner of fuch tobacco the fum of twenty fhillings.

To give receipts for tobacco when brought.

XL. AND be it further enacted, that all the penalties and forfeitures in this act contained, and not herein before particularly appropriated, fhall be one moiety to the commonwealth, to be applied towards defraying the charges of the execution of this act, and the other half for the perfon who fhall inform and fue for the fame, and fhall be recovered, with cofts, by action of debt or information, in any court of record within this ftate, where the penalty or forfeiture exceeds twenty five fhillings or two hundred pounds of tobacco; and where the fame does not exceed thofe fums, before any Juftice of the Peace for the county where the offence fhall be committed.

Penalties how to be recovered and applied.

XLI. AND whereas recoveries and forfeitures inflicted by this act are liable to be evaded by mafters or commanders and fkippers of veffels and other perfons leaving this ftate, before any action or fuit brought for fuch recovery can be determined: For remedy thereof, Be it enacted, that upon the ap-pearance of the defendant in any action or fuit brought againft any mafter, commander, or fkipper of any veffel, or any other perfon, for a breach of this act, where the plaintiff fhall move that the defendant may be held to fpecial bail, the court may, if they fee caufe, rule him to give fpecial bail accordingly, or commit him in cuftody of the fheriff until fuch bail be given; any law, cuftom, or ufage, to the con-trary notwithftanding.

Mafters of veffels fued may be ruled to bail.

XLII. AND whereas, the act of Affembly paffed in October one thoufand feven hundred and feventy eight, for reviving feveral public warehoufes for the infpection of tobacco, hath expired, and it is necef-fary the fame fhould be revived and continued; Be it therefore enacted, that the faid recited act fhall be and is hereby revived and continued until the laft day of September next, except fo much thereof as makes it felony for any perfon or perfons to forge, counterfeit, alter or erafe, any infpector or infpectors receipt or ftamp; and in lieu thereof fo much of this act as inflicts the punifhment on perfons guilty of the offences aforefaid, or either of them, is hereby declared to be in force from the paffing the fame.

The act of Oct. 1778, ch. 10, re-vived and continued till September. Exception.

XLIII. AND whereas the feveral amendatory acts of Affembly for the infpection of tobacco, paffed fubfequent to the aforefaid act of one thoufand feven hundred and feventy eight, will expire at the end of this feffion of Affembly, and it is expedient the fame fhould be further continued; Be it therefore enacted, that all and every act or acts, paffed as aforefaid, fhall continue and be in force until the laft day of September next, and no longer.

Other fubfequent acts continued to fame time.

XLIV. AND be it further enacted, that all acts and proceedings of the infpectors, made and done in purfuance of the directions of the faid recited act, or any or either of them, fhall, notwithftanding the expiration thereof, be held and deemed good and valid in law. And all fuch infpectors are hereby ex-onerated and difcharged of and from all cofts, damages, pains and penalties, by them incurred or to be incurred, for any thing by them done in purfuance of the faid acts by reafon of the expiration thereof.

Infpectors indem-nified.

XLV. AND be it further enacted, that in cafe any of the warehoufes herein before named fhall not after the firft day of October next, and before the firft day of October one thoufand feven hundred and eighty five, receive a fufficient quantity of tobacco to pay the infpectors falaries and rents of the ware-houfes, the infpection of tobacco at fuch warehoufes refpectively fhall be thenceforth difcontinued, unlefs the fame fhall be fupported at private expence. Provided, that this claufe fhall not extend to the dif-continuance at one time of two or more warehoufes which may be in the fame county, or county next adjacent, but in fuch cafes, that warehoufe fhall be difcontinued to which the fmalleft quantity of tobacco may be brought in the years aforefaid.

Warehoufes to be difcontinued Octo-ber 1, 1785, if the infpection tax don't pay the falaries and rent.
Exception.

XLVI. AND be it enacted, that the public printer fhall furnifh one copy of this act to the infpectors at each of the warehoufes herein mentioned; and alfo to each of the Naval Officers within this ftate. This act fhall commence and be in force from and after the firft day of October next, and not fooner, except fuch parts as are declared to be in force from the paffing thereof.

Commencement of this act.

XLVII. AND be it further enacted, that the acting infpectors of tobacco at the feveral warehoufes be, and they are hereby exempted from militia duty, except in cafe of actual invafion or infurrection.

Infpectors exempt from militia duty.

A. D. 1783.

See May 1782, ch. 2.

CHAP. XI.

An act to amend the act for appropriating the public revenue.

Preamble.

I. WHEREAS the General Assembly of this commonwealth did, during the last session, pass an an act, entitled *An act to amend and reduce the several acts of Assembly for ascertaining certain taxes and duties, and for establishing a permanent revenue, into one act*; which act hath been amended by an act passed the present session of Assembly, entitled *An act to amend an act to amend and reduce the several acts of Assembly for ascertaining certain taxes and duties, and for establishing a permanent revenue, into one act*: And whereas the operation of the said acts, as well as the present circumstances of this state, render it necessary that the act entitled *An act for appropriating the public revenue*, should be amended: *Be it therefore enacted*, that all the revenue arising under the said first recited act, as now

Land tax appropriated.

amended, shall be appropriated as herein after directed; and the same shall be paid accordingly, the respective claims being previously audited, and warrants drawn by the Auditors of public accounts accordingly. The land tax arising within the borough of *Norfolk* shall be applied towards the payment of the debt due from the state to the said borough, for public buildings destroyed by order of Convention: There shall also be a sufficient sum out of the land tax applied towards the discharge of the interest due on certificates for paper money funded agreeable to the directions of an act entitled *An act for calling in and funding the paper money of this state*: And there shall also be reserved, one tenth part of the said land tax toward the redemption of the money issued by authority of this state, agreeable to the recommendation of Congress of the eighteenth day of *March*, one thousand seven hundred and eighty: And all the rest of the tax on land arising from the said recited acts, shall be applied to the use of Congress, towards paying this state's quota of the interest of the debt due by the United States.

Slave tax.

II. AND be it further enacted, that the money arising from the tax on slaves, shall be applied towards the payment of this state's debt due to the army, agreeable to the directions of an act, entitled *An act to establish permanent and adequate funds for the redemption of the certificates granted the officers and soldiers for their arrears of pay and depreciation*; and also that the money arising from the said tax, shall be applied towards making good to Congress any deficiency which may arise in this state's quota of interest due on the debts of the United States, so as to make good to Congress the annual sum of four hundred thousand dollars.

III. AND to prevent all doubts respecting the apportionment of the said slave tax, *Be it enacted*, that the Treasurer shall, as the same may be paid into the public treasury, apply one half of the money so paid towards the discharge of the aforesaid debt due to the army, if so much shall be requisite to make good the annual claim of the army, agreeable to the aforesaid act, entitled *An act to establish permanent and adequate funds for the redemption of the certificates granted the officers and soldiers for their arrears of pay and depreciation*; and the other half of the tax on slaves, as the same may be paid into the treasury, shall be applied towards making good any deficiency which may arise to make good this state's quota of the interest of the debt due by the United States, so as to make up annually the aforesaid sum of four hundred thousand dollars; and if the said revenue arising from the tax on slaves shall exceed the sums requisite to compleat such payments to the army and to Congress, such overplus or excess shall be applied towards the payment of any debts, either foreign or domestic, due by this state, for the payment whereof no other provision hath been or shall be made by law; such payments to be made by the Treasurer, agreeable to order of the Executive, who shall direct the payment of the same to such public creditors as in their opinion have the most pressing and meritorious demands against the public for the same.

All other taxes.

IV. AND be it further enacted, that all the revenue arising from the tax on free male tithables, and all taxable property included in the said revenue law, and not before appropriated, shall be applied as follows: Five tenths thereof to the support of civil government; one tenth towards the payment of debts due on the military fund; one tenth thereof to the payment of military pensioners, and the sums voted for the immediate relief of wounded or disabled officers and soldiers; one other tenth to be applied towards the contingent expences of government, to be paid to the orders of the Executive; and the remaining two tenths to be reserved in the treasury, subject to the future direction of the General Assembly.

Tonnage duty.

V. AND be it further enacted, that all the duties and tonnage arising under the said revenue act, and all the money arising under the law for recruiting this state's quota of troops to serve in the continental army, and not heretofore appropriated by any act or resolution of the General Assembly, shall be applied in aid of the fund for the support of civil government; and if the said fund shall be more than sufficient for the purpose, the excess or overplus shall be applied in aid of the fund for the contingent charges of government, at the disposition of the Executive.

Auditors to furnish the Treasurer with distinct accounts of each branch of taxes.

VI. AND be it further enacted, that the Auditors shall furnish the Treasurer with an account of the sums to be paid into the Treasury by the sheriffs for taxes collected under the said revenue law, at the time of paying the same, distinguishing the tax paid for land, for slaves, and on free male tithables, and other property.

Repealing clause.

VII. AND be it further enacted, that all and every other act or acts, as comes within the purview of this act, shall be hereby repealed.

CHAP. XII.

See May 1779. ch. 16, and notes.

An act to repeal so much of any act or acts of Assembly as declares the Delegates to Congress eligible to either House of Assembly.

Preamble.

Repealing clause.

I. WHEREAS it is improper that a Delegate to Congress should, at the same time, be a member of the General Assembly: *Be it therefore enacted*, that so much of any act or acts of Assembly as declares that the Delegates to Congress shall be eligible to either House of Assembly, shall be, and the same is hereby repealed.

Acceptance of appointment to Congress, vacates the seat of a member of Assembly.

II. AND be it further enacted, that if any member of either House of Assembly shall accept of an appointment to Congress, the seat of such member, in either House of Assembly, shall be thereby vacated.

CHAP. XIII.

Private.

An act for clearing Roanoke *river.*

CHAP. XIV.

An act to repeal so much of any act or acts of Assembly as subject the people called Quakers and Menonists to penalties or disabilities for non-juring.

See May 1777, ch. 3.

I. WHEREAS by an act entitled *An act to oblige the free male inhabitants of this state above a certain age to give assurance of allegiance to the same, and for other purposes,* non-jurors are prohibited from purchasing lands, suing for debts, and are subject to other disabilities; which said prohibition is greatly oppressive on those peaceable and industrious people of the community, known by the names of Quakers and Menonists, who from conscientious scruples have declined giving that assurance of allegiance which is enjoined by the above recited act: For remedy whereof, *Be it enacted,* that so much of the said act, and any other law, as does disable any person or persons that are *bona fide* in religious fellowship with the said people called Quakers, or with the people called Menonists, from exercising and enjoying the rights and privileges they might have done in case the said act or acts had never been passed, shall be, and the same is hereby repealed.

Preamble.

Repealing clause.

II. AND *be it further enacted,* that where any Quaker or Quakers, Menonist or Menonists, shall have purchased lands or other property, such purchases shall be deemed valid, and held in the same manner as if the above recited act or acts had never been made.

Confirmation of their purchases.

CHAP. XV.

An act for granting pardon to John Holland.

Private.

CHAP. XVI.

An act concerning Peter Heron, *a subject of his Most Christian Majesty.*

Private.

CHAP. XVII.

An act to authorize the Auditors to grant new warrants and certificates in certain cases.

I. BE *it enacted by the General Assembly,* that it shall be lawful for the Auditors of public accounts, and they are hereby directed and required, upon application, to issue other warrants and certificates where former ones by them granted shall be lost and not paid; and where any such warrants or certificates shall have been granted for paper money, to reduce and liquidate the same agreeable to the legal scale of depreciation.

New warrants, &c. instead of those lost.

II. PROVIDED *always, and it is further enacted,* that every person making application as aforesaid, shall before other warrants or certificates be issued, take an oath to be administered by either of the Auditors, or before the court of his or her county, that he or she hath lost such warrant or certificate, as the case may be, and hath not directly or indirectly received any satisfaction for the same; and shall moreover enter into bond with sufficient security, in double the sum contained in such warrant or certificate, payable to the Governor in behalf of the commonwealth, to indemnify the state against the warrant or certificate so lost; and where such bond and security shall be given in the county court, the same shall be transmitted, together with the certificate of the court, to the Auditors.

Oath to be made and bond given.

CHAP. XVIII.

An act authorizing the Justices of the county of Monongalia *to appoint a place for holding courts for the said county and for other purposes.*

Private.

CHAP. XIX.

An act to alter the place of holding courts in the county of Brunswick.

Private.

CHAP. XX.

An act to repeal so much of an act entitled An act to suspend in part the operation of the act concerning escheats and forfeitures from British subjects, and for other purposes, as empowers the Governor and Council to draw warrants on the Treasurer in favour of George Harmer.

Private. See May 1780, ch. 27, Oct. 1780, ch. 24.

CHAP. XXI.

An act to amend and reduce into one act the several acts of Assembly for the appointment of Naval Officers and and ascertaining their fees.

I. WHEREAS it is expedient and necessary to amend and reduce into one act, the several acts of Assembly for the appointment of Naval Officers, and ascertaining their fees: *Be it therefore enacted,* that there shall be a Naval Officer for each of the following districts, that is to say: For the lower district of *James* river, extending from *Hampton* to the mouth of *Kyth's* or *Lawn's* creek; for the upper district of the said river, extending from *Kyth's* or *Lawn's* creek upwards; for the district of *Elizabeth* river, extending to *Chuccatuck* creek; for the district of *South Quay*; for the district of *York* river; for the district of *Rappahannock*; for the district of *South Potowmack*, and a deputy for the said district to reside at *Alexandria*; and two for the district of the *Eastern Shore,* namely, one in the county of *Accomack,* and one in the county of *Northampton*; to be hereafter appointed, in case of vacancies, by joint ballot of both Houses of Assembly, and commissioned by the Governor. The Naval Office for the lower district on *James* river shall be kept at *Hampton*; the one for the upper district at *Burwell's* ferry; the one for the district of *Elizabeth* river at *Norfolk*; the one for the district of *York* river at *York* town; the one for the district of *Rappahannock* at *Urbanna*; the one for the district of *South Potowmack* at the mouth of *Yocomico*; the one for the county of *Accomack* at *Accomack* court-house; and the one for the county of *Northampton* at *Bridge* town. And if any Naval Officer shall not keep his office at the

Preamble.

Districts.

How Naval Officers to be appointed.

Where the offices are to be kept, or the office forfeited.

A. D. 1783.

To give bond and be sworn.

The oath.

Vacancies to be temporarily supplied by Governor and Council.

place herein fixed for the same, he shall forfeit his office, and another Naval Officer shall be appointed in like manner as is herein after directed in the case of death, resignation, or other disability. Every Naval Officer, at the time of receiving his commission, shall enter into bond with good and sufficient security, in the penalty of five thousand pounds, for the due and faithful discharge of his office according to law; and moreover take the following oath, to be administered by the Governor in Council, to wit: I A. B. *do swear that I will be faithful and true to the commonwealth of Virginia, and will well and truly discharge the duty of Naval Officer for the district of*   *according to law, and the best of my skill and judgment, without favour, affection, or partiality. So help me God.* Vacancies occasioned by the death, resignation, or other disability, of any of the said Naval Officers, shall be supplied by the Governor, with the advice of the Council, to continue in office until the end of the next session of Assembly. Every Naval Officer shall, upon application, grant a permit, under his hand and seal, to the owner or master of a vessel within his district, to export out of this commonwealth any commodities whatsoever.

Rules for observing embargoes.

II. AND to prevent the dangerous consequences that may arise from the breach and contempt of embargoes, *Be it further enacted,* that every master of a ship or vessel, when he makes his entry, shall give bond with security, in the penalty of one thousand pounds, that he will not depart this commonwealth when an embargo is laid, during the continuance thereof; and every Naval Officer upon receipt of the order for such embargo, shall forthwith give notice thereof to the masters of vessels within his district; and no bond given, respecting such embargo, shall be adjudged, deemed, or taken to be forfeited, unless notice be given as aforesaid. Every Naval Officer at the time of, and before clearing out any vessel, shall administer to the master thereof the following oath (and if a Quaker he shall affirm) that is to say: I A. B. *master of the vessel*   *, do swear (or affirm, as the case may be) that I will make diligent enquiry and search in my said vessel, and will not knowingly or willingly carry or suffer to be carried in my said vessel, out of this commonwealth, without such pass as is directed by law, any person or persons whatsoever, that I shall know to be removing hence in order to defraud his or their creditors; or any servant or slave that is not attending his or her master or owner.* And the master of every vessel who unloaded ballast, shall, at the time of clearing, produce to the Naval Officer a certificate as herein after mentioned, that such ballast was unloaded and brought on shore according to law; and on failure thereof, he shall forfeit and pay the sum of fifty pounds to the use of the commonwealth. That every Naval Officer, at the time of granting a permit to load or trade, shall take bond of the master of the vessel, in the penalty of two hundred pounds, conditioned that he will not crop, cut away the bulge, draw the staves, or otherwise abuse or injure any tobacco cask freighted in his vessel, or cause or suffer the same to be done with his knowledge, privity, or procurement, without the consent of the freighter or freighters; and if the Naval Officer shall neglect to take such bond, he shall forfeit and pay the sum of two hundred pounds, to be recovered by information and applied, one moiety to the use of the commonwealth, and the other to the informer.

Oath to be taken by masters of vessels at clearing.

And certificates as to ballast produced.

Bond to be taken on granting a permit to trade.

Naval Officers fees.

III. AND be it further enacted, that the fees of the Naval Officers shall be as follows: For entering and clearing and all necessary papers for any vessel under sixty tons, except vessels transporting goods from one district to another, thirty shillings; for entering and clearing any vessel above sixty and under one hundred tons, forty shillings; for entering and clearing any vessel above one hundred tons and under two hundred tons, fifty shillings; for entering and clearing any vessel above two hundred tons, sixty shillings; to be paid in the current money of this state. If any Naval Officer shall presume to demand or take, directly or indirectly, any greater or other fee or fees, recompence or reward, than is allowed by this act, or shall connive at a false entry, and be thereof lawfully convicted, he shall be for ever after rendered incapable of holding such office, and another Naval Officer shall be appointed in his stead, in like manner as is directed in the case of resignation.

Penalty for over charging, or conniving at a false entry.

To be prosecuted within one year.

Tables of fees to be set up in his office in English, French, and Dutch.

IV. PROVIDED always, and it is further enacted, that no Naval Officer shall be impeached or questioned for or concerning any offence aforesaid, unless he be prosecuted for the same within one year. Every Naval Officer shall set up, or cause to be set up, in the most public place in his office, and constantly kept there, three fair written tables or copies of the fees allowed by this act, that is to say, one in the *English*, one in the *French*, and one other in the *Dutch* language; and also a table in each of the said languages, shewing plainly and clearly the duties payable on all goods imported, and the tonnage payable on vessels; and upon receiving any fee or fees of office, shall, if required, give a receipt to the person paying, expressing the amount thereof, and the time the same was paid, under the penalty of ten pounds, to be recovered, with costs, by the party grieved. No vessel shall be cleared out unless the master thereof produces to the Naval Officer a manifest of the cargo on board, and makes oath (or affirms if a Quaker) that the commodities to be exported have been inspected, stamped, and branded, according to law; and if the Naval Officer gives a clearance without such manifest being produced to him, and oath or affirmation made as aforesaid, he shall forfeit and pay the sum of fifty pounds, to the use of the commonwealth. Every Naval Officer shall and may go on board any vessel in which any commodities shall be laden, and seize, secure, and bring on shore, any goods that have not been inspected, stamped, or branded, according to law; provided he shall have previously received information, on oath, of the same; which goods so seized may, on due proof before two Justices (one being of the quorum) that they were shipped contrary to this act, be ordered for sale, and the money arising therefrom applied, one half to the use of the commonwealth, and the other half to the informer.

What shall be done previous to clearing out a vessel.

Penalty on Naval Officer.

His power to seize goods on board, not inspected or branded

Registers their form.

V. AND be it further enacted, that no vessel belonging to any inhabitant or inhabitants of this state, shall be qualified to trade to any foreign parts or islands, until the owner or owners shall have registered his or their vessel in the tenour following: "*Virginia* to wit, Jurat A. B. that the ship   , of   , whereof   is at present master, being a   , of   tons, was built at   , in the year   , and that   , of   , and   , of   , at present are sole owners thereof." Which oath shall be attested by the Naval Officer under his hand, and the seal of his office affixed thereto, and being registered by the Naval Officer, in a book to be kept for that purpose, shall be delivered to the master or owner of the vessel for the security of her navigation; and the Naval Officer may demand and receive the sum of ten shillings for registering and recording the same; and for every endorsement thereon two shillings and six pence. Every Naval Officer shall enter in a book to be kept for that purpose, a fair list of the entries, and in one other book a fair list of the clearances, of all vessels with their cargoes; and once in three months transmit a copy thereof to the Governor, under the like pains for a neglect thereof as is herein before prescribed in the case of his demanding or taking exorbitant fees.

Fees for them.

Books to be kept of entries and clearances.

VI. AND be it further enacted, that the bonds directed to be taken by this act, shall be made payable to the Governor for the time being, and his successors, for the use of the commonwealth.

Regulations for unlading ballast.

VII. AND whereas the casting of ballast into rivers or creeks must prove dangerous and destructive to navigation: For prevention whereof, *Be it enacted,* that immediately after the commencement of this act; the court of every county adjoining any navigable river or creek, shall appoint one or more fit person or persons, residing convenient to the places where vessels usually ride in such river or creek, to be directors of the delivery of ballast from on board any vessel within their district; and the clerk of the court shall forthwith issue and deliver to the sheriff of his county, an attested copy of such appointment, to be by him served on every person appointed, or left at his place of abode, of which the sheriff shall make due return to the next court, when and where every person so appointed shall appear, and make oath in open court, *That he will, when required, diligently attend the delivery of ballast from on board any vessel within his district, and will not knowingly permit the same, or any part thereof, to be cast into the water where navigable, but will direct, and to the best of his power cause all such ballast to be brought and laid on shore at some convenient place or places where it may not obstruct navigation, nor be washed into the channel; and that he will truly and faithfully execute his office without favour, partiality, or malice.* If any person so appointed, and having notice, shall fail to appear before the said court, unless hindered by sickness or other legal disability, or being there, shall refuse to be sworn, he shall be fined twenty pounds; and the court shall, upon every such failure or refusal, or in case of death, removal, or other legal disability, of any person appointed, proceed to appoint another in his room, who shall take the same oath, and upon failure or refusal shall pay the same fine; which the court is hereby empowered and required to cause the sheriff to levy, and to be accounted for and paid by him to the Treasurer. Every person so appointed and sworn, shall, upon notice given him by the master of any vessel intending to discharge ballast, forthwith go on board, and attend until the same be delivered in manner directed by this act, and thereupon he shall give the master a certificate that the ballast on board his vessel has been duly unladen and brought on shore according to law; and for his attendance may demand and receive five shillings for every day he shall attend; to be paid by the master before certificate given; and if any such officer shall neglect to perform his duty as by this act directed, he shall forfeit and pay twenty pounds for every neglect or failure.

VIII. *AND be it further enacted,* that if the master or commander of any ship or vessel within this state, suffer any ballast to be discharged from on board his vessel, without having a ballast master on board, he shall forfeit and pay the sum of fifty pounds; one half of which to the informer, and the other to the use of the commonwealth.

IX. *AND be it further enacted,* that any master of a vessel who shall be sued for any forfeiture accruing by this act, the court, in which such suit shall be brought, shall rule every such master to give special bail, in the same manner as by law heretofore they could do.

> *Masters of vessels sued for forfeitures under this act may be ruled to give bail.*

X. *AND be it further enacted,* that any master or skipper of a vessel transporting goods, wares, or merchandize, liable to a duty, from one district to another, shall produce a permit from the Naval Officer of the district from whence such goods were transported, certifying the duties were secured to be paid agreeable to law, and shall obtain a permit from the Naval Officer of the district to land them; and failing so to do, such goods, wares, and merchandize, shall be subject to the same forfeitures as goods, wares, and merchandizes are liable to which are not legally entered and the duties secured to be paid; and for such permit each Naval Officer shall be entitled to receive two shillings and six pence.

> *Transporting goods from one district to another.*

XI. *AND be it further enacted,* that every ship or vessel, which shall at any time hereafter be entered in any district or port within this commonwealth, in order to unlade the goods or merchandizes imported in her, or in order to lade and take on board any tobacco or other goods or merchandize for exportation out of this commonwealth, that are subject by the laws now in force to pay tonnage, shall be gauged and measured in the manner following, that is to say: Every ship or vessel shall be measured by the length of the gun-deck, deducting three fifths of the greatest breadth from outside to outside, and multiplying the product by the breadth from out to out (and not within board) and that product again by half the said breadth, and that product divided by ninety four, which will give the true contents of the tonnage, according to which method and rule all ships and vessels shall be measured, and the said tonnage shall be computed and collected accordingly; any custom practice or usage, to the contrary notwithstanding. And the Naval Officer of each district, where he has reason to suspect that any ship or vessel is registered at less tonnage than her real burthen, shall be empowered to go on board the said ship or vessel and make a measurement of her as above directed.

> *How the tonnage of vessels shall be ascertained.*

XII. *AND be it further enacted,* that if any Naval Officer, sheriff, constable, or any other person, shall be sued or molested for any thing done in execution of the powers given them by any act or acts of Assembly, for imposing duties and imposts upon any goods, wares, or merchandize, brought within this commonwealth, such Naval Officer, sheriff, constable, or other person (as the case may be) may plead the general issue and give this act in evidence; and the defendant shall recover double costs, if the plaintiff be cast in such suit; in all actions, suits, or informations to be brought, or when any seizure of liquors, goods, wares, or merchandize, shall be made, if the property thereof be claimed by any person as the owner or importer thereof, the *onus probandi* shall lie upon such owner or claimer thereof.

> *Officers sued here indemnified.*

CHAP. XXII.

An act directing the Auditors to issue warrants in certain cases.

I. BE it enacted by the General Assembly, that the Auditors shall, yearly, issue to such of the officers of the state line and navy as are by law entitled to half pay, their warrants for the same.

II. *AND be it further enacted,* that the Auditors shall make a return of the amount of the said warrants to the next session of Assembly, or as soon after as may be, that adequate funds may be provided for the discharge thereof.

> *For half pay to the officers of the state line and navy, intitled thereto.*
>
> *To return the amount of them to the Assembly.*

CHAP. XXIII.

An act giving certain powers to the trustees of the town of Portsmouth.

> *Private.*

CHAP. XXIV.

An act for paying the soldiers late from the southern army belonging to the Virginia continental line three months wages.

> *Repealed, ch. 43*

> A. D. 1783.

A. D. 1783.

Had its effect.

CHAP. XXV.

An act to amend the act entitled An act to amend the act for calling in and redeeming certain certificates.

CHAP. XXVI.

Private.

An act for establishing a town in the county of Princess Anne.

CHAP. XXVII.

See Oct. 1776, ch. 23

An act to amend an act entitled An act declaring tenants of lands or slaves in taille, to hold the same in fee simple.

Preamble.

Lands or slaves escheated by virtue of the act, to go according to the donation.

Not to restrain a tenant from conveying, nor exempt them from debts.

I. WHEREAS by the operation of an act entitled *An act declaring tenants of lands or slaves in taille to hold the same in fee simple*, the conditional provisions made by many persons for the several branches of their families may be defeated, and the estates intended as such provisions become escheated to the commonwealth: For remedy whereof, Be it enacted, that all estates in lands or slaves, which by virtue of the said act have become, or shall hereafter become escheatable to the commonwealth, for defect of blood, shall descend and be deemed to have descended, agreeable to the limitations of the deed or will creating such estates. *Provided always*, that nothing in this act contained shall be construed to restrain any tenant of such lands or slaves from selling, or conveying the same by deed, in his or her life time, or disposing thereof by his or her last will and testament; and that all such estates shall remain liable to the debts of the tenants, in the same manner as lands and slaves held in *fee simple*. *Provided also*, that this act shall not extend to any lands or slaves which have been escheated and sold for the use of the commonwealth.

CHAP. XXVIII.

Private.

An act for incorporating the trustees of Hampden Sidney.

CHAP. XXIX.

An act to legalize certain proceedings of the county court of Cumberland, and for other purposes.

Preamble.

Proceedings declared valid.

I. WHEREAS in consequence of the destruction of the court-house of the county of *Cumberland* by fire, the Justices of the said county convened and held a monthly meeting of the court, in the month of *February* last, at the place where the said court-house formerly stood, and proceeded to the business before them, without any previous adjournment of time or place, and doubts have arisen whether the proceedings then and there had by the said court are not thereby rendered illegal: Be it therefore enacted by the General Assembly, that the proceedings of the Justices of the said county court of *Cumberland*, at a court by them held in the month of *February* last, at the place aforesaid, shall be, and the same are hereby declared to be valid and effectual in law, in like manner as if the same had been held and done with due adjournment of time and place.

Any court whose courthouse is burnt, may sit elsewhere.

II. AND for preventing the inconveniencies which might otherwise result from the like accidents, Be it further enacted, that where the court-house of any county hath been, or may be destroyed or rendered unfit for use, the court of the county, or a majority of them, shall be, and they are hereby authorized, to hold their sessions at any place they may appoint, until such court-house can be re-built or repaired.

CHAP. XXX.

An act directing the enlistment of guards for the public prison and stores.

Preamble.

Governor and Council to inlist guards.

Proviso.

I. WHEREAS it is necessary that proper guards should be kept at this time over the public prison and certain places where public stores are deposited, and it is meant by this Assembly to take measures for relieving the militia from such duty as soon as possible: Be it therefore enacted, that it shall and may be lawful for the Governor, with advice of Council, to cause as many men, not exceeding twenty five, with proper officers, to be enlisted as guards for public service, as he, the said Governor, with advice of Council, may deem necessary, and may retain the same in service so long as the public exigencies may require. *Provided always*, that if the Delegates representing this state in General Congress, shall, on application, procure such a number of the soldiers of the line of this state, enlisted for three years in the continental army, as may be sufficient for the purpose aforesaid, then the said guards and officers enlisted to command the same, shall be discharged.

CHAP. XXXI.

Private. See May 1780, ch. 25.

An act to suspend the sale of certain escheated lands late the property of John Connolly.

CHAP. XXXII.

See Oct. 1782, ch 40 Oct. 1783, ch. 2

An act to amend an act entitled An act concerning the appointment of sheriffs.

Preamble.

I. WHEREAS by an act, entitled *An act concerning the appointment of sheriffs*, it is enacted, that the court of every county within this commonwealth, shall annually between the last day of *March* and the last day of *May*, nominate to the Governor or Chief Magistrate for the time being, two persons named in the commission of the peace for their county, one of which persons so nominated, shall be commissioned by the Governor to execute the office of sheriff of that county; and shall qualify to his commission at the court to be held for the county in *November*, or if no court shall be then held, or he shall be unable to attend, at the next succeeding court; which, in one instance, is contrary to the constitution or form of government, and in another, unnecessarily abridges the time which sheriffs were by

Repeal of part of former act.

law authorized to continue in office: Be it therefore enacted, that the said act so far as it directs the county courts of this commonwealth annually, to nominate to the Governor or Chief Magistrate for the time being, two persons named in the commission of the peace for their county, and that one of those persons, so nominated, shall be commissioned by the Governor, to execute the office of sheriff of that county, shall be, and the same is hereby repealed.

II. *AND be it further enacted*, that the courts of the several counties of this commonwealth, shall nominate sheriffs in the months of *April* or *May*, in all cases where heretofore they ought to have been nominated in the month of *August*: and the sheriffs so nominated shall be commissioned by the Governor, in manner as by the said act is directed.

III. *BE it further enacted*, that where the Justices of any county or counties have neglected to nominate sheriffs, between the last day of *March* and the first day of *June*, in the present year, agreeable to the directions of the said act, it shall and may be lawful for such Justices, at their respective courts to be held for the month of *August* or *September* next, to nominate sheriffs in the same manner as if the said act had never passed.

A. D. 1783.

When courts are to nominate for sheriffs.

C H A P.   XXXIII.

An act for dissolving the vestry of the parish of Lynnhaven, *in the county of* Princess Anne.

Private.

C H A P.   XXXIV.

An act for the payment of wages to the members of the present General Assembly

Occasional.

C H A P.   XXXV.

An act to authorize and confirm marriages in certain cases.

See Oct. 1780, *ch.* 6.

I. WHEREAS it hath been represented to this present General Assembly, that many of the good people in the remote parts of this commonwealth are destitute of any persons, authorized by law, to solemnize marriages amongst them: *Be it enacted*, that where it shall appear to the court of any county, on the western waters, that there is not a sufficient number of clergymen authorized to celebrate marriages therein, such court is hereby empowered to nominate so many sober and discreet laymen as will supply the deficiency; and each of the persons so nominated, upon taking the oath of allegiance to this state, shall receive a license to celebrate the rites of matrimony according to the forms and customs of the church, of which he is reputed a member, between any persons regularly applying to him therefor within the said county, that is to say, the parties so applying shall produce a marriage license, obtained as the law requires, or a certificate that their intention of marriage has been thrice published, agreeable to the directions of this act, and no legal objection made against their joining together as husband and wife, given under the hand of the person by whom such publications were made, and witnessed by a Magistrate or commissioned officer of the militia.

Preamble.

Courts on the western waters may licence laymen to marry.

Parties to produce a licence, or certificate of publication.

II. *AND be it further enacted*, that all publications of banns of matrimony, on the said western waters, shall be made on three several days, and not in less time than two weeks, in open and public assemblies, convened for religious worship or other lawful purposes, within the bounds of the respective congregations or militia companies, in which the parties to be married severally reside. For a certificate of publication, the person making the same may demand and receive three shillings; and for the celebration of a marriage, the licenced minister or layman may demand and receive six shillings, and no more; and any person who shall certify a publication of such banns, or celebrate a marriage, contrary to the directions of this act, shall forfeit and pay the sum of five hundred pounds, to be recovered with costs, in any court of record, the one half to the informer, and the other half to the overseers of the poor for the use of the parish, and shall moreover suffer one year's imprisonment, without bail or mainprize.

How publication of banns shall be made.

Fees.

Penalties for illegal publication of marriage.

III. AND whereas some Magistrates and others, not authorized by law, have been induced, by the want of ministers, to solemnize marriages on the said western waters: *Be it enacted*, that all such marriages, heretofore openly and solemnly made, or which shall be so made before this act shall take effect, and have been consumated by the parties cohabiting together as husband and wife, shall be taken, and they are hereby declared good and valid in law; and all and every person or persons solemnizing such marriages, are, and shall be, exonerated from all pains and penalties therefor, as if they had been authorized ministers. *Provided always*, that nothing herein contained shall extend or be construed to extend, to confirm any marriages heretofore celebrated, or which may hereafter be celebrated, between parties within the degrees of consanguinity or affinity, forbidden by law, or where either of the parties were bound by a former marriage to a husband or wife then alive.

Former marriages confirmed.

Proviso to restrain incests and polygamy

C H A P.   XXXVI.

An act to amend an act, entitled An act to vest certain escheated lands in the county of Kentucky *in trustees for a public school.*

Private. See May 1780, *ch.* 20.

C H A P.   XXXVII.

An act to authorize the United States in Congress Assembled to procure ten acres of land in this State, for the use of the United States.

I. BE it enacted, that the Congress of the United States shall be, and they are hereby authorized and empowered, to procure ten acres of land in any part of this state, for the purpose of erecting magazines for the use of the United States, by purchase, from any person or persons willing to sell the same; and in case a convenient seat cannot be procured by that means, it shall and may be lawful for the Governor with the advice of Council, to cause to be surveyed and laid off any quantity of land, not exceeding ten acres, in such place as Major General Lincoln, or any other person appointed by Congress shall judge proper, and shall cause the same to be valued on oath, by twelve disinterested freeholders of the said county, where such land may be; which survey and valuation shall be certified by the persons making the same, to the court of such county, and there recorded, and upon payment or tender of the sum, to which such land shall be valued, to the owner or owners thereof, the same shall be vested in the United States for ever, for the purpose aforesaid.

May purchase of any willing to sell.

If none willing how it may be taken

CHAP. XXXVIII.

A. D. 1783.
See Oct. 1782,
ch 8.

Preamble.

Repeal of the act allowing commutables. Revived Oct. 1783, ch. 1

Of the duty upon wine and spirits; and of the tonnage of Virginia vessels and small vessels of Maryland.

Northern-Neck quitrents restored to the proprietor.

Courts having neglected to assign assessors, district, are to do it.

General Court to meet in Feb. to give judgments against sheriffs. Altered, Oct. 1783, ch 1.

Principal of officers certificates not to be discounted for their taxes.

Lists of tithables to be taken for levies.

An act to amend the act to amend and reduce the several acts of Assembly for ascertaining certain taxes and duties, and for establishing a permanent revenue, into one act.

I. WHEREAS great loss has been incurred by the state from the receipt of the articles made commutable by an act *To amend and reduce the several acts of Assembly for ascertaining certain taxes and duties, and for establishing a permanent revenue into one act*

II. AND whereas from the present situation of the country, it is unnecessary longer to continue that regulation; *Be it therefore enacted by the General Assembly,* that so much of the said recited act as makes tobacco, hemp, flour, or deer-skins, receivable in payment of the taxes imposed by the said act, shall be, and the same is hereby repealed.

III. AND be it further enacted, that so much of the said recited act as relates to the duty upon wine and spirits, imported or brought into this commonwealth, shall be, and the same is hereby repealed: *Provided always,* that no ship or other vessel, belonging to any citizen or citizens of this commonwealth, and no ship or other vessel, under the burthen of sixty tons, belonging to any citizen or citizens of the state of *Maryland,* shall be subject to the duty on tonnage.

IV. AND whereas by the said recited act, all persons who were indebted for quitrents due within the Northern-Neck, were permitted to retain the same in their hands until the future directions of the Assembly.

V. AND whereas it is unjust that the executors of the late proprietor of the Northern Neck, should be any longer prevented from receiving what was due to the said proprietor at the time of his death: *Be it further enacted,* that so much of the said recited act as permit the persons indebted as aforesaid, to retain in their hands the sums due at the time of the death of the said proprietor, shall be, and the same is hereby repealed.

VI. AND be it further enacted, that the court of every county, where the same hath not been done pursuant to the said act, shall, on or before the first day of *October* next, divide their respective counties into convenient precincts, and proceed to take lists of the enumerated articles, in the same manner, and within the same periods of time, and under the like penalties for neglect of duty, as is prescribed and inflicted by the said act.

VII. AND whereas by an act of the present session, distress upon the collection of the taxes, due by virtue of the said recited act, is suspended until the month of *November* next, and no provision has been made to compel the several sheriffs and collectors to make speedy payment to the public treasury: *Be it further enacted,* that the respective sheriffs shall account for, and pay the amount of their several collections, made pursuant to the said act, into the public treasury, on or before the twentieth day of *January* next. And the Judges of the General Court shall hold an additional sessions on the second *Monday* in *February* next, for the sole purpose of receiving and hearing motions against delinquent sheriffs or collectors, and rendering judgment, and awarding execution thereupon, in like manner and effect as by law they can now do at the usual quarterly sessions of the said court, to continue until the business before them shall be finished.

VIII AND whereas by an act of the present session of Assembly, entitled *An act to establish certain and adequate funds for the redemption of certificates granted to the officers and soldiers for their arrears of pay and depreciation,* provision is made for the payment of interest, and part of the principal annually, of the said certificates whereby it becomes unnecessary that any part of the principal of the said certificates may be discounted in taxes: *Be it further enacted,* that no discount of principal of any certificate issued or to be issued, to any officer or soldier, shall be allowed in discharge of the taxes imposed by the act *To amend and reduce the several acts of Assembly for ascertaining certain taxes and duties, and for establishing a permanent revenue into one act.*

IX. AND be it further enacted, that nothing in the said act contained, shall be construed to prevent the several county courts from causing lists to be taken of all free male tithables, between the ages of sixteen and twenty one years, and of imposing taxes upon all such, for the purposes of county or parish levies. This act shall commence and be in force from and after the first day of *July* next.

CHAP. XXXIX.

See May 1779.
ch. 12, *and notes.*

Preamble.

Time allowed for those;

and for returning surveys to the register.

All plats in Kentucky to be first lodged with the deputy Register.

An act for giving further time to enter certificates for settlement rights, and to locate warrants upon preemption rights, and for other purposes.

I. WHEREAS sundry persons have been hitherto prevented, by unavoidable accidents, from making entries upon their certificates for settlement rights, with the surveyor of the county wherein the lands lie, and from obtaining and locating warrants for lands due to them upon preemption rights: *Be it therefore enacted,* that the further time of nine months, from and after the end of this present session of Assembly, shall be allowed for making all entries upon certificates for settlement rights, and for locating warrants upon preemption rights, as specially described in the certificates by which such rights are held.

II. AND whereas on account of the like accidents, some plats and certificates of survey have not been returned to the Register's office, within the time limited by law; and it is doubtful whether such plats and certificates of survey can now be received by the Register of the Land Office: *Be it therefore enacted,* that the Register of the Land Office, or his deputy, shall be obliged to receive such plats and certificates of survey; and the lands shall not be liable to forfeiture, on account of such failure, before the first day of *June* next: *Provided,* that nothing herein contained, shall be construed to affect any caveats now entered or which shall be entered, before the end of this present session of Assembly.

III. AND whereas the good purposes for which a Deputy Register was appointed in the western country, will not be fully attained, unless all plats and certificates of surveys, made in the district of *Kentucky,* are registered in his office: *Be it therefore enacted,* that from and after the first day of *November* next, the Register of the Land Office shall not receive any plat and certificate of survey, made in the district of *Kentucky,* before it has been registered and transmitted to him by his deputy in that country, agreeable to an act entitled *An act to empower the Register of the Land Office to appoint a deputy on the western waters,* and no patent shall issue until such survey has been registered six months in the principal Land Office.

IV. AND whereas a practice hath too often prevailed of entering friendly caveats, upon lands actually liable to forfeiture, and of taking out summons's on such friendly caveats, without any design of executing the same, whereby such caveats are continued for a great length of time, and much lands covered from taxation: Be it enacted, that no caveat shall be entered after the first day of January next, unless the person, at the time of entering such caveat, shall file with the Register or his deputy, an affidavit that such caveat is really and bona fide made with an intention of procuring the lands for the person in whose name such caveat is entered, and not in trust for the benefit of the person against whom such caveat is entered; and all caveats entered contrary to the directions of this act, shall be absolutely null and void. And wherever a summons upon a caveat shall either not be returned at all, or be returned not executed, the caveat upon which such summons shall have issued shall be dismissed with costs; unless the court, before whom such caveat shall be depending, shall be satisfied that the said summons, not having been executed, did not proceed from the neglect of the party who entered such caveat.

To prevent friendly caveats, and acts in real.

V. AND be it further enacted, that the clerk of the General Court, within one month after the end of every session of the said court, shall return to the Register of the Land Office an attested list of all caveats that were dismissed or determined at the said preceding court, which the Register shall compare with the caveat book; and in all cases where he shall find that the caveats have been dismissed, or determined in favour of the defendant, he shall make out grants for such lands, as if no such caveats had been entered in his office. And the clerk of the supreme court of the district of Kentucky, shall, in like manner, return to the Deputy Register in that country, within one month after the end of every session of the said court, an attested list of all caveats that were dismissed or determined at the said preceding court, which the Deputy Register shall compare with his caveat book; and in all cases where he shall find that the caveats have been dismissed, or determined in favour of the defendant, he shall record and transmit the said list to the principal Register, together with the plats and certificates of survey that have been detained in his office by such caveats, that grants may issue thereupon, as if no such caveats had been entered.

List of caveats ended, to be returned to the Register after every General Court. And the like to the deputy in the Kentucky district.

C H A P. XL.

An act to enable the General Court to settle and adjust costs.

I. WHEREAS doubts have arisen whether the General Court of this commonwealth can by law award costs except in particular cases: For removing such doubts in future, Be it enacted, that it shall be lawful for the General Court, on giving judgment in any cause removed by appeal, writ of error, supersedeas, or certiorari, from the inferior courts, either for the appellant, appellee, plaintiff, or defendant, and in any cause originating in the General Court, where the verdict or judgment shall be given for the defendant, to award costs to the party or parties in whose favour such judgment shall be given; and on all motions it shall be lawful for the said court to give or refuse costs, at their discretion; and in all other causes where the plaintiff shall recover debt or damages, the costs shall be governed by the laws now in force.

*Preamble.
Where costs shall be recovered.
Where discretionary.
Where be refer'd to former laws.*

C H A P. XLI.

An act to give further time for the probation of deeds and other instruments of writing, and for other purposes.

Repeal'd. Oct. 1783, ch. 23.

C H A P. XLII.

An act to continue and amend an act entitled An act for the relief of certain persons now resident on the western frontier.

Private. See May 1781, ch. 19.

C H A P. XLIII.

An act to repeal the act entitled An act for paving the soldiers late from the southern army, belonging to the Virginia continental line, three months wages.

See ch. 24.

At a GENERAL ASSEMBLY begun and held at the Public Buildings in the City of *Richmond*, on *Monday* the 20th day of *October*, in the Year of our Lord 1783.

C H A P. I.

An act to amend the several acts of Assembly for ascertaining certain taxes and duties, and for establishing a permanent revenue.

*See Oct. 1777, ch. 2, and notes.
Preamble.*

I. WHEREAS application hath been made to this present General Assembly, that the produce of the country may be received in payment of the taxes imposed by an act entitled *An act to amend and reduce the several acts of Assembly for ascertaining certain taxes and duties, and for establishing a permanent revenue into one act:* Be it therefore enacted, that one half of the tax directed under the aforesaid act, to be paid for the present year, and distrainable for on the twentieth day of November, on lands and lots, free male persons above the age of twenty one years, slaves, cattle, horses, mares, colts, mules, wheels for riding carriages, billiard tables, and ordinary licences, may be paid at the option of the payer, either in specie, tobacco, hemp, flour, or deer-skins, to wit: In

Commodities to be taken for half the tax.

A. D. 1783.

Price and various regulations.

inspectors receipts or notes, for good merchantable crop tobacco, not less than nine hundred and fifty nett weight, which shall have been inspected or re-inspected since the first day of October, in the present year, at the rate of thirty shillings *per* hundred, or in transfer receipts or notes for tobacco at the rate of one hundred and six pounds for one hundred pounds of crop tobacco, at any public inspection within this commonwealth, or in inspectors receipts or notes for sound, clean, and merchantable hemp, delivered at the warehouses provided or to be provided for the reception thereof, at the towns of *Alexandria, Dumfries, Falmouth, Fredericksburg, Louisville, Smithfield, Winchester, Staunton,* and *Stone House,* in *Botetourt, Richmond, Manchester, Blandford,* and *West-Point. Provided,* that hemp and skins as herein after described, shall be the only articles receivable at the towns of *Staunton* and *Winchester,* and at the *Stone-House,* in *Botetourt;* which said notes or receipts for hemp, shall be received in discharge of taxes according to this act, at the rate of thirty shillings *per* hundred, except hemp delivered at *Winchester,* which shall be at twenty six shillings, at *Staunton,* twenty four shillings, and at the *Stone-House,* twenty two shillings *per* hundred; or in receipts for sound and merchantable flour, inspected since the first day of October, in the present year, in casks, delivered at the warehouses provided or to be provided by the inspectors and receivers of hemp, at the aforesaid towns, at the rate of fourteen shillings *per* hundred, with an allowance of two shillings and six pence for cask and inspection; or in receipts for skins of deer in the hair, well skinned, cleaned, and trimmed, restricted to the seasons of red, blue, and short grey, delivered at the houses to be provided for that purpose, at the said towns of *Staunton, Winchester, Lou-*

Sheriffs to give receipts expressing how taxes are paid

isville, and at the *Stone-House,* in the county of *Botetourt,* at the price of one shilling and eight pence for grey skins, and two shillings *per* pound for red and blue skins. And any person or persons chargeable with taxes by the said recited act, and paying the same in manner herein directed, shall be discharged thereof, and may demand and receive of the sheriff or collector a receipt, specifying in what articles such person paid his tax, whether it be specie or commutables, particularizing the warehouse from

And return a list to the clerk's office, who shall set up a copy in the courthouse

which the tobacco notes he may have received shall have issued. And every sheriff shall, moreover, return a list on oath of such payments, to the clerk of the court of his county, immediately after his collection, copies of which list shall be fixed up in the said courthouse for the inspection of the people. And the Auditors are hereby required not to settle finally with any sheriff, for the taxes collected under

To pay commutables to Treasurer.
Penalty.
Former payments in coin regulated.

this and the said recited act, except the said sheriff do produce to them a copy of such list, certified by the clerk; and the Auditors shall, upon settlement with the sheriff, give their order to the Treasurer to receive such specie or commutables from the sheriff, agreeable to the said list; and every sheriff failing to pay the same accordingly, shall forfeit and pay the sum of five hundred pounds, to be recovered in like manner as is prescribed in the case of delinquent sheriffs. *Provided,* that any person having before the publication of the said act, paid to any sheriff or collector, in gold or silver coin, more than one moiety of his taxes, shall on tendering to the same sheriff or collector any article hereby declared to be commutable therefor, be entitled to a restitution of all such surplus.

Tobacco payments restricted to certain warehouses;

II. AND that the several sheriffs and collectors of taxes may be prevented from injuring the public revenue, by speculating in the payments made them of the taxes aforesaid; *Be it enacted,* that every person chargeable with such taxes, who may pay any part thereof in tobacco agreeable to this act, shall only be permitted to discharge the same in inspectors receipts or notes, issued from those warehouses where the person chargeable therewith may by law pay parish and county levies and officers fees, agreeable to an act entitled, *An act to amend and reduce the several acts of Assembly for the inspection of tobacco into one act;* and the several sheriffs and collectors shall account for the same on oath, and shall make payment thereof at the treasury, but shall not be suffered to make payment at any other warehouses

and hemp to certain places.

whatsoever. *Provided nevertheless,* that nothing in this act contained shall entitle any person whatsoever to pay the commutable of hemp in discharge of taxes, except the property for which such taxes are due shall lie and be on the western side of the mountain commonly called the *Blue Ridge,* or the person rendering the same shall make oath that it is the growth of the estate for the taxes on which it is offered in payment. *And provided also,* that the receipts from the warehouses hereafter mentioned, shall pass in the payment of taxes in the counties following, that is to say: In the counties of *Frederick, Hampshire, Berkeley, Shenandoah, Rockingham, Ohio,* and *Monongalia,* at any of the warehouses in *Fairfax, Prince William, Stafford,* or *Spotsylvania;* in the counties of *Augusta, Botetourt, Rockbridge, Greenbrier, Washington,* and *Montgomery,* at any of the warehouses in the counties of *Henrico* or *Chesterfield.*

Inspectors of flour to return accounts.
Penalty.

III. AND that the flour so paid in discharge of the taxes may be converted to the purposes by this act intended, before the same should be injured or lost, *Be it enacted,* that the inspectors or receivers of flour, shall, on or before the fifteenth day of *March* next, make out and transmit to the Treasurer a fair and accurate list of the quantity of flour by him or them received, and for whom; and on failure so to do, he or they shall forfeit and pay the sum of fifty pounds, to be recovered by motion in the General Court, or the court of the county where such inspections may be, with costs, to the use of the commonwealth, and thereupon execution shall issue, provided the party has ten days previous notice of such

Treasurer to sell commutables.

motion. And the Treasurer for the time being shall sell the said tobacco, hemp, skins, and flour, from time to time, as occasion may require, for current gold or silver coin, or otherwise dispose of the said tobacco, hemp, skins, and flour, in payment of the debts and contracts of this commonwealth, on the best terms that can be obtained, in like manner as if the same had been current gold and silver coin actually paid into the treasury, having due regard to the appropriations which are or shall be made of the revenue of the commonwealth. And the courts of the counties respectively in which the aforesaid towns

Courts to provide houses to store hemp, flour, and deer-skins.

of *Alexandria, Dumfries, Falmouth, Fredericksburg, Harrodsburg, Richmond, Manchester, Blandford, Staunton, Smithfield, Winchester,* and *West Point,* and the said *Stone-House,* are, shall be, and are hereby authorized and required, to provide good and sufficient warehouses for the storage of hemp, flour, or deer-skins, as the same are respectively made receivable at the said towns, and *Stone-House* in the county

And appoint one or two receivers at each place.

of *Botetourt,* in the manner herein before directed, and to appoint one or two reputable persons, as the case may require, within the said towns respectively, and at the *Stone-House* in the county of *Botetourt,* for the receiving, safe keeping, and delivery of the said hemp, flour, or deer-skins, on public account, and for inspecting the said hemp, who, in the receipts given by them, or either of them, shall

Their duty;

specify the names of the persons or owners delivering the same, the number and quantity of each bundle of hemp, and the warehouse, number, and nett weight of each barrel of inspected flour received, for which the inspectors manifest shall be produced, and filed at the said warehouse, as a voucher to prove the inspection thereof, before the delivery by the owner; and the said courts respectively are hereby autho-

and allowance.

rized to allow to the inspectors or receivers aforesaid, for their risk and trouble, five *per cent.* in money, valuing the articles by them received at the price they are estimated at in this act, which they shall certify to the Auditors of public accounts; and all other expences attending the said warehouses for the receiving and delivering of the hemp and flour aforesaid, shall be allowed and certified in like manner, and shall be paid out of the money in the public treasury arising from the sale thereof; and the said receivers or inspectors of hemp and flour, or deer skins, shall before entering upon the duties of their office, give

To give bond.

bond in a reasonable penalty, payable to the Treasurer for the time being, or to his successors, for the use of the commonwealth, conditioned for the true and faithful performance of the duties required of them by law in the execution of their said office; and in case of failure in any court to appoint an inspector or receiver respectively as aforesaid, such court shall be liable to the same penalties as is provided in the case of the Justices neglecting or refusing to take and return lists of the enumerated articles, to be recovered and applied in like manner; and such inspector or receiver shall be liable to damages upon the action of the party grieved, and shall moreover forfeit and pay the sum of one hundred pounds, recoverable on information in any court, for the use of the commonwealth.

Penalty on courts failing; and on receivers.

IV. AND *be it further enacted*, that hemp, flour, and all other articles directed to be paid by this act, shall be weighed by the nett weight or short hundred, and that the several certificates for hemp and flour shall be separate, so that the several commutable articles may appear in a clear and distinct view.

How commutables to be weighed.

V. AND *be it further enacted*, that the Treasurer shall and may receive from any sheriff or collector, who shall obtain the certificate of the Auditors of any partial settlement made with them, such sums of money, or quantities of tobacco, hemp, flour, or deer skins, or sums in warrants and certificates receivable by law, as such sheriff or collector shall tender him in payment for the same, and grant his receipts accordingly.

Treasurer may receive partial payments.

VI. AND whereas very great loss has been heretofore sustained by the article of hemp, owing to the carelessness of the inspectors or receivers thereof, or other causes: That the like may in future be prevented, Be it *enacted*, that the purchaser or person receiving the notes for hemp, from the public, may at his own proper cost and charges upon delivery thereof, giving notice to the inspector or receiver, open and review the hemp so to him delivered, and if the same shall appear unmerchantable or damaged, it shall and may be lawful for any two Justices of the Peace for the county in which such hemp shall have been stored, upon application of the person demanding the same, to issue their warrant, directed to seven men well skilled in the quality of hemp, who, or any five of them, having first taken an oath to do impartial justice between the person demanding the hemp, and the public inspector or receiver, shall examine the quality and condition thereof, and if it shall be found by them that the same is not sound, clean, and merchantable, they shall make report thereof, and such hemp shall, by order of two Justices (upon such report to them presented) be directed to be sold at public vendue, for ready money, upon such notice as to them shall seem reasonable; and if the said hemp shall not sell for the current price of good merchantable hemp (which price shall be affixed by any two Justices before the sale) the difference between the prices shall be paid by such inspector or public receiver to the person demanding the said hemp; and upon refusal to make payment, it shall be lawful for the court of the county in which such hemp shall have been stored, and they are hereby required, upon motion to them, reasonable notice having been given, to give judgment and award execution for the amount thereof, together with costs, and the charges necessarily expended by the person demanding the said hemp; and the sheriff shall levy and account for the same as by law in other cases of execution is directed.

Hemp may be reviewed by the purchaser. Proceeding thereon.

What satisfaction shall be made by receiver.

VII. AND whereas the time fixed by the act of the last session, for payment into the public treasury by the sheriffs, will not in many of the counties give the sheriffs opportunity to make the collections compleat, and it is not necessary that the Judges of the General Court should hold an additional sessions for rendering judgments against delinquent sheriffs: Be it *enacted*, that so much of the said act as compels the respective sheriffs to account for, and pay into the public treasury, the amount of their several collections, on or before the twentieth day of *January* next, and the Judges of the General Court to hold an additional sessions on the second *Monday* in *February*, shall be, and the same is hereby repealed.

Repeal as to time sheriffs are to account, and for an additional sessions of the Judges.

VIII. AND *be it further enacted*, that the respective sheriffs shall account for and pay the amount of their several collections into the public treasury, on or before the first day of *March* next; and in case any sheriff or collector shall fail to account for, as by law is directed, and pay into the public treasury by the said first day of *March*, the money, or other articles in lieu thereof, by him received for taxes, every such delinquent sheriff or collector shall be liable to a judgment against him, on motion, with damages and interest, as by the former act directed, at the General Court in *April* next, or any succeeding court; provided the party shall have had legal notice of the same.

Sheriffs to account and pay the first of March.

IX. AND *be it further enacted*, that none of the articles made commutable by this act, shall be received by the sheriffs or collectors from the persons chargeable with taxes, after the first day of *March* next. And that it shall be at the option of the Treasurer to receive the same, or any part thereof (flour excepted, which he is hereby directed not to receive) from the sheriffs or collectors after the first day of *April* next.

Commutables not to be received by sheriffs after that day. Treasurer may receive them or not after 1st of April.

X. AND to explain what shall be legal notice, Be it *enacted*, that in all cases of delinquency by the sheriffs or collectors of the public revenue, when a motion is intended to be made against them, affidavit before any Justice of the Peace within this commonwealth, that notice of such intended motion shall have been made, either by delivery thereof to the party, or in case he shall not be found at his usual place of abode, by leaving the same thereat for him, ten days before such motion is to be made, shall be held, deemed, and taken as sufficient and legal notice.

How notice may be given to sheriffs and proved.

XI. AND *be it further enacted*, that distress for the money and commutables, hereby made receivable in payment of taxes, shall be suspended until the first day of *January* next, any law to the contrary notwithstanding. And that after the said first day of *January*, distress may be made by the respective sheriffs and collectors within this commonwealth, in the manner directed by the act, entitled *An act to amend and reduce the several acts of Assembly for ascertaining certain taxes and duties, and for establishing a permanent revenue, into one act.*

Distress for taxes suspended.

CHAP. II.

An act to amend the several acts of Assembly concerning the appointment of sheriffs.

See Oct. 1784, ch. 40. May 1783, ch. 2.

I. WHEREAS by two acts of Assembly, one entitled *An act concerning the appointment of sheriffs*, and the other *An act to amend an act entitled An act concerning the appointment of sheriffs*, the county courts are directed to proceed to the nomination of sheriffs within certain limited periods. And whereas several county courts have not made such nomination according to the said recited acts: For remedy whereof, Be it *enacted*, that in all cases wherein the county courts have failed to make such nomination within the periods prescribed by the said recited acts, the said county courts shall and may, and they are hereby empowered, to proceed to a nomination of two persons proper to fill the office of sheriff within their county, at any session of their court subsequent to the periods mentioned in the said recited acts; and one of the persons so to be nominated shall be commissioned by the Governor, in the same manner as if the nomination had been made according to the directions of the said recited acts.

Preamble.

Courts may yet nominate where they have failed.

A. D. 1783.

Irregular nomi-
nations to be regard-
ed.

II. AND be it further enacted, that where the court of any county hath already recommended persons as proper to fill the office of sheriff, not within the periods prescribed by the said recited act, the Governor is hereby empowered to commission one of the persons so recommended to act as sheriff for the said county.

If sheriffs fail to
give security for tax-
es a new sheriff to
be appointed.

III. AND whereas it sometimes happens that sheriffs neglect or fail to give security for the collection of the taxes, yet are willing to enjoy the other emoluments and profits of the office attended with less risk : Be it therefore enacted, that where any sheriff now in commission, hath failed to give security for the collection of the taxes, or where any sheriff hereafter commissioned, shall fail to give such security at the next court to be held for his county, the clerk of every county court respectively, where any such failure shall happen, shall certify the same to the Governor, who is hereby authorized and required to issue a commission for the next person nominated by the court, which to all intents and purposes shall supersede and annul the former commission. And if the second person so commissioned, shall also neglect or refuse to give security as aforesaid for the collection of the taxes, the Governor with advice of Council, is hereby authorized to commission any other Justice of the Peace for the said county, who shall be nominated by the court thereof.

When courts are
to recommend.

IV. AND be it further enacted, that the court of every county shall hereafter, in the month of *June* or *July* annually, nominate two persons named in the commission of the peace for their county, one of whom shall be commissioned by the Governor, to execute the office of sheriff, any law to the contrary notwithstanding.

Deputies to be in-
eligible to Assembly
for two years after
their quietus.

V. AND be it further enacted, that no deputy sheriff shall be eligible to either House of Assembly, until he has been two years out of office, and has made up his collections of the public taxes, and paid into the Treasury all arrearages, and has obtained a *quietus* for the same.

CHAP. III.

An act directing the emancipation of certain slaves who have served as soldiers in this state, and for the emancipation of the slave Aberdeen.

Preamble.

I. WHEREAS it hath been represented to the present General Assembly, that during the course of the war, many persons in this state had caused their slaves to enlist in certain regiments or corps raised within the same, having tendered such slaves to the officers appointed to recruit forces within this state, as substitutes for free persons, whose lot or duty it was to serve in such regiment or corps, at the same time representing to such recruiting officers that the slaves so enlisted by their direction and concurrence were free-men; and it appearing further to this Assembly, that on the expiration of the term of enlistment of such slaves, that the former owners have attempted again to force them to return to a state of servitude, contrary to the principles of justice, and to their own solemn promise.

Slaves enlisted by
appointment of their
masters, and serv-
ing, to be free.

II. AND whereas it appears just and reasonable that all persons enlisted as aforesaid, who have faithfully served agreeable to the terms of their enlistment, and have thereby of course contributed towards the establishment of *American* liberty and independence, should enjoy the blessings of freedom as a reward for their toils and labours: Be it therefore enacted, that each and every slave, who by the appointment and direction of his owner, hath enlisted in any regiment or corps raised within this state, either on continental or state establishment, and hath been received as a substitute for any free person whose duty or lot it was to serve in such regiment or corps, and hath served faithfully during the term of such enlistment, or hath been discharged from such service by some officer duly authorized to grant such discharge, shall from and after the passing of this act, be fully and compleatly emancipated, and shall be held and deemed free in as full and ample a manner as if each and every of them were specially named in this act;

And may sue in
forma pauperis and
recover damages.

and the Attorney-General for the commonwealth, is hereby required to commence an action, *in forma pauperis*, in behalf of any of the persons above described, who shall after the passing of this act be detained in servitude by any person whatsoever; and if upon such prosecution it shall appear that the pauper is entitled to his freedom in consequence of this act, a jury shall be empannelled to assess the damages for his detention.

Aberdeen declar-
ed free.

III. AND whereas it has been represented to this General Assembly, that *Aberdeen*, a negro man slave, hath laboured a number of years in the public service at the lead mines, and for his meritorious services is entitled to freedom; Be it therefore enacted, that the said slave *Aberdeen* shall be, and he is hereby emancipated and declared free in as full and ample a manner as if he had been born free.

CHAP. IV.

An act for surveying the lands given by law to the officers and soldiers on continental and state establishments, and for other purposes.

Preamble.

Deputation of offi-
cers to choose super-
intendants and sur-
veyors.

I. FOR the better locating and surveying the lands given by law to the officers and soldiers on continental and state establishments; Be it enacted by the General Assembly, that it shall and may be lawful for the deputations of officers, consisting of Major-General *Peter Muhlenburg*, Major-General *Charles Scott*, Major-General *George Weedon*, Brigadier General *Daniel Morgan*, Brigadier General *James Wood*, Colonel *William Heth*, Lieutenant-Colonels *Towles, Hopkins, Clarke*, and *Temple*, Captain *Nathaniel Burwell*, and Captain *Mayo Carrington*, of the continental line, or any five of them; and Brigadier-General *Clarke*, Colonels *Brent, Muter*, and *Dabney*, Major *Meriwether*, Captains *Roan, Rogers*, and *Boswell*, of the state line, or any three of them, to appoint superintendants on behalf of the respective lines, or jointly, for the purpose of regulating the surveying of the lands appropriated by law as bounties for the said officers and soldiers; and that the said deputations of officers shall have power to nominate and appoint two principal surveyors, to be commissioned as other surveyors within this commonwealth, and contract with them for their fees, who shall appoint their deputies, to be approved by the superintendants; and in case of their death, or inability to act, the superintendants shall have power

One sixth of sur-
veyors fees reserved
to Wm. & Mary
college.

to appoint, from time to time, a successor or successors, as the case may require. Provided, that one sixth part of the fees received by such surveyor or surveyors, shall be accounted for to the use of the College of *William & Mary*, in the same manner as other surveyors are directed to account for their fees, upon surveys made by them within this commonwealth. That the holder or holders of land warrants

Warrants for boun-
ty lands to be deli-
vered by March 15.

for military bounties, given by law as aforesaid, on or before the fifteenth day of *March* next, deliver the same to the principal surveyors, at such place or places as they shall, with the advice of the deputations, direct, endorsing on the back of each warrant, the number of surveys the same shall be laid off in, specifying the quantity of each survey. *Provided*, that a General Officer shall not be allowed more than six, a Field Officer five, and a Captain and Subaltern four surveys, in their respective apportionments of land, and the staff in proportion. The non-commissioned officers and soldiers warrants shall be put into classes, as near as circumstances will admit, of one thousand acres each, numbered previous to the drawing; and the number of the lot drawn shall be endorsed on every such class; and the persons interested in each class, shall determine their choice by lot, in the same manner as shall be done by classes, and the same to be divided accordingly by the surveyors.

A. D. 1783.
Limitation as to the number of surveys.
Warrants to be classed and drawn for.
Priority of location.

II. AND be it further enacted, that the priority of location shall be determined by lot, as soon as may be, after the said fifteenth day of *March* next, under the direction and management of the principal surveyors and the superintendants, or any three of them, according to such regulations as shall be fixed on by the present deputation, from the officers on the continental and state establishments respectively. That all warrants delivered to the principal surveyors before the sixteenth of *March* next, shall be first surveyed, and those delivered upon that, or any subsequent day, shall be surveyed in the same order of priority, as they may be respectively delivered to the principal surveyors. And if the proprietor of any warrant shall, either by himself or agent, decline or refuse to locate and survey agreeable to the number of lot or lots drawn thereto, such proprietor shall be postponed to those who do not refuse to locate and survey according to rotation.

III. AND be it further enacted, that every officer and soldier, or their legal representatives, may attend in person, or by another authorized for the purpose, to the locating and surveying their respective portions of land; and the portions of such officers and soldiers not being transferred, who may not be represented, shall be located and surveyed under the direction of the superintendants, agreeable to their number or rotation; but the superintendants shall not be compelled to attend to the locating and surveying of lands claimed by purchase, unless such claimant attend in person, or by an agent duly authorized for that purpose. And that every person or persons holding officers or soldiers warrants by assignment, shall pay down to the principal surveyors at the time of delivering such warrant or warrants, one dollar for every hundred acres thereof, exclusive of the legal surveyors fees, towards raising a fund for the purpose of supporting all contingent expences, or at the option of such holder or holders, the same may be held up until the warrants of all the original grantees have been surveyed; the said surveyors to account for all the money so received, to such person or persons as the said deputations may direct.

Locations and surveys to be made under the direction of the superintendants.
Transfer'd rights.

IV. AND be it further enacted, that the surveyors under the direction of the superintendants, and the claimants having a right to survey from the priority of their numbers, shall proceed in the first place to survey all the good lands, to be adjudged of by the superintendants, in that tract of country lying on the *Cumberland* and *Teniffee* rivers, as set apart by law for the said officers and soldiers, and then proceed in the like manner to survey on the north-west side of the river *Ohio*, between the rivers *Scioto* and the *Little Miami*, until the deficiency of all military bounties in lands shall be fully and amply made up. *Provided always*, that in such surveys, the same proportions be observed in length and breadth as are directed by law in other surveys within this commonwealth, and shall be closed and marked on all sides. And whatever lands may happen to be left within the tract of country reserved for the army on this side the *Ohio* and *Mississippi*, shall be saved, subject to the order and particular disposition of the Legislature of this state. And that the Governor with advice of Council, be, and he is hereby empowered and required to furnish the superintendants with such military aid, at such time, and in such manner, as he may judge necessary for the purpose of carrying this act into execution. *Provided*, that the aid to be ordered shall be from the *Kentucky* country, and not exceeding one hundred men.

Where and how the lands are to be surveyed.
Governor if necessary may furnish military aid.
Limitation thereof.

V. AND whereas the deputations of officers aforesaid, have represented to this Assembly that a certain tract of country, lying on the *Mississippi* and the waters thereof, is from its situation and other advantages, of too much importance to be subject to fall to the lot of any individual, and it now being the request of the said lines, through their respective deputations as aforesaid, that four thousand acres of land should be laid off on the *Mississippi* and the waters thereof, within the said tracts of country for a town and other public purposes, for the common benefit and interest of the whole: *Be it therefore enacted*, that the said deputations jointly, be, and they are hereby empowered, to cause four thousand acres of land to be laid off in such manner and form as they may judge most beneficial for a town, without being confined to any certain length or breadth as in other surveys, and vested in trustees, at such place on the said river *Mississippi* and the waters thereof, as the said trustees may agree upon, and in such manner as the said deputations may direct for the purposes aforesaid, saving to all persons whatsoever, other than the said officers and soldiers, all right and title to the said four thousand acres of land as fully as if this act had never been made.

Deputations may lay off 4000 acres for a town.
Saving the rights of others.

CHAP. V.

An act to authorize the Congress of the United States to adopt certain regulations respecting the British trade.

I. WHEREAS it appears by an order of the King of *Great Britain* in council, bearing date the second day of *July* last, made under the express authority of his Parliament, that the growth or produce of any of the United States of *America*, are prohibited from being carried to any of the *British West India* islands, by any other than *British* subjects, in *British* built ships, owned by *British* subjects, and navigated according to the laws of that kingdom.

Preamble.

II. AND whereas this proceeding, though but a temporary expedient, exhibits a disposition in *Great Britain* to gain partial advantages, injurious to the rights of free commerce, and is repugnant to the principles of reciprocal interest and convenience, which are found by experience to form the only permanent foundation of friendly intercourse between states: *Be it therefore enacted*, that the United States in Congress assembled, shall be, and they are hereby authorized and empowered to prohibit the importation of the growth or produce of the *British West India* islands, into these United States, in *British* vessels, or to adopt any other mode which may most effectually tend to counteract the designs of *Great Britain*, with respect to the American commerce, so long as the said restriction shall be continued on the part of *Great Britain*. *Provided*, that this act shall not be in force until all the states in the Union shall have passed similar laws.

Congress impowered to prohibit the importations from the West Indies in British vessels, &c.
Suspension of the act.

CHAP. VI.

An act concerning fairs in the town of Fredericksburg, *and the Court of Hustings thereof and for other purposes.*

Private.

A. D. 1783.

Private.

C H A P.   VII.

An act for altering the court days of the counties of Pittsylvania, Botetourt, Montgomery, and Spotsylvania

C H A P.   VIII.

Private.

An act for admitting certain persons to the rights of citizenship.

C H A P.   IX.

Private.

An act to revive an act entitled An act concerning pensioners.

C H A P.   X.

Temporary.

An act for further continuing an act entitled An act to ascertain the losses and injuries sustained from the depredations of the enemy within this commonwealth.

C H A P.   XI.

Private.

An act to authorize the sheriff of Monongalia to hold elections of a Senator and Delegates for the said county at two different places within the same.

C H A P.   XII.

An act making certain receipts and warrants payable in taxes.

Preamble.

I. WHEREAS by an act of Assembly passed in *October,* one thousand seven hundred and eighty two, entitled *An act to amend and reduce the several acts of Assembly for ascertaining certain taxes and duties, and for establishing a permanent revenue, into one act,* tobacco, hemp, flour, and deer-skins, were, under certain restrictions and limitations, made commutable with specie in the payment of the taxes imposed by the said act.

II. AND whereas by one other act passed in *May,* one thousand seven hundred and eighty three, entitled *An act to amend the act entitled An act to amend and reduce the several acts of Assembly for ascertaining certain taxes and duties, and for establishing a permanent revenue, into one act,* so much of the first recited act as makes tobacco, hemp, flour, or deer-skins, receivable in the payment of taxes imposed by the said act was repealed.

III. AND whereas it is represented to this present General Assembly, that many citizens of this commonwealth, in conformity to the first recited act, delivered to the receivers of hemp and flour, before the passing of the last recited act, the whole or a part of their taxes, in the said specifics, and obtained receipts for the same, which it is doubted cannot legally be received or paid in discharge of the taxes now

Receipts not transfer'd for hemp or flour delivered according to act Oct. 1782, ch. 8. for taxes, to be now received.

due, notwithstanding the greater part of such hemp and flour has been applied to the use of the public: For removing such doubts, *Be it enacted,* that all receipts which have not been returned to the officer granting the same, or transferred for hemp and flour delivered pursuant to the directions of the said first recited act, shall be received by the sheriffs or collectors in discharge of one half of the taxes of the persons delivering such hemp or flour, at the rate or price affixed thereto by the said act; and such receipts shall be allowed the sheriffs and collectors in the settlement of their accounts for the collection of the public taxes; any law to the contrary, or seeming to the contrary, notwithstanding.

Auditors to issue warrants to veniremen and witnesses for their allowance.

IV. AND be it further enacted, that the Auditors of public accounts shall be, and they are hereby empowered and authorized, to issue warrants to each sheriff, witness, and venire-man, that shall hereafter attend the General Court on any criminal prosecution, in which their allowance is to be paid by the commonwealth, and such warrants, when issued, shall be receivable in taxes now due, or that hereafter may become due.

C H A P.   XIII.

An act to amend the act for establishing Pilots, and regulating their fees.

See May 1783, ch. 1.

Preamble.

Rate of pilotage increased for large vessels.

Four pilots may be in partnership.

I. WHEREAS it is represented to this present General Assembly, that the prices allowed for pilotage of vessels, by the act entitled *An act for establishing pilots, and regulating their fees,* are inadequate to their services: *Be it therefore enacted,* that every pilot may demand and take for each vessel drawing upwards of ten feet water, one fifth more in addition to the sums respectively allowed by the foot in the said recited act. That instead of two pilots only being in partnership, as by the said act is directed, it shall and may be lawful for any number of pilots, not exceeding four, to be in partnership.

C H A P.   XIV.

Private.

An act to empower the county court of Stafford to levy the tobacco due to Henry Tyler, deceased, late clerk of the said court.

C H A P.   XV.

Private. See May 1780, ch. 25.

An act for repealing in part the act for establishing the town of Louisville.

CHAP. XVI.

An act for the admission of emigrants and declaring their rights to citizenship.

I. WHEREAS it is the policy of all infant states to encourage population, among other means, by an easy mode for the admission of foreigners to the rights of citizenship; yet wisdom and safety suggest the propriety of guarding against the introduction of secret enemies, and of keeping the offices of government in the hands of citizens intimately acquainted with the spirit of the constitution and the genius of the people, as well as permanently attached to the common interest: *Be it therefore enacted by the General Assembly*, that all free persons, born within the territory of this commonwealth; all persons not being natives, who have obtained a right to citizenship under the act entitled *An act declaring who shall be deemed citizens of this commonwealth*; and also all children wheresoever born, whose fathers or mothers are or were citizens at the time of the birth of such children, shall be deemed citizens of this commonwealth, until they relinquish that character in manner herein after mentioned; and that all persons, other than alien enemies, who shall migrate into this state, and shall before some court of record give satisfactory proof by oath (or being Quakers or Menonists, by affirmation) that they intend to reside therein, and also take the legal oath, or affirmation, for giving assurance of fidelity to the commonwealth (which oaths, or affirmations, the clerk of the court shall enter on record, and give a certificate thereof to the person taking the same, for which he shall receive the fee of one dollar) shall be entitled to all the rights, privileges, and advantages of citizens, except that they shall not be capable of election or appointment to any office, legislative, executive, or judiciary, until an actual residence in the state of two years from the time of taking such oaths, or affirmations, as aforesaid, nor until they shall have evinced a permanent attachment to the state, by having intermarried with a citizen of this commonwealth, or a citizen of any other of the United States, or purchased lands to the value of one hundred pounds therein.

Preamble.

Who shall be deemed citizens.

Exception as to holding offices.

II. PROVIDED *always, and be it further enacted*, that no person whatsoever, having or holding any place or pension from any foreign state or potentate, shall be eligible to any office. legislative. executive, or judiciary, within this commonwealth.

III. AND in order to preserve to the citizens of this commonwealth, that natural right which all men have of relinquishing the society in which birth or accident may have thrown them, and of seeking subsistence and happiness elsewhere, and to declare explicitly what shall be deemed evidence of an intention in any citizen to exercise that right; *Be it further enacted*, that whensoever any citizen of this commonwealth shall, by deed in writing, under his hand and seal, executed in the presence of, and subscribed by three witnesses, and by them or two of them proved in the General Court, or the court of the county wherein he resides, or by open verbal declaration made in either of the said courts (to be by them entered of record) declare that he relinquishes the character of a citizen, and shall depart out of this commonwealth; such person shall, from the time of his departure, be considered as having exercised his right of expatriation, and shall thenceforth be deemed no citizen.

How a citizen may expatriate himself.

IV. AND *be it further enacted*, that the act of Assembly passed in the year one thousand seven hundred and seventy nine, entitled *An act declaring who shall be deemed citizens of this commonwealth*, shall be, and the same is hereby repealed.

Repeal of act of May 1779, ch. 55.

CHAP. XVII.

An act prohibiting the migration of certain persons to this commonwealth, and for other purposes.

I. WHEREAS it is just and necessary to prevent the admission into this state of those persons, who being either citizens or natives of some of the United States, have withdrawn themselves from their country, and actually been in arms, aiding and abetting the common enemy in their endeavours to subvert the rights and liberties of *America*: *Be it therefore enacted*, that all persons who having accepted a military commission from the United States, or any of them, or who having taken the oath of fidelity to any of the United States, or who having been natives of, or residents in any of the United States, on the nineteenth day of *April*, in the year one thousand seven hundred and seventy five, or at any time since, have at any time during the late war, voluntarily joined themselves to the fleets or armies of the King of *Great Britain*, and have borne arms against the United States, or any of them, within their territories or on their coasts, or who being inhabitants of any of the United States, on the nineteenth day of *April*, one thousand seven hundred and seventy five, or at any time since, and have been owner, or part owners, of any privateer, or other armed vessel, cruising against the United States, or any of them, shall be, and they are hereby prohibited from migrating to, or becoming citizens of this state.

Preamble.

Description of persons prohibited.

II. AND *be it further enacted*, that all and every person or persons, who at any time acted as a member of the board, commonly called the Board of Refugee Commissioners at *New York*, or who hath acted under the authority, or by the direction of the said board, shall be, and they are hereby prohibited from migrating to, or becoming citizens of this state.

III. AND *be it further enacted*, that all persons resident in this or any other of the United States, on the said nineteenth day of *April*, and not included in the above descriptions, who are at present prohibited by law from migrating to this state, shall be, and they are hereby permitted to migrate into, and enjoy all the rights of citizenship, except that they shall not be capable of voting for members to either House of Assembly, or of holding or exercising any office of trust or profit, civil or military: *Provided*, that nothing herein contained shall be construed so as to contravene the treaty of peace with *Great Britain*, lately concluded.

All other former residents allowed to return;
But not to vote in elections.
Not to contravene the treaty of peace.

IV. AND *be it further enacted*, that full and ample protection shall be given to all persons who shall come into this commonwealth upon lawful business, except those who are prohibited by this act from migrating into this state.

Protection to all, not prohibited, coming on lawful business.

V. AND *be it further enacted*, that the act, entitled *An act to prohibit intercourse with, and the admission of, British subjects into this state*, and also so much of every other act or acts of Assembly, as comes within the meaning of this act, shall be, and the same are hereby repealed.

Repealing clause.

CHAP. XVIII.

An act to authorize the Delegates of this state in Congress, to convey to the United States in Congress assembled, all the right of this commonwealth to the territory north westward of the river Ohio.

Preamble.

I. WHEREAS the Congress of the United States did, by their act of the sixth day of *September*, in the year one thousand seven hundred and eighty, recommend to the several states in the union, having claims to waste and unappropriated lands in the western country, a liberal cession to the United States of a portion of their respective claims for the common benefit of the union:

II. AND whereas this commonwealth did, on the second day of *January*, in the year one thousand seven hundred and eighty one, yield to the Congress of the United States, for the benefit of the said states, all right, title, and claim, which the said commonwealth had to the territory north-west of the river *Ohio*, subject to the conditions annexed to the said act of cession.

III. AND whereas the United States in Congress assembled, have by their act of the thirteenth of *September* last, stipulated the terms on which they agree to accept the cession of this state, should the Legislature approve thereof, which terms, although they do not come fully up to the propositions of this commonwealth, are conceived on the whole, to approach so nearly to them, as to induce this state to accept thereof, in full confidence that Congress will, in justice to this state for the liberal cession she hath made, earnestly press upon the other states claiming large tracts of waste and uncultivated territory, the propriety of making cessions equally liberal for the common benefit and support of the union: *Be it enacted by the General Assembly*, that it shall and may be lawful for the Delegates of this state to the Congress of the United States, or such of them as shall be assembled in Congress, and the said Delegates, or such of them so assembled, are hereby fully authorized and empowered, for and on behalf of this state, by proper deeds or instrument in writing, under their hands and seals, to convey, transfer, assign, and make over unto the United States in Congress assembled, for the benefit of the said states, all right, title, and claim, as well of soil as jurisdiction, which this commonwealth hath to the territory or tract of country within the limits of the *Virginia* charter, situate, lying, and being to the north-west of the river *Ohio*, subject to the terms and conditions contained in the before recited act of Congress of the thirteenth day of *September* last, that is to say: Upon condition that the territory so ceded shall be laid out and formed into states, containing a suitable extent of territory, not less than one hundred, nor more than one hundred and fifty miles square, or as near thereto as circumstances will admit; and that the states so formed, shall be distinct republican states, and admitted members of the fœderal union, having the same rights of sovereignty, freedom, and independence, as the other states; that the necessary and reasonable expences incurred by this state in subduing any *British* posts, or in maintaining forts or garrisons within and for the defence, or in acquiring any part of the territory so ceded or relinquished, shall be fully reimbursed by the United States; and that one commissioner shall be appointed by Congress, one by this commonwealth, and another by those two Commissioners, who, or a majority of them, shall be authorized and empowered to adjust and liquidate the account of the necessary and reasonable expences incurred by this state, which they shall judge to be comprized within the intent and meaning of the act of Congress of the tenth of *October*, one thousand seven hundred and eighty, respecting such expences. That the *French* and *Canadian* inhabitants, and other settlers of the *Kaskaskies*, *St. Vincents*, and the neighbouring villages, who have professed themselves citizens of *Virginia*, shall have their possessions and titles confirmed to them, and be protected in the enjoyment of their rights and liberties. That a quantity not exceeding one hundred and fifty thousand acres of land, promised by this state, shall be allowed and granted to the then Colonel, now General *George Rogers Clarke*, and to the officers and soldiers of his regiment, who marched with him when the posts of *Kaskaskies* and *St. Vincents* were reduced, and to the officers and soldiers that have been since incorporated into the said regiment, to be laid off in one tract, the length of which not to exceed double the breadth, in such place on the north-west side of the *Ohio* as a majority of the officers shall choose, and to be afterwards divided among the said officers and soldiers in due proportion according to the laws of *Virginia*. That in case the quantity of good lands on the south-east side of the *Ohio*, upon the waters of *Cumberland* river, and between the *Green* river and *Tenisee* river, which have been reserved by law for the *Virginia* troops upon continental establishment, should, from the *North Carolina* line bearing in further upon the *Cumberland* lands than was expected, prove insufficient for their legal bounties, the deficiency should be made up to the said troops in good lands to be laid off between the rivers *Scioto* and *Little Miami*, on the north-west side of the river *Ohio*, in such proportions as have been engaged to them by the laws of *Virginia*. That all the lands within the territory so ceded to the United States, and not reserved for or appropriated to any of the before mentioned purposes, or disposed of in bounties to the officers and soldiers of the *American* army, shall be considered as a common fund for the use and benefit of such of the United States as have become, or shall become members of the confederation or fœderal alliance of the said states, *Virginia* inclusive, according to their usual respective proportions in the general charge and expenditure, and shall be faithfully and *bona fide* disposed of for that purpose, and for no other use or purpose whatsoever. *Provided*, that the trust hereby reposed in the Delegates of this state shall not be executed unless three of them, at least, are present in Congress.

Delegates empowered to convey.

Conditions.

Reservations.

All the lands ceded to be a common fund for the members of the fœderal alliance, and for no otheruse. Three members at least to execute the trust.

CHAP. XIX.

An act to oblige vessels coming from foreign parts to perform quarantine.

Preamble.

How rules for performing quarantine shall be made and observed.

I. WHEREAS it is necessary to compel vessels arriving in this country from foreign parts of the world, to perform quarantine in certain cases: *Be it enacted by the General Assembly*, that vessels, persons, and merchandize, coming or brought into any place within this commonwealth, from any other part of the world, whence the Governor with advice of his Council shall judge it probable that any plague or other infectious disease may be brought, shall be obliged to make their quarantine in such place, during such time, and in such manner as shall be directed by the Governor, by his order in Council, notified by proclamation, to be published in the *Virginia* gazette; and until they shall be discharged from the quarantine, no such persons or merchandize shall come or be brought on shore, or go or be put on board of any other vessel in the commonwealth, but in such manner in such cases, and by such licence, as shall be permitted by the order; and the vessels and persons receiving goods out of her, shall be subject to the orders concerning quarantine, and for preventing infection, which shall be made by the Governor and Council and notified as aforesaid. The master of a vessel coming from sea, on board of which there shall be a person infected with the plague or other pestilential disease, shall immediately make the case known to some Naval Officer, who shall send intelligence thereof with all speed to the Governor, that measures may be taken for support of the crew, and precautions used to prevent the spreading of the infection; and the master shall not enter into any port, but shall remain in some open road, and fhall avoid and hinder all intercourfe with other veffels or perfons; nor fhall any of the paffengers or crew go on fhore until the order of the Governor and Council fhall be received by the mafter. Whofoever fhall offend againft this act in either or any of the aforementioned inftances, fhall be amerced the fum of five hundred pounds. When a place fhall be infected with the plague or other peftilential difeafe, or when the Governor with advice of the Council fhall have notified by proclamation publifhed in the *Virginia* gazette, that it is judged probable the plague or other peftilential difeafe may be brought from any place, if a veffel from fuch place fhall be coming into a port of the commonwealth, the Naval Officer, or perfon who fhall be authorized to fee quarantine performed, fhall go off or caufe fome other to go off to the veffel, and at a convenient diftance require the commander to declare what is his name, at what places the cargo was taken on board, at what places the veffel touched in her paffage, whether any of thofe places were infected with the plague or any other peftilential difeafe, how long the veffel had been in her paffage, how many perfons were on board when fhe fet fail, whether any on board during the voyage had been infected with the plague or other peftilential difeafe, and who they are, how many died in the voyage, and of what diftemper, what veffels he or any of his company with his privity went on board of, and whether any of their company had been on board of his veffel in their voyage, and to what places thofe veffels belonged, and what are the contents of his lading. And if it fhall appear by the examination that the veffel ought to perform quarantine, the officers of the fhips of war and forts and garrifons, or other officers civil or military, of the commonwealth, having notice thereof, and other perfons called to their affiftance, may force fuch veffel by violence, and if neceffary by firing guns at her, to go to the place appointed for quarantine. The mafter of a veffel coming from a place infected with the plague or other peftilential difeafe, or having any perfon on board fo infected, who fhall conceal it, or who fhall not give true anfwers to the queftions fo to be propounded to him, fhall be amerced the fum of five hundred pounds. The mafter of a veffel ordered to perform quarantine, when he fhall be required, after his arrival at the place appointed, fhall deliver to the officer authorized to fee it performed there, the bills of health and manifefts he fhall have received during the voyage, with his log-book and journal; and refufing or neglecting fo to do, or to repair in convenient time after notice to the place appointed, or efcaping from thence before quarantine performed, fhall be amerced the fum of five hundred pounds. Perfons ordered to perform quarantine, if they fhall efcape, may be compelled to return, or if they fhall attempt to efcape, may be detained by the perfons who fhall be authorized to fee the quarantine performed, and who may employ force and call for the affiftance of others, if it be neceffary, for this purpofe. Any perfon going on board a veffel or into a place under quarantine, without licence from the fuperintendant thereof, may be compelled to remain there, in the fame manner as he might have been if he had been one of the crew of the veffel. A Naval Officer, or perfon authorized to execute an order concerning quarantine, guilty of wilful breach or neglect of duty, fhall be amerced the fum of one thoufand pounds. And any perfon embezzling or wilfully damaging goods performing quarantine under his direction, fhall be liable to the party injured for treble the value of the damages fuftained thereby. The veffel, perfons, and goods, after quarantine performed, certificate thereof, and that they are free from infection, being given by the fuperintendant, fhall be no further reftrained by virtue of this act. A perfon authorized to fee quarantine performed, or a watchman upon any veffel, place, or goods under quarantine, deferting his duty, or willingly permitting a perfon, veffel, or goods, to depart, or be conveyed away from the place where the quarantine ought to be performed, without a lawful licence; or a perfon empowered to give a certificate of the performance of quarantine, knowingly giving a falfe certificate, fhall be amerced the fum of one hundred pounds. The forfeitures inflicted by this act fhall be to the ufe of the commonwealth, and fhall be recovered by action of debt, in which action the defendant fhall be ruled to give fpecial bail.

II. *AND be it further enacted,* that the Governor in Council, fhall direct the Auditors to iffue their warrants on the Treafurer for fuch fums of money as may be neceffary for the fupport of the perfons performing quarantine and thofe appointed to fee it performed, who is directed to pay the fame out of the public money in his hands, appropriated to defray the contingent charges of government, and fhall be repaid by the mafter or owner of the veffel, after quarantine performed.

A. D. 1783.

Penalty for breach. Enquiry when veffels come from infected places.

Various penalties.

C H A P. XX.

An act for cutting a navigable canal from the waters of Elizabeth *river to the waters of* North *river.*

Private.

C H A P. XXI.

An act for furveying and apportioning the lands granted to the Illinois *regiment, and eftablifhing a town within the faid grant.*

Preamble.

I. FOR locating and furveying the one hundred and fifty thoufand acres of land granted by a refolution of Affembly to Colonel *George Rogers Clarke,* and the officers and foldiers who affifted in the reduction of the *Britifh* pofts in the *Illinois; Be it enacted by the General Affembly,* that William Fleming, *John Edwards, John Campbell, Walker Daniel,* gentlemen, and *George Rogers Clarke, John Montgomery, Abraham Chaplain, John Bailey, Robert Todd,* and *William Clarke,* officers in the *Illinois* regiment, fhall be, and they are hereby conftituted a board of Commiffioners; and that they or the major part of them, fhall fettle and determine the claims to land under the faid refolution. That the refpective claimants fhall give in their claims to the faid commiffioners on or before the firft day of *April,* one thoufand feven hundred and eighty four, and if approved and allowed, fhall pay down to the faid commiffioners one dollar for every hundred acres of fuch claim, to enable them to furvey and apportion the faid lands. The faid commiffioner fhall appoint a principal furveyor, who fhall have power to appoint his deputies, to be approved by the faid commiffioners, and to contract with him for his fees. That from and after the faid firft day of *April,* one thoufand feven hundred and eighty four, the faid commiffioners or the major part of them, fhall proceed with the furveyor to lay off the faid one hundred and fifty thoufand acres of land on the north-weft fide of the *Ohio* river, the length of which fhall not exceed double the breadth; and after laying out one thoufand acres at the moft convenient place therein for a town, fhall proceed to lay out and furvey the refidue, and divide the fame by fair and equal lot among the claimants; but no lot or furvey fhall exceed five hundred acres. That the faid commiffioners in their apportionments of the faid land, fhall govern themfelves by the allowances made by law to the officers and foldiers in the continental army. That the faid commiffioners fhall, as foon as may be, after the faid one hundred and forty nine thoufand acres fhall be furveyed, caufe a plat thereof, certified on oath, to be returned to the Regifter's office, and thereupon a patent fhall iffue to the faid commiffioners or the furvivors of them, who fhall hold the fame in truft for the refpective claimants; and they, or the major part of them, fhall thereafter upon application, execute good and fufficient deeds for conveying the feveral portions of land to the faid officers and foldiers.

Commiffioners appointed to fettle their claims.

When claims to be given in and contribution to be made for expences.

A furveyor and deputies to be appointed.

When and how the lands fhall be furveyed, divided, patented, and conveyed.

A D. 1783.

A town to be laid off named Clarkſville.

II. *AND be it further enacted,* that a plat of the ſaid one thouſand acres of land laid off for a town, ſhall be returned by the ſurveyor to the court of the county of *Jefferſon,* to be by the clerk thereof recorded, and thereupon the ſame ſhall be, and is hereby veſted in *William Fleming, John Edwards, John Campbell, Walker Daniel, George Rogers Clarke, John Montgomery, Abraham Chaplin, John Bailey, Robert Todd,* and *William Clarke,* gentlemen, truſtees, to be by them, or any five of them, laid off into lots of half an acre each, with convenient ſtreets and public lots, which ſhall be, and the ſame is hereby eſtabliſhed a town by the name of *Clarkſville.* That after the ſaid lands ſhall be laid off into lots and ſtreets, the ſaid truſtees, or any five of them, ſhall proceed to ſell the ſame, or ſo many as they ſhall judge expedient, at public auction, for the beſt price that can be had, the time and place of ſale being previouſly advertiſed two months at the courthouſes of the adjacent counties; the purchaſers reſpectively

Lots to be ſold for the benefit of the inhabitants.

to hold their ſaid lots, ſubject to the condition of building on each a dwelling-houſe twenty feet by eighteen at leaſt, with a brick or ſtone chimney, to be finiſhed within three years from the day of ſale; and the ſaid truſtees, or any five of them, are hereby empowered to convey the ſaid lots to the purchaſers thereof in *fee ſimple,* ſubject to the condition aforeſaid; and the money ariſing from ſuch ſale ſhall be applied by the ſaid truſtees in ſuch manner as they may judge moſt beneficial for the inhabitants of the ſaid town; that the ſaid truſtees, or the major part of them, ſhall have power from time to time to ſettle

Subject to the condition of building thereon,

and determine all diſputes concerning the bounds of the ſaid lots, and to ſettle ſuch rules and orders for the regular building thereon as to them ſhall ſeem beſt and moſt convenient; and in caſe of the death, removal out of the county, or other legal diſability, of any of the ſaid truſtees, the remaining truſtees ſhall ſupply ſuch vacancies, by electing others from time to time, who ſhall be veſted with the ſame powers as thoſe particularly nominated in this act. The purchaſers of the ſaid lots, ſo ſoon as they ſhall have ſaved the ſame according to their reſpective deeds of conveyance, ſhall have and enjoy all the rights, privileges, and immunities, which the freeholders and inhabitants of other towns in this ſtate,

and ſold again, if forfeited.

not incorporated, hold and enjoy. If the purchaſer of any lot ſhall fail to build thereon within the time before limited, the ſaid truſtees, or a major part of them, may thereupon enter into ſuch lot, and may either ſell the ſame again and apply the money towards repairing the ſtreets, or in any other way for the benefit of the ſaid town, or appropriate ſuch lot to the public uſe of the inhabitants of the ſaid town.

C H A P. XXII.

Temporary.

An act to revive and amend an act entitled An act for adjuſting claims for property impreſſed or taken for public ſervice.

C H A P. XXIII.

Private.

An act to repeal a former act, and to enable the court of Botetourt *county to levy a ſum of money due to the Reverend* Adam Smyth.

C H A P. XXIV.

Had its effect. See May 1783, ch. 41.

An act to repeal an act, entitled An act to give further time for the probation of deeds and other inſtruments of writing, and for other purpoſes.

C H A P. XXV.

Private.

An act appointing certain perſons to receive ſubſcriptions and contract with undertakers for the clearing of James *river through the South Mountain.*

C H A P. XXVI.

See Oct. 1777. ch. 15, 17, & notes. Preamble.

An act to amend the acts for eſtabliſhing the High Court of Chancery and General Court.

I. WHEREAS great inconvenience may ariſe to the ſuitors in the ſeveral courts of this commonwealth, who are litigant with perſons reſiding without this commonwealth, and have not agents or attornies within the ſame, by the death or removal of witneſſes whoſe depoſitions cannot legally be taken for want of notice to ſuch abſent perſons. And whereas the acts eſtabliſhing the High Court of Chancery and General Court, require ſome amendments: *Be it therefore enacted,* that

How commiſſions to examine witneſſes againſt a party out of the ſtate, may be obtained.

when any commiſſion to take the depoſition of a witneſs, in a ſuit depending in any of the courts of this commonwealth, where the plaintiff or defendant in ſuch ſuit doth not reſide within the ſame, or hath not an agent or attorney within the ſame, to whom notice of the time and place of taking ſuch depoſition can be given, then the perſon obtaining ſuch commiſſion, having publiſhed in the *Virginia* gazette, four weeks ſucceſſively, the time and place when and where the witneſs is to be examined, and the name of the witneſs, together with the names of the parties to the ſuit in which ſuch witneſs is to be examined, it ſhall and may be lawful for any plaintiff or defendant as aforeſaid, to proceed to take any depoſition authorized by the commiſſion iſſuing from the court agreeable to law, where the ſuit depends as aforeſaid; and ſuch depoſition, when taken and returned to the clerk's office agreeable to the rules of the court from whence the commiſſion iſſued, ſhall there be filed and allowed to be read in evidence, in the ſame manner and under the like reſtrictions, as if notice had been duly given to the oppoſite party,

Printer's fee for publication.

any law, uſage, or cuſtom, to the contrary in any wiſe notwithſtanding. And the Printer may demand and receive the ſum of twelve ſhillings for publiſhing ſuch advertiſement four weeks, which ſhall be taxed in the bill of coſts if the party chargeable therewith ſhall prevail in the ſuit.

Clerk of the General Court, upon affidavit filed to iſſue commiſſions.

II. *AND be it further enacted,* that where a plaintiff or defendant in any action or ſuit depending in the General Court, or which may hereafter be commenced in the General Court, ſhall produce to the clerk of the General Court an affidavit or affidavits for the purpoſe of obtaining a commiſſion to take the depoſition of a witneſs, the ſaid clerk may, and he is hereby authorized and empowered, to iſſue a commiſſion in the ſame manner and under the like reſtrictions as any Judges of the General Court might or could do in vacation time.

III. AND whereas the mode of trial in order to aſcertain all material facts, affirmed by the one party and denied by the other, in the ſuits depending, or that may hereafter be commenced, in the High

Court of Chancery by jury upon *viva voce* testimony in the said court, hath been found to be expensive to the parties, and inconvenient to witnesses: *Be it therefore enacted*, that so much of the twenty sixth rule prescribed by the act for establishing an High Court of Chancery, as directs such matters of fact to be tried by jury in the said court, upon *viva voce* testimony, shall be, and the same is hereby repealed; and henceforward the mode of trial in all causes now depending before the High Court of Chancery, as well as in such as may hereafter be commenced, shall be the same as heretofore used and practised in the Courts of Chancery within the colony of *Virginia* under the former government.

Ordinary trials by jury in Chancery repealed.

Former mode of trial revived.

C H A P. XXVII.

An act to amend the several acts for regulating public ferries.

See 1769, ch 2 §, and notes.

I. WHEREAS it has been represented to this Assembly, that a public ferry across the rivers *Staunton* and *Dan*, near the confluence of the said rivers, in the county of *Mecklenburg*, from the land of Sir *Peyton Skipwith* on the north side, to his land on the south side, will be of great advantage to travellers and others: *Be it therefore enacted*, that a public ferry shall be constantly kept at the aforesaid place, and that the rates for crossing, and penalties for neglect of duty, shall be the same as is directed in the case of other ferries established by law in the said county.

Preamble.

A new ferry appointed and the rates.

II. AND whereas the acts now in force for regulating ferries, are insufficient to restrain those living near public ferries from setting over passengers from their lands, across rivers and creeks where such ferries are established, to the great injury of the keepers thereof; *Be it enacted*, that if any person, other than a ferry keeper, shall hereafter, for reward, set any person or persons over any river or creek whereon public ferries are established, or shall permit or allow any person or persons living on the opposite shore of such river or creek, to take passengers from their lands contiguous to a public ferry, he or she so offending, shall forfeit and pay five pounds current money for every such offence, one moiety to the ferry keeper nearest the place where such offence shall be committed, the other moiety to the informer; and if such ferry keeper shall be the informer, he shall be entitled to the whole penalty; to be recovered with costs, by action of debt or information in any county court within this commonwealth.

Penalty on private persons ferrying over others for reward.

II. AND *be it further enacted*, that all and every act and acts, contrary to the meaning of this act, shall be, and the same are hereby repealed.

Repeal.

C H A P. XXVIII.

An act for establishing inspections of tobacco on the western waters, at Portsmouth, *in the county of* Norfolk, *and at* Gibson's, *in the county of* King George.

See May 1783, ch. 10.

I. WHEREAS it is represented to this present General Assembly, that the erecting of warehouses for the inspection of tobacco in the county of *Lincoln*, on *Kentucky* river, at the mouth of *Hickman's* creek, on the lands of *James Hogans*; also in the county of *Jefferson*, at the falls of the *Ohio* river, on the lands of *John Campbell*; also in the county of *Fayette*, at *Lee's* town, on the *Kentucky* river, on the lands of *Hancock Lee*; in the county of *Norfolk*, on the public lands in the town of *Portsmouth*; and also in the county of *King George*, on the lot of land belonging to *John Gravett* and *William Shropshire*, will be of public benefit: *Be it therefore enacted*, that the said inspections of tobacco shall be, and they are hereby established at the places aforesaid, that is to say: The inspection in the county of *Lincoln*, shall be called and known by the name of *Hickman's*; the inspection in the county of *Jefferson*, shall be called and known by the name of *Campbell's*; the inspection in the county of *Fayette*, shall be called and known by the name of *Lee's*; in the county of *Norfolk*, shall be called *Portsmouth*; and the inspection in the county of *King George*, shall be called and known by the name of *Gibson's*. And the courts of the said counties shall observe the same rules and regulations in erecting the said warehouses, and recommending of inspectors, as are prescribed by the act, entitled *An act to amend and reduce the several acts of Assembly for the inspection of tobacco, into one act;* and that the transfer notes issued by the inspectors at the warehouses in the said counties of *Lincoln, Jefferson*, and *Fayette*, shall be payable in the said counties for all county and parish levies, and also all clerks, sheriffs, and other officers fees, within the same; and the transfer notes issued by the inspectors at *Gibson's* warehouse, shall be payable in like manner as those formerly issued by the inspectors at *Gibson's* warehouse in the said county of *King George*.

Preamble.

Several warehouses appointed.

Courts to build warehouses and recommend inspectors. Currency of their transfer notes.

II. AND *be it further enacted*, that the acting inspectors attending the said warehouses, shall be entitled to, and receive the following salaries, that is to say: At *Hickman's* warehouse, the sum of twenty five pounds each; the inspectors at *Campbell's* warehouse, the sum of twenty five pounds each; at *Lee's* warehouse, the sum of twenty five pounds each; at *Portsmouth*, thirty pounds each; and at *Gibson's* warehouse, the sum of thirty pounds each. And the surplus money remaining in their hands, after paying their wages and other contingent charges of the warehouses, shall be accounted for in the same manner as is directed by the said recited act.

Inspectors salaries

III. AND *be it enacted*, that for all tobacco which shall be delivered out of the warehouses aforesaid, there shall be paid to the inspector, by the person demanding the same, ten shillings for every hogshead so delivered, and one shilling and three pence for every hundred weight which may be put up in any lesser package; which money shall be the fund for payment of the inspectors salaries as well as for supporting the respective warehouses.

Inspection tax.

C H A P. XXIX.

An act to ascertain the mode of obtaining grants to certain lands on the western waters.

See May 1779, ch 12.

I. WHEREAS, in obedience to an act of Assembly entitled, *An act for adjusting and settling the titles of claimers to unpatented lands, previous to the establishment of the commonwealth's Land Office*, the commissioners thereby appointed, proceeded to issue certificates to different claimants under the said act.

Preamble.

II. AND whereas many surveys made in conformity to the said certificates, include other surveys made for the same persons under the sanction, and in the name of several companies who obtained grants under the former government, and which have since been confirmed by the High Court of Appeals: For the preservation of the rights of such companies, and convenience of those who have obtain-

A. D. 1783.

Patents to be issued to those who purchased of companies, and have certificates from commissioners; to pay the companies 3 l. per hundred and interest from May 15, 1779. After 25th Dec. 1784, distress may be made of the land, for arrears of purchase money.

ed surveys under the decision of the said commissioners, *Be it enacted*, that all persons who have obtained certificates from the respective commissioners acting under the above recited act, for land they also claimed by purchase from the grantees, may return their surveys made in conformity to such certificates to the Land Office, and the Register is hereby authorized and required to issue grants upon all such surveys, within six months after they have been returned into his office. *Provided always*, that the proprietor of such surveys shall account with the grantees or their agents, for so much of the lands as were surveyed to the said companies, prior to the year one thousand seven hundred and seventy six, agreeable to the decree of the Court of Appeals, that is to say, they shall pay the said companies or their agents, the sum of three pounds per hundred acres, for all land confirmed to the said grantees as aforesaid, with lawful interest from the fifteenth day of *May* one thousand seven hundred and seventy nine, and no more.

III. AND in lieu of forfeiture of lands in case of non-payment, which is unreasonable, and shall hereafter cease; *Be it further enacted*, that for all arrearages which shall be due, and have been previously demanded by the said companies or their agents, on or before the twenty fifth day of *December*, one thousand seven hundred and eighty four, previous to which no distress shall be made, the sheriffs of the counties wherein such lands lie, the price of which may be due, at the request of the different companies or their agents, may, and are hereby directed to lay off in a compact body, so much of the said land, to be pointed out by the tenant or proprietor, as shall be the value of such debt, and shall proceed to sell the same, charging the debtor with the usual commission thereon, and the expence of surveying such dividend or quantity of land; provided that he gives thirty days public notice of the time and place of such sale.

Public to repay the expence of ascertaining titles before commissioners, since evicted by Court of Appeals.

IV. AND whereas many of the citizens of this commonwealth, have paid considerable sums of money to commissioners, clerks, and surveyors, for ascertaining their titles to lands, which titles have since been evicted by a decree of the Court of Appeals: *Be it therefore enacted*, that the clerks and surveyors belonging to the different districts laid off by the above recited act, shall immediately upon the receipt of this act, ascertain the amount of all surveys made prior to the year one thousand seven hundred and seventy six, which are included in the certificates granted by the commissioners, and the disbursements in specie of the proprietors of the said land respectively, to the said commissioners, clerks, and surveyors, in procuring certificates for and re-surveying the same; which accounts shall be duly proved before any county court of the district, and certified by the clerk of such court to the Auditors of public accounts, who shall issue their warrants for the same; which warrants shall be receivable in taxes under the act for calling in and redeeming certain certificates.

V. AND be it further enacted, that all acts coming within the purview of this act, shall be, and the same are hereby repealed.

CHAP. XXX.

See Nov. 1781, ch. 23. May 1782, ch. 44. Oct. 1782, ch. 45.

Preamble.

An act to revive and continue the several acts of Assembly for suspending the issuing of executions on certain judgments until December, one thousand seven hundred and eighty three.

I. WHEREAS the present scarcity of specie in this state, causes an utter inability in debtors to discharge their debts, unless they are still permitted to pay them in the produce of the country, or by transferring property to their creditors, and it is therefore wise, just, and necessary, that the act, entitled *An act to amend an act entitled An act to repeal so much of a former act as suspends the issuing of executions on certain judgments until* December *one thousand seven hundred and eighty three*, (which provides a remedy for the said mischief) and expired on the first day of the present month, should be revived and further continued: *Be it therefore enacted*, that the said recited act, entitled *An act to amend an act entitled An act to repeal so much of a former act as suspends the issuing of executions on certain judgments until* December *one thousand seven hundred and eighty three*, be, and the same is hereby revived and further continued, from the day on which it expired, for and during the term of four months, and from thence to the end of the next session of Assembly.

Act of Oct. 1782, revived and continued.

Also act of May 1782.

II. AND whereas the said before recited act, entitled *An act to repeal so much of a former act as suspends the issuing of executions upon certain judgments until* December *one thousand seven hundred and eighty three*, hath also expired: *Be it further enacted*, that the said last recited act, entitled *An act to repeal so much of a former act as suspends the issuing of executions upon certain judgments until* December *one thousand seven hundred and eighty three*, shall be, and the same is hereby also revived, and shall continue and be in force for and during the term of four months, and from thence to the end of the next session of Assembly.

CHAP. XXXI.

Preamble.

An act to provide certain and adequate funds for the payment of this state's quota of the debts contracted by the United States

I. WHEREAS the United States in Congress assembled, did, by their act of the eighteenth day of *April* in the present year, recommend to the several states as indispensably necessary to the restoration of public credit, and to the punctual and honorable discharge of the public debts, to invest the United States in Congress assembled, with a power to levy for the use of the United States, certain duties upon goods imported into the said states from any foreign port, island, or plantation, as therein enumerated, and upon all other goods, a duty of *five per centum ad valorem*, at the time and place of importation, subject to such limitations and restrictions as in the said act are particularly mentioned.

Congress empowered to levy a duty on goods imported, and make regulations for collecting it. Duty on particular articles. 5 per cent. ad valorem on all other goods.

II. AND whereas the raising a general revenue throughout the United States by duties imposed on commodities imported, and appropriated to the discharge of the principal and interest of the public debts, may contribute to lighten the burthen of taxes on real and personal property, and thereby prove a great ease and relief to the people: *Be it enacted*, that the United States in Congress assembled, shall be, and they are hereby vested with full power and authority, to levy for the use of the United States, upon goods imported into this state from any foreign port, island, or plantation, the following duties, to be collected under such regulations as the United States in Congress assembled shall direct, to wit: Upon all rum of *Jamaica* proof, *per* gallon, four ninetieths of a dollar; upon all other spirituous liquors, three ninetieths of a dollar; upon *Madeira* wine, twelve ninetieths of a dollar; upon all other wines, six ninetieths of a dollar; upon common bohea tea, *per* pound, six ninetieths of a dollar; upon all other teas, twenty four ninetieths of a dollar; upon pepper, *per* pound, three ninetieths of a dollar; upon brown fugar, *per* pound, half a ninetieth of a dollar; upon loaf fugar, two ninetieths of a dollar; upon all other fugars, one ninetieth of a dollar; upon molaffes, *per* gallon, one ninetieth of a dollar; upon cocoa and coffee, *per* pound, one ninetieth of a dollar; and upon all other goods, a duty of five *per centum ad valorem*, at the time and place of importation. *Provided*, that the faid duties fhall be applied to the difcharging the intereft and principal of the debts contracted on the faith of the United States for fupporting the late war, and on no account diverted to any other ufe or purpofe, nor to be continued for a longer term than twenty five years. *And provided alfo*, that an account of the proceeds and application of the faid duties, be made out and tranfmitted annually to the feveral ftates, diftinguifhing the proceeds of the feveral articles, and the amount of the whole revenue received from each ftate, together with the allowances made to the feveral officers employed in the collection of the faid revenue.

III. *AND be it further enacted*, that the Governor of this commonwealth, for the time being, with the advice of the Council, fhall be, and he is hereby authorized and empowered in the firft inftance, and as there fhall be occafion, from time to time, to appoint the collectors of the duties aforefaid, which collectors fo appointed, fhall be amenable to, and removable by, the United States in Congrefs affembled, alone; and in cafe the Governor, as aforefaid, fhall fail to make fuch appointment, within one month after notice given to him by Congrefs for that purpofe, the appointments may then be made by the United States in Congrefs affembled; provided fuch appointment be made to a citizen of this ftate.

IV. *AND be it further enacted*, that this act fhall commence and be in force, fo foon as each and every of the other ftates in the union fhall pafs laws conformable to the act of Congrefs herein before recited, and official communication thereof be made by the United States in Congrefs affembled, to the Governor of this commonwealth, who, on receipt thereof, fhall promulgate the fame by proclamation, which he is hereby authorized and directed to iffue, and thereupon the refpective grants of the ftates fhall be confidered and deemed by this ftate as forming a mutual compact among all the ftates, and be irrevocable by any one or more of them without the concurrence of the whole, or a majority of the United States in Congrefs affembled. *Provided always*, that nothing herein contained fhall give the United States in Congrefs affembled, a power to direct any regulations for collecting the aforefaid duties, which fhall extend fo far as to fubject any perfon or perfons committing a breach of this act within this commonwealth, to be carried out of the fame for trial, or to compel him to anfwer any action out of the ftate, or to deprive him of a trial according to the conftitution and laws of this commonwealth, or to convict him criminally, without a trial by jury, or his own voluntary confeffion in open court, or to impofe exceffive fines, or to break open any dwelling-houfe, ftore, or warehoufe, at any other time than the day time, between the rifing and fetting of the fun, nor then, without a warrant from a lawful Magiftrate, and iffued upon the oath of the party requefting the fame. *And alfo provided*, that the trial on all feizures arifing within this commonwealth, under this act, fhall be before the Court of Amiralty of this ftate, and from the judgment of the faid court, either party fhall be allowed an appeal to the Court of Appeals of this ftate, before whom a trial fhall in all cafes be final; and that in no cafe the forfeiture fhall exceed the goods feized and the veffel in which the faid goods may be imported.

Commencement and continuance of the act.

Collectors not to be carried for trial or compelled to anfwer a fuit, out of the ftate. Other regulations.

Trials upon feizures here, to be in the Court of Admiralty and appeals to the Court of Appeals. Limitation of forfeitures.

CHAP. XXXII.

An act for reducing the feveral acts of Affembly concerning furveyors into one act, and for paying clerks and other officers fees.

I. FOR reducing the feveral acts of Affembly concerning furveyors into one act, and for defining as well their duties as for eftablifhing and regulating their fees in future, *Be it enacted*, that every perfon who fhall hereafter defire to become a furveyor, fhall be nominated by the court of his county, examined and certified able by the prefident and profeffors of *William* and *Mary* college, and if of good character, commiffioned by the Governor, with a refervation in fuch commiffion to the faid profeffors, for the ufe of the college, of one fixth part of the legal fees that fhall be received by fuch furveyor, for the yearly payment of which he fhall give bond with fufficient fecurity to the prefident and mafters of the faid college; he fhall hold his office during good behaviour; and before he fhall be capable of entering upon the execution of his office, fhall, before the court of the fame county, take an oath, and give bond with two fufficient fecurities to the Governor and his fucceffors, in fuch fum as he, with advice of his Council, fhall have directed, for the faithful execution of his office. All deputy furveyors fhall be recommended by their principals to the court of the county of which fuch principal may be furveyor; the court fhall thereupon appoint and direct one or more fit perfons to examine into the capacity, ability, and fitnefs, of the perfon or perfons fo recommended, and upon a certificate of fuch examination and report of the capacity, ability, and fitnefs, of the perfon or perfons fo recommended, the faid court is hereby empowered and directed to appoint him or them to act as deputy or deputies, for whofe conduct in every refpect touching his office, the principal furveyor fhall be anfwerable; and all deputies fo appointed, fhall have power and authority to act and do in all things and to every intent and purpofe, as the principal furveyor, except in cafes otherwife provided by this act, and fhall thereupon be entitled to one half the fees received for fervices performed by them refpectively, after deducting the proportion thereof due to the college. If any principal furveyor fhall fail to nominate a fufficient number of deputies to perform the fervices of his office in due time, the court of the county fhall direct what number he fhall nominate, and in cafe of failure, fhall nominate for him. And if any deputy furveyor, or any other on his behalf and with his privity, fhall pay or agree to pay any greater part of the profits of his office, fum of money in grofs, or other valuable confideration, to his principal for his recommendation or intereft in procuring the deputation, fuch deputy and principal fhall be thereby rendered forever incapable of ferving in fuch office. Every perfon having a land warrant, and being defirous of locating the fame on any particular wafte and unappropriated lands, fhall lodge fuch warrant with the chief furveyor of the county wherein the faid lands or the greater part of them lie, who fhall give a receipt for it if required. The party fhall direct the location thereof fo fpecially and precifely as that others may be enabled with certainty to locate other warrants on the adjacent refiduum; which location fhall bear date the day on which it fhall be made, and fhall be entered by the furveyor in a book to be kept for that purpofe, in which there fhall be left no blank leaves or fpaces between the different entries. And if feveral perfons fhall apply with their warrants at the office of any furveyor at the fame time, to make entries, they fhall be preferred according to the priority of the dates of their warrants, but if fuch warrants be dated on the fame day, the furveyor fhall fettle the right of priority between fuch perfons by lot. And every furveyor fhall, at the time of making entries for perfons not being inhabitants of his county, appoint a time for furveying their land, and give notice thereof in writing to the perfons making the fame; and if on fuch application at his office, the furveyor fhall refufe to enter fuch location, under pretence of a prior entry for the fame lands made by fome other perfons, he fhall have a right to demand of the faid furveyor a view of the original of fuch prior entry in his book, and alfo an attefted copy of it. Any chief furveyor having a warrant for lands, and defirous to locate the fame within his own county, fhall enter fuch location with the clerk of the county, who fhall return the fame to his next court, to be there

Preamble.

Surveyors how to be appointed. To give bond to the college. Tenure of office. To be fworn and give bond in court.

How deputies fhall be appointed.

Their power and reward.

Penalty for giving principal more.

Land warrants to be lodged with principal furveyor. Locations to be precifely made and entered in book.

Preference where different applications to locate the fame land. Notice of time of furveying to perfons out of the county. How a furveyor may locate his own warrants.

A. D. 1783.

When and how surveys of located lands are to be made.

recorded; and the said surveyor shall proceed to have the survey made as soon as may be, or within six months at farthest, by some one of his deputies, or if he hath no deputy, then by any surveyor or deputy surveyor of an adjacent county, and in case of failure his entry shall be void, and the land liable to the entry of any other person. Every chief surveyor shall proceed with all practicable dispatch to survey all lands entered for in his office, and shall, if the party live within his county, either give him personal notice of the time at which he will attend to make such survey, or shall publish such notice by fixing an advertisement thereof on the door of the court-house of the county, on two several court days; which time, so appointed, shall be at least one month after personal notice given, or after the last advertisement so published; and if the surveyor shall accordingly attend, and the party, or some one for him, shall fail to appear at the time, with proper chain carriers, and a person to mark the lines, if necessary, his entry shall become void, the land thereafter subject to the entry of any other person, and the surveyor shall return him the warrant, which may, notwithstanding, be located anew upon any other waste or unappropriated lands, or again upon the same lands where it hath not in the mean time been entered for by another person. Where the chief surveyor doth not mean to survey himself he shall immediately after the entry made, direct a deputy surveyor to perform the duty, who shall proceed as is before directed in the case of the chief surveyor. The persons employed to carry the chain on any survey shall

Chain carriers to be sworn.
Surveys to be closed, lines marked, and of proportioned length and breadth. Exception.
A plat and certificate to be delivered within three months and warrant re-delivered.
Provided the fees be paid.
The plats, &c. to be examined and entered in the book of principal surveyor.
Lists of all surveys to be annually returned to the college and clerk of the court
None to be clerk and surveyor of the same county.
How surveyors may be punished for neglect.
Surveyors office to be annually inspected.

be sworn by the surveyor, whether principal or deputy, to measure justly and exactly to the best of their abilities, and to deliver a true account thereof to such surveyor, and shall be paid for their trouble by the party for whom the survey is made. The surveyor, at the time of making the survey, shall not leave any open lines, but shall see the same bounded plainly by marked trees, except where a water course or ancient marked line shall be the boundary, and shall make the breadth of each survey at least one third of its length in every part, unless where such breadth shall be restrained on both sides by mountains unfit for cultivation, by water courses, or the bounds of lands before appropriated. He shall, as soon as it can conveniently be done, and within three months at farthest after making the survey, deliver to his employer or his order, a fair and true plat and certificate of such survey, the quantity contained, the hundred (where hundreds are established in the county wherein it lies) the courses and descriptions of the several boundaries, natural and artificial, ancient and new, expressing the proper names of such natural boundaries where they have any, and the name of every person whose former lines made a boundary, and also the nature of the warrant and rights on which such survey was made; and shall at the same time re-deliver the said warrant to the party. The said surveyor may nevertheless detain the said certificates and warrants until the payment of his fees. The said plats and certificates shall be examined and tried by the said principal surveyor whether truly made and legally proportioned as to length and breadth, and shall be entered within three months at farthest, after the survey is made, in a book well bound, to be provided by the court of his county at the county charge; and he shall, in the month of July every year, return to the president and professors of William and Mary college, and also to the clerk's office of his county court, a true list of all surveys made by him or his deputies in the preceding twelve months, with the names of the persons for whom they were respectively made, and the quantities contained in each, there to be recorded by such clerk; and no person shall hereafter hold the offices of clerk of a county court and surveyor of a county, nor shall a deputy in either office act as deputy or chief in the other. Any surveyor, whether principal or deputy, failing in any of the duties aforesaid, shall be liable to be indicted in the General Court and punished by amercement or deprivation of his office, and incapacity to take it again, at the discretion of a jury; and shall moreover be liable to any party injured, for all damages he may sustain by such failure. Every county court shall once in every year, and oftener if they see cause, appoint two or more capable persons to examine the books of entries and surveys in possession of their chief surveyor, and to report in what condition and order the same are kept; and on his death or removal shall have power to take the same into their possession, and deliver them to the succeeding chief surveyor.

No plat to be delivered but to the owner within a year; except to a caveat or upon certificate of a caveat entered.
Penalty.

II. AND for preventing hasty and surreptitious grants, and avoiding controversies and expensive law suits, Be it enacted, that no surveyor shall, at any time within twelve months after the survey made, issue or deliver any certificate, copy, or plat of land, by him surveyed, except only to the person or persons for whom the same was surveyed, or to his, her, or their order, unless a caveat shall have been entered against a grant to the person claiming under such survey, to be proved by an authentic certificate of such caveat from the clerk of the General Court produced to the surveyor; and if any surveyor shall presume to issue any certificate, copy, or plat, as aforesaid, to any other than the person or persons entitled thereto, every surveyor so offending shall forfeit and pay to the party injured, his or her legal representatives or assigns, thirty pounds for every hundred acres of land contained in the survey whereof a certificate, copy, or plat, shall be so issued, or shall be liable to the action of the party injured at the common law for his or her damages, at the election of the party.

Fees in tobacco.

III. AND for declaring what fees a surveyor shall be entitled to, Be it enacted, that every surveyor shall be entitled to receive the following fees, for the services herein after mentioned, to be paid by the person employing him, and no other fees whatsoever, that is to say: For every survey by him plainly bounded as the law directs, and for a plat of such survey, after the delivery of such plat, where the survey shall not exceed four hundred acres of land, two hundred and fifty pounds of tobacco; for every hundred acres contained in one survey above four hundred, twelve pounds of tobacco; for surveying a lot in a town, twenty pounds of tobacco; and where the surveyor shall be stopped or hindered from finishing a survey by him begun, to be paid by the party who required the survey to be made, one hundred and twenty five pounds of tobacco; for running a dividing line, one hundred pounds of tobacco; for surveying an acre of land for a mill, fifty pounds of tobacco; for every survey of land formerly patented, and which shall be required to be surveyed, and for a plat thereof delivered as aforesaid, the same fee as for land not before surveyed; and where a survey shall be made of any lands which are to be added to other lands, in an inclusive patent, the surveyor shall not be paid a second fee for the land first surveyed, but shall only receive what the survey of the additional land shall amount to; and where any surveys have been actually made of several parcels of land adjoining and several plats delivered, if the party shall desire one inclusive plat thereof, the surveyor shall make out such plat for fifty pounds of tobacco; for running a dividing line between any county or parish, to be paid by such respective counties or parishes in proportion to the number of tithables, if ten miles or under, five hundred pounds of tobacco; and for every mile above ten, fifteen pounds of tobacco; for receiving a warrant of survey and giving a receipt therefor, eight pounds of tobacco; for recording a certificate from the commissioners of any district of a claim to land allowed by them, to be paid by the claimant, eight pounds of tobacco; for making an entry for land, or for a copy thereof, eight pounds of tobacco; for a copy of a plat of land, or of a certificate of survey, twelve pounds of tobacco.

May be discharged in money at penny half-penny.

IV. AND be it further enacted, that all persons who are now chargeable with any surveyor's fees, for services under the act of Assembly, entitled An act for regulating the fees of the Register of the Land Office and for other purposes, or who shall hereafter become chargeable with any tobacco for any of the services mentioned in this act, shall at their election, discharge the same either in transfer tobacco notes or in specie at the rate of twelve shillings and six pence for every hundred pounds of gross tobacco.

V. *AND be it further enacted*, that the surveyor of every county shall hereafter cause to be set up in some public place in his office, and there constantly kept, a fair table of his fees herein before mentioned, on pain of forfeiting one hundred pounds, which penalty shall be to the person or persons who shall inform or sue for the same. And if any surveyor who now is or shall hereafter become entitled to fees under this or the said recited act, shall ask or demand of any person whatsoever more than twelve shillings and six pence *per* hundred for such tobacco fees, or shall ask or demand larger fees than are allowed by this act, every person so offending shall forfeit and pay ten times the amount of the fees so charged, to the party or parties injured.

Table of fees to be set up in office under penalty. Penalty for overcharging.

VI. *AND be it further enacted*, that every surveyor of lands shall hereafter be resident in the county whereof he is surveyor, during the time he shall continue in office, under the penalty of forfeiting two hundred pounds current money for every month he shall reside out of the same, unless detained by such business as the court of the county shall judge reasonable, one moiety of which shall be to the commonwealth, for the better support of this government and the contingent charges thereof, and the other moiety to the informer.

Surveyors to be resident in their county, under a monthly penalty.

VII. *AND be it further enacted*, that all the several penalties and forfeitures by this act laid, given or inflicted, shall and may be recovered with costs, by action of debt or information, in any court of record within this commonwealth wherein such penalty shall be cognizable; and that all and every other act and acts, clause and clauses, heretofore made, for or concerning any matter or thing within the purview of this act, shall be, and are hereby repealed.

How penalties may be recovered. Repeal of former acts.

VIII. *AND be it further enacted*, that all persons who now are, or hereafter shall be chargeable with any tobacco fees due to clerks, sheriffs, and other public officers, may discharge the same either in tobacco or specie at the rate of twelve shillings and six pence *per* hundred, upon the gross tobacco.

Officers fees may be paid at one penny half-penny.

A. D. 1783.

POSTSCRIPT.

IN many parts of the foregoing collection the punctuation is inaccurate, and in some there are mistakes, and the sentences seem defective, perplexed, and obscure. Errors of this kind are copied from the acts, which were printed after every session, and with which alone the over-lookers could compare this work, residing at too great a distance from the place where the rolls are kept to have access to them. Such of these errors, or supposed errors, as they noted, occur in the following places:

Pages.	Lines.		Pages.	Lines.		Pages.	Lines.	
98	47	51	149	63		192	41	49
99	16		155	38		194	54	
101	3	8	161	42		195	14	41
102	32	33 59	168	23		198	77	
103	36		172	2		203	29	
106	34	51 55	173	52		206	26	
113	51		175	23		213	52	
115	59		176	12		215	67	
117	58		181	22		216	48	
119	27		183	12		218	42	
128	38							

SOME notes, and the numbers of some chapters referred to, in the margin, which are erroneous, may be corrected, the one by adverting to the text, and the other by consulting the table, and recuring to the acts there indicated.

THE session of *October* 1781, mentioned in some of the marginal references, should stand *November* 1781.

THE act of *March* 1781, exempting artificers in iron works from military duty, which was left out because the subsequent acts continuing it had not been attended to, until it was too late to print it in the proper place, is in these words:

" *BE it enacted by the General Assembly*, that every artificer actually and necessarily employed at any " iron-works in this state, shall be exempted from all military duty, during the time they are so em- " ployed; and that such and so many waggons, or other carriages, with their teams and drivers, as " are also actually and necessarily employed at such works, shall be exempted from all impresses for " public service, during such employment; any law to the contrary notwithstanding. This act shall " continue, and be in force, until the end of the next session of Assembly, and no longer."

THE other errors may be thus corrected:

Pages.	Lines.	
157	55	For "fum or" read "fum of"
159	61	For "or emancipation" read "of emancipation"
161		read the 46th line as if it had been inserted between the 48th and 49th
166	32	Before "injunctions" for "obtained" read "obtain"
168	25	For "in such" read "on such"
175	27	Leave out from "them" to "such" in the next following line.
190	78	Leave out from "yearly" to "or" in the line next following.
191	28	For "on" read "or"
192	3	For "recommend" read "recommended"
195	76 77	Leave out "and the sheriff or any constable of his county"
215	66	For "commissioner" read "commissioners"

T A B L E

Of the principal matters contained in the preceding collection.

F I N I S.